Table of Contents

Foreword

When we look back to the end of the 20th Century we will recall that period as the beginning of a new industrial revolution led by the Internet. How significant will it be? You have to reach back to the harnessing of electricity to find something so energizing to the world's economy. The Internet has improved virtually every aspect of the economy, from manufacturing to distribution. It has cut costs of production and allowed new businesses to be launched that have changed the landscape and decimated traditional bricks and mortar players in a host of industries.

Fortunes have been made by companies and individuals who have pioneered and invested in Net properties. The spectrum of Net stocks, from retailers to communications to technological enhancers, is so broad that it can no longer be easily summarized or captured.

While the tendency is to believe that the "easy" money has been had in the sector, the plethora of publicly traded entities present unprecedented opportunities for those who can distinguish between those companies that can dominate in the new Millennium and those that may struggle, be acquired or ultimately fail.

Ahh, but that's where the difficulty comes in. Who has the financial wherewithal to compete with the Yahoo!s and the America Onlines? Who will capture the most ad dollars? Who will capture the most business-to-business profits? Who has multiple revenue streams and a diversified set of businesses that would thrive with or without a continued Net explosion?

That's why this handbook can be a most valuable companion for those trying to understand where the next wave of solid investment ideas might come from. As someone who has successfully invested in the Net, both as an entrepreneur and as a stock picker, I can tell you that this sector has lacked even the most remote guideposts until now.

Here you will find a compendium of financials that will allow you to value the sector on an "apples to apples" basis, something that is currently unavailable anywhere else. And unlike so much of the Wall Street research that is out there, this Net bible isn't dictated from the underwriting forces on high. It is objective, rational and simple to use.

So often you hear of a company that might be the next big Net stock. If you are like me, you will want to check how it stacks up in this book before you pull the trigger. I know I will.

James J. Cramer
Co-Founder
TheStreet.com
September, 1999

Introduction

The frothy market for Internet stocks will surely be remembered as the investment phenomenon of the 1990s. At first, as prices for initial public offerings shot upwards on their first days of trading like corks from Champagne bottles, it seemed that investors were eager to own anything with a dot-com suffix. Companies with positive earnings were a rarity and company fundamentals appeared to be beside the point as investors bid up the market. Other investors hovered perplexed on the outskirts of the action, unsure how to evaluate the new companies or the industry's future.

The fizz began to subside in mid-1999, as prices moderated – and occasionally crashed – for the pure-play Internet stocks. As the mania has ebbed, a more realistic and discriminating attitude has taken hold. Investors are turning to fundamentals once again, and are seeking to broaden their understanding of this sometimes-arcane young industry.

One thing hasn't changed: the sense of enormous opportunity for the companies – and the investors – that correctly stake out the direction in which this nascent industry will grow.

Mergent FIS recognizes this opportunity, and the hunger for information on these companies. Accordingly, we are proud to present the **Handbook of Internet Stocks**. In these pages you will find profiles of 200 publicly held companies representing various aspects of the Internet. Those included range from many cutting-edge young companies pioneering their corners of Internet enterprise (more than 70 offered their stock to the public for the first time in 1999) to a handful of large, well-established, diversified companies that stand to benefit powerfully from the continuing Internet boom (AT&T Corp., for example, ranks itself as the largest direct Internet service provider to consumers in the U.S.). Companies profiled range from those retailing products and services to consumers over the Internet (Amazon.com, Inc. is perhaps the most familiar example), to those that provide the software, hardware, and communications infrastructure that make the Internet a resource for millions. Also included are the major Internet-access companies, a sampling of subscription – and advertising – supported Internet information companies, electronic financial-service providers, and consultants who assist companies in setting up Web sites.

This book may serve as a primer to demystify Internet companies for the newcomer, or as a convenient one-stop reference for the experienced Internet investor. As the Internet becomes a part of all of our lives and its potential is fully explored, the investment craze of the 1990s will still have plenty to offer in the next millennium.

Suzanne Wittebort
Asst. V.P., Equity Analysis
Mergent FIS Inc.
Charlotte, NC
September, 1999

Alphabetical Listing of Companies

Company	Ticker Symbol	Web Site
About.com, Inc.	BOUT	www.about.com
AboveNet Communications Inc.	ABOV	www.abovenet.com
AdForce, Inc.	ADFC	www.adforce.com
Allaire Corp.	ALLR	www.allaire.com
Alloy Online, Inc.	ALOY	www.alloy.com
Amazon.com, Inc.	AMZN	www.amazon.com
America Online, Inc.	AOL	www.aol.com
AmeriTrade Holding Corp.	AMTD	www.amtd.com
AppNet Systems, Inc.	APNT	www.appnet.net
Ariba, Inc.	ARBA	www.ariba.com
Asymetrix Learning Systems, Inc.	ASYM	www.asymetrix.com
At Home Corp.	ATHM	www.home.net
AT&T Corp.	T	www.att.com
Audiohighway.com	AHWY	www.audiohighway.com
Autobytel.com Inc.	ABTL	www.autobytel.com
Autoweb.com, Inc.	AWEB	www.autoweb.com
AXENT Technologies Inc.	AXNT	www.axent.com
Beyond.com Corp.	BYND	www.beyond.com
Bluefly, Inc.	BFLY	www.bluefly.com
Bottomline Technologies Inc.	EPAY	www.bottomline.com
Broadcom Corp.	BRCM	www.broadcom.com
BroadVision Inc.	BVSN	www.broadvision.com
C-ME.com	CMEE	www.c-me.com
CareerBuilder, Inc.	CBDR	www.careerbuilder.com
CDnow, Inc.	CDNW	www.cdnow.com
Cheap Tickets, Inc.	CTIX	www.cheaptickets.com
CheckFree Holdings Corp.	CKFR	www.checkfree.com
Cisco Systems, Inc.	CSCO	www.cisco.com
Citrix Systems, Inc.	CTXS	www.citrix.com
CMGI Inc.	CMGI	www.cmgi.com
CNet Inc.	CNET	www.cnet.com
Compaq Computer Corp.	CPQ	www.compaq.com
Comps.com, Inc.	CDOT	www.comps.com
Concentric Network Corp.	CNCX	www.concentric.com
Conexant Systems Inc.	CNXT	www.conexant.com
ConnectInc.com, Co.	CNKT	www.connectinc.com
Copper Mountain Networks, Inc.	CMTN	www.coppermountain.com
Covad Communications Group, Inc.	COVD	www.covad.com
Critical Path, Inc.	CPTH	www.cp.net
Crosswalk.com, Inc.	AMEN	www.crosswalk.com

Alphabetical Listing of Companies (cont.)

Company	Ticker Symbol	Web Site
CyberCash, Inc.	CYCH	www.cybercash.com
Cyberian Outpost, Inc.	COOL	www.outpost.com
Cybershop International, Inc.	CYSP	www.cybershop.com
CyberSource Corp.	CYBS	www.cybersource.com
Cylink Corp.	CYLK	www.cylink.com
Dell Computer Corp.	DELL	www.dell.com
Digital Lava Inc.	DGV	www.digitallava.com
Digital River, Inc.	DRIV	www.digitalriver.com
DoubleClick, Inc.	DCLK	www.doubleclick.com
drkoop.com Inc.	KOOP	www.drkoop.com
E*Trade Group, Inc.	EGRP	www.etrade.com
e4L, Inc.	ETV	www.e4l.com
Earthlink Network, Inc.	ELNK	www.earthlink.com
EarthWeb Inc.	EWBX	www.earthweb.com
eBay Inc.	EBAY	www.ebay.com
EDGAR Online, Inc.	EDGR	www.edgar-online.com
Edify Corp.	EDFY	www.edify.com
eFax.com Inc.	EFAX	www.efax.com
Egghead.com, Inc.	EGGS	www.egghead.com
Emusic.com, Inc.	EMUS	www.emusic.com
Entrust Technologies, Inc.	ENTU	www.entrust.com
eToys Inc.	ETYS	www.etoys.com
Exodus Communications, Inc.	EXDS	www.exodus.net
FatBrain.com, Inc.	FATB	www.fatbrain.com
Fine.com International Corp.	FDOT	www.fine.com
FlashNet Communications Inc.	FLAS	www.flash.net
Flycast Communications Corp.	FCST	www.flycast.com
Frontline Communications Corp.	FCCN	www.frontline.net
FVC.com, Inc.	FVCX	www.fvc.com
Gateway Inc.	GTW	www.gateway.com
GenesisIntermedia.com Inc.	GENI	www.genesisintermedia.com
Getty Images, Inc.	GETY	www.getty-images.com
Go2net Inc.	GNET	www.go2net.com
GoTo.com, Inc.	GOTO	www.goto.com
Harbinger Corp.	HRBC	www.harbinger.com
Healtheon Corp.	HLTH	www.healtheon.com
Hollywood Entertainment Corp.	HLYW	www.hollywoodvideo.com
HomeCom Communications Inc.	HCOM	www.homecom.com
Hoover's Inc.	HOOV	www.hoovers.com
IDT Corp.	IDTC	www.idt.net

Company	Ticker Symbol	Web Site
IMALL, Inc.	IMAL	www.imall.com
Infonautics, Inc.	INFO	www.infonautics.com
Infoseek Corp.	SEEK	www.infoseek.com
InfoSpace.com Inc.	INSP	www.infospace.com
Inktomi Corp.	INKT	www.inktomi.com
Intel Corp.	INTC	www.intel.com
Intelligent Life Corp.	ILIF	www.bankrate.com
International Business Machines Corp.	IBM	www.ibm.com
Internet America, Inc.	GEEK	www.airmail.net
Internet Financial Services Inc.	IFSX	www.abwatley.com
InterVU Inc.	ITVU	www.intervu.net
Intraware Inc.	ITRA	www.intraware.com
Intuit Inc.	INTU	www.intuit.com
ISS Group, Inc.	ISSX	www.iss.net
iTurf Inc.	TURF	www.iturf.com
iVillage Inc.	IVIL	www.ivillage.com
iXL Enterprises, Inc.	IIXL	www.ixl.com
Juno Online Services, Inc.	JWEB	www.juno.com
Launch Media, Inc.	LAUN	www.launch.com
Litronic Inc.	LTNX	www.litronic.com
Log On America, Inc.	LOAX	www.loa.com
Lycos, Inc.	LCOS	www.lycos.com
Macromedia, Inc.	MACR	www.macromedia.com
Mail.com, Inc.	MAIL	www.mail.com
MapQuest.com, Inc.	MQST	www.mapquest.com
Marimba, Inc.	MRBA	www.marimba.com
MarketWatch.com Inc.	MKTW	cbs.marketwatch.com
MCI WORLDCOM, Inc.	WCOM	www.wcom.com
Media Metrix, Inc.	MMXI	www.mediametrix.com
MERANT Plc	MRNT	www.merant.com
Metricom, Inc.	MCOM	www.metricom.com
Micro Warehouse, Inc.	MWHS	www.warehouse.com
Microsoft Corp.	MSFT	www.microsoft.com
MindSpring Enterprises, Inc.	MSPG	www.mindspring.com
Modem Media.Poppe Tyson, Inc.	MMPT	www.modemmedia.com
Mpath Interactive, Inc.	MPTH	www.mpath.com
Multex.com, Inc.	MLTX	www.multex.com
NAVIDEC, Inc.	NVDC	www.navidec.com
Neon Systems, Inc.	NESY	www.neonsys.com
Net.B@nk, Inc.	NTBK	www.netbank.com

Alphabetical Listing of Companies (cont.)

Company	Ticker Symbol	Web Site
NetGravity, Inc.	NETG	www.netgravity.com
NetSpeak Corp.	NSPK	www.netspeak.com
Network Computing Devices, Inc.	NCDI	www.ncd.com
Network Solutions, Inc.	NSOL	www.netsol.com
Network-1 Security Solutions, Inc.	NSSI	www.network-1.com
Networks Associates, Inc.	NETA	www.nai.com
NewsEDGE Corp.	NEWZ	www.newsedge.com
NextCard, Inc.	NXCD	www.nextcard.com
NorthPoint Communications Group, Inc.	NPNT	www.northpointcom.com
OneMain.com, Inc.	ONEM	www.onemain.com
OneSource Information Services, Inc.	ONES	www.onesource.com
Onsale, Inc.	ONSL	www.onsale.com
Open Market, Inc.	OMKT	www.openmarket.com
Open Text Corp.	OTEX	www.opentext.com
Oracle Corp.	ORCL	www.oracle.com
pcOrder.com, Inc.	PCOR	www.pcorder.com
Peapod, Inc.	PPOD	www.peapod.com
Phone.com Inc.	PHCM	www.phone.com
Pilot Network Services, Inc.	PILT	www.pilot.net
Portal Software, Inc.	PRSF	www.portal.com
Preview Travel, Inc.	PTVL	www.previewtravel.com
Priceline.com, Inc.	PCLN	www.priceline.com
Prodigy Communications Corp.	PRGY	www.prodigy.com
Progress Software Corp.	PRGS	www.progress.com
Proxicom Inc.	PXCM	www.proxicom.com
PSINet Inc.	PSIX	www.psinet.com
Qwest Communications International, Inc.	QWST	www.qwest.com
Rambus Inc.	RMBS	www.rambus.com
Ramp Networks, Inc.	RAMP	www.rampnet.com
Razorfish, Inc.	RAZF	www.razorfish.com
RCN Corp.	RCNC	www.rcn.com
RealNetworks, Inc.	RNWK	www.real.com
Rhythms NetConnections, Inc.	RTHM	www.rhythms.com
Rogue Wave Software, Inc.	RWAV	www.roguewave.com
RoweCom Inc.	ROWE	www.rowe.com
Sagent Technology, Inc.	SGNT	www.sagent.com
Sapient Corp.	SAPE	www.sapient.com
Schwab (Charles) Corp.	SCH	www.schwab.com
Secure Computing Corp.	SCUR	www.securecomputing.com
Security Dynamics Technologies, Inc.	SDTI	www.securitydynamics.com

Alphabetical Listing of Companies (cont.)

Company	Ticker Symbol	Web Site
Security First Technologies Corp.	SONE	www.s1.com
Silknet Software, Inc.	SILK	www.silknet.com
Software.com Inc.	SWCM	www.software.com
SportsLine USA, Inc.	SPLN	cbs.sportsline.com
Spyglass, Inc.	SPYG	www.spyglass.com
Sterling Commerce, Inc.	SE	www.sterlingcommerce.com
Student Advantage, Inc.	STAD	www.studentadvantage.com
Sun Microsystems, Inc.	SUNW	www.sun.com
Sybase, Inc.	SYBS	www.sybase.com
Teligent, Inc.	TGNT	www.teligent.com
Terayon Communication Systems, Inc.	TERN	www.terayon.com
theglobe.com, Inc.	TGLO	www.theglobe.com
TheStreet.com, Inc.	TSCM	www.thestreet.com
THINK New Ideas, Inc.	THNK	www.thinkinc.com
3Com Corp.	COMS	www.3com.com
Ticketmaster Online-CitySearch, Inc.	TMCS	www.ticketmaster.com
TMP Worldwide Inc.	TMPW	www.tmpw.com
TMSSequoia	TMSS	www.tmssequoia.com
Tut Systems Inc.	TUTS	www.tutsys.com
24/7 Media, Inc.	TFSM	www.247media.com
uBid Inc.	UBID	www.ubid.com
USInternetworking, Inc.	USIX	www.usi.net
USWeb Corp.	USWB	www.usweb.com
V-One Corp.	VONE	www.v-one.com
Value America, Inc.	VUSA	www.valueamerica.com
Verio Inc.	VRIO	www.verio.com
Verisign Inc.	VRSN	www.verisign.com
VerticalNet, Inc.	VERT	www.verticalnet.com
Viant Corp.	VIAN	www.viant.com
Vignette Corp.	VIGN	www.vignette.com
Visual Data Corp.	VDAT	www.vdat.com
Wavo Corp.	WAVO	www.wavo.com
WebTrends Corp.	WEBT	www.webtrends.com
White Pine Software, Inc.	WPNE	www.wpine.com
WinStar Communications, Inc.	WCII	www.winstar.com
Wit Capital Group, Inc.	WITC	www.witcapital.com
WorldGate Communications, Inc.	WGAT	www.wgate.com
Xoom.com Inc.	XMCM	www.xoom.com
Yahoo! Inc.	YHOO	www.yahoo.com
Ziff-Davis, Inc.	ZD	www.ziffdavis.com

Ranking by 1999 Stock Performance

Rank	Company	7/31/99 Price ($)	12/31/98 Price ($)	% Change
1.	Go2net Inc.	58.7500	8.8438	+564.31
2.	Metricom, Inc.	25.4375	5.1875	+390.36
3.	AmeriTrade Holding Corp.	24.9375	5.2495	+375.05
4.	RealNetworks, Inc.	76.3125	17.9375	+325.44
5.	Conexant Systems Inc.	62.8750	16.7500	+275.37
6.	Exodus Communications, Inc.	60.0315	16.0625	+273.74
7.	DoubleClick, Inc.	81.0000	22.2500	+264.04
8.	CMGI Inc.	92.1875	26.6250	+246.24
9.	AboveNet Communications Inc.	35.4060	10.5000	+237.20
10.	Verio Inc.	35.6565	11.1875	+218.72
11.	CNet Inc.	40.0000	13.3125	+200.47
12.	InterVU Inc.	37.2500	12.7500	+192.16
13.	White Pine Software, Inc.	6.7500	2.3750	+184.21
14.	E*Trade Group, Inc.	30.1250	11.6953	+157.58
15.	Teligent, Inc.	72.1250	28.7500	+150.87
16.	Verisign Inc.	74.1250	29.5625	+150.74
17.	MERANT Plc	22.5000	*b*9.0000	+150.00
18.	PSINet Inc.	51.7190	20.8750	+147.76
19.	InfoSpace.com Inc.	45.9375	19.0625	+140.98
20.	NAVIDEC, Inc.	12.0625	5.0625	+138.27
21.	RCN Corp.	42.0000	17.6875	+137.46
22.	Net.B@nk, Inc.	21.5000	9.1658	+134.57
23.	Security First Technologies Corp.	34.8750	15.2500	+128.69
24.	Visual Data Corp.	15.2500	6.8750	+121.82
25.	BroadVision Inc.	69.6875	32.0000	+117.77
26.	VerticalNet, Inc.	43.9375	*b*20.6250	+113.03
27.	Bottomline Technologies Inc.	39.7500	*b*21.0000	+89.29
28.	Copper Mountain Networks, Inc.	121.0000	*e*64.0000	+89.06
29.	Healtheon Corp.	50.2500	*b*27.0000	+86.11
30.	eFax.com Inc.	12.1250	*b*6.8750	+76.36
31.	CyberSource Corp.	25.8125	*f*14.7500	+75.00
32.	Cheap Tickets, Inc.	57.8750	*c*33.6250	+72.12
33.	Harbinger Corp.	13.5000	8.0000	+68.75
34.	HomeCom Communications Inc.	5.8125	3.5000	+66.07

a - from 1/31/99   *c* - from 3/31/99   *e* - from 5/31/99

b - from 2/28/99   *d* - from 4/30/99   *f* - from 6/30/99

1999 Stock Performance (cont.)

Rank	Company	7/31/99 Price ($)	12/31/98 Price ($)	% Change
35.	Juno Online Services, Inc.	20.0625	e12.2500	+63.78
36.	Schwab (Charles) Corp.	44.0625	28.0940	+56.84
37.	Infonautics, Inc.	7.0000	4.5000	+55.56
38.	Proxicom Inc.	34.7500	d22.4375	+54.87
39.	WorldGate Communications, Inc.	43.5000	d28.5000	+52.63
40.	GoTo.com, Inc.	42.3750	f28.0000	+51.34
41.	Gateway Inc.	76.1250	51.1875	+48.72
42.	Lycos, Inc.	41.3125	27.7815	+48.71
43.	SportsLine USA, Inc.	22.8750	15.5625	+46.99
44.	Concentric Network Corp.	24.1250	16.6250	+45.11
45.	Software.com Inc.	33.6250	f23.1875	+45.01
46.	Student Advantage, Inc.	13.6250	f9.5000	+43.42
47.	Fine.com International Corp.	3.7190	2.6250	+41.68
48.	drkoop.com Inc.	22.2500	f15.9375	+39.61
49.	Audiohighway.com	15.1250	10.8750	+39.08
50.	TMSSequoia	0.3900	0.2810	+38.79
51.	Sybase, Inc.	10.2500	7.4060	+38.40
52.	Cylink Corp.	5.0000	3.6250	+37.93
53.	International Business Machines Corp.	125.6875	92.1875	+36.34
54.	Xoom.com Inc.	44.6250	33.0000	+35.23
55.	WinStar Communications, Inc.	52.5000	39.0000	+34.62
56.	Cisco Systems, Inc.	62.1250	46.4065	+33.87
57.	Oracle Corp.	38.0625	28.7514	+32.38
58.	Ramp Networks, Inc.	18.8750	f14.3125	+31.88
59.	WebTrends Corp.	33.0000	b25.1250	+31.34
60.	Covad Communications Group, Inc.	46.0000	a35.1684	+30.80
61.	Frontline Communications Corp.	8.7500	6.7185	+30.24
62.	Edify Corp.	10.7500	8.3125	+29.32
63.	NetGravity, Inc.	21.5625	16.7500	+28.73
64.	Asymetrix Learning Systems, Inc.	5.6250	4.3750	+28.57
65.	IDT Corp.	19.7500	15.3750	+28.46
66.	THINK New Ideas, Inc.	12.2500	9.5625	+28.10
67.	Preview Travel, Inc.	23.3750	18.4375	+26.78
68.	CheckFree Holdings Corp.	29.5625	23.3750	+26.47
69.	Entrust Technologies, Inc.	30.0000	23.8750	+25.65
70.	America Online, Inc.	97.1250	77.5625	+25.22

a - from 1/31/99   *c* - from 3/31/99   *e* - from 5/31/99
b - from 2/28/99   *d* - from 4/30/99   *f* - from 6/30/99

1999 Stock Performance (cont.)

Rank	Company	7/31/99 Price ($)	12/31/98 Price ($)	% Change
71.	Microsoft Corp.	85.8125	69.3440	+23.75
72.	Bluefly, Inc.	12.5000	10.1250	+23.46
73.	At Home Corp.	45.6875	37.1250	+23.06
74.	Peapod, Inc.	8.3125	6.8125	+22.02
75.	eBay Inc.	97.6875	80.4086	+21.49
76.	NextCard, Inc.	36.1250	e29.9375	+20.67
77.	AppNet Systems, Inc.	15.8750	f13.4375	+18.14
78.	Qwest Communications International, Inc.	29.5000	25.0000	+18.00
79.	Vignette Corp.	64.0000	b54.2500	+17.97
80.	Intraware Inc.	22.2500	b18.8750	+17.88
81.	Intel Corp.	69.0000	59.2815	+16.39
82.	Open Market, Inc.	13.5000	11.6875	+15.51
83.	Yahoo! Inc.	136.4375	118.4690	+15.17
84.	MCI WORLDCOM, Inc.	82.5000	71.7500	+14.98
85.	Open Text Corp.	27.6875	24.3125	+13.88
86.	Beyond.com Corp.	23.6250	20.7500	+13.86
87.	Intuit Inc.	81.8125	72.5000	+12.84
88.	TMP Worldwide Inc.	46.9375	42.0000	+11.76
89.	Dell Computer Corp.	40.8750	36.5940	+11.70
90.	24/7 Media, Inc.	31.2500	28.0000	+11.61
91.	IMALL, Inc.	20.3125	18.2500	+11.30
92.	Ziff-Davis, Inc.	17.5625	15.8125	+11.07
93.	Phone.com Inc.	62.1875	f56.0000	+11.05
94.	iXL Enterprises, Inc.	29.7500	f26.8750	+10.70
95.	MindSpring Enterprises, Inc.	33.5625	30.5315	+9.93
96.	CDnow, Inc.	19.7500	18.0000	+9.72
97.	Modem Media.Poppe Tyson, Inc.	29.1250	b26.8750	+8.37
98.	Citrix Systems, Inc.	52.0625	48.5315	+7.28
99.	Terayon Communication Systems, Inc.	39.1250	37.0000	+5.74
100.	Getty Images, Inc.	18.1250	17.1875	+5.45
101.	Crosswalk.com, Inc.	10.3750	9.8750	+5.06
102.	NetSpeak Corp.	11.8125	11.2500	+5.00
103.	Macromedia, Inc.	34.8750	33.6875	+3.53
104.	Sagent Technology, Inc.	9.8125	d9.5000	+3.29
105.	AT&T Corp.	52.1250	50.5025	+3.21
106.	EarthWeb Inc.	40.0000	38.8750	+2.89

a - from 1/31/99   *c - from 3/31/99*   *e - from 5/31/99*
b - from 2/28/99   *d - from 4/30/99*   *f - from 6/30/99*

1999 Stock Performance (cont.)

Rank	Company	7/31/99 Price ($)	12/31/98 Price ($)	% Change
107.	Pilot Network Services, Inc.	9.1250	8.9375	+2.10
108.	ConnectInc.com, Co.	2.7810	2.7500	+1.13
109.	GenesisIntermedia.com Inc.	6.1250	f6.1250	---
110.	Broadcom Corp.	120.5000	120.7500	-0.21
111.	EDGAR Online, Inc.	9.0625	e9.1250	-0.68
112.	Sapient Corp.	55.2500	56.0000	-1.34
113.	Alloy Online, Inc.	11.7500	e12.1250	-3.09
114.	Network Solutions, Inc.	62.2500	65.4375	-4.87
115.	Mail.com, Inc.	17.8750	f18.8125	-4.98
116.	Amazon.com, Inc.	50.0315	53.5363	-6.55
117.	Viant Corp.	32.6875	f35.0000	-6.61
118.	Rambus Inc.	89.0625	96.2500	-7.47
119.	Ariba, Inc.	89.5940	f97.2500	-7.87
120.	Comps.com, Inc.	7.6875	e8.3750	-8.21
121.	Priceline.com, Inc.	75.5625	c82.8750	-8.82
122.	OneSource Information Services, Inc.	8.5000	e9.4375	-9.93
123.	MapQuest.com, Inc.	14.9375	e16.7500	-10.82
124.	theglobe.com, Inc.	14.2500	16.4375	-13.31
125.	Allaire Corp.	44.1250	a51.3750	-14.11
126.	Silknet Software, Inc.	32.2030	e37.5000	-14.13
127.	Portal Software, Inc.	41.8440	e49.1250	-14.82
128.	Earthlink Network, Inc.	48.3125	57.0000	-15.24
129.	Inktomi Corp.	108.4375	129.3750	-16.18
130.	Digital Lava Inc.	5.1250	b6.1250	-16.33
131.	Media Metrix, Inc.	38.3750	e47.5625	-19.32
132.	CareerBuilder, Inc.	9.4375	e11.7500	-19.68
133.	Flycast Communications Corp.	22.9375	e28.6250	-19.87
134.	V-One Corp.	2.3750	2.9690	-20.01
135.	AdForce, Inc.	23.1875	e29.0000	-20.04
136.	USWeb Corp.	20.9375	26.3750	-20.62
137.	Security Dynamics Technologies, Inc.	18.2500	23.0000	-20.65
138.	Sun Microsystems, Inc.	67.8750	85.6250	-20.73
139.	ISS Group, Inc.	21.7500	27.5000	-20.91
140.	Progress Software Corp.	26.6250	33.7500	-21.11
141.	Internet Financial Services Inc.	12.4375	d15.8125	-21.34
142.	Litronic Inc.	8.0000	f10.2500	-21.95

a - from 1/31/99   *c* - from 3/31/99   *e* - from 5/31/99
b - from 2/28/99   *d* - from 4/30/99   *f* - from 6/30/99

1999 Stock Performance (cont.)

Rank	Company	7/31/99 Price ($)	12/31/98 Price ($)	% Change
143.	Infoseek Corp.	38.0625	49.3750	-22.91
144.	pcOrder.com, Inc.	36.0000	b47.1250	-23.61
145.	TheStreet.com, Inc.	27.2500	e35.7500	-23.78
146.	About.com, Inc.	31.3750	e41.3750	-24.17
147.	Razorfish, Inc.	32.9375	d43.5000	-24.28
148.	Network Computing Devices, Inc.	5.1875	7.0000	-25.89
149.	Cybershop International, Inc.	8.3125	11.3750	-26.92
150.	Wit Capital Group, Inc.	24.5000	f34.0000	-27.94
151.	Rogue Wave Software, Inc.	6.0940	8.7500	-30.35
152.	CyberCash, Inc.	10.3750	15.0000	-30.83
153.	NewsEDGE Corp.	7.7500	11.6250	-33.33
154.	eToys Inc.	39.9375	e60.6875	-34.19
155.	FatBrain.com, Inc.	15.0000	c22.8750	-34.43
156.	OneMain.com, Inc.	23.6875	c36.2500	-34.66
157.	Intelligent Life Corp.	5.7500	e8.8750	-35.21
158.	Hollywood Entertainment Corp.	17.6250	27.2500	-35.32
159.	Digital River, Inc.	22.7500	35.5000	-35.92
160.	Network-1 Security Solutions, Inc.	4.1250	6.6250	-37.74
161.	Spyglass, Inc.	13.5000	22.0000	-38.64
162.	e4L, Inc.	5.1250	c8.3750	-38.81
163.	Neon Systems, Inc.	32.8750	c55.0000	-40.23
164.	Ticketmaster Online-CitySearch, Inc.	32.6875	56.0000	-41.63
165.	Sterling Commerce, Inc.	26.2500	45.0000	-41.67
166.	Compaq Computer Corp.	24.0625	42.0000	-42.71
167.	NorthPoint Communications Group, Inc.	24.3750	e42.5625	-42.73
168.	MarketWatch.com Inc.	39.6250	a69.5000	-42.99
169.	Internet America, Inc.	16.5000	29.0000	-43.10
170.	Prodigy Communications Corp.	21.8750	b38.8750	-43.73
171.	3Com Corp.	24.1250	44.8125	-46.16
172.	Log On America, Inc.	15.8750	d29.5000	-46.19
173.	USInternetworking, Inc.	27.3750	d51.1250	-46.45
174.	Rhythms NetConnections, Inc.	43.5000	d82.5000	-47.27
175.	Tut Systems Inc.	29.8750	a57.5000	-48.04
176.	Wavo Corp.	4.0625	8.0310	-49.41
177.	FlashNet Communications Inc.	19.6250	c41.1250	-52.28
178.	Launch Media, Inc.	11.8750	d25.2500	-52.97

a - from 1/31/99   *c - from 3/31/99*   *e - from 5/31/99*

b - from 2/28/99   *d - from 4/30/99*   *f - from 6/30/99*

1999 Stock Performance (cont.)

Rank	Company	7/31/99 Price ($)	12/31/98 Price ($)	% Change
179.	AXENT Technologies Inc.	14.0000	30.5625	-54.19
180.	RoweCom Inc.	19.5000	c43.6250	-55.30
181.	FVC.com, Inc.	6.8750	15.7500	-56.35
182.	Critical Path, Inc.	33.5000	e77.0000	-56.49
183.	Mpath Interactive, Inc.	17.0000	d39.3750	-56.83
184.	Marimba, Inc.	26.1875	d60.7500	-56.89
185.	Autobytel.com Inc.	17.9375	c41.8750	-57.16
186.	Micro Warehouse, Inc.	14.1250	33.8125	-58.23
187.	Egghead.com, Inc.	8.6875	20.8125	-58.26
188.	Onsale, Inc.	16.1875	40.0625	-59.59
189.	iVillage Inc.	40.3750	c100.5000	-59.83
190.	Cyberian Outpost, Inc.	10.7500	27.5000	-60.91
191.	Value America, Inc.	14.6250	d39.4375	-62.92
192.	Autoweb.com, Inc.	12.9375	c35.6250	-63.68
193.	iTurf Inc.	13.7500	d39.0000	-64.74
194.	Multex.com, Inc.	20.2500	c62.5000	-67.60
195.	Networks Associates, Inc.	17.5000	66.2500	-73.58
196.	uBid Inc.	23.1250	106.6250	-78.31
197.	Secure Computing Corp.	3.0310	19.0625	-84.10
---	C-ME.com	6.3750	N/A	---
---	Emusic.com, Inc.	16.0000	N/A	---
---	Hoover's Inc.	13.3750	N/A	---

a - from 1/31/99 *c - from 3/31/99* *e - from 5/31/99*
b - from 2/28/99 *d - from 4/30/99* *f - from 6/30/99*

Note: C-ME.com, Emusic.com, Inc., and Hoover's Inc. began trading in July 1999.

This ranking reflects each company's stock price movement from 12/31/98 to 7/31/99. Where 12/31/98 prices are not available, the earliest available 1999 month-end prices are used, as noted.

Rankings by Market Capitalization and Total Assets

Rank	Company	Mkt. Cap. ($mill.)	Assets Rank	Assets ($mill.)
1.	Microsoft Corp.	437,974.9	4	37,156.0
2.	Intel Corp.	228,252.0	5	31,471.0
3.	International Business Machines Corp.	227,380.0	2	86,100.0
4.	Cisco Systems, Inc.	200,234.2	8	8,916.7
5.	AT&T Corp.	166,574.8	3	59,550.0
6.	MCI WORLDCOM, Inc.	154,531.6	1	86,401.0
7.	America Online, Inc.	107,622.3	13	5,348.0
8.	Dell Computer Corp.	103,858.2	12	6,877.0
9.	Oracle Corp.	53,927.2	11	7,259.7
10.	Sun Microsystems, Inc.	52,525.9	9	8,420.4
11.	Compaq Computer Corp.	40,906.3	6	23,051.0
12.	Schwab (Charles) Corp.	36,034.3	7	22,264.4
13.	Yahoo! Inc.	35,336.6	33	621.9
14.	Qwest Communications International, Inc.	21,998.2	10	8,067.6
15.	Amazon.com, Inc.	16,870.8	32	648.5
16.	At Home Corp.	16,808.6	28	780.6
17.	eBay Inc.	12,564.6	79	92.5
18.	Broadcom Corp.	11,984.8	53	237.4
19.	Gateway Inc.	11,922.1	16	2,890.4
20.	Priceline.com, Inc.	10,754.1	96	66.6
21.	CMGI Inc.	8,786.7	52	237.5
22.	3Com Corp.	8,493.0	14	4,495.4
23.	E*Trade Group, Inc.	7,065.8	17	1,968.9
24.	Conexant Systems Inc.	6,128.3	22	1,418.0
25.	RealNetworks, Inc.	5,570.9	66	128.1
26.	Inktomi Corp.	5,456.4	89	70.6
27.	Intuit Inc.	5,092.1	21	1,498.6
28.	Exodus Communications, Inc.	4,995.2	44	293.3
29.	eToys Inc.	4,588.4	127	30.7
30.	Citrix Systems, Inc.	4,572.7	36	431.4
31.	AmeriTrade Holding Corp.	4,350.0	23	1,290.4
32.	Ariba, Inc.	4,070.7	143	19.2
33.	Teligent, Inc.	3,888.8	29	763.4
34.	Verisign Inc.	3,753.5	98	64.3

Market Capitalization and Total Assets (cont.)

Rank	Company	Mkt. Cap. ($mill.)	Assets Rank	Assets ($mill.)
35.	Lycos, Inc.	3,604.9	49	248.8
36.	Healtheon Corp.	3,573.2	82	79.9
37.	PSINet Inc.	3,353.1	24	1,284.2
38.	Covad Communications Group, Inc.	3,300.1	63	139.4
39.	DoubleClick, Inc.	3,222.2	57	183.6
40.	RCN Corp.	3,186.1	18	1,907.6
41.	Rhythms NetConnections, Inc.	3,174.7	60	171.7
42.	Portal Software, Inc.	3,152.8	126	32.3
43.	NorthPoint Communications Group, Inc.	2,959.2	100	60.5
44.	CNet Inc.	2,916.0	80	88.4
45.	WinStar Communications, Inc.	2,863.6	19	1,663.2
46.	Copper Mountain Networks, Inc.	2,815.5	119	36.2
47.	Verio Inc.	2,717.6	27	933.7
48.	Networks Associates, Inc.	2,432.3	20	1,536.7
49.	Infoseek Corp.	2,381.0	72	101.7
50.	Sterling Commerce, Inc.	2,318.4	25	967.0
51.	InfoSpace.com Inc.	2,177.5	71	102.3
52.	MindSpring Enterprises, Inc.	2,129.3	50	247.6
53.	Rambus Inc.	2,097.3	75	97.9
54.	Network Solutions, Inc.	2,075.6	51	243.9
55.	GoTo.com, Inc.	1,930.8	140	20.0
56.	iXL Enterprises, Inc.	1,920.1	62	143.0
57.	Phone.com Inc.	1,896.7	64	138.9
58.	Ziff-Davis, Inc.	1,813.9	15	3,433.8
59.	BroadVision Inc.	1,781.3	73	101.6
60.	Vignette Corp.	1,778.8	134	22.8
61.	TMP Worldwide Inc.	1,768.2	34	608.1
62.	Wit Capital Group, Inc.	1,763.6	135	22.3
63.	NextCard, Inc.	1,660.0	112	45.5
64.	Go2net Inc.	1,634.2	162	11.3
65.	USWeb Corp.	1,600.3	39	403.2
66.	Earthlink Network, Inc.	1,551.3	47	266.3
67.	Sapient Corp.	1,529.4	56	184.9
68.	CheckFree Holdings Corp.	1,529.2	48	252.8
69.	Macromedia, Inc.	1,494.5	55	194.6
70.	VerticalNet, Inc.	1,489.2	158	12.3

Market Capitalization and Total Assets (cont.)

Rank	Company	Mkt. Cap. ($mill.)	Assets Rank	Assets ($mill.)
71.	Software.com Inc.	1,371.6	144	19.0
72.	Prodigy Communications Corp.	1,336.8	83	78.3
73.	Entrust Technologies, Inc.	1,330.5	69	107.8
74.	Critical Path, Inc.	1,278.2	137	20.7
75.	Cheap Tickets, Inc.	1,243.3	156	13.2
76.	AboveNet Communications Inc.	1,100.8	41	383.9
77.	USInternetworking, Inc.	1,089.0	70	106.5
78.	Concentric Network Corp.	999.6	43	298.3
79.	iVillage Inc.	983.9	111	46.8
80.	Security First Technologies Corp.	962.5	110	48.3
81.	WorldGate Communications, Inc.	932.7	182	5.6
82.	Proxicom Inc.	860.2	136	22.1
83.	Beyond.com Corp.	849.8	68	109.9
84.	Sybase, Inc.	837.8	30	696.6
85.	ISS Group, Inc.	826.2	84	78.0
86.	Terayon Communication Systems, Inc.	818.3	115	42.1
87.	Razorfish, Inc.	811.0	160	12.1
88.	Xoom.com Inc.	809.1	95	66.9
89.	Hollywood Entertainment Corp.	806.2	26	934.4
90.	Mail.com, Inc.	773.2	138	20.3
91.	Security Dynamics Technologies, Inc.	709.3	45	280.9
92.	Viant Corp.	698.0	130	29.8
93.	Juno Online Services, Inc.	694.8	153	14.7
94.	IDT Corp.	671.6	37	417.2
95.	TheStreet.com, Inc.	667.9	133	27.6
96.	Media Metrix, Inc.	664.0	146	16.1
97.	drkoop.com Inc.	657.8	200	0.4
98.	Value America, Inc.	649.8	101	60.1
99.	Getty Images, Inc.	642.3	35	462.9
100.	24/7 Media, Inc.	632.1	99	62.7
101.	Net.B@nk, Inc.	631.7	40	388.4
102.	Marimba, Inc.	603.4	152	14.9
103.	CDnow, Inc.	591.7	92	69.0
104.	Open Text Corp.	584.2	46	270.6
105.	CyberSource Corp.	567.3	151	15.0
106.	pcOrder.com, Inc.	559.6	159	12.3

Market Capitalization and Total Assets (cont.)

Rank	Company	Mkt. Cap. ($mill.)	Assets Rank	Assets ($mill.)
107.	MarketWatch.com Inc.	545.0	190	4.5
108.	Intraware Inc.	535.3	120	35.0
109.	Metricom, Inc.	535.2	123	34.5
110.	OneMain.com, Inc.	534.1	178	6.3
111.	SportsLine USA, Inc.	520.4	65	137.7
112.	Harbinger Corp.	520.3	58	178.4
113.	Allaire Corp.	520.1	167	10.0
114.	InterVU Inc.	519.9	129	30.4
115.	Micro Warehouse, Inc.	505.7	31	666.5
116.	AppNet Systems, Inc.	493.7	67	118.4
117.	MapQuest.com, Inc.	490.4	161	11.5
118.	Open Market, Inc.	487.8	76	95.0
119.	Silknet Software, Inc.	483.0	97	64.7
120.	Student Advantage, Inc.	474.1	168	9.9
121.	Digital River, Inc.	467.7	81	80.3
122.	AdForce, Inc.	463.6	141	19.9
123.	Ticketmaster Online-CitySearch, Inc.	455.9	38	416.7
124.	Progress Software Corp.	450.4	54	206.7
125.	Multex.com, Inc.	442.5	131	28.0
126.	WebTrends Corp.	418.3	192	3.4
127.	Bottomline Technologies Inc.	415.3	102	55.1
128.	AXENT Technologies Inc.	391.1	61	161.3
129.	NetGravity, Inc.	383.0	125	33.4
130.	Ramp Networks, Inc.	382.9	170	8.9
131.	About.com, Inc.	381.3	148	15.7
132.	Mpath Interactive, Inc.	379.1	180	6.2
133.	theglobe.com, Inc.	378.0	118	38.1
134.	EarthWeb Inc.	376.0	128	30.5
135.	IMALL, Inc.	371.0	154	14.5
136.	Tut Systems Inc.	348.8	150	15.3
137.	Flycast Communications Corp.	333.1	163	10.8
138.	Autoweb.com, Inc.	324.1	174	7.2
139.	Modem Media.Poppe Tyson, Inc.	323.3	88	71.3
140.	Preview Travel, Inc.	323.1	86	72.2
141.	Autobytel.com Inc.	320.7	124	34.2
142.	Onsale, Inc.	317.5	90	69.4

Market Capitalization and Total Assets (cont.)

Rank	Company	Mkt. Cap. ($mill.)	Assets Rank	Assets ($mill.)
143.	Neon Systems, Inc.	291.0	**107**	52.6
144.	FlashNet Communications Inc.	273.8	**169**	9.7
145.	Egghead.com, Inc.	267.4	**59**	176.2
146.	Emusic.com, Inc.	251.1	**105**	54.2
147.	Sagent Technology, Inc.	247.9	**175**	7.2
148.	Cyberian Outpost, Inc.	247.7	**87**	71.5
149.	iTurf Inc.	238.3	**196**	1.2
150.	Spyglass, Inc.	223.1	**122**	34.6
151.	CareerBuilder, Inc.	222.2	**181**	6.0
152.	uBid Inc.	211.8	**121**	34.6
153.	CyberCash, Inc.	209.6	**78**	93.3
154.	RoweCom Inc.	197.1	**139**	20.3
155.	Edify Corp.	190.6	**93**	67.0
156.	FatBrain.com, Inc.	168.8	**117**	39.6
157.	e4L, Inc.	167.4	**74**	98.8
158.	Alloy Online, Inc.	167.2	**173**	7.4
159.	Hoover's Inc.	162.4	**165**	10.1
160.	eFax.com Inc.	155.8	**145**	16.2
161.	NetSpeak Corp.	152.9	**108**	51.7
162.	Launch Media, Inc.	150.4	**157**	13.2
163.	Cylink Corp.	147.3	**77**	94.3
164.	Peapod, Inc.	145.2	**114**	43.0
165.	NewsEDGE Corp.	134.4	**91**	69.2
166.	Visual Data Corp.	125.6	**177**	6.4
167.	Pilot Network Services, Inc.	124.5	**116**	42.1
168.	THINK New Ideas, Inc.	123.4	**94**	66.9
169.	Log On America, Inc.	121.4	**197**	1.1
170.	Wavo Corp.	117.5	**106**	53.0
171.	FVC.com, Inc.	114.0	**109**	51.2
172.	Internet America, Inc.	113.7	**142**	19.4
173.	EDGAR Online, Inc.	104.6	**198**	0.8
174.	Internet Financial Services Inc.	98.7	**183**	5.5
175.	Comps.com, Inc.	90.9	**171**	8.4
176.	NAVIDEC, Inc.	89.2	**186**	5.3
177.	OneSource Information Services, Inc.	84.9	**132**	27.6
178.	Audiohighway.com	84.2	**155**	13.5

Market Capitalization and Total Assets (cont.)

Rank	Company	Mkt. Cap. ($mill.)	Assets Rank	Assets ($mill.)
179.	Network Computing Devices, Inc.	83.9	85	75.1
180.	Infonautics, Inc.	81.9	164	10.2
181.	Asymetrix Learning Systems, Inc.	79.3	113	43.6
182.	Litronic Inc.	77.9	194	2.8
183.	Intelligent Life Corp.	77.3	193	3.1
184.	Crosswalk.com, Inc.	72.7	188	4.9
185.	White Pine Software, Inc.	71.9	147	16.0
186.	Cybershop International, Inc.	71.6	149	15.4
187.	Rogue Wave Software, Inc.	63.5	103	54.5
188.	Secure Computing Corp.	63.1	104	54.3
189.	Bluefly, Inc.	61.3	176	7.2
190.	ConnectInc.com, Co.	41.3	184	5.5
191.	V-One Corp.	39.9	191	3.9
192.	HomeCom Communications Inc.	38.8	189	4.6
193.	C-ME.com	36.7	199	0.5
194.	GenesisIntermedia.com Inc.	32.5	166	10.0
195.	Frontline Communications Corp.	31.4	179	6.3
196.	Digital Lava Inc.	23.8	195	1.2
197.	Network-1 Security Solutions, Inc.	18.0	172	8.2
198.	Fine.com International Corp.	10.0	187	5.1
199.	TMSSequoia	5.3	185	5.3
---	MERANT Plc	N/A	42	323.1

Note: Sufficient data were not available to calculate market capitalization for MERANT Plc, a U.K. company.

Market capitalization is calculated by multiplying the 7/31/99 closing stock price by the number of shares outstanding as stated on the most recent SEC quarterly report filing available.

Rankings by Revenues and Net Income

Rev. Rank	Company	Revenues ($000)	Net Inc. Rank	Net Inc. ($000)
1.	International Business Machines Corp.	81,667,000	2	6,328,000
2.	AT&T Corp.	53,223,000	4	5,235,000
3.	Compaq Computer Corp.	31,169,000	200	-2,743,000
4.	Intel Corp.	26,273,000	3	6,068,000
5.	Microsoft Corp.	19,747,000	1	7,785,000
6.	Dell Computer Corp.	18,243,000	5	1,460,000
7.	MCI WORLDCOM, Inc.	17,678,000	199	-2,540,000
8.	Sun Microsystems, Inc.	11,726,297	8	1,031,334
9.	Oracle Corp.	8,827,252	7	1,289,758
10.	Cisco Systems, Inc.	8,458,777	6	1,350,072
11.	Gateway Inc.	7,467,925	12	346,399
12.	3Com Corp.	5,772,149	10	403,874
13.	America Online, Inc.	4,777,000	9	762,000
14.	Schwab (Charles) Corp.	2,736,221	11	348,462
15.	Qwest Communications International, Inc.	2,242,700	198	-844,000
16.	Micro Warehouse, Inc.	2,220,018	16	30,178
17.	Conexant Systems Inc.	1,200,000	195	-262,000
18.	Ziff-Davis, Inc.	1,108,892	183	-77,809
19.	Networks Associates, Inc.	990,045	14	36,438
20.	Sybase, Inc.	867,469	186	-93,128
21.	Hollywood Entertainment Corp.	763,908	176	-50,464
22.	Amazon.com, Inc.	609,996	190	-124,546
23.	Intuit Inc.	592,736	116	-12,157
24.	Sterling Commerce, Inc.	490,302	180	-61,156
25.	TMP Worldwide Inc.	406,769	31	4,250
26.	MERANT Plc	374,202	158	-28,532
27.	IDT Corp.	335,373	76	-6,263
28.	e4L, Inc.	327,850	174	-48,474
29.	PSINet Inc.	259,636	194	-261,869
30.	CheckFree Holdings Corp.	250,131	26	10,457
31.	Citrix Systems, Inc.	248,636	13	61,102
32.	E*Trade Group, Inc.	245,282	48	-712
33.	WinStar Communications, Inc.	244,447	197	-419,750
34.	Progress Software Corp.	239,890	19	22,532

Revenues and Net Income (cont.)

Rev. Rank	Company	Revenues ($000)	Net Inc. Rank	Net Inc. ($000)
35.	USWeb Corp.	228,600	192	-188,281
36.	RCN Corp.	210,940	193	-204,801
37.	Onsale, Inc.	207,751	127	-14,666
38.	Yahoo! Inc.	203,270	18	25,588
39.	Broadcom Corp.	203,095	15	36,398
40.	Getty Images, Inc.	185,084	169	-35,553
41.	Earthlink Network, Inc.	175,941	179	-59,782
42.	Security Dynamics Technologies, Inc.	171,334	17	29,415
43.	Cheap Tickets, Inc.	171,114	39	1,065
44.	AmeriTrade Holding Corp.	164,194	43	210
45.	Sapient Corp.	160,372	23	13,699
46.	Macromedia, Inc.	149,886	21	19,784
47.	Egghead.com, Inc.	148,721	167	-34,423
48.	Prodigy Communications Corp.	136,140	181	-65,083
49.	Harbinger Corp.	135,151	89	-8,527
50.	Verio Inc.	120,653	188	-111,854
51.	MindSpring Enterprises, Inc.	114,673	25	10,544
52.	Network Computing Devices, Inc.	105,596	94	-9,103
53.	AXENT Technologies Inc.	101,019	27	7,679
54.	Network Solutions, Inc.	93,652	24	11,235
55.	Open Text Corp.	92,537	20	20,170
56.	CMGI Inc.	91,484	22	16,553
57.	Cyberian Outpost, Inc.	85,203	153	-25,220
58.	Concentric Network Corp.	82,807	185	-85,148
59.	DoubleClick, Inc.	80,188	142	-18,173
60.	NewsEDGE Corp.	79,532	137	-17,228
61.	Edify Corp.	70,886	79	-6,675
62.	Peapod, Inc.	69,265	147	-21,565
63.	RealNetworks, Inc.	64,839	135	-16,414
64.	iXL Enterprises, Inc.	64,767	175	-48,866
65.	Open Market, Inc.	62,145	162	-30,472
66.	Secure Computing Corp.	61,442	63	-3,262
67.	CNet Inc.	56,432	34	2,600
68.	CDnow, Inc.	56,395	172	-43,769
69.	Lycos, Inc.	56,060	187	-96,917
70.	Exodus Communications, Inc.	52,738	182	-66,442

Revenues and Net Income (cont.)

Rev. Rank	Company	Revenues ($000)	Net Inc. Rank	Net Inc. ($000)
71.	BroadVision Inc.	50,911	33	4,039
72.	Infoseek Corp.	50,715	74	-5,694
73.	THINK New Ideas, Inc.	49,797	87	-8,308
74.	Entrust Technologies, Inc.	48,988	151	-23,828
75.	Healtheon Corp.	48,838	178	-54,048
76.	uBid Inc.	48,232	102	-10,169
77.	At Home Corp.	48,045	191	-144,179
78.	eBay Inc.	47,352	35	2,398
79.	Rogue Wave Software, Inc.	44,439	37	2,177
80.	Cylink Corp.	42,760	138	-17,356
81.	Modem Media.Poppe Tyson, Inc.	42,544	62	-3,203
82.	Proxicom Inc.	42,405	145	-20,642
83.	Value America, Inc.	41,544	177	-53,616
84.	Bottomline Technologies Inc.	39,303	32	4,051
85.	Verisign Inc.	38,930	144	-19,743
86.	Intraware Inc.	38,417	114	-12,033
87.	Rambus Inc.	37,864	29	6,788
88.	FVC.com, Inc.	37,251	85	-8,016
89.	Beyond.com Corp.	36,650	164	-31,073
90.	ISS Group, Inc.	35,929	69	-4,102
91.	Priceline.com, Inc.	35,237	189	-112,242
92.	Asymetrix Learning Systems, Inc.	33,352	71	-5,159
93.	Terayon Communication Systems, Inc.	31,696	150	-23,228
94.	SportsLine USA, Inc.	30,551	168	-35,509
95.	OneSource Information Services, Inc.	30,428	28	6,988
96.	eFax.com Inc.	30,233	52	-1,501
97.	eToys Inc.	29,959	160	-28,558
98.	Ticketmaster Online-CitySearch, Inc.	27,873	136	-17,219
99.	FlashNet Communications Inc.	26,892	103	-10,265
100.	Portal Software, Inc.	26,669	139	-17,408
101.	Software.com Inc.	25,618	81	-7,382
102.	MapQuest.com, Inc.	24,717	61	-3,155
103.	Security First Technologies Corp.	24,180	159	-28,558
104.	Autobytel.com Inc.	23,826	143	-19,398
105.	Wavo Corp.	22,296	157	-28,485
106.	Copper Mountain Networks, Inc.	21,821	104	-10,331

Revenues and Net Income (cont.)

Rev. Rank	Company	Revenues ($000)	Net Inc. Rank	Net Inc. ($000)
107.	pcOrder.com, Inc.	21,714	98	-9,638
108.	Juno Online Services, Inc.	21,694	165	-31,626
109.	Digital River, Inc.	20,911	124	-13,798
110.	Allaire Corp.	20,512	105	-10,770
111.	Spyglass, Inc.	20,494	86	-8,016
112.	Inktomi Corp.	20,426	149	-22,355
113.	Viant Corp.	20,043	78	-6,487
114.	Neon Systems, Inc.	20,016	36	2,252
115.	24/7 Media, Inc.	19,863	152	-24,723
116.	FatBrain.com, Inc.	19,780	100	-9,892
117.	RoweCom Inc.	19,053	82	-7,629
118.	Net.B@nk, Inc.	18,771	30	4,464
119.	Internet America, Inc.	18,119	59	-2,463
120.	AppNet Systems, Inc.	17,674	126	-14,379
121.	Pilot Network Services, Inc.	17,522	141	-18,095
122.	Student Advantage, Inc.	17,443	70	-5,115
123.	Marimba, Inc.	17,085	73	-5,681
124.	Sagent Technology, Inc.	17,043	122	-13,701
125.	Vignette Corp.	16,205	154	-26,197
126.	Metricom, Inc.	15,859	184	-84,164
127.	iVillage Inc.	15,012	171	-43,654
128.	Infonautics, Inc.	14,925	140	-17,448
129.	GenesisIntermedia.com Inc.	14,906	38	1,427
130.	Preview Travel, Inc.	14,008	148	-22,078
131.	AboveNet Communications Inc.	13,968	155	-26,555
132.	Silknet Software, Inc.	13,918	97	-9,374
133.	Razorfish, Inc.	13,843	44	-1
134.	Phone.com Inc.	13,442	146	-20,763
135.	Multex.com, Inc.	13,182	99	-9,868
136.	Autoweb.com, Inc.	13,041	111	-11,484
137.	Comps.com, Inc.	12,900	53	-1,659
138.	CyberCash, Inc.	12,588	163	-30,944
139.	NetGravity, Inc.	11,557	109	-11,293
140.	Tut Systems Inc.	10,555	123	-13,747
141.	Alloy Online, Inc.	10,210	77	-6,364
142.	Ramp Networks, Inc.	9,858	119	-13,418

Revenues and Net Income (cont.)

Rev. Rank	Company	Revenues ($000)	Net Inc. Rank	Net Inc. ($000)
143.	InfoSpace.com Inc.	9,414	92	-9,056
144.	Hoover's Inc.	9,229	57	-2,255
145.	Internet Financial Services Inc.	9,119	47	-632
146.	NAVIDEC, Inc.	8,555	68	-3,933
147.	Ariba, Inc.	8,363	107	-10,953
148.	Xoom.com Inc.	8,318	106	-10,798
149.	Flycast Communications Corp.	8,029	96	-9,307
150.	Mpath Interactive, Inc.	8,027	112	-11,951
151.	WebTrends Corp.	8,008	42	219
152.	White Pine Software, Inc.	7,793	88	-8,424
153.	NetSpeak Corp.	7,719	115	-12,063
154.	TMSSequoia	7,355	40	489
155.	MarketWatch.com Inc.	7,027	117	-12,413
156.	CareerBuilder, Inc.	7,006	113	-11,987
157.	Litronic Inc.	6,653	51	-1,406
158.	ConnectInc.com, Co.	6,479	84	-7,904
159.	Media Metrix, Inc.	6,330	80	-7,159
160.	V-One Corp.	6,260	95	-9,193
161.	Fine.com International Corp.	6,133	66	-3,566
162.	theglobe.com, Inc.	5,510	132	-16,046
163.	Covad Communications Group, Inc.	5,326	173	-48,121
164.	Launch Media, Inc.	5,014	120	-13,419
165.	Go2net Inc.	4,831	58	-2,371
166.	Cybershop International, Inc.	4,814	83	-7,888
167.	TheStreet.com, Inc.	4,623	134	-16,358
168.	AdForce, Inc.	4,286	128	-15,020
169.	USInternetworking, Inc.	4,122	166	-32,453
170.	iTurf Inc.	4,014	41	425
171.	About.com, Inc.	3,722	130	-15,578
172.	Intelligent Life Corp.	3,469	55	-2,095
173.	CyberSource Corp.	3,384	101	-10,085
174.	EarthWeb Inc.	3,349	91	-8,970
175.	HomeCom Communications Inc.	3,292	50	-1,204
176.	VerticalNet, Inc.	3,135	121	-13,594
177.	Wit Capital Group, Inc.	2,038	90	-8,794
178.	EDGAR Online, Inc.	2,003	56	-2,221

Revenues and Net Income (cont.)

Rev. Rank	Company	Revenues ($000)	Net Inc. Rank	Net Inc. ($000)
179.	Visual Data Corp.	1,881	64	-3,435
180.	Network-1 Security Solutions, Inc.	1,831	75	-5,777
181.	InterVU Inc.	1,712	131	-15,710
182.	IMALL, Inc.	1,596	108	-11,086
183.	Mail.com, Inc.	1,495	118	-12,525
184.	Digital Lava Inc.	1,464	67	-3,731
185.	NextCard, Inc.	1,199	133	-16,064
186.	Crosswalk.com, Inc.	1,083	65	-3,459
187.	WorldGate Communications, Inc.	1,022	156	-27,122
188.	Teligent, Inc.	960	196	-281,471
189.	NorthPoint Communications Group, Inc.	931	161	-28,847
190.	Critical Path, Inc.	897	110	-11,461
191.	GoTo.com, Inc.	822	125	-14,023
192.	Log On America, Inc.	760	45	-422
193.	Frontline Communications Corp.	575	54	-1,744
194.	Rhythms NetConnections, Inc.	528	170	-36,334
195.	Bluefly, Inc.	243	60	-2,478
196.	Audiohighway.com	139	72	-5,442
197.	Emusic.com, Inc.	92	129	-15,140
198.	C-ME.com	66	46	-571
199.	drkoop.com Inc.	43	93	-9,084
---	OneMain.com, Inc.	---	49	-765

Figures are for the most recent fiscal year for which figures were available, up to and including 6/30/99 fiscal year-ends.

Classification by Industry

Financial Services

AmeriTrade Holding Corp.
E*Trade Group, Inc.
Internet Financial Services Inc.
Net.B@nk, Inc.
NextCard, Inc.
Schwab (Charles) Corp.
Wit Capital Group, Inc.

Information Services (Advertising/Subscription-Supported)

About.com, Inc.
AdForce, Inc.
Audiohighway.com
CareerBuilder, Inc.
CNet Inc.
Comps.com, Inc.
Crosswalk.com, Inc.
DoubleClick, Inc.
drkoop.com Inc.
EarthWeb Inc.
EDGAR Online, Inc.
eFax.com Inc.
e4L, Inc.
Flycast Communications Corp.
GenesisIntermedia.com Inc.
Go2net Inc.
GoTo.com, Inc.
Hoover's Inc.
Infonautics, Inc.
Infoseek Corp.
InfoSpace.com Inc.
Intelligent Life Corp.
iVillage Inc.
Launch Media, Inc.
Lycos, Inc.
Mail.com, Inc.
MapQuest.com, Inc.
MarketWatch.com Inc.
Media Metrix, Inc.
Multex.com, Inc.
NewsEDGE Corp.
OneSource Information Services, Inc.
SportsLine USA, Inc.
Student Advantage, Inc.

theglobe.com, Inc.
TheStreet.com, Inc.
TMP Worldwide Inc.
24/7 Media, Inc.
VerticalNet, Inc.
Visual Data Corp.
Wavo Corp.
Xoom.com Inc.
Yahoo! Inc.
Ziff-Davis, Inc.

Infrastructure-Carriers

AT&T Corp.
Copper Mountain Networks, Inc.
Covad Communications Group, Inc.
Exodus Communications, Inc.
IDT Corp.
MCI WORLDCOM, Inc.
NorthPoint Communications Group, Inc.
PSINet Inc.
Qwest Communications International, Inc.
RCN Corp.
Rhythms NetConnections, Inc.
Teligent, Inc.
Tut Systems Inc.
WinStar Communications, Inc.
WorldGate Communications, Inc.

Infrastructure-Hardware

Broadcom Corp.
Compaq Computer Corp.
Conexant Systems Inc.
Cylink Corp.
Dell Computer Corp.
Gateway Inc.
Intel Corp.
International Business Machines Corp.
Litronic Inc.
Metricom, Inc.
Network Computing Devices, Inc.
Rambus Inc.
Security Dynamics Technologies, Inc.
Sun Microsystems, Inc.
Terayon Communication Systems, Inc.
3Com Corp.
V-One Corp.

Classification by Industry (cont.)

Infrastructure-Software

Allaire Corp.
Ariba, Inc.
AXENT Technologies Inc.
Bottomline Technologies Inc.
BroadVision Inc.
CheckFree Holdings Corp.
Citrix Systems, Inc.
CMGI Inc.
ConnectInc.com, Co.
CyberCash, Inc.
Digital Lava Inc.
Edify Corp.
HomeCom Communications Inc.
Inktomi Corp.
InterVU Inc.
Intraware Inc.
Intuit Inc.
ISS Group, Inc.
Macromedia, Inc.
Marimba, Inc.
Microsoft Corp.
Neon Systems, Inc.
NetGravity, Inc.
Network-1 Security Solutions, Inc.
Networks Associates, Inc.
Open Market, Inc.
Open Text Corp.
Oracle Corp.
pcOrder.com, Inc.
Phone.com Inc.
Pilot Network Services, Inc.
Portal Software, Inc.
Progress Software Corp.
RealNetworks, Inc.
Rogue Wave Software, Inc.
Sagent Technology, Inc.
Security First Technologies Corp.
Silknet Software, Inc.
Software.com Inc.
Sterling Commerce, Inc.
Sybase, Inc.
TMSSequoia
USInternetworking, Inc.
Vignette Corp.
White Pine Software, Inc.

Internet Access Providers

America Online, Inc.
At Home Corp.
Earthlink Network, Inc.
FlashNet Communications Inc.
Frontline Communications Corp.
Internet America, Inc.
Log On America, Inc.
MindSpring Enterprises, Inc.
OneMain.com, Inc.
Prodigy Communications Corp.

Retail-Products & Services

Alloy Online, Inc.
Amazon.com, Inc.
Autobytel.com Inc.
Autoweb.com, Inc.
Beyond.com Corp.
Bluefly, Inc.
CDnow, Inc.
Cheap Tickets, Inc.
Cyberian Outpost, Inc.
Cybershop International, Inc.
eBay Inc.
Egghead.com, Inc.
Emusic.com, Inc.
eToys Inc.
FatBrain.com, Inc.
Getty Images, Inc.
Hollywood Entertainment Corp.
iTurf Inc.
Micro Warehouse, Inc.
Onsale, Inc.
Peapod, Inc.
Preview Travel, Inc.
Priceline.com, Inc.
Ticketmaster Online-CitySearch, Inc.
uBid Inc.
Value America, Inc.

Web Services, Consulting & Internet Presence Providers

AboveNet Communications Inc.
AppNet Systems, Inc.
Asymetrix Learning Systems, Inc.

Classification by Industry (cont.)

Web Services, Consulting & Internet Presence Providers (cont.)

C-ME.com
Cisco Systems, Inc.
Concentric Network Corp.
Critical Path, Inc.
CyberSource Corp.
Digital River, Inc.
Entrust Technologies, Inc.
Fine.com International Corp.
FVC.com, Inc.
Harbinger Corp.
Healtheon Corp.
IMALL, Inc.
iXL Enterprises, Inc.
Juno Online Services, Inc.
MERANT Plc

Modem Media.Poppe Tyson, Inc.
Mpath Interactive, Inc.
NAVIDEC, Inc.
NetSpeak Corp.
Network Solutions, Inc.
Proxicom Inc.
Ramp Networks, Inc.
Razorfish, Inc.
RoweCom Inc.
Sapient Corp.
Secure Computing Corp.
Spyglass, Inc.
THINK New Ideas, Inc.
USWeb Corp.
Verio Inc.
Verisign Inc.
Viant Corp.
WebTrends Corp.

HOW TO USE THIS BOOK

The presentation of background information plus current and historical data provides the answers to three basic questions for each company:

1. What does the company do? (See G.)
2. How has it done in the past? (See B, D, E, I, J.)
3. How is it doing now? (See D, E, F, H.)

The following information is highlighted:

A. CAPSULE STOCK INFORMATION – This section shows the stock symbol, plus the approximate yield afforded by the indicated dividend, based on a recent price, and the price earnings ratio calculated on earnings from the most recent four quarters.

B. LONG-TERM PRICE CHART – This chart illustrates the pattern of monthly stock price movements, fully adjusted for stock dividends and splits. The chart points out the degree of volatility in the price movement of the company's stock and reveals its long-term trend. It indicates areas of price support and resistance, plus other technical points to be considered by the investor. The bars at the base of the long-term price chart indicate the monthly trading volume.

C. PRICE SCORES – Below each company's price/volume chart are its *Mergent FIS Price Scores*. These are basic measures of the stock's performance. Each stock is measured against the New York Stock Exchange Composite Index.

A score of 100 indicates that the stock did as well as the New York Stock Exchange Composite Index during the time period. A score of less than 100 means that the stock did not do as well; a score of more than 100 means that the stock outperformed the NYSE Composite Index.

The *7 YEAR PRICE SCORE* mirrors the common stock's price growth over the previous seven years. The higher the price score, the better the relative performance. It is based

on the ratio of the latest 12-month average price to the current seven year average. This ratio is then indexed against the same ratio for the market as a whole (the New York Stock Exchange Composite Index), which is taken as 100.

The *12 MONTH PRICE SCORE* is a similar measurement but for a shorter period of time. It is based on the ratio of the latest two-month average price to the current 12-month average. As was done for the Long-Term Price Score, this ratio is also indexed to the same ratio for the market as a whole. In both cases, all prices are adjusted for all stock dividends and splits.

D. INTERIM EARNINGS (Per Share) – Figures are reported before effect of extraordinary items, discontinued operations and cumulative effects of accounting changes (unless otherwise noted). Each figure is for the quarterly period indicated, unless otherwise noted. These figures are essentially as reported by the company, although all figures are adjusted for all stock dividends and splits. See 'Earnings Per Share' below.

E. INTERIM DIVIDENDS (Per Share) – The cash dividends are the actual dollar amounts declared by the company. No adjustments have been made for stock dividends and splits. **Ex-Dividend Date**: a stockholder must purchase the stock prior to this date in order to be entitled to the dividend. The **Record Date** indicates the date on which the shareholder had to have been a holder of record in order to have qualified for the dividend. The **Payable Date** indicates the date the company paid or intends to pay the dividend. The cash amount shown in the first column is followed by a letter (example ''Q'' for quarterly) to indicate the frequency of the dividend.

Indicated Dividend – This is the annualized amount (fully adjusted for splits) of the latest regular cash dividend.

F. CAPITALIZATION – These are certain items in the company's capital account. Both

35

ILLUSTRATIVE, INC.

YIELD 0.4%
P/E RATIO 19.6

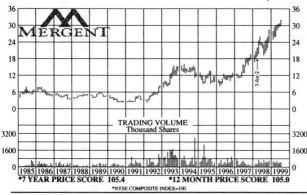

INTERIM EARNINGS (Per Share):				
Qtr.	Mar.	June	Sept.	Dec.
1996	0.20	0.26	0.17	0.21
1997	0.14	0.29	0.25	0.37
1998	0.27	0.30	0.31	0.40
1999	0.34	0.29	...	...

INTERIM DIVIDENDS (Per Share):				
Amt.	Decl.	Ex.	Rec.	Pay.
0.075S	11/24/97	11/26/97	11/28/97	12/12/97
3-for-2	1/23/98	3/02/98	2/13/98	2/27/98
0.055S	5/12/98	5/27/98	5/29/98	6/19/98
0.055S	11/22/98	11/23/98	11/25/98	12/06/98
0.055S	5/10/99	5/17/99	5/21/99	5/30/99

Indicated div.: $0.11

TRADING VOLUME
Thousand Shares

*7 YEAR PRICE SCORE 105.4   *12 MONTH PRICE SCORE 105.0
*NYSE COMPOSITE INDEX=100

CAPITALIZATION (12/31/98):		
	($000)	(%)
Long-Term Debt	15,456	18.1
Common & Surplus	69,762	81.9
Total	85,218	100.0

RECENT DEVELOPMENTS: On 6/5/99, ILLU announced that it had signed a letter of intent to purchase Bratton, Inc. and Lakeside Systems Co., Inc. Both companies provide integrated security systems used in transportation and marine operations. The acquisitions are expected to be completed during the second half of 1999. For the three months ended 6/30/99, net earnings soared 94.2% to $3.6 million, or

$0.29 per share (diluted). Net sales climbed 68.3% to $60.6 million versus $36.0 million the previous year. Railroad mergers have spurred market demand for services and products due to the resulting consolidation of operating systems. Gross profit surged 51.9% to $12.4 million from $8.2 million a year ago. Order backlog at 6/30/99 advanced to $187.4 million from $102.2 million in 1997.

BUSINESS

ILLUSTRATIVE, INC. is a major supplier of transportation, communication and security products in North America. The Company manufactures an extensive line of railroad and marine signal and communication equipment, traffic control systems, grade crossing hardware, and allied components. In addition, ILLU designs complete security programs for industrial and scientific corporations. It provides custom-designed data protection programs for clients and manufactures security products from sensors to virus-prevention software. The Company operates six facilities. Three are in Illinois and the others are in Tijeras, New Mexico; Silver Spring, Maryland, and New Haven, Connecticut.

QUARTERLY DATA

12/31/98 ($000)	REV	INC
First Quarter	35,988	1,448
Second Quarter.........	47,621	2,987
Third Quarter............	56,125	2,639
Fourth Quarter	73,796	3,889

ANNUAL FINANCIAL DATA

	12/31/98	12/31/97	12/31/96	12/31/95	12/31/94	12/31/93	12/31/92
Earnings Per Share	1.06	0.91	0.67	0.77	0.74	①②0.58	①0.38
Cash Flow Per Share	1.60	1.40	1.05	1.04	0.97	0.82	0.65
Tang. Book Val. Per Share	5.80	4.91	4.07	3.48	3.48	1.86	0.94
Dividends Per Share	0.10	0.10	0.10	0.10	...	...	...
Dividend Payout %	9.4	11.0	14.9	12.9	...	...	...
INCOME STATEMENT (IN THOUSANDS):							
Total Revenues	213,530	175,440	136,780	119,703	99,295	81,899	70,934
Costs & Expenses	189,244	154,901	121,153	104,217	85,729	71,656	61,198
Depreciation & Amort.	5,639	5,004	3,906	2,621	2,121	1,936	2,022
Operating Income	18,380	15,578	11,787	12,899	11,465	8,304	6,768
Net Interest Inc./(Exp.)	d1,219	d724	d741	d264	d427	d1,318	d2,160
Income Before Income Taxes	17,583	15,105	11,180	12,685	11,077	7,076	4,608
Income Taxes	6,622	5,775	4,294	5,046	4,193	2,498	1,688
Equity Earnings/Minority Int.	d330	...	...	...	...	...	...
Net Income	10,961	9,330	6,886	7,639	6,884	①②4,578	①2,920
Cash Flow	16,600	14,334	10,792	10,260	9,005	6,514	4,942
Average Shs. Outstg.	10,374	10,266	10,241	9,851	9,318	7,913	7,599
BALANCE SHEET (IN THOUSANDS):							
Cash & Cash Equivalents	6,748	...	...	250	3,065	443	357
Total Current Assets	96,352	73,030	56,841	42,730	37,030	25,586	23,336
Net Property	24,029	17,932	14,177	11,069	9,023	7,454	7,117
Total Assets	135,769	104,677	86,845	68,395	53,000	38,488	36,575
Total Current Liabilities	46,029	39,401	21,827	21,060	16,240	14,846	13,676
Long-Term Obligations	15,456	3,412	12,090	733	439	4,898	11,915
Net Stockholders' Equity	69,762	57,939	49,232	43,063	33,086	15,197	7,377
Net Working Capital	50,323	33,629	35,014	21,670	20,790	10,740	9,660
Year-end Shs. Outstg.	10,521	10,244	10,209	10,092	9,492	8,076	7,497
STATISTICAL RECORD:							
Operating Profit Margin %	8.6	8.9	8.6	10.8	11.5	10.1	9.5
Net Profit Margin %	5.1	5.3	5.0	6.4	6.9	5.6	4.1
Return on Equity %	15.7	16.1	14.0	17.7	20.8	30.1	39.6
Return on Assets %	8.1	8.9	7.9	11.2	13.0	11.9	8.0
Debt/Total Assets %	11.4	3.3	13.9	1.1	0.8	12.7	32.6
Price Range	31¹¹/₁₆-11	13-8	13¹¹/₁₆-8¹¹/₁₆	16³/₁₆-11	15¹/₂-7³/₄	8⁷/₁₆-2¹/₄	4¹³/₁₆-2⁵/₁₆
P/E Ratio	18.6-10.4	14.3-8.8	20.3-13.2	20.9-14.2	20.9-10.5	14.5-3.9	12.7-6.1
Average Yield %	0.7	1.0	0.9	0.7	...	...	...

Statistics are as originally reported. Adj. for stk. split: 3-for-2, 2/27/98 ① Bef. disc. oper. gain 12/31/92: $165,000 ($0.02/sh.); 12/31/91: $2.5 mill. ($0.33/sh.) ② Bef. extraord. credit $273,000 ($0.03/sh.)

OFFICERS:
S. E. Wells, Chmn.
C. E. Willis, C.E.O. & Pres.
S. M. Scott, Exec. V.P., Treas. & Sec.

INVESTOR CONTACT: J. Miller, V.P., Investor Relations, (312) 555-3384

PRINCIPAL OFFICE: 5555 North Shore Parkway, Chicago, IL 60611

TELEPHONE NUMBER: (312) 555-1234
FAX: (312) 555-5678
WEB: www.illustrative.com

NO. OF EMPLOYEES: 3,200

SHAREHOLDERS: 1,200 (approx.)

ANNUAL MEETING: In April

INCORPORATED: IL, 1951

INSTITUTIONAL HOLDINGS:
No. of Institutions: 63
Shares Held: 4,184,110
% Held: 39.8

INDUSTRY: Communications equipment, nec (SIC: 3669)

TRANSFER AGENT(S): First Union National Bank, Charlotte, NC

the dollar amounts and their respective percentages are given.

Long-term Debt is the total amount of debt owed by the company which is due beyond one year.

Capital Lease Obligations is shown as a separate caption when indicated on the balance sheet as such.

Deferred Income Taxes represents the company's tax liability arising from accelerated depreciation and investment tax credit.

Preferred Stock is the sum of equity issues, exclusive of common stock, the holders of which have a prior claim, ahead of the common shareholders, to the income of the company while it continues to operate and to the assets in the event of dissolution.

Minority Interest in this instance is a capital item which reflects the share of ownership by an outside party in a consolidated subsidiary of the company.

Common and Surplus is the sum of the stated or par value of the common stock, plus additional paid-in capital and retained earnings less the dollar amount of treasury shares.

G. COMPANY BUSINESS – This section explains what the company does: the products or services it sells, its markets and production facilities.

H. RECENT DEVELOPMENTS – This section keeps you up to date on what has happened in the most recent quarter for which results are available. In addition to analysis of recently released sales and earnings figures, items covered include, where applicable and available, new product introductions, capital expenditures, expanded operations, acquisitions, divestitures, labor developments, equity or debt financing, substantial stock repurchases, the rate of incoming orders and the level of backlog.

I. ANNUAL FINANCIAL DATA – These figures are fully adjusted for all stock dividends and stock splits.

Earnings Per Share are as reported by the company except for adjustment for certain items as footnoted. Earnings per share

reported after 12/15/97 a re presented on a diluted basis, as described by Financial Accounting Standards Board Statement 128. Earnings per share reported prior to that date are shown on a primary basis.

Cash Flow Per Share is computed by dividing the total of net income and non-cash depreciation and amortization charges, less preferred dividends, by average shares outstanding.

Tangible Book Value Per Share is calculated by dividing tangible assets at fiscal year-end by shares outstanding. It demonstrates the underlying value of each common share if the company were to be liquidated as of that date.

Dividends Per Share represent the sum of all cash payments on a calendar year basis. Any fiscal year ending prior to June 30, for example, is shown with dividends for the prior calendar year.

Dividend Payout % is the percentage of cash paid out of **Earnings Per Share**.

J. INCOME STATEMENT, BALANCE SHEET AND STATISTICAL RECORD – Here is pertinent earnings and balance sheet information essential to analyzing a corporation's performance. The comparisons, each year shown as originally reported, provide the necessary historical perspective to intelligently review the various operating and financial trends. Generic definitions follow.

INCOME STATEMENT:

Total Revenues is the total income from operations including non-operating revenues.

Costs and Expenses is the total of all costs related to the operation of the business – including cost of sales, selling, and general and administrative expenses. Excluded items are depreciation, interest and non-operating expenses.

Depreciation and Amortization includes all non-cash charges such as depletion and amortization as well as depreciation.

Operating Income is the profit remaining after deducting depreciation as well as all operating costs and expenses from the company's net sales and revenues. This figure is *before* interest expenses, extraordinary gains and charges, and income and expense items of a non-operating nature.

Net Interest Income/(Expense) is the net amount of interest paid and received by a company during the fiscal year.

Income Before Income Taxes is the remaining income *after* deducting all costs, expenses, property charges, interest, etc. but *before* deducting income taxes.

Equity Earnings/Minority Interest is the net amount of profits allocated to minority owners or affiliates.

Income Taxes are shown as reported by the company and include both the amount of current taxes actually paid out and the amount deferred to future years.

Net Income is as reported by the corporation, before extraordinary gains and losses, discontinued operations and accounting changes, which are appropriately footnoted.

Cash Flow is the sum of net income and non-cash depreciation and amortization charges, less preferred dividends.

Average Shares Outstanding is the weighted average number of shares including common equivalent shares outstanding during the year, as reported by the corporation and fully adjusted for all stock dividends and splits. The use of *average shares* minimizes the distortion in *earnings per share* which could result from issuance of a large amount of stock or the company's purchase of a large amount of its own stock during the year.

BALANCE SHEET:

All balance sheet items are shown as reported by the corporation in its annual report. Because of the limited amount of space available and in an effort to simplify and standardize accounts, some items have been combined.

Cash & Cash Equivalents comprise unrestricted cash and temporary investments in marketable securities, such as U.S. Government securities, certificates of deposit and short-term investments.

Total Current Assets are all of the company's short-term assets, including cash, mar-

ketable securities, inventories, certain receivables, etc., as reported.

Net Property is total fixed assets, including all property, land, plants, buildings, equipment, fixtures, etc., less accumulated depreciation.

Total Assets represent the sum of all tangible and intangible assets as reported by the company.

Total Current Liabilities are all of the obligations of the company due within one year, as reported.

Long-term Obligations are total long-term debts (due beyond one year) reported by the company, including bonds, capital lease obligations, notes, mortgages, debentures, etc.

Net Stockholders' Equity is the sum of all capital stock accounts – stated values of preferred and common stock, paid-in capital, earned surplus (retained earnings), etc., net of all treasury stock.

Net Working Capital is derived by subtracting Current Liabilities from Current Assets.

Year-end Shares Outstanding are the number of shares outstanding as of the date of the company's annual report, exclusive of treasury stock and adjusted for subsequent stock dividends and splits.

STATISTICAL RECORD:

Operating Profit Margin indicates operating profit as a percentage of net sales or revenues.

Net Profit Margin is the percentage of total revenues remaining after the deduction of all non-extraordinary costs, including interest and taxes.

Return on Equity is one of several measures of profitability. It is the ratio of net income to net stockholders' equity, expressed as a percentage. This ratio illustrates how effectively the investment of the stockholders is being utilized to earn a profit.

Return on Assets is another means of measuring profitability. It is the ratio of net income to total assets, expressed as a percentage. This indicates how effectively the corporate assets are being used to generate profits.

Debt/Total Assets represents the ratio of long-term obligations to total assets as a percentage.

Price/Earnings Ratio is shown as a range. The figures are calculated by dividing the stock's highest price for the year and its lowest price by the year's earnings per share. Prices are for calendar years. Earnings used in the calculation for a particular calendar year are for the fiscal year in which the majority of the company's business took place. As a rule, for companies whose fiscal years end before June 30, the ratio is calculated by using the price range of the prior calendar year. For those with fiscal years ending on June 30 or later, the current year's price range is used.

Average Yield is the ratio (expressed as a percentage) of the annual dividend to the mean price of the common stock (average of the high and low for the year). Both prices and dividends are for calendar years.

EDITOR'S NOTE: In order to preserve the historical relationships between prices, earnings and dividends, figures are not restated to reflect subsequent events.

K. ADDITIONAL INFORMATION – For each stock, listings are provided for the company's officers, date of incorporation, its address, telephone number, fax number and website (when available), annual meeting date, the number of employees, the number of stockholders, institutional holdings, and transfer agent.

Institutional Holdings indicates the number of investment companies, insurance companies, bank trust and college endowment funds holding the stock and the total number of shares held as last reported. Coverage includes investment companies, mutual funds, insurance companies, and banks reporting under rule 13(F) to the Securities & Exchange Commission.

ABBREVIATIONS
AND
SYMBOLS

d	Deficit
E	Extra
M	Monthly
N.M.	Not Meaningful
p	Preliminary
P.F.	Pro Forma
Q.	Quarterly
r.	Revised
S	Semi-annual
Sp	Special Dividend
Y	Year-end Dividend

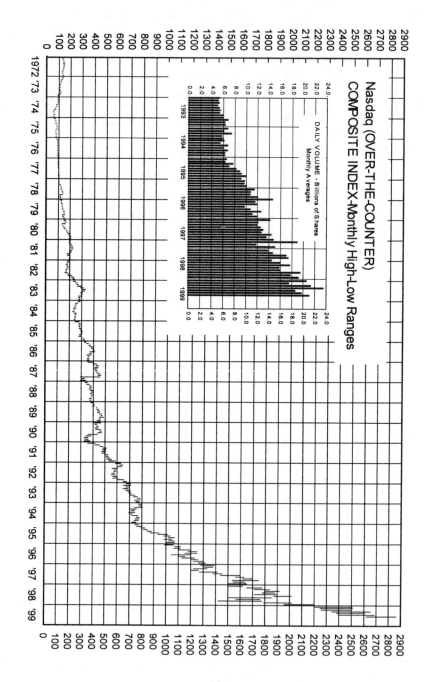

Nasdaq (OVER-THE-COUNTER)
COMPOSITE INDEX-Monthly High-Low Ranges

DAILY VOLUME - Billions of Shares
Monthly Averages

40

NASDAQ SYMBOL BOUT
Rec. Pr. 31⅜ (7/31/99)

ABOUT.COM, INC.

YIELD ...
P/E RATIO ...

INTERIM EARNINGS (Per Share):

Qtr.	Mar.	June	Sept.	Dec.
1997	----------------d4.94----------------			
1998	----------------d9.71----------------			
1999	d4.07	d1.71	...	...

INTERIM DIVIDENDS (Per Share):

Amt.	Decl.	Ex.	Rec.	Pay.
	No dividends paid.			

TRADING VOLUME
Thousand Shares

*7 YEAR PRICE SCORE N/A   *12 MONTH PRICE SCORE N/A

*NYSE COMPOSITE INDEX=100

CAPITALIZATION (12/31/98):

	($000)	(%)
Long-Term Debt	621	7.6
Capital Lease Obligations..	149	1.8
Redeemable Pfd. Stock	32,072	392.1
Common & Surplus	d24,662	-301.5
Total	8,180	100.0

RECENT DEVELOPMENTS: For the quarter ended 6/30/99, the Company reported a net loss of $20.7 million versus a net loss of $2.8 million in the corresponding 1998 period. Results included non-cash compensation charges of $242,000 in 1999 versus $31,000 in 1998. Revenues surged to $3.7 million from $396,000 the year before. Gross profit improved to $779,000 versus a gross loss of $348,000 the year before. During the quarter, BOUT acquired Vantage Net, Inc., a provider of polling services on the Internet. In June, through an agreement with Broadcast.com, BOUT launched a live, all-talk Internet radio program ''Talking ABOUT This Week'' showcasing the expertise of the Company's network of guides. In May 1999, BOUT entered into an e-commerce alliance with Borders.com to develop co-branded bookstores across the About.com network.

BUSINESS

ABOUT.COM, Inc. (formerly MiningCo.com) is an Internet news, information and entertainment service. The Company's service is a network of over 650 Web sites, each of which focuses on a specific topic and is overseen by a professional guide. Through these GuideSites™, the guides create and maintain Internet directories that include approximately 400,000 pre-screened links to other Web sites, which are summarized by the guides, enabling users to find relevant Internet content. The GuideSite network also provides original content, consisting primarily of text, that is created regularly by the guides on thousands of subjects.

ANNUAL FINANCIAL DATA

	12/31/98	12/31/97	① 12/31/96
Earnings Per Share	d9.71	d4.94	d1.20
Cash Flow Per Share	d8.97	d4.77	d1.18
INCOME STATEMENT (IN THOUSANDS):			
Total Revenues	3,722	391	...
Costs & Expenses	17,331	8,429	2,351
Depreciation & Amort.	1,282	303	29
Operating Income	d14,892	d8,341	d2,381
Net Interest Inc./(Exp.)	d686	d649	d57
Income Before Income Taxes	d15,578	d8,640	d2,438
Net Income	d15,578	d8,640	d2,438
Cash Flow	d15,526	8,337	d2,409
Average Shs. Outstg.	1,732	1,749	2,035
BALANCE SHEET (IN THOUSANDS):			
Cash & Cash Equivalents	10,644	303	...
Total Current Assets	11,662	422	...
Net Property	3,302	748	...
Total Assets	15,658	1,357	...
Total Current Liabilities	7,430	3,519	...
Long-Term Obligations	770	8,733	...
Net Stockholders' Equity	d24,662	d10,944	...
Net Working Capital	4,231	d3,098	...
Year-end Shs. Outstg.	2,203	1,475	...
STATISTICAL RECORD:			
Debt/Total Assets %	4.9	643.5	...

Statistics are as originally reported. ① Period from 6/27/96 (inception) to 12/31/96.

OFFICERS:
S. P. Kurnit, Chmn., Pres., C.E.O.
A. P. Blaustein, Sr. V.P., Gen. Couns.
T. B. Sloan, C.F.O.
W. C. Day, C.O.O.

INVESTOR CONTACT: Lorraine Sahagian, (212) 849-2000

PRINCIPAL OFFICE: 220 East 42nd Street, 24th Floor, New York, NY 10017

TELEPHONE NUMBER: (212) 849-2000
FAX: (212) 818-1376
WEB: www.about.com

NO. OF EMPLOYEES: 113

SHAREHOLDERS: 59

ANNUAL MEETING: N/A

INCORPORATED: NY, Jun., 1996; reincorp., DE, Dec., 1998

No. of Institutions: 35
Shares Held: 935,870
% Held: 7.8

INDUSTRY: Computer integrated systems design (SIC: 7373)

TRANSFER AGENT(S): American Stock Transfer & Trust Company, New York, NY

ABOVENET COMMUNICATIONS INC.

YIELD ...
P/E RATIO ...

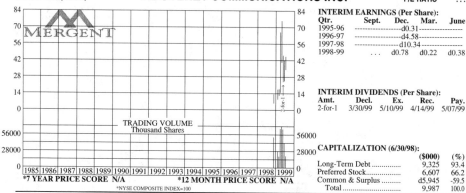

INTERIM EARNINGS (Per Share):

Qtr.	Sept.	Dec.	Mar.	June
1995-96		d0.31		
1996-97		d4.58		
1997-98		d10.34		
1998-99	...	d0.78	d0.22	d0.38

INTERIM DIVIDENDS (Per Share):

Amt.	Decl.	Ex.	Rec.	Pay.
2-for-1	3/30/99	5/10/99	4/14/99	5/07/99

CAPITALIZATION (6/30/98):

	($000)	(%)
Long-Term Debt	9,325	93.4
Preferred Stock	6,607	66.2
Common & Surplus	d5,945	-59.5
Total	9,987	100.0

TRADING VOLUME
Thousand Shares

*7 YEAR PRICE SCORE N/A   *12 MONTH PRICE SCORE N/A

*NYSE COMPOSITE INDEX=100

RECENT DEVELOPMENTS: On 6/23/99, the Company announced that it had entered into an agreement to be acquired by Metromedia Fiber Network, Inc., an international provider of dedicated fiber optic networks. Under the terms of the agreement, each share of ABOV common stock will be exchanged for 1.175 shares of Metromedia class A common stock. The transaction is expected to be completed during the third quarter of 1999, subject to approval by shareholders of both companies and other customary closing conditions. For the fiscal year ended 6/30/99, net loss totaled $26.6 million versus a loss of $5.4 million the year before. Results in the recent period included one-time charges of $3.4 million stemming from accelerated telecommunications costs and merger-related expenses. Revenues jumped to $14.0 million from $3.4 million in the previous year.

BUSINESS

ABOVENET COMMUNICATIONS INC. is a provider of high performance, managed co-location and Internet connectivity services for companies that depend on the Web to do business. The Company has developed the Internet Service Exchange™, a network that brings together Internet service providers and content providers in a centralized facility featuring direct-route backbone connectivity, access to ABOV's huge bandwidth and co-located clients, optimal routing programs, and security. The Company derives most of its revenues from bandwidth charges, with additional revenues generated from charges to access ABOV's network, proprietary tools and management services, and one-time installation fees.

ANNUAL FINANCIAL DATA

	6/30/98	6/30/97	[1] 6/30/96
Earnings Per Share	d10.34	[2] d4.58	d0.31
Cash Flow Per Share	d9.43	d4.25	d0.10
INCOME STATEMENT (IN THOUSANDS):			
Total Revenues	3,436	552	79
Costs & Expenses	8,288	2,223	105
Depreciation & Amort.	476	133	52
Operating Income	d5,327	d1,804	d78
Net Interest Inc./(Exp.)	d98	1	...
Net Income	d5,425	[2] d1,803	d78
Cash Flow	d4,949	d1,670	d26
Average Shs. Outstg.	525	393	250
BALANCE SHEET (IN THOUSANDS):			
Cash & Cash Equivalents	8,141	331	...
Total Current Assets	8,768	372	...
Net Property	4,436	766	...
Total Assets	13,693	1,171	...
Total Current Liabilities	3,707	1,318	...
Long-Term Obligations	9,325	116	...
Net Stockholders' Equity	661	d262	...
Net Working Capital	5,061	d946	...
Year-end Shs. Outstg.	729	406	...
STATISTICAL RECORD:			
Debt/Total Assets %	68.1	9.9	...
Price Range	13⁷/16-5¾	...	...

Statistics are as originally reported. Adj. for 2-for-1 stk. split, 5/7/99. [1] From inception, 3/8/96 through 6/30/96. [2] Incl. non-recurr. chrg. $431,100.

OFFICERS:
S. Tuan, Chmn., C.E.O.
P. C. Chen, Vice-Chmn.
W. J. Kaplan, Pres., C.O.O.
D. F. Larson, Sr. V.P., C.F.O.

PRINCIPAL OFFICE: 50 W. San Fernando Street, Suite 1010, San Jose, CA 95113

TELEPHONE NUMBER: (408) 367-6666
WEB: www.abovenet.com

NO. OF EMPLOYEES: 78 (avg.)

SHAREHOLDERS: 91

ANNUAL MEETING: N/A

INCORPORATED: CA, Mar., 1996; reincorp., DE, Nov., 1998

INSTITUTIONAL HOLDINGS:
No. of Institutions: 48
Shares Held: 4,914,934
% Held: 15.8

INDUSTRY: Computer programming services (SIC: 7371)

TRANSFER AGENT(S): Boston Equiserve L.P., Canton, MA.

ADFORCE, INC.

YIELD ...
P/E RATIO ...

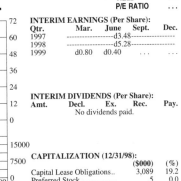

7 YEAR PRICE SCORE N/A   **12 MONTH PRICE SCORE N/A**
*NYSE COMPOSITE INDEX=100

TRADING VOLUME
Thousand Shares

1985|1986|1987|1988|1989|1990|1991|1992|1993|1994|1995|1996|1997|1998|1999

INTERIM EARNINGS (Per Share):

Qtr.	Mar.	June	Sept.	Dec.
1997		d3.48		
1998		d5.28		
1999	d0.80	d0.40	...	...

INTERIM DIVIDENDS (Per Share):

Amt.	Decl.	Ex.	Rec.	Pay.
	No dividends paid.			

CAPITALIZATION (12/31/98):

	($000)	(%)
Capital Lease Obligations..	3,089	19.2
Preferred Stock.................	5	0.0
Common & Surplus	12,976	80.7
Total	16,070	100.0

RECENT DEVELOPMENTS: For the second quarter ended 6/30/99, the Company recorded a net loss of $5.2 million compared with a net loss of $4.1 million in the corresponding quarter the year before. Net revenue soared to $4.2 million from $784,000 in the comparable quarter a year earlier. Net revenue growth was primarily due to the increased volume of ads delivered on behalf of customers, partially offset by a decrease in the average rate charged. The rate decline was due to competitive pressures and discounts for high-volume customers. Ad volumes skyrocketed to 18.4 billion versus 1.6 billion due to ad volume growth among existing customers and the addition of new customers. Ad volume was partially offset by the loss of a major customer, GeoCities, which contributed approximately 12.0% of the Company's revenue. Gross profit as a percentage of revenue improved to 24.4% versus a negative 95.0% due to higher ad delivery and lower fixed costs.

BUSINESS

ADFORCE, INC. provides centralized, outsourced advertising management and delivery services that enable on-line publishers, rep firms, advertising agencies, and advertisers to utilize the Internet as the first fully interactive medium. The Company distributes advanced scalable technology, supported by large data centers, which delivers billions of ad impressions for its customers. The Company offers a suite of products that allows advertisers and publishers to target, deliver, track, measure and analyze Internet advertising programs. In May 1999, the Company completed its initial public offering of common stock. The Company's three largest customers are AdSmart, 24/7 Media, and NetScape.

ANNUAL FINANCIAL DATA

	12/31/98	12/31/97
Earnings Per Share	d5.28	d3.48
Cash Flow Per Share	d7.20	d2.90
INCOME STATEMENT (IN THOUSANDS):		
Total Revenues	4,286	320
Costs & Expenses	24,620	5,119
Depreciation & Amort.	d5,465	797
Operating Income	d14,869	d5,596
Net Interest Inc./(Exp.)	d151	d108
Income Before Income Taxes	d15,020	d5,704
Net Income	d15,020	d5,704
Cash Flow	d20,485	d4,907
Average Shs. Outstg.	2,844	1,693
BALANCE SHEET (IN THOUSANDS):		
Cash & Cash Equivalents	10,045	1,680
Total Current Assets	11,780	2,323
Net Property	4,208	1,946
Total Assets	19,875	4,269
Total Current Liabilities	3,805	1,150
Long-Term Obligations	3,089	1,744
Net Stockholders' Equity	12,981	1,375
Net Working Capital	7,975	1,173
Year-end Shs. Outstg.	14,484	...
STATISTICAL RECORD:		
Debt/Total Assets %	15.5	40.9

Statistics are as originally reported.

OFFICERS:
C. W. Berger, Chmn., C.E.O. & Pres.
J. A. Tanner, Exec. V.P. & C.F.O.
R. S. Jackson, V.P., Sec. & Gen. Couns.

INVESTOR CONTACT: Sheryl Draisen, (408) 873-3693

PRINCIPAL OFFICE: 10101 North De Anza Boulevard, Suite 210, Cupertino, CA 95014

TELEPHONE NUMBER: (408) 873-3680
FAX: (408) 873-3693
WEB: www.adforce.com

NO. OF EMPLOYEES: 97 (avg.)

SHAREHOLDERS: 147
ANNUAL MEETING: N/A

INCORPORATED: CA, Jan., 1996; reincorp., DE, Mar., 1999

INSTITUTIONAL HOLDINGS:
No. of Institutions: 3
Shares Held: 79,300
% Held: 0.0

INDUSTRY: Communication services, nec (SIC: 4899)

TRANSFER AGENT(S): ChaseMellon Shareholder Services, Ridgefield Park, NJ

NASDAQ SYMBOL ALLR
Rec. Pr. 44⅛ (7/31/99)

ALLAIRE CORP.

YIELD ...
P/E RATIO ...

INTERIM EARNINGS (Per Share):

Qtr.	Mar.	June	Sept.	Dec.
1996			d0.97	
1997			d4.40	
1998			d3.67	
1999	d0.19	d0.26	...	...

INTERIM DIVIDENDS (Per Share):

Amt.	Decl.	Ex.	Rec.	Pay.
	No dividends paid.			

TRADING VOLUME
Thousand Shares

1985|1986|1987|1988|1989|1990|1991|1992|1993|1994|1995|1996|1997|1998|1999
*7 YEAR PRICE SCORE N/A   *12 MONTH PRICE SCORE N/A
*NYSE COMPOSITE INDEX=100

CAPITALIZATION (12/31/98):

	($000)	(%)
Long-Term Debt	1,034	...
Capital Lease Obligations..	159	...
Redeemable Pfd. Stock	12,673	...
Preferred Stock..................	751	...
Common & Surplus	d19,226	...
Total	d-4,609	100.0

RECENT DEVELOPMENTS: For the quarter ended 6/30/99, the Company reported a net loss of $2.9 million versus a net loss of $3.8 million in the corresponding period of the prior year. The recent quarter's net loss included merger costs of $2.7 million related to the recent acquisitions of Bright Tiger Technologies, Inc. and Live Software, Inc. Total revenues more than doubled to $13.1 million from $4.8 million the year before. Gross profit more than tripled to $10.6 million, or 81.7% of total revenue, versus $3.5 million, or 72.9% of total revenue, in the prior-year quarter. During the second quarter, ALLR's technology was adopted by industry-leading companies including Sony Pictures Entertainment/Columbia Tri-Star Interactive, Cheap Tickets, Inc., AT&T Wireless Services, Travelscape.com and Bank of America. During the second quarter, ALLR also announced ColdFusion Express, a free limited functionality edition of its Web application server.

BUSINESS

ALLAIRE CORPORATION develops, markets and supports software for a wide range of Web development, from building static Web pages to developing high-volume, interactive Web applications. ALLR's products and services enable organizations to link their information systems to the Web, as well as to develop new Web-based business applications in areas such as electronic commerce, content management and personalization. The Company's products operate with emerging Web application technologies as well as key enterprise information system technologies. COLDFUSION is the Company's key product line. It is designed to employ an easy-to-learn software development language that allows developers to quickly and efficiently create Web applications.

REVENUES

12/31/1998	($000)	(%)
Software license fees.	17,187	83.7
Services	3,325	16.3
Total revenue.............	20,512	100.0

ANNUAL FINANCIAL DATA

	12/31/98	12/31/97	12/26/96
Earnings Per Share	d3.67	d4.40	d0.97
Cash Flow Per Share	d3.20	d3.97	d0.92
INCOME STATEMENT (IN THOUSANDS):			
Total Revenues	20,512	7,650	2,358
Costs & Expenses	29,870	14,536	3,976
Depreciation & Amort.	1,378	726	94
Operating Income	d10,736	d7,612	d1,712
Net Interest Inc./(Exp.)	d34	187	14
Income Before Income Taxes	d10,770	d7,425	d1,698
Net Income	d10,770	d7,425	d1,698
Cash Flow	d9,392	d6,699	d1,604
Average Shs. Outstg.	2,938	1,687	1,743
BALANCE SHEET (IN THOUSANDS):			
Cash & Cash Equivalents	1,847	5,521	526
Total Current Assets	6,049	7,170	1,230
Net Property	3,484	2,209	568
Total Assets	9,953	9,697	2,038
Total Current Liabilities	14,562	5,678	1,006
Long-Term Obligations	1,193	499	...
Net Stockholders' Equity	d18,475	d9,153	d1,768
Net Working Capital	d8,513	1,492	224
Year-end Shs. Outstg.	4,145	3,002	3,002
STATISTICAL RECORD:			
Debt/Total Assets %	12.0	5.1	...
Statistics are as originally reported.			

OFFICERS:
J. J. Allaire, Chmn. , Exec. V.P., Products
D. J. Orfao, Pres., C.E.O.
D. A. Gerth, V.P., C.F.O., Treas.

INVESTOR CONTACT: JoAnne Trayer, Investor Relations, (617)761-2020

PRINCIPAL OFFICE: One Alewife Center, Cambridge, MA 02140

TELEPHONE NUMBER: (617) 761-2000
FAX: (617) 761-2001
WEB: www.allaire.com

NO. OF EMPLOYEES: 165 (avg.)

SHAREHOLDERS: 146

ANNUAL MEETING: In June

INCORPORATED: MN, 1996

INSTITUTIONAL HOLDINGS:
No. of Institutions: 35
Shares Held: 3,246,430
% Held: 31.0

INDUSTRY: Prepackaged software (SIC: 7372)

TRANSFER AGENT(S): Boston Equiserve L.P. Canton, MA

NASDAQ SYMBOL ALOY
Rec. Pr. 11¾ (7/31/99)

ALLOY ONLINE, INC.

YIELD ...
P/E RATIO ...

INTERIM EARNINGS (Per Share):

Qtr.	Apr.	July	Oct.	Jan.
1996-97		d0.03		
1997-98		d0.31		
1998-99		d0.72		
1999-00	d0.26	...	...	...

INTERIM DIVIDENDS (Per Share):

Amt.	Decl.	Ex.	Rec.	Pay.
		No dividends paid.		

CAPITALIZATION (1/31/99):

	($000)	(%)
Long-Term Debt	3,945	68.3
Capital Lease Obligations..	40	0.7
Redeemable Pfd. Stock	4,836	83.7
Common & Surplus	d3,046	-52.7
Total	5,775	100.0

RECENT DEVELOPMENTS: For the quarter ended 4/30/99, the Company recorded a net loss of $2.3 million compared with a net loss of $1.3 million in the corresponding quarter the year before. Net revenues jumped 88.6% to $2.6 million from $1.4 million a year earlier. Net merchandise revenues grew 76.8% to $2.4 million from $1.4 million primarily due to growth in orders fueled by the Company's expanded database of buyers and prospects. Sponsorship and other revenues totaled $163,000 compared with immaterial revenues in the equivalent 1998 quarter. Gross profit as a percentage of net revenues increased to 51.1% versus 33.1% in the previous year. This increase was the result of strong retail demand for the Company's merchandise, efficient inventory control, and the growth of high margin sponsorship and other revenues. As of 4/30/99, the Company's on-line user base had grown 90.0% to 570,000 registrants versus 300,000 registrants on 1/31/99. The Company is currently adding approximately 3,000 registrants per day.

BUSINESS

ALLOY ONLINE, INC. is a Web site and direct marketer serving the interests of Generation Y (10 through 24 year olds) consumers by providing community, content, and commerce services. Through these services, young adults can interact, share information, explore various content, and shop for apparel, accessories, footwear, music, cosmetics and magazine subscriptions. The Company completed its initial public offering in May 1999.

ANNUAL FINANCIAL DATA

	1/31/99	1/31/98	1/31/97
Earnings Per Share	d0.72	d0.31	d0.03
Cash Flow Per Share	d0.71	d0.31	d0.03
Tang. Book Val. Per Share	...	0.32	...
INCOME STATEMENT (IN THOUSANDS):			
Total Revenues	10,210	1,800	25
Costs & Expenses	16,228	3,697	143
Depreciation & Amort.	107	2	...
Operating Income	d6,125	d1,899	d118
Net Interest Inc./(Exp.)	d239	34	...
Income Before Income Taxes	d6,364	d1,865	d118
Net Income	d6,364	d1,865	d118
Cash Flow	d6,257	d1,863	d118
Average Shs. Outstg.	8,869	6,007	4,061
BALANCE SHEET (IN THOUSANDS):			
Cash & Cash Equivalents	2,983	2,321	...
Total Current Assets	6,898	3,138	...
Net Property	178	23	...
Total Assets	7,407	3,166	...
Total Current Liabilities	1,632	687	...
Long-Term Obligations	3,985	...	...
Net Stockholders' Equity	d3,046	2,479	...
Net Working Capital	5,266	2,451	...
Year-end Shs. Outstg.	8,480	7,768	...
STATISTICAL RECORD:			
Debt/Total Assets %	53.8	...	...

Statistics are as originally reported.

OFFICERS:
M. C. Diamond, Chmn. & C.E.O.
J. K. Johnson Jr., Pres. & C.O.O.
S. A. Gradess, C.F.O. & Sec.

INVESTOR CONTACT: Investor Relations, (877)-Alloy-IR

PRINCIPAL OFFICE: 115 West 30th Street, #201, New York, NY 10001

TELEPHONE NUMBER: (212) 244-4307
WEB: www.alloy.com

NO. OF EMPLOYEES: 45

SHAREHOLDERS: N/A

ANNUAL MEETING: N/A

INCORPORATED: DE, Jan. 1996

INSTITUTIONAL HOLDINGS:
No. of Institutions: N/A
Shares Held: N/A
% Held: N/A

INDUSTRY: Misc. general merchandise stores (SIC: 5399)

TRANSFER AGENT(S): American Stock Transfer & Trust Company, New York, NY

AMAZON.COM, INC.

YIELD ...
P/E RATIO ...

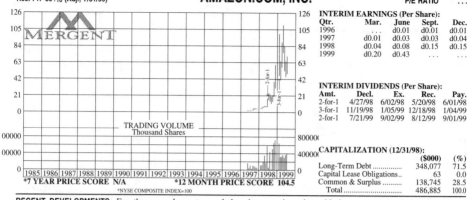

7 YEAR PRICE SCORE N/A   **12 MONTH PRICE SCORE 104.5**
*NYSE COMPOSITE INDEX=100

TRADING VOLUME
Thousand Shares

INTERIM EARNINGS (Per Share):

Qtr.	Mar.	June	Sept.	Dec.
1996	...	d0.01	d0.01	d0.01
1997	d0.01	d0.03	d0.03	d0.04
1998	d0.04	d0.08	d0.15	d0.15
1999	d0.20	d0.43	...	...

INTERIM DIVIDENDS (Per Share):

Amt.	Decl.	Ex.	Rec.	Pay.
2-for-1	4/27/98	6/02/98	5/20/98	6/01/98
3-for-1	11/19/98	1/05/99	12/18/98	1/04/99
2-for-1	7/21/99	9/02/99	8/12/99	9/01/99

CAPITALIZATION (12/31/98):

	($000)	(%)
Long-Term Debt	348,077	71.5
Capital Lease Obligations..	63	0.0
Common & Surplus	138,745	28.5
Total	486,885	100.0

RECENT DEVELOPMENTS: For the second quarter ended 6/30/99, the Company incurred a net loss of $138.0 million compared with a net loss of $22.6 million in the corresponding quarter the year before. Results for the 1999 and 1998 quarters included $50.6 million and $5.4 million in pre-tax charges, respectively, associated with merger and acquisition related costs. Net sales increased 171.1% to $314.4 million compared with $116.0 million in the comparable prior-year period. Sales growth was attributed to an increase in units sold due to growth of the Company's customer base, and repeat purchases from existing customers. Cumulative customer accounts amounted to 10.7 million, up 224.2% from 3.3 million at 6/30/98. Gross profit as a percentage of net sales decreased to 21.5% versus 22.6% in the equivalent 1998 quarter. On 7/13/99, the Company launched Amazon.com Electronics and Amazon.com Toys and Games.

BUSINESS

AMAZON.COM, INC. is a major on-line retailer of books, music CDs, DVD, videos, computer games, and other titles. On its Web site, the Company offers more than 4.7 million titles, search and browse features, e-mail services, free electronic greeting cards, personalized shopping services, Web-based credit card payments and direct shipping to customers. The Company strives to offer high value through innovative technology, broad selection, high-quality content, competitive pricing and personalized services. In the fourth quarter of 1998, the Company launched Amazon.co.uk in the United Kingdom and amazon.de in Germany. During the first quarter of 1999, the Company introduced customers to purchase and sell products via Amazon.Com Auctions. On 6/8/99, the Company launched an area where users can download free digital recordings of new song releases.

ANNUAL FINANCIAL DATA

	12/31/98	12/31/97	12/31/96	12/31/95	12/31/94
Earnings Per Share	d0.42	d0.11	d0.02	...	...
Cash Flow Per Share	d0.38	d0.09	d0.02	...	...
Tang. Book Val. Per Share	...	0.10	0.01	...	...
INCOME STATEMENT (IN THOUSANDS):					
Total Revenues	609,996	147,758	15,746	511	...
Costs & Expenses	709,878	172,225	21,439	796	47
Depreciation & Amort.	12,078	4,742	286	19	5
Operating Income	d111,960	d29,209	d5,979	d304	d52
Net Interest Inc./(Exp.)	d12,586	1,619	202	1	...
Income Before Income Taxes	d124,546	d27,590	d5,777	d303	d52
Net Income	d124,546	d27,590	d5,777	d303	d52
Cash Flow	d112,468	d22,848	d5,491	d284	d47
Average Shs. Outstg.	296,344	259,812	271,860	340,794	319,140
BALANCE SHEET (IN THOUSANDS):					
Cash & Cash Equivalents	373,445	125,066	6,248	996	...
Total Current Assets	424,254	137,335	7,140	1,027	...
Net Property	29,791	9,265	985	57	...
Total Assets	648,460	149,006	8,271	1,084	...
Total Current Liabilities	161,575	43,818	4,870	107	...
Long-Term Obligations	348,140	76,702	...	...	...
Net Stockholders' Equity	138,745	28,486	3,401	977	...
Net Working Capital	262,679	93,517	2,270	920	...
Year-end Shs. Outstg.	318,534	287,244	286,200	261,990	...
STATISTICAL RECORD:					
Debt/Total Assets %	53.7	51.5	...	...	...
Price Range	60⁵⁄₁₆-4⅛	5½-1⁵⁄₁₆	...	...	...

Statistics are as originally reported. Adj. for stk. splits: 2-for-1, 9/2/99; 3-for-1, 1/4/99; 2-for-1, 6/1/98

OFFICERS:
J. P. Bezos, Chmn. & C.E.O.
J. Galli, Pres. & C.O.O.
J. D. Covey, V.P., C.F.O. & Sec.
R. L. Dalzell, V.P. & C.I.O.

PRINCIPAL OFFICE: 1516 Second Avenue, 4th Floor, P. O. Box 80387, Seattle, WA 98101

TELEPHONE NUMBER: (206) 622-2335
FAX: (206) 622-2405
WEB: www.amazon.com
NO. OF EMPLOYEES: 2,100 (approx.)
SHAREHOLDERS: 2,304
ANNUAL MEETING: In May
INCORPORATED: WA, Jul., 1994; reincorp., DE, Jun., 1996

INSTITUTIONAL HOLDINGS:
No. of Institutions: 234
Shares Held: 76,806,348 (Adj.)
% Held: 23.8

INDUSTRY: Catalog and mail-order houses (SIC: 5961)

TRANSFER AGENT(S): ChaseMellon Shareholder Services, Ridgefield Park, NJ

NYSE SYMBOL AOL
Rec. Pr. 97 1/8 (7/31/99)

AMERICA ONLINE, INC.

YIELD ...
P/E RATIO 145.0

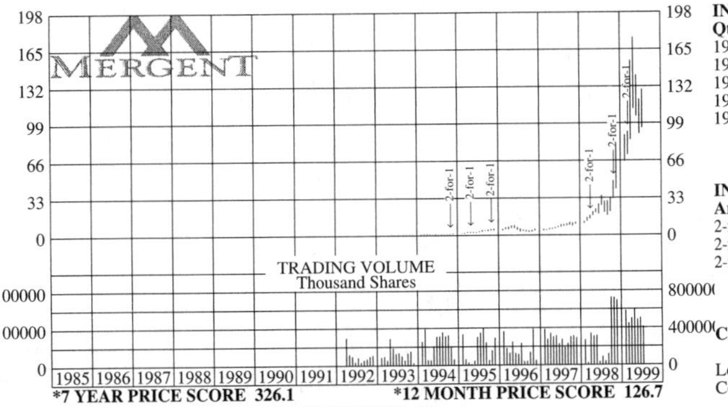

*7 YEAR PRICE SCORE 326.1 *12 MONTH PRICE SCORE 126.7

*NYSE COMPOSITE INDEX=100

INTERIM EARNINGS (Per Share):

Qtr.	Sept.	Dec.	Mar.	June
1994-95	0.01	d0.08	d0.01	0.01
1995-96	d0.02	0.02	0.02	0.02
1996-97	d0.48	d0.17	d0.01	d0.02
1997-98	0.02	0.03	0.02	0.03
1998-99	0.10	0.11	0.33	0.13

INTERIM DIVIDENDS (Per Share):

Amt.	Decl.	Ex.	Rec.	Pay.
2-for-1	2/10/98	3/17/98	2/23/98	3/16/98
2-for-1	10/27/98	11/18/98	11/03/98	11/17/98
2-for-1	1/27/99	2/23/99	2/08/99	2/22/99

CAPITALIZATION (6/30/98):

	($000)	(%)
Long-Term Debt	372,000	38.4
Common & Surplus	598,000	61.6
Total	970,000	100.0

RECENT DEVELOPMENTS: For the year ended 6/30/99, net income jumped to $762.0 million compared with $74.0 million in 1998. Results in 1999 included $567.0 million in pre-tax gains and $160.0 million in pre-tax charges. Revenues soared 54.5% to $4.78 billion from $3.09 billion in the previous year. Results reflected solid profits through increased advertising and commerce revenues as well as the successful integrations of acquired companies. The Company announced an agreement with EarthLink, an Internet service provider, under which EarthLink will distribute a co-branded version of AOL Instant Messenger to its members. Meanwhile, AOL Latin America and Big Entertainment signed a multi-year agreement in which Big Entertainment's movie Web site, Hollywood.com, will become part of AOL's services in Latin America.

BUSINESS

AMERICA ONLINE, INC. is a leading provider of on-line services, offering its subscribers a wide variety of services including electronic mail, conferencing, entertainment, software, computing support, interactive magazines and newspapers, and on-line classes, as well as access to services of the Internet. In addition, the Company is a provider of data network services and multimedia and CD-ROM production services. AOL has the largest subscriber base of any on-line service provider, serving 17.6 million members worldwide as of June 1999 and about two million members through CompuServe, a wholly-owned subsidiary. AOL generates revenues principally through membership and usage fees, and increasingly from advertising and merchandise sales, transaction fees, royalties, and the provision of network and production services to enterprises. In March 1999, AOL acquired Netscape Communications Corporation.

ANNUAL FINANCIAL DATA

	6/30/98	6/30/97	6/30/96	6/30/95	6/30/94	6/30/93	6/30/92
Earnings Per Share	[3] **0.09**	[2] **d0.65**	**0.04**	**d0.06**	**0.04**	[1] **0.01**	[1] **Nil**
Cash Flow Per Share	**0.19**	**d0.49**	**0.22**	**0.07**	**0.07**	**0.05**	**0.01**
Tang. Book Val. Per Share	**0.25**	**0.09**	**0.62**	**0.26**	**0.21**	**0.06**	**0.03**
INCOME STATEMENT (IN MILLIONS):							
Total Revenues	2,600.0	1,685.2	1,093.9	394.3	115.7	52.0	26.6
Costs & Expenses	2,422.0	2,067.1	869.2	341.5	76.0	27.0	18.1
Depreciation & Amort.	100.0	123.8	159.4	72.1	20.4	8.5	5.2
Operating Income	78.0	d505.6	65.2	d19.3	4.2	1.7	3.3
Net Interest Inc./(Exp.)	...	...	...	2.9	...	...	...
Income Before Income Taxes	92.0	d499.3	62.3	d18.5	10.0	5.0	3.6
Income Taxes	...	...	32.5	15.2	3.8	1.9	1.4
Net Income	[3] 92.0	[2] d499.3	29.8	d33.6	6.2	[1] 4.2	[1] 2.2
Cash Flow	192.0	d375.6	189.3	38.4	38.0	22.6	7.4
Average Shs. Outstg. (000)	1,036,000	764,856	864,776	543,776	552,280	468,576	622,208
BALANCE SHEET (IN MILLIONS):							
Cash & Cash Equivalents	631.0	124.6	129.1	64.1	67.7	14.3	14.0
Total Current Assets	930.0	323.5	270.6	132.9	105.3	25.4	19.2
Net Property	363.0	233.1	101.3	70.5	18.4	2.4	1.2
Total Assets	2,214.0	846.7	958.8	406.5	155.2	39.3	23.6
Total Current Liabilities	894.0	554.5	289.9	133.3	40.4	8.6	4.6
Long-Term Obligations	372.0	50.0	19.3	19.5	5.8	...	...
Net Stockholders' Equity	598.0	128.0	512.5	217.9	98.9	23.8	18.9
Net Working Capital	36.0	d231.0	d19.3	d0.5	65.0	16.8	14.7
Year-end Shs. Outstg. (000)	878,564	801,512	741,008	600,880	463,680	377,088	701,568
STATISTICAL RECORD:							
Operating Profit Margin %	3.0	...	6.0	...	3.6	3.3	12.5
Net Profit Margin %	3.5	...	2.7	...	5.3	8.1	8.3
Return on Equity %	15.4	...	5.8	...	6.3	17.6	11.7
Return on Assets %	4.2	...	3.1	...	11.3	10.7	9.4
Debt/Total Assets %	16.8	5.9	2.0	4.8	3.9	...	...
Price Range	80-10 5/16	11 7/16-3	8 7/8-2 13/16	5 3/4-1 9/16	1 13/16-0 3/4	1 1/8-0 1/4	0 7/16-0 3/16
P/E Ratio	918.5-118.4	...	252.8-79.7	...	445.9-182.0	994.3-252.3	147.5-54.2

Statistics are as originally reported. Adj. for 2-for-1 split, 11/94, 4/95, 11/95, 3/98, 11/98 & 2/99. [1] Bef. cr$1.1 mill. tax benefit fr. net op. loss car. fwd., 1993; cr$1.3 mill., 1992. [2] Incl. $1.0 mill. non-recur. chg., 1998; $482.6 mill., 1997. [3] Incl. $132.0 mill. restr., acq. R&D, & settlement chgs.

OFFICERS:
S. M. Case, Chmn., C.E.O.
K. J. Novack, Vice-Chmn.
R. W. Pittman, Pres., C.O.O.
J. M. Kelly, Sr. V.P., C.F.O., Treas.

INVESTOR CONTACT: Richard E. Hanlon, VP -Investor Relations, (703) 448-8700

PRINCIPAL OFFICE: 22000 AOL Way, Dulles, VA 20166-9323

TELEPHONE NUMBER: (703) 448-8700
FAX: (703) 506-1942
WEB: www.aol.com

NO. OF EMPLOYEES: 8,500

SHAREHOLDERS: 4,408 (approx.) 237,000 beneficial holders

ANNUAL MEETING: In Oct.

INCORPORATED: DE, May, 1985

INSTITUTIONAL HOLDINGS:
No. of Institutions: 720
Shares Held: 555,722,260
% Held: 51.3

INDUSTRY: Information retrieval services (SIC: 7375)

TRANSFER AGENT(S): The First National Bank of Boston, Boston, MA.

AMERITRADE HOLDING CORP.

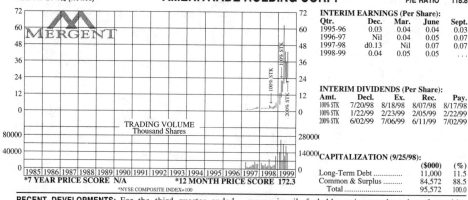

INTERIM EARNINGS (Per Share):

Qtr.	Dec.	Mar.	June	Sept.
1995-96	0.03	0.04	0.04	0.03
1996-97	Nil	0.04	0.05	0.07
1997-98	d0.13	Nil	0.07	0.07
1998-99	0.04	0.05	0.05	...

INTERIM DIVIDENDS (Per Share):

Amt.	Decl.	Ex.	Rec.	Pay.
100% STK	7/20/98	8/18/98	8/07/98	8/17/98
100% STK	1/22/99	2/23/99	2/05/99	2/22/99
200% STK	6/02/99	7/06/99	6/11/99	7/02/99

TRADING VOLUME
Thousand Shares

7 YEAR PRICE SCORE N/A   **12 MONTH PRICE SCORE 172.3**
*NYSE COMPOSITE INDEX=100

CAPITALIZATION (9/25/98):

	($000)	(%)
Long-Term Debt	11,000	11.5
Common & Surplus	84,572	88.5
Total	95,572	100.0

RECENT DEVELOPMENTS: For the third quarter ended 6/25/99, net income increased 50.1% to $8.9 million compared with $5.9 million in the corresponding quarter the year before. Total revenues increased 88.1% to $90.1 million from $47.9 million in the comparable quarter a year earlier. Commissions and clearing fees more than doubled to $56.1 million versus $24.0 million in the equivalent 1998 quarter. Interest revenue grew 65.6% to $31.2 million from $18.9 million the previous year. The higher revenues were primarily fueled by an increased number of securities transactions processed. During the 1999 quarter, the Company opened 84,000 new accounts, while average trades per day increased 179.0% to 59,648. Assets in customer accounts totaled $22.60 billion. Advertising expenses rose 130.9% to $12.1 million compared with $5.2 million the year before. On 7/29/99, the Company announced it would not conduct the planned public offering of class A stock.

BUSINESS

AMERITRADE HOLDING CORP. and its subsidiaries provide discount brokerage and clearing services to their customers. The Company is focused on providing retail customers with products and services at a significantly reduced price compared with traditional broker commissions. Customers are able to trade securities through various avenues, including the popular Internet channel. Core accounts numbered approximately 505,000 as of 6/25/99. The Company's discount brokerage operations are composed of Ameritrade Inc., Accutrade Inc., and Amerivest Inc. Advanced Clearing Inc. is the Company's securities clearing firm. Currently under development, OMoney Financial Services Corporation will provide on-line financial services.

ANNUAL FINANCIAL DATA

	9/25/98	9/26/97	9/27/96	9/29/95	9/30/94
Earnings Per Share	Nil	0.08	0.07	0.05	0.03
Cash Flow Per Share	0.02	0.10	0.08	0.05	0.03
Tang. Book Val. Per Share	0.45	0.35	0.16	0.08	...
INCOME STATEMENT (IN THOUSANDS):					
Total Revenues	164,194	95,667	65,379	42,882	31,361
Costs & Expenses	160,301	72,186	45,549	31,447	23,558
Depreciation & Amort.	3,362	2,056	1,412	605	354
Operating Income	531	21,425	18,418	10,830	7,450
Income Before Income Taxes	531	21,425	18,418	10,830	7,450
Income Taxes	321	7,603	7,259	3,799	2,619
Net Income	210	13,822	11,158	7,031	4,831
Cash Flow	3,572	15,879	12,570	7,636	5,184
Average Shs. Outstg.	174,465	165,227	153,766	153,766	154,271
BALANCE SHEET (IN THOUSANDS):					
Cash & Cash Equivalents	527,982	373,286	191,436	125,456	...
Total Current Assets	1,200,836	716,517	372,608	265,598	...
Net Property	26,116	8,710	3,746	3,691	...
Total Assets	1,290,402	757,357	401,679	287,105	...
Total Current Liabilities	1,194,830	690,368	366,164	260,504	...
Long-Term Obligations	11,000	...	4,853	7,097	...
Net Stockholders' Equity	84,572	66,989	30,662	19,504	...
Net Working Capital	6,007	26,150	6,443	5,094	...
Year-end Shs. Outstg.	174,157	174,214	153,766	153,766	...
STATISTICAL RECORD:					
Operating Profit Margin %	0.3	22.4	28.2	25.3	23.8
Net Profit Margin %	0.1	14.4	17.1	16.4	15.4
Return on Equity %	0.2	20.6	36.4	36.1	...
Return on Assets %	...	1.8	2.8	2.4	...
Debt/Total Assets %	0.9	...	1.2	2.5	...
Price Range	6½-1⅞	3¼-0	...	...	...
P/E Ratio	3,094.9-885.4	39.1-11.8	...	...	...

Statistics are as originally reported. Adj. for stk. splits: 3-for-1, 7/2/99; 2-for-1, 8/18/98; 2-for-1, 2/22/99

QUARTERLY DATA

09/25/98 ($000)	Rev	Inc
1st Quarter................	31,365	(11,249)
2nd Quarter...............	36,762	(271)
3rd Quarter	47,926	5,940
4th Quarter................	48,141	5,790

OFFICERS:
J. J. Ricketts, Chmn., C.E.O. & C.O.O.
T. K. Lewis Jr., Co-C.E.O.
J. A. Konen, Pres.
R. T. Slezak, V.P., C.F.O. & Treas.
INVESTOR CONTACT: J. Joe Ricketts, Chmn., (402) 597-5654
PRINCIPAL OFFICE: 4211 South 102nd Street, Omaha, NE 68127

TELEPHONE NUMBER: (402) 331-7856
FAX: (402) 597-7789
WEB: www.amtd.com
NO. OF EMPLOYEES: 1,353
SHAREHOLDERS: 143 class A stock; approx. 9,100 beneficial owners of class A
ANNUAL MEETING: In Feb.
INCORPORATED: NE, Dec., 1981; reincorp., DE, Oct., 1996

INSTITUTIONAL HOLDINGS:
No. of Institutions: 64
Shares Held: 5,280,556
% Held: 9.1
INDUSTRY: Security brokers and dealers (SIC: 6211)
TRANSFER AGENT(S): The Bank of New York, New York, NY

APPNET SYSTEMS, INC.

YIELD ...
P/E RATIO ...

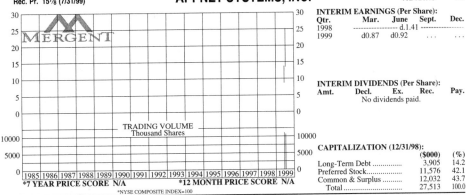

INTERIM EARNINGS (Per Share):

Qtr.	Mar.	June	Sept.	Dec.
1998	---------------- d.1.41 ----------------			
1999	d0.87	d0.92	...	...

INTERIM DIVIDENDS (Per Share):

Amt.	Decl.	Ex.	Rec.	Pay.
	No dividends paid.			

TRADING VOLUME
Thousand Shares

| 1985 | 1986 | 1987 | 1988 | 1989 | 1990 | 1991 | 1992 | 1993 | 1994 | 1995 | 1996 | 1997 | 1998 | 1999 |

*7 YEAR PRICE SCORE N/A   *12 MONTH PRICE SCORE N/A

*NYSE COMPOSITE INDEX=100

CAPITALIZATION (12/31/98):

	($000)	(%)
Long-Term Debt	3,905	14.2
Preferred Stock	11,576	42.1
Common & Surplus	12,032	43.7
Total	27,513	100.0

RECENT DEVELOPMENTS: For the three months ended 6/30/99, the Company reported a net loss of $18.9 million compared with a net loss of $19.7 million in the corresponding period of the prior year. Earnings in both periods included charges for acquisition-related expenses of $3.0 million in 1999 and $4.2 million in 1998. Revenues increased 64.9% to $25.1 million from $15.2 million. Gross profit jumped 80.7% to $10.8 million, or 43.3% of revenues, versus $6.0 million, or 39.5% of revenues, in the comparable 1998 quarter. The Company has launched its transaction-based outsourcing service, called outsourceEC, where the Company designs, hosts, operates and maintains commerce-enabled Web sites for customers. Initial customers include WeddingChannel.com, Burton Snowboards, and The National Oceanic and Atmospheric Agency. APNT has also launched an image awareness campaign that will incorporate both print and interactive media.

BUSINESS

APPNET SYSTEMS, INC. provides Internet and electronic commerce professional services and solutions to medium-sized and large businesses. The Company develops electronic commerce tools that facilitate and promote communication and commerce between businesses and consumers as well as among businesses and their trading partners. The Company creates these tools by providing a range of professional services, including strategic consulting, interactive media services, Internet-based application development, electronic commerce systems integration, and electronic commerce outsourcing. The Company announced its initial public offering on 6/18/99.

ANNUAL FINANCIAL DATA

	12/31/98
Earnings Per Share	① d1.41
Cash Flow Per Share	d0.47

INCOME STATEMENT (IN THOUSANDS):

Total Revenues	17,674
Costs & Expenses	20,327
Depreciation & Amort.	10,151
Operating Income	d12,804
Net Interest Inc./(Exp.)	d1,052
Income Before Income Taxes	d14,579
Income Taxes	cr200
Net Income	① d14,379
Cash Flow	d5,101
Average Shs. Outstg.	10,785

BALANCE SHEET (IN THOUSANDS):

Cash & Cash Equivalents	2,447
Total Current Assets	14,803
Net Property	3,012
Total Assets	118,370
Total Current Liabilities	12,074
Long-Term Obligations	3,905
Net Stockholders' Equity	23,608
Net Working Capital	2,729
Year-end Shs. Outstg.	19,504

STATISTICAL RECORD:

Debt/Total Assets %	3.3

Statistics are as originally reported. ① Incl. credit for acquisition comp. of $1.2 mill.

OFFICERS:
K. S. Bajaj, Chmn., Pres., C.E.O.
J. Pearlstein, Sr. V.P., C.F.O., Treas.
W. S. Dawson, V.P., Gen. Couns., Sec.

INVESTOR CONTACT: Jack Pearlstein, C.F.O, (301) 493-8900

PRINCIPAL OFFICE: 6707 Democracy Boulevard, Suite 1000, Bethesda, MD 20817

TELEPHONE NUMBER: (301) 493-8900
FAX: (301) 581-2488
WEB: www.appnet.net

NO. OF EMPLOYEES: 755 (approx.)

SHAREHOLDERS: 133 (common); 5 (Class A preferred); 11 (Class B preferred)

ANNUAL MEETING: N/A

INCORPORATED: DE, Nov., 1997

INSTITUTIONAL HOLDINGS:
No. of Institutions: N/A
Shares Held: N/A
% Held: N/A

INDUSTRY: Business services, nec (SIC: 7389)

TRANSFER AGENT(S): BankBoston, N.A., Boston, MA

ARIBA, INC.

YIELD ...
P/E RATIO ...

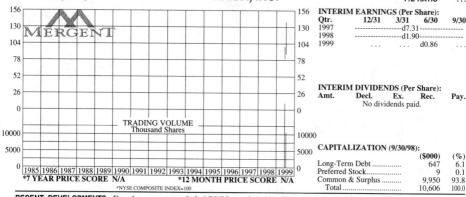

*7 YEAR PRICE SCORE N/A   *12 MONTH PRICE SCORE N/A

*NYSE COMPOSITE INDEX=100

INTERIM EARNINGS (Per Share):

Qtr.	12/31	3/31	6/30	9/30
1997	----------------d7.31----------------			
1998	----------------d1.90----------------			
1999	...	...	d0.86	...

INTERIM DIVIDENDS (Per Share):

Amt.	Decl.	Ex.	Rec.	Pay.
	No dividends paid.			

CAPITALIZATION (9/30/98):

	($000)	(%)
Long-Term Debt	647	6.1
Preferred Stock.................	9	0.1
Common & Surplus	9,950	93.8
Total	10,606	100.0

RECENT DEVELOPMENTS: For the quarter ended 6/30/99, the Company reported a net loss of $11.3 million compared with a net loss of $3.0 million in the equivalent 1998 quarter. Revenues were $11.9 million, up from $2.5 million a year earlier. The improvement in revenues was primarily attributed to the Company's extending its base of major buyers. During July, ARBA announced a strategic expansion of its operations into the international market. Ariba has opened five regional hubs in Germany, the Netherlands, Sweden, Switzerland, and the United Kingdom to provide pan-European support for its clients. During July, MCI WorldCom signed a client agreement to use the Ariba® business-to-business eCommerce solution. MCI WorldCom expects to use the intranet- and Internet-based Ariba solution to aggregate and direct company-wide operating resource spending through the Ariba Network™ eCommerce service to preferred suppliers.

BUSINESS

ARIBA, INC. is a provider of Internet-based business-to-business electronic commerce products and services for acquiring and managing operating resources. The Company's offerings connect buyers to suppliers to deliver an automated solution for improving the acquisition and management of goods and services required to operate a company. The Ariba ORMS application enables organizations to automate the procurement cycle within their intranets. The Ariba Network, a global business-to-business electronic commerce network for operating resources, enables buyers and suppliers to automate transactions on the Internet. Together, the Ariba ORMS application and the Ariba Network provide a business-to-business electronic commerce solution for operating resources designed to benefit both buyers and suppliers. The Ariba ORMS application has been licensed by large, multinational and public sector organizations including General Motors, Cisco Systems, FedEx, Hewlett-Packard Company, Philips, US WEST and Visa.

ANNUAL FINANCIAL DATA

	9/30/98	9/30/97
Earnings Per Share	d1.90	d7.31
Cash Flow Per Share	d1.62	d7.06
Tang. Book Val. Per Share	0.52	0.80
INCOME STATEMENT (IN THOUSANDS):		
Total Revenues	8,363	760
Costs & Expenses	18,284	5,550
Depreciation & Amort.	1,600	162
Operating Income	d11,521	d4,952
Income Before Income Taxes	d10,953	d4,679
Net Income	d10,953	d4,679
Cash Flow	d9,353	d4,517
Average Shs. Outstg.	5,762	640
BALANCE SHEET (IN THOUSANDS):		
Cash & Cash Equivalents	13,932	15,471
Total Current Assets	16,787	15,828
Net Property	2,217	861
Total Assets	19,242	16,800
Total Current Liabilities	8,636	2,143
Long-Term Obligations	647	140
Net Stockholders' Equity	9,959	14,517
Net Working Capital	8,151	13,685
Year-end Shs. Outstg.	19,092	18,227
STATISTICAL RECORD:		
Debt/Total Assets %	3.4	0.8

Statistics are as originally reported.

OFFICERS:
K. J. Krach, Chmn., Pres., C.E.O.
E. P. Kinsey, V.P., C.F.O., Sec.

PRINCIPAL OFFICE: 1314 Chesapeake Terrace, Sunnyvale, CA 94089

TELEPHONE NUMBER: (408) 543-3800
FAX: (408) 543-3900
WEB: www.ariba.com

NO. OF EMPLOYEES: 221

SHAREHOLDERS: 159 (approx.)

ANNUAL MEETING: N/A

INCORPORATED: DE, Sept., 1996

INSTITUTIONAL HOLDINGS:
No. of Institutions: 5
Shares Held: 172,550
% Held: 0.4

INDUSTRY: Prepackaged software (SIC: 7372)

TRANSFER AGENT(S): BankBoston, N.A., Canton, MA

ASYMETRIX LEARNING SYSTEMS, INC.

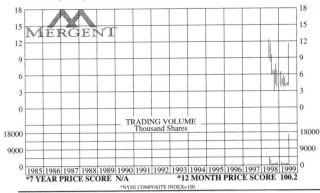

*7 YEAR PRICE SCORE N/A   *12 MONTH PRICE SCORE 100.2

*NYSE COMPOSITE INDEX=100

TRADING VOLUME
Thousand Shares

1985 1986 1987 1988 1989 1990 1991 1992 1993 1994 1995 1996 1997 1998 1999

INTERIM EARNINGS (Per Share):

Qtr.	Mar.	June	Sept.	Dec.
1996		d6.78		
1997	d0.43	d0.35	d.1.07	d0.35
1998	d0.05	d0.32	d0.07	d0.17
1999	d.017	d0.14	...	...

INTERIM DIVIDENDS (Per Share):

Amt.	Decl.	Ex.	Rec.	Pay.
	No dividends paid.			

CAPITALIZATION (12/31/98):

	($000)	(%)
Common & Surplus	37,010	100.0
Total	37,010	100.0

RECENT DEVELOPMENTS: For the quarter ended 6/30/99, the Company reported a net loss of $2.0 million versus a net loss of $2.1 million in the corresponding period of the previous year. Total revenues increased 2.1% to $8.6 million from $8.4 million the year before. Total product revenue improved 7.5% to $3.6 million, while service revenue slipped 1.4% to $5.0 million. The Company has outlined plans for a new business-to-business and consumer learning portal, click2learn.com. This Internet learning destination, which complements the Company's existing line of products, will be conduit to Web-delivered courseware and ancillary products, as well as a free publishing vehicle for on-line course content. On 7/21/99, ASYM and Go2Net, Inc., a network of branded, technology- and community-driven Web sites, announced a memorandum of understanding for a comprehensive, three-year marketing, distribution, licensing and co-branding partnership.

BUSINESS

ASYMETRIX LEARNING SYS-TEMS, INC. provides a single source on-line learning tool that includes both a technology platform for on-line learning and related professional services that enable customers to create, distribute and manage learning applications throughout an enterprise. ASYM provides its customers with needs analysis and consulting, on-line learning authoring and management products, custom content development, off-the-shelf content, and learning systems integration services. The Company's products and services serve the financial services, accounting, health care, insurance, computer hardware and software, manufacturing, networking, telecommunications, government, and education industries.

ANNUAL FINANCIAL DATA

	12/31/98	12/31/97	12/31/96	12/31/95
Earnings Per Share	d0.62	③ d2.17	①② d4.01	② d6.78
Cash Flow Per Share	d0.46	d1.99	d3.72	d6.06
Tang. Book Val. Per Share	1.94	0.23	2.08	...
INCOME STATEMENT (IN THOUSANDS):				
Total Revenues	33,352	24,064	17,255	18,164
Costs & Expenses	39,609	35,873	38,780	35,141
Depreciation & Amort.	1,662	1,118	1,696	2,086
Operating Income	d7,919	d12,927	d23,221	d19,063
Net Interest Inc./(Exp.)	609	484	1,102	d574
Income Before Income Taxes	d7,328	d13,077	d23,359	d19,637
Income Taxes	...	38	196	78
Equity Earnings/Minority Int.	2,169	d634	d112	...
Net Income	d5,159	③ d13,115	①② d23,555	② d19,715
Cash Flow	d4,867	d11,997	d21,859	d17,629
Average Shs. Outstg.	10,599	6,038	5,879	2,907
BALANCE SHEET (IN THOUSANDS):				
Cash & Cash Equivalents	21,713	2,454	3,763	...
Total Current Assets	31,257	10,760	16,264	...
Net Property	2,320	1,834	1,182	...
Total Assets	43,622	21,564	18,727	...
Total Current Liabilities	6,344	10,153	6,417	...
Net Stockholders' Equity	37,010	9,762	12,310	...
Net Working Capital	24,913	607	9,847	...
Year-end Shs. Outstg.	13,948	6,625	5,915	...
STATISTICAL RECORD:				
Price Range	12⅜-2⅞	...	...	...

Statistics are as originally reported. ① Incl. loss of $2.8 mill. on impairment of assets. ② Incl. restructuring chrg. of $1.1 mill., 1996; $3.3 mill., 1995 ③ Incl. expense of $4.1 mill. for acquisition of in-process research and development.

REVENUES

(12/31/1998)	($000)	(%)
Online Learning Products	10,828	32.5
Other Products	4,365	13.1
Service Revenues	18,159	54.4
Total	33,352	100.0

OFFICERS:
B. Kolde, Chmn.
J. A. Billmaier, C.E.O.
K. M. Oakes, Pres.
J. D. Atherly, C.F.O., V.P., Fin., Admin.

PRINCIPAL OFFICE: 110-110th Avenue NE, Suite 700, Bellevue, WA 98004-5840

TELEPHONE NUMBER: (425) 462-0501
FAX: (425) 455-3071
WEB: www.asymetrix.com
NO. OF EMPLOYEES: 317
SHAREHOLDERS: 313 (approx.)
ANNUAL MEETING: In May
INCORPORATED: WA, Dec., 1984; reincorp., DE, Jun., 1998

INSTITUTIONAL HOLDINGS:
No. of Institutions: 11
Shares Held: 2,282,987
% Held: 16.8
INDUSTRY: Computer programming services (SIC: 7371)
TRANSFER AGENT(S): ChaseMellon Shareholder Services, L.L.C., South Hackensack, NJ

AT HOME CORP.

YIELD ...
P/E RATIO ...

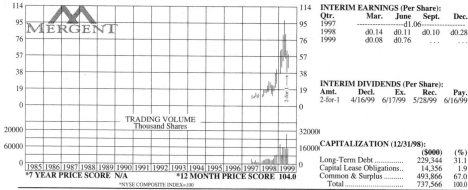

INTERIM EARNINGS (Per Share):

Qtr.	Mar.	June	Sept.	Dec.
1997		d1.06		
1998	d0.14	d0.11	d0.10	d0.28
1999	d0.08	d0.76	...	...

INTERIM DIVIDENDS (Per Share):

Amt.	Decl.	Ex.	Rec.	Pay.
2-for-1	4/16/99	6/17/99	5/28/99	6/16/99

CAPITALIZATION (12/31/98):

	($000)	(%)
Long-Term Debt	229,344	31.1
Capital Lease Obligations..	14,356	1.9
Common & Surplus	493,866	67.0
Total	737,566	100.0

TRADING VOLUME
Thousand Shares

*7 YEAR PRICE SCORE N/A   *12 MONTH PRICE SCORE 104.0
*NYSE COMPOSITE INDEX=100

RECENT DEVELOPMENTS: For the quarter ended 6/30/99, the Company incurred a net loss of $217.9 million compared with a net loss of $24.8 million in the corresponding prior-year quarter. Results in 1999 include one-time merger and related charges totaling $218.2 million. Total revenue was $70.5 million versus $9.2 million the year before. Comparisons were made with restated prior-year results. ATHM's subscriber base grew to over 620,000 cable users from about 146,000 subscribers the year before. The @Home service was launched in 21 new markets, bringing the total to 89 worldwide. Traffic on the Company's Internet portal excite.com totaled 81.0 million page views per day, while registered users for Excite services totaled 38.0 million. During the quarter, ATHM launched 4 new products. Excite Voicemail and Excite Voicechat provide Internet-related voicemail services. Excite Planner and Excite Assistant bring updated Internet content to the desktop. In July 1999, ATHM announced an agreement to buy iMall, Inc. for approximately $425.0 million.

BUSINESS

AT HOME CORP. is a provider of Internet services over the cable television infrastructure and leased digital telecommunication lines to consumers and businesses. The Company's primary offering, the @Home service, allows residential subscribers to connect their personal computers via cable modems to a high-speed Internet backbone network developed by the Company. This service enables subscribers to receive the ''@Home Experience,'' which includes Internet service over hybrid fiber co-axial cable with ''always on'' connection. For businesses, ATHM's @Work services provide a platform for Internet, intranet and extranet connectivity solutions and networked business applications over both cable infrastructures and digital telecommunications lines. In May 1999, the Company completed the acquisition of Excite.com. The Excite subsidiary operates two Internet portal sites, excite.com and webcrawler.com, which are currently accessible on the World Wide Web.

ANNUAL FINANCIAL DATA

	12/31/98	12/31/97	12/31/96	12/31/95
Earnings Per Share	① d0.63	① d1.06	d0.13	d0.01
Cash Flow Per Share	d0.34	d1.01	d0.12	...
Tang. Book Val. Per Share	1.62	0.50	...	...
INCOME STATEMENT (IN THOUSANDS):				
Total Revenues	48,045	7,437	676	...
Costs & Expenses	132,017	220,619	23,800	2,844
Depreciation & Amort.	66,620	8,913	1,903	42
Operating Income	d150,592	d222,095	d25,027	d2,886
Net Interest Inc./(Exp.)	6,413	3,033	514	130
Income Before Income Taxes	d144,179	d219,062	d24,513	d2,756
Net Income	① d144,179	① d219,062	d24,513	d2,756
Cash Flow	d77,559	d210,149	d22,610	d2,714
Average Shs. Outstg.	228,480	207,086	192,240	...
BALANCE SHEET (IN THOUSANDS):				
Cash & Cash Equivalents	419,289	120,379	16,770	6,907
Total Current Assets	433,328	125,440	18,315	7,156
Net Property	49,240	33,061	14,328	921
Total Assets	780,631	160,583	33,388	8,124
Total Current Liabilities	43,004	24,050	7,742	912
Long-Term Obligations	243,700	15,735	5,654	...
Net Stockholders' Equity	493,866	119,062	18,317	7,212
Net Working Capital	390,324	101,390	10,573	6,244
Year-end Shs. Outstg.	246,546	237,206	23,710	...
STATISTICAL RECORD:				
Debt/Total Assets %	31.2	9.8	16.9	...
Price Range	42⅜-10¼	15⁵⁄₁₆-8⁵⁄₁₆	...	...

Statistics are as originally reported. Adj. for stk. split: 2-for-1, 6/16/99 ① Incl. non-recurr. chrg. 12/31/98: $104.1 mill.; 12/31/97: $172.6 mill.

QUARTERLY DATA

12/31/98 ($000)	Rev	Inc
1st Quarter	5,773	(31,216)
2nd Quarter	9,220	(24,772)
3rd Quarter	13,815	(23,287)
4th Quarter	19,237	(64,904)

OFFICERS:
T. A. Jermoluk, Chmn., C.E.O.
W. R. Hearst III, Vice-Chmn.
G. Bell, Pres.
K. A. Goldman, Sr. V.P., C.F.O.

PRINCIPAL OFFICE: 425 Broadway Street, Redwood City, CA 94063

TELEPHONE NUMBER: (650) 569-5000
WEB: www.home.net
NO. OF EMPLOYEES: 570
SHAREHOLDERS: 911
ANNUAL MEETING: N/A
INCORPORATED: DE, Mar., 1995

INSTITUTIONAL HOLDINGS:
No. of Institutions: 296
Shares Held: 103,723,928
% Held: 31.4
INDUSTRY: Computer related services, nec (SIC: 7379)
TRANSFER AGENT(S): Boston EquiServe, Boston, MA

AT&T CORP.

YIELD	1.7%
P/E RATIO	21.8

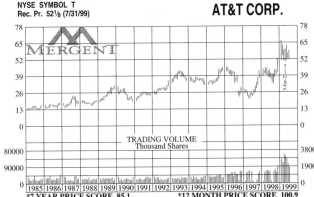

INTERIM EARNINGS (Per Share):

Qtr.	3/31	6/30	9/30	12/31
1995	0.51	0.57	0.11	d1.11
1996	0.60	0.63	0.56	0.51
1997	0.46	0.39	0.47	0.54
1998	0.53	d0.06	0.77	0.75
1999	0.38	0.49	...	...

INTERIM DIVIDENDS (Per Share):

Amt.	Decl.	Ex.	Rec.	Pay.
0.33Q	9/18/98	9/28/98	9/30/98	11/02/98
0.33Q	12/16/98	12/29/98	12/31/98	2/01/99
0.33Q	3/17/99	3/29/99	3/31/99	5/01/99
3-for-2	3/17/99	4/16/99	3/31/99	4/15/99
0.22Q	6/16/99	6/28/99	6/30/99	8/02/99

Indicated div.: $0.88 (Div. Reinv. Plan)

TRADING VOLUME
Thousand Shares

CAPITALIZATION (12/31/98):

	($000)	(%)
Long-Term Debt	5,556,000	15.2
Deferred Income Tax	5,453,000	14.9
Common & Surplus	25,522,000	69.9
Total	36,531,000	100.0

*7 YEAR PRICE SCORE 85.1   *12 MONTH PRICE SCORE 100.9
*NYSE COMPOSITE INDEX=100

RECENT DEVELOPMENTS: For the second quarter ended 6/30/99, net income was $1.58 billion compared with a loss from continuing operations of $161.0 million in the corresponding quarter a year earlier. Results for 1999 benefited from improved operating performance, lower costs and a net pre-tax restructuring benefit of $29.0 million. Earnings for 1998 included one-time restructuring and other charges of $2.74 billion. Total revenues increased 18.8% to $15.69

billion from $13.21 billion in the comparable 1998 quarter, propelled by revenue growth in wireless services, business services and outsourcing sources. Revenues from the Company's broadband and Internet services unit increased 7.6% to $1.42 billion on a pro forma basis. The pro forma revenues exclude all closed cable partnerships and the results of At Home, which is now accounted for as a equity investment.

BUSINESS

AT&T CORP. (formerly American Telephone & Telegraph Co.) is a global company that provides voice, data and video communications services and products, serving more than 80.0 million customers including consumers, large and small businesses, and government entities. The Company, and its subsidiaries, furnish domestic long distance, international long distance, regional, local and wireless telecommunications services and cable television, and provide billing, directory and calling card services to support its communications operations. Also, the Company is a supplier of data and Internet services for businesses and is the largest direct Internet service provider to consumers in the U.S. On 3/9/99, the Company acquired Tele-Communications, Inc., a provider of domestic cable and telecommunications services, and its interests in At Home Corp.

ANNUAL FINANCIAL DATA

	12/31/98	12/31/97	12/31/96	12/31/95	12/31/94	12/31/93	12/31/92
Earnings Per Share	① 1.94	② 1.83	② 2.31	③ 0.06	③ 2.01	④ 1.96	③ 1.91
Cash Flow Per Share	3.65	3.39	3.44	2.09	3.73	3.74	3.68
Tang. Book Val. Per Share	6.68	5.88	5.02	3.85	5.81	6.83	9.41
Dividends Per Share	0.88	0.88	0.88	0.88	0.88	0.88	0.88
Dividend Payout %	45.4	48.2	38.0	N.M.	43.8	44.9	46.1
INCOME STATEMENT (IN MILLIONS):							
Total Revenues	53,223.0	51,319.0	52,184.0	79,609.0	75,094.0	67,156.0	64,904.0
Costs & Expenses	41,107.0	40,524.0	40,634.0	73,549.0	63,025.0	57,292.0	55,095.0
Depreciation & Amort.	4,629.0	3,827.0	2,740.0	4,845.0	4,039.0	3,626.0	3,540.0
Operating Income	7,487.0	6,968.0	8,810.0	1,215.0	8,030.0	6,238.0	6,269.0
Net Interest Inc./(Exp.)	d427.0	d191.0	d334.0	d738.0	d748.0	d566.0	d663.0
Income Before Income Taxes	8,307.0	7,193.0	8,866.0	935.0	7,518.0	6,204.0	5,958.0
Income Taxes	3,072.0	2,721.0	3,258.0	796.0	2,808.0	2,230.0	2,151.0
Net Income	① 5,235.0	② 4,472.0	② 5,608.0	③ 139.0	③ 4,710.0	④ 3,974.0	③ 3,807.0
Cash Flow	9,864.0	8,299.0	8,348.0	4,984.0	8,749.0	7,600.0	7,347.0
Average Shs. Outstg. (000)	2,700,000	2,445,000	2,424,000	2,388,000	2,346,000	2,029,500	1,998,000
BALANCE SHEET (IN MILLIONS):							
Cash & Cash Equivalents	3,160.0	145.0	134.0	908.0	1,208.0	532.0	1,310.0
Total Current Assets	14,118.0	16,179.0	18,310.0	39,509.0	37,611.0	29,736.0	26,514.0
Net Property	26,903.0	22,710.0	19,794.0	22,264.0	22,035.0	19,397.0	19,358.0
Total Assets	59,550.0	58,635.0	55,552.0	88,884.0	79,262.0	60,766.0	57,188.0
Total Current Liabilities	15,442.0	16,942.0	16,318.0	39,372.0	30,930.0	25,334.0	21,386.0
Long-Term Obligations	5,556.0	6,826.0	7,883.0	11,635.0	11,358.0	6,812.0	8,604.0
Net Stockholders' Equity	25,522.0	22,647.0	20,295.0	17,274.0	17,921.0	13,850.0	18,921.0
Net Working Capital	d1,324.0	d763.0	1,992.0	137.0	6,681.0	4,404.0	5,128.0
Year-end Shs. Outstg. (000)	2,631,000	2,434,500	2,434,500	2,394,008	2,353,509	2,028,597	2,009,746
STATISTICAL RECORD:							
Operating Profit Margin %	14.1	13.6	16.9	1.5	10.7	9.3	9.7
Net Profit Margin %	9.8	8.7	10.7	0.2	6.3	5.9	5.9
Return on Equity %	20.5	19.7	27.6	0.8	26.3	28.7	20.1
Return on Assets %	8.8	7.6	10.1	0.2	5.9	6.5	6.7
Debt/Total Assets %	9.3	11.6	14.2	13.1	14.3	11.2	15.0
Price Range	52¹¹/₁₆-32¼	42¹¹/₁₆-20½	45¹⁵/₁₆-23⅝	45¹¹/₁₆-31¾	38¹/₁₆-31¾	43⁵/₁₆-33⁷/₁₆	35⁷/₁₆-24⁷/₁₆
P/E Ratio	27.1-16.6	23.4-11.2	19.9-9.6	759.9-528.3	19.0-15.7	22.1-17.0	18.6-12.8
Average Yield %	2.1	2.8	2.6	2.3	2.5	2.3	2.9

Statistics are as originally reported. Adj. for stock split: 3-for-2, 4/15/99 ① Incls. nonrecurr. pre-tax chrg. of $2.51 bill.; bef. gain of $1.29 bill. from disc. ops. & extraord. chrg. of $137.0 mill. ② Bef. disc. ops. credit 12/31/97: $166.0 mill.; credit 12/31/96: $300.0 mill. ③ Incls. non-recurr. chrg. 12/31/95: $7.85 bill.; chrg. 12/31/94: $169.0 mill.; chrgs. 12/31/92: $132.0 mill. ④ Bef. acctg. adj. of $7.77 bill.; & incls. credit of $217.0 mill. & restr. chrg. of $498.0 mill.

OFFICERS:
C. M. Armstrong, Chmn., C.E.O.
J. D. Zeglis, Pres.
D. E. Somers, Sr. Exec. V.P., C.F.O.
E. M. Dwyer, V.P., Treas.

PRINCIPAL OFFICE: 32 Avenue Of The Americas, New York, NY 10013-2412

TELEPHONE NUMBER: (212) 387-5400
WEB: www.att.com

NO. OF EMPLOYEES: 107,800 (approx.)

SHAREHOLDERS: 3,200,000

ANNUAL MEETING: In May

INCORPORATED: NY, Mar., 1885

INSTITUTIONAL HOLDINGS:
No. of Institutions: 1,083
Shares Held: 1,577,275,571
% Held: 49.6

INDUSTRY: Telephone communications, exc. radio (SIC: 4813)

TRANSFER AGENT(S): Boston EquiServe Trust Company, N.A.

AUDIOHIGHWAY.COM

YIELD ...
P/E RATIO ...

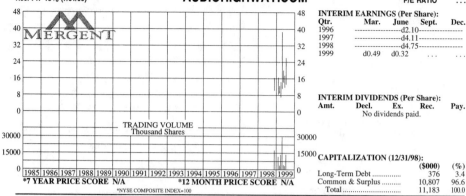

INTERIM EARNINGS (Per Share):

Qtr.	Mar.	June	Sept.	Dec.
1996	------------------d2.10-----------------			
1997	------------------d4.11-----------------			
1998	------------------d4.75-----------------			
1999	d0.49	d0.32	...	...

INTERIM DIVIDENDS (Per Share):

Amt.	Decl.	Ex.	Rec.	Pay.
	No dividends paid.			

CAPITALIZATION (12/31/98):

	($000)	(%)
Long-Term Debt	376	3.4
Common & Surplus	10,807	96.6
Total	11,183	100.0

TRADING VOLUME
Thousand Shares

1985 1986 1987 1988 1989 1990 1991 1992 1993 1994 1995 1996 1997 1998 1999
*7 YEAR PRICE SCORE N/A   *12 MONTH PRICE SCORE N/A
*NYSE COMPOSITE INDEX=100

RECENT DEVELOPMENTS: For the second quarter ended 6/30/99, the Company reported a net loss of $1.7 million compared with a loss of $966,000 in the corresponding quarter the year before. Revenues increased to $249,000 from $10,000 in the comparable quarter a year earlier. Revenues increased 51.0% over revenues in the first quarter of 1999. Total costs and expenses grew 196.0% to $2.1 million from $709,000 in the equivalent 1998 quarter. For the six months ended 6/30/99, the Company posted a net loss of $4.0 million compared with a loss of $1.7 million in the corresponding prior-year period. Revenues jumped to $414,000 from $52,000 in the comparable 1998 period. Total costs and expenses grew 211.8% to $4.1 million from $1.3 million in the equivalent six-month period of 1998.

BUSINESS

AUDIOHIGHWAY.COM offers a proprietary information and entertainment service that enables its users to download and play back selected audio content from the Internet via the Company's AudioCast System. Through licensing agreements with audio content providers such as National Public Radio, Penguin Books USA and Newsweek on Air, AHWY has a digital library of more than 3,500 titles, including frequently-updated news programs, audio books, and music. The digital library can be accessed from the Company's Web site free of charge. AHWY's revenues are derived from advertising.

ANNUAL FINANCIAL DATA

	12/31/98	12/31/97	12/31/96
Earnings Per Share	① d4.75	d4.11	d2.10
Cash Flow Per Share	d2.96	d2.76	d2.00
Tang. Book Val. Per Share	2.63	...	...
INCOME STATEMENT (IN THOUSANDS):			
Total Revenues	139	4	...
Costs & Expenses	1,702	1,263	1,428
Depreciation & Amort.	2,048	1,240	76
Operating Income	d3,611	d2,499	d1,504
Net Interest Inc./(Exp.)	d1,845	d1,292	d77
Income Before Income Taxes	d5,442	d3,791	d1,581
Net Income	① d5,442	d3,791	d1,581
Cash Flow	d3,394	d2,551	d1,505
Average Shs. Outstg.	1,146	923	752
BALANCE SHEET (IN THOUSANDS):			
Cash & Cash Equivalents	13,007	5	...
Total Current Assets	13,134	50	...
Net Property	333	378	...
Total Assets	13,467	428	...
Total Current Liabilities	2,284	1,791	...
Long-Term Obligations	376	1,082	...
Net Stockholders' Equity	10,807	d2,445	...
Net Working Capital	10,850	d1,741	...
Year-end Shs. Outstg.	4,103	944	832
STATISTICAL RECORD:			
Debt/Total Assets %	2.8	252.8	...
Price Range	16⅜-10¼	...	...

Statistics are as originally reported. ① Bef. extraord. chrg. $425,000.

OFFICERS:
N. M. Schulhof, Pres. & C.E.O.
G. Sutyak, C.F.O.
G. Jasmin, Exec. V.P., C.O.O. & Sec.

PRINCIPAL OFFICE: 20600 Mariani Avenue, Cupertino, CA 95014

TELEPHONE NUMBER: (408) 255-5301
FAX: (408) 255-5591
WEB: www.audiohighway.com

NO. OF EMPLOYEES: 24

SHAREHOLDERS: 202 (approx.)

ANNUAL MEETING: N/A

INCORPORATED: CA, 1994

INSTITUTIONAL HOLDINGS:
No. of Institutions: 5
Shares Held: 16,456
% Held: 0.3

INDUSTRY: Data processing and preparation (SIC: 7374)

TRANSFER AGENT(S): U.S. Stock Transfer Corporation, Glendale, CA.

AUTOBYTEL.COM INC.

YIELD ...
P/E RATIO ...

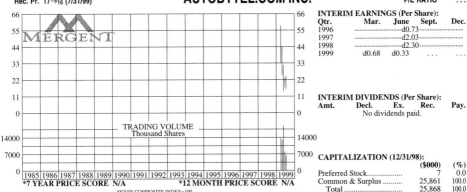

INTERIM EARNINGS (Per Share):

Qtr.	Mar.	June	Sept.	Dec.
1996	------------------d0.73------------------			
1997	------------------d2.03------------------			
1998	------------------d2.30------------------			
1999	d0.68	d0.33	...	...

INTERIM DIVIDENDS (Per Share):

Amt.	Decl.	Ex.	Rec.	Pay.
	No dividends paid.			

*7 YEAR PRICE SCORE N/A   *12 MONTH PRICE SCORE N/A
*NYSE COMPOSITE INDEX=100

CAPITALIZATION (12/31/98):

	($000)	(%)
Preferred Stock.............	7	0.0
Common & Surplus	25,861	100.0
Total	25,868	100.0

RECENT DEVELOPMENTS: For the three months ended 6/30/99, the Company reported a net loss of $6.0 million compared with a net loss of $3.1 million in the corresponding period of the prior year. Total revenues jumped 70.3% to $9.2 million from $5.4 million in the comparable 1998 period. The growth in revenues reflects the number of new paying dealers that joined the network, as well as the revenues derived from new business sectors. The number of paying dealers increased 11.9% to 2,865 from 2,560. On 7/29/99, the Company announced that it has entered into a definitive agreement to acquire privately-held W.G. Nichols, a publisher of Chilton series of automobile repair manuals. During the quarter, ABTL added programs to its network, including an insurance center where consumers can compare quotes in real-time and purchase a policy from one of four auto insurers, as well as a service and maintenance site that provides service reminders and allows consumers to schedule dealer visits.

BUSINESS

AUTOBYTEL.COM INC. is a branded Internet site for new and pre-owned vehicle information and purchasing services. Through www.autobytel.com, consumers can research pricing, specifications and other information regarding new and pre-owned vehicles. When consumers indicate they are ready to buy, they can be connected to Autobytel.com's network of over 2,700 participating dealers in North America, with each dealer representing a particular vehicle make. Dealers participate in the network by entering into non-exclusive contracts with ATBL. In addition, consumers can apply for and receive insurance, financing, leasing and warranty proposals as well as other services and information through the Web site.

ANNUAL FINANCIAL DATA

	12/31/98	12/31/97	12/31/96
Earnings Per Share	d2.30	d2.03	d0.73
Cash Flow Per Share	d2.15	d1.92	d0.70
Tang. Book Val. Per Share	3.04	1.59	...
INCOME STATEMENT (IN THOUSANDS):			
Total Revenues	23,826	15,338	5,025
Costs & Expenses	43,213	31,868	10,945
Depreciation & Amort.	1,256	885	239
Operating Income	d20,643	d17,415	d6,159
Income Before Income Taxes	d19,363	d16,795	d6,035
Income Taxes	35	15	...
Net Income	d19,398	d16,810	d6,035
Cash Flow	d18,142	d15,925	d5,796
Average Shs. Outstg.	8,423	8,291	8,252
BALANCE SHEET (IN THOUSANDS):			
Cash & Cash Equivalents	27,984	15,813	...
Total Current Assets	31,652	18,101	...
Net Property	2,208	2,317	...
Total Assets	34,207	20,513	...
Total Current Liabilities	8,216	7,163	...
Net Stockholders' Equity	25,868	13,259	...
Net Working Capital	23,436	10,938	...
Year-end Shs. Outstg.	8,506	8,324	...

Statistics are as originally reported.

QUARTERLY DATA

(12/31/1998) ($000)	Rev	Inc
1st Quarter................	4,632	(6,898)
2nd Quarter...............	5,405	(3,071)
3rd Quarter	6,462	(5,543)
4th Quarter................	7,327	(3,886)

OFFICERS:
M. J. Fuchs, Chmn.
M. W. Lorimer, C.E.O., Pres.
H. Printer, Sr. V.P., C.F.O.
A. Amir, V.P., Gen. Couns.

PRINCIPAL OFFICE: 18872 MacArthur Boulevard, Irvine, CA 92612-1400

TELEPHONE NUMBER: (949) 225-4500
FAX: (949) 757-8937
WEB: www.autobytel.com
NO. OF EMPLOYEES: 180
SHAREHOLDERS: 49
ANNUAL MEETING: In July
INCORPORATED: DE, 1996

INSTITUTIONAL HOLDINGS:
No. of Institutions: 31
Shares Held: 672,091
% Held: 3.8

INDUSTRY: Computer related services, nec (SIC: 7379)

TRANSFER AGENT(S): U.S. Stock Transfer Corporation, Glendale, CA

AUTOWEB.COM, INC.

YIELD ...
P/E RATIO ...

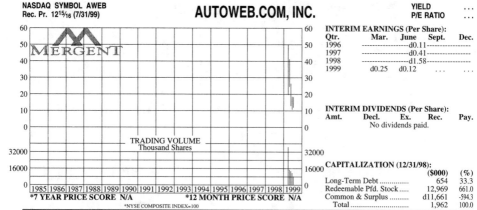

*7 YEAR PRICE SCORE N/A   *12 MONTH PRICE SCORE N/A
*NYSE COMPOSITE INDEX=100

INTERIM EARNINGS (Per Share):

Qtr.	Mar.	June	Sept.	Dec.
1996	------------------d0.11------------------			
1997	------------------d0.41------------------			
1998	------------------d1.58------------------			
1999	d0.25	d0.12	...	...

INTERIM DIVIDENDS (Per Share):

Amt.	Decl.	Ex.	Rec.	Pay.
	No dividends paid.			

CAPITALIZATION (12/31/98):

	($000)	(%)
Long-Term Debt	654	33.3
Redeemable Pfd. Stock	12,969	661.0
Common & Surplus	d11,661	-594.3
Total	1,962	100.0

RECENT DEVELOPMENTS: For the quarter ended 6/30/99, the Company reported a net loss of $3.0 million compared with a net loss of $2.1 million in the corresponding period of 1998. Net revenues more than doubled to $7.0 million from $2.8 million in the prior year. The top line benefited from growth in AWEB's dealer network and a substantial increase in visitors to its internet site. During the quarter, AWEB entered into advertising agreements with Yahoo!, America Online, and Hotbot, which is expected to further expand its visibility, broaden its reach and drive traffic to its site. In July 1999, AWEB acquired SalesEnhancer.com, an Internet-based auto dealer support service from Solution Management, Inc. SalesEnhancer.com provides sales management tools that enables dealers to better manage purchase inquiries, improve customer response time and sell more cars.

BUSINESS

AUTOWEB.COM, INC. is a consumer automotive Internet service. With an extensive collection of automotive-related community, content and commerce offerings, Autoweb.com™ guides consumers through every stage of the vehicle ownership process from browsing and buying, to maintaining or selling. Autoweb.com™ process connects mass market consumers to real-world buying alternatives through a network of member dealers and other commerce partners.

ANNUAL FINANCIAL DATA

	12/31/98	12/31/97	12/31/96
Earnings Per Share	d1.58	d0.41	d0.11
Cash Flow Per Share	d1.51	d0.39	d0.11
INCOME STATEMENT (IN THOUSANDS):			
Total Revenues	13,041	3,492	307
Costs & Expenses	23,915	6,305	1,102
Depreciation & Amort.	551	158	40
Operating Income	d11,425	d2,971	d835
Income Before Income Taxes	d11,484	d2,920	d845
Net Income	d11,484	d2,920	d845
Cash Flow	d11,823	d3,038	d813
Average Shs. Outstg.	7,850	7,794	7,497
BALANCE SHEET (IN THOUSANDS):			
Cash & Cash Equivalents	2,714	1,819	...
Total Current Assets	6,023	2,819	...
Net Property	1,162	475	...
Total Assets	7,185	3,294	...
Total Current Liabilities	5,223	2,046	...
Long-Term Obligations	654	17	...
Net Stockholders' Equity	d11,661	d4,030	...
Net Working Capital	800	773	...
Year-end Shs. Outstg.	8,063	7,812	7,794
STATISTICAL RECORD:			
Debt/Total Assets %	9.1	0.5	...

Statistics are as originally reported.

OFFICERS:
F. Zamani, Chmn., Sec.
D. A. DeBiase, Pres., C.E.O.
S. M. Hedgpeth III, V.P., Fin., Admin.,
C.F.O., Treas.,

PRINCIPAL OFFICE: 3270 Jay Street,
Building 6, Santa Clara, CA 95054

TELEPHONE NUMBER: (408) 554-9552
WEB: www.autoweb.com

NO. OF EMPLOYEES: 81 (avg.)

SHAREHOLDERS: 58

ANNUAL MEETING: N/A

INCORPORATED: CA, Oct., 1995; reincorp.,
DE, Mar., 1999

INSTITUTIONAL HOLDINGS:
No. of Institutions: 20
Shares Held: 556,832
% Held: 2.2

INDUSTRY: Automotive services, nec (SIC: 7549)

TRANSFER AGENT(S): American Securities
Transfer & Trust, Inc.

AXENT TECHNOLOGIES INC.

YIELD ...
P/E RATIO 73.7

| 1985 | 1986 | 1987 | 1988 | 1989 | 1990 | 1991 | 1992 | 1993 | 1994 | 1995 | 1996 | 1997 | 1998 | 1999 |

TRADING VOLUME
Thousand Shares

*7 YEAR PRICE SCORE N/A　　　　***12 MONTH PRICE SCORE 54.9**

*NYSE COMPOSITE INDEX=100

INTERIM EARNINGS (Per Share):

Qtr.	Mar.	June	Sept.	Dec.
1995	---------------d0.30----------------			
1996	0.01	0.11	0.05	0.14
1997	d2.32	0.11	0.12	0.31
1998	d0.41	0.16	0.18	0.32
1999	d0.23	0.08	...	...

INTERIM DIVIDENDS (Per Share):

Amt.	Decl.	Ex.	Rec.	Pay.
	No dividends paid.			

CAPITALIZATION (12/31/98):

	($000)	(%)
Common & Surplus	134,437	100.0
Total	134,437	100.0

RECENT DEVELOPMENTS: For the quarter ended 6/30/99, the Company reported a net loss of $2.2 million compared with a net loss of $4.0 million in the equivalent quarter of 1998. Results for the second quarter of 1999 included a $1.3 million non-recurring charge for amortization of intangible assets. Total net revenues rose 17.3% to $26.4 million from $22.5 million in the prior-year period. Gross profit increased 11.7% to $22.7 million compared with $20.3 million a year ago. The Company unveiled an e-security strategy, leveraging its products and Lifecycle Security™ services, designed to allow companies to safely execute e-business and e-commerce activities. AXNT also introduced the Smart Security Architecture, which helps align the appropriate level of security for each customer's business needs. In addition, AXNT introduced NetProwler™ 3.0, a network intrusion detection software system that allows companies to protect against attacks and secure proprietary systems in real-time.

BUSINESS

AXENT TECHNOLOGIES INC. is a developer and provider of information security products for organizations using enterprise computer networks, including systems that utilize the Internet, internal networks, individual servers, workstations and desktop and laptop computers. AXNT's products provide security assessment and policy management, host- and network-based intrusion detection, systems and network access control, data confidentiality, user administration, activity monitoring, security authentication solutions for remote network access and virtual private networking capabilities for remote users and remote sites. Some of AXNT's products include Enterprise Security Manager™, NetRecon™, Intruder Alert™ and NetProwler™. These products allow customers to create systems and networks that are protected from access, theft and damage by unauthorized users. The Company operates four software development centers in Utah, New Hampshire, California, and Massachusetts. The Company's information security products are used by more than 5,000 companies and government agencies.

ANNUAL FINANCIAL DATA

	12/31/98	12/31/97	12/31/96	12/31/95	12/31/94	12/31/93
Earnings Per Share	④ 0.30	③ d1.65	① 0.31	① d0.30	② d0.36	① 0.06
Cash Flow Per Share	0.41	d1.52	0.38	d0.25	d0.28	0.12
Tang. Book Val. Per Share	5.28	3.47	3.40	0.37	0.24	...
INCOME STATEMENT (IN THOUSANDS):						
Total Revenues	101,019	41,661	22,097	14,728	8,594	6,075
Costs & Expenses	89,670	60,964	21,296	19,048	13,210	5,877
Depreciation & Amort.	2,920	1,569	743	392	697	535
Operating Income	8,429	d20,872	58	d4,712	d5,313	d337
Net Interest Inc./(Exp.)	4,506	1,760	1,065	d129	...	...
Income Before Income Taxes	7,679	d9,098	5,603	d6,987	d7,353	d1,243
Net Income	④ 7,679	③ d19,696	① 3,285	① d2,695	② d3,273	① 569
Cash Flow	10,599	d18,127	4,028	d2,303	d2,576	1,104
Average Shs. Outstg.	25,990	11,927	10,662	9,118	9,065	9,021
BALANCE SHEET (IN THOUSANDS):						
Cash & Cash Equivalents	111,742	40,890	35,890	6,083	6,612	...
Total Current Assets	144,262	52,867	41,284	11,492	9,317	...
Net Property	7,446	2,240	1,417	1,097	590	...
Total Assets	161,263	56,475	44,001	12,646	10,009	...
Total Current Liabilities	26,826	13,416	9,553	9,544	6,951	...
Long-Term Obligations	...	...	...	...	865	...
Net Stockholders' Equity	134,437	43,059	34,448	2,976	1,944	...
Net Working Capital	117,436	39,451	31,731	1,948	2,366	...
Year-end Shs. Outstg.	25,460	12,397	10,130	7,953	7,944	...
STATISTICAL RECORD:						
Operating Profit Margin %	8.3	...	0.3	...	...	...
Net Profit Margin %	7.6	...	14.9	...	...	9.4
Return on Equity %	5.7	...	9.5	...	...	...
Return on Assets %	4.8	...	7.5	...	...	...
Debt/Total Assets %	...	...	...	...	8.6	...
Price Range	32⅝-12	25½-10⅜	24¼-9⅜	...	...	...
P/E Ratio	108.7-40.0	...	78.2-30.2	...	...	...

Statistics are as originally reported. ① Bef. disc. ops. income 12/31/96, $2.4 mill.; income 12/31/95, $5.1 mill.; income 12/31/93, $1.7 mill. ② Incls. one-time pre-tax chrg. of $4.3 mill.; bef. income from disc. ops. of $3.8 mill. ③ Incls. one-time pre-tax chrg. of $25.9 mill.; bef. inc. of $255,000 from disc. ops. ④ Incls. one-time pre-tax chrg. of $17.0 mill.

OFFICERS:
J. C. Becker, Chmn., C.E.O.
B. M. Jackson, Pres., C.O.O.
R. B. Edwards Jr., V.P., C.F.O., Treas.
G. M. Ford, V.P., Gen. Couns., Sec.

PRINCIPAL OFFICE: 2400 Research Blvd., Ste. 200, Rockville, MD 20850

TELEPHONE NUMBER: (301) 258-5043
FAX: (301) 330-5756
WEB: www.axent.com

NO. OF EMPLOYEES: 527 (avg.)

SHAREHOLDERS: 310 (approx. holders of record); 19,000(approx. bene. holders)

ANNUAL MEETING: In Jun.

INCORPORATED: DE, 1991

INSTITUTIONAL HOLDINGS:
No. of Institutions: 107
Shares Held: 16,067,319
% Held: 57.7

INDUSTRY: Prepackaged software (SIC: 7372)

TRANSFER AGENT(S): Boston EquiServe, Boston, MA.

BEYOND.COM CORP.

YIELD ...
P/E RATIO ...

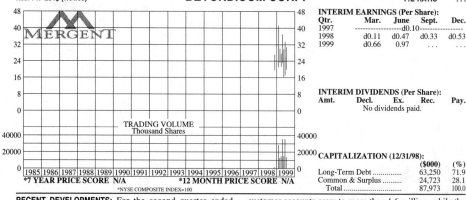

*7 YEAR PRICE SCORE N/A   *12 MONTH PRICE SCORE N/A

*NYSE COMPOSITE INDEX=100

INTERIM EARNINGS (Per Share):

Qtr.	Mar.	June	Sept.	Dec.
1997	------------------d0.10------------------			
1998	d0.11	d0.47	d0.33	d0.53
1999	d0.66	0.97	...	...

INTERIM DIVIDENDS (Per Share):

Amt.	Decl.	Ex.	Rec.	Pay.
	No dividends paid.			

CAPITALIZATION (12/31/98):

	($000)	(%)
Long-Term Debt	63,250	71.9
Common & Surplus	24,723	28.1
Total	87,973	100.0

RECENT DEVELOPMENTS: For the second quarter ended 6/30/99, the Company reported a net loss of $34.2 million compared with a net loss of $5.6 million in the corresponding quarter of the previous year. Earnings in the 1999 quarter included goodwill and deferred compensation charges totaling $12.3 million. Revenue more than tripled to $26.3 million versus $7.6 million the year before. Operating losses totaled $34.4 million versus an operating loss of $5.4 million in the previous year. Overall cumulative customer accounts grew to more than 1.6 million, while the Company's affiliates program, which enables commercial sites to promote and sell BYND's products, increased to 34,400 affiliates. During the quarter, BYND was awarded a three-year, $6.1 million contract with the U.S. Patent and Trademark Office. The Company also won a 65-month, $120.0 million contract with the IRS to electronically deliver upgrades of Microsoft products.

BUSINESS

BEYOND.COM CORP. is engaged in the online reselling of commercial off-the-shelf computer software. Through its on-line store, the Company offers consumers, corporations, and government agencies software as well as related computer products, customer service, website design consultation, and marketing support. In addition to the traditional delivery of standardized media and computer products, BYND offers digital delivery of software on demand.

QUARTERLY DATA

12/31/98 ($000)	REV	INC
1st Quarter	6,192	(2,227)
2nd Quarter	7,577	(5,564)
3rd Quarter	9,742	(8,898)
4th Quarter	13,139	(14,384)

ANNUAL FINANCIAL DATA

	12/31/98	12/31/97	12/31/96	12/31/95
Earnings Per Share	d1.65	① d0.21	① d0.10	d0.07
Cash Flow Per Share	d1.21	d0.20	d0.10	d0.07
Tang. Book Val. Per Share	0.90	...	...	...
INCOME STATEMENT (IN THOUSANDS):				
Total Revenues	36,650	16,806	5,858	1,003
Costs & Expenses	59,495	18,637	6,703	1,507
Depreciation & Amort.	8,291	79	19	14
Operating Income	d31,136	d1,910	d864	d518
Net Interest Inc./(Exp.)	63	167	85	7
Income Before Income Taxes	d31,073	d1,743	d779	d511
Net Income	d31,073	① d1,743	① d779	d511
Cash Flow	d22,833	d1,765	d861	d598
Average Shs. Outstg.	18,900	9,000	9,000	9,000
BALANCE SHEET (IN THOUSANDS):				
Cash & Cash Equivalents	81,548	2,571	3,737	...
Total Current Assets	102,059	9,206	5,143	...
Net Property	3,150	380	66	...
Total Assets	109,904	9,586	5,691	...
Total Current Liabilities	21,931	8,113	1,600	...
Long-Term Obligations	63,250	99	105	...
Net Stockholders' Equity	24,723	d11,191	d2,409	...
Net Working Capital	80,128	1,093	3,543	...
Year-end Shs. Outstg.	27,425	9,070	9,000	...
STATISTICAL RECORD:				
Debt/Total Assets %	57.6	1.0	1.8	...
Price Range	27¼-19⁹⁄₁₆	...	...	...

Statistics are as originally reported. ① Bef. disc. oper. loss $3.6 mill., 12/97; $736,000, 12/96

OFFICERS:
W. S. McKiernan, Chmn.
M. L. Breier, Pres., C.E.O.
M. J. Praisner, V.P., C.F.O.
R. Scudellari, Sec.

INVESTOR CONTACT: Investor Relations, (408) 616-4200

PRINCIPAL OFFICE: 1195 West Fremont Ave., Sunnyvale, CA 94087

TELEPHONE NUMBER: (408) 616-4200
WEB: www.software.net or www.beyond.com

NO. OF EMPLOYEES: 137 (avg.)

SHAREHOLDERS: 105 (approx.)

ANNUAL MEETING: In Apr.

INCORPORATED: CA, Aug., 1994; reincorp., DE, Jun., 1998

INSTITUTIONAL HOLDINGS:
No. of Institutions: 43
Shares Held: 10,798,326
% Held: 30.2

INDUSTRY: Prepackaged software (SIC: 7372)

TRANSFER AGENT(S): BankBoston, N.A., Canton, MA.

BLUEFLY, INC.

YIELD ...
P/E RATIO ...

INTERIM EARNINGS (Per Share):

Qtr.	Mar.	June	Sept.	Dec.
1997	0.02	d0.27	d0.06	0.13
1998	d0.11	d0.15	d0.25	d0.38
1999	d0.27	0.61	...	...

INTERIM DIVIDENDS (Per Share):

Amt.	Decl.	Ex.	Rec.	Pay.
	No dividends paid.			

TRADING VOLUME
Thousand Shares

1985 1986 1987 1988 1989 1990 1991 1992 1993 1994 1995 1996 1997 1998 1999

*7 YEAR PRICE SCORE N/A   ***12 MONTH PRICE SCORE N/A**

*NYSE COMPOSITE INDEX=100

CAPITALIZATION (12/31/98):

	($000)	(%)
Common & Surplus	6,392	100.0
Total	6,392	100.0

RECENT DEVELOPMENTS: For the second quarter ended 6/30/99, the Company reported a net loss of $3.0 million compared with a loss from continuing operations of $397,000 in the corresponding prior-year period. Results for the 1998 quarter excluded a loss of $1.1 million related to the discontinued golf sportswear division. The Company reported net sales of $802,000. The growth in sales was attributed to the Company's strategic marketing relationships, its print advertising campaign, and the increased breadth of its inventory. During the quarter, the Company launched a completely redesigned version of its Web site, adding two new departments and a host of improvements to its customer interface. In addition, BFLY entered into an agreement with an investor group led by affiliates of Soros Private Equity Partners. The agreement provides for a $10.0 million investment in the Company.

BUSINESS

BLUEFLY, INC. (formerly Pivot Rules, Inc.) is an Internet retailer of designer fashions at outlet store prices. BFLY opened its virtual doors to the public on September 8, 1998. The Company's Web site, Bluefly.com, offers approximately 3,400 styles of products from over 90 different top, name-brand designers. As of 6/30/99, the total number of registered users was approximately 85,370. The Company has entered into strategic marketing relationships which provides it with highly targeted, prominent positioning on nine of the top twelve most visited Web sites or portals (i.e. America Online, Excite, Go Network, Lycos, MSN, Netcenter, Tripod, Women.com and Yahoo!), and has been featured in numerous national publications and several television reports. In 9/98, the Company disposed of its golf sportswear division. In 10/98, the Company changed its name to Bluefly, Inc. in an effort to concentrate on its Internet retail operations.

ANNUAL FINANCIAL DATA

	12/31/98	12/31/97	12/31/96	12/31/95
Earnings Per Share	① d0.89	d0.18	0.11	d0.17
Cash Flow Per Share	d0.85	0.03	0.16	d0.14
Tang. Book Val. Per Share	1.86	2.24	0.34	...
INCOME STATEMENT (IN THOUSANDS):				
Total Revenues	243	10,323	8,596	6,337
Costs & Expenses	2,785	9,959	8,018	6,241
Depreciation & Amort.	128	452	55	43
Operating Income	d2,670	d88	523	53
Net Interest Inc./(Exp.)	142	d220	d443	d418
Income Before Income Taxes	d2,528	d563	205	d297
Income Taxes	cr50	cr182	70	cr89
Net Income	① d2,478	d381	135	d208
Cash Flow	d2,350	71	190	d165
Average Shs. Outstg.	2,771	2,149	1,200	1,200
BALANCE SHEET (IN THOUSANDS):				
Cash & Cash Equivalents	2,830	55	33	...
Total Current Assets	6,653	6,222	1,255	...
Net Property	497	774	89	...
Total Assets	7,165	7,151	1,636	...
Total Current Liabilities	773	1,101	1,092	...
Long-Term Obligations	...	...	135	...
Net Stockholders' Equity	6,392	6,050	409	...
Net Working Capital	5,880	5,121	163	...
Year-end Shs. Outstg.	3,433	2,700	1,200	...
STATISTICAL RECORD:				
Operating Profit Margin %	...	...	6.1	0.8
Net Profit Margin %	...	...	1.6	...
Return on Equity %	...	...	33.0	...
Return on Assets %	...	...	8.3	...
Debt/Total Assets %	...	...	8.3	...
Price Range	24½-3⅜	...	...	...

Statistics are as originally reported. ① Bef. disc. oper. loss $1.2 mill., but incl. non-recurr. chrg. $332,000.

OFFICERS:
E. K. Seiff, Chmn., Pres., C.E.O. & Treas.
P. C. Barry, Exec. V.P. & C.F.O.
J. B. Morris, Exec. V.P. & Sec.

PRINCIPAL OFFICE: 42 West 39th St., New York, NY 10018

TELEPHONE NUMBER: (212) 944-8000
WEB: www.bluefly.com

NO. OF EMPLOYEES: 27 full-time; 2 part-time

SHAREHOLDERS: 64 (of record); 300 (approx. beneficial)

ANNUAL MEETING: In Oct.
INCORPORATED: NY, 1991

INSTITUTIONAL HOLDINGS:
No. of Institutions: 6
Shares Held: 320,307
% Held: 6.6

INDUSTRY: Men's and boys' clothing (SIC: 5136)

TRANSFER AGENT(S): American Stock Transfer & Trust Company, New York, NY

BOTTOMLINE TECHNOLOGIES INC.

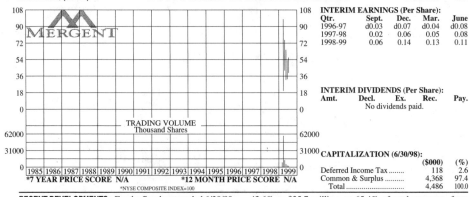

INTERIM EARNINGS (Per Share):

Qtr.	Sept.	Dec.	Mar.	June
1996-97	d0.03	d0.07	d0.04	d0.08
1997-98	0.02	0.06	0.05	0.08
1998-99	0.06	0.14	0.13	0.11

INTERIM DIVIDENDS (Per Share):

Amt.	Decl.	Ex.	Rec.	Pay.
		No dividends paid.		

CAPITALIZATION (6/30/98):

	($000)	(%)
Deferred Income Tax	118	2.6
Common & Surplus	4,368	97.4
Total	4,486	100.0

7 YEAR PRICE SCORE N/A   **12 MONTH PRICE SCORE N/A**

*NYSE COMPOSITE INDEX=100

RECENT DEVELOPMENTS: For the fiscal year ended 6/30/99, net income soared to $4.1 million from $1.6 million the year before. Diluted earnings per share amounted to $0.43 versus $0.20 a year earlier. Total revenues advanced 35.4% to $39.3 million from $29.0 million in the prior year. Software licenses revenues jumped 60.7% to $15.9 million from $9.9 million in the previous year, while service and maintenance revenues increased 28.0% to $12.4 million compared with $9.7 million in 1998. Gross profit improved 42.6% to $25.7 million, or 65.4% of total revenues, from $18.0 million, or 62.1% of total revenues, in the prior year. On 7/13/99, the Company acquired NetTransact, an Internet/electronic bill presentment system, from The Northern Trust Company. Along with the acquisition, the Company entered into a marketing agreement with Northern Trust, whereby Northern Trust will market the product to its corporate treasury management clients.

BUSINESS

BOTTOMLINE TECHNOLOGIES INC. provides software that is used to make and manage corporate payments. The Company's products and services enable organizations to make the transition from the traditional paper check process to electronic payments and electronic commerce. The Company's software complements and integrates with existing corporate payment applications, such as accounts payable, payroll, travel expenses and insurance claims, and offers a single solution to control, manage and issue all payments. EPAY also offers consulting services and related equipment and supplies to help customers plan, design and implement transition from paper to electronic payments. The Company has more than 2,000 customers, representing every major industry sector, including The Charles Schwab Corporation, Dow Jones & Company, Inc., The Federal Reserve System, Microsoft Corporation and Nissan Motor Acceptance Corporation.

ANNUAL FINANCIAL DATA

	6/30/98	6/30/97	6/30/96
Earnings Per Share	0.20	d0.23	0.14
Cash Flow Per Share	0.33	d0.01	0.29
Tang. Book Val. Per Share	0.69	0.42	...
INCOME STATEMENT (IN THOUSANDS):			
Total Revenues	29,037	22,126	18,067
Costs & Expenses	25,380	22,684	15,730
Depreciation & Amort.	827	1,174	784
Operating Income	2,830	d1,732	1,553
Net Interest Inc./(Exp.)	d50	d56	d6
Income Before Income Taxes	2,780	d1,788	1,547
Income Taxes	1,177	cr536	664
Net Income	1,603	d1,252	883
Cash Flow	2,430	d78	1,667
Average Shs. Outstg.	7,316	5,986	5,693
BALANCE SHEET (IN THOUSANDS):			
Cash & Cash Equivalents	1,362	827	...
Total Current Assets	9,346	8,742	...
Net Property	1,865	1,446	...
Total Assets	11,301	10,481	...
Total Current Liabilities	5,462	6,266	...
Long-Term Obligations	...	54	...
Net Stockholders' Equity	4,368	2,680	...
Net Working Capital	3,884	2,476	...
Year-end Shs. Outstg.	6,360	6,306	5,844
STATISTICAL RECORD:			
Operating Profit Margin %	9.7	...	8.6
Net Profit Margin %	5.5	...	4.9
Return on Equity %	36.7	...	...
Return on Assets %	14.2	...	...
Debt/Total Assets %	...	0.5	...

Statistics are as originally reported.

OFFICERS:
D. M. McGurl, Chmn., Pres., C.E.O.
R. A. Eberle, Exec. V.P., C.F.O., Treas.
J. L. Mullen, Exec. V.P.

PRINCIPAL OFFICE: 155 Fleet Street, Portsmouth, NH 03801

TELEPHONE NUMBER: (603) 436-0700
FAX: (603) 436-0300
WEB: www.bottomline.com

NO. OF EMPLOYEES: 238

SHAREHOLDERS: N/A

ANNUAL MEETING: N/A

INCORPORATED: NH, 1989; reincorp., DE, Aug., 1997

INSTITUTIONAL HOLDINGS:
No. of Institutions: 38
Shares Held: 897,192
% Held: 8.6

INDUSTRY: Prepackaged software (SIC: 7372)

TRANSFER AGENT(S): State Street Bank and Trust Company, Canton, MA

BROADCOM CORP.

YIELD ...
P/E RATIO 256.4

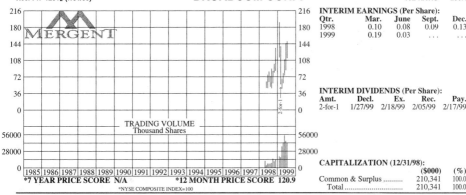

*7 YEAR PRICE SCORE N/A *12 MONTH PRICE SCORE 120.9
*NYSE COMPOSITE INDEX=100

TRADING VOLUME
Thousand Shares

INTERIM EARNINGS (Per Share):

Qtr.	Mar.	June	Sept.	Dec.
1998	0.10	0.08	0.09	0.13
1999	0.19	0.03	...	...

INTERIM DIVIDENDS (Per Share):

Amt.	Decl.	Ex.	Rec.	Pay.
2-for-1	1/27/99	2/18/99	2/05/99	2/17/99

CAPITALIZATION (12/31/98):

	($000)	(%)
Common & Surplus	210,341	100.0
Total	210,341	100.0

RECENT DEVELOPMENTS: For the quarter ended 6/30/99, net income dropped 41.9% to $2.8 million compared with $4.9 million in the corresponding quarter of the previous year. Earnings in 1999 included merger-related charges of $11.1 million and litigation settlement charges of $17.0 million. Revenues climbed sharply to $116.3 million from $45.2 million in the previous year. Gross profit soared to $69.2 million from $24.8 million the year before. During the quarter, BRCM introduced the Broadcom BCM5400, a transceiver which will enable business networking makers to deliver data at gigabit speeds over cable wire. On 5/31/99, the Company completed the acquisition of three companies, Maverick Networks, Epigram, Inc. and Armedia, Inc. In July 1999, BRCM acquired HotHaus Technologies Inc., a telecommunications software company specializing in voice over Internet protocol, for about $280.0 million in stock. In August 1999, BRCM acquired AltoCom, Inc., a PC modem technology company.

BUSINESS

BROADCOM CORP. is a provider of highly integrated silicon products that enable broadband digital transmission of voice, data and video content to and throughout the home and within the business enterprise. Using proprietary technologies, the company designs, develops and supplies integrated circuits for various broadband communications markets, including the markets for cable set-top boxes, cable modems, high-speed office networks, home networking, direct broadcast satellite and terrestrial digital broadcast, and digital subscriber line.

REVENUES

12/31/98	($000)	(%)
Product Revenue	198,481	97.7
Development Revenue.................	4,614	2.3
Total Revenue	203,095	100.0

ANNUAL FINANCIAL DATA

	12/31/98	12/31/97	12/31/96	12/31/95
Earnings Per Share	0.39	d0.02	0.06	Nil
Cash Flow Per Share	0.48	0.04	0.08	0.01
Tang. Book Val. Per Share	2.34	0.08	0.06	...
INCOME STATEMENT (IN THOUSANDS):				
Total Revenues	203,095	36,955	21,370	6,107
Costs & Expenses	142,046	36,088	16,171	5,769
Depreciation & Amort.	8,819	3,105	897	451
Operating Income	52,230	d2,238	4,302	d113
Income Before Income Taxes	55,997	d1,948	4,515	7
Income Taxes	19,599	cr775	1,499	3
Net Income	36,398	d1,173	3,016	4
Cash Flow	45,217	1,932	3,913	455
Average Shs. Outstg.	93,664	52,903	49,879	43,460
BALANCE SHEET (IN THOUSANDS):				
Cash & Cash Equivalents	62,629	22,116	4,657	...
Total Current Assets	157,295	36,519	9,979	...
Net Property	28,286	8,449	4,298	...
Total Assets	237,444	45,244	14,367	...
Total Current Liabilities	27,103	10,257	4,450	...
Long-Term Obligations	...	1,595	147	...
Net Stockholders' Equity	210,341	33,392	9,770	...
Net Working Capital	130,192	26,262	5,529	...
Year-end Shs. Outstg.	90,065	63,004	58,808	...
STATISTICAL RECORD:				
Operating Profit Margin %	25.7	...	20.1	...
Net Profit Margin %	17.9	...	14.1	0.1
Return on Equity %	17.3	...	30.9	...
Return on Assets %	15.3	...	21.0	...
Debt/Total Assets %	...	3.5	1.0	...
Price Range	135-47	...	...	...
P/E Ratio	346.1-120.5	...	...	...

Statistics are as originally reported. Adj. for stk. split: 2-for-1, 2/17/99

OFFICERS:
H. T. Nicholas III, Co-Chmn., Pres., C.E.O.
H. Samueli Ph.D, Co-Chmn., V.P.
W. J. Ruehle, V.P., C.F.O.
D. A. Dull, V.P., Gen. Couns.

INVESTOR CONTACT: Investor Relations, (949) 585-5660

PRINCIPAL OFFICE: 16215 Alton Parkway, Irvine, CA 92618-3616

TELEPHONE NUMBER: (949) 450-8700
FAX: (949) 450-8710
WEB: www.broadcom.com
NO. OF EMPLOYEES: 411 full-time; 25 part-time (approx.)
SHAREHOLDERS: 319 (class A, approx.); 229 (class B, approx.).
ANNUAL MEETING: In May
INCORPORATED: CA, Aug., 1991

INSTITUTIONAL HOLDINGS:
No. of Institutions: 119
Shares Held: 15,464,619
% Held: 40.0

INDUSTRY: Semiconductors and related devices (SIC: 3674)

TRANSFER AGENT(S): U.S. Stock Transfer Corporation, Glendale, CA.

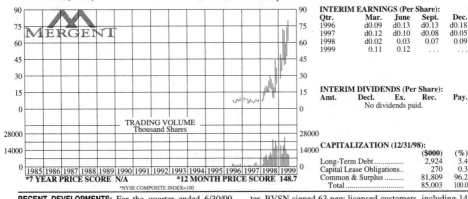

NASDAQ SYMBOL BVSN
Rec. Pr. 69¹¹⁄₁₆ (7/31/99)

BROADVISION, INC.

YIELD ...
P/E RATIO 178.7

INTERIM EARNINGS (Per Share):

Qtr.	Mar.	June	Sept.	Dec.
1996	d0.09	d0.13	d0.13	d0.18
1997	d0.12	d0.10	d0.08	d0.05
1998	d0.02	0.03	0.07	0.09
1999	0.11	0.12	...	...

INTERIM DIVIDENDS (Per Share):

Amt.	Decl.	Ex.	Rec.	Pay.
	No dividends paid.			

TRADING VOLUME
Thousand Shares

CAPITALIZATION (12/31/98):

	($000)	(%)
Long-Term Debt	2,924	3.4
Capital Lease Obligations..	270	0.3
Common & Surplus	81,809	96.2
Total	85,003	100.0

*7 YEAR PRICE SCORE N/A   *12 MONTH PRICE SCORE 148.7
*NYSE COMPOSITE INDEX=100

RECENT DEVELOPMENTS: For the quarter ended 6/30/99, net income totaled $3.3 million compared with $693,000 in the corresponding prior-year period. Total revenues more than doubled to $23.5 million from $11.4 million a year earlier. Software license revenues soared 93.1% to $15.5 million. Service revenues jumped to $8.0 million versus $3.4 million in 1998. Gross profit climbed 96.2% to $17.8 million from $9.1 million. Operating income totaled $2.9 million compared with $28,000 in 1998. During the quar-

ter, BVSN signed 63 new licensed customers, including 14 partner organizations, bringing the total to more than 350 accounts worldwide. BVSN also introduced the latest versions of the BroadVision One-To-One™ Commerce family. TELUS Interactive, a new service providing enhanced opportunities for companies to do e-business more cost effectively, is based on BVSN's core application. BVSN has expanded its international operations to Latin American markets.

BUSINESS

BROADVISION, INC. develops, markets and supports application software products for one-to-one relationship management for the extended enterprise. These products are designed to enable businesses to use the Internet as a cost-effective platform to conduct e-commerce, provide self-service, and deliver targeted information for the financial services, retail, distribution, high technology, telecommunications, and travel industries. The BROADVISION ONE-TO-ONE™ product family allows businesses to tailor World Wide Web site content to the needs and interests of individual users by personalizing each visit on a real-time basis.

ANNUAL FINANCIAL DATA

	12/31/98	12/31/97	12/31/96	12/31/95	12/31/94	12/31/93
Earnings Per Share	0.16	d0.36	d0.54	d0.23	...	...
Cash Flow Per Share	0.31	d0.26	d0.47	d0.22	...	...
Tang. Book Val. Per Share	3.30	0.74	1.06	0.67	0.38	...
INCOME STATEMENT (IN THOUSANDS):						
Total Revenues	50,911	27,105	10,882	540	...	...
Costs & Expenses	45,193	32,702	20,313	4,798	1,688	140
Depreciation & Amort.	3,794	2,041	1,266	220	83	3
Operating Income	1,924	d7,638	d10,697	d4,478	d1,771	d143
Net Interest Inc./(Exp.)	...	...	...	191	101	7
Income Before Income Taxes	3,960	d7,373	d10,145	d4,318	d1,670	d136
Income Taxes	cr79	...	...	...	...	...
Net Income	4,039	d7,373	d10,145	d4,318	d1,670	d136
Cash Flow	7,833	d5,332	d8,879	d4,098	d1,587	d133
Average Shs. Outstg.	25,653	20,208	18,815	18,543	...	...
BALANCE SHEET (IN THOUSANDS):						
Cash & Cash Equivalents	61,878	10,473	19,720	4,507	2,297	...
Total Current Assets	80,828	20,625	25,585	4,926	2,322	...
Net Property	8,034	6,467	3,024	868	309	...
Total Assets	101,562	27,342	28,930	5,857	2,640	...
Total Current Liabilities	16,508	9,140	7,327	1,010	114	...
Long-Term Obligations	3,194	3,005	495	516	...	...
Net Stockholders' Equity	81,809	15,121	21,016	4,254	2,526	...
Net Working Capital	64,320	11,485	18,258	3,916	2,208	...
Year-end Shs. Outstg.	24,796	20,343	19,908	6,308	6,720	5,700
STATISTICAL RECORD:						
Operating Profit Margin %	3.8	...	...	...	...	...
Net Profit Margin %	7.9	...	...	...	...	...
Return on Equity %	4.9	...	...	...	...	...
Return on Assets %	4.0	...	...	...	...	...
Debt/Total Assets %	3.1	11.0	1.7	8.8	...	...
Price Range	44¼-6	10⅜-4⅛	10-5¼	...	...	...
P/E Ratio	276.4-37.5	...	...	...	...	...

Statistics are as originally reported.

REVENUES

(12/31/98)	($000)	(%)
Software Licenses	36,067	70.8
Services	14,844	29.2
Total	50,911	100.0

OFFICERS:
P. Chen, Chmn., C.E.O.
R. C. Bolten, V.P., C.F.O.,

PRINCIPAL OFFICE: 585 Broadway,
Redwood City, CA 94063

TELEPHONE NUMBER: (650) 261-5100
FAX: (650) 261-5900
WEB: www.broadvision.com

NO. OF EMPLOYEES: 271

SHAREHOLDERS: 9,845

ANNUAL MEETING: In May

INCORPORATED: DE, May, 1993

INSTITUTIONAL HOLDINGS:
No. of Institutions: 124
Shares Held: 13,667,159
% Held: 54.0

INDUSTRY: Prepackaged software (SIC: 7372)

TRANSFER AGENT(S): American Securities Transfer, Inc., Denver, CO

C-ME.COM

YIELD ...
P/E RATIO ...

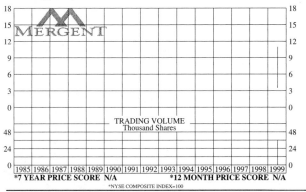

INTERIM EARNINGS (Per Share):

Qtr.	Sept.	Dec.	Mar.	June
1996-97	------------------d0.14------------------			
1997-98	------------------d0.11------------------			
1998-99	------------ d0.07 ------------			...

INTERIM DIVIDENDS (Per Share):

Amt.	Decl.	Ex.	Rec.	Pay.
	No dividends paid.			

CAPITALIZATION (6/30/98):

	($000)	(%)
Common & Surplus	421	100.0
Total	421	100.0

RECENT DEVELOPMENTS: On 7/22/99, the Company completed the initial public offering of 2.5 million shares of CMEE common stock. Proceeds of approximately $3.0 million will be used to expand the Company's relationships with current retail customers, including Burlington Coat Factory and Family Bargain Corporation, and to gain new customers through increased marketing efforts. For the nine months ended 3/31/99, the Company reported a net loss of $389,468 compared with a net loss of $415,892 in the corresponding period a year earlier. Revenues, consisting primarily of fees paid by users of the Company's Virtual Trade Show, Web design services and Internet Sourcing Network users, slid 24.0% to $41,146 from $54,168 a year earlier. Operating loss totaled $407,054 versus a loss of $426,721 the year before, reflecting lower operating costs and expenses.

BUSINESS

CYBER MERCHANTS EXCHANGE, INC., which does business as C-ME.com, is a business-to-business electronic commerce company serving the worldwide retail industry. The Company provides its customers with an Internet-based communications system that enables retailers and suppliers to conduct negotiations and to facilitate electronically the purchase and sale of merchandise. The Company has developed three interrelated services to meet the general merchandising needs of retailers and their vendor suppliers—a virtual trade show, an Internet Sourcing Network and Internet EDI. The Virtual Trade Show consists of a continuous, revolving product showcase that features vendors' products and allows buyers to customize product searches. The Internet Sourcing Network is a private network that links the Company's retail customers with their vendors and handles buyer product inquiries and vendor responses via e-mail. Internet EDI provides retailers a platform for sending purchase orders to vendors, while giving vendors the ability to send real-time invoices, packing lists and shipping information to retailers.

ANNUAL FINANCIAL DATA

	6/30/98	6/30/97
Earnings Per Share	**d0.11**	**d0.14**
Cash Flow Per Share	**d0.10**	**d0.13**
Tang. Book Val. Per Share	**0.07**	**0.10**
INCOME STATEMENT (IN THOUSANDS):		
Total Revenues	66	36
Costs & Expenses	614	648
Depreciation & Amort.	39	25
Operating Income	d587	d637
Net Interest Inc./(Exp.)	16	50
Income Before Income Taxes	d571	d587
Income Taxes	1	1
Net Income	d571	d588
Cash Flow	d533	d563
Average Shs. Outstg.	5,282	4,223
BALANCE SHEET (IN THOUSANDS):		
Cash & Cash Equivalents	82	4
Total Current Assets	389	439
Net Property	79	98
Total Assets	472	541
Total Current Liabilities	51	49
Net Stockholders' Equity	421	492
Net Working Capital	338	390
Year-end Shs. Outstg.	5,750	4,750

Statistics are as originally reported.

OFFICERS:
F. S. Yuan, Chmn., Pres., C.E.O.
H. W. Moore, Vice-Chmn.
D. Rau, C.F.O.

PRINCIPAL OFFICE: 320 S. Garfield Avenue, Suite 318, Alhambra, CA 91801

TELEPHONE NUMBER: (626) 588-3660
FAX: (626) 588-3655
WEB: www.c-me.com

NO. OF EMPLOYEES: 6

SHAREHOLDERS: 520

ANNUAL MEETING: N/A

INCORPORATED: CA, 1996

INSTITUTIONAL HOLDINGS:
No. of Institutions: 7
Shares Held: 690,000
% Held: 12.0

INDUSTRY: Computer programming services (SIC: 7371)

TRANSFER AGENT(S): U.S. Stock Transfer Corporation, Glendale, CA

CAREERBUILDER, INC.

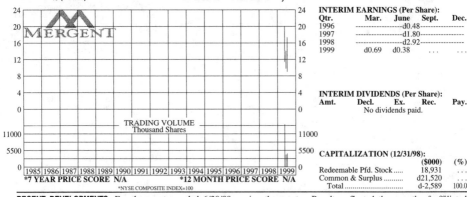

*7 YEAR PRICE SCORE N/A *12 MONTH PRICE SCORE N/A

*NYSE COMPOSITE INDEX=100

INTERIM EARNINGS (Per Share):

Qtr.	Mar.	June	Sept.	Dec.
1996		d0.48		
1997		d1.80		
1998		d2.92		
1999	d0.69	d0.38	...	...

INTERIM DIVIDENDS (Per Share):

Amt.	Decl.	Ex.	Rec.	Pay.
		No dividends paid.		

CAPITALIZATION (12/31/98):

	($000)	(%)
Redeemable Pfd. Stock	18,931	...
Common & Surplus	d21,520	...
Total	d-2,589	100.0

RECENT DEVELOPMENTS: For the quarter ended 6/30/99, the Company reported a net loss of $5.2 million compared with a loss of $3.0 million in the equivalent quarter of 1998. Total revenues more than doubled to $3.3 million from $1.5 million in the prior-year period. Revenues benefited from strong demand for subscription advertising, on-line recruiting services, and job postings. In addition, agreements made with Microsoft, NBC, ComputerJobs, and Ticketmaster Online-CitySearch contributed to results during the quarter. Results reflected the growth of affiliated web sites to 26 from 22 in the first quarter, as well as the increase of U.S. subscribers to 815 from 645 in the first quarter. CBDR announced a marketing agreement with Lycos Network members HotBot, Wired News, HotWired, Webmonkey, and Suck.com. Under the agreement, CBDR will have a prominent place on each web site and provide visitors with direct access to job opportunities via the Company's Mega Job Search™ site.

BUSINESS

CAREERBUILDER, INC. is a provider of comprehensive on-line recruitment offerings for employers and job seekers. Through a network of more than 500 subscribers, job seekers have registered with over 320,000 personal search agents and 18 interactive media companies. The Company provides employers with the ability to advertise jobs and manage their on-line recruiting efforts on a network of integrated sites. Job seekers are provided with tools to find, explore, evaluate, and compare job opportunities. The Company operates three on-line recruitment services: The Career-Builder Network, CareerBuilder.com, and TeamBuilder.

ANNUAL FINANCIAL DATA

	12/31/98	12/31/97	12/31/96
Earnings Per Share	d2.92	d1.80	d0.48
Cash Flow Per Share	d2.72	d1.72	d0.47
INCOME STATEMENT (IN THOUSANDS):			
Total Revenues	7,006	1,925	138
Costs & Expenses	18,153	9,012	2,501
Depreciation & Amort.	871	334	49
Operating Income	d12,018	d7,421	d2,412
Net Interest Inc./(Exp.)	31	107	d4
Income Before Income Taxes	d11,987	d7,314	d2,416
Net Income	d11,987	d7,314	d2,416
Cash Flow	d12,244	d7,529	d2,438
Average Shs. Outstg.	4,494	4,366	5,133
BALANCE SHEET (IN THOUSANDS):			
Cash & Cash Equivalents	2,709	1,909	...
Total Current Assets	4,732	2,510	...
Net Property	1,213	1,000	...
Total Assets	6,042	3,589	...
Total Current Liabilities	8,631	2,641	...
Net Stockholders' Equity	d21,520	d9,752	...
Net Working Capital	d3,899	d131	...
Year-end Shs. Outstg.	4,855	4,371	5,876
STATISTICAL RECORD:			
Statistics are as originally reported.			

REVENUES

(12/31/1998)	($000)	(%)
Service fees	6,648	94.9
Sotware license fees ..	358	5.1
Total	7,006	100.0

OFFICERS:
R. J. McGovern, Chmn., Pres., C.E.O.
J. A. Tholen, Sr. V.P., C.F.O., Sec., Dir.
J. A. Winchester, Sr. V.P., C.T.O.

PRINCIPAL OFFICE: 11495 Sunset Hills Road, Suite 210, Reston, VA 20190

TELEPHONE NUMBER: (703) 709-1001
WEB: www.careerbuilder.com

NO. OF EMPLOYEES: 113 (avg.)

SHAREHOLDERS: 101

ANNUAL MEETING: N/A

INCORPORATED: DE, Nov., 1995

INSTITUTIONAL HOLDINGS:
No. of Institutions: 2
Shares Held: 27,800
% Held: 0.1

INDUSTRY: Information retrieval services
(SIC: 7375)

TRANSFER AGENT(S): American Stock Transfer & Trust Company, New York, NY.

CDNOW, INC.

YIELD ...
P/E RATIO ...

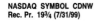

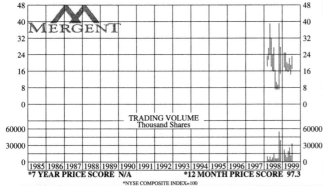

TRADING VOLUME
Thousand Shares

| 1985 | 1986 | 1987 | 1988 | 1989 | 1990 | 1991 | 1992 | 1993 | 1994 | 1995 | 1996 | 1997 | 1998 | 1999 |

*7 YEAR PRICE SCORE N/A   *12 MONTH PRICE SCORE 97.3

*NYSE COMPOSITE INDEX=100

INTERIM EARNINGS (Per Share):

Qtr.	Mar.	June	Sept.	Dec.
1997	d0.07	d0.13	d0.36	d0.86
1998	d0.78	d0.55	d0.74	d0.73
1999	d0.96	d1.06	...	...

INTERIM DIVIDENDS (Per Share):

Amt.	Decl.	Ex.	Rec.	Pay.
	No dividends paid.			

CAPITALIZATION (12/31/98):

	($000)	(%)
Long-Term Debt	1,751	3.3
Common & Surplus	51,139	96.7
Total	52,890	100.0

RECENT DEVELOPMENTS: On 7/13/99, CDNW entered into a definitive agreement with Sony Corporation of America and Time Warner Inc. to merge with Columbia House, a direct marketer of music and videos. For the quarter ended 6/30/99, the Company reported a net loss of $31.7 million compared with a net loss of $8.9 million a year earlier. Included in the current quarter's loss is an $8.1 million charge for amortization of goodwill and other intangibles. Net sales surged to $34.6 million from $11.6 million in the corresponding quarter of 1998. Gross profit rose to $6.6 million from $2.3 million in 1998. Operating loss more than tripled to $32.4 million versus $9.5 million in the prior year, primarily due to significant increases in sales and marketing expenses. During the quarter, CDNW added 332,000 new customers and completed the migration of Music Boulevard with the launch of the new CDNOW store. The Company will begin later in the year to offer digitial downloads of singles, full albums, and compilations.

BUSINESS

CDNOW, INCORPORATED is an on-line retailer of CDs and other music-related products. The Company's on-line store, cdnow.com, offers a broad selection, informative content, easy-to-use navigation and search capabilities, and personalized merchandising and recommendations. To assist customers in making music selections, the CDnow store contains approximately 500,000 product notes, reviews and related articles and 500,000 sound samples.

ANNUAL FINANCIAL DATA

	12/31/98	12/31/97	12/31/96	12/31/95
Earnings Per Share	d2.79	d1.42	...	...
Cash Flow Per Share	d2.66	d1.29	...	...
Tang. Book Val. Per Share	2.87	...	0.07	...
INCOME STATEMENT (IN THOUSANDS):				
Total Revenues	56,395	17,373	6,300	2,176
Costs & Expenses	100,140	26,883	7,991	2,343
Depreciation & Amort.	2,130	1,067	105	33
Operating Income	d45,875	d10,577	d1,796	d200
Net Interest Inc./(Exp.)	2,106	d170	d15	d1
Income Before Income Taxes	d43,769	d10,747	d1,810	d201
Net Income	d43,769	d10,747	① d1,810	d201
Cash Flow	d41,755	d10,091	d1,705	d168
Average Shs. Outstg.	15,713	7,846	...	...
BALANCE SHEET (IN THOUSANDS):				
Cash & Cash Equivalents	49,041	11,689	1,022	...
Total Current Assets	58,204	14,471	1,202	...
Net Property	6,644	1,884	362	...
Total Assets	69,044	16,448	1,575	...
Total Current Liabilities	15,796	15,689	970	...
Long-Term Obligations	1,751	962	91	...
Net Stockholders' Equity	51,139	d9,752	514	...
Net Working Capital	42,408	d1,218	231	...
Year-end Shs. Outstg.	17,843	7,846	7,846	...
STATISTICAL RECORD:				
Debt/Total Assets %	2.5	5.8	5.8	...

Statistics are as originally reported. ① Incl. non-recurr. chrg. $1.0 mill.

OFFICERS:
J. Olim, Chmn., Pres., C.E.O.
J. Sussman, V.P., C.F.O.
M. Olim, Treas., Sec.,
D. Capozzi, V.P., Gen. Couns.

PRINCIPAL OFFICE: 1005 Virginia Drive, Fort Washington, PA 19034

TELEPHONE NUMBER: (215) 619-9900
WEB: www.cdnow.com
NO. OF EMPLOYEES: 191 full-time; 20 part-time
SHAREHOLDERS: 171
ANNUAL MEETING: In March
INCORPORATED: PA, Apr., 1995

INSTITUTIONAL HOLDINGS:
No. of Institutions: 26
Shares Held: 2,651,358
% Held: 9.0
INDUSTRY: Record & prerecorded tape stores (SIC: 5735)
TRANSFER AGENT(S): StockTrans, Inc., Ardmore, PA.

CHEAP TICKETS, INC.

YIELD ...
P/E RATIO ...

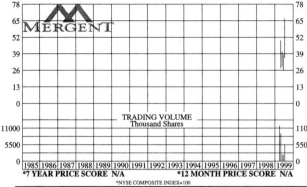

7 YEAR PRICE SCORE N/A   **12 MONTH PRICE SCORE N/A**

*NYSE COMPOSITE INDEX=100

INTERIM EARNINGS (Per Share):

Qtr.	Mar.	June	Sept.	Dec.
1999	0.01	0.15	...	...

INTERIM DIVIDENDS (Per Share):

Amt.	Decl.	Ex.	Rec.	Pay.
	No dividends paid.			

CAPITALIZATION (12/31/98):

	($000)	(%)
Long-Term Debt	586	8.7
Capital Lease Obligations..	652	9.7
Redeemable Pfd. Stock	4,136	61.2
Common & Surplus	1,385	20.5
Total	6,759	100.0

RECENT DEVELOPMENTS: For the quarter ended 6/30/99, net income soared to $3.2 million compared with $644,000 in the corresponding quarter of the previous year. Total revenue more than doubled to $102.6 million from $48.2 million the year before. Gross bookings from non-published fares totaled $97.4 million compared with $45.7 million in the prior-year period. Published fares revenue grew 53.3% to $37.9 million from $24.7 million in 1998.

Internet booking revenue totaled $27.1 million and accounted for 29.7% of gross bookings versus 6.9% the year before. The increase in Internet revenue was positively affected by increased Web site efficiency, increased advertising, and a higher level of consumer awareness. Gross profits advanced to $19.5 million from $9.2 million in the corresponding prior-year period. During the quarter, the Company added 450,661 Internet users.

BUSINESS

CHEAP TICKETS, INC. is a retail seller of discount tickets for domestic air travel, cruises, auto rental, and hotel reservations. The Company sells tickets through call centers, retail stores and its Internet site at www.cheaptickets.com. CTIX sells both published and non-published fares for regularly scheduled domestic routes. Non-published fares are tickets that the Company buys from airlines and resells to consumers at significant discounts off published fares. CTIX has the rights to buy these fares under contracts from over 25 airline carriers, including America West, American, Continental, TWA and US Airways. CTIX also offers a full complement of regularly published fares, giving customers a variety of choice in leisure travel tickets at competitive prices.

ANNUAL FINANCIAL DATA

	12/31/98	12/31/97	12/31/96
Earnings Per Share	0.03	d0.09	0.05
Cash Flow Per Share	0.06	d0.06	0.06
Tang. Book Val. Per Share	0.10	0.05	...
INCOME STATEMENT (IN THOUSANDS):			
Total Revenues	171,114	102,849	64,596
Costs & Expenses	168,966	104,091	63,315
Depreciation & Amort.	512	370	205
Operating Income	1,636	d1,612	1,076
Net Interest Inc./(Exp.)	226	d2	d10
Income Before Income Taxes	1,806	d1,615	1,113
Income Taxes	740	cr607	439
Net Income	1,065	d1,009	674
Cash Flow	1,064	d895	878
Average Shs. Outstg.	17,921	14,847	14,249
BALANCE SHEET (IN THOUSANDS):			
Cash & Cash Equivalents	7,909	6,254	...
Total Current Assets	9,846	7,961	...
Net Property	2,999	2,520	...
Total Assets	13,226	11,204	...
Total Current Liabilities	6,373	5,605	...
Long-Term Obligations	1,238	948	...
Net Stockholders' Equity	1,385	812	...
Net Working Capital	3,473	2,356	...
Year-end Shs. Outstg.	14,474	14,847	...
STATISTICAL RECORD:			
Operating Profit Margin %	1.0	...	1.7
Net Profit Margin %	0.6	...	1.0
Return on Equity %	76.9	...	...
Return on Assets %	8.1	...	...
Debt/Total Assets %	9.4	8.5	...

Statistics are as originally reported.

REVENUES

(12/31/1998)	($000)	(%)
Non-published fares ..	159,846	93.4
Published fare commission............	11,268	6.6
Total	171,114	100.0

OFFICERS:
M. J. Hartley, Chmn., C.E.O., Pres.
D. K. Jorgenson, V.P., C.F.O.
F. M. Bartholomew, C.O.O.

PRINCIPAL OFFICE: 1440 Kapiolani Boulevard, Honolulu, HI 96814

TELEPHONE NUMBER: (808) 945-7439
WEB: www.cheaptickets.com

NO. OF EMPLOYEES: 590 (approx.)

SHAREHOLDERS: 4

ANNUAL MEETING: N/A

INCORPORATED: HI, Aug., 1986; reincorp., DE, Feb., 1999

INSTITUTIONAL HOLDINGS:
No. of Institutions: 32
Shares Held: 1,283,209
% Held: 6.1

INDUSTRY: Passenger transport arrangement, nec (SIC: 4729)

TRANSFER AGENT(S): American Securities Transfer and Trust, New York, NY

CHECKFREE HOLDINGS CORP.

YIELD ...
P/E RATIO 268.8

*7 YEAR PRICE SCORE N/A   *12 MONTH PRICE SCORE 105.1
*NYSE COMPOSITE INDEX=100

INTERIM EARNINGS (Per Share):

Qtr.	Sept.	Dec.	Mar.	June
1995-96	...	...	...	d0.89
1996-97	d0.19	d0.13	d2.83	d0.29
1997-98	0.17	d0.03	d0.32	0.10
1998-99	d0.03	0.22	d0.01	0.02

INTERIM DIVIDENDS (Per Share):

Amt.	Decl.	Ex.	Rec.	Pay.
No dividends paid.				

CAPITALIZATION (6/30/98):

	($000)	(%)
Capital Lease Obligations..	6,467	3.4
Common & Surplus	183,854	96.6
Total	190,321	100.0

RECENT DEVELOPMENTS: For the fiscal year ended 6/30/99, the Company reported net income of $10.5 million compared with a loss of $3.7 million in the previous year. Results in fiscal 1998 included non-recurring charges totaling $36.5 million. Total revenue advanced 7.0% to $250.1 million versus $233.9 million the year before. Processing and servicing revenue climbed 16.1% to $201.1 million from $159.3 million in the prior year. License fees fell to $16.0 million versus $29.0 million in the previous year, while maintenance fees dropped to $15.4 million versus $25.9 million. Loss from operations improved to $3.7 million compared with a loss of $7.2 million in the prior year. The Company signed contracts for electronic billing and payment services with 43 billers, two-and-one-half times more than the year before, and ended the year with nearly 3.0 million subscribers, up from 2.4 million at the end of 1998.

BUSINESS

CHECKFREE HOLDINGS CORPORATION is a provider of electronic commerce services, institutional portfolio management services, and financial application software for financial institutions, businesses and their customers. The Company designs, develops and markets services that enable its customers to make electronic payments and collections, receive electronic bills and on-line banking offerings, and automate paper-based recurring financial transactions. The Company's EC Solutions division assists customers with the education and implementation of electronic billing and payment solutions. The Company's customers include more than 2.8 million consumers, 1,000 businesses and 850 financial institutions.

ANNUAL FINANCIAL DATA

	6/30/98	6/30/97 ②	6/30/96	12/31/95	12/31/94	12/31/93	12/31/92
Earnings Per Share	① d0.07	① d3.44③	③ d3.69	d0.01	0.02	0.04	Nil
Cash Flow Per Share	0.44	d2.81	d3.51	0.08	0.09	0.09	0.04
Tang. Book Val. Per Share	2.52	1.17	1.82	3.08	0.59	0.10	...
INCOME STATEMENT (IN THOUSANDS):							
Total Revenues	233,864	176,445	51,040	49,330	39,267	30,892	22,201
Costs & Expenses	249,251	327,987	192,208	48,511	35,962	28,014	21,285
Depreciation & Amort.	27,962	29,857	6,997	2,485	1,922	1,377	1,097
Operating Income	d7,176	d175,149	d148,165	d1,665	1,383	1,502	d180
Net Interest Inc./(Exp.)	2,832	1,319	1,334	1,490	d497	d114	d59
Income Before Income Taxes	d4,344	d173,830	d146,831	d175	886	1,388	d239
Income Taxes	cr641	cr12,017	cr8,629	40	400	368	cr159
Net Income	① d3,703	① d161,813	①⑪⑪ d138,203	d215	486	1,020	d80
Cash Flow	24,259	d131,956	d131,206	2,269	2,408	2,397	1,017
Average Shs. Outstg.	55,087	46,988	37,420	28,219	27,103	26,886	27,127
BALANCE SHEET (IN THOUSANDS):							
Cash & Cash Equivalents	61,068	36,517	39,076	84,852	14,774	2,132	...
Total Current Assets	136,700	86,223	90,799	90,467	17,615	5,790	...
Net Property	50,920	44,027	36,567	13,559	12,156	10,835	...
Total Assets	250,112	223,836	196,230	115,642	30,512	17,669	...
Total Current Liabilities	58,462	66,221	45,303	8,675	5,684	5,167	...
Long-Term Obligations	6,467	8,401	8,324	7,282	8,213	8,968	...
Net Stockholders' Equity	183,854	148,644	137,675	99,325	16,372	2,985	...
Net Working Capital	78,238	20,002	45,496	81,792	11,931	623	...
Year-end Shs. Outstg.	56,365	55,546	41,517	32,107	26,862	23,355	23,415
STATISTICAL RECORD:							
Operating Profit Margin %	...	...	...	...	3.5	4.9	...
Net Profit Margin %	...	...	...	...	1.2	3.3	...
Return on Equity %	...	...	...	...	3.0	34.2	...
Return on Assets %	...	...	...	...	1.6	5.8	...
Debt/Total Assets %	2.6	...	3.8	4.2	6.3	26.9	50.8	...
Price Range	31½-5³/₄	31⁷/₁₆-9½	26³/₈-10½	29³/₈-16	...	...	...

Statistics are as originally reported. ① Incl. non-recurr. chrg. 6/30/98: $33.5 mill; 6/30/97: $140 mill.; 1996: $122.4 mill. ② For 6 mos. due to fiscal year-end change ③ Bef. extraord. chrg. $364,374

CISCO SYSTEMS, INC.

YIELD ...
P/E RATIO 101.8

INTERIM EARNINGS (Per Share):

Qtr.	Oct.	Jan.	Apr.	July
1995-96	0.07	0.07	0.09	0.09
1996-97	0.06	0.11	0.13	0.05
1997-98	0.10	0.14	0.02	0.15
1998-99	0.15	0.09	0.19	0.18

INTERIM DIVIDENDS (Per Share):

Amt.	Decl.	Ex.	Rec.	Pay.
3-for-2	11/03/97	12/17/97	11/18/97	12/16/97
3-for-2	8/04/98	9/16/98	8/14/98	9/15/98
2-for-1	5/11/99	6/22/99	5/24/99	6/21/99

CAPITALIZATION (7/25/98):

	($000)	(%)
Minority Interest	43,107	0.6
Common & Surplus	7,106,618	99.4
Total	7,149,725	100.0

7 YEAR PRICE SCORE 206.0 **12 MONTH PRICE SCORE 122.2**
NYSE COMPOSITE INDEX=100

RECENT DEVELOPMENTS: For the year ended 7/31/99, net income increased 55.6% to $2.10 billion compared with $1.35 billion in the previous year. Diluted earnings per share were $0.62 versus $0.42 in 1998. Net sales advanced 43.2% to $12.15 billion from $8.49 billion in the prior year. Gross margin as a percentage of net sales declined slightly to 65.1% from 65.6% a year earlier. Operating income grew 28.4% to $3.47 billion from $2.70 billion the year before. On 8/16/99, the Company entered into a definitive agreement to acquire privately-held Calista Inc. in Bucks, England and San Jose, California for $55.0 million in stock. The transaction is expected to close in the first quarter of CSCO's fiscal year 2000. Calista Inc. is a developer of Internet technology that allows different business phones to work together over an open Internet-based infrastructure.

BUSINESS

CISCO SYSTEMS, INC. develops, manufactures, markets, and supports high-performance multiprotocol internetworking systems that enable its customers to build large-scale integrated networks. The Company's products connect and manage communications among local and wide area networks that employ a variety of network protocols, media interfaces, network topologies and cabling systems. Cisco's principal products, a family of multiprotocol routers that support a wide variety of network protocols and media, simultaneously offer routing and bridging functions at rapid speeds, and offer a high level of network intelligence through Cisco's Internetwork Operating System software.

ANNUAL FINANCIAL DATA

	7/25/98	7/26/97	7/28/96	7/30/95	7/31/94	7/25/93	7/26/92
Earnings Per Share	① 0.42	① 0.34	0.30	0.17	0.13	0.07	0.04
Cash Flow Per Share	0.52	0.41	0.35	0.19	0.14	0.08	0.04
Tang. Book Val. Per Share	2.27	1.42	0.97	0.56	0.37	0.21	0.11
INCOME STATEMENT (IN MILLIONS):							
Total Revenues	8,458.8	6,440.2	4,096.0	1,978.9	1,243.0	649.0	339.6
Costs & Expenses	6,027.1	4,600.7	2,562.6	1,277.5	724.0	371.9	203.5
Depreciation & Amort.	327.3	212.2	132.6	58.5	30.8	13.6	6.7
Operating Income	2,104.4	1,627.3	1,400.8	642.9	488.1	263.6	129.4
Income Before Income Taxes	2,302.5	1,888.9	1,464.8	679.0	509.5	275.1	136.1
Income Taxes	952.4	840.2	551.5	258.0	194.6	103.2	51.7
Net Income	① 1,350.1	① 1,048.7	913.3	421.0	314.9	172.0	84.4
Cash Flow	1,677.4	1,260.9	1,045.9	479.5	345.7	185.5	91.1
Average Shs. Outstg. (000)	3,216,346	3,101,936	2,999,637	2,495,682	2,385,459	2,323,206	2,286,648
BALANCE SHEET (IN MILLIONS):							
Cash & Cash Equivalents	1,691.5	1,275.6	1,038.2	439.5	182.8	89.0	156.4
Total Current Assets	3,761.9	3,101.3	2,159.6	996.0	507.7	268.3	247.1
Net Property	595.3	466.4	331.3	136.6	77.4	48.7	28.0
Total Assets	8,916.7	5,452.0	3,630.2	1,757.3	1,053.7	595.2	323.9
Total Current Liabilities	1,767.0	1,120.1	769.4	337.8	205.5	120.0	78.3
Net Stockholders' Equity	7,106.6	4,289.6	2,819.6	1,378.7	848.2	475.2	245.6
Net Working Capital	1,994.9	1,981.2	1,390.3	658.2	302.2	148.3	168.8
Year-end Shs. Outstg. (000)	3,125,164	3,018,506	2,921,778	2,450,214	2,319,273	2,226,744	2,163,996
STATISTICAL RECORD:							
Operating Profit Margin %	24.9	25.3	34.2	32.5	39.3	40.6	38.1
Net Profit Margin %	16.0	16.3	22.3	21.3	25.3	26.5	24.8
Return on Equity %	19.0	24.4	32.4	30.5	37.1	36.2	34.4
Return on Assets %	15.1	19.2	25.2	24.0	29.9	28.9	26.1
Price Range	48⅞-17³⁄₁₆	20³⁄₁₆-10¹⁄₁₆	15⅜-7⅛	9¹⁵⁄₁₆-3⅝	4½-2¹⁄₁₆	3⅝-2⅛	2¼-0⅞
P/E Ratio	116.3-40.9	59.7-29.7	50.5-23.3	58.7-21.3	34.3-15.8	49.3-28.6	60.5-24.2

Statistics are as originally reported. Adj. for stk. splits: 2-for-1, 6/21/99; 3-for-2, 9/15/98; 3-for-2, 12/16/97; 2-for-1, 2/16/96; 2-for-1, 3/15/94; 2-for-1, 3/19/93; 2-for-1, 3/23/92 ① Incl. non-recurr. net chrg. 7/25/98: $588.3 mill. ($0.38/sh.); credit 7/26/97: $152.7 million (0.15/sh.)

OFFICERS:
J. P. Morgridge, Chmn.
J. T. Chambers, Pres. & C.E.O.
L. B. Carter, C.F.O.

INVESTOR CONTACT: Randi Feigin, Investor Relations, (408) 527-1099

PRINCIPAL OFFICE: 170 West Tasman Drive, San Jose, CA 95134

TELEPHONE NUMBER: (408) 526-4000
FAX: (408) 526-4100
WEB: www.cisco.com

NO. OF EMPLOYEES: 18,700

SHAREHOLDERS: 12,880 (approx.)

ANNUAL MEETING: In Nov.

INCORPORATED: CA, Dec., 1984

INSTITUTIONAL HOLDINGS:
No. of Institutions: 1,063
Shares Held: 1,976,284,639
% Held: 60.8

INDUSTRY: Computer peripheral equipment, nec (SIC: 3577)

TRANSFER AGENT(S): First National Bank of Boston, Boston, MA

CITRIX SYSTEMS, INC.

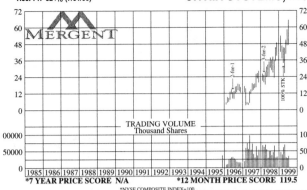

*7 YEAR PRICE SCORE N/A   *12 MONTH PRICE SCORE 119.5
*NYSE COMPOSITE INDEX=100

TRADING VOLUME
Thousand Shares

INTERIM EARNINGS (Per Share):

Qtr.	Mar.	June	Sept.	Dec.
1996	0.04	0.04	0.07	0.08
1997	0.09	0.10	0.14	0.14
1998	0.14	0.11	0.19	0.24
1999	0.28	0.29	...	

INTERIM DIVIDENDS (Per Share):

Amt.	Decl.	Ex.	Rec.	Pay.
3-for-2	1/26/98	2/23/98	2/12/98	2/20/98
100% STK	3/01/99	3/26/99	3/17/99	3/25/99

CAPITALIZATION (12/31/98):

	($000)	(%)
Common & Surplus	297,454	100.0
Total	297,454	100.0

RECENT DEVELOPMENTS:

For the second quarter ended 6/30/99, net income surged to $27.8 million compared with $9.6 million in the comparable prior-year quarter. Earnings for 1998 included a charge of $10.7 million for in-process research and development. Net revenues increased 68.0% to $94.4 million from $56.2 million a year earlier. Results reflected an increasing level of visibility for server-based computing within the market. Gross margin as a percentage of net revenue improved to 96.7% from 91.7% in the previous year. On 7/27/99, CTXS acquired ViewSoft, Inc., a firm specializing in software for multi-tier and Web-based application development and deployment, for approximately $32.0 million. In the third quarter of 1999, CTXS expects to incur a one-time charge of approximately $2.0 million related to the acquisition.

BUSINESS

CITRIX SYSTEMS, INC. is a supplier of server-based computing products and technologies that enable enterprise-wide deployment and management of applications designed for Microsoft Corporation Windows® operating systems. The Company's MetaFrame™ and WinFrame® product lines, developed under license and strategic alliance agreements with Microsoft, permit organizations to deploy and manage Windows applications without regard to location, network connection, or type of client hardware platform. These product lines utilize CTXS's proprietary Independent Computing Architecture, which allows an application's graphical user interface to be displayed on a client while its logic is executed on a server, thereby providing a bandwidth-efficient solution. CTXS's products enable the broad deployment of Windows applications in a variety of environments, including: low bandwidth connections, such as dial-up, wide area networks and wireless; the Internet, accessed through widely-available browser technology; existing Intel-based computer systems; non-Intel platforms, such as UNIX workstations, Java, X-Terminals and Macintosh systems; and emerging platforms, such as hand-held wireless devices, information kiosks, and Windows-based terminals and network computers.

ANNUAL FINANCIAL DATA

	12/31/98	12/31/97	12/31/96	12/31/95	12/31/94	12/31/93	12/31/92
Earnings Per Share	⚀ 0.67	⚀ 0.48	0.23	0.03	d0.05	d0.51	...
Cash Flow Per Share	0.84	0.49	0.23	0.03	d0.05	d0.51	...
Tang. Book Val. Per Share	2.92	2.37	1.77	0.61	...	...	...
INCOME STATEMENT (IN THOUSANDS):							
Total Revenues	248,636	123,933	44,527	14,568	10,086	5,164	1,801
Costs & Expenses	147,959	67,493	26,434	12,568	9,833	7,865	5,520
Depreciation & Amort.	15,173	1,712	376	185	55	21	17
Operating Income	85,504	54,728	17,718	1,815	197	d2,723	d3,736
Net Interest Inc./(Exp.)	9,968	9,894	4,545	173	45	1	52
Income Before Income Taxes	95,472	64,622	22,263	1,988	242	d2,722	d3,686
Income Taxes	34,370	23,264	3,562	93	...	...	...
Net Income	⚀ 61,102	⚀ 41,358	18,701	1,895	242	d2,722	d3,686
Cash Flow	76,275	43,070	19,077	2,080	d419	d4,166	d3,670
Average Shs. Outstg.	91,296	87,262	81,909	61,210	9,124	8,158	...
BALANCE SHEET (IN THOUSANDS):							
Cash & Cash Equivalents	184,480	229,192	137,342	43,471	1,913	1,066	...
Total Current Assets	244,016	258,362	147,498	46,353	3,718	2,145	...
Net Property	14,183	6,678	2,082	302	214	47	...
Total Assets	431,380	282,668	149,580	46,715	3,932	2,306	...
Total Current Liabilities	85,116	35,445	7,720	3,665	1,729	1,779	...
Long-Term Obligations	...	...	...	8	88	68	...
Net Stockholders' Equity	297,454	196,848	141,851	42,962	d16,473	d16,103	...
Net Working Capital	158,900	222,916	139,778	42,688	1,990	366	...
Year-end Shs. Outstg.	85,924	82,946	80,041	70,953	6,523	3,456	2,874
STATISTICAL RECORD:							
Operating Profit Margin %	34.4	44.2	39.8	12.5	2.0	...	...
Net Profit Margin %	24.6	33.4	42.0	13.0	2.4	...	...
Return on Equity %	20.5	21.0	13.2	4.4	...	...	...
Return on Assets %	14.2	14.6	12.5	4.1	6.1	...	...
Debt/Total Assets %	...	...	...	0.2	1.7	...	...
Price Range	48⅞-18³⁄₁₆	28³⁄₁₆-3¼	18¹⁵⁄₁₆-3¹⁵⁄₁₆	...	...	...	...
P/E Ratio	72.9-27.1	59.3-6.8	83.3-17.2	...	...	...	...

Statistics are as originally reported. Adj. for stk. splits: 100% div., 3/25/99; 3-for-2, 2/20/98; 2-for-1, 6/4/96; 2-for-3 reverse, 12/7/95 ⚀ Incl. non-recurr. chrg. 12/31/98: $18.4 mill.; 12/31/97: $4.0 mill.

OFFICERS:

E. E. Iacobucci Jr., Chmn.
M. B. Templeton, Pres. & C.E.O.
R. W. Roberts, C.E.O.
J. J. Felcyn Jr., C.F.O. & V.P.

TELEPHONE NUMBER: (954) 267-3000
FAX: (954) 341-6880
WEB: www.citrix.com

NO. OF EMPLOYEES: 620 (approx.)

SHAREHOLDERS: 449 (approx.)

ANNUAL MEETING: In May

INCORPORATED: DE, Apr., 1989

PRINCIPAL OFFICE: 6400 N.W. 6th Way, Ft. Lauderdale, FL 33309

INSTITUTIONAL HOLDINGS:
No. of Institutions: 215
Shares Held: 71,655,368
% Held: 82.1

INDUSTRY: Prepackaged software (SIC: 7372)

TRANSFER AGENT(S): First National Bank of Boston, Boston, MA

NASDAQ SYMBOL CMGI
Rec. Pr. 92³/₁₆ (7/31/99)

CMGI INC.

YIELD ...
P/E RATIO 151.1

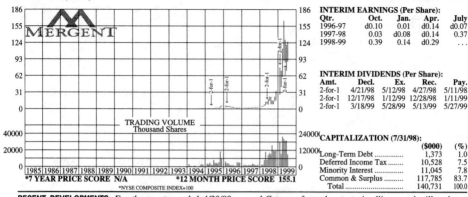

186

155

124

93

62

31

0

MERGENT

2-for-1

2-for-1

2-for-1

TRADING VOLUME
Thousand Shares

40000

20000

0

| 1985 | 1986 | 1987 | 1988 | 1989 | 1990 | 1991 | 1992 | 1993 | 1994 | 1995 | 1996 | 1997 | 1998 | 1999 |

*7 YEAR PRICE SCORE N/A   ***12 MONTH PRICE SCORE 155.1**

*NYSE COMPOSITE INDEX=100

INTERIM EARNINGS (Per Share):

Qtr.	Oct.	Jan.	Apr.	July
1996-97	d0.10	0.01	d0.14	d0.07
1997-98	0.03	d0.08	d0.14	0.37
1998-99	0.39	0.14	d0.29	...

INTERIM DIVIDENDS (Per Share):

Amt.	Decl.	Ex.	Rec.	Pay.
2-for-1	4/21/98	5/12/98	4/27/98	5/11/98
2-for-1	12/17/98	1/12/99	12/28/98	1/11/99
2-for-1	3/18/99	5/28/99	5/13/99	5/27/99

CAPITALIZATION (7/31/98):

	($000)	(%)
Long-Term Debt	1,373	1.0
Deferred Income Tax	10,528	7.5
Minority Interest	11,045	7.8
Common & Surplus	117,785	83.7
Total	140,731	100.0

RECENT DEVELOPMENTS: For the quarter ended 4/30/99, CMGI reported a loss from continuing operations of $27.2 million compared with income from continuing operations of $8.1 million in the corresponding period of 1998. Results included pre-tax charges of $4.5 million in 1999 and $9.3 million in 1998 for in-process research and development. Results also included pre-tax gains of $859,000 in 1999 and $49.1 million in 1998 on the sale of stock. Net revenues more than doubled to $43.7 million from $18.1 million in the year-earlier quarter. Separately, the Company and Gateway formed a strategic alliance and will seek out collaborative and investment opportunities on the Internet. Additionally, Gateway agreed to invest $200.0 million for an ownership stake in CMGI, subject to certain closing conditions. On 6/29/99, the Company and Compaq entered into a comprehensive strategic partnership that will enable both companies to aggressively pursue Internet-related business and market opportunities. As per the terms of the agreement, CMGI will acquire control of Compaq's AltaVista business and its related properties.

BUSINESS

CMGI INC. (formerly CMG Information Services, Inc.) develops and operates Internet and direct marketing companies as well as venture funds focused on the Internet. The CMG Internet Group includes majority-owned subsidiaries: ADSmart Corporation develops and markets on-line ad sales and ad serving services; Engage Technologies, Inc. develops and markets precision on-line marketing services; Accipiter, Inc. specializes in Internet advertising management services; InfoMation Publishing Corporation develops and markets a Web-based product for corporate knowledge management; NaviSite Internet Services Corporation provides Web hosting and server management services; Planet Direct Corporation, a personalized Web service with over 400 Internet Service Provider partners, tailors members' on-line experience to their interests and local community; and Password Internet Publishing Corporation, which provides tools for the creation of a personalized mini-web. Compaq, Microsoft, Intel and Sumitomo hold minority positions in CMGI.

ANNUAL FINANCIAL DATA

	7/31/98	7/31/97	7/31/96	7/31/95	7/31/94	7/31/93	7/31/92
Earnings Per Share	② 0.19	② d0.29	② 0.19	① 0.05	0.02	0.02	0.01
Cash Flow Per Share	0.26	d0.22	0.22	0.06	0.03	0.03	0.02
Tang. Book Val. Per Share	0.74	0.16	0.70	0.77	0.08	...	...
INCOME STATEMENT (IN THOUSANDS):							
Total Revenues	91,484	70,607	28,485	11,207	19,388	16,548	13,827
Costs & Expenses	163,702	118,409	46,236	9,501	15,445	13,328	11,984
Depreciation & Amort.	6,793	5,307	2,823	569	942	925	814
Operating Income	d79,011	d53,109	d20,574	1,137	3,000	2,295	1,029
Net Interest Inc./(Exp.)	d870	1,749	2,691	302	d96	d324	d382
Income Before Income Taxes	46,340	d24,989	30,995	5,979	2,905	1,832	664
Income Taxes	29,787	cr2,962	16,673	2,177	1,103	627	279
Equity Earnings/Minority Int.	d11,849	d769	d746	d292	...	...	...
Net Income	② 16,553	② d22,027	② 14,322	① 3,801	1,801	1,206	385
Cash Flow	23,346	d16,720	17,145	4,371	2,743	2,130	1,200
Average Shs. Outstg.	90,060	75,432	77,456	75,126	93,500	75,719	74,705
BALANCE SHEET (IN THOUSANDS):							
Cash & Cash Equivalents	67,301	65,707	76,546	65,651	2,955	...	250
Total Current Assets	105,085	106,691	90,566	72,390	9,319	4,465	4,068
Net Property	13,973	11,144	8,461	1,321	2,351	2,147	2,087
Total Assets	237,460	148,354	109,503	79,361	12,740	7,260	6,835
Total Current Liabilities	92,301	68,136	18,557	23,189	3,643	5,906	6,143
Long-Term Obligations	1,373	9,550	...	93	165	315	902
Net Stockholders' Equity	117,785	29,448	53,992	55,490	8,867	152	d1,015
Net Working Capital	12,784	38,555	72,009	49,201	5,676	d1,441	d2,075
Year-end Shs. Outstg.	92,136	77,276	73,336	70,710	105,201	48,584	47,869
STATISTICAL RECORD:							
Operating Profit Margin %	...	...	...	10.1	15.5	13.9	7.4
Net Profit Margin %	18.1	...	50.3	33.9	9.3	7.3	2.8
Return on Equity %	14.1	...	26.5	6.9	20.3	791.9	...
Return on Assets %	7.0	...	13.1	4.8	14.1	16.6	5.6
Debt/Total Assets %	0.6	6.4	...	0.1	1.3	4.3	13.2
Price Range	33⁷/₈-3³/₈	3⁷/₈-1³/₈	5⁷/₈-1¹/₈	6¹/₄-0¹¹/₁₆	0-0¹/₄	...	...
P/E Ratio	183.0-18.3	...	31.9-6.2	122.9-13.5	50.7-13.6	...	...

Statistics are as originally reported. Adj. for 2-for-1 sock splits, 5/99, 1/99, 5/98, 2/96 & 5/95. ① Bef. disc. opers. gain $24.4 mill. & incl. non-recurr. credit $4.8 mill. ② Incl. non-recurr. credit $118.9 mill., 7/98; $25.8 mill., 7/97; $46.9 mill., 7/96.

OFFICERS:
D. S. Wetherell, Chmn., Pres., C.E.O.
A. J. Hajducky III, C.F.O., Treas., C.A.O.

PRINCIPAL OFFICE: 100 Brickstone Square, Andover, MA 01810

TELEPHONE NUMBER: (978) 684-3600
WEB: www.cmgi.com

NO. OF EMPLOYEES: 1,024

SHAREHOLDERS: 374

ANNUAL MEETING: In Dec.

INCORPORATED: DE, 1986

INSTITUTIONAL HOLDINGS:
No. of Institutions: 166
Shares Held: 38,362,662
% Held: 40.2

INDUSTRY: Direct mail advertising services (SIC: 7331)

TRANSFER AGENT(S): Boston Financial Data Services, Inc., North Quincy, MA

NASDAQ SYMBOL CNET
Rec. Pr. 40 (7/31/99)

CNET INC.

YIELD ...
P/E RATIO 81.6

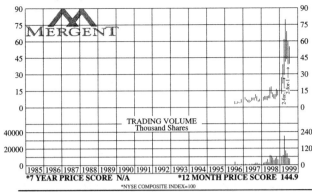

TRADING VOLUME
Thousand Shares

| 1985 | 1986 | 1987 | 1988 | 1989 | 1990 | 1991 | 1992 | 1993 | 1994 | 1995 | 1996 | 1997 | 1998 | 1999 |

*7 YEAR PRICE SCORE N/A   ***12 MONTH PRICE SCORE 144.9**
*NYSE COMPOSITE INDEX=100

INTERIM EARNINGS (Per Share):

Qtr.	Mar.	June	Sept.	Dec.
1996	...	...	d0.09	d0.08
1997	d0.25	0.09	d0.12	d0.19
1998	d0.10	0.01	0.06	0.06
1999	0.31	0.11	...	...

INTERIM DIVIDENDS (Per Share):

Amt.	Decl.	Ex.	Rec.	Pay.
2-for-1	2/10/99	3/09/99	2/22/99	3/08/99
2-for-1	4/21/99	6/01/99	5/10/99	5/28/99

CAPITALIZATION (12/31/98):

	($000)	(%)
Long-Term Debt	569	0.7
Common & Surplus	76,603	99.3
Total	77,172	100.0

RECENT DEVELOPMENTS: For the three months ended 6/30/99, net income soared to $9.2 million, up from $341,000 in the corresponding quarter of the previous year. The 1999 earnings include a $4.7 million gain on investments. Total revenue jumped 92.2% to $25.6 million from $13.3 million the year before, primarily due to the Company's on-line division. Gross profit more than tripled to $16.3 million from $5.6 million the previous year. CNET's Internet traffic increased to 10.8 million daily page views and 130,000 lead generations per day. During the quarter,

the Company acquired Sumo, Inc., an Internet service directory company. In May 1999, CNET launched CNET Auctions, an on-line auction service for technology products. In July 1999, CNET acquired GDT, S.A., a Switzerland-based database specialist, for $50.0 million in stock and cash. In addition, CNET announced that it will spend $100.0 million over the next 18 months on a targeted marketing campaign which will encompass television, radio, print, outdoor and on-line advertising

BUSINESS

CNET INCORPORATED provides consumers with information on-line and on television regarding computers, the Internet and digital technologies. CNET seeks to use its editorial, technical, product database and programming expertise to engage consumers and attract advertisers. The Company maintains eight on-line technology-focused sites, produces four television series and operates Snap.com, a free Internet search engine.

REVENUES

(12/31/98)	($000)	(%)
Internet	49,374	87.5
Television	7,058	12.5
Total	56,432	100.0

ANNUAL FINANCIAL DATA

	12/31/98	12/31/97	12/31/96	12/31/95	12/31/94	12/31/93
Earnings Per Share	0.04	⊡ d0.45	d0.25	d0.15	d0.06	d0.03
Cash Flow Per Share	0.21	d0.24	d0.15	d0.09	d0.05	d0.03
Tang. Book Val. Per Share	1.12	0.69	0.42	0.17	0.07	...
INCOME STATEMENT (IN THOUSANDS):						
Total Revenues	56,432	33,640	14,830	3,500	...	...
Costs & Expenses	41,759	56,174	23,764	8,340	2,022	941
Depreciation & Amort.	12,143	11,604	6,602	3,631	750	...
Operating Income	2,530	d34,138	d15,535	d8,470	d2,772	d941
Net Interest Inc./(Exp.)	1,416	611	452	d137	d54	d5
Income Before Income Taxes	2,600	d24,728	d16,949	d8,607	d2,827	d946
Net Income	2,600	⊡ d24,728	d16,949	d8,607	d2,827	d946
Cash Flow	14,743	d13,124	d10,347	d4,977	d2,076	d946
Average Shs. Outstg.	69,706	54,447	67,439	55,296	44,722	32,399
BALANCE SHEET (IN THOUSANDS):						
Cash & Cash Equivalents	52,479	24,153	20,156	703	1,224	...
Total Current Assets	70,969	34,438	26,389	2,110	1,288	...
Net Property	15,326	19,554	11,743	2,393	288	...
Total Assets	88,354	58,262	39,842	4,657	1,609	...
Total Current Liabilities	11,182	15,007	6,166	1,391	417	...
Long-Term Obligations	569	2,612	578	467	...	...
Net Stockholders' Equity	76,603	40,643	33,098	2,799	1,192	...
Net Working Capital	59,787	19,431	20,223	719	871	...
Year-end Shs. Outstg.	68,240	58,649	79,689	16,200	16,200	...
STATISTICAL RECORD:						
Operating Profit Margin %	4.5	...	...	...	...	...
Net Profit Margin %	4.6	...	...	...	...	...
Return on Equity %	3.4	...	...	...	...	...
Return on Assets %	2.9	...	...	...	...	...
Debt/Total Assets %	0.6	4.5	1.4	10.0	...	...
Price Range	18⅝-5⅞	11⅝-3¹⁵⁄₁₆	7¼-2¹⁵⁄₁₆	...	...	...
P/E Ratio	530.6-166.5	...	...	...	...	...

Statistics are as originally reported. Adj. for stk. splits: 2-for-1, 5/28/99; 2-for-1, 3/8/99.
⊡ Incl. non-recurr. net chrg. 1.7mil

OFFICERS:
H. M. Minor, Chmn., Pres.
R. J. Marino, C.E.O.
D. N. Woodrum, C.F.O.
S. W. Bonnie, Exec. V.P., C.O.O., Sec.

PRINCIPAL OFFICE: 150 Chestnut Street, San Francisco, CA 94111

TELEPHONE NUMBER: (415) 395-7800
WEB: www.cnet.com

NO. OF EMPLOYEES: 491

SHAREHOLDERS: 226

ANNUAL MEETING: In May

INCORPORATED: DE, Dec., 1992

INSTITUTIONAL HOLDINGS:
No. of Institutions: 106
Shares Held: 22,965,296
% Held: 33.0

INDUSTRY: Motion picture & video production (SIC: 7812)

TRANSFER AGENT(S): Harris Trust Company of California, Chicago, IL

COMPAQ COMPUTER CORP.

YIELD 0.3%
P/E RATIO 43.0

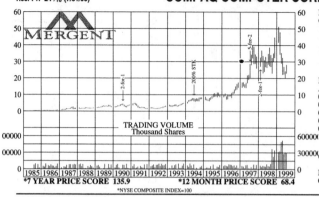

INTERIM EARNINGS (Per Share):

Qtr.	Mar.	June	Sept.	Dec.
1995	0.16	0.18	0.18	0.06
1996	0.17	0.20	0.25	0.33
1997	0.28	0.17	0.34	0.43
1998	0.01	d2.33	0.07	0.43
1999	0.16	d0.10	...	...

INTERIM DIVIDENDS (Per Share):

Amt.	Decl.	Ex.	Rec.	Pay.
0.015Q	6/12/98	6/26/98	6/30/98	7/20/98
0.015Q	9/14/98	9/28/98	9/30/98	10/20/98
0.02Q	12/10/98	12/29/98	12/31/98	1/20/99
0.02Q	3/24/99	3/29/99	3/31/99	4/20/99
0.02Q	6/23/99	6/28/99	6/30/99	7/20/99

Indicated div.: $0.08

CAPITALIZATION (12/31/98):

	($000)	(%)
Minority Interest	422,000	3.6
Common & Surplus	11,351,000	96.4
Total	11,773,000	100.0

7 YEAR PRICE SCORE 135.9 **12 MONTH PRICE SCORE 68.4**
*NYSE COMPOSITE INDEX=100

RECENT DEVELOPMENTS: For the quarter ended 6/30/99, the Company reported a net loss of $184.0 million versus a loss of $3.63 billion in 1998. Results in 1998 included $3.63 billion in restructuring and other charges. Total revenues soared 61.5% to $9.42 billion from $5.83 billion in the prior-year period. Results were negatively affected by pricing pressures in the personal computer division and a non-competitive cost structure. Gross margin fell to 20.5% versus 24.8% the year before. CPQ plans to incur a restructur-

ing charge of $700.0 million to $900.0 million in the third quarter, which will include costs related to terminating nearly 8,000 employees and closing some facilities. CPQ anticipates faster recovery in the Asia-Pacific region, especially in Korea, due to strong performances in revenues and unit shipment growth in the second quarter. CPQ has formed a sales and marketing alliance with AltiGen Communications Inc., a provider of LAN- and IP-based computer telephony solutions.

BUSINESS

COMPAQ COMPUTER CORP. designs, develops, manufactures and markets a wide range of personal computing products, including desktop personal computers, portable computers, and tower PC servers and peripheral products that store and manage data in network environments. In addition to its core products, CPQ provides NT professional workstations, Internet products and services, mobile computing for home and schools, high-speed network connections, and computer equipment financing. Compaq products are sold in more than 100 countries. On 8/18/99, the Company became the largest outside shareholder of CMGI, Inc. through a strategic partnership that allows both companies to pursue cooperative Internet-related business opportunities.

ANNUAL FINANCIAL DATA

	12/31/98	12/31/97	12/31/96	12/31/95	12/31/94	12/31/93	12/31/92
Earnings Per Share	③ d1.71	② 1.19	0.94	① 0.58	0.65	0.36	0.17
Cash Flow Per Share	d1.15	1.53	1.15	0.73	0.77	0.49	0.30
Tang. Book Val. Per Share	6.73	6.21	4.49	3.45	2.82	2.10	1.68
Dividends Per Share	0.06	...	...	...	...	...	...
INCOME STATEMENT (IN MILLIONS):							
Total Revenues	31,169.0	24,584.0	18,109.0	14,755.0	10,866.0	7,191.0	4,099.8
Costs & Expenses	33,007.0	21,304.0	15,947.0	13,258.0	9,431.0	6,343.0	3,617.1
Depreciation & Amort.	893.0	545.0	285.0	214.0	169.0	156.0	159.5
Operating Income	d2,731.0	2,735.0	1,877.0	1,283.0	1,266.0	692.0	323.2
Income Before Income Taxes	d2,662.0	2,758.0	1,876.0	1,188.0	1,172.0	616.0	295.4
Income Taxes	81.0	903.0	563.0	399.0	305.0	154.0	97.5
Equity Earnings/Minority Int.	...	...	...	...	...	...	15.2
Net Income	③ d2,743.0	② 1,855.0	1,313.0	① 789.0	867.0	462.0	213.2
Cash Flow	d1,850.0	2,400.0	1,598.0	1,003.0	1,036.0	618.0	372.7
Average Shs. Outstg. (000)	1,608,000	1,564,000	1,391,500	1,368,000	1,343,000	1,270,500	1,239,620
BALANCE SHEET (IN MILLIONS):							
Cash & Cash Equivalents	4,091.0	6,762.0	3,993.0	745.0	471.0	627.0	356.7
Total Current Assets	15,167.0	12,017.0	9,169.0	6,527.0	5,158.0	3,291.0	2,319.0
Net Property	2,902.0	1,985.0	1,172.0	1,110.0	944.0	779.0	807.7
Total Assets	23,051.0	14,631.0	10,756.0	8,042.0	6,345.0	4,270.0	3,318.2
Total Current Liabilities	10,733.0	5,202.0	3,852.0	2,680.0	2,013.0	1,244.0	959.9
Long-Term Obligations	...	...	300.0	300.0	300.0	...	...
Net Stockholders' Equity	11,351.0	9,429.0	6,144.0	4,614.0	3,674.0	2,654.0	2,006.7
Net Working Capital	4,434.0	6,815.0	5,317.0	3,847.0	3,145.0	2,047.0	1,359.1
Year-end Shs. Outstg. (000)	1,687,000	1,519,000	1,368,000	1,335,500	1,305,000	1,265,220	1,197,450
STATISTICAL RECORD:							
Operating Profit Margin %	...	11.1	10.4	8.7	11.7	9.6	7.9
Net Profit Margin %	...	7.5	7.3	5.3	8.0	6.4	5.2
Return on Equity %	...	19.7	21.4	17.1	23.6	17.4	10.6
Return on Assets %	...	12.7	12.2	9.8	13.7	10.8	6.4
Debt/Total Assets %	...	...	2.8	3.7	4.7	...	...
Price Range	44¾-22¹⁵/₁₆	39¹³/₁₆-14⁵/₁₆	17⁷/₁₆-7³/₁₆	11³/₈-6¹/₄	8⁷/₁₆-4¹³/₁₆	5¹/₁₆-2¹³/₁₆	3⁵/₁₆-1¹/₂
P/E Ratio	...	33.4-11.9	18.5-7.6	19.7-10.8	13.0-7.5	13.9-7.6	19.3-8.6
Average Yield %	0.2	...	...	...	...	...	...

Statistics are as originally reported. Adj. for 2-for-1 split, 1/98; 3-for-1 split, 6/94; 5-for-2 split, 11/97. ① Incl. $241.0 mill. ($0.44/sh.) non-tax deduct. chg. ② Incl. $252.0 mill. non-recur. chg. ③ Incl. $3.20 bill. chg. for in-process tech. & $393.0 mill. restr. & asset impairment chgs.

OFFICERS:
B. M. Rosen, Chmn.
M. D. Capellas, C.E.O., Pres.
B. Wells, V.P., Treas., C.F.O. (acting)

INVESTOR CONTACT: Tarrant Hancock, Dir.
Invest. Rel., (281) 374-1459

PRINCIPAL OFFICE: 20555 State Hwy. 249, Houston, TX 77070

TELEPHONE NUMBER: (281) 370-0670
FAX: (281) 514-0570
WEB: www.compaq.com

NO. OF EMPLOYEES: 71,000 full-time (approx.); 19,000 part-time (approx.)

SHAREHOLDERS: 89,000 (approx.)

ANNUAL MEETING: In Apr.

INCORPORATED: DE, Feb., 1982

INSTITUTIONAL HOLDINGS:
No. of Institutions: 781
Shares Held: 830,601,093
% Held: 48.9

INDUSTRY: Electronic computers (SIC: 3571)

TRANSFER AGENT(S): BankBoston, N.A., c/o Boston EquiServe, Boston, MA.

COMPS.COM, INC.

YIELD ...
P/E RATIO ...

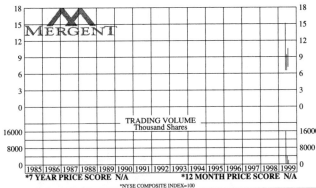

INTERIM EARNINGS (Per Share):

Qtr.	Mar.	June	Sept.	Dec.
1996			d0.74	
1997			d0.53	
1998			d0.60	
1999	d0.49	d0.30	...	...

INTERIM DIVIDENDS (Per Share):

Amt.	Decl.	Ex.	Rec.	Pay.
		No dividends paid.		

CAPITALIZATION (12/31/98):

	($000)	(%)
Long-Term Debt	1,101	421.4
Capital Lease Obligations..	23	8.7
Redeemable Pfd. Stock	7,009	2683.5
Common & Surplus	d7,871	-3013.6
Total	261	100.0

*7 YEAR PRICE SCORE N/A   *12 MONTH PRICE SCORE N/A

*NYSE COMPOSITE INDEX=100

RECENT DEVELOPMENTS: For the quarter ended 6/30/99 the Company reported a net loss of $2.3 million compared with a net loss of $11,000 in the same period of 1998. Results included pre-tax stock-based charges of $249,000 in 1999 and $3,000 in 1998. The bottom line was adversely affected by an 11.7 percentage point increase in cost of revenues as a percentage of revenues to 50.7% versus 39.0% in 1998. Net revenues grew 16.3% to $3.9 million from $3.3 million in the prior year. Approximately 11.0% of revenues were derived from Internet-related transactions, resulting in total Internet-related revenues accounting for approximately 37.0% of net revenues. Loss from operations amounted to $2.3 million in 1999 compared with income from operations of $62,000 a year earlier. On 6/18/99, the Company acquired the assets of Inside Prospects of California for an undisclosed amount. Inside Prospects, which is based in San Diego and operates in San Diego and Orange counties, markets proprietary tenant information to commercial real estate firms and other businesses.

BUSINESS

COMPS.COM, INC. is a national provider of comprehensive commercial real estate sales information and services both off-line and on the Internet. Via the Company's database, Comps.com matches buyers with brokers' property listings by posting such listings on its Web site and sending summary announcements by fax and e-mail to property owners and investors contained in its database. The Company completed its public offering on 5/10/99.

ANNUAL FINANCIAL DATA

	12/31/98	12/31/97	12/31/96
Earnings Per Share	d0.60	d0.53	d0.74
Cash Flow Per Share	d0.36	d0.27	d0.45
INCOME STATEMENT (IN THOUSANDS):			
Total Revenues	12,900	10,867	8,707
Costs & Expenses	13,459	11,259	9,927
Depreciation & Amort.	840	914	1,020
Operating Income	d1,399	d1,306	d2,240
Net Interest Inc./(Exp.)	d260	d252	d125
Income Before Income Taxes	d1,659	d1,557	d2,307
Net Income	d1,659	d1,557	d2,307
Cash Flow	d1,273	d942	d1,586
Average Shs. Outstg.	3,517	3,502	3,502
BALANCE SHEET (IN THOUSANDS):			
Cash & Cash Equivalents	378	352	...
Total Current Assets	3,728	2,796	...
Net Property	1,471	1,204	...
Total Assets	8,414	4,091	...
Total Current Liabilities	8,082	5,849	...
Long-Term Obligations	1,123	1,822	...
Net Stockholders' Equity	d7,871	d9,505	...
Net Working Capital	d4,354	d3,053	...
Year-end Shs. Outstg.	3,534	3,502	...
STATISTICAL RECORD:			
Debt/Total Assets %	13.3	44.5	...

Statistics are as originally reported.

OFFICERS:
C. A. Crane, Chmn., C.E.O.
J. D. Sharfman, Pres.
K. Goodrum, V.P., Fin., Admin., C.F.O., Sec.

PRINCIPAL OFFICE: 9888 Carroll Centre Road, Suite 100, San Diego, CA 92126

TELEPHONE NUMBER: (619) 578-3000
WEB: www.comps.com
NO. OF EMPLOYEES: 220 full-time (approx.); 45 part-time (approx.)
SHAREHOLDERS: N/A
ANNUAL MEETING: In July
INCORPORATED: CA, Jan., 1992; reincorp., DE, 1994

INSTITUTIONAL HOLDINGS:
No. of Institutions: 1
Shares Held: 247,500
% Held: 2.1
INDUSTRY: Data processing and preparation (SIC: 7374)
TRANSFER AGENT(S): American Stock Transfer & Trust Company, New York, NY.

NASDAQ SYMBOL CNCX
Rec. Pr. 24⅛ (7/31/99)

CONCENTRIC NETWORK CORPORATION

YIELD ...
P/E RATIO ...

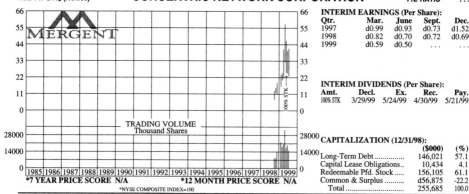

*7 YEAR PRICE SCORE N/A   *12 MONTH PRICE SCORE N/A
*NYSE COMPOSITE INDEX=100

INTERIM EARNINGS (Per Share):

Qtr.	Mar.	June	Sept.	Dec.
1997	d0.99	d0.93	d0.73	d1.52
1998	d0.82	d0.70	d0.72	d0.69
1999	d0.59	d0.50	...	...

INTERIM DIVIDENDS (Per Share):

Amt.	Decl.	Ex.	Rec.	Pay.
100% STK	3/29/99	5/24/99	4/30/99	5/21/99

CAPITALIZATION (12/31/98):

	($000)	(%)
Long-Term Debt	146,021	57.1
Capital Lease Obligations..	10,434	4.1
Redeemable Pfd. Stock.....	156,105	61.1
Common & Surplus	d56,875	-22.2
Total.............................	255,685	100.0

RECENT DEVELOPMENTS: For quarter ended 6/30/99, the Company reported a net loss of $20.5 million compared with a net loss of $20.2 million in comparable 1998 quarter. The 1999 results included non-recurring charges of $1.4 million versus $2.1 million in the year-earlier quarter. Revenue increased 68.0% to $33.0 million from $19.7 million in the prior-year quarter. The Company benefited from continued revenue growth across all enterprise-related product lines. Loss from operations totaled $17.8 million versus a loss of $16.2 million the year before. During the quarter, the Company entered into several key strategic agreements, including the Microsoft portal and WebTV service agreements and marketing relationships with regis-ter.com and MySoftware.

BUSINESS

CONCENTRIC NETWORK COR-PORATION provides tailored, value-added Internet Protocol-based network services for businesses and consumers. The Company's service offerings for enterprises include Virtual Private Networks, Dedicated Access Facilities, Digital Subscriber Lines, remote access and Web hosting. These services enable enterprises to take advantage of standard Internet tools such as browsers and high-performance services for customized data communications within an enterprise and between an enterprise and its suppliers, partners and customers. Among the current enterprise customers are Intuit, SBC, Teligent and WebTV. The Company's service offerings for consumers and small office/home office customers include local Internet dial-up access, DSL and applications hosting.

ANNUAL FINANCIAL DATA

	12/31/98	12/31/97	12/31/96	12/31/95	12/31/94
Earnings Per Share	① d2.93	d4.17	d5.94	...	...
Cash Flow Per Share	d1.78	d2.73	d5.09	...	...
Tang. Book Val. Per Share	...	1.13	...	...	...
INCOME STATEMENT (IN THOUSANDS):					
Total Revenues	82,807	45,457	15,648	2,483	442
Costs & Expenses	120,192	76,471	69,299	21,574	4,506
Depreciation & Amort.	33,418	19,230	9,470	2,196	169
Operating Income	d70,803	d50,244	d63,121	d21,287	d4,233
Net Interest Inc./(Exp.)	d13,595	d6,571	d3,260	d721	d57
Income Before Income Taxes	d85,148	d55,582	d66,381	d22,008	d4,290
Net Income	① d85,148	d55,582	d66,381	d22,008	d4,290
Cash Flow	d63,688	d36,352	d56,911	d19,812	d4,121
Average Shs. Outstg.	29,094	13,330	11,180	...	...
BALANCE SHEET (IN THOUSANDS):					
Cash & Cash Equivalents	170,339	139,084	17,657	19,054	...
Total Current Assets	187,111	148,772	21,228	20,337	...
Net Property	64,268	53,710	47,927	16,289	...
Total Assets	298,257	244,489	70,722	37,235	...
Total Current Liabilities	42,572	33,399	32,096	11,345	...
Long-Term Obligations	156,455	179,172	30,551	11,047	...
Net Stockholders' Equity	d56,875	31,918	d92,290	d25,932	...
Net Working Capital	144,539	115,373	d10,868	8,992	...
Year-end Shs. Outstg.	30,288	28,278	2,786	2,776	...
STATISTICAL RECORD:					
Debt/Total Assets %	52.5	73.3	43.2	29.7	...
Price Range	18⅝-7¼	...	...	...	...

Statistics are as originally reported. Adj. for stk. splits: 2-for-1, 5/21/99 ① Incl. pre-tax chrg. $3.8 mill. for amort. of good will and other intangible assets, a pre-tax chrg. of $1.3 mill. for acq.-related exps., and a pre-tax chrg. of $5.2 mill. for write-off of in-process tech.; excl. $3.0 mill. extraord. gain on early retirem

OFFICERS:
H. R. Nothhaft, Chmn., Pres., C.E.O.
M. F. Anthofer, Sr. V.P., C.F.O.

PRINCIPAL OFFICE: 1400 Parkmoor Avenue, San Jose, CA 95126

TELEPHONE NUMBER: (408) 817-2800
WEB: www.concentric.com

NO. OF EMPLOYEES: 508

SHAREHOLDERS: 271; 4,388 beneficial (approx.)

ANNUAL MEETING: In May

INCORPORATED: FL, 1991; reincorp., DE, Jun., 1997

INSTITUTIONAL HOLDINGS:
No. of Institutions: 100
Shares Held: 23,631,702
% Held: 78.0

INDUSTRY: Telephone communications, exc. radio (SIC: 4813)

TRANSFER AGENT(S): ChaseMellon Shareholder Services LLC, Ridgefield Park, NJ

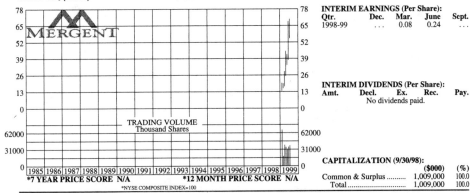

CONEXANT SYSTEMS INC.

INTERIM EARNINGS (Per Share):

Qtr.	Dec.	Mar.	June	Sept.
1998-99	...	0.08	0.24	...

INTERIM DIVIDENDS (Per Share):

Amt.	Decl.	Ex.	Rec.	Pay.
	No dividends paid.			

*7 YEAR PRICE SCORE N/A   *12 MONTH PRICE SCORE N/A

*NYSE COMPOSITE INDEX=100

CAPITALIZATION (9/30/98):

	($000)	(%)
Common & Surplus	1,009,000	100.0
Total	1,009,000	100.0

RECENT DEVELOPMENTS: For the quarter ended 6/30/99, the Company reported net income of $24.4 million compared with a net loss of $33.4 million in the corresponding period of 1998. Net revenues advanced 36.9% to $380.3 million from $277.8 million a year earlier. Revenues in the personal computing business platform rose 8.2% to $154.4 million, while revenues in the network access business platform more than doubled to $82.6 million from $38.9 million in 1998. Revenues in the wireless communications business platform increased 68.2% to $70.0 million. Gross margin leapt 74.1% to $164.2 million from 94.3 million in the prior year. The Company anticipates revenue growth of more than 10.0% in the fourth quarter based on current design wins and sales order momentum. Gross margin is anticipated to be in the range of 43.0% to 45.0%. Moreover, the Company expects revenues to grow more than 15.0% in its expansion platform businesses in the fourth quarter.

BUSINESS

CONEXANT SYSTEMS INC. commenced operations as an independent entity in January 1999 after Rockwell International Corporation spun off its semiconductor systems business to its shareowners. Conexant focuses exclusively on providing semiconductor products for communications electronics. The Company uses mixed-signal processing to deliver integrated systems and semiconductor products for a range of communications applications. These products facilitate communications worldwide through wireline voice and data communications networks, cordless and cellular wireless telephony systems, personal imaging devices and equipment, and emerging cable and wireless broadband communications networks. The Company aligns its business into five product platforms: network access, wireless communications, digital infotainment, personal imaging and personal computing. The continuing expansion of the worldwide Internet infrastructure has driven growth in CNXT's network access division, which accounted for 22.0% of total revenues at 6/30/99 versus 14.0% at 6/30/98.

ANNUAL FINANCIAL DATA

	9/30/98	9/30/97	9/30/96	9/30/95
INCOME STATEMENT (IN MILLIONS):				
Total Revenues	1,200.0	1,412.0	1,470.0	784.0
Costs & Expenses	1,424.0	1,064.0	1,143.0	616.0
Depreciation & Amort.	220.0	181.0	132.0	61.0
Operating Income	d444.0	167.0	195.0	107.0
Income Before Income Taxes	d430.0	180.0	198.0	111.0
Income Taxes	cr168.0	54.0	114.0	35.0
Net Income	d262.0	126.0	84.0	76.0
Cash Flow	d42.0	307.0	216.0	137.0
BALANCE SHEET (IN MILLIONS):				
Cash & Cash Equivalents	14.0	14.0	14.0	...
Total Current Assets	587.0	521.0	616.0	...
Net Property	713.0	802.0	656.0	...
Total Assets	1,418.0	1,486.0	1,383.0	...
Total Current Liabilities	331.0	299.0	387.0	...
Net Stockholders' Equity	1,009.0	1,107.0	899.0	...
Net Working Capital	256.0	222.0	229.0	...
STATISTICAL RECORD:				
Operating Profit Margin %	...	11.8	13.3	13.6
Net Profit Margin %	...	8.9	5.7	9.7
Return on Equity %	...	11.4	9.3	...
Return on Assets %	...	8.5	6.1	...

Statistics are as originally reported.

OFFICERS:
D. W. Decker, Chmn., C.E.O.
B. S. Iyer, Sr. V.P., C.F.O., Sec.
K. K. Petry, V.P., Treas.

PRINCIPAL OFFICE: 4311 Jamboree Road, Newport Beach, CA 92660-3095

TELEPHONE NUMBER: (949) 221-4600
WEB: www.conexant.com

NO. OF EMPLOYEES: 6,300 (approx.)

SHAREHOLDERS: N/A

ANNUAL MEETING: N/A

INCORPORATED: DE, Sep., 1996

INSTITUTIONAL HOLDINGS:
No. of Institutions: 211
Shares Held: 41,405,587
% Held: 42.9

INDUSTRY: Electronic parts and equipment (SIC: 5065)

TRANSFER AGENT(S): ChaseMellon Shareholder Services. L.L.C.

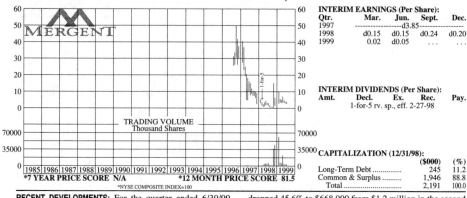

NASDAQ SYMBOL CNKT
Rec. Pr. 2¾ (7/31/99)

CONNECTINC.COM, CO.

YIELD ...
P/E RATIO ...

INTERIM EARNINGS (Per Share):

Qtr.	Mar.	Jun.	Sept.	Dec.
1997	-------------------d3.85------------------			
1998	d0.15	d0.15	d0.24	d0.20
1999	0.02	d0.05	...	...

INTERIM DIVIDENDS (Per Share):

Amt.	Decl.	Ex.	Rec.	Pay.
	1-for-5 rv. sp., eff. 2-27-98			

TRADING VOLUME
Thousand Shares

1985 1986 1987 1988 1989 1990 1991 1992 1993 1994 1995 1996 1997 1998 1999
*7 YEAR PRICE SCORE N/A   ***12 MONTH PRICE SCORE 81.5**
*NYSE COMPOSITE INDEX=100

CAPITALIZATION (12/31/98):

	($000)	(%)
Long-Term Debt	245	11.2
Common & Surplus	1,946	88.8
Total	2,191	100.0

RECENT DEVELOPMENTS: For the quarter ended 6/30/99, the Company reported a net loss of $728,000 compared with a net loss of $1.9 million in the corresponding quarter the year before. Total revenue declined 27.3% to $1.2 million from $1.7 million in the prior-year quarter. License revenue jumped 21.7% to $560,000 compared with $460,000 in the year-earlier quarter. The increase in license revenue was due to the fact that CNKT began shipment of MarketStream 2.0 during this period. Service revenue dropped 45.6% to $668,000 from $1.2 million in the second quarter of 1998. The service revenue decline was influenced by the fact that many of CNKT's engineers were involved with the development of the new MarketStream product while simultaneously working on customer implementations. During the quarter, CNKT signed several new customers. Revenues over the next four quarters should benefit as a result.

BUSINESS

CONNECTINC.COM, CO. (formerly Connect, Inc.) develops, markets and supports its packaged application product, MarketStream™, an electronic commerce application that provides a broad technology foundation for e-business. Targeted specifically at companies looking to establish an e-business as an extension of their existing business model, or at new start-up companies, MarketStream is designed to help provide accelerated time-to-market. MarketStream includes support for integrated cross-supplier catalog search, product-specific attributes, tiered or customized pricing, buyer profiling and personalization, back-end system integration and robust reporting capabilities.

REVENUES

(12/31/1998)	($000)	(%)
License	1,828	28.2
Service	4,650	71.8
Total	6,478	100.0

ANNUAL FINANCIAL DATA

	12/31/98	12/31/97	12/31/96	12/31/95	12/31/94	12/31/93
Earnings Per Share	① d0.74	d3.85	d4.50	d3.95	d0.65	d0.70
Cash Flow Per Share	d0.62	d3.38	d4.03	d3.69	d0.47	d0.61
Tang. Book Val. Per Share	0.15	...	3.60	...	...	...
INCOME STATEMENT (IN THOUSANDS):						
Total Revenues	6,479	9,362	10,180	8,573	7,972	3,862
Costs & Expenses	13,049	22,093	24,833	20,779	9,039	5,230
Depreciation & Amort.	1,262	1,788	1,705	988	473	280
Operating Income	d7,833	d14,518	d16,358	d13,194	d1,540	d1,648
Net Interest Inc./(Exp.)	d352	d414	d331	d1,003	d240	d205
Income Before Income Taxes	d7,904	d14,585	d16,142	d14,165	d1,739	d1,921
Income Taxes				cr26	26	
Net Income	① d7,904	d14,585	d16,142	d14,139	d1,765	d1,921
Cash Flow	d6,641	d12,797	d14,437	d13,151	d1,291	d1,641
Average Shs. Outstg.	10,682	3,784	3,582	3,563	2,719	2,703
BALANCE SHEET (IN THOUSANDS):						
Cash & Cash Equivalents	3,965	9,644	12,214	12,929	1,594	...
Total Current Assets	4,790	12,837	15,354	14,410	2,747	...
Net Property	609	2,442	3,647	3,263	2,146	...
Total Assets	5,453	15,364	19,154	18,063	5,161	...
Total Current Liabilities	3,262	5,404	5,009	3,108	5,533	...
Long-Term Obligations	245	939	790	1,636	1,167	...
Net Stockholders' Equity	1,946	d633	13,355	13,318	d1,538	...
Net Working Capital	1,528	7,434	10,344	11,302	d2,786	...
Year-end Shs. Outstg.	13,214	3,828	3,706	80	74	...
STATISTICAL RECORD:						
Debt/Total Assets %	4.5	6.1	4.1	9.1	22.6	...
Price Range	15¹¹/₁₆-0¼	40⅝-2½	50-25⅝	...	...	...

Statistics are as originally reported. Adj. for 1-for-5 reverse stk. split, 2/98. ① Incl. non-recurr. chrg. $1.1 mill.

OFFICERS:
C. D. Norris, Pres., C.E.O.
K. J. Berry, C.F.O., V.P., Fin.

PRINCIPAL OFFICE: 515 Ellis Street, Mountain View, CA 94043-2242

TELEPHONE NUMBER: (650) 254-4000
WEB: www.connectinc.com.
NO. OF EMPLOYEES: 35
SHAREHOLDERS: 217 (approx.)
ANNUAL MEETING: In Aug.
INCORPORATED: CA, Apr., 1987; reincorp., DE, Jul., 1996

INSTITUTIONAL HOLDINGS:
No. of Institutions: 8
Shares Held: 1,151,498
% Held: 7.8
INDUSTRY: Prepackaged software (SIC: 7372)
TRANSFER AGENT(S): U.S. Stock Transfer Corporation, Glendale, CA

COPPER MOUNTAIN NETWORKS, INC.

YIELD ...
P/E RATIO ...

*7 YEAR PRICE SCORE N/A   *12 MONTH PRICE SCORE N/A

*NYSE COMPOSITE INDEX=100

TRADING VOLUME
Thousand Shares

1985 1986 1987 1988 1989 1990 1991 1992 1993 1994 1995 1996 1997 1998 1999

INTERIM EARNINGS (Per Share):

Qtr.	Mar.	June	Sept.	Dec.
1996			d11.67	
1997			d15.62	
1998			d7.75	
1999	d0.03	0.09	...	...

INTERIM DIVIDENDS (Per Share):

Amt.	Decl.	Ex.	Rec.	Pay.
	No dividends paid.			

CAPITALIZATION (12/31/98):

	($000)	(%)
Long-Term Debt	1,965	6.8
Preferred Stock	44,502	154.5
Common & Surplus	d17,659	-61.3
Total	28,808	100.0

RECENT DEVELOPMENTS: For the second quarter ended 6/30/99, net income amounted to $2.3 million. This compares with a net loss of $3.5 million in the corresponding quarter the year before. Net revenues skyrocketed to $22.9 million from $1.3 million in the comparable quarter a year earlier. The net revenue increase was primarily due to the increase in sales of the Company's CE200 DSL access concentrators and related DSL CPE. During the quarter, sales to North Point Communications and Rhythms Net-Connections were $8.5 million and $11.1 million; respectively. Gross profit as a percentage of net revenue increased to 52.7% from 37.9% in the equivalent 1998 quarter. This increase was the result of higher unit volumes, and to a lesser extent due to decreased unit costs associated with improved overhead absorption and a favorable product mix. Total operating expenses more than doubled to $9.5 million from $4.0 million in the second quarter of 1998.

BUSINESS

COPPER MOUNTAIN NET-WORKS, INC. supplies digital subscriber line, or DSL, based communications products that allow high-speed internetworking over existing copper facilities. The Company generates its revenue primarily from the sales of its central office based equipment, such as CopperEdge 200 DSL access concentrators (CE200), the related wide-area network cards, line cards, and DSL CPE. The Company sells the majority of its products directly to telecommunications service providers. In 1998, sales to the Company's two largest customers, NorthPoint Communications, Inc. and Rhythms Net-Connections Inc., accounted for 61.0% and 18.0% of net revenues, respectively. On 5/18/99, the Company completed its initial public offering of 4.6 million shares of common stock.

ANNUAL FINANCIAL DATA

	12/31/98	12/31/97	① 12/31/96
Earnings Per Share	d7.75	d15.62	d11.67
Cash Flow Per Share	d6.83	d14.90	d11.08
INCOME STATEMENT (IN THOUSANDS):			
Total Revenues	21,821	211	...
Costs & Expenses	31,114	10,887	2,116
Depreciation & Amort.	1,231	511	109
Operating Income	d10,524	d11,187	d2,225
Net Interest Inc./(Exp.)	193	171	44
Income Before Income Taxes	d10,331	d11,016	d2,181
Net Income	d10,331	d11,016	d2,181
Cash Flow	d9,100	d10,505	d2,072
Average Shs. Outstg.	1,333	705	187
BALANCE SHEET (IN THOUSANDS):			
Cash & Cash Equivalents	18,529	9,517	...
Total Current Assets	31,699	10,181	...
Net Property	3,214	1,905	...
Total Assets	36,209	12,332	...
Total Current Liabilities	7,373	2,528	...
Long-Term Obligations	1,965	735	...
Net Stockholders' Equity	26,843	9,069	...
Net Working Capital	24,326	7,653	...
Year-end Shs. Outstg.	2,517	2,231	...
STATISTICAL RECORD:			
Debt/Total Assets %	5.4	6.0	...

Statistics are as originally reported. ① Period from 3/11/96 (inception) to 12/31/96

OFFICERS:
J. D. Markee, Chmn. & Chief Technical Off.
R. S. Gilbert, Pres. & C.E.O.
J. A. Creelman, V.P., C.F.O. & Sec.

INVESTOR CONTACT: Investor Relations Dept., (877) 463-6268

PRINCIPAL OFFICE: 2470 Embarcadero Way, Palo Alto, CA 94303

TELEPHONE NUMBER: (650) 858-8500
FAX: (650) 858-8085
WEB: www.coppermountain.com.
NO. OF EMPLOYEES: 154 (approx.)
SHAREHOLDERS: N/A
ANNUAL MEETING: N/A
INCORPORATED: CA, Mar., 1996; reincorp., DE, Apr., 1999

INSTITUTIONAL HOLDINGS:
No. of Institutions: 9
Shares Held: 431,420
% Held: 1.9
INDUSTRY: Telephone and telegraph apparatus (SIC: 3661)
TRANSFER AGENT(S): ChaseMellon Shareholder Services, L.L.C., Ridgefield Park, NJ

COVAD COMMUNICATIONS GROUP, INC.

YIELD ...
P/E RATIO ...

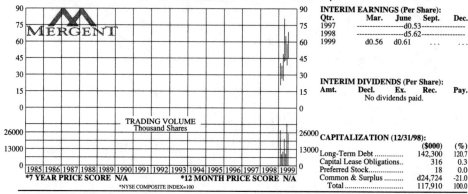

INTERIM EARNINGS (Per Share):

Qtr.	Mar.	June	Sept.	Dec.
1997		----------d0.53----------		
1998		----------d5.62----------		
1999	d0.56	d0.61	...	...

INTERIM DIVIDENDS (Per Share):

Amt.	Decl.	Ex.	Rec.	Pay.
	No dividends paid.			

CAPITALIZATION (12/31/98):

	($000)	(%)
Long-Term Debt	142,300	120.7
Capital Lease Obligations..	316	0.3
Preferred Stock.................	18	0.0
Common & Surplus	d24,724	-21.0
Total	117,910	100.0

7 YEAR PRICE SCORE N/A   **12 MONTH PRICE SCORE N/A**
*NYSE COMPOSITE INDEX=100

RECENT DEVELOPMENTS: For the three months ended 6/30/99, the Company reported a net loss of $41.9 million versus a loss of $8.9 million in the corresponding quarter a year earlier. Revenues jumped to $10.8 million from $809,000 the year before. Loss from operations was $34.6 million compared with a loss of $5.6 million in the prior year. As of 6/30/99, subscriber lines totaled over 16,700, up 94.0% from approximately 8,600 lines at 3/31/99. During the second quarter and early in the third quarter, the Company launched service in Atlanta, Baltimore, Chicago, Denver, Detroit, Minneapolis/St. Paul and Portland. This brings COVD's coverage to 37 metropolitan statistical areas (''MSAs''). The Company expects to cover 51 MSAs by the end of 1999.

BUSINESS

COVAD COMMUNICATIONS GROUP, INC. is a provider of high-speed Internet and network access. The Company offers digital subscriber line (DSL) services to large enterprise customers and through Internet Service Providers to small- and medium-sized businesses and home users. COVD's services are provided over standard copper telephone lines at speeds of up to 1.5 megabits per second and through over 4,000 DSL lines.

ANNUAL FINANCIAL DATA

	12/31/98	12/31/97
Earnings Per Share	d5.62	d0.53
Cash Flow Per Share	d2.89	d0.46
Tang. Book Val. Per Share	...	0.15
INCOME STATEMENT (IN THOUSANDS):		
Total Revenues	5,326	26
Costs & Expenses	19,596	2,428
Depreciation & Amort.	23,412	365
Operating Income	d37,682	d2,767
Net Interest Inc./(Exp.)	d10,439	155
Net Income	d48,121	d2,612
Cash Flow	d24,709	d2,247
Average Shs. Outstg.	8,564	4,908
BALANCE SHEET (IN THOUSANDS):		
Cash & Cash Equivalents	64,450	4,378
Total Current Assets	69,689	4,819
Net Property	59,145	3,014
Total Assets	139,419	8,074
Total Current Liabilities	21,509	1,022
Long-Term Obligations	142,616	554
Net Stockholders' Equity	d24,706	6,498
Net Working Capital	48,180	3,797
Year-end Shs. Outstg.	17,661	43,667
STATISTICAL RECORD:		
Debt/Total Assets %	102.3	6.9

Statistics are as originally reported.

OFFICERS:
C. McMinn, Chmn.
R. Knowling, Jr., Pres., C.E.O.
T. Laehy, V.P., Fin., C.F.O.

INVESTOR CONTACT: Nick Kormeluk, V.P.-
Investor Relations, (408) 844-7500

PRINCIPAL OFFICE: 2330 Central
Expressway, Santa Clara, CA 95050

TELEPHONE NUMBER: (408) 844-7500
WEB: www.covad.com

NO. OF EMPLOYEES: 335

SHAREHOLDERS: 335 (holders of record); 5
(holders of class B common stock)

ANNUAL MEETING: N/A

INCORPORATED: DE, Jul., 1997

INSTITUTIONAL HOLDINGS:
No. of Institutions: 83
Shares Held: 15,088,101
% Held: 21.3

INDUSTRY: Telephone and telegraph
apparatus (SIC: 3661)

TRANSFER AGENT(S): BankBoston N.A.,
Boston, MA

CRITICAL PATH, INC.

YIELD ...
P/E RATIO ...

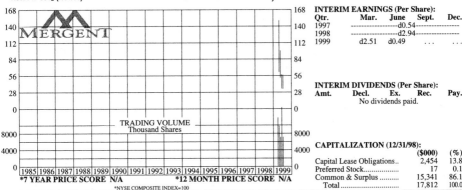

*7 YEAR PRICE SCORE N/A   *12 MONTH PRICE SCORE N/A
*NYSE COMPOSITE INDEX=100

INTERIM EARNINGS (Per Share):

Qtr.	Mar.	June	Sept.	Dec.
1997		--------------d0.54--------------		
1998		--------------d2.94--------------		
1999	d2.51	d0.49	...	...

INTERIM DIVIDENDS (Per Share):

Amt.	Decl.	Ex.	Rec.	Pay.
	No dividends paid.			

CAPITALIZATION (12/31/98):

	($000)	(%)
Capital Lease Obligations..	2,454	13.8
Preferred Stock.................	17	0.1
Common & Surplus	15,341	86.1
Total	17,812	100.0

RECENT DEVELOPMENTS: On 7/21/99, the Company completed the acquisition of dotOne. For the second quarter ended 6/30/99, the Company recorded a net loss of $16.3 million compared with a net loss of $1.8 million in the corresponding quarter the year before. Results for the 1999 quarter included an $8.2 million charge associated with stock-based expenses. Net revenues sky-rocketed to $2.0 million from $66,000 in the comparable quarter a year earlier. The growth in revenues was due to an aggressive growth strategy, which has increased the Company's customer base and number of mailboxes served domestically and internationally. During the quarter, the Company signed 169 long-term contracts with companies and organizations, including British Telecom, CompuServe, Comcast, and Sina.com, China's largest portal. On 6/30/99, total active mailboxes increased 196.0% to 4.2 million compared with the previous quarter. On 6/23/99, the Company agreed to acquire Amplitude Software Corp.

BUSINESS

CRITICAL PATH, INC. is a provider of business-to-business Internet messaging services for corporations, Internet service providers, Web hosting companies, and Web portals. The Company has constructed a global infrastructure with data centers connected to Internet exchange points, and currently reaches millions of end-users. The Company offers secure and scalable e-mail, and a flexible suite of enhanced messaging services to partners such as E*TRADE, CompuServ, Network Solutions, US West, Sprint, and ICQ.

ANNUAL FINANCIAL DATA

	12/31/98	12/31/97
Earnings Per Share	**d2.94**	**d0.54**
Cash Flow Per Share	**d1.91**	**d0.53**
Tang. Book Val. Per Share	**1.85**	...
INCOME STATEMENT (IN THOUSANDS):		
Total Revenues	897	...
Costs & Expenses	8,342	1,030
Depreciation & Amort.	4,003	26
Operating Income	d11,448	d1,056
Net Interest Inc./(Exp.)	d13	d18
Income Before Income Taxes	d11,461	d1,074
Net Income	d11,461	d1,074
Cash Flow	d7,458	d1,048
Average Shs. Outstg.	3,899	1,994
BALANCE SHEET (IN THOUSANDS):		
Cash & Cash Equivalents	15,116	1
Total Current Assets	15,375	5
Net Property	4,687	501
Total Assets	20,663	550
Total Current Liabilities	2,851	1,529
Long-Term Obligations	2,454	42
Net Stockholders' Equity	15,358	d1,021
Net Working Capital	12,524	d1,524
Year-end Shs. Outstg.	8,294	2,394
STATISTICAL RECORD:		
Debt/Total Assets %	11.9	7.6
Statistics are as originally reported.		

OFFICERS:
D. C. Hayden, Chmn.
D. T. Hickey, Pres. & C.E.O.
D. A. Thatcher, Exec. V.P. & C.F.O.

PRINCIPAL OFFICE: 320 1st Street, San Francisco, CA 94105

TELEPHONE NUMBER: (415) 808-8800
WEB: www.cp.net.

NO. OF EMPLOYEES: 182

SHAREHOLDERS: 369 (approx.)

ANNUAL MEETING: N/A

INCORPORATED: CA, Feb., 1997

INSTITUTIONAL HOLDINGS:
No. of Institutions: 65
Shares Held: 2,917,478
% Held: 7.7

INDUSTRY: Business services, nec (SIC: 7389)

TRANSFER AGENT(S): American Securities Transfer & Trust, New York, NY

CROSSWALK.COM, INC.

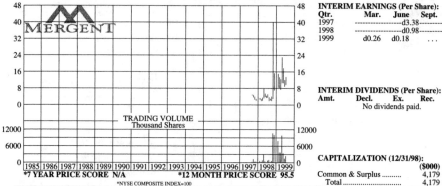

INTERIM EARNINGS (Per Share):

Qtr.	Mar.	June	Sept.	Dec.
1997	-------------------d3.38------------------			
1998	-------------------d0.98------------------			
1999	d0.26	d0.18	...	...

INTERIM DIVIDENDS (Per Share):

Amt.	Decl.	Ex.	Rec.	Pay.
	No dividends paid.			

TRADING VOLUME
Thousand Shares

7 YEAR PRICE SCORE N/A   **12 MONTH PRICE SCORE 95.5**

*NYSE COMPOSITE INDEX=100

CAPITALIZATION (12/31/98):

	($000)	(%)
Common & Surplus	4,179	100.0
Total	4,179	100.0

RECENT DEVELOPMENTS: On 8/2/99, shares of AMEN began traading on the Nasdaq National Market System. The Company's stock previously traded on the Nasdaq Small-cap System. For the second quarter ended 6/30/99, the Company reported a net loss of $1.3 million compared with a net loss of $747,598 in the corresponding prior-year quarter. Total revenues jumped to $1.7 million from $166,309 a year earlier. Gross profit margin as a percentage of total revenues grew to 48.0% from 39.0% in the previous year.

Crosswalk operating expenses surged to $892,908 from $321,952 the year before. On 6/2/99, the Company acquired Wike Associates, Inc., the parent company of Media Management, a Christian publishing and direct mail company that is the owner and developer of GOSHEN.net, a Web site and e-mail service that primarily serves Christian leaders. On 5/24/99, the Company changed its name to Crosswalk.com, Inc. from Didax Inc.

BUSINESS

CROSSWALK.COM, INC. (formerly Didax Inc.) is a portal Web site that provides information, resources and retail sales opportunities that the Company believes generally appeals to the Christian community. Members and site visitors with Internet access may currently enter crosswalk.com free of charge to view channels on the Web site targeting music, personal finance, careers, and home schooling; lifestyle channels focusing on men, women, and spiritual life; and services ranging from free Web access filtering and a full-Web filtered search engine to on-line shopping, family-friendly movie reviews, games, chat, forums, local events, news, free email and more. Content and site resources are developed and offered both by AMEN and by ministries, secular retailers, and publishers. The Company generates revenues through the sale of sponsorships and advertising, the on-line retailing of Christian and family-friendly products, sales of subscriptions, royalties and referral fees, and the provision of technology services.

ANNUAL FINANCIAL DATA

	12/31/98	12/31/97	12/31/96	12/31/95
Earnings Per Share	d0.98	d3.38	d4.35	d1.58
Cash Flow Per Share	d0.94	d3.13	d4.15	d1.56
Tang. Book Val. Per Share	1.02	1.28	...	...
INCOME STATEMENT (IN THOUSANDS):				
Total Revenues	1,083	345	181	...
Costs & Expenses	4,628	2,414	2,464	704
Depreciation & Amort.	135	306	119	7
Operating Income	d3,679	d2,375	d2,402	d711
Net Interest Inc./(Exp.)	214	d1,750	d66	4
Income Before Income Taxes	d3,459	d4,125	d2,465	d707
Net Income	d3,459	d4,125	d2,465	d707
Cash Flow	d3,325	d3,819	d2,346	d699
Average Shs. Outstg.	3,535	1,220	565	448
BALANCE SHEET (IN THOUSANDS):				
Cash & Cash Equivalents	3,978	5,430	2	247
Total Current Assets	4,478	5,533	99	291
Net Property	322	132	167	60
Total Assets	4,903	5,758	282	361
Total Current Liabilities	677	207	1,199	118
Net Stockholders' Equity	4,179	3,792	d2,705	d357
Net Working Capital	3,801	5,326	d1,101	173
Year-end Shs. Outstg.	4,035	2,968	595	547

Statistics are as originally reported.

OFFICERS:
J. G. Buick, Chmn.
R. C. Varney, Vice-Chmn.
W. M. Parker, Pres. & C.E.O.
G. A. Struzik, C.F.O. & Sec.

PRINCIPAL OFFICE: 4206F Techonology Court, Chantilly, VA 20151

TELEPHONE NUMBER: (703) 968-4808
FAX: (703) 968-4819
WEB: www.crosswalk.com
NO. OF EMPLOYEES: 33 full-time; 4 part-time
SHAREHOLDERS: 6,100
ANNUAL MEETING: In May
INCORPORATED: DE, Jan., 1997

INSTITUTIONAL HOLDINGS:
No. of Institutions: 10
Shares Held: 151,122
% Held: 2.3

INDUSTRY: Computer programming services (SIC: 7371)

TRANSFER AGENT(S): American Stock Transfer & Trust Co., New York, NY

CYBERCASH, INC.

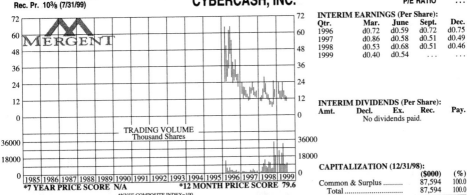

YIELD ...
P/E RATIO ...

INTERIM EARNINGS (Per Share):

Qtr.	Mar.	June	Sept.	Dec.
1996	d0.72	d0.59	d0.72	d0.75
1997	d0.86	d0.58	d0.51	d0.49
1998	d0.53	d0.68	d0.51	d0.46
1999	d0.40	d0.54	...	...

INTERIM DIVIDENDS (Per Share):

Amt.	Decl.	Ex.	Rec.	Pay.
	No dividends paid.			

TRADING VOLUME
Thousand Shares

*7 YEAR PRICE SCORE N/A   *12 MONTH PRICE SCORE 79.6
*NYSE COMPOSITE INDEX=100

CAPITALIZATION (12/31/98):

	($000)	(%)
Common & Surplus	87,594	100.0
Total	87,594	100.0

RECENT DEVELOPMENTS: For the three months ended 6/30/99, the Company recorded a net loss of $11.0 million compared with a net loss of $9.6 million in the second quarter of 1998. Results for the 1998 quarter included a restructuring charge of $608,755. Net revenues nearly doubled to $4.2 million from $2.4 million the year before. Gross profit rose 6.9% to $918,877 from $859,519 in the prior-year quarter. During the quarter, CYCH increased the number of merchants using the CashRegister service to about 13,000, adding over 1,100 per month. CYCH also launched its CashRegister OnDemand™ service, a Web-based payment system targeting first-time on-line and physical world merchants seeking entry into electronic commerce on the Internet. In addition, CYCH acquired Tellan Software, Inc., a producer of payment processing software for merchants to use in physical and Internet point-of-sale. CYCH is focusing on the distribution of its electronic wallets and the InstaBuy service to consumers through key channel partners.

BUSINESS

CYBERCASH, INC. provides secure, convenient payment technologies and services, enabling e-commerce across the entire market spectrum from electronic retailing environments to the Internet. CYCH provides a complete line of software products and services allowing merchants, billers, financial institutions and consumers to conduct secure transactions using the broadest array of popular payment forms. Credit, debit, purchase cards, cash, checks, smart cards and alternative payments types are all supported by the Company's payment solutions. Leading brands include Instabuy™, ICVERIFY®, PCVERIFY™, CashRegister, NetVERIFY™, CyberCoin®, and PayNow™. Leading brands of its subsidiary, Tellan Software, Inc., include WebAuthorize™, PCAuthorize® and MacAuthorize®.

REVENUES

(12/31/1998)	($000)	(%)
Product Sales	6,478	51.5
Service Offerings	6,109	48.5
Total	12,587	100.0

ANNUAL FINANCIAL DATA

	12/31/98	12/31/97	12/31/96	12/31/95	12/31/94
Earnings Per Share	① d2.15	① d2.43	d2.77	d2.50	d0.29
Cash Flow Per Share	d1.54	d2.19	d2.63	d2.41	d0.28
Tang. Book Val. Per Share	1.17	1.50	3.56	...	...
INCOME STATEMENT (IN THOUSANDS):					
Total Revenues	12,588	4,487	127	...	...
Costs & Expenses	36,029	28,861	27,536	9,805	1,155
Depreciation & Amort.	8,317	2,403	1,344	344	13
Operating Income	d31,758	d26,777	d28,752	d10,149	d1,168
Net Interest Inc./(Exp.)	915	1,461	2,197	143	14
Income Before Income Taxes	d30,843	d25,316	d26,555	d10,006	d1,153
Equity Earnings/Minority Int.	d101	d905	...	...	...
Net Income	① d30,944	① d26,222	d26,555	d10,006	d1,153
Cash Flow	d22,628	d23,819	d25,211	d9,663	d1,140
Average Shs. Outstg.	14,708	10,898	9,585	4,002	4,002
BALANCE SHEET (IN THOUSANDS):					
Cash & Cash Equivalents	11,250	22,265	33,937	5,295	1,473
Total Current Assets	16,512	25,789	34,783	5,694	1,484
Net Property	9,050	4,671	5,630	1,567	224
Total Assets	93,324	31,017	41,050	7,386	1,719
Total Current Liabilities	5,730	1,659	2,881	2,265	379
Net Stockholders' Equity	87,594	16,593	38,109	d10,981	d1,027
Net Working Capital	10,782	24,130	31,902	3,429	1,105
Year-end Shs. Outstg.	19,110	11,055	10,712	2,063	...
STATISTICAL RECORD:					
Price Range	27¾-5⅞	24¼-10½	64¾-20¾	...	...

Statistics are as originally reported. ① Incl. non-recurr. chrg. 12/31/98: $608,755; 12/31/97: $2.2 mill.

OFFICERS:
W. M. Melton, Chmn., C.E.O.
J. J. Condon, Pres., C.O.O.
D. N. Cavender, C.F.O.
R. B. Stevenson Jr., Sr. V.P., Gen. Coun.
INVESTOR CONTACT: Jordanna M. Taffel
PRINCIPAL OFFICE: 2100 Reston Parkway, 3rd Floor, Reston, VA 20191

TELEPHONE NUMBER: (703) 620-4200
WEB: www.cybercash.com
NO. OF EMPLOYEES: 337
SHAREHOLDERS: 367
ANNUAL MEETING: In June
INCORPORATED: DE, Aug., 1994

INSTITUTIONAL HOLDINGS:
No. of Institutions: 29
Shares Held: 1,162,768
% Held: 5.8
INDUSTRY: Computer integrated systems design (SIC: 7373)
TRANSFER AGENT(S): Bank of Boston c/o Boston EquiServe, LP, Boston, MA

CYBERIAN OUTPOST, INC.

YIELD ...
P/E RATIO ...

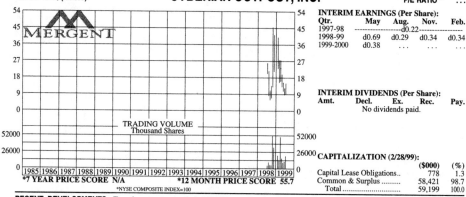

*7 YEAR PRICE SCORE N/A *12 MONTH PRICE SCORE 55.7
*NYSE COMPOSITE INDEX=100

INTERIM EARNINGS (Per Share):

Qtr.	May	Aug.	Nov.	Feb.
1997-98		d0.22		
1998-99	d0.69	d0.29	d0.34	d0.34
1999-2000	d0.38	...	...	...

INTERIM DIVIDENDS (Per Share):

Amt.	Decl.	Ex.	Rec.	Pay.
		No dividends paid.		

CAPITALIZATION (2/28/99):

	($000)	(%)
Capital Lease Obligations..	778	1.3
Common & Surplus	58,421	98.7
Total	59,199	100.0

RECENT DEVELOPMENTS: For the quarter ended 5/31/99, COOL reported a net loss of $8.9 million compared with a net loss of $4.2 million a year earlier. Net sales soared to $32.7 million from $11.6 million in 1998. Strong sales were the result of increases in the Company's customer base and repeat purchases from existing customers, which accounted for approximately 43.0% of net sales. Gross profit as a percentage of sales increased to 10.4% versus 9.0% the year before. The higher gross profit was achieved despite delayed shipments from Apple for the PowerBook G3 and the temporary halt of Compaq Computer deliveries. During the quarter, COOL was authorized to sell Compaq's commercial products as a participant in Compaq's Authorized Internet Reseller Pilot Program. The Company has formed a joint venture with electronics retailer Tweeter Home Entertainment Group, Inc. to market Tweeter's merchandise via the Internet.

BUSINESS

CYBERIAN OUTPOST, INC. operates an Internet-only superstore for computer products from its Web site at Outpost.com. The Connecticut-based company provides consumers and small office purchasers search capabilities and product information on more than 160,000 hardware, software, and peripheral products. The virtual store offers consumers the ability to browse its categorized inventory or find specific products via its interactive search engine.

ANNUAL FINANCIAL DATA

	2/28/99	2/28/98	2/28/97	2/29/96
Earnings Per Share	d1.64	d0.22	d0.22	d0.07
Cash Flow Per Share	d1.52	d1.04	d0.20	d0.07
Tang. Book Val. Per Share	2.54	...	...	...
INCOME STATEMENT (IN THOUSANDS):				
Total Revenues	85,203	22,681	10,790	1,852
Costs & Expenses	111,604	28,436	12,034	2,193
Depreciation & Amort.	1,111	713	95	27
Operating Income	d27,512	d6,468	d1,339	d368
Net Interest Inc./(Exp.)	2,288	d658	d4	d2
Income Before Income Taxes	d25,220	d7,092	d1,338	d372
Net Income	d25,220	d7,092	d1,338	d372
Cash Flow	d24,109	d6,379	d1,244	d345
Average Shs. Outstg.	15,886	6,145	6,145	5,244
BALANCE SHEET (IN THOUSANDS):				
Cash & Cash Equivalents	55,563	7,325	41	...
Total Current Assets	65,119	9,308	556	...
Net Property	5,937	1,611	199	...
Total Assets	71,464	10,940	755	...
Total Current Liabilities	12,265	8,484	1,892	...
Long-Term Obligations	778	136	23	...
Net Stockholders' Equity	58,421	d3,671	d1,161	...
Net Working Capital	52,854	824	d1,336	...
Year-end Shs. Outstg.	23,004	6,680	6,452	6,000
STATISTICAL RECORD:				
Debt/Total Assets %	1.1	1.2	3.0	...
Price Range	45½-5¹⁵⁄₁₆	...	...	...

Statistics are as originally reported.

OFFICERS:
D. Peck, Pres., C.E.O.
K. N. Vick, Exec. V.P., C.F.O.

PRINCIPAL OFFICE: 27 North Main Street, Kent, CT 06757
FAX: (860) 927-8375

TELEPHONE NUMBER: (860) 927-2050
WEB: www.outpost.com
NO. OF EMPLOYEES: 156 full-time; 8 part-time
SHAREHOLDERS: 453 (approx.)
ANNUAL MEETING: In July
INCORPORATED: CT, Mar., 1995; reincorp., DE, Jul., 1998

INSTITUTIONAL HOLDINGS:
No. of Institutions: 21
Shares Held: 940,436
% Held: 4.4

INDUSTRY: Computer and software stores (SIC: 5734)

TRANSFER AGENT(S): American Stock Transfer & Trust Company, New York, NY

CYBERSHOP INTERNATIONAL, INC.

YIELD ...
P/E RATIO ...

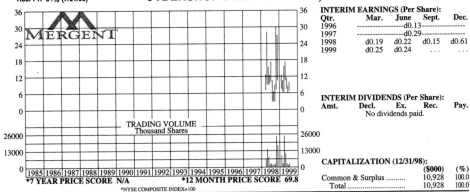

7 YEAR PRICE SCORE N/A   **12 MONTH PRICE SCORE 69.8**
*NYSE COMPOSITE INDEX=100

INTERIM EARNINGS (Per Share):

Qtr.	Mar.	June	Sept.	Dec.
1996	---------------d0.13---------------			
1997	---------------d0.29---------------			
1998	d0.19	d0.22	d0.15	d0.61
1999	d0.25	d0.24	...	...

INTERIM DIVIDENDS (Per Share):

Amt.	Decl.	Ex.	Rec.	Pay.
No dividends paid.				

CAPITALIZATION (12/31/98):

	($000)	(%)
Common & Surplus	10,928	100.0
Total	10,928	100.0

RECENT DEVELOPMENTS: For the three months ended 6/30/99, the Company reported a net loss of $1.9 million compared with a net loss of $1.6 million in the corresponding period of the previous year. The loss for the current quarter included a $259,000 charge for merger and acquisition related costs. Total revenues soared to $2.1 million from $553,000 in the comparable 1998 quarter. Product sales almost quadrupled to $2.1 million from $523,000 in the prior-year period, while revenues from advertising and set-up fees fell to $9,000 from $30,000 the year before. Gross profit jumped to $610,000, or 29.5% of total revenues, versus $159,000, or 28.8% of total revenues in the previous year. During the quarter, the Company completed the acquisition of Magellan Group, an on-line and direct response company that sells products on toolsforliving.com. This acquisition has expanded CYSP's customer base and will increase the Company's branding and distribution capabilities.

BUSINESS

CYBERSHOP INTERNATIONAL, INC. and subsidiaries is an on-line retailer that offers brand name products through its on-line stores located at cybershop.com, egift.com and electronics.net, and from its store located on America Online. The Company's on-line department store accessed at cybershop.com provides color pictures and detailed information relating to products that are conveniently organized into departments by brand and category. Cybershop.com offers a broad selection of branded merchandise at a guaranteed competitive price. The Company has pursued strategic alliances which are intended to generate additional referral traffic to each on-line store.

ANNUAL FINANCIAL DATA

	12/31/98	12/31/97	12/31/96	12/31/95
Earnings Per Share	d1.22	d0.29	d0.13	d0.13
Cash Flow Per Share	d1.19	d0.45	d0.19	d0.21
Tang. Book Val. Per Share	1.51	...	...	...
INCOME STATEMENT (IN THOUSANDS):				
Total Revenues	4,814	1,495	513	140
Costs & Expenses	13,506	3,234	1,111	744
Depreciation & Amort.	200	89	56	43
Operating Income	d8,892	d1,828	d653	d647
Net Interest Inc./(Exp.)	619	22	3	6
Income Before Income Taxes	d8,273	d1,806	d650	d641
Equity Earnings/Minority Int.	385	...	...	...
Net Income	d7,888	d1,806	d650	d641
Cash Flow	d7,688	d1,717	d594	d598
Average Shs. Outstg.	6,462	3,781	3,097	2,873
BALANCE SHEET (IN THOUSANDS):				
Cash & Cash Equivalents	12,285	787	510	...
Total Current Assets	13,285	884	549	...
Net Property	1,924	132	116	...
Total Assets	15,351	1,227	670	...
Total Current Liabilities	4,374	1,211	406	...
Long-Term Obligations	...	15	12	...
Net Stockholders' Equity	10,928	d5	251	...
Net Working Capital	8,911	d327	143	...
Year-end Shs. Outstg.	7,243	4,000	...	...
STATISTICAL RECORD:				
Debt/Total Assets %	...	1.2	1.8	...
Price Range	30-2¾	...	...	...
Statistics are as originally reported.				

REVENUES

(12/31/98)	($000)	(%)
Product Sales	4,683	97.3
Advg & Set-up Fees	131	3.7
Total	4,814	100.0

OFFICERS:
J. S. Tauber, Chmn., Pres., C.E.O.
J. Leist, Sr. V.P., C.O.O., C.F.O.

PRINCIPAL OFFICE: 116 Newark Avenue, Jersey City, NJ 07302

TELEPHONE NUMBER: (201) 234-5000
FAX: (201) 234-5099
WEB: www.cybershop.com
NO. OF EMPLOYEES: 42 full-time; 3 part-time
SHAREHOLDERS: 64 (approx.)
ANNUAL MEETING: In June
INCORPORATED: DE, Oct., 1997

INSTITUTIONAL HOLDINGS:
No. of Institutions: 14
Shares Held: 1,678,957
% Held: 22.1

INDUSTRY: Catalog and mail-order houses (SIC: 5961)

TRANSFER AGENT(S): American Stock Transfer & Trust Co., New York, NY

NASDAQ SYMBOL CYBS
Rec. Pr. 25¹³⁄₁₆ (7/31/99)

CYBERSOURCE CORPORATION

YIELD ...
P/E RATIO ...

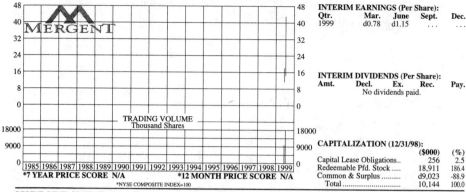

7 YEAR PRICE SCORE N/A **12 MONTH PRICE SCORE N/A**
*NYSE COMPOSITE INDEX=100

INTERIM EARNINGS (Per Share):

Qtr.	Mar.	June	Sept.	Dec.
1999	d0.78	d1.15	...	...

INTERIM DIVIDENDS (Per Share):

Amt.	Decl.	Ex.	Rec.	Pay.
	No dividends paid.			

CAPITALIZATION (12/31/98):

	($000)	(%)
Capital Lease Obligations..	256	2.5
Redeemable Pfd. Stock	18,911	186.4
Common & Surplus	d9,023	-88.9
Total	10,144	100.0

RECENT DEVELOPMENTS: On 6/24/99, the Company completed its initial public offering of 4.0 million shares of common stock, which generated net proceeds of approximately $46.0 million. For the three months ended 6/30/99, net loss totaled $6.9 million compared with a loss of $2.0 million a year earlier. Revenues jumped to $2.5 million from $699,000 the year before. Transactions processed in the second quarter surged to a record 8.0 million versus 1.2 million in the same quarter a year earlier. Results benefited from the addition of over 150 new Internet merchants using the Company's Internet Commerce Suite. Gross profit advanced to $300,000 from $44,000 the prior year. Loss from operations was $6.8 million compared with a loss of $2.0 million in 1998.

BUSINESS

CYBERSOURCE CORPORATION develops and provides real-time e-commerce transaction services. Through its CyberSource Internet Commerce Suite, the Company offers services to on-line merchants for global payment processing, fraud prevention, tax calculation, export compliance, territory management, delivery address verification and fulfillment management. The Company's services are designed to enable customers to reduce overall operating costs, speed their time to market and help distinguish themselves in areas such as Web site content and marketing.

ANNUAL FINANCIAL DATA

	12/31/98	12/31/97	12/31/96
Earnings Per Share	d2.05	...	...
Cash Flow Per Share	d1.89	...	...
Tang. Book Val. Per Share	...	0.23	...
INCOME STATEMENT (IN THOUSANDS):			
Total Revenues	3,384	968	144
Costs & Expenses	12,625	4,968	1,214
Depreciation & Amort.	796	325	73
Operating Income	d10,037	d4,325	d1,143
Net Interest Inc./(Exp.)	d48	d13	...
Net Income	d10,085	d4,338	d1,143
Cash Flow	d9,289	d4,013	d1,070
Average Shs. Outstg.	4,918	...	...
BALANCE SHEET (IN THOUSANDS):			
Cash & Cash Equivalents	11,111	2,000	...
Total Current Assets	12,385	2,584	...
Net Property	2,300	1,151	...
Total Assets	14,975	3,735	...
Total Current Liabilities	4,831	568	...
Long-Term Obligations	256	33	...
Net Stockholders' Equity	d9,023	1,037	...
Net Working Capital	7,554	2,016	...
Year-end Shs. Outstg.	5,407	4,535	...
STATISTICAL RECORD:			
Debt/Total Assets %	1.7	0.9	...
Statistics are as originally reported.			

OFFICERS:
W. S. McKiernan, Chmn., Pres., C.E.O.
C. E. Noreen, Jr., V.P., C.F.O.
R. Scudellari, Sec.

PRINCIPAL OFFICE: 550 S. Winchester
Blvd., Suite 301, San Jose, CA 95128

TELEPHONE NUMBER: (408) 556-9100
WEB: www.cybersource.com

NO. OF EMPLOYEES: 146

SHAREHOLDERS: N/A

ANNUAL MEETING: N/A

INCORPORATED: DE, Dec., 1998

INSTITUTIONAL HOLDINGS:
No. of Institutions: N/A
Shares Held: N/A
% Held: N/A

INDUSTRY: Data processing and preparation
(SIC: 7374)

TRANSFER AGENT(S): American Stock
Transfer and Trust Co., New York, NY

NASDAQ SYMBOL CYLK
Rec. Pr. 5 (7/31/99)

CYLINK CORP.

YIELD ...
P/E RATIO ...

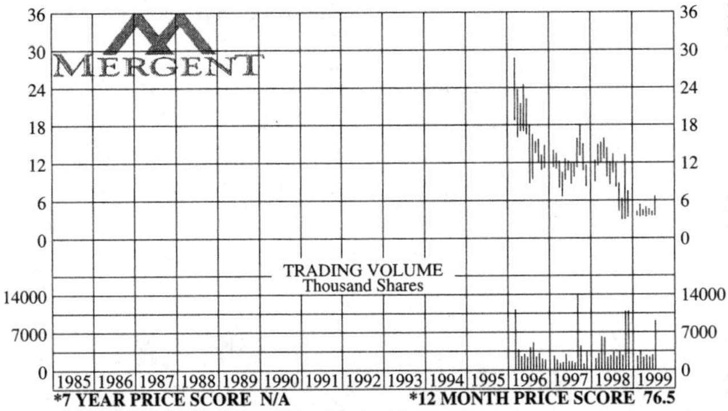

MERGENT
36
30
24
18
12
6
0
TRADING VOLUME
Thousand Shares
14000
7000
0
1985 1986 1987 1988 1989 1990 1991 1992 1993 1994 1995 1996 1997 1998 1999

*7 YEAR PRICE SCORE N/A *12 MONTH PRICE SCORE 76.5

*NYSE COMPOSITE INDEX=100

INTERIM EARNINGS (Per Share):

Qtr.	Mar.	June	Sept.	Dec.
1996	d0.05	0.01	0.05	0.04
1997	0.04	0.05	d2.37	d0.04
1998	d0.12	d0.06	d0.20	d0.23
1999	d0.14	d0.10	...	...

INTERIM DIVIDENDS (Per Share):

Amt.	Decl.	Ex.	Rec.	Pay.

No dividends paid.

CAPITALIZATION (12/31/98):

	($000)	(%)
Capital Lease Obligations..	147	0.2
Common & Surplus	75,221	99.8
Total	75,368	100.0

RECENT DEVELOPMENTS: For the quarter ended 6/27/99, the Company reported a net loss of $3.1 million compared with a loss of $1.7 million in the corresponding period of the previous year. Revenues advanced 23.0% to $15.2 million from $12.4 million the year before. Gross margin advanced to $10.4 million versus $8.4 million in the prior-year period. Operating loss was $3.7 million versus a loss of $3.1 million a year ago. The increase in operating loss was the result of restructuring efforts in sales management and new sales channels that the new management team undertook beginning in the fourth quarter of 1998. During the quarter, the Company announced the general availability of the CYLINK FRAME ENCRYPTOR™. In July 1999, CYLK acquired Security Design International, Inc., a security consulting company specializing in network vulnerablity assessments. Comparisons were made with restated 1998 results.

BUSINESS

CYLINK CORP. develops and delivers products for secure transactions and communications over local area networks, wide area networks, the Internet, and broadcast networks. Cylink's network security portfolio consists of hardware and software encryption platforms, certificate servers, remote access gateways, network security management systems, toolkits, public key processors, advanced smart cards and smart card operating systems, card readers and conditional access technology for broadcast networks. The Company's products are designed to offer an integrated solution for transforming any portion of an enterprise's network into a virtual private network and providing secure access for local and remote authorized users.

REVENUES

(12/31/98)	($000)	(%)
United States	25,334	78.6
South America...........	1,752	5.4
Europe	3,855	12.0
Asia...........................	1,303	4.0
Total	32,244	100.0

ANNUAL FINANCIAL DATA

	12/31/98	12/31/97	12/31/96	12/31/95	12/31/94	12/31/93
Earnings Per Share	**[1] d0.60**	**[1] [2] d2.37**	**[1] 0.05**	**[1] d0.06**	**d0.06**	**0.10**
Cash Flow Per Share	**d0.38**	**d2.26**	**0.10**	**d0.01**	**...**	**0.12**
Tang. Book Val. Per Share	**2.40**	**2.13**	**3.80**	**0.77**	**0.80**	**...**
INCOME STATEMENT (IN THOUSANDS):						
Total Revenues	42,760	49,333	51,958	34,902	26,646	26,294
Costs & Expenses	65,306	112,745	52,366	37,673	28,467	23,250
Depreciation & Amort.	6,312	2,914	1,350	919	728	494
Operating Income	d28,858	d66,326	d1,758	d3,690	d2,549	2,550
Net Interest Inc./(Exp.)	2,281	2,697	3,303	50	198	179
Income Before Income Taxes	d26,511	d63,312	1,448	d1,834	d1,152	3,028
Income Taxes	cr9,155	...	251	cr755	cr452	1,127
Net Income	[1] d17,356	[1] [2] d63,312	[1] 1,197	[1] d1,079	d700	1,901
Cash Flow	d11,044	d60,398	2,547	d160	28	2,395
Average Shs. Outstg.	29,009	26,703	25,761	19,572	19,351	19,901
BALANCE SHEET (IN THOUSANDS):						
Cash & Cash Equivalents	46,575	22,977	78,849	6,098	6,626	...
Total Current Assets	79,537	63,472	103,142	20,246	18,265	...
Net Property	5,731	6,699	3,760	2,295	1,958	...
Total Assets	94,318	82,593	107,088	22,725	20,663	...
Total Current Liabilities	18,950	13,222	9,624	7,642	6,223	...
Long-Term Obligations	147	256	241	291	...	...
Net Stockholders' Equity	75,221	69,102	97,211	14,605	14,149	...
Net Working Capital	60,587	50,250	93,518	12,604	12,042	...
Year-end Shs. Outstg.	29,115	28,695	25,597	19,087	17,624	...
STATISTICAL RECORD:						
Operating Profit Margin %	...	...	...	...	...	9.7
Net Profit Margin %	...	...	2.3	...	...	7.2
Return on Equity %	...	...	1.2	...	...	...
Return on Assets %	...	...	1.1	...	...	...
Debt/Total Assets %	0.2	0.3	0.2	1.3	...	...
Price Range	15 7/8-2 15/16	17 7/8-6 5/8	28 3/4-8 3/4	...	...	...
P/E Ratio	...	...	573.9-174.7	...	...	...

Statistics are as originally reported. [1] Bef. disc. oper. gain net 12/31/98: $22.5 mill.; 12/31/97: $3.2 mill.; 12/31/97: $6.7 mill.; 1996: 3.2 mill. [2] Incl. non-recurr. chrg. $63.9 mill.

OFFICERS:
W. P. Crowell, Pres., C.E.O.
R. A. Barnes, V.P., C.F.O.
R. B. Fougner, Sec., Gen. Couns.

PRINCIPAL OFFICE: 910 Hermosa Court, Sunnyvale, CA 94086

TELEPHONE NUMBER: (408) 735-5800
FAX: (408) 735-6643
WEB: www.cylink.com

NO. OF EMPLOYEES: 325 (avg.)

SHAREHOLDERS: 126 (approx.)

ANNUAL MEETING: In May

INCORPORATED: CA, 1989

INSTITUTIONAL HOLDINGS:
No. of Institutions: 29
Shares Held: 4,818,648
% Held: 16.5

INDUSTRY: Computer peripheral equipment, nec (SIC: 3577)

TRANSFER AGENT(S): Boston EquiServe LP., Canton, MA

DELL COMPUTER CORP.

NASDAQ SYMBOL DELL
Rec. Pr. 40⅞ (7/31/99)

YIELD ...
P/E RATIO 61.0

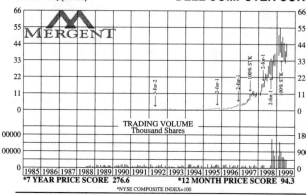

7 YEAR PRICE SCORE 276.6   **12 MONTH PRICE SCORE 94.3**
*NYSE COMPOSITE INDEX=100

TRADING VOLUME
Thousand Shares

INTERIM EARNINGS (Per Share):

Qtr.	Apr.	July	Oct.	Jan.
1996-97	0.03	0.04	0.05	0.04
1997-98	0.07	0.07	0.09	0.10
1998-99	0.11	0.13	0.14	0.17
1999-00	0.17	0.19	...	...

INTERIM DIVIDENDS (Per Share):

Amt.	Decl.	Ex.	Rec.	Pay.
2-for-1	2/18/98	3/09/98	2/27/98	3/06/98
2-for-1	8/18/98	9/08/98	8/28/98	9/04/98
100% STK	2/16/99	3/08/99	2/26/99	3/05/99

CAPITALIZATION (1/29/99):

	($000)	(%)
Long-Term Debt	512,000	18.1
Common & Surplus	2,321,000	81.9
Total	2,833,000	100.0

RECENT DEVELOPMENTS: For the quarter ended 7/30/99, net income increased 46.5% to $507.0 million compared with $346.0 million in the prior-year quarter. Net revenue advanced 41.8% to $6.14 billion from $4.33 billion a year earlier. The Americas experienced revenue growth of 48.0% led by sales of computer systems to consumers, small businesses and government agencies. European reve-

nues rose 24.0% and Asia-Pacific and Japan experienced revenue growth of 52.0%, led by strong results in China. Sales via the Company's Web site surpassed $30.0 million per day in July, and accounted for 40.0% of total revenue. On 8/10/99, Amazon.com announced that it has selected DELL's OptiPlex® corporate PC line as its desktop computing standard.

BUSINESS

DELL COMPUTER CORPORATION, together with its subsidiaries, designs, develops, manufactures, markets, services and supports a wide range of computer systems, including desktops, notebooks and network servers, and also markets software, peripherals and service and support programs. With revenue of approximately $18.24 billion for fiscal 1998 (which ended on 1/29/99), the Company is a major direct computer systems company. DELL designs and customizes products and services to end-user requirements, and offers an extensive selection of peripherals and software. DELL's complete range of computer systems include Dell Dimension® and OptiPlex® desktop computers, Inspiron® and Latitude® notebook computers, Precision® workstation and PowerEdge® network servers. The Internet has become a major retail channel for DELL, accounting for half of U.S. customers shipments and a total of $30.0 million per day in orders, in July 1999. The Company's products and services are sold in more than 170 countries and territories to customers ranging from major corporations, government agencies, and medical and education institutions to small businesses and individuals.

ANNUAL FINANCIAL DATA

	1/29/99	2/1/98	2/2/97	1/28/96	1/29/95	1/30/94	1/31/93
Earnings Per Share	0.53	0.32	⑪ 0.17	0.08	0.05	d0.02	0.04
Cash Flow Per Share	0.56	0.34	0.19	0.10	0.07	...	0.05
Tang. Book Val. Per Share	0.91	0.50	0.29	0.32	0.13	0.12	0.16
INCOME STATEMENT (IN MILLIONS):							
Total Revenues	18,243.0	12,327.0	7,759.0	5,296.0	3,475.3	2,873.2	2,013.9
Costs & Expenses	16,094.0	10,944.0	6,998.0	4,881.0	3,192.9	2,881.5	1,855.2
Depreciation & Amort.	103.0	67.0	47.0	38.0	33.1	30.6	19.6
Operating Income	2,046.0	1,316.0	714.0	377.0	249.3	d39.0	139.1
Net Interest Inc./(Exp.)	...	...	d7.0	d15.0	...	...	...
Income Before Income Taxes	2,084.0	1,368.0	747.0	383.0	213.0	d38.8	143.3
Income Taxes	624.0	424.0	216.0	111.0	63.8	cr2.9	41.7
Net Income	1,460.0	944.0	⑪ 531.0	272.0	149.2	d35.8	101.6
Cash Flow	1,563.0	1,011.0	578.0	298.0	173.6	d7.1	121.2
Average Shs. Outstg. (000)	2,772,000	2,952,000	3,068,800	3,107,200	2,659,200	2,389,312	2,511,040
BALANCE SHEET (IN MILLIONS):							
Cash & Cash Equivalents	3,181.0	1,844.0	1,352.0	646.0	527.2	337.0	95.3
Total Current Assets	6,339.0	3,912.0	2,747.0	1,957.0	1,470.4	1,048.4	852.8
Net Property	523.0	342.0	235.0	179.0	117.0	86.9	70.5
Total Assets	6,877.0	4,268.0	2,993.0	2,148.0	1,594.0	1,140.5	927.0
Total Current Liabilities	3,695.0	2,697.0	1,658.0	939.0	751.4	538.0	493.8
Long-Term Obligations	512.0	17.0	18.0	113.0	113.4	100.0	48.4
Net Stockholders' Equity	2,321.0	1,293.0	806.0	973.0	340.5	300.3	369.2
Net Working Capital	2,644.0	1,215.0	1,089.0	1,018.0	719.0	510.4	358.9
Year-end Shs. Outstg. (000)	2,543,000	2,576,000	2,768,752	2,990,304	2,539,520	2,427,456	2,358,912
STATISTICAL RECORD:							
Operating Profit Margin %	11.2	10.7	9.2	7.1	7.2	...	6.9
Net Profit Margin %	8.0	7.7	6.8	5.1	4.3	...	5.0
Return on Equity %	62.9	73.0	65.9	28.0	43.8	...	27.5
Return on Assets %	21.2	22.1	17.7	12.7	9.4	...	11.0
Debt/Total Assets %	7.4	0.4	0.6	5.3	7.1	8.8	5.2
Price Range	37¹⁵/₁₆-9¹⁵/₁₆	12-3¹/₈	4-0¾	1⁹/₁₆-0⁵/₈	0¾-0⁵/₈	0¾-0³/₈	0¾-0¹/₄
P/E Ratio	71.5-18.7	40.6-9.7	23.2-4.2	18.3-7.3	13.9-5.6	...	18.4-5.7

Statistics are as originally reported. Adj. for stk. splits: 2-for-1, 3/5/99; 2-for-1, 9/4/98; 2-for-1, 3/6/98; 2-for-1, 7/25/97; 2-for-1, 12/6/96; 2-for-1, 10/27/95 ⑪ Bef. extraord. chrg. $13.0 mill. ($0.02/sh.).

OFFICERS:
M. S. Dell, Chmn. & C.E.O.
M. L. Topfer, Vice-Chmn.
K. B. Rollins, Vice-Chmn.
J. Gesmar-Larsen, Sr. V.P. & Pres.

PRINCIPAL OFFICE: One Dell Way, Round Rock, TX 78682-2244

TELEPHONE NUMBER: (512) 338-4400
FAX: (512) 728-3653
WEB: www.dell.com

NO. OF EMPLOYEES: 24,400 (approx.)

SHAREHOLDERS: 26,173

ANNUAL MEETING: In July

INCORPORATED: TX, May, 1984; reincorp., DE, Oct., 1987

INSTITUTIONAL HOLDINGS:
No. of Institutions: 609
Shares Held: 976,309,140
% Held: 38.4

INDUSTRY: Electronic computers (SIC: 3571)

TRANSFER AGENT(S): American Stock Transfer and Trust Company, New York, NY

DIGITAL LAVA INC.

YIELD ...
P/E RATIO ...

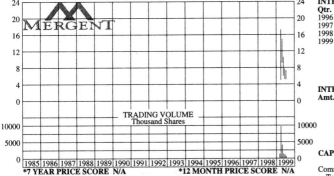

*7 YEAR PRICE SCORE N/A   *12 MONTH PRICE SCORE N/A

*NYSE COMPOSITE INDEX=100

TRADING VOLUME
Thousand Shares

INTERIM EARNINGS (Per Share):

Qtr.	Mar.	June	Sept.	Dec.
1996		-----d93.00-----		
1997		-----d31.14-----		
1998		-----d25.22-----		
1999	d0.99	d0.26	...	...

INTERIM DIVIDENDS (Per Share):

Amt.	Decl.	Ex.	Rec.	Pay.
	No dividends paid.			

CAPITALIZATION (12/31/98):

	($000)	(%)
Common & Surplus	d6,081	...
Total	d-6,081	100.0

RECENT DEVELOPMENTS: For the quarter ended 6/30/99, the Company incurred a net loss of $1.2 million compared with a net loss of $1.5 million in the corresponding period of the previous year. Revenues declined 29.1% to $195,419 from $275,671 the year before. Gross profit as a percentage of revenues grew to 92.9% from 83.5% a year earlier. Loss from operations totaled $1.4 million versus a loss from operations of $1.2 million in the prior year. During the quarter, the Company introduced its VIDEOVISOR WEB™ product for both the WINDOWS MEDIA™ and REALNETWORKS G2™ players. Going forward, the Company intends to focus on increasing its sales force, forming additional strategic partnerships and expanding its customer base. In addition, DGV plans to continue to participate in trade shows, such as MultiMediaCom, Online Learning 99 and TechLearn 99.

BUSINESS

DIGITAL LAVA INC. is a provider of software products and services related to the use of video for corporate training, communications, research and other applications. Digital Lava's product line includes vPRISM™ and VIDEOVISOR™ software. vPRISM™ allows users to organize and manage video, link video to other types of data and publish video, together with linked data, as VIDEO-CAPSULE™ files on compact discs and digital video discs, or stream the video information over private intranets or the Internet. Streaming technology allows an Internet or intranet user to access information in a file before the file is completely downloaded. As a result, large files containing audio and video can be heard or seen almost immediately, even with slower connections.

REVENUES

12/31/1998	($000)	(%)
Software Licenses	1,058	72.3
Consulting & Services	406	27.7
Total	1,464	100.0

ANNUAL FINANCIAL DATA

	12/31/98	12/31/97	12/31/96
Earnings Per Share	d25.22	d31.14	d93.00
Cash Flow Per Share	d19.91	d25.11	d76.30
INCOME STATEMENT (IN THOUSANDS):			
Total Revenues	1,464	565	...
Costs & Expenses	3,049	3,064	1,516
Depreciation & Amort.	785	821	428
Operating Income	d2,371	d3,321	d1,944
Net Interest Inc./(Exp.)	d1,359	d925	d451
Income Before Income Taxes	d3,731	d4,245	d2,385
Net Income	d3,731	d4,245	d2,385
Cash Flow	d2,945	d3,424	d1,956
Average Shs. Outstg.	148	136	26
BALANCE SHEET (IN THOUSANDS):			
Cash & Cash Equivalents	31	173	...
Total Current Assets	1,140	430	...
Total Assets	1,217	526	...
Total Current Liabilities	7,297	4,143	...
Net Stockholders' Equity	d6,081	d3,617	...
Net Working Capital	d6,157	d3,713	...
Year-end Shs. Outstg.	132	132	111
STATISTICAL RECORD:			
Statistics are as originally reported.			

OFFICERS:
J. W. Stigler, Chmn.
R. F. Greene, C.E.O.
J. D. Sharfman, Pres.
D. Gampe, C.F.O.

PRINCIPAL OFFICE: 10850 Wilshire Boulevard, Suite 1260, Los Angeles, CA 90024

TELEPHONE NUMBER: (310) 470-1169
WEB: www.digitallava.com

NO. OF EMPLOYEES: 21 (avg.)

SHAREHOLDERS: 92

ANNUAL MEETING: In July

INCORPORATED: NJ, Jul., 1995; reincorp., DE, Nov., 1996

INSTITUTIONAL HOLDINGS:
No. of Institutions: 11
Shares Held: 447,534
% Held: 9.7

INDUSTRY: Computer programming services (SIC: 7371)

TRANSFER AGENT(S): American Stock Transfer & Trust Company, New York, NY

DIGITAL RIVER, INC.

YIELD ...
P/E RATIO ...

MERGENT

TRADING VOLUME
Thousand Shares

| 1985 | 1986 | 1987 | 1988 | 1989 | 1990 | 1991 | 1992 | 1993 | 1994 | 1995 | 1996 | 1997 | 1998 | 1999 |

*7 YEAR PRICE SCORE N/A   ***12 MONTH PRICE SCORE 92.5**

*NYSE COMPOSITE INDEX=100

INTERIM EARNINGS (Per Share):

Qtr.	Mar.	June	Sept.	Dec.
1996	----------------d0.13----------------			
1997	----------------d0.46----------------			
1998	----------------d1.01----------------			
1999	d0.27	d0.33	...	...

INTERIM DIVIDENDS (Per Share):

Amt.	Decl.	Ex.	Rec.	Pay.
	No dividends paid.			

CAPITALIZATION (12/31/98):

	($000)	(%)
Common & Surplus	74,587	100.0
Total	74,587	100.0

RECENT DEVELOPMENTS: For the quarter ended 6/30/99, DRIV incurred a net loss of $6.7 million versus a net loss of $3.8 million for the corresponding period of the prior year. Earnings for the 1999 quarter included amortization of goodwill and acquisition-related costs of $1.3 million. Sales advanced to $15.8 million from $3.5 million a year earlier. The Company continues to benefit from the strong market for electronic software delivery. Separately, DRIV acquired three e-commerce providers, Maagnum Internet Group, Public Software Library Ltd., and Universal Commerce, Inc. for $2.5 million, $5.2 million, and $2.0 million, respectively. The acquisitions mark the Company's entry into the shareware market, and expand its client base to more than 6,000 clients. On 7/11/99, DRIV announced a definitive agreement for the acquisition of the assets of Tech Squared, Inc. in a stock-for-stock exchange. The transaction is expected to be completed in the fourth quarter of 1999.

BUSINESS

DIGITAL RIVER, INC. is a provider of electronic commerce outsourcing solutions to software publishers and on-line retailers. The Company also provides data mining and merchandising services to assist clients in increasing Internet page view traffic to, and sales through, their Web stores. The Company provides more than 6,000 software publisher clients and on-line retailers with its technology for Internet delivery of more than 100,000 digital products, including 30,000 software products and applications. The Company's clients include IBM, Corel Corporation, Cyberian Outpost, Inc., Lotus Development Corporation, Micro Warehouse, Inc., Network Associates, Inc., Symantec Corporation, Kmart Corporation, CompUSA, Inc. and Wal-Mart Stores, Inc.

ANNUAL FINANCIAL DATA

	12/31/98	12/31/97	12/31/96	12/31/95
Earnings Per Share	d1.01	d0.46	d0.13	d0.03
Cash Flow Per Share	d0.96	d0.44	d0.12	d0.03
Tang. Book Val. Per Share	3.82	0.25	...	...
INCOME STATEMENT (IN THOUSANDS):				
Total Revenues	20,911	2,472	111	...
Costs & Expenses	35,000	5,815	773	160
Depreciation & Amort.	604	195	35	5
Operating Income	d14,693	d3,538	d697	d165
Net Interest Inc./(Exp.)	895	53	8	22
Income Before Income Taxes	d13,798	d3,485	d689	d143
Net Income	d13,798	d3,485	d689	d143
Cash Flow	d13,194	d3,290	d654	d138
Average Shs. Outstg.	13,691	7,514	5,333	5,333
BALANCE SHEET (IN THOUSANDS):				
Cash & Cash Equivalents	74,397	2,126	800	...
Total Current Assets	76,304	2,320	809	...
Net Property	3,914	903	107	...
Total Assets	80,328	3,405	1,202	...
Total Current Liabilities	5,741	1,076	1,260	...
Net Stockholders' Equity	74,587	2,329	d58	...
Net Working Capital	70,563	1,244	d451	...
Year-end Shs. Outstg.	19,545	9,242	5,333	...
STATISTICAL RECORD:				
Price Range	44-5	...	...	...
Statistics are as originally reported.				

OFFICERS:
J. A. Ronning, C.E.O.
P. W. Steiner, Pres.
R. E. Strawman, C.F.O., Treas.
G. R. Smith, Sec., Contr.

PRINCIPAL OFFICE: 9625 West 76th St., Eden Prairie, MN 55344

TELEPHONE NUMBER: (612) 253-1234
WEB: www.digitalriver.com

NO. OF EMPLOYEES: 148 (avg.)

SHAREHOLDERS: 190 (approx.)

ANNUAL MEETING: In Apr.

INCORPORATED: DE, Feb., 1994; reincorp., DE, Dec., 1997

DOUBLECLICK, INC.

INTERIM EARNINGS (Per Share):				
Qtr.	Mar.	June	Sept.	Dec.
1998	d0.16	d0.14	d0.14	d0.13
1999	d0.18	d0.14	...	...

INTERIM DIVIDENDS (Per Share):				
Amt.	Decl.	Ex.	Rec.	Pay.
2-for-1	3/11/99	4/05/99	3/22/99	4/05/99

TRADING VOLUME
Thousand Shares

1985 1986 1987 1988 1989 1990 1991 1992 1993 1994 1995 1996 1997 1998 1999
7 YEAR PRICE SCORE N/A   **12 MONTH PRICE SCORE 147.0**
*NYSE COMPOSITE INDEX=100

CAPITALIZATION (12/31/98):	($000)	(%)
Capital Lease Obligations..	242	0.2
Common & Surplus	148,338	99.8
Total	148,580	100.0

RECENT DEVELOPMENTS: For the second quarter ended 6/30/99, the Company reported a net loss of $5.6 million compared with a net loss of $4.7 million in the corresponding quarter of the previous year. Revenue jumped to $31.0 million from $17.3 million the year before. Revenue from the Company's international operations grew 58.0% to $7.7 million. Gross profit soared to $16.1 million versus $5.6 million in the prior-year quarter. Operating loss totaled $7.0 million compared with a loss of $5.5 million in the previous year. During the quarter, DCLK launched a shopping and services program that offers e-commerce advertisers a targeted way to reach consumers through syndicated programs in the Company's network. In June 1999, DCLK agreed to acquire Abacus Direct Corp., a provider of marketing information, for about $1.00 billion in stock. In July 1999, DCLK signed a merger agreement with NetGravity Inc., a provider of on-line advertising and direct marketing software, valued at $530.0 million in cash and stock.

BUSINESS

DOUBLECLICK, INC. is a provider of comprehensive Internet advertising services for advertisers and Web publishers worldwide. DoubleClick currently has six principal service offerings: DoubleClick Network, DoubleClick DART Service, DoubleClick Select, DoubleClick Direct, DoubleClick International, and DoubleClick Local. DCLK's DoubleClick Network provides server-based ad sales, delivery, and services to website publishers. The Company's DoubleClick DART Service allows web site publishers and advertisers to control the delivery, measurement, and analysis of their marketing campaigns. The Company maintains offices in 14 countries.

ANNUAL FINANCIAL DATA

	12/31/98	12/31/97	12/31/96
Earnings Per Share-	d0.59	d0.61	d0.35
Cash Flow Per Share	d0.50	d0.55	d0.35
Tang. Book Val. Per Share	3.79	0.77	...
INCOME STATEMENT (IN THOUSANDS):			
Total Revenues	80,188	30,597	6,514
Costs & Expenses	98,267	38,183	9,576
Depreciation & Amort.	2,849	879	46
Operating Income	d20,928	d8,465	d3,108
Net Interest Inc./(Exp.)	2,755	109	d84
Income Before Income Taxes	d18,173	d8,356	d3,192
Net Income	d18,173	d8,356	d3,192
Cash Flow	d15,324	d7,477	d3,146
Average Shs. Outstg.	30,441	13,717	9,059
BALANCE SHEET (IN THOUSANDS):			
Cash & Cash Equivalents	136,814	8,546	...
Total Current Assets	169,025	19,391	4,079
Net Property	13,741	1,997	446
Total Assets	183,621	21,742	4,526
Total Current Liabilities	34,907	11,880	7,117
Long-Term Obligations	242	...	...
Net Stockholders' Equity	148,338	9,400	d2,592
Net Working Capital	134,118	7,512	d3,038
Year-end Shs. Outstg.	39,136	12,238	9,059
STATISTICAL RECORD:			
Debt/Total Assets %	0.1	...	...
Price Range	38⁹/₁₆-6¾	...	...

Statistics are as originally reported. Adj. for stk. split: 2-for-1, 4/5/99.

QUARTERLY DATA

(12/31/98)($000)	Rev	Inc
First Quarter	13,004	(4,427)
Second Quarter	17,293	(4,674)
Third Quarter.............	20,777	(4,714)
Fourth Quarter	29,114	(4,357)

OFFICERS:
K. J. O'Connor, Chmn., C.E.O.
K. P. Ryan, Pres., C.O.O.
S. R. Collins, C.F.O.

INVESTOR CONTACT: Llona Nemeth, Dir. Invest. Rel., (212) 683-0001

PRINCIPAL OFFICE: 41 Madison Avenue,, 32nd Floor, New York, NY 10010

TELEPHONE NUMBER: (212) 683-0001
WEB: www.doubleclick.com

NO. OF EMPLOYEES: 482

SHAREHOLDERS: 27,340

ANNUAL MEETING: N/A

INCORPORATED: DE, Jan., 1996

INSTITUTIONAL HOLDINGS:
No. of Institutions: 129
Shares Held: 19,860,832
% Held: 50.2
INDUSTRY: Advertising agencies (SIC: 7311)
TRANSFER AGENT(S): American Stock Transfer and Trust Company, New York, NY

DRKOOP.COM INC.

YIELD ...
P/E RATIO ...

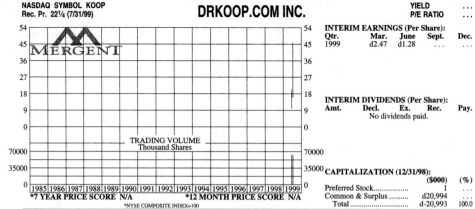

*7 YEAR PRICE SCORE N/A   *12 MONTH PRICE SCORE N/A
*NYSE COMPOSITE INDEX=100

INTERIM EARNINGS (Per Share):

Qtr.	Mar.	June	Sept.	Dec.
1999	d2.47	d1.28	...	...

INTERIM DIVIDENDS (Per Share):

Amt.	Decl.	Ex.	Rec.	Pay.
	No dividends paid.			

CAPITALIZATION (12/31/98):

	($000)	(%)
Preferred Stock.................	1	...
Common & Surplus	d20,994	...
Total	d-20,993	100.0

RECENT DEVELOPMENTS: For the quarter ended 6/30/99, the Company reported a net loss of $11.4 million compared with a net loss of $1.4 million in the equivalent 1998 quarter. Revenues were $1.0 million compared with none in the 1998 period. KOOP's revenues benefited from the addition of seven contracts during the quarter bringing the total to fifteen as of 6/30/99. In August, KOOP entered into an agreement to be the health channel for its ABC LocalNet® program. This agreement establishes KOOP as the exclusive health content provider for over 100 of ABC's local television stations' Web sites as well. Also in August, KOOP announced that it will be launching a global branding effort, for which it has selected an advertising agency and public relations firm. Effective 7/1/99, the Company and America Online, Inc. signed a four-year Interactive Services Agreement pursuant to which the Company was designated as AOL's premier provider of healthcare content. The agreement obligates KOOP to make portal payments aggregating $89.0 million and to provide AOL warrants to purchase drkoop.com common stock.

BUSINESS

DRKOOP.COM is an Internet-based consumer healthcare network led by Dr. C. Everett Koop, former U.S. Surgeon General. The network consists of a consumer-focused interactive Web site that provides users with comprehensive healthcare information and services, as well as affiliate relationships with portals, other Web sites, healthcare organizations and traditional media outlets. The Web site is a healthcare portal that integrates healthcare content on a wide variety of subjects, interactive communities and tools as well as opportunities to purchase healthcare-related products and services on-line.

ANNUAL FINANCIAL DATA

	12/31/98
Earnings Per Share	d2.89

INCOME STATEMENT (IN THOUSANDS):

Total Revenues	43
Costs & Expenses	8,989
Depreciation & Amort.	171
Operating Income	d9,117
Net Interest Inc./(Exp.)	34
Income Before Income Taxes	d9,084
Net Income	d9,084
Cash Flow	d8,913
Average Shs. Outstg.	8,100

BALANCE SHEET (IN THOUSANDS):

Total Current Assets	62
Net Property	307
Total Assets	380
Total Current Liabilities	2,968
Net Stockholders' Equity	d20,993
Net Working Capital	d2,905
Year-end Shs. Outstg.	8,550

STATISTICAL RECORD:
Statistics are as originally reported.

OFFICERS:
D. W. Hackett, C.E.O., Pres.

PRINCIPAL OFFICE: 8920 Business Park Rd., Austin, TX 78759

TELEPHONE NUMBER: (512) 726-5110
FAX: (512) 726-5130
WEB: www.drkoop.com
NO. OF EMPLOYEES: 37
SHAREHOLDERS: N/A
ANNUAL MEETING: N/A
INCORPORATED: DE, 1997

INSTITUTIONAL HOLDINGS:
No. of Institutions: 6
Shares Held: 272,343
% Held: 1.0
INDUSTRY: Computer integrated systems design (SIC: 7373)
TRANSFER AGENT(S): American Stock and Transfer Co., New York, NY

E*TRADE GROUP, INC.

YIELD ...
P/E RATIO ...

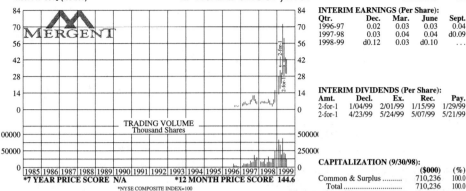

INTERIM EARNINGS (Per Share):

Qtr.	Dec.	Mar.	June	Sept.
1996-97	0.02	0.03	0.03	0.04
1997-98	0.03	0.04	0.04	d0.09
1998-99	d0.12	0.03	d0.10	...

INTERIM DIVIDENDS (Per Share):

Amt.	Decl.	Ex.	Rec.	Pay.
2-for-1	1/04/99	2/01/99	1/15/99	1/29/99
2-for-1	4/23/99	5/24/99	5/07/99	5/21/99

TRADING VOLUME
Thousand Shares

7 YEAR PRICE SCORE N/A   **12 MONTH PRICE SCORE 144.6**
*NYSE COMPOSITE INDEX=100

CAPITALIZATION (9/30/98):

	($000)	(%)
Common & Surplus	710,236	100.0
Total	710,236	100.0

RECENT DEVELOPMENTS: For the three months ended 6/30/99, the Company reported a net loss of $24.2 million compared with a net income of $5.1 million in the corresponding period of the previous year. Results for the 1999 quarter included merger-related expenses totaling $3.7 million. Net revenues more than doubled to $151.7 million from $66.5 million in the prior-year quarter. Transaction revenues surged to $106.1 million from $43.4 million the year before. Transactions totaled 5.1 million compared with 1.8 million a year ago. Operating loss totaled $42.7 million compared with operating income of $8.6 million the year before. On 4/21/99, the Company acquired ClearStation Inc., a financial media web site that combines technical and fundamental investment analysis with community discussion to supply ideas, analysis and opinions to individual investors. On 6/1/99, EGRP announced a definitive agreement to merge with Telebanc to create the first pure-play Internet company to unite banking and brokerage services.

BUSINESS

E*TRADE GROUP, INC., through its wholly-owned subsidiary, E*TRADE Securities, Inc., is a provider of on-line investing services. The Company offers automated order placement and execution, along with a suite of products and services that can be personalized, including portfolio tracking, Java-based charting and quote applications, real-time market commentary and analysis, news, and other information services. The Company provides these services 24 hours a day, seven days a week by means of the Internet, touch-tone telephone, including interactive voice recognition, on-line service providers (America Online, AT&T WorldNet, CompuServe, Microsoft Network and Prodigy) and direct modem access.

REVENUES

(09/30/98)	($000)	(%)
Transaction		
Revenues	162,097	66.1
Interest	56,019	22.8
International	7,031	2.9
Other Revenues	20,135	8.2
Total	245,282	100.0

ANNUAL FINANCIAL DATA

	9/30/98	9/30/97	9/30/96	9/30/95	9/30/94	9/30/93
Earnings Per Share	...	0.10	d0.01	0.03	0.01	...
Cash Flow Per Share	0.07	0.13	...	0.03	0.01	...
Tang. Book Val. Per Share	3.14	1.82	0.59	0.19	...	...
INCOME STATEMENT (IN MILLIONS):						
Total Revenues	245.3	142.7	51.6	23.3	10.9	3.0
Costs & Expenses	234.4	115.8	52.1	18.8	10.6	2.9
Depreciation & Amort.	12.5	3.6	0.9	0.2	0.1	...
Operating Income	d1.7	23.3	d1.4	4.3	0.2	0.1
Income Before Income Taxes	d1.7	23.3	d1.4	4.3	0.2	0.1
Income Taxes	cr1.0	9.4	cr0.6	1.7	cr0.5	...
Net Income	d0.7	13.9	d0.8	2.6	0.8	0.1
Cash Flow	11.8	17.5	...	2.8	0.9	0.1
Average Shs. Outstg. (000)	169,140	138,296	114,256	105,924	104,744	106,708
BALANCE SHEET (IN MILLIONS):						
Cash & Cash Equivalents	529.4	228.2	85.1	9.6	0.7	...
Total Current Assets	1,851.2	957.5	280.6	12.0	1.9	...
Net Property	48.1	18.8	9.2	1.5	0.3	...
Total Assets	1,968.9	989.9	294.9	14.2	2.2	...
Total Current Liabilities	1,258.7	699.2	225.6	3.0	2.2	...
Long-Term Obligations	...	9.4	...	...	0.1	...
Net Stockholders' Equity	710.2	281.3	69.3	11.1	d0.1	...
Net Working Capital	592.6	258.3	55.0	9.1	d0.3	...
Year-end Shs. Outstg. (000)	226,413	154,629	118,157	59,564	59,816	...
STATISTICAL RECORD:						
Operating Profit Margin %	...	16.3	...	18.5	2.2	3.5
Net Profit Margin %	...	9.7	...	11.1	7.2	3.3
Return on Equity %	...	4.9	...	23.2	...	...
Return on Assets %	...	1.4	...	18.2	36.3	...
Debt/Total Assets %	...	0.9	...	0.3	3.0	...
Price Range	16¼-2½	11¹⁵/₁₆-2¾	3½-2¹/₁₆	...	...	...
P/E Ratio	...	119.3-27.5	...	...	...	...

Statistics are as originally reported. Adj. for stk. split: 2-for-1, 5/21/99; 2-for-1, 1/29/99

OFFICERS:
C. M. Cotsakos, Chmn., C.E.O.
K. Levinson, Pres., C.O.O.
L. C. Purkis, Exec. V.P., C.F.O., C.A.O.

PRINCIPAL OFFICE: Four Embarcadero Place, 2400 Geng Road, Palo Alto, CA 94303

TELEPHONE NUMBER: (650) 842-2500
FAX: (650) 842-2552
WEB: www.etrade.com
NO. OF EMPLOYEES: 833
SHAREHOLDERS: 409
ANNUAL MEETING: In Mar.
INCORPORATED: CA, 1982; reincorp., DE, Jul., 1996

INSTITUTIONAL HOLDINGS:
No. of Institutions: 154
Shares Held: 73,321,230
% Held: 31.4

INDUSTRY: Security brokers and dealers (SIC: 6211)

TRANSFER AGENT(S): American Stock Transfer & Trust Company, New York, NY.

EARTHLINK NETWORK INC.

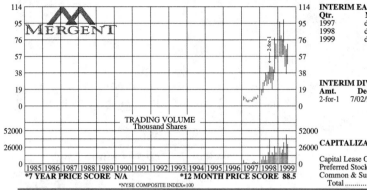

7 YEAR PRICE SCORE N/A   **12 MONTH PRICE SCORE 88.5**

NYSE COMPOSITE INDEX=100

INTERIM EARNINGS (Per Share):

Qtr.	Mar.	June	Sept.	Dec.
1997	d0.46	d0.40	d0.36	d0.29
1998	d0.28	d0.53	d0.78	d0.89
1999	d0.82	d0.88	...	...

INTERIM DIVIDENDS (Per Share):

Amt.	Decl.	Ex.	Rec.	Pay.
2-for-1	7/02/98	7/21/98	7/15/98	7/20/98

CAPITALIZATION (12/31/98):

	($000)	(%)
Capital Lease Obligations..	7,701	3.8
Preferred Stock..............	41	0.0
Common & Surplus	197,303	96.2
Total	205,045	100.0

RECENT DEVELOPMENTS: For the quarter ended 6/30/99, the Company reported a net loss of $24.5 million compared with a loss of $12.0 million in the corresponding quarter of the previous year. Earnings in the 1999 and 1998 periods include amortization and transaction costs of $17.7 million and $7.2 million, respectively. Total revenue more than doubled to $78.0 million from $38.0 million in the prior year. The Company reported 180,000 net new members, a 125.0% increase over the second quarter of 1998, bringing its membership base to 1.4 million. Operating income totaled a loss of $28.5 million versus a loss of $11.8 million the year before. During the quarter, ELNK added six new partners, including, BigStar.com, Ebay, E-TRADE, Mail.com, MarketWatch and The Weather Channel. In August 1999, ELNK will be the official Internet service provider used by all FreeMac.com customers.

BUSINESS

EARTHLINK NETWORK INC. is an Internet Service Provider. ELNK provides its EarthLink Sprint Internet service to more than 1.3 million individuals and businesses internationally through a telecommunications network of leased, high-speed, dedicated data lines and over more than 2,300 dial-up access sites. ELNK owns and operates dial-up access sites in Southern California and leases dial-up access sites from UUNET, Sprint, and PSINet. ELNK's Internet service can be accessed through a local telephone call or by cable, ADSL, ISDN, frame relay and other high-speed access technologies. Under an alliance entered into with Sprint Corporation in June 1998, ELNK is co-branded as Sprint's exclusive consumer Internet access provider. As part of the alliance, Sprint committed to generating at least 150,000 new members for ELNK during each of the next five years.

ANNUAL FINANCIAL DATA

	12/31/98	12/31/97	12/31/96	12/31/95	12/31/94
Earnings Per Share	① d2.58	d1.49	d2.25	d0.62	d0.05
Cash Flow Per Share	d0.48	d1.03	d2.19	d0.59	d0.05
Tang. Book Val. Per Share	4.03	0.23	...	0.02	...
INCOME STATEMENT (IN THOUSANDS):					
Total Revenues	175,941	79,174	32,503	3,028	111
Costs & Expenses	183,454	98,251	58,608	8,741	252
Depreciation & Amort.	54,726	9,377	4,153	305	7
Operating Income	d62,239	d28,454	d30,258	d6,018	d148
Net Interest Inc./(Exp.)	2,457	d1,462	d891	d102	...
Income Before Income Taxes	d59,782	d29,916	d31,149	d6,120	d148
Net Income	① d59,782	d29,916	d31,149	d6,120	d148
Cash Flow	d12,657	d20,539	d26,996	d5,815	d141
Average Shs. Outstg.	26,157	20,002	12,338	9,806	3,100
BALANCE SHEET (IN THOUSANDS):					
Cash & Cash Equivalents	140,864	17,700	5,080	1,790	...
Total Current Assets	150,565	22,082	9,073	2,253	27
Net Property	35,206	23,398	17,401	2,551	90
Total Assets	266,341	46,887	27,119	4,874	186
Total Current Liabilities	61,296	32,594	28,279	4,229	89
Long-Term Obligations	7,701	8,218	6,088	355	...
Net Stockholders' Equity	197,344	6,075	d21,261	290	97
Net Working Capital	89,269	d10,512	d19,206	d1,976	d62
Year-end Shs. Outstg.	29,070	22,500	12,046	10,114	5,882
STATISTICAL RECORD:					
Debt/Total Assets %	2.9	17.5	22.4	7.3	...
Price Range	78½-12¼	12½-4⁵⁄₁₆	...	...	...

Statistics are as originally reported. Adj. for stk. split: 2-for-1, 7/20/98. ① Incl. non-recurr. chrg. $42.6 mill.

REVENUES

12/31/98	($000)	(%)
Recurring Revenues ..	164,723	93.6
Other Revenues	6,547	3.7
Incremental Revenues	4,671	2.7
Total	175,941	100.0

OFFICERS:
S. D. Dayton, Chmn.
C. G. Betty, Pres., C.E.O.
G. L. Hoberg, Sr. V.P., C.F.O.

INVESTOR CONTACT: Erika L. Barnes, Asst. Man., Investor Relations, (626) 296-5949

PRINCIPAL OFFICE: 3100 New York Drive, Suite 210, Pasadena, CA 91107

TELEPHONE NUMBER: (626) 296-2400
FAX: (626) 296-2470
WEB: www.earthlink.com

NO. OF EMPLOYEES: 1,343

SHAREHOLDERS: 310 (approx.)

ANNUAL MEETING: In May

INCORPORATED: CA, May, 1994; reincorp., DE, Jun., 1996

INSTITUTIONAL HOLDINGS:
No. of Institutions: 91
Shares Held: 12,277,848
% Held: 38.5

INDUSTRY: Prepackaged software (SIC: 7372)

TRANSFER AGENT(S): American Stock Transfer & Trust Company, New York, NY

EARTHWEB INC.

YIELD ...
P/E RATIO ...

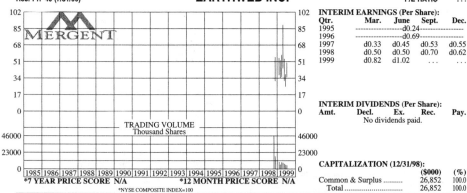

*7 YEAR PRICE SCORE N/A   *12 MONTH PRICE SCORE N/A
*NYSE COMPOSITE INDEX=100

TRADING VOLUME
Thousand Shares

INTERIM EARNINGS (Per Share):

Qtr.	Mar.	June	Sept.	Dec.
1995	----------------d0.24----------------			
1996	----------------d0.69----------------			
1997	d0.33	d0.45	d0.53	d0.55
1998	d0.50	d0.50	d0.70	d0.62
1999	d0.82	d1.02	...	...

INTERIM DIVIDENDS (Per Share):

Amt.	Decl.	Ex.	Rec.	Pay.
	No dividends paid.			

CAPITALIZATION (12/31/98):

	($000)	(%)
Common & Surplus	26,852	100.0
Total	26,852	100.0

RECENT DEVELOPMENTS: For the quarter ended 6/30/99, the Company reported a net loss of $9.2 million compared with a loss of $1.5 million in 1998. Results for the second quarter of 1999 included a one-time operating charge of $672,000, which included a $500,000 non-cash charge related to the MicroHouse acquisition. Revenues soared to $7.2 million from $666,000 in the prior-year period. Revenues reflected the expansion of EWBX's business-to-business services. Gross profit was $4.6 million compared with $268,000 in the previous year. The Company recently introduced a new set of on-line services in Europe, Asia and Latin America. These new services are a strategic effort for EWBX to take advantage of international advertising and e-commerce opportunities. The Company also introduced the browser-based Java version of Support-Source. SupportSource 2000 is the next generation of electronic reference library of hardware, networking and applications information.

BUSINESS

EARTHWEB INC. is a provider of Internet-based on-line services to the global information technology (IT) industry. The Company offers a range of technical materials, such as resource directories, tutorials and a reference library; community areas, such as bulletin boards and question and answer services; and commerce services, which provide a single on-line source for IT professionals. The Company also provides recruitment services to allow technical recruiters and IT managers to locate skilled IT professionals. EWBX primarily develops and maintains Web sites and on-line commerce infrastructures. The Company derives substantially all of its revenues from advertising sales.

ANNUAL FINANCIAL DATA

	12/31/98	12/31/97	12/31/96	12/31/95
Earnings Per Share	d1.53	① d1.13	d0.69	d0.24
Cash Flow Per Share	d1.34	d0.94	d0.65	d0.23
Tang. Book Val. Per Share	3.26	2.03	1.45	...
INCOME STATEMENT (IN THOUSANDS):				
Total Revenues	3,349	1,135	472	...
Costs & Expenses	11,511	5,947	2,437	662
Depreciation & Amort.	1,116	893	101	42
Operating Income	d9,277	d5,704	d2,066	d704
Income Before Income Taxes	d8,970	d5,437	d2,004	d704
Net Income	d8,970	① d5,437	d2,004	d704
Cash Flow	d7,854	d4,544	d1,903	d663
Average Shs. Outstg.	5,880	4,812	2,925	2,925
BALANCE SHEET (IN THOUSANDS):				
Cash & Cash Equivalents	25,579	5,287	3,779	...
Total Current Assets	27,265	6,301	4,614	...
Net Property	2,069	1,651	819	...
Total Assets	30,477	8,514	5,652	...
Total Current Liabilities	3,559	1,984	1,299	...
Net Stockholders' Equity	26,852	6,445	4,259	...
Net Working Capital	23,705	4,317	3,315	...
Year-end Shs. Outstg.	7,899	2,925	2,925	...
STATISTICAL RECORD:				
Price Range	85¹/₁₆-31	...	...	...

Statistics are as originally reported. ① Incl. about $337,000 chg. rel. to impairment of intangible assets fr. acq.; bef. disc. oper. loss $2.4 mill.

OFFICERS:
J. D. Hidary, Pres., C.E.O.
M. Hidary, Exec. V.P., Sec., Treas.
I. Math, V.P. Fin.
W. Gollan, Sr. V.P.

PRINCIPAL OFFICE: 3 Park Ave., New York, NY 10016

TELEPHONE NUMBER: (212) 725-6550
FAX: (212) 725-6559
WEB: www.earthweb.com
NO. OF EMPLOYEES: 121
SHAREHOLDERS: 115
ANNUAL MEETING: In May
INCORPORATED: NY, Apr., 1996; reincorp., DE, Jun., 1997

INSTITUTIONAL HOLDINGS:
No. of Institutions: 27
Shares Held: 1,488,944
% Held: 15.9

INDUSTRY: Data processing and preparation (SIC: 7374)

TRANSFER AGENT(S): American Stock Transfer & Trust Co., New York, NY.

NASDAQ SYMBOL EBAY
Rec. Pr. 97¹¹/₁₆ (7/31/99)

EBAY INC.

YIELD ...
P/E RATIO 888.1

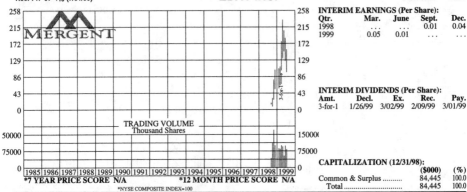

TRADING VOLUME
Thousand Shares

| 1985 | 1986 | 1987 | 1988 | 1989 | 1990 | 1991 | 1992 | 1993 | 1994 | 1995 | 1996 | 1997 | 1998 | 1999 |

*7 YEAR PRICE SCORE N/A   *12 MONTH PRICE SCORE N/A
*NYSE COMPOSITE INDEX=100

INTERIM EARNINGS (Per Share):

Qtr.	Mar.	June	Sept.	Dec.
1998	...	...	0.01	0.04
1999	0.05	0.01	...	...

INTERIM DIVIDENDS (Per Share):

Amt.	Decl.	Ex.	Rec.	Pay.
3-for-1	1/26/99	3/02/99	2/09/99	3/01/99

CAPITALIZATION (12/31/98):

	($000)	(%)
Common & Surplus	84,445	100.0
Total	84,445	100.0

RECENT DEVELOPMENTS: For the quarter ended 6/30/99, EBAY reported net income of $816,000 versus $2.7 million in the same quarter of 1998. Revenues soared to $49.4 million from $19.5 million in the previous year, primarily due to increased traffic on EBAY's Web site. Revenues are net of $3.9 million in credits given to users for the 6/10/99 outage of the Company's Web site. Gross profit, as a percentage of sales, slipped to 77.8% from 83.1% the year before. Income from operations fell to a loss of $4.6 million

from income of $4.2 million in the prior year. Operating results were negatively affected by increases in personnel, infrastructure and marketing expenses. During the quarter, the number of registered users increased to 5.6 million, up from 3.9 million the prior year. The Company hosted 24.9 million auctions with gross merchandise sales of $622.0 million. In June, EBAY acquired alando.de AG, Germany's largest on-line trading company, for approximately $42.8 million.

BUSINESS

EBAY INCORPORATED is the world's largest person-to-person trading community on the Internet, based on the number of items listed, the number of users and minutes of usage per month. The Company offers a Web-based community in which buyers and sellers are brought together in an auction format to buy and sell items such as antiques, coins, collectibles, computers, memorabilia, stamps and toys. The eBay service permits sellers to list items for sale, buyers to bid on items of interest and all users to browse through listed items. The Company has more than 2.4 million items for sale in more than 1,600 categories, with approximately 300,000 items being added daily. As of 6/30/99, EBAY had more than 5.6 million registered users.

QUARTERLY DATA

12/31/1998($000)	Rev	Inc
First Quarter	5,981	148
Second Quarter	8,941	67
Third Quarter	12,935	663
Fourth Quarter	19,495	1,520

ANNUAL FINANCIAL DATA

	12/31/98	12/31/97	12/31/96
Earnings Per Share	0.02	0.01	0.02
Cash Flow Per Share	0.06	0.01	0.02
Tang. Book Val. Per Share	0.69	0.02	...
INCOME STATEMENT (IN THOUSANDS):			
Total Revenues	47,352	5,744	372
Costs & Expenses	36,841	4,158	117
Depreciation & Amort.	4,350	99	2
Operating Income	6,161	1,487	253
Net Interest Inc./(Exp.)	d39	d3	...
Income Before Income Taxes	7,030	1,543	254
Income Taxes	4,632	669	106
Net Income	2,398	874	148
Cash Flow	6,748	973	150
Average Shs. Outstg.	114,590	82,659	6,375
BALANCE SHEET (IN THOUSANDS):			
Cash & Cash Equivalents	72,191	3,723	103
Total Current Assets	83,385	4,967	285
Net Property	7,831	652	23
Total Assets	92,483	5,619	308
Total Current Liabilities	8,038	1,124	91
Long-Term Obligations	...	305	...
Net Stockholders' Equity	84,445	1,015	162
Net Working Capital	75,347	3,843	194
Year-end Shs. Outstg.	120,760	61,200	61,200
STATISTICAL RECORD:			
Operating Profit Margin %	13.0	25.9	68.0
Net Profit Margin %	5.1	15.2	39.8
Return on Equity %	2.8	86.1	91.4
Return on Assets %	2.6	15.6	48.1
Debt/Total Assets %	...	5.4	...
Price Range	103¾-8⁷/₁₆	...	...
P/E Ratio	5,161.2-418.7	...	...

Statistics are as originally reported. Adj. for stk. split: 3-for-1, 3/1/99

OFFICERS:
P. M. Omidyar, Chmn.
M. C. Whitman, Pres., C.E.O.
G. F. Bengier, V.P., Oper., C.F.O.
M. R. Jacobson, V.P., Gen. Couns., Sec.

PRINCIPAL OFFICE: 2005 Hamilton Avenue, Suite 350, San Jose, CA 95125

TELEPHONE NUMBER: (408) 558-7400
WEB: www.ebay.com

NO. OF EMPLOYEES: 138

SHAREHOLDERS: 500

ANNUAL MEETING: In May

INCORPORATED: CA, May, 1996; reincorp., DE, Mar., 1998

INSTITUTIONAL HOLDINGS:
No. of Institutions: 96
Shares Held: 14,347,024
% Held: 11.5

INDUSTRY: Business services, nec (SIC: 7389)

TRANSFER AGENT(S): ChaseMellon Shareholder Services, L.L.C., Ridgefield Park, NJ

EDGAR ONLINE, INC.

YIELD ...
P/E RATIO ...

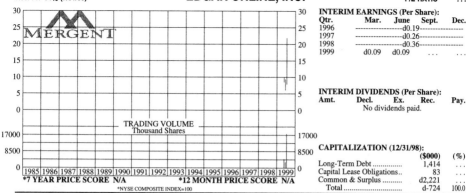

INTERIM EARNINGS (Per Share):

Qtr.	Mar.	June	Sept.	Dec.
1996			d0.19	
1997			d0.26	
1998			d0.36	
1999	d0.09	d0.09	...	...

INTERIM DIVIDENDS (Per Share):

Amt.	Decl.	Ex.	Rec.	Pay.
		No dividends paid.		

CAPITALIZATION (12/31/98):

	($000)	(%)
Long-Term Debt	1,414	...
Capital Lease Obligations..	83	...
Common & Surplus	d2,221	...
Total	d-724	100.0

RECENT DEVELOPMENTS: For the quarter ended 6/30/99, the Company reported a net loss of $807,000 compared with a net loss of $175,000 in 1998. Total revenues jumped to $1.04 million from $498,000 in the prior-year period. Revenues benefited from strong performances in all three of the Company's revenue sources, subscriptions, corporate contracts and advertising. Gross profit increased to $605,000 compared with $218,000 in the year before. Results in upcoming quarters should benefit from increased sales and marketing initiatives. On 5/26/99, EDGR completed its initial public offering of 3.6 million shares at a price of $9.50 per share, for gross proceeds of $34.2 million. The Company agreed to acquire FreeEDGAR.com, a developer of products that automatically structure and deliver financial data by transforming flat text and HTML formats into interactive data analysis and interpretation tools, for approximately 950,000 shares of EDGR's stock.

BUSINESS

EDGAR ONLINE, INC. is an Internet-based commercial provider of business, financial, and competitive information contained in corporate filings made by public companies with the Securities Exchange Commission. These services are designed to meet the needs of individuals and businesses for timely and cost-effective access to over 15,000 U.S. public companies, and include a range of navigation tools, personalized features, E-mail, and Web-based alerts. The Company's proprietary software enhances SEC filings by organizing and processing them into an easily accessible and searchable format. Revenues are derived from three primary sources: individual subscriptions, corporate contracts and advertising. A portion of revenues is also derived from barter transactions. Currently, the Company utilizes access to more than 60 widely used Web sites including Yahoo!, Infoseek's GO Network, MSNBC, and TheStreet.com.

ANNUAL FINANCIAL DATA

	12/31/98	12/31/97	12/31/96
Earnings Per Share	d0.36	d0.26	d0.19
Cash Flow Per Share	d0.34	d0.21	d0.18
INCOME STATEMENT (IN THOUSANDS):			
Total Revenues	2,003	1,044	170
Costs & Expenses	3,958	1,938	878
Depreciation & Amort.	134	305	55
Operating Income	d2,089	d1,199	d763
Net Interest Inc./(Exp.)	d132	d299	d73
Income Before Income Taxes	d2,221	d1,498	d836
Net Income	d2,221	d1,498	d836
Cash Flow	d2,088	d1,193	d781
Average Shs. Outstg.	6,129	5,655	4,302
BALANCE SHEET (IN THOUSANDS):			
Cash & Cash Equivalents	148	17	...
Total Current Assets	290	67	...
Net Property	412	287	...
Total Assets	785	366	...
Total Current Liabilities	731	1,406	...
Long-Term Obligations	1,497	...	...
Net Stockholders' Equity	d2,221	d1,589	...
Net Working Capital	d441	d1,339	...
Year-end Shs. Outstg.	6,331	6,074	...
STATISTICAL RECORD:			
Debt/Total Assets %	190.8	...	...
Statistics are as originally reported.			

OFFICERS:
M. Strausberg, Chmn., C.I.O.
S. Strausberg, C.E.O., Sec.
T. Vos, Pres., C.O.O.
G. D. Adams, C.F.O.

PRINCIPAL OFFICE: 50 Washington Street, Norwalk, CT 06854

TELEPHONE NUMBER: (203) 852-5666
WEB: www.edgar-online.com

NO. OF EMPLOYEES: 20

SHAREHOLDERS: N/A

ANNUAL MEETING: N/A

INCORPORATED: DE, Nov., 1995

INSTITUTIONAL HOLDINGS:
No. of Institutions: 2
Shares Held: 371,800
% Held: 0.0

INDUSTRY: Business services, nec (SIC: 7389)

TRANSFER AGENT(S): American Stock Transfer & Trust Company, New York, NY.

NASDAQ SYMBOL EDFY
Rec. Pr. 10¾ (7/31/99)

EDIFY CORP.

YIELD ...
P/E RATIO ...

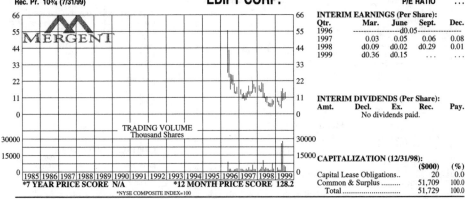

*7 YEAR PRICE SCORE N/A   *12 MONTH PRICE SCORE 128.2
*NYSE COMPOSITE INDEX=100

INTERIM EARNINGS (Per Share):

Qtr.	Mar.	June	Sept.	Dec.
1996		d0.05		
1997	0.03	0.05	0.06	0.08
1998	d0.09	d0.02	d0.29	0.01
1999	d0.36	d0.15	...	...

INTERIM DIVIDENDS (Per Share):

Amt.	Decl.	Ex.	Rec.	Pay.
		No dividends paid.		

CAPITALIZATION (12/31/98):

	($000)	(%)
Capital Lease Obligations..	20	0.0
Common & Surplus	51,709	100.0
Total	51,729	100.0

RECENT DEVELOPMENTS: On 5/17/99, the Company entered into a definite agreement to be acquired by Security First Technologies. Under the agreement, each EDFY share will be exchanged for 0.330969 shares of Security First common stock. For the quarter ended 6/30/99, the Company reported a net loss of $2.9 million compared with a loss of $295,000 in the corresponding quarter of the previous year. Net revenue advanced 12.9% to $20.2 million from $17.9 million in the prior-year period. Service and other revenue increased to $11.0 million versus $8.7 million the year before, while license revenue stayed essentially flat at $9.2 million. Operating loss totaled $2.6 million compared with a loss of $766,000 in 1998. In July 1999, EDFY released Electronic Workforce 6.1, a new version featuring SMART options, speaker verification and enhanced connectivity. On 7/15/99, the Company sold its Employee Relationship Management Group assets to Workscape Inc.

BUSINESS

EDIFY CORPORATION is a supplier of self-service software that enables organizations to deploy automated services accessed by customers and employees via the Internet, corporate intranets and the telephone. EDFY's software is targeted at large organizations where there is a need to process substantial numbers of customer or employee service transactions efficiently. The Company currently offers two self-service software products: the Electronic Workforce and the Electronic Banking System. The Electronic Workforce allows the incorporation of multiple media, enabling service applications through Web browsers, telephones, facsimiles, electronic mail and alphanumeric pagers. The Electronic Banking System is a software application product that offers financial institutions the means to deploy a suite of automated banking services via the World Wide Web.

REVENUES

(12/31/98)	($000)	(%)
License	37,375	52.8
Services & Other	33,511	47.2
Total	70,886	100.0

ANNUAL FINANCIAL DATA

	12/31/98	12/31/97	12/31/96	12/31/95	12/31/94	12/31/93
Earnings Per Share	① d0.39	0.22	d0.05	d0.01	...	...
Cash Flow Per Share	d0.12	0.41	0.08	0.07	...	...
Tang. Book Val. Per Share	2.98	3.36	3.05	...	...	...
INCOME STATEMENT (IN THOUSANDS):						
Total Revenues	70,886	57,052	33,017	16,003	8,363	4,043
Costs & Expenses	74,626	51,235	33,224	15,210	9,462	8,175
Depreciation & Amort.	4,615	3,474	1,979	963	677	543
Operating Income	d8,355	2,343	d2,186	d170	d1,776	d4,675
Net Interest Inc./(Exp.)	1,805	1,953	1,475	85	54	139
Income Before Income Taxes	d6,550	4,296	d711	d85	d1,722	d4,536
Income Taxes	125	344	44	19	22	7
Net Income	① d6,675	3,952	d755	d104	d1,744	d4,543
Cash Flow	d2,060	7,426	1,224	859	d1,067	d4,000
Average Shs. Outstg.	17,090	18,063	15,033	13,154	...	...
BALANCE SHEET (IN THOUSANDS):						
Cash & Cash Equivalents	34,837	43,161	44,840	7,154	2,587	...
Total Current Assets	59,386	61,286	54,697	13,435	5,131	...
Net Property	7,329	6,953	5,790	1,822	1,035	...
Total Assets	67,004	68,480	60,721	15,372	6,214	...
Total Current Liabilities	15,225	12,332	10,827	4,443	3,003	...
Long-Term Obligations	20	340	707	510	148	...
Net Stockholders' Equity	51,709	55,808	49,187	10,419	3,063	...
Net Working Capital	44,161	48,954	43,870	8,992	2,128	...
Year-end Shs. Outstg.	17,363	16,607	16,102	2,431	2,256	...
STATISTICAL RECORD:						
Operating Profit Margin %	...	4.1	...	...	...	...
Net Profit Margin %	...	6.9	...	...	...	...
Return on Equity %	...	7.1	...	...	...	...
Return on Assets %	...	5.8	...	...	...	...
Debt/Total Assets %	...	0.5	1.2	3.3	2.4	...
Price Range	20⅞-4⅝	22⅛-8⅞	55¾-13⅜	...	...	...
P/E Ratio	...	100.5-40.3	...	...	...	...

Statistics are as originally reported. ① Incl. non-recurr. chrg. $5.0 mill.

OFFICERS:
J. M. Crowe, Pres., C.E.O.

PRINCIPAL OFFICE: 2840 San Tomas Expressway, Santa Clara, CA 95051

TELEPHONE NUMBER: (408) 982-2000
FAX: (408) 982-0777
WEB: www.edify.com
NO. OF EMPLOYEES: 442 (avg.)
SHAREHOLDERS: 351 (approx.)
ANNUAL MEETING: In May
INCORPORATED: CA, Oct., 1989; reincorp., DE, Apr., 1996

INSTITUTIONAL HOLDINGS:
No. of Institutions: 23
Shares Held: 6,248,601
% Held: 35.4

INDUSTRY: Prepackaged software (SIC: 7372)

TRANSFER AGENT(S): Bank Boston, NA c/o Boston EquiServe, LP, Boston, MA

EFAX.COM INC.

YIELD ...
P/E RATIO ...

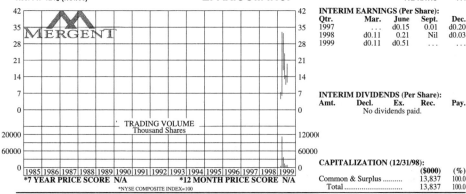

INTERIM EARNINGS (Per Share):

Qtr.	Mar.	June	Sept.	Dec.
1997	...	d0.15	0.01	d0.20
1998	d0.11	0.21	Nil	d0.03
1999	d0.11	d0.51	...	...

INTERIM DIVIDENDS (Per Share):

Amt.	Decl.	Ex.	Rec.	Pay.
No dividends paid.				

CAPITALIZATION (12/31/98):

	($000)	(%)
Common & Surplus	13,837	100.0
Total	13,837	100.0

*7 YEAR PRICE SCORE N/A   *12 MONTH PRICE SCORE N/A
*NYSE COMPOSITE INDEX=100

RECENT DEVELOPMENTS: For the quarter ended 6/30/99, the Company reported a net loss of $6.2 million compared with income of $114,000 in the corresponding quarter of the previous year. Total revenue fell 18.6% to $6.3 million from $7.7 million the year before. Product revenue dropped 18.4% to $5.0 million from $6.1 million in the prior year, while development fees fell to $253,000 compared with $1.6 million the year before. Operating income totaled a loss of $6.2 million versus income of $64,000 a year ago.

The decrease in operating income was attributed to increased sales and marketing expenses associated with the promotion of the e-fax service. During the quarter, EFAX launched two co-branded websites for Xoom and FindLaw. Additionally, the Company signed new partnerships with eGroups and Fortune City. In June, the Company launched eFax Plus, which allows users to send faxes while on-line, in addition to storing faxes on the Web and converting faxes into editable text documents.

BUSINESS

EFAX COM CORP. (formerly Jetfax, Inc.) is a provider of Internet document communications services. Through its website, eFax.com, the Company offers a free, fax-to-e-mail service targeting mobile professionals, small business users, and home office workers. Users can receive faxes that include text and graphics via a personalized fax number. The fax is received at the Company's Service Center, compressed and forwarded to the users' e-mail address.

ANNUAL FINANCIAL DATA

	12/31/98	12/31/97	12/31/96	3/31/96	3/31/95
Earnings Per Share	d0.13	d0.61	d0.14	...	...
Cash Flow Per Share	d0.07	d0.56	d0.12	...	...
Tang. Book Val. Per Share	1.17	1.30	0.16	1.37	...
INCOME STATEMENT (IN THOUSANDS):					
Total Revenues	30,233	23,020	12,862	13,187	7,752
Costs & Expenses	31,314	28,655	13,669	15,561	8,323
Depreciation & Amort.	705	539	143	250	115
Operating Income	d1,786	d6,174	d950	d2,624	d686
Net Interest Inc./(Exp.)	319	190	22	d273	d68
Income Before Income Taxes	d1,421	d6,063	d937	d2,894	d754
Income Taxes	80	96	105	35	...
Net Income	d1,501	d6,159	d1,042	d2,929	d754
Cash Flow	d796	d5,688	d1,015	d2,776	d639
Average Shs. Outstg.	11,784	10,170	8,454	...	...
BALANCE SHEET (IN THOUSANDS):					
Cash & Cash Equivalents	4,113	7,224	106	3,452	...
Total Current Assets	13,281	16,350	4,940	9,420	...
Net Property	1,339	1,160	615	174	...
Total Assets	16,215	18,856	6,121	9,619	...
Total Current Liabilities	2,353	3,536	2,978	5,640	...
Long-Term Obligations	...	...	198	...	...
Net Stockholders' Equity	13,837	15,271	219	1,369	...
Net Working Capital	10,928	12,814	1,962	3,780	...
Year-end Shs. Outstg.	11,874	11,741	996	954	...
STATISTICAL RECORD:					
Debt/Total Assets %	...	...	3.2	...	...
Statistics are as originally reported.					

QUARTERLY DATA

12/31/98 ($000)	REV	INC
1st Quarter	7,698	(1,325)
2nd Quarter	7,722	64
3rd Quarter	7,748	(85)
4th Quarter	7,064	(441)

OFFICERS:
E. R. Prince III, Chmn., C.E.O.
A. K. Jones, V.P., C.F.O., V.P.

INVESTOR CONTACT: Jennifer Myers, Investor Relations, (650) 688-6887

PRINCIPAL OFFICE: 1378 Willow Road, Menlo Park, CA 94025

TELEPHONE NUMBER: (650) 324-0600
FAX: (650) 326-6003
WEB: www.efax.com

NO. OF EMPLOYEES: 116 (avg.)

SHAREHOLDERS: 236 (approx.); 28,000(beneficial approx.)

ANNUAL MEETING: In May
INCORPORATED: DE, Aug., 1988

INSTITUTIONAL HOLDINGS:
No. of Institutions: 18
Shares Held: 964,548
% Held: 7.8

INDUSTRY: Computer peripheral equipment, nec (SIC: 3577)

TRANSFER AGENT(S): American Stock Transfer & Trust, New York, NY

E4L, INC.

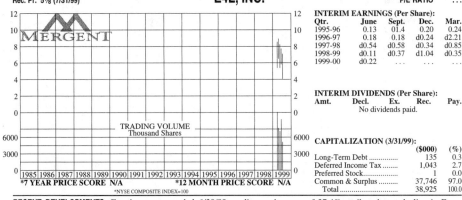

INTERIM EARNINGS (Per Share):

Qtr.	June	Sept.	Dec.	Mar.
1995-96	0.13	01.4	0.20	0.24
1996-97	0.18	0.18	d0.24	d2.21
1997-98	d0.54	d0.58	d0.34	d0.85
1998-99	d0.11	d0.37	d1.04	d0.35
1999-00	d0.22	...	...	...

INTERIM DIVIDENDS (Per Share):

Amt.	Decl.	Ex.	Rec.	Pay.
		No dividends paid.		

TRADING VOLUME
Thousand Shares

CAPITALIZATION (3/31/99):

	($000)	(%)
Long-Term Debt	135	0.3
Deferred Income Tax	1,043	2.7
Preferred Stock	1	0.0
Common & Surplus	37,746	97.0
Total	38,925	100.0

*7 YEAR PRICE SCORE N/A   *12 MONTH PRICE SCORE N/A

*NYSE COMPOSITE INDEX=100

RECENT DEVELOPMENTS: For the quarter ended 6/30/99, ETV incurred a net loss of $5.9 million compared with a net loss of $3.2 million in the equivalent 1998 quarter. Net revenues were $68.2 million, down 18.0% from $83.2 million a year earlier. Results for 1998 exclude the reversal of unusual charges of $1.2 million. The decline in revenues was primarily attributed to a decrease in U.S. revenue directly related to a $9.0 million backlog decrease for ETV's Ab Rocker, which debuted at the beginning of the quarter. In addition, international revenues were $24.6 million, a decrease of 27.4% attributed to a decline in European net revenue caused by the termination of two media contracts during the fourth quarter of fiscal year 1999. This was offset by a 46.6% increase in net revenue in Japan. During the quarter, the Company completed the jointly formed BuyItNow.com LLC transaction and produced the new format designed to drive viewers to its 48% owned subsidiary's Web site. BuyItNow.com is a Web Plaza™ of product-focused Internet stores.

BUSINESS

E4L, INC. (formerly National Media Corporation) is a direct-response television company involved in the growing world of electronic commerce. The Company broadcasts more than 3,000 half-hours of programming each week, reaches 100 percent of television homes in the United States, and brings its programming to more than 370 million television households in more than 70 countries worldwide. ETV broadcasts the Everything4Less Show each week over network radio and simultaneously cybercasts the Show through broadcast.com over the Internet.

REVENUES

(03/31/99)	($000)	(%)
Product	321,052	97.9
Retail royalties	221	0.1
Commission & other	6,577	2.0
Total	327,850	100.0

ANNUAL FINANCIAL DATA

	3/31/99	3/31/98	3/31/97	3/31/96	3/31/95	3/31/94	3/31/93
Earnings Per Share	① d1.88	② d2.31	③ d2.07	0.74	d0.05	d0.72	0.48
Cash Flow Per Share	d1.52	d1.97	d1.60	0.82	0.08	d0.59	0.63
Tang. Book Val. Per Share	0.51	0.73	1.57	2.37	1.55	0.41	1.05
INCOME STATEMENT (IN THOUSANDS):							
Total Revenues	327,850	278,474	358,179	292,607	176,167	172,602	141,997
Costs & Expenses	371,837	323,458	389,981	268,990	174,050	179,373	133,269
Depreciation & Amort.	7,375	7,628	10,450	2,498	1,800	1,628	2,022
Operating Income	d51,362	d52,612	d42,252	21,119	317	d8,399	6,706
Net Interest Inc./(Exp.)	d3,216	d3,457	d1,542	d1,015	d689	d300	d371
Income Before Income Taxes	d48,034	d56,069	d43,794	20,104	d372	d8,699	6,335
Income Taxes	440	700	1,897	3,525	300	...	76
Net Income	① d48,474	② d56,769	③ d45,691	16,579	d672	d8,699	6,259
Cash Flow	d41,099	d49,141	d35,241	19,077	1,128	d7,071	8,281
Average Shs. Outstg.	27,054	24,904	22,072	23,176	14,024	12,078	13,046
BALANCE SHEET (IN THOUSANDS):							
Cash & Cash Equivalents	8,098	18,315	4,058	18,405	13,467	1,595	2,848
Total Current Assets	67,818	92,926	93,898	92,384	54,151	36,849	35,705
Net Property	8,119	12,338	14,182	6,954	4,443	4,809	4,494
Total Assets	98,801	143,091	165,632	116,548	64,143	47,475	46,771
Total Current Liabilities	54,586	83,484	74,130	53,662	32,070	35,472	27,710
Long-Term Obligations	135	469	959	4,054	3,613	448	1,090
Net Stockholders' Equity	37,747	54,327	88,560	56,462	26,625	10,571	17,630
Net Working Capital	13,232	9,442	19,768	38,722	22,081	1,377	7,995
Year-end Shs. Outstg.	31,473	25,375	24,045	17,490	14,193	13,651	11,581
STATISTICAL RECORD:							
Operating Profit Margin %	...	...	...	7.2	0.2	...	4.7
Net Profit Margin %	...	...	...	5.7	...	...	4.4
Return on Equity %	...	...	...	29.4	...	...	35.5
Return on Assets %	...	...	...	14.2	...	...	13.4
Debt/Total Assets %	0.1	0.3	0.6	3.5	5.6	0.9	2.3

Statistics are as originally reported. ① Excl. extraord. gain of $4.9 mill., restruct. & incl. unusual chrgs. of $20.2 mill., a gain on sale of an investment in comon stock of $6.5 mill. & a writedown of impaired goodwill of $11.3 mill. ② Incl. unusual chrg. of $1.9 mill. & a writedown of goodwill of $14.5 mill. ③ Incl. unusual chrg. of $750,000.

OFFICERS:
S. C. Lehman, Chmn., C.E.O.
E. R. Weiss, Vice-Chmn., C.O.O.
J. W. Kirby, Pres.
D. M. Yukelson, Exec. V.P., C.F.O., Sec.

PRINCIPAL OFFICE: 15821 Ventura Boulevard, 5th Floor, Los Angeles, CA 91436

TELEPHONE NUMBER: (818) 461-6400
FAX: (818) 461-6530
WEB: www.e4l.com
NO. OF EMPLOYEES: 320 (approx.)
SHAREHOLDERS: 825 (approx.)
ANNUAL MEETING: N/A
INCORPORATED: DE, 1986

INSTITUTIONAL HOLDINGS:
No. of Institutions: 37
Shares Held: 7,945,921
% Held: 26.0
INDUSTRY: Catalog and mail-order houses (SIC: 5961)
TRANSFER AGENT(S): ChaseMellon Shareholder Services, Ridgefield Park, NJ

EGGHEAD.COM, INC.

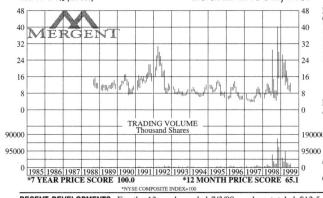

*7 YEAR PRICE SCORE 100.0   *12 MONTH PRICE SCORE 65.1
*NYSE COMPOSITE INDEX=100

INTERIM EARNINGS (Per Share):

Qtr.	June	Sept.	Dec.	Mar.
1995-96	d0.18	d0.20	d0.05	d0.22
1996-97	d0.43	d0.27	0.09	d2.17
1997-98	d0.21	d0.24	d0.29	d1.70
1998-99	d0.24	d0.30	d0.36	d0.50
1999-00	d0.34	. . .	. . .	. . .

INTERIM DIVIDENDS (Per Share):

Amt.	Decl.	Ex.	Rec.	Pay.
	No dividends paid.			

CAPITALIZATION (4/3/99):

	($000)	(%)
Common & Surplus	140,994	100.0
Total	140,994	100.0

RECENT DEVELOPMENTS:

For the 13 weeks ended 7/3/99, the Company reported a net loss of $10.5 million compared with a net loss of $5.5 million in the corresponding period of the previous year. Net sales increased 37.4% to $40.6 million from $29.5 million in the prior-year quarter. Gross margin declined 6.1% to $2.9 million from $3.1 million in the prior-year quarter. Gross margin was negatively affected by some competitors' selling current version goods below or marginally above their acquisition cost. Operating loss totaled $12.5 million compared with a loss of $6.6 million a year ago. On 7/14/99, EGGS announced the signing of a definitive agreement to merge with and into Onsale, Inc. EGGS shareholders will recieve 0.565 Onsale common shares for each Egghead share held. The combination, subject to shareholder and regulatory approval, will create a leader in on-line retailing of technology products and related categories.

BUSINESS

EGGHEAD.COM, INC. is an on-line retailer of personal computer hardware, software, peripherals and accessories. In addition to computer-related products, EGGS sells consumer electronics and other consumer and business goods. In February 1998, EGGS shifted its business emphasis to Internet commerce and closed its national retail network of over 200 stores. The Company's on-line stores offer a three-format experience. The Egghead Superstores, which include Egghead Computer and Egghead Software, offer customers a large selection of new, current-version computer hardware and software products at competitive prices. The Egghead SurplusDirect liquidation center offers customers excess, close-out, refurbished and reconditioned merchandise at liquidation prices. Egghead Auctions offers customers computer and consumer goods and the opportunity to influence prices through auction-style bidding.

ANNUAL FINANCIAL DATA

	4/3/99	3/28/98	3/29/97	3/30/96	4/1/95	4/2/94	4/3/93
Earnings Per Share	d1.40	d2.40	�धd2.78	⌧d0.64	⌧d0.19	⌧d0.49	0.41
Cash Flow Per Share	d1.22	d2.09	d2.38	d0.02	0.42	0.11	0.91
Tang. Book Val. Per Share	3.57	2.25	5.69	7.94	8.53	8.38	8.42
INCOME STATEMENT (IN THOUSANDS):							
Total Revenues	148,721	293,079	360,715	403,841	434,021	373,510	725,447
Costs & Expenses	185,147	339,829	401,217	413,740	431,218	376,859	704,367
Depreciation & Amort.	4,560	10,721	7,099	10,721	10,468	10,250	9,083
Operating Income	d40,986	d57,471	d47,601	d20,620	d7,665	d13,599	12,397
Net Interest Inc./(Exp.)	. . .	. . .	. . .	. . .	. . .	270	42
Income Before Income Taxes	d34,423	d54,531	d48,961	d18,151	d5,397	d13,700	11,360
Income Taxes	. . .	. . .	4,788	cr7,030	cr2,106	cr5,343	4,430
Net Income	d34,423	d54,531	⌧d48,961	⌧d11,121	⌧d3,291	⌧d8,357	6,530
Cash Flow	d29,863	d43,810	d41,862	d400	7,177	1,893	15,613
Average Shs. Outstg.	24,569	20,967	17,581	17,437	17,281	17,088	17,090
BALANCE SHEET (IN THOUSANDS):							
Cash & Cash Equivalents	119,467	67,381	83,473	49,590	42,592	25,677	26,386
Total Current Assets	135,141	95,020	154,593	247,168	241,033	230,826	239,333
Net Property	9,196	2,806	19,710	29,495	21,925	19,351	21,214
Total Assets	176,185	131,387	175,520	284,232	270,141	256,010	263,216
Total Current Liabilities	35,191	45,297	75,035	143,780	122,305	110,988	117,622
Long-Term Obligations	. . .	. . .	. . .	. . .	. . .	106	1,097
Net Stockholders' Equity	140,994	86,087	100,047	139,269	146,416	143,416	142,990
Net Working Capital	99,950	49,723	79,558	103,388	118,728	119,838	121,711
Year-end Shs. Outstg.	30,675	23,493	17,591	17,547	17,166	17,121	16,983
STATISTICAL RECORD:							
Operating Profit Margin %	. . .	. . .	. . .	. . .	. . .	. . .	1.7
Net Profit Margin %	. . .	. . .	. . .	. . .	. . .	. . .	0.9
Return on Equity %	. . .	. . .	. . .	. . .	. . .	. . .	4.6
Return on Assets %	. . .	. . .	. . .	. . .	. . .	. . .	2.5
Debt/Total Assets %	. . .	. . .	. . .	. . .	. . .	0.1	0.4
Price Range	40¼-4⁵/₁₆	11⅛-3⅝	13⅞-4¾	14¼-5¾	12⅛-6⅛	11¼-6⅝	30¾-7¾
P/E Ratio	. . .	. . .	. . .	. . .	. . .	. . .	75.0-18.9

Statistics are as originally reported. ⌧ Bef. disc. oper. credit 3/29/97: $10.0 mill. ($0.57/sh.); 3/30/96: $376,000 ($0.02/sh.); 4/1/95: $6.0 mill. ($0.34/sh.); 4/2/94: $7.8 mill. ($0.46/sh.).

OFFICERS:
G. P. Orban, Chmn., C.E.O.
B. W. Bender, V.P., C.F.O., C.A.O., Sec.

PRINCIPAL OFFICE: 521 S.E. Chkalov Drive, Vancouver, WA 98683

TELEPHONE NUMBER: (360) 883-3447
WEB: www.egghead.com

NO. OF EMPLOYEES: 295 (approx.)

SHAREHOLDERS: 1,310 (approx.)

ANNUAL MEETING: In Sept.

INCORPORATED: WA, Jun., 1984; reincorp., WA, Apr., 1988

INSTITUTIONAL HOLDINGS:
No. of Institutions: 38
Shares Held: 6,344,532
% Held: 21.3

INDUSTRY: Computers, peripherals & software (SIC: 5045).

TRANSFER AGENT(S): ChaseMellon Shareholder Services, Seattle, WA.

EMUSIC.COM, INC.

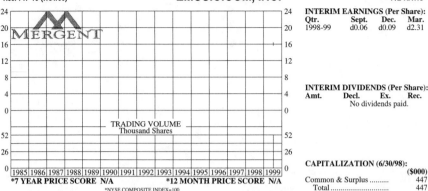

*7 YEAR PRICE SCORE N/A   *12 MONTH PRICE SCORE N/A
*NYSE COMPOSITE INDEX=100

TRADING VOLUME
Thousand Shares

INTERIM EARNINGS (Per Share):

Qtr.	Sept.	Dec.	Mar.	Jun.
1998-99	d0.06	d0.09	d2.31	d1.06

INTERIM DIVIDENDS (Per Share):

Amt.	Decl.	Ex.	Rec.	Pay.
		No dividends paid.		

CAPITALIZATION (6/30/98):

	($000)	(%)
Common & Surplus	447	100.0
Total	447	100.0

RECENT DEVELOPMENTS: For the year ended 6/30/99, the Company reported a net loss of $15.1 million compared with a net loss of $1.2 million in the previous year. Diluted loss per share was $3.52 versus a loss of $0.12 in fiscal 1998. Total revenues were $92,000 in the current year. Operating loss totaled $15.5 million versus $1.2 million in the prior year. Operating expenses jumped to $15.5 million from $1.2 million a year earlier. Comparisons with fiscal 1998 are not meaningful given the Company's early stage of operations in fiscal 1998. On 6/18/99, the Company completed the acquisition of Internet Underground Music Archive, Inc. (IUMA) for approximately $9.0 million in cash and stock. IUMA will become a wholly-owned subsidiary of the Company.

BUSINESS

EMUSIC.COM, INC. is a provider of downloadable music over the Internet. Through its Web site, the Company offers music consumers a selection of music from which they may discover, sample, and purchase recordings for immediate digital delivery. The Company has exclusive, multi-year, digital download licenses to over 300,000 titles, from over 75 record labels and over 1,200 recording artists, including such well known artists as The Offspring, They Might be Giants, Jimi Hendrix and Ella Fitzgerald. The Company has over 13,000 titles available for download on its Web site. In addition, the Company's subsidiary, IUMA, offers customers access to over 3,700 unsigned artists. On 1/31/99, the Company acquired Creative Fulfillment, Inc.

ANNUAL FINANCIAL DATA

	6/30/98
Earnings Per Share	d0.12
Cash Flow Per Share	d0.12
Tang. Book Val. Per Share	0.03
INCOME STATEMENT (IN THOUSANDS):	
Costs & Expenses	1,177
Depreciation & Amort.	3
Operating Income	d1,180
Income Before Income Taxes	d1,180
Net Income	d1,180
Cash Flow	d1,177
Average Shs. Outstg.	10,234
BALANCE SHEET (IN THOUSANDS):	
Cash & Cash Equivalents	510
Total Current Assets	531
Net Property	34
Total Assets	582
Total Current Liabilities	135
Net Stockholders' Equity	447
Net Working Capital	396
Year-end Shs. Outstg.	14,715

STATISTICAL RECORD:
Statistics are as originally reported.

OFFICERS:
R. H. Kohn, Chmn., Sec.
G. Hoffman Jr., Pres., C.E.O.
J. H. Howell, Exec. V.P., C.F.O.
P. M. Aztiz, Exec. V.P., Gen. Couns.

PRINCIPAL OFFICE: 1991 Broadway, Suite 200, Redwood City, CA 94063

TELEPHONE NUMBER: (650) 216-0200
WEB: www.emusic.com

NO. OF EMPLOYEES: 63

SHAREHOLDERS: 201

ANNUAL MEETING: In July

INCORPORATED: DE, Jan., 1998

INSTITUTIONAL HOLDINGS:
No. of Institutions: N/A
Shares Held: N/A
% Held: N/A

INDUSTRY: Communications equipment, nec (SIC: 3669)

TRANSFER AGENT(S): Interwest, Salt Lake City, UT

ENTRUST TECHNOLOGIES, INC.

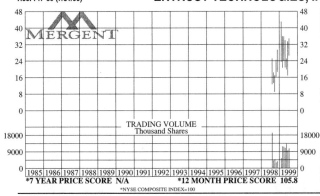

*7 YEAR PRICE SCORE N/A   *12 MONTH PRICE SCORE 105.8
*NYSE COMPOSITE INDEX=100

TRADING VOLUME
Thousand Shares

INTERIM EARNINGS (Per Share):

Qtr.	Mar.	June	Sept.	Dec.
1997	0.01	Nil	Nil	Nil
1998	Nil	d0.70	d0.04	d0.02
1999	0.01	0.02	...	...

INTERIM DIVIDENDS (Per Share):

Amt.	Decl.	Ex.	Rec.	Pay.
		No dividends paid.		

CAPITALIZATION (12/31/98):

	($000)	(%)
Long-Term Debt	32	0.0
Common & Surplus	87,059	100.0
Total	87,091	100.0

RECENT DEVELOPMENTS: For the quarter ended 6/30/99, the Company reported net income of $871,000 compared with a net loss of $21.6 million in the corresponding period of the prior year. Earnings for the 1999 and 1998 quarters included acquired in-process research and development and goodwill amortization of $178,000 and $20.2 million, respectively. Total revenues climbed 79.4% to $19.8 million from $11.0 million the year before. License revenues improved 70.4% to $13.9 million, while services and main- tenance revenues increased to $5.8 million from $2.9 mil- lion a year earlier. The Company achieved record results in all areas of its business, fueled by e-commerce growth in global organizations. On 5/25/99, ENTU formed a new company and Web site, Entrust.net, to provide security service for Web servers. Separately, the Company intro- duced its Electronic Business Security Services, which offer corporations tight security framework for large-scale, business-to-business Web transactions.

BUSINESS

ENTRUST TECHNOLOGIES, INC. develops and supports managed pub- lic-key infrastructure solutions, which combine encryption and digital signa- ture capabilities with automated key and certificate management to allow enterprises to more effectively man- age trusted, secure electronic commu- nications and transactions over advanced networks, including the Internet, extranets and intranets. The Company operates offices across North America and in London, the United Kingdom, Zurich, and Frankfurt.

REVENUES

12/31/98	($000)	(%)
License	8,689	67.9
Services and Maintenance	4,113	32.1
Total	12,802	100.0

ANNUAL FINANCIAL DATA

	12/31/98	12/31/97	12/31/96	12/31/95
Earnings Per Share	☐ d0.68	0.01	...	...
Cash Flow Per Share	d0.64	0.02	...	...
Tang. Book Val. Per Share	1.97	0.35	...	...
INCOME STATEMENT (IN THOUSANDS):				
Total Revenues	48,988	25,006	12,802	3,973
Costs & Expenses	73,522	25,136	12,542	6,253
Depreciation & Amort.	1,261	360	204	144
Operating Income	d25,795	d490	56	d2,424
Net Interest Inc./(Exp.)	1,807	723	...	...
Income Before Income Taxes	d23,988	233	56	d2,424
Income Taxes	cr160	cr281	cr331	cr301
Net Income	☐ d23,828	514	387	d2,123
Cash Flow	d22,567	874	591	d1,979
Average Shs. Outstg.	35,255	41,743	...	...
BALANCE SHEET (IN THOUSANDS):				
Cash & Cash Equivalents	81,067	12,638	...	...
Total Current Assets	98,176	22,334	2,542	...
Net Property	4,874	1,680	1,145	...
Total Assets	107,829	24,757	3,687	2,190
Total Current Liabilities	20,738	8,627	3,728	...
Long-Term Obligations	32	1,468	...	...
Net Stockholders' Equity	87,059	14,662	d60	1,672
Net Working Capital	77,438	13,707	d1,186	...
Year-end Shs. Outstg.	42,493	42,493	...	...
STATISTICAL RECORD:				
Operating Profit Margin %	...	...	0.4	...
Net Profit Margin %	...	2.1	3.0	...
Return on Equity %	...	3.5	...	...
Return on Assets %	...	2.1	10.5	...
Debt/Total Assets %	...	5.9	...	...
Price Range	29⁷/₁₆-9	...	...	...

Statistics are as originally reported. ☐ Incl. acquired in-process research & dev. & goodwill amortization of $20.6 mill.

OFFICERS:
F. W. Conner, Chmn.
J. A. Ryan, Pres., C.E.O.
M. L. Axelson, Sr. V.P., C.F.O..

PRINCIPAL OFFICE: One Preston Park South, 4975 Preston Park Blvd., Plano, TX 75093

TELEPHONE NUMBER: (972) 943-7300
WEB: www.entrust.com

NO. OF EMPLOYEES: 456

SHAREHOLDERS: 131 (approx.)

ANNUAL MEETING: In May

INCORPORATED: MD, Dec., 1996

INSTITUTIONAL HOLDINGS:
No. of Institutions: 31
Shares Held: 9,857,699
% Held: 23.2

INDUSTRY: Computer programming services (SIC: 7371)

TRANSFER AGENT(S): American Securities Transfer & Trust, Inc., Denver, CO

ETOYS INC.

YIELD ...
P/E RATIO ...

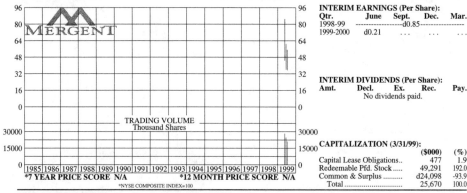

TRADING VOLUME
Thousand Shares

INTERIM EARNINGS (Per Share):

Qtr.	June	Sept.	Dec.	Mar.
1998-99	------------------d0.85-----------------			
1999-2000	d0.21	...	...	...

INTERIM DIVIDENDS (Per Share):

Amt.	Decl.	Ex.	Rec.	Pay.
		No dividends paid.		

CAPITALIZATION (3/31/99):

	($000)	(%)
Capital Lease Obligations..	477	1.9
Redeemable Pfd. Stock	49,291	192.0
Common & Surplus	d24,098	-93.9
Total	25,670	100.0

RECENT DEVELOPMENTS: For the quarter ended 6/30/99, the Company reported a net loss of $20.8 million versus a loss of $2.2 million in the corresponding quarter of the previous year. Earnings in 1999 included a non-cash deferred compensation charge of $3.8 million. Net sales surged to $8.0 million from $381,000 in the prior-year quarter. Cumulative customer accounts grew to 467,000, while repeat customers accounted for approximately 40.0% of net sales. Operating income totaled a loss of $21.7 mil-

lion compared with a loss of $2.7 million the year before. During the quarter, the Company entered into warehouse agreements in Utah and Virginia, adding over 1.4 million square feet of capacity. In July 1999, ETYS completed the acquisition of BabyCenter Inc., an on-line company providing information and products to new and expecting parents. The Company also launched an on-line children's book store. In August 1999, ETYS signed a three-year, $18.0 million marketing agreement with AOL Inc.

BUSINESS

ETOYS INC. is a Web-based retailer focused exclusively on children's products, including toys, video games, software, videos and music. The Company's on-line store, etoys.com, offers a selection of competitively priced children's products, with over 9,500 stock keeping units representing more than 750 brands. The Company provides a selection of both traditional, well-known brands such as MATTEL, HASBRO and LEGO, and specialty brands, such as PLAYMOBIL and LEARNING CURVE. The Company's Web site features detailed product information and merchandising through easy-to-use Web pages. In addition, ETYS provides customers with shopping services such as birthday reminders, wish lists, product reviews, recommendations and gift suggestions.

QUARTERLY DATA

03/31/1999	Rev	Inc
First Quarter	381	(2,171)
Second Quarter..........	608	(3,383)
Third Quarter.............	22,910	(9,822)
Fourth Quarter...........	6,059	(13,182)

ANNUAL FINANCIAL DATA

	3/31/99	3/31/98
Earnings Per Share	**d0.85**	**d0.09**
Cash Flow Per Share	**d0.66**	**d0.09**
INCOME STATEMENT (IN THOUSANDS):		
Total Revenues	29,959	687
Costs & Expenses	52,514	2,937
Depreciation & Amort.	6,544	20
Operating Income	d29,099	d2,270
Net Interest Inc./(Exp.)	542	3
Income Before Income Taxes	d28,557	d2,267
Income Taxes	1	1
Net Income	d28,558	d2,268
Cash Flow	d22,014	d2,248
Average Shs. Outstg.	33,428	25,130
BALANCE SHEET (IN THOUSANDS):		
Cash & Cash Equivalents	20,173	1,552
Total Current Assets	26,817	1,811
Net Property	2,136	160
Total Assets	30,666	2,927
Total Current Liabilities	4,996	355
Long-Term Obligations	477	...
Net Stockholders' Equity	d24,098	d1,345
Net Working Capital	21,821	1,456
Year-end Shs. Outstg.	34,535	32,799
STATISTICAL RECORD:		
Debt/Total Assets %	1.6	...
Statistics are as originally reported.		

OFFICERS:
E. C. Lenk, Chmn., Pres., C.E.O.
S. J. Schoch, Sr. V.P., C.F.O.

PRINCIPAL OFFICE: 3100 Ocean Park Blvd., Suite 300, Santa Monica, CA 90405

TELEPHONE NUMBER: (310) 664-8100
WEB: www.etoys.com

NO. OF EMPLOYEES: 306

SHAREHOLDERS: 127

ANNUAL MEETING: N/A

INCORPORATED: DE, Nov., 1996

INSTITUTIONAL HOLDINGS:
No. of Institutions: 6
Shares Held: 823,980
% Held: 0.8
INDUSTRY: Hobby, toy, and game shops (SIC: 5945)
TRANSFER AGENT(S): ChaseMellon Shareholder Services, L.L.C., Los Angeles, CA

EXODUS COMMUNICATIONS, INC.

YIELD   ...
P/E RATIO   ...

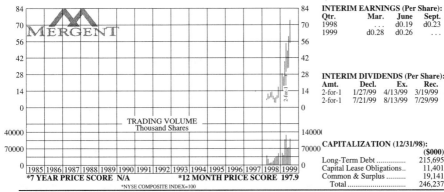

INTERIM EARNINGS (Per Share):

Qtr.	Mar.	June	Sept.	Dec.
1998	...	d0.19	d0.23	d0.27
1999	d0.28	d0.26	...	...

INTERIM DIVIDENDS (Per Share):

Amt.	Decl.	Ex.	Rec.	Pay.
2-for-1	1/27/99	4/13/99	3/19/99	4/12/99
2-for-1	7/21/99	8/13/99	7/29/99	8/12/99

CAPITALIZATION (12/31/98):

	($000)	(%)
Long-Term Debt	215,695	87.6
Capital Lease Obligations..	11,401	4.6
Common & Surplus	19,141	7.8
Total	246,237	100.0

*7 YEAR PRICE SCORE N/A   *12 MONTH PRICE SCORE 197.9

*NYSE COMPOSITE INDEX=100

RECENT DEVELOPMENTS: For the quarter ended 6/30/99, EXDS incurred a net loss of $20.9 million compared with a loss of $14.1 million in the corresponding period of the prior year. Revenues soared to $42.5 million from $10.1 million in the comparable prior-year quarter. Gross margin jumped to $7.9 million compared with a loss of $2.9 million in 1998. Operating income slipped to a loss of $14.5 million versus a loss of $13.8 million the year before. The Company added 327 customers and increased the average annualized revenue per hosting customer to $157,000. EXDS opened five new Data Centers and opened the Company's first international Data Center in London. The Company plans to open six additional Internet Data Centers by the end of 1999. During the quarter, the Company introduced a new Internet Service Provider program designed to cut costs for service providers on Internet infrastructure and improve customer access. In July 1999, EXDS acquired Cohesive Technology Solutions, Inc.

BUSINESS

EXODUS COMMUNICATIONS, INC. is a provider of Internet system and network management services for enterprises with mission-critical Internet operations. The Company's services include Internet Data Centers, network services and managed services. Exodus delivers its services from eight geographically distributed Internet Data Centers that are connected through a high-performance dedicated and redundant backbone network. Four more Data Centers are being planned. Exodus' Internet services are designed to provide enterprises with the high performance, scalability and expertise they need to optimize their mission-critical Internet operations.

REVENUES

(12/31/1998)($000)	Rev	(%)
Service Revenues	2,454	78.4
Equipment Revenues.	676	21.6
Total Revenues	3,130	100.0

ANNUAL FINANCIAL DATA

	12/31/98	12/31/97	12/31/96	12/31/95
Earnings Per Share	① d2.19	d3.46	d0.54	d0.25
Cash Flow Per Share	d1.70	d2.88	d0.48	d0.24
Tang. Book Val. Per Share	0.48	...	...	...
INCOME STATEMENT (IN THOUSANDS):				
Total Revenues	52,738	12,408	3,130	1,408
Costs & Expenses	94,267	32,682	6,763	2,616
Depreciation & Amort.	15,156	4,518	461	65
Operating Income	d56,685	d24,792	d4,094	d1,273
Net Interest Inc./(Exp.)	d9,757	d506	d39	d38
Income Before Income Taxes	d66,442	d25,298	d4,133	d1,311
Net Income	① d66,442	d25,298	d4,133	d1,311
Cash Flow	d53,300	d22,193	d3,672	d1,246
Average Shs. Outstg.	31,286	7,712	7,656	5,260
BALANCE SHEET (IN THOUSANDS):				
Cash & Cash Equivalents	150,891	10,270	3,715	...
Total Current Assets	166,742	13,484	4,357	...
Net Property	68,306	25,170	3,410	...
Total Assets	293,286	40,973	8,289	...
Total Current Liabilities	47,049	17,191	2,465	...
Long-Term Obligations	227,096	15,135	1,449	...
Net Stockholders' Equity	19,141	d30,600	d5,234	...
Net Working Capital	119,693	d3,707	1,892	...
Year-end Shs. Outstg.	40,134	8,268	7,784	...
STATISTICAL RECORD:				
Debt/Total Assets %	77.4	36.9	17.5	...
Price Range	17⁷/₁₆-3⁷/₈	...	...	...

Statistics are as originally reported. Adj. for stk. split: 2-for-1, 8/13/99; 2-for-1, 3/19/1999 ① Incl. net non-recurr. chrg. $2.0 mill.

OFFICERS:
K. B. Chandrasekhar, Chmn., C.E.O.
E. M. Hancock, Pres., C.E.O.
R. S. Stoltz, C.O.O., C.F.O.

INVESTOR CONTACT: Investor Relations, (408) 346-2191

PRINCIPAL OFFICE: 2831 Mission College Blvd., Santa Clara, CA 95054

TELEPHONE NUMBER: (408) 346-2200
WEB: www.exodus.net

NO. OF EMPLOYEES: 472 (avg.)

SHAREHOLDERS: 284
ANNUAL MEETING: In June

INCORPORATED: Aug., 1992; reincorp., DE, Feb., 1998

INSTITUTIONAL HOLDINGS:
No. of Institutions: 138
Shares Held: 54,772,712 (Adj.)
% Held: 66.5

INDUSTRY: Telephone communications, exc. radio (SIC: 4813)

TRANSFER AGENT(S): Boston EquiServe Limited Partnership, Boston, MA

FATBRAIN.COM, INC.

YIELD ...
P/E RATIO ...

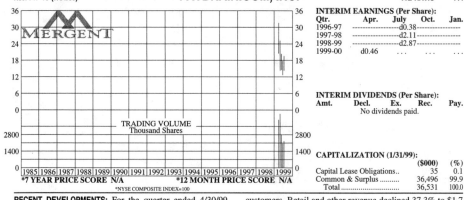

*7 YEAR PRICE SCORE N/A   *12 MONTH PRICE SCORE N/A

*NYSE COMPOSITE INDEX=100

INTERIM EARNINGS (Per Share):

Qtr.	Apr.	July	Oct.	Jan.
1996-97		d0.38		
1997-98		d2.11		
1998-99		d2.87		
1999-00	d0.46	...	...	...

INTERIM DIVIDENDS (Per Share):

Amt.	Decl.	Ex.	Rec.	Pay.
		No dividends paid.		

CAPITALIZATION (1/31/99):

	($000)	(%)
Capital Lease Obligations..	35	0.1
Common & Surplus	36,496	99.9
Total	36,531	100.0

RECENT DEVELOPMENTS: For the quarter ended 4/30/99, the Company reported a net loss of $5.2 million versus a net loss of $1.7 million in the comparable prior-year period. Total revenues increased 39.8% to $6.1 million from $4.4 million a year ago. On-line revenue more than doubled to $4.5 million from $1.8 million the year before. The improvement in on-line revenue was attributed to a significant increase in the customer base to 103,057 versus 29,115 a year earlier, as well as repeat purchases from existing customers. Retail and other revenue declined 37.3% to $1.7 million from $2.6 million in the prior-year quarter. This decrease was due to the increased focus of sales and marketing on the on-line business, as well as the closure of two retail stores, located in Cupertino, CA and Vienna, VA, at the end of fiscal 1999. Gross profit as a percentage of total revenues fell to 23.3% from 31.4% due to the increase in lower-margin on-line sales, as well as the implementation of a competitive pricing policy.

BUSINESS

FATBRAIN.COM, INC. (formerly Computer Literacy, Inc.) is an on-line retailer of information resources focused on business and technical professionals. The Company offers its customers on-line access to a broad and comprehensive selection of technical and professional books, technology-based training tools, product manuals, research reports and other information resources. The Company also operates two physical retail stores that complement its on-line product offering. FATB has established co-branded on-line stores with a number of technology companies, including Microsoft, Sun Microsystems, Cisco Systems, Hewlett-Packard Company, 3Com and Hughes. On May 31, 1997, the Company acquired all of the outstanding capital stock of Computer Literacy Bookshops, Inc. for approximately $5.1 million.

ANNUAL FINANCIAL DATA

	1/31/99	1/31/98	1/31/97
Earnings Per Share	d2.87	d2.11	d0.38
Cash Flow Per Share	d2.67	d1.92	d0.37
Tang. Book Val. Per Share	3.02	4.56	...
INCOME STATEMENT (IN THOUSANDS):			
Total Revenues	19,780	10,948	180
Costs & Expenses	29,393	13,834	789
Depreciation & Amort.	692	297	13
Operating Income	d10,305	d3,183	d622
Income Before Income Taxes	d9,892	d3,190	d567
Net Income	d9,892	d3,190	d567
Cash Flow	d9,200	d2,893	d554
Average Shs. Outstg.	3,441	1,509	1,504
BALANCE SHEET (IN THOUSANDS):			
Cash & Cash Equivalents	14,685	4,974	...
Total Current Assets	20,225	9,250	...
Net Property	2,097	1,182	...
Total Assets	39,614	13,598	...
Total Current Liabilities	3,083	3,620	...
Long-Term Obligations	35	53	...
Net Stockholders' Equity	36,496	9,925	...
Net Working Capital	17,142	5,630	...
Year-end Shs. Outstg.	11,172	1,527	1,504
STATISTICAL RECORD:			
Debt/Total Assets %	0.1	0.4	...

Statistics are as originally reported.

BUSINESS LINE ANALYSIS

01/31/99	Rev(%)	Inc(%)
Internet commerce.....	53.9	41.4
Retail stores..............	45.5	58.2
Unallocated................	0.6	0.4
Total	100.0	100.0

OFFICERS:
C. MacAskill, Chmn., C.E.O., Pres.
D. P. Alvarez, C.F.O., V.P.
K. Orumchian, Sec., V.P.

INVESTOR CONTACT: Alex Wellins, Jennifer Jarmin Morgan-Walke Associates, (415) 296-7383

PRINCIPAL OFFICE: 1308 Orleans Drive, Sunnyvale, CA 94089

TELEPHONE NUMBER: (408) 541-2020
FAX: (408) 752-9919
WEB: www.fatbrain.com

NO. OF EMPLOYEES: 170 (approx.)

SHAREHOLDERS: 86 (approx.)

ANNUAL MEETING: In June

INCORPORATED: CA, Nov., 1994; reincorp., DE, Jul., 1998

INSTITUTIONAL HOLDINGS:
No. of Institutions: 12
Shares Held: 485,031
% Held: 4.3

INDUSTRY: News dealers and newsstands (SIC: 5994)

TRANSFER AGENT(S): U.S. Stock Transfer Corporation Glendale, CA

FINE.COM INTERNATIONAL CORP.

YIELD ...
P/E RATIO ...

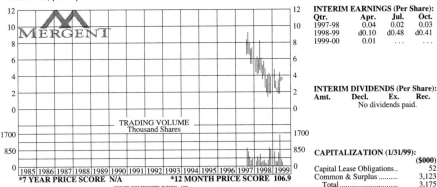

7 YEAR PRICE SCORE N/A   **12 MONTH PRICE SCORE 106.9**
*NYSE COMPOSITE INDEX=100

TRADING VOLUME
Thousand Shares

INTERIM EARNINGS (Per Share):

Qtr.	Apr.	Jul.	Oct.	Jan.
1997-98	0.04	0.02	0.03	d0.03
1998-99	d0.10	d0.48	d0.41	d0.35
1999-00	0.01	...	...	...

INTERIM DIVIDENDS (Per Share):

Amt.	Decl.	Ex.	Rec.	Pay.
		No dividends paid.		

CAPITALIZATION (1/31/99):

	($000)	(%)
Capital Lease Obligations..	52	1.6
Common & Surplus	3,123	98.4
Total	3,175	100.0

RECENT DEVELOPMENTS: For the quarter ended 4/30/99, net income totaled $15,524 compared with a net loss of $368,428 in the corresponding quarter the year before. Gross revenues improved 40.8% to $1.9 million from $1.3 million in the prior-year quarter. Results benefited from restructuring initiatives which included growing sales, adding strategic consulting services, increasing internal productivity and lowering FDOT's overhead cost structure. On 5/17/99, the Company entered into an agreement to be acquired by ARIS Corporation, a provider of international IT consulting, training and software. On 8/5/99, FDOT announced an amended merger agreement under which ARIS has agreed to pay FDOT's shareholders ARIS common stock or ARIS common stock and cash equal to $4.5531 per share of FDOT stock. The amended terms continue to value FDOT at approximately $12.3 million. The acquisition is expected to close in the third quarter of 1999.

BUSINESS

FINE.COM INTERNATIONAL CORP. provides strategic consulting, technical development and graphic design services and solutions to allow its clients to utilize Web-based interactive technologies. The Company's Web application development process combines marketing expertise with state-of-the-art interactive database compilation and dissemination techniques and technologies. Also, the Company develops marketing-driven, interactive, database-oriented Web applications for business clients who seek to establish a commercial presence on, or conduct Internet commerce over, the Web. Corporate clients for whom the Company has built and implemented such Internet, Extranet and Intranet sites include: Amway Corporation, Fluke Corporation, Fuji Photo Film Co. Ltd., General Electric Company, Intel Corporation, Japan Airlines Company, Inc., Mann Packing Company, Marriott International, Inc., Microsoft Corporation, Mitsui and Co., Ltd., the Nasdaq-Amex Stock Market, Optiva Corporation, Penford Corporation, Safeway Inc., Twentieth Century Fox Home Entertainment, Inc., Wall Data, Inc., the State of Washington, Windermere Services Company and WOWFactor.

ANNUAL FINANCIAL DATA

	1/31/99	1/31/98	1/31/97	1/31/96
Earnings Per Share	d1.34	0.05	0.11	0.03
Cash Flow Per Share	d1.21	0.10	0.13	0.05
Tang. Book Val. Per Share	1.17	2.83	0.20	0.09
INCOME STATEMENT (IN THOUSANDS):				
Total Revenues	6,133	3,448	1,486	532
Costs & Expenses	9,594	3,373	1,259	459
Depreciation & Amort.	345	88	30	25
Operating Income	d3,807	d13	198	48
Net Interest Inc./(Exp.)	139	140	d9	d3
Income Before Income Taxes	d3,668	127	189	45
Income Taxes	cr102	47	64	15
Net Income	d3,566	81	124	30
Cash Flow	d3,220	169	154	56
Average Shs. Outstg.	2,668	1,764	1,155	1,155
BALANCE SHEET (IN THOUSANDS):				
Cash & Cash Equivalents	1,521	3,013	198	16
Total Current Assets	3,579	4,310	716	103
Net Property	1,414	436	81	46
Total Assets	5,070	7,352	869	150
Total Current Liabilities	1,895	618	414	58
Long-Term Obligations	52	...	...	...
Net Stockholders' Equity	3,123	6,734	455	90
Net Working Capital	1,684	3,692	302	46
Year-end Shs. Outstg.	2,670	2,380	1,056	1,056
STATISTICAL RECORD:				
Operating Profit Margin %	...	...	13.3	9.0
Net Profit Margin %	...	2.3	8.4	5.7
Return on Equity %	...	1.2	27.3	33.3
Return on Assets %	...	1.1	14.3	20.1
Debt/Total Assets %	1.0	...	...	...
Price Range	8¼-1⅜	9¼-5⅜	...	...
P/E Ratio	...	184.6-107.3	...	...

Statistics are as originally reported.

OFFICERS:
D. M. Fine, Chmn., C.E.O.
T. J. Carrol, Exec. V.P.

TELEPHONE NUMBER: (206) 292-2888
FAX: (206) 292-2889
WEB: www.fine.com

NO. OF EMPLOYEES: 69

SHAREHOLDERS: 47 (of record)

ANNUAL MEETING: In June

PRINCIPAL OFFICE: 1525 Fourth Ave., Suite 800, Seattle, WA 98101

INCORPORATED: WA, Oct., 1994

INSTITUTIONAL HOLDINGS:
No. of Institutions: N/A
Shares Held: N/A
% Held: N/A

INDUSTRY: Data processing and preparation (SIC: 7374)

TRANSFER AGENT(S): ChaseMellon Shareholder Services, LLC, SouthHackensack, NJ.

FLASHNET COMMUNICATIONS INC.

YIELD ...
P/E RATIO ...

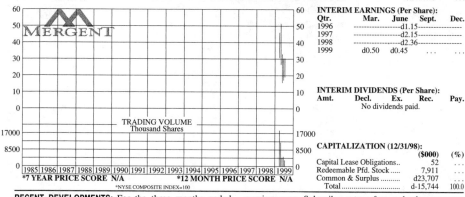

*7 YEAR PRICE SCORE N/A   *12 MONTH PRICE SCORE N/A

*NYSE COMPOSITE INDEX=100

INTERIM EARNINGS (Per Share):

Qtr.	Mar.	June	Sept.	Dec.
1996	---------------d1.15---------------			
1997	---------------d2.15---------------			
1998	---------------d2.36---------------			
1999	d0.50	d0.45	...	...

INTERIM DIVIDENDS (Per Share):

Amt.	Decl.	Ex.	Rec.	Pay.
No dividends paid.				

CAPITALIZATION (12/31/98):

	($000)	(%)
Capital Lease Obligations..	52	...
Redeemable Pfd. Stock	7,911	...
Common & Surplus	d23,707	...
Total	d-15,744	100.0

RECENT DEVELOPMENTS: For the three months ended 6/30/99, the Company reported a net loss of $6.2 million compared with a net loss of $2.6 million in the corresponding period of the prior year. Revenues increased 53.0% to $9.5 million from $6.2 million. Consumer access services revenues grew 45.6% to $7.4 million from $5.1 million the year before. The improvement in access service revenues was primarily attributed to an increase in the Company's subscriber base of 38% to 220,000 from 160,000 in the previous year. Subscriber set-up fees and other revenues more than doubled to $1.7 million versus $791,000 the year before. This growth was the result of the reintroduction of set-up fees on all products in March 1999 and non-refundable shipping revenues. Gross profit climbed 52.4% to $4.9 million from $3.2 million in the year-ago quarter. During the quarter, FLAS formed strategic relationships with companies including eBay, Intellesale.com, Cideo, iPin, PCWarehouse and Broadcast.com.

BUSINESS

FLASHNET COMMUNICATIONS INC. is a nationwide provider of consumer Internet access and business services. The Internet access services are provided through a national network with 621 "points of presence," or local telephone numbers through which the Company's subscribers can access the Internet. The business services consist of high speed Internet access services and other services that enable customers to outsource their Internet and electronic commerce activities. As of 6/30/99, the Company had accumulated a subscriber base of approximately 219,000 users, including approximately 3,100 customers for its business services.

ANNUAL FINANCIAL DATA

	12/31/98	12/31/97	12/31/96
Earnings Per Share	d2.36	d2.15	d1.15
Cash Flow Per Share	d1.46	d1.73	d1.04
INCOME STATEMENT (IN THOUSANDS):			
Total Revenues	26,892	17,537	3,654
Costs & Expenses	29,739	26,235	8,976
Depreciation & Amort.	4,961	2,276	588
Operating Income	d7,809	d10,974	d5,910
Net Interest Inc./(Exp.)	d2,456	d714	d144
Income Before Income Taxes	d10,265	d11,688	d6,054
Net Income	d10,265	d11,688	d6,054
Cash Flow	d8,044	d9,413	d5,466
Average Shs. Outstg.	5,505	5,449	5,266
BALANCE SHEET (IN THOUSANDS):			
Cash & Cash Equivalents	1,038	1,570	...
Total Current Assets	2,720	2,442	...
Net Property	6,821	8,396	...
Total Assets	9,733	11,000	...
Total Current Liabilities	25,477	19,277	...
Long-Term Obligations	52	5,159	...
Net Stockholders' Equity	d23,707	d13,436	...
Net Working Capital	d22,757	d16,835	...
Year-end Shs. Outstg.	5,529	5,487	5,421
STATISTICAL RECORD:			
Debt/Total Assets %	0.5	46.9	...

Statistics are as originally reported.

REVENUES

(12/31/1998)	($000)	(%)
Consumer access services..................	21,979	81.7
Business services.......	1,597	5.9
Set-up fees & other....	3,316	12.4
Total	26,892	100.0

OFFICERS:
A. L. Thurburn, Chmn.
M. S. Leslie, Pres., C.E.O., C.O.O., Sec.
A. N. Jent, C.F.O.

PRINCIPAL OFFICE: 1812 North Forest Park Boulevard, Ft.Worth, TX 76102

TELEPHONE NUMBER: (817) 332-8883
FAX: (817) 332-3934
WEB: www.flash.net
NO. OF EMPLOYEES: 248 (avg.)
SHAREHOLDERS: N/A
ANNUAL MEETING: N/A
INCORPORATED: TX, Sep., 1995

INSTITUTIONAL HOLDINGS:
No. of Institutions: 25
Shares Held: 783,650
% Held: 5.6

INDUSTRY: Telephone communications, exc. radio (SIC: 4813)

TRANSFER AGENT(S): BancBoston, N.A., Boston, MA.

NASDAQ SYMBOL FCST
Rec. Pr. 22¹⁵/₁₆ (7/31/99)

FLYCAST COMMUNICATIONS CORPORATION

YIELD ...
P/E RATIO ...

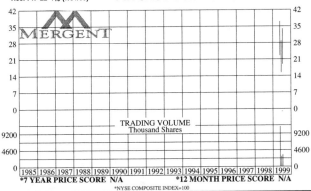

INTERIM EARNINGS (Per Share):

Qtr.	Mar.	June	Sept.	Dec.
1997	----------------d31.80----------------			
1998	----------------d11.93----------------			
1999	d4.04	d0.54	...	...

INTERIM DIVIDENDS (Per Share):

Amt.	Decl.	Ex.	Rec.	Pay.
No dividends paid.				

9200
4600
0

1985 1986 1987 1988 1989 1990 1991 1992 1993 1994 1995 1996 1997 1998 1999

TRADING VOLUME
Thousand Shares

*7 YEAR PRICE SCORE N/A   *12 MONTH PRICE SCORE N/A

*NYSE COMPOSITE INDEX=100

CAPITALIZATION (12/31/98):

	($000)	(%)
Long-Term Debt	3,682	61.6
Capital Lease Obligations	1,022	17.1
Redeemable Pfd. Stock	13,855	231.7
Common & Surplus	d12,578	-210.3
Total	5,981	100.0

RECENT DEVELOPMENTS: For the quarter ended 6/30/99, FCST incurred a net loss of $6.2 million compared with a net loss of $1.8 million in the equivalent 1998 quarter. Revenues were $6.4 million from $1.2 million in the corresponding period of 1998. The improvement in revenues was primarily attributed to an increase in the number of advertisers purchasing advertisements on the Flycast Network and an increase in purchases made by existing advertisers. In July, the Company announced a comprehensive email strategy. Flycast has created a new e-mail marketing division, Flycast eDispatch, which, in conjuction with the Flycast Network, will provide direct response and e-commerce marketers with an integrated suite of tools and services designed to maximize the effectiveness of on-line marketing initiatives. FCST will package and manage e-mail advertising campaigns across thousands of individual vehicles. In addition, eDispatch will centralize buying, trafficking and performance tracking, and support both text and graphical publications and advertising.

BUSINESS

FLYCAST COMMUNICATIONS CORPORATION delivers Web-based advertising solutions designed to maximize the return on investment for response-oriented advertisers, direct marketers and electronic commerce companies. By combining unsold advertising space from over 1,000 Web sites, the Flycast Network offers advertisers a large audience of Web users and high-quality advertising space at favorable prices. Additionally, by selling advertising space on an unnamed basis, Flycast creates a supplemental revenue opportunity for Web sites that does not conflict with their other sales efforts.

ANNUAL FINANCIAL DATA

	12/31/98	12/31/97	12/31/96
Earnings Per Share	d11.93	d31.80	d445.00
Cash Flow Per Share	d11.26	d30.17	d426.96
INCOME STATEMENT (IN THOUSANDS):			
Total Revenues	8,029	630	...
Costs & Expenses	16,393	3,857	427
Depreciation & Amort.	531	184	18
Operating Income	d8,895	d3,411	d445
Net Interest Inc./(Exp.)	d412	d6	...
Income Before Income Taxes	d9,307	d3,417	d445
Net Income	d9,307	d3,417	d445
Cash Flow	d9,432	d3,439	d427
Average Shs. Outstg.	838	114	1
BALANCE SHEET (IN THOUSANDS):			
Cash & Cash Equivalents	5,193	3,560	...
Total Current Assets	8,898	3,996	...
Net Property	1,785	661	...
Total Assets	10,791	4,675	...
Total Current Liabilities	4,810	498	...
Long-Term Obligations	4,704	40	...
Net Stockholders' Equity	d12,578	d4,058	...
Net Working Capital	4,088	3,498	...
Year-end Shs. Outstg.	2,657	2,352	...
STATISTICAL RECORD:			
Debt/Total Assets %	43.6	0.9	...
Statistics are as originally reported.			

OFFICERS:
G. R. Garrick, Chmn., Pres., C.E.O.
R. J. Harms, C.F.O., Asst. Sec.

PRINCIPAL OFFICE: 181 Fremond Street, San Francisco, CA 94105

TELEPHONE NUMBER: (415) 977-1000
WEB: www.flycast.com
NO. OF EMPLOYEES: 86
SHAREHOLDERS: 123
ANNUAL MEETING: N/A
INCORPORATED: CA, Feb., 1994; reincorp., DE, Apr., 1999

INSTITUTIONAL HOLDINGS:
No. of Institutions: 2
Shares Held: 375,760
% Held: 2.7
INDUSTRY: Advertising, nec (SIC: 7319)
TRANSFER AGENT(S): U.S. Stock Transfer Corporation, Glendale, CA

FRONTLINE COMMUNICATIONS CORP.

YIELD ...
P/E RATIO ...

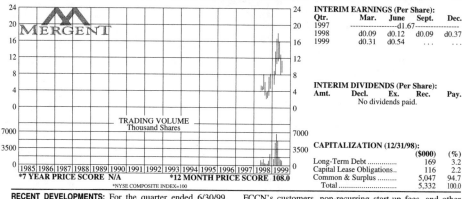

*7 YEAR PRICE SCORE N/A   *12 MONTH PRICE SCORE 108.0
*NYSE COMPOSITE INDEX=100

INTERIM EARNINGS (Per Share):

Qtr.	Mar.	June	Sept.	Dec.
1997	------------------d1.67------------------			
1998	d0.09	d0.12	d0.09	d0.37
1999	d0.31	d0.54	...	...

INTERIM DIVIDENDS (Per Share):

Amt.	Decl.	Ex.	Rec.	Pay.
	No dividends paid.			

CAPITALIZATION (12/31/98):

	($000)	(%)
Long-Term Debt	169	3.2
Capital Lease Obligations..	116	2.2
Common & Surplus	5,047	94.7
Total	5,332	100.0

RECENT DEVELOPMENTS: For the quarter ended 6/30/99, the Company reported a net loss of $1.9 million compared with a loss of $265,822 in 1998. Results for the second quarter of 1999 included a non-cash compensation charge of $712,220. Revenues soared to $758,561 from $124,113 in the prior-year period. Revenues are derived primarily from Internet access charges to individual and business subscribers and comprised of recurring revenues from FCCN's customers, non-recurring start-up fees, and other ancillary services. The number of subscribers for 1999 increased to 15,000 from 2,000 subscribers in 1998. The increase in subscriber base was primarily due to acquisitions. Webprime, FCCN's Web development division, has been selected to design and develop a Web site for Tri State Health System, a healthcare delivery system in New York, New Jersey, and Pennsylvania.

BUSINESS

FRONTLINE COMMUNICATIONS CORP. is an Internet service provider that offers e-commerce and Internet access to individual and business subscribers located in the Northeastern U.S. The Company provides subscribers with direct access to a wide range of Internet applications and resources, including electronic mail, Web hosting and design, dedicated circuits, e-commerce solutions, access to World Wide Web sites and regional/local information and data services. The Company provides Internet services through its three e-commerce brands; Frontline.net, WOWFactor.com, and Channel iShop.com. The Company has approximately 15,000 subscribers. On 5/27/99, the Company completed the acquisition of WebPrime, Inc., a Web design and development company serving numerous Fortune 500 Companies.

ANNUAL FINANCIAL DATA

	12/31/98	12/31/97	12/31/96
Earnings Per Share	d0.72	① d1.67	d0.11
Cash Flow Per Share	d0.63	d1.64	d0.09
Tang. Book Val. Per Share	0.63	...	...
INCOME STATEMENT (IN THOUSANDS):			
Total Revenues	575	322	99
Costs & Expenses	2,175	2,285	139
Depreciation & Amort.	221	45	10
Operating Income	d1,820	d2,008	d50
Net Interest Inc./(Exp.)	76	d29	d4
Income Before Income Taxes	d1,744	d2,037	d54
Net Income	d1,744	① d2,037	d54
Cash Flow	d1,524	d1,993	d44
Average Shs. Outstg.	2,435	1,218	512
BALANCE SHEET (IN THOUSANDS):			
Cash & Cash Equivalents	1,995	40	2
Total Current Assets	2,200	290	6
Net Property	982	179	47
Total Assets	6,286	486	54
Total Current Liabilities	955	713	74
Long-Term Obligations	284	218	37
Net Stockholders' Equity	5,047	d445	d56
Net Working Capital	1,246	d423	d68
Year-end Shs. Outstg.	3,130	1,408	...
STATISTICAL RECORD:			
Debt/Total Assets %	4.5	44.8	67.7
Price Range	8¼-2⅛	...	...

Statistics are as originally reported. ① Includes non-recurring charge of $1.5 million.

OFFICERS:
S. J. Cole-Hatchard, Chmn., C.E.O., Pres.
V. Thatham, C.F.O., V.P.
A. Wagner-Mele, Exec. V.P., Sec., Gen. Couns.

INVESTOR CONTACT: Stephen J. Cole-Hatchard, Chairman, (919) 623-8553

PRINCIPAL OFFICE: One Blue Plaza, 6th Floor, Pearl River, NY 10965

TELEPHONE NUMBER: (914) 623-8553
FAX: (914) 623-8669
WEB: www.frontline.net

NO. OF EMPLOYEES: 65

SHAREHOLDERS: 54 (approx.)

ANNUAL MEETING: In June

INCORPORATED: DE, Feb., 1997

INSTITUTIONAL HOLDINGS:
No. of Institutions: 3
Shares Held: 41,400
% Held: 1.2

INDUSTRY: Information retrieval services (SIC: 7375)

TRANSFER AGENT(S): American Securities Transfer & Trust Co., Inc., Denver, Co.

NASDAQ SYMBOL FVCX
Rec. Pr. 6⅞ (7/31/99)

FVC.COM, INC.

YIELD ...
P/E RATIO ...

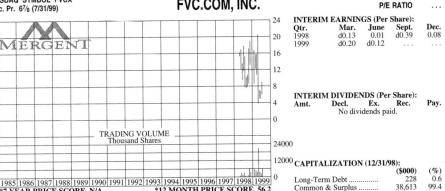

INTERIM EARNINGS (Per Share):

Qtr.	Mar.	June	Sept.	Dec.
1998	d0.13	0.01	d0.39	0.08
1999	d0.20	0.12	...	...

INTERIM DIVIDENDS (Per Share):

Amt.	Decl.	Ex.	Rec.	Pay.
	No dividends paid.			

CAPITALIZATION (12/31/98):

	($000)	(%)
Long-Term Debt	228	0.6
Common & Surplus	38,613	99.4
Total	38,841	100.0

*7 YEAR PRICE SCORE N/A   *12 MONTH PRICE SCORE 56.2
*NYSE COMPOSITE INDEX=100

RECENT DEVELOPMENTS: For the quarter ended 6/30/99, the Company incurred a net loss of $2.0 million compared with income of $121,000 in the corresponding quarter of the previous year. Revenue slipped 3.3% to $10.6 million from $11.0 million in the previous year. Gross profit increased to $5.1 million, or 47.9% of revenue, versus $5.0 million, or 45.7% of revenue, the year before. Operating loss was $2.0 million compared with operating income of $301,000 in 1998, primarily due to a substantial increase in selling, general and administrative expenses. During the quarter, FVCX introduced the V-Gate 4000, which enables seamless videoconferencing between IP/Ethernet, ATM, and ISDN standards. In July 1999, the Company purchased a 52.0% ownership in its UK partner operation to expand the company's presence in the UK and Middle East markets.

BUSINESS

FVC.COM, INC is a manufacturer of enterprise video networking products and services. The Company's video access products facilitate the connection of traditional room systems, desktop video equipment and personal computers to enterprise networks. The Company's video server products provide a range of video services such as multicasting, recording, storage and translation across the Internet and corporate intranets. Integrated with voice and data, these products enable applications such as distance learning, corporate communications, virtual meetings and telemedicine to be delivered over broadband IP and legacy networks.

ANNUAL FINANCIAL DATA

	12/31/98	12/31/97	12/31/96	12/31/95
Earnings Per Share	① d0.69	d1.44	d1.14	d5.30
Cash Flow Per Share	d0.52	d1.25	d0.96	d5.15
Tang. Book Val. Per Share	2.36	0.39	0.42	...
INCOME STATEMENT (IN THOUSANDS):				
Total Revenues	37,251	18,771	12,093	3,670
Costs & Expenses	43,264	22,317	14,021	8,903
Depreciation & Amort.	1,961	566	342	156
Operating Income	d7,974	d4,112	d2,270	d5,389
Net Interest Inc./(Exp.)	d1,057	d295	d91	79
Income Before Income Taxes	d8,016	d4,328	d2,243	d5,310
Net Income	① d8,016	d4,328	d2,243	d5,310
Cash Flow	d6,055	d3,762	d1,901	d5,154
Average Shs. Outstg.	11,541	3,012	1,974	1,001
BALANCE SHEET (IN THOUSANDS):				
Cash & Cash Equivalents	26,748	2,500	676	...
Total Current Assets	45,263	9,774	4,302	...
Net Property	2,400	1,043	913	...
Total Assets	51,165	11,104	5,432	...
Total Current Liabilities	12,324	7,883	3,256	...
Long-Term Obligations	228	1,312	102	...
Net Stockholders' Equity	38,613	1,909	2,074	...
Net Working Capital	32,939	1,891	1,046	...
Year-end Shs. Outstg.	16,389	4,825	4,864	...
STATISTICAL RECORD:				
Debt/Total Assets %	0.4	11.8	1.9	...
Price Range	19-7½	...	...	...

Statistics are as originally reported. ① Incl. non-recurr. chrg. $4.7 mill.

GEOGRAPHIC DATA

(12/31/98)	REV%
United States	79.0
Asia	9.0
Europe	12.0
Total	100.0

OFFICERS:
R. K. Ungermann, Chmn.
R. M. Beyer, Pres., C.E.O.
T. Cole, V.P., Oper., C.F.O.

INVESTOR CONTACT: Investor Relations, (408) 567-7200

PRINCIPAL OFFICE: 3393 Octavius Drive, Suite 102, Santa Clara, CA 95054

TELEPHONE NUMBER: (408) 567-7200
FAX: (408) 988-7077
WEB: www.fvc.com

NO. OF EMPLOYEES: 100 (approx.)

SHAREHOLDERS: 250 approx.

ANNUAL MEETING: In June

INCORPORATED: CA, Oct., 1993; reincorp., DE, Dec., 1997

INSTITUTIONAL HOLDINGS:
No. of Institutions: 24
Shares Held: 3,976,704
% Held: 24.0

INDUSTRY: Computer integrated systems design (SIC: 7373)

TRANSFER AGENT(S): American Securities Transfer & Trust Inc., Denver, CO

GATEWAY INC.

YIELD ...
P/E RATIO 30.2

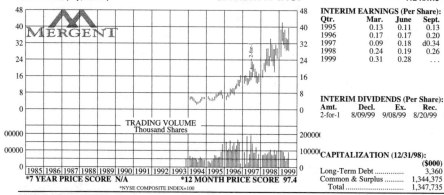

INTERIM EARNINGS (Per Share):

Qtr.	Mar.	June	Sept.	Dec.
1995	0.13	0.11	0.13	0.19
1996	0.17	0.17	0.20	0.28
1997	0.09	0.18	d0.34	0.30
1998	0.24	0.19	0.26	0.41
1999	0.31	0.28	...	...

INTERIM DIVIDENDS (Per Share):

Amt.	Decl.	Ex.	Rec.	Pay.
2-for-1	8/09/99	9/08/99	8/20/99	9/07/99

CAPITALIZATION (12/31/98):

	($000)	(%)
Long-Term Debt	3,360	0.2
Common & Surplus	1,344,375	99.8
Total	1,347,735	100.0

RECENT DEVELOPMENTS: For the quarter ended 6/30/99, net income jumped 46.9% to $89.2 million versus $60.7 million in 1998. Net sales were $1.91 billion, up 18.1% from $1.62 billion in the prior-year period. Revenues reflected strong demand for the Company's PC products and continued strength from Asian-Pacific operations. Strong growth in the U.S. market may have been triggered by new marketing strategies and programs initiated by GTW. Operating income increased 46.4% to $122.9 million versus $83.9 million a year ago. The number of units shipped rose 36.0% to 1,003,900 units during the quarter. Results benefited from the rapid growth of GTW's Internet service provider, Gateway.net. The service was introduced in 1997 and began bundling with most computers this February, which resulted in the doubling of subscribers to over 400,000. GTW announced a strategic alliance with GE Capital Information Technology Solutions to jointly offer products and services for enterprise infrastructures.

BUSINESS

GATEWAY INC. (formerly Gateway 2000, Inc.), together with its subsidiary companies, is a direct marketer of personal computers and related products and services. Gateway develops, manufactures, markets, and supports a broad line of desktop and portable PCs, digital media (convergence) PCs, servers, workstations and PC-related products used by individuals, families, businesses, government agencies and educational institutions. Gateway sells its products directly to PC customers through three complementary distribution channels including phone sales, its Internet Web site, and its Gateway Country® stores. Gateway began offering nationwide Internet provider service directly to its customers in November 1997. In February 1999, Gateway purchased a minority interest in the e-commerce operations of NECX Direct, with an option to acquire the remaining shares in the future.

ANNUAL FINANCIAL DATA

	12/31/98	12/31/97	12/31/96	12/31/95	12/31/94	12/31/93	12/31/92
Earnings Per Share	1.09	① 0.35	0.31	0.55	0.31	0.35	0.26
Cash Flow Per Share	1.42	0.63	0.99	0.67	0.36	0.56	0.41
Tang. Book Val. Per Share	4.08	2.62	2.41	1.67	1.20	0.96	0.53
INCOME STATEMENT (IN MILLIONS):							
Total Revenues	7,467.9	6,293.7	5,035.2	3,676.3	2,701.2	1,731.7	1,107.1
Costs & Expenses	6,868.2	5,916.6	4,617.4	3,389.2	2,542.2	1,574.6	998.9
Depreciation & Amort.	105.5	86.8	61.8	38.1	18.0	8.0	4.9
Operating Income	494.2	176.4	356.1	249.0	141.0	149.1	103.2
Income Before Income Taxes	541.2	203.6	382.7	262.1	146.1	154.0	106.0
Income Taxes	194.8	93.8	132.0	89.1	50.1	2.8	...
Net Income	346.4	① 109.8	250.7	173.0	96.0	151.2	106.0
Cash Flow	451.9	196.6	312.4	211.1	114.0	159.2	110.9
Average Shs. Outstg. (000)	317,858	312,402	314,624	315,976	314,624	283,812	272,388
BALANCE SHEET (IN MILLIONS):							
Cash & Cash Equivalents	1,328.5	632.2	516.4	169.4	243.9	132.2	16.4
Total Current Assets	2,228.2	1,544.7	1,318.3	866.2	654.2	500.5	246.0
Net Property	531.0	336.5	242.4	170.3	89.3	60.4	23.3
Total Assets	2,890.4	2,039.3	1,673.4	1,124.0	770.6	564.3	269.3
Total Current Liabilities	1,429.7	1,003.9	799.8	525.3	348.9	254.8	126.6
Long-Term Obligations	3.4	7.2	7.2	10.8	27.1	29.1	13.8
Net Stockholders' Equity	1,344.4	930.0	815.5	555.5	376.0	280.3	129.0
Net Working Capital	798.5	540.8	518.6	340.9	305.3	245.7	119.5
Year-end Shs. Outstg. (000)	313,138	308,256	307,024	298,212	289,584	289,536	242,664
STATISTICAL RECORD:							
Operating Profit Margin %	6.6	2.8	7.1	6.8	5.2	8.6	9.3
Net Profit Margin %	4.6	1.7	5.0	4.7	3.6	8.7	9.6
Return on Equity %	25.8	11.8	30.7	31.1	25.5	53.9	82.2
Return on Assets %	12.0	5.4	15.0	15.4	12.5	26.8	39.4
Debt/Total Assets %	0.1	0.4	0.4	1.0	3.5	5.2	5.1
Price Range	34³/₈-15¹/₂	23¹/₈-11¹³/₁₆	16⁹/₁₆-4¹/₂	9³/₈-4	6³/₁₆-2⁵/₁₆	...	...
P/E Ratio	31.5-14.2	66.1-33.7	54.3-14.8	17.1-7.3	20.3-7.6	...	...

Statistics are as originally reported. Adj. for 2-for-1 split, 9/99 & 6/97. ① Incl. $95.0 mill. after-tax non-recur. chg.

OFFICERS:
T. W. Waitt, Chmn., C.E.O.
J. Weitzen, Pres., C.O.O.
J. J. Todd, Sr. V.P., C.F.O., Treas.

INVESTOR CONTACT: Investor Relations, (605) 232-2757

PRINCIPAL OFFICE: 4545 Towne Centre Court, San Diego, CA 92121

TELEPHONE NUMBER: (619) 799-3401
FAX: (619) 799-3459
WEB: www.gateway.com
NO. OF EMPLOYEES: 19,300 (approx.)
SHAREHOLDERS: 4,226
ANNUAL MEETING: In May
INCORPORATED: IA, 1986; reincorp., DE, Dec., 1991

INSTITUTIONAL HOLDINGS:
No. of Institutions: 262
Shares Held: 117,102,124 (Adj.)
% Held: 37.4

INDUSTRY: Electronic computers (SIC: 3571)

TRANSFER AGENT(S): UMB Bank, NA, Kansas City, MO.

GENESISINTERMEDIA.COM INC.

YIELD ...
P/E RATIO ...

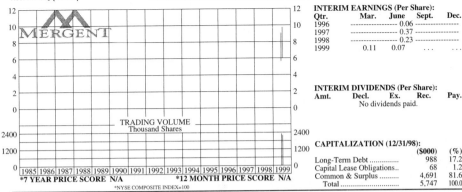

7 YEAR PRICE SCORE N/A **12 MONTH PRICE SCORE N/A**

NYSE COMPOSITE INDEX=100

INTERIM EARNINGS (Per Share):

Qtr.	Mar.	June	Sept.	Dec.
1996	------------------ 0.06 ------------------			
1997	------------------ 0.37 ------------------			
1998	------------------ 0.23 ------------------			
1999	0.11	0.07	...	...

INTERIM DIVIDENDS (Per Share):

Amt.	Decl.	Ex.	Rec.	Pay.
	No dividends paid.			

CAPITALIZATION (12/31/98):

	($000)	(%)
Long-Term Debt	988	17.2
Capital Lease Obligations..	68	1.2
Common & Surplus	4,691	81.6
Total	5,747	100.0

RECENT DEVELOPMENTS: For the quarter ended 6/30/99, net income fell 25.3% to $248,280 from $332,242 in the corresponding period of the previous year. Total revenues jumped 76.0% to $6.1 million from $3.4 million in the comparable 1998 quarter. The increase in revenues was attributed to the improvement in product sales, which almost tripled to $4.7 million compared with $1.2 million in the year-ago period. Income from operations advanced 45.3% to $520,827 versus $358,477 the year before. On 7/19/99, the Company signed an agreement to acquire cyberXpo.com™, Inc., a privately-held multimedia and e-commerce marketing company. GENI will acquire cyberXpo.com, its cyberCenter® interactive e-commerce network and all of cyberXpo's outstanding contracts. On 6/22/99, GENI also acquired from Global Leisure Travel, Inc. the rights to the Contour System, a customized computer system for integrating marketing and sales of multi-brand and multi-component travel products.

BUSINESS

GENESISINTERMEDIA.COM INC. is an integrated marketing company that utilizes conventional media and emerging, interactive multimedia technologies to market its products and its clients' products. The interactive multimedia technologies the Company uses include the Internet, CD-ROMs and DVDs. The Company markets products and services, which it develops, licenses exclusively or distributes for third parties. The Company uses conventional marketing (network and cable television, radio, newspapers, magazines), as well as interactive multimedia, the Internet and the Company's CENTERLINQ network. The Company's proprietary marketing system, CENTERLINQ, is a network of Internet portals that provide direct access to the Internet via freestanding kiosks with touch-screen computer terminals, combined with place-based video advertising in the high-traffic areas of shopping malls, such as food courts.

ANNUAL FINANCIAL DATA

	12/31/98	12/31/97	12/31/96
Earnings Per Share	0.37	0.61	0.10
Cash Flow Per Share	0.41	0.62	0.10
Tang. Book Val. Per Share	1.41	0.90	...
INCOME STATEMENT (IN THOUSANDS):			
Total Revenues	14,906	18,164	14,342
Costs & Expenses	13,171	15,692	13,947
Depreciation & Amort.	143	38	8
Operating Income	1,592	2,435	386
Net Interest Inc./(Exp.)	d135	d33	...
Income Before Income Taxes	1,457	2,402	386
Income Taxes	30	35	...
Net Income	1,427	2,367	386
Cash Flow	1,569	2,404	394
Average Shs. Outstg.	3,847	3,884	3,883
BALANCE SHEET (IN THOUSANDS):			
Cash & Cash Equivalents	1,842	280	...
Total Current Assets	6,690	5,523	...
Net Property	2,054	1,192	...
Total Assets	9,988	6,714	...
Total Current Liabilities	4,241	2,486	...
Long-Term Obligations	1,056	610	...
Net Stockholders' Equity	4,691	3,619	...
Net Working Capital	2,449	3,037	...
Year-end Shs. Outstg.	3,060	4,000	4,000
STATISTICAL RECORD:			
Operating Profit Margin %	10.7	13.4	2.7
Net Profit Margin %	9.6	13.0	2.7
Return on Equity %	30.4	65.4	...
Return on Assets %	14.3	35.2	...
Debt/Total Assets %	10.6	9.1	...

Statistics are as originally reported.

OFFICERS:
R. E. Batrawi, Chmn., C.E.O
D. E. Jacobson, C.F.O.
C. T. Dinkel, C.O.O.

PRINCIPAL OFFICE: 13063 Ventura Boulevard, Studio City, CA 91604-2238

TELEPHONE NUMBER: (818) 464-7270
WEB: www.genesisintermedia.com

NO. OF EMPLOYEES: 146

SHAREHOLDERS: N/A

ANNUAL MEETING: N/A

INCORPORATED: DE, Oct., 1993

INSTITUTIONAL HOLDINGS:
No. of Institutions: N/A
Shares Held: N/A
% Held: N/A

INDUSTRY: Advertising, nec (SIC: 7319)

TRANSFER AGENT(S): U.S. Stock Transfer Corporation, Glendale, California.

GETTY IMAGES, INC.

YIELD ...
P/E RATIO ...

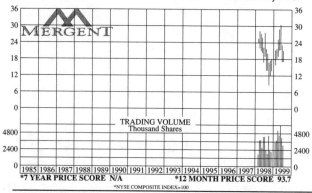

INTERIM EARNINGS (Per Share):

Qtr.	Mar.	June	Sept.	Dec.
1996	---------- 0.06 ----------			
1997	---------- 0.11 ----------			
1998	---------- d1.22 ----------			
1999	d0.26	d0.47	...	...

INTERIM DIVIDENDS (Per Share):

Amt.	Decl.	Ex.	Rec.	Pay.
	No dividends paid.			

CAPITALIZATION (12/31/98):

	($000)	(%)
Long-Term Debt	72,354	17.4
Common & Surplus	343,927	82.6
Total	416,281	100.0

7 YEAR PRICE SCORE N/A   **12 MONTH PRICE SCORE 93.7**
NYSE COMPOSITE INDEX=100

RECENT DEVELOPMENTS: For the quarter ended 6/30/99, the Company reported a net loss of $15.8 million versus a net loss of $14.1 million in 1998. The 1998 results included a nonrecurring charge of $9.1 million and excluded an extraordinary charge of $830,000. Sales grew 14.2% to $55.0 million from $48.1 million a year earlier. Gross profit jumped 17.5% to $40.2 million from $34.2 million in 1998. Operating loss was $14.1 million versus $14.3 million in 1998. On 8/9/99, the Company announced the acquisition of EyeWire, Inc., a provider of royalty-free photography, video, audio, typefaces, software and other design resources to creative professionals and business users. Under the terms of the all-stock transaction, EyeWire shareholders will receive 1.9 million newly issued shares of Getty Images common stock. The acquisition supports and accelerates GETY's strategy of migrating the visual content industry from an analog to a digital platform. EyeWire will be integrated into Getty Images' recently formed Creative Professional division.

BUSINESS

GETTY IMAGES, INC., with 30 million photographs and more than 13,000 hours of film, is an international provider of visual content to a diverse range of professionals in advertising and graphic design, magazine, book and newspaper publishing, broadcasting, production and new media publishing. The Company markets rights to images and footage through its web sites, its international network of wholly-owned offices in 17 countries, and agents in more than 50 countries. The Company has e-commerce enabled Web sites, which allow its customers to shop for, purchase and receive the Company's image products. The Company also promotes its products through print and CD-ROM catalogs, which are distributed to existing and potential customers and through print and Web advertising.

ANNUAL FINANCIAL DATA

	12/31/98	12/31/97	12/31/96	12/31/95
Earnings Per Share	① d1.22	② 0.11	③ 0.06	③ 0.04
Cash Flow Per Share	0.54	0.40	0.15	0.12
Tang. Book Val. Per Share	0.59	1.37	1.12	...
INCOME STATEMENT (IN THOUSANDS):				
Total Revenues	185,084	100,797	54,475	33,918
Costs & Expenses	163,489	81,450	49,370	30,951
Depreciation & Amort.	51,358	11,467	...	...
Operating Income	d29,763	7,880	5,105	2,967
Net Interest Inc./(Exp.)	d2,986	1,187	1,250	891
Income Before Income Taxes	d32,873	7,895	3,659	2,057
Income Taxes	2,680	3,873	1,911	1,187
Net Income	① d35,553	② 4,022	③ 4,248	③ 2,652
Cash Flow	15,805	15,489	4,248	2,652
Average Shs. Outstg.	29,160	38,765	27,832	23,057
BALANCE SHEET (IN THOUSANDS):				
Cash & Cash Equivalents	16,150	29,234	34,441	1,223
Total Current Assets	69,209	60,504	48,684	14,924
Net Property	62,757	39,853	19,692	7,789
Total Assets	462,863	171,638	95,544	45,745
Total Current Liabilities	46,582	37,442	18,741	22,741
Long-Term Obligations	72,354	14,657	10,466	5,606
Net Stockholders' Equity	343,927	119,539	66,167	17,414
Net Working Capital	22,627	23,062	29,943	d7,817
Year-end Shs. Outstg.	30,575	38,317	37,388	23,057
STATISTICAL RECORD:				
Operating Profit Margin %	...	7.8	9.4	8.7
Net Profit Margin %	...	4.0	7.8	7.8
Return on Equity %	...	3.4	6.4	15.2
Return on Assets %	...	2.3	4.4	5.8
Debt/Total Assets %	15.6	8.5	11.0	12.3
Price Range	28¼-8⅝	...	...	...

Statistics are as originally reported. ① Incl. non-recurr. integration & restruct. chrgs. of $13.8 mill. & amort. of intangibles of $37.0 mill.; bef. extraord. loss of $830,000. ② Incl. exps. fr. legal settlement of $974,000 & amort. of intangibles of $3.3 mill. ③ Incl. amort. of intangibles of $1.4 mill., 1996; $1.3 mill., 1995.

OFFICERS:
M. H. Getty, Exec. Chmn.
M. Torrance, Non Exec. Vice-Chmn.
J. D. Klein, C.E.O.
C. J. Roling, C.F.O., Treas.

PRINCIPAL OFFICE: 2101 Fourth Avenue, Fifth Floor, Seattle, WA 98121

TELEPHONE NUMBER: (206) 695-3400
WEB: www.getty-images.com

NO. OF EMPLOYEES: 1,345

SHAREHOLDERS: 76 (approx.)

ANNUAL MEETING: In May

INCORPORATED: DE, Feb., 1998

INSTITUTIONAL HOLDINGS:
No. of Institutions: 67
Shares Held: 12,584,460
% Held: 35.9
INDUSTRY: Business services, nec (SIC: 7389)
TRANSFER AGENT(S): The Bank of New York, New York, NY

GO2NET INC.

YIELD ...
P/E RATIO ...

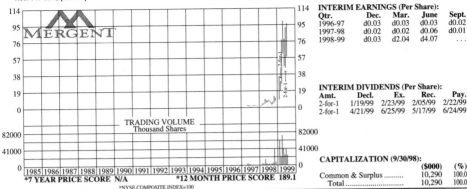

MERGENT

TRADING VOLUME
Thousand Shares

| 1985 | 1986 | 1987 | 1988 | 1989 | 1990 | 1991 | 1992 | 1993 | 1994 | 1995 | 1996 | 1997 | 1998 | 1999 |

*7 YEAR PRICE SCORE N/A   *12 MONTH PRICE SCORE 189.1
*NYSE COMPOSITE INDEX=100

INTERIM EARNINGS (Per Share):

Qtr.	Dec.	Mar.	June	Sept.
1996-97	d0.03	d0.03	d0.03	d0.02
1997-98	d0.02	d0.02	d0.06	d0.01
1998-99	d0.03	d2.04	d4.07	...

INTERIM DIVIDENDS (Per Share):

Amt.	Decl.	Ex.	Rec.	Pay.
2-for-1	1/19/99	2/23/99	2/05/99	2/22/99
2-for-1	4/21/99	6/25/99	5/17/99	6/24/99

CAPITALIZATION (9/30/98):

	($000)	(%)
Common & Surplus	10,290	100.0
Total	10,290	100.0

RECENT DEVELOPMENTS:

For the quarter ended 6/30/99, GNET reported a net loss of $566,946 versus a net loss of $1.36 million in 1998. Results in 1999 included a $883,441 stock compensation charge and a $2.7 million charge for amortization of intangibles. Results in 1998 included a charge of $1.2 million. Revenues soared to $5.7 million from $2.0 million in the prior-year period. Acquisitions completed during the quarter contributed to the improved results. GNET signed a licensing agreement with Intershop Communications, Inc., a supplier of sell-side electronic commerce hosting solutions. Intershop will provide interfaces for setting up on-line storefronts to members of GNET's HyperMart and Virtual Avenue. Also, GNET and Vulcan Ventures Inc. will invest $20.0 million in CommTouch Software, Ltd., and CommTouch will develop e-mail and related services for GNET. The Company completed the acquisitions of Virtual Avenue, USA Online, IQC.com, Haggle Online, and Authorize.Net.

BUSINESS

GO2NET INC. offers a network of branded, technology and community-driven Web sites concentrated in the areas of personal finance, search, commerce and on-line games. GNET operates the following six network properties: Silicon Investor, a financial discussion site; StockSite, which offers articles, portfolio tracking tools, company research and news relating to business and finance; MetaCrawler, an index guide that combines various guides into one service; HyperMart, a provider of free business hosting services; WebMarket, a comparison shopping service; and PlaySite, a multi-player on-line games site. The Go2Net Labs division develops technologies for use on GNET sites and is licensed to other Internet companies. The Company derives revenues through relationships with over 225 advertisers.

ANNUAL FINANCIAL DATA

	9/30/98	9/30/97	② 12/31/96	9/30/96
Earnings Per Share	① d0.10	d0.12	d0.03	d0.04
Cash Flow Per Share	d0.07	d0.11	d0.03	d0.04
Tang. Book Val. Per Share	0.43	0.65	0.08	...
INCOME STATEMENT (IN THOUSANDS):				
Total Revenues	4,831	254	...	...
Costs & Expenses	6,946	2,072	348	412
Depreciation & Amort.	765	171	22	19
Operating Income	d2,880	d1,989	d370	d431
Net Interest Inc./(Exp.)	508	270	7	13
Income Before Income Taxes	d2,371	d1,718	d363	d418
Net Income	① d2,371	d1,718	d363	d418
Cash Flow	d1,606	d1,547	d341	d398
Average Shs. Outstg.	23,128	13,858	10,577	10,195
BALANCE SHEET (IN THOUSANDS):				
Cash & Cash Equivalents	8,415	10,892	693	866
Total Current Assets	9,771	11,096	701	874
Net Property	1,221	509	184	179
Total Assets	11,334	12,620	921	1,066
Total Current Liabilities	1,045	185	33	45
Net Stockholders' Equity	10,290	12,434	888	1,021
Net Working Capital	8,726	10,911	669	829
Year-end Shs. Outstg.	23,757	18,021	10,628	6,476
STATISTICAL RECORD:				
Price Range	12¹⁵/₁₆-1¾	2³/₄-1⁵/₁₆	...	...

Statistics are as originally reported. Adj. for 2-for-1 split, 2/99 & 6/99. ① Incl. $1.4 mill. non-recur., non-cash chgs. rel. to merger & write-down of technology. ② For three months.

OFFICERS:
R. C. Horowitz, Chmn., C.E.O., C.F.O.
J. Keister, Pres.
M. J. Riccio Jr., C.O.O.

PRINCIPAL OFFICE: 999 Third Avenue, Suite 4700, Seattle, WA 98104

TELEPHONE NUMBER: (206) 447-1595
FAX: (206) 447-1625
WEB: www.go2net.com

NO. OF EMPLOYEES: 69 (avg.)

SHAREHOLDERS: 66 (approx.)

ANNUAL MEETING: In Mar.

INCORPORATED: DE, Feb., 1996

INSTITUTIONAL HOLDINGS:
No. of Institutions: 44
Shares Held: 2,585,527 (Adj.)
% Held: 10.0

INDUSTRY: Computers, peripherals & software (SIC: 5045)

TRANSFER AGENT(S): Continental Stock Transfer & Trust Company, New York, NY.

GOTO.COM, INC.

YIELD ...
P/E RATIO ...

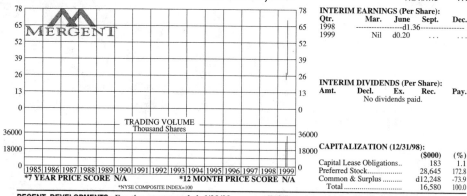

*7 YEAR PRICE SCORE N/A   *12 MONTH PRICE SCORE N/A

*NYSE COMPOSITE INDEX=100

TRADING VOLUME
Thousand Shares

INTERIM EARNINGS (Per Share):

Qtr.	Mar.	June	Sept.	Dec.
1998	------------------d1.36------------------			
1999	Nil	d0.20	...	...

INTERIM DIVIDENDS (Per Share):

Amt.	Decl.	Ex.	Rec.	Pay.
	No dividends paid.			

CAPITALIZATION (12/31/98):

	($000)	(%)
Capital Lease Obligations..	183	1.1
Preferred Stock.................	28,645	172.8
Common & Surplus	d12,248	-73.9
Total	16,580	100.0

RECENT DEVELOPMENTS: For the quarter ended 6/30/99, the Company reported a net loss of $7.0 million compared with $1.7 million in the equivalent 1998 period. Revenue surged to $3.6 million from $19,000 a year earlier. The Company reported gross profit as a percentage of net sales of 63.0% in the 1999 quarter. The Company reported a loss from operations of $8.0 million versus a loss of $1.7 million in the previous year. GOTO raised $120.0 million through its initial public offering and the earlier mezzanine round of financing, which will allow the Company to continue to support the growth it has seen in its advertiser, affiliate and consumer bases. As of 6/30/99, the Company had more than 10,000 advertisers, 80,000 network affiliate locations in its Search Syndication Network™, and an estimated 10.0 million users who benefited from the utilization of GoTo.com, both from its stand-alone site and other sites across its network.

BUSINESS

GOTO.COM, INC. created and operates an on-line marketplace that brings together consumers and advertisers. The Company serves the needs of three constituencies: Internet consumers, advertisers and destination Web sites. GOTO aims to improve a consumer's ability to quickly and easily find relevant search listings for advertisers of information, products and services while also providing advertisers with a cost-effective way to target potential consumers. Consumers conduct keyword searches using the GoTo.com search service at its Web site and at thousands of network affiliate sites across the Internet. Advertisers bid in an ongoing auction for priority placement in the keyword search results, with the highest bidder's site appearing first in the results. Each advertiser pays GOTO the amount of its bid whenever a consumer clicks on an advertiser's listing in the search results. In addition, the Company outsources its search service to destination Web sites as part of its Search Syndication Network.

ANNUAL FINANCIAL DATA

	12/31/98	12/31/97
Earnings Per Share	**d1.36**	**d0.01**
Cash Flow Per Share	**d1.22**	**d0.01**
Tang. Book Val. Per Share	...	0.01
INCOME STATEMENT (IN THOUSANDS):		
Total Revenues	822	22
Costs & Expenses	13,667	136
Depreciation & Amort.	1,493	5
Operating Income	d14,338	d119
Net Interest Inc./(Exp.)	316	...
Income Before Income Taxes	d14,022	d119
Income Taxes	1	1
Net Income	d14,023	d120
Cash Flow	d12,530	d115
Average Shs. Outstg.	10,296	9,869
BALANCE SHEET (IN THOUSANDS):		
Cash & Cash Equivalents	16,357	87
Total Current Assets	18,604	109
Net Property	1,336	54
Total Assets	19,969	214
Total Current Liabilities	3,389	91
Long-Term Obligations	183	...
Net Stockholders' Equity	16,397	123
Net Working Capital	15,215	18
Year-end Shs. Outstg.	10,444	10,017
STATISTICAL RECORD:		
Debt/Total Assets %	0.9	...
Statistics are as originally reported.		

OFFICERS:
R. M. Kavner, Chmn.
J. S. Brewer, C.E.O.
T. Meisel, Pres. & C.O.O.
T. Tappin, C.F.O.

PRINCIPAL OFFICE: 140 West Union Street, Pasadena, CA 91103

TELEPHONE NUMBER: (626) 685-5600
WEB: www.goto. com

NO. OF EMPLOYEES: 83

SHAREHOLDERS: 100 (approx.)

ANNUAL MEETING: N/A

INCORPORATED: DE, Sep., 1997

INSTITUTIONAL HOLDINGS:
No. of Institutions: 5
Shares Held: 230,050
% Held: 0.5
INDUSTRY: Business services, nec (SIC: 7389)
TRANSFER AGENT(S): ChaseMellon Shareholder Services L.L.C., Ridgefield Park, NJ

HARBINGER CORPORATION

YIELD ...
P/E RATIO ...

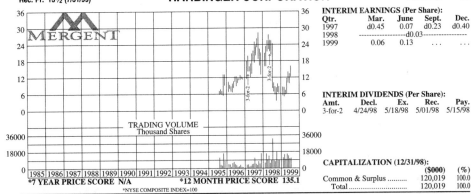

INTERIM EARNINGS (Per Share):

Qtr.	Mar.	June	Sept.	Dec.
1997	d0.45	0.07	d0.23	d0.40
1998		--------------d0.03--------------		
1999	0.06	0.13	...	...

INTERIM DIVIDENDS (Per Share):

Amt.	Decl.	Ex.	Rec.	Pay.
3-for-2	4/24/98	5/18/98	5/01/98	5/15/98

TRADING VOLUME
Thousand Shares

*7 YEAR PRICE SCORE N/A   *12 MONTH PRICE SCORE 135.1
*NYSE COMPOSITE INDEX=100

CAPITALIZATION (12/31/98):

	($000)	(%)
Common & Surplus	120,019	100.0
Total	120,019	100.0

RECENT DEVELOPMENTS: For the quarter ended 6/30/99, net income more than doubled to $5.3 million compared with income from continuing operations of $2.6 million in the corresponding period of 1998. The 1998 results included a nonrecurring pre-tax charge of $5.0 million and excluded a loss of $637,000 from discontinued operations. Total revenues jumped 16.7% to $38.7 million from $33.2 million in 1998. Service revenues improved 20.8% to $26.4 million, while software revenues rose 8.9% to $12.3 mil-

lion. During the quarter, HRBC announced the introduction of HARBINGER® KNOWBILITY™ LOGIC, a data dictionary. KNOWBILITY™ LOGIC is a foundation for structured, accessible data resulting in easier catalog maintenance for suppliers and improved catalog performance for buyers. Separately, the Company invested $15.0 million on revamping its information technology infrastructure to support growth expectations.

BUSINESS

HARBINGER CORPORATION is a worldwide provider of business-to-business electronic commerce products and services and offers comprehensive, customizable standards-based electronic commerce tools. The Company develops, markets and supports software products and provides communication and consulting services that help businesses automate the cycle of transactions for the exchange of goods and services. The Company's core competency is building and managing trading communities for its customers who electronically communicate with each other.

REVENUES

(12/31/1998)	($000)	(%)
Services	88,067	65.2
Software	47,084	34.8
Total	135,151	100.0

ANNUAL FINANCIAL DATA

	12/31/98	12/31/97	12/31/96	12/31/95	12/31/94	12/31/93
Earnings Per Share	③ d0.35	② d1.02	① d0.35	0.05	① d0.14	0.21
Cash Flow Per Share	0.05	d0.56	d0.19	0.14	d0.08	0.26
Tang. Book Val. Per Share	2.53	2.78	0.81	0.93	0.24	0.15
INCOME STATEMENT (IN THOUSANDS):						
Total Revenues	135,151	120,675	41,725	23,117	13,652	10,536
Costs & Expenses	137,109	142,686	39,138	18,316	15,432	8,747
Depreciation & Amort.	10,694	11,005	3,773	1,666	918	647
Operating Income	d12,652	d33,016	d1,186	3,135	d2,698	1,142
Net Interest Inc./(Exp.)	4,830	3,902	156	65	d38	d103
Income Before Income Taxes	d7,822	d29,414	d8,103	1,934	d2,963	998
Income Taxes	705	3,093	146	687	cr1,052	cr2,571
Equity Earnings/Minority Int.	...	d300	d7,073	d1,266	d227	d41
Net Income	③ d8,527	② d32,507	① d8,249	1,247	① d1,911	3,569
Cash Flow	2,167	d21,502	d4,504	2,714	d1,193	3,889
Average Shs. Outstg.	41,557	38,162	24,098	20,097	15,440	15,174
BALANCE SHEET (IN THOUSANDS):						
Cash & Cash Equivalents	92,307	102,144	8,395	11,918	4,642	1,802
Total Current Assets	137,653	147,848	22,516	20,772	10,045	6,710
Net Property	23,150	18,167	6,845	2,107	1,637	
Total Assets	178,369	183,559	42,457	40,260	15,661	12,201
Total Current Liabilities	58,350	53,541	11,164	6,452	7,319	2,920
Long-Term Obligations	...	...	...	...	...	1,978
Net Stockholders' Equity	120,019	130,018	31,293	29,133	5,399	4,337
Net Working Capital	79,303	94,307	11,352	14,320	2,726	3,790
Year-end Shs. Outstg.	40,751	40,829	24,435	21,806	16,643	15,183
STATISTICAL RECORD:						
Operating Profit Margin %	...	...	...	13.6	...	10.8
Net Profit Margin %	...	...	...	5.4	...	33.9
Return on Equity %	...	...	...	4.3	...	82.3
Return on Assets %	...	...	...	3.1	...	29.3
Debt/Total Assets %	...	...	...	...	...	16.2
Price Range	27⁹/₁₆-3½	28⁵/₁₆-11¹¹/₁₆	12⁷/₈-6¹¹/₁₆	13¹/₈-5⁷/₁₆	...	...
P/E Ratio	...	...	...	246.9-102.5	...	...

Statistics are as originally reported. Adjusted for 3-for-2 stock splits 1/31/97 & 5/15/98. ① Incl. nonrecurr. chrg. $4.3 mill., 12/94; $8.8 mill., 12/96. ② Bef. disc. oper. loss $4.1 mill. & extraord. chrg. $2.4 mill., incl. non-recurr. chrg. $51.7 mill. ③ Bef. disc. oper. loss $6.2 mill., but Incl. non-recurr. chrg. $27.0 mill.

OFFICERS:
C. T. Howle, Chmn., C.E.O.
D. T. Leach, Pres., C.O.O.
J. K. McCormick, C.F.O., C.A.O.
J. G. Katz, V.P., Sec.

PRINCIPAL OFFICE: 1277 Lenox Pk. Blvd., Atlanta, GA 30319

TELEPHONE NUMBER: (404) 467-3000
FAX: (404) 841-4364
WEB: www.harbinger.com

NO. OF EMPLOYEES: 975 (approx.)

SHAREHOLDERS: 260 (approx.)

ANNUAL MEETING: In Apr.

INCORPORATED: GA, 1988

INSTITUTIONAL HOLDINGS:
No. of Institutions: 70
Shares Held: 14,284,055
% Held: 37.2

INDUSTRY: Computer programming services (SIC: 7371)

TRANSFER AGENT(S): American Stock Transfer and Trust Company, New York, NY

HEALTHEON CORP.

YIELD   ...
P/E RATIO   ...

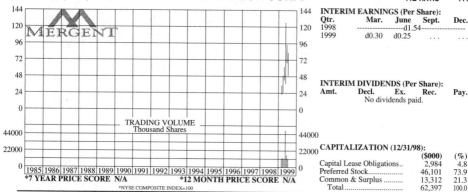

*7 YEAR PRICE SCORE N/A   ***12 MONTH PRICE SCORE N/A**

*NYSE COMPOSITE INDEX=100

TRADING VOLUME
Thousand Shares

INTERIM EARNINGS (Per Share):

Qtr.	Mar.	June	Sept.	Dec.
1998	------------------d1.54----------------			
1999	d0.30	d0.25	...	...

INTERIM DIVIDENDS (Per Share):

Amt.	Decl.	Ex.	Rec.	Pay.
	No dividends paid.			

CAPITALIZATION (12/31/98):

	($000)	(%)
Capital Lease Obligations..	2,984	4.8
Preferred Stock..................	46,101	73.9
Common & Surplus	13,312	21.3
Total	62,397	100.0

RECENT DEVELOPMENTS: For the quarter ended 6/30/99, the Company reported a net loss of $17.6 million compared with a loss of $12.7 million in the corresponding quarter of the previous year. Revenue totaled $22.7 million versus $9.8 million the year before. Operating income decreased to a loss of $18.2 million compared with a loss of $12.8 million the year before. Gross margin, as a percentage of revenue, dropped to 78.9% from 85.8% in the prior-year period. On 4/21/99, HLTH signed an agreement to acquire MedE America. On 5/20/99, the Company signed an agreement to acquire WebMD, Inc., a provider of on line healthcare information and services for physicians and consumers. On 7/1/99, HLTH agreed to acquire Greenberg News Networks, Inc. All three mergers are expected to simultaneously close in the third quarter of 1999. Through co-branded content relationships, Lycos has begun offering WebMD content to its portal visitors, with MSN and Excite to start in August and September, respectively.

BUSINESS

HEALTHEON CORP. offers a suite of healthcare transaction and information services delivered over the Internet or over private intranets and other networks. The Company has designed an Internet-based information and transaction platform that allows it to create Virtual Healthcare Networks that facilitate and streamline interactions among participants in the healthcare industry. Healtheon VHNs enable the secure exchange of healthcare information and support a broad range of healthcare transactions, including enrollment, eligibility determination, referrals and authorizations, laboratory and diagnostic test ordering, clinical data retrieval and claims processing. Healtheon provides its own applications on the Healtheon Platform and also enables third-party applications to operate on its platform.

REVENUES

(12/31/1998)	($000)	(%)
Services	27,102	55.5
Services to rel parties	20,956	42.9
Software licenses.......	780	1.6
Total	48,838	100.0

ANNUAL FINANCIAL DATA

	12/31/98	12/31/97	12/31/96	12/31/95
Earnings Per Share	**d1.54**	**d3.88**	**d2.83**	**d0.85**
Cash Flow Per Share	**d0.89**	**d2.51**	**d1.86**	**d0.78**
INCOME STATEMENT (IN THOUSANDS):				
Total Revenues	48,838	13,390	11,013	2,175
Costs & Expenses	79,830	28,932	21,188	5,752
Depreciation & Amort.	22,956	9,881	6,366	359
Operating Income	d53,948	d25,423	d16,541	d3,936
Net Interest Inc./(Exp.)	790	288	483	202
Income Before Income Taxes	d54,048	d28,005	d18,606	d3,734
Net Income	d54,048	d28,005	d18,606	d3,734
Cash Flow	d24,783	d18,124	d12,240	d4,099
Average Shs. Outstg.	34,987	7,223	6,583	5,246
BALANCE SHEET (IN THOUSANDS):				
Cash & Cash Equivalents	36,817	21,804	7,539	...
Total Current Assets	45,477	26,587	10,677	...
Net Property	12,285	5,500	4,534	...
Total Assets	79,940	53,747	34,407	...
Total Current Liabilities	17,543	11,797	8,172	...
Long-Term Obligations	2,984	932	1,210	...
Net Stockholders' Equity	59,413	d9,930	d14,553	...
Net Working Capital	27,934	14,790	2,505	...
Year-end Shs. Outstg.	54,463	9,437	8,652	8,250
STATISTICAL RECORD:				
Debt/Total Assets %	3.7	1.7	3.5	...
Statistics are as originally reported.				

OFFICERS:
J. H. Clark, Chmn.
W. M. Long, C.E.O.
M. K. Hoover, Pres.
J. L. Westermann III, V.P., C.F.O., Sec., Treas.

PRINCIPAL OFFICE: 4600 Patrick Henry Drive, Santa Clara, CA 95054

TELEPHONE NUMBER: (408) 876-5000
FAX: (408) 876-5010
WEB: www.healtheon.com
NO. OF EMPLOYEES: 648 (avg.)
SHAREHOLDERS: 373
ANNUAL MEETING: In June
INCORPORATED: DE, Dec., 1995

INSTITUTIONAL HOLDINGS:
No. of Institutions: 45
Shares Held: 5,417,381
% Held: 7.6

INDUSTRY: Data processing and preparation (SIC: 7374)

TRANSFER AGENT(S): American Stock Transfer Trust Company, New York, NY

NASDAQ SYMBOL HLYW
Rec. Pr. $17\frac{5}{8}$ (7/31/99)

HOLLYWOOD ENTERTAINMENT CORPORATION

YIELD . . .
P/E RATIO . . .

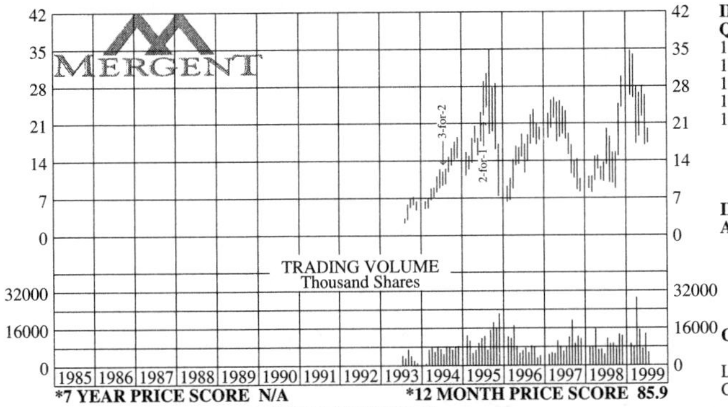

*7 YEAR PRICE SCORE N/A *12 MONTH PRICE SCORE 85.9

*NYSE COMPOSITE INDEX=100

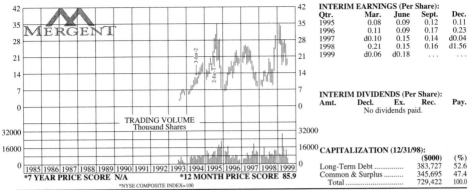

INTERIM EARNINGS (Per Share):

Qtr.	Mar.	June	Sept.	Dec.
1995	0.08	0.09	0.12	0.11
1996	0.11	0.09	0.17	0.23
1997	d0.10	0.15	0.14	d0.04
1998	0.21	0.15	0.16	d1.56
1999	d0.06	d0.18	. . .	. . .

INTERIM DIVIDENDS (Per Share):

Amt.	Decl.	Ex.	Rec.	Pay.

No dividends paid.

CAPITALIZATION (12/31/98):

	($000)	(%)
Long-Term Debt	383,727	52.6
Common & Surplus	345,695	47.4
Total	729,422	100.0

RECENT DEVELOPMENTS: For the three months ended 6/30/99, the Company reported a net loss of $8.3 million compared with net income of $5.7 million in the corresponding period of the previous year. Total revenues advanced 50.2% to $250.4 million from $166.7 million in the prior-year quarter. Rental revenue was $205.6 million, up 45.2% versus $141.6 million a year ago. Product sales jumped 77.8% to $44.7 million from $25.2 million the year before. Hollywood Video reported revenue of $242.0 million, while the Company's Web site Reel.com reported revenue of $8.4 million. During the second quarter, the Company opened 81 new stores and had a total of 1,403 video superstores in 43 states and the District of Columbia.

BUSINESS

HOLLYWOOD ENTERTAINMENT CORPORATION owns and operates Hollywood Video, the second largest video store chain in the U.S. with 1,260 retail superstores in 42 states, and Reel.com, an on-line video only retailer. The Company's superstores are an average size of 7,200 square feet and carry over 12,000 videocassettes. Reel.com (www.reel.com) offers over 100,000 VHS titles and 2,300 DVD titles for sale. In addition, the Web site offers proprietary information about movies including descriptions, ratings, critics' reviews, recommendations and links to star filmographics, which entertain consumers and help them select and purchase movies via the Internet. At 12/31/98, the Company's on-line customer base was estimated to be more than 400,000.

REVENUES

(12/31/98)	($000)	(%)
Hollywood Video	756,658	99.1
Reel.com	7,250	0.9
Total	763,908	100.0

ANNUAL FINANCIAL DATA

	12/31/98	12/31/97	12/31/96	12/31/95	12/31/94	12/31/93	12/31/92
Earnings Per Share	**[4] d1.30**	**[3] 0.15**	**0.59**	**[2] 0.36**	**0.32**	**0.14**	**[1] 0.09**
Cash Flow Per Share	**3.77**	**3.86**	**3.06**	**1.79**	**1.09**	**0.39**	**0.34**
Tang. Book Val. Per Share	**3.64**	**5.33**	**6.75**	**3.14**	**2.58**	**0.73**	**0.18**
INCOME STATEMENT (IN THOUSANDS):							
Total Revenues	763,908	500,501	302,342	149,430	73,288	17,339	11,044
Costs & Expenses	604,972	318,619	176,809	84,601	40,852	9,760	6,318
Depreciation & Amort.	196,849	140,201	87,115	47,292	19,826	3,936	2,456
Operating Income	d37,913	41,681	38,418	17,537	12,610	3,643	2,270
Net Interest Inc./(Exp.)	d31,752	d13,464	d4,136	1,124	d109	d237	d321
Income Before Income Taxes	d69,665	9,343	34,282	18,661	12,502	3,407	1,957
Income Taxes	cr19,201	3,784	13,652	6,875	4,359	1,400	cr50
Net Income	[4] d50,464	[3] 5,559	20,630	[2] 11,786	8,143	2,007	2,007
Cash Flow	146,385	145,760	107,745	59,078	27,969	5,943	4,148
Average Shs. Outstg.	38,844	37,718	35,159	32,962	25,578	15,357	12,936
BALANCE SHEET (IN THOUSANDS):							
Cash & Cash Equivalents	3,975	3,909	12,849	29,980	39,017	9,606	1,013
Total Current Assets	115,058	111,445	87,121	73,680	54,060	11,483	2,146
Net Property	328,182	234,497	115,812	65,958	14,606	3,550	1,793
Total Assets	934,434	689,123	449,783	334,660	142,861	22,791	7,475
Total Current Liabilities	179,879	143,843	80,728	55,947	26,322	6,458	3,325
Long-Term Obligations	383,727	231,155	82,156	355	2,470	1,636	1,332
Net Stockholders' Equity	345,695	289,896	274,703	217,783	110,765	13,303	2,283
Net Working Capital	d64,821	d32,398	6,393	17,733	27,738	5,025	d1,179
Year-end Shs. Outstg.	43,933	36,786	26,006	36,007	28,984	18,152	12,975
STATISTICAL RECORD:							
Operating Profit Margin %	. . .	8.3	12.7	11.7	17.2	21.0	20.6
Net Profit Margin %	. . .	1.1	6.8	7.9	11.1	11.6	18.2
Return on Equity %	. . .	1.9	7.5	5.4	7.4	15.1	87.9
Return on Assets %	. . .	0.8	4.6	3.5	5.7	8.8	26.8
Debt/Total Assets %	41.1	33.5	18.3	0.1	1.7	7.2	17.8
Price Range	$29\frac{7}{8}$-8	$25\frac{7}{8}$-$8\frac{1}{8}$	$23\frac{5}{8}$-$6\frac{1}{4}$	35-$7\frac{3}{8}$	$18\frac{7}{16}$-5	$7\frac{1}{4}$-$2\frac{5}{16}$	. . .
P/E Ratio	. . .	172.4-54.1	40.0-10.6	97.2-20.5	57.6-15.6	51.7-16.7	. . .

Statistics are as originally reported. Adj. for stk. splits: 2-for-1, 7/28/95; 3-for-2, 7/8/94 [1] Pro forma [2] Bef. acctg. change chrg. $2.6 mill. ($0.08/sh.) [3] Incl. non-recurr. chrg. $18.9 mill; bef. extraord. chrg. $563,000 [4] Bef. nonrecurr. chrg. $101.8 mill.

OFFICERS:
M. J. Wattles, Chmn., C.E.O.
J. B. Yapp, Pres., C.O.O.
D. G. Martin, Exec. V.P., C.F.O.
D. J. Ekman, Sr. V.P., Sec., Gen. Couns.

PRINCIPAL OFFICE: 9275 SW Peyton Lane, Wilsonville, OR 97070

TELEPHONE NUMBER: (503) 570-1600
FAX: (503) 570-1681
WEB: www.hollywoodvideo.com

NO. OF EMPLOYEES: 22,197 (approx.)

SHAREHOLDERS: 211

ANNUAL MEETING: N/A

INCORPORATED: OR, Jun., 1988

INSTITUTIONAL HOLDINGS:
No. of Institutions: 98
Shares Held: 26,244,880
% Held: 57.6

INDUSTRY: Video tape rental (SIC: 7841)

TRANSFER AGENT(S): Continental Stock Transfer & Trust Company, New York, New York.

NASDAQ SYMBOL HCOM
Rec. Pr. 5¹³/₁₆ (7/31/99)

HOMECOM COMMUNICATIONS INC.

YIELD ...
P/E RATIO ...

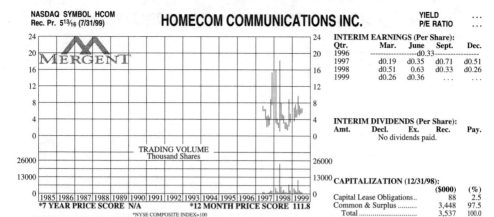

*7 YEAR PRICE SCORE N/A   *12 MONTH PRICE SCORE 111.8

*NYSE COMPOSITE INDEX=100

INTERIM EARNINGS (Per Share):

Qtr.	Mar.	June	Sept.	Dec.
1996	--------------------d0.33--------------------			
1997	d0.19	d0.35	d0.71	d0.51
1998	d0.51	0.63	d0.33	d0.26
1999	d0.26	d0.36	...	...

INTERIM DIVIDENDS (Per Share):

Amt.	Decl.	Ex.	Rec.	Pay.
No dividends paid.				

CAPITALIZATION (12/31/98):

	($000)	(%)
Capital Lease Obligations..	88	2.5
Common & Surplus	3,448	97.5
Total	3,537	100.0

RECENT DEVELOPMENTS: For the quarter ended 6/30/99, the Company reported a net loss of $2.4 million compared with net income of $2.8 million in the equivalent quarter of 1998. Results in 1998 included a $4.4 million non-operating gain from the sale of HCOM's HostAmerica business. Revenues jumped to $2.0 million from $900,000 in the prior-year period. Revenues benefited from the inclusion of First Institutional Marketing, Inc., which was acquired on 3/24/99, and stronger sales from the FAST custom applica-

tion development group. On 8/10/99, the Company announced that it reached an agreement with AlternetWorx, Inc., in which HCOM will be the exclusive provider of on-line insurance services for Passport-to-Wealth™, a fully-interactive benefits and resource membership program. Also, the Company agreed to provide an Internet distribution channel for The AIG Life Insurance Companies life insurance and annuity products. Terms of the agreements were not disclosed.

BUSINESS

HOMECOM COMMUNICATIONS INC. is a developer and marketer of specialized software applications, products and services which provide consumers and financial institutions the technology necessary to develop and integrate an on-line marketplace. The Company focuses on financial applications and solutions targeted for the financial services market, including banking, insurance, and securities brokerage firms. The Company operates in four integrated business units: HomeCom Financial Applications, Solutions and Technology; HomeCom's Financial Solutions; HomeCom Internet Security Services; and HomeCom's InsureRate™. On 3/24/99, the Company acquired First Institutional Marketing, Inc., a provider of insurance products and marketing programs for the commercial banking industry.

REVENUES

(12/31/98)	($000)	(%)
Service Sales	2,941	89.3
Equipment Sales........	351	10.7
Total	3,292	100.0

ANNUAL FINANCIAL DATA

	12/31/98	12/31/97	12/31/96	12/31/95	[1] 12/31/94
Earnings Per Share	[2] d0.44	d1.88	d0.33	Nil	d0.01
Cash Flow Per Share	d0.22	d1.52	d0.29	...	d0.01
Tang. Book Val. Per Share	0.61	0.65	...	4.81	...
INCOME STATEMENT (IN THOUSANDS):					
Total Revenues	3,292	2,879	2,299	328	...
Costs & Expenses	7,672	6,386	2,792	326	17
Depreciation & Amort.	949	924	88	4	...
Operating Income	d5,328	d4,431	d581	d2	d17
Net Interest Inc./(Exp.)	d445	d543	d51	d3	...
Income Before Income Taxes	d1,204	d4,881	d626	d5	d17
Net Income	[2] d1,204	d4,881	d626	d5	d17
Cash Flow	d922	d3,958	d538	d2	d17
Average Shs. Outstg.	4,287	2,603	1,880	1,850	1,850
BALANCE SHEET (IN THOUSANDS):					
Cash & Cash Equivalents	2,542	3,188	332	129	...
Total Current Assets	3,228	3,659	821	216	...
Net Property	797	628	359	30	...
Total Assets	4,565	4,665	1,727	247	...
Total Current Liabilities	962	937	2,126	82	...
Long-Term Obligations	88	1,652	148	161	...
Net Stockholders' Equity	3,448	1,957	d621	5	...
Net Working Capital	2,266	2,722	d1,305	134	...
Year-end Shs. Outstg.	5,072	2,956	1,923	1	...
STATISTICAL RECORD:					
Debt/Total Assets %	1.9	35.4	8.6	65.0	...
Price Range	18¼-1⅛	15⅜-2⅛	...	...	...

Statistics are as originally reported. [1] For one month only. [2] Incl. $4.4 mill. non-operating gain.

H. W. Sax, Pres., C.E.O.
N. H. Smith, V.P., C.F.O.
N. Stricklen, Sr. V.P.
K. Puri, Exec. V.P.

PRINCIPAL OFFICE: Building 14, Suite 100, 3535 Piedmont Road, Atlanta, GA 30305

TELEPHONE NUMBER: (404) 237-4646
FAX: (404) 237-3060
WEB: www.homecom.com
NO. OF EMPLOYEES: 103
SHAREHOLDERS: N/A
ANNUAL MEETING: In Jun.
INCORPORATED: DE, Dec., 1994

No. of Institutions: 3
Shares Held: 134,244
% Held: 2.0

INDUSTRY: Computer programming services (SIC: 7371)

TRANSFER AGENT(S): American Stock Transfer & Trust Company, New York, NY.

HOOVER'S INC.

YIELD ...
P/E RATIO ...

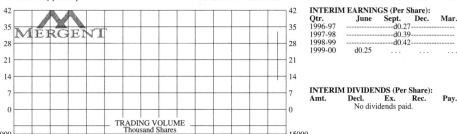

*7 YEAR PRICE SCORE N/A   *12 MONTH PRICE SCORE N/A

*NYSE COMPOSITE INDEX=100

INTERIM EARNINGS (Per Share):

Qtr.	June	Sept.	Dec.	Mar.
1996-97		----------------d0.27----------------		
1997-98		----------------d0.39----------------		
1998-99		----------------d0.42----------------		
1999-00	d0.25	...	...	...

INTERIM DIVIDENDS (Per Share):

Amt.	Decl.	Ex.	Rec.	Pay.
		No dividends paid.		

CAPITALIZATION (3/31/99):

	($000)	(%)
Long-Term Debt	98	1.4
Capital Lease Obligations..	70	1.0
Common & Surplus	6,760	97.6
Total	6,928	100.0

RECENT DEVELOPMENTS: For the quarter ended 6/30/99, HOOV reported a net loss of $1.8 million versus a net loss of $700,000 in 1998. This reflects increased spending for sales and marketing, product development and technology. Meanwhile, total revenues advanced 68.4% to $3.2 million versus $1.9 million in 1998, driven by an 82.0% increase in on-line information sales and a 174.0% jump in advertising, e-commerce and sponsership revenues. On 7/13/99, HOOV announced that it expanded its relationship with Dow Jones & Company to include e-commerce, content licensing to Dow Jones and advertising on Hoover's Online. Under the terms of the agreement, HOOV's Company Information will be featured within Dow Jones Interactive (www.djinteractive.com). As part of the agreement, Hoover's Online is integrating the content of the Dow Jones Interactive's Publications Library, a searchable archive of more than 6,000 publications, into the Hoover's Web site. Also, HOOV will supply Dow Jones Interactive with in-depth officer, product, sales and competitive information for major entities throughout the world.

BUSINESS

HOOVER'S INC. is an Internet provider of proprietary company and industry information designed to meet the diverse needs of business organizations, businesspeople and investment professionals worldwide. The Company's core asset is its proprietary editorial content, which includes information on nearly 14,000 public and private enterprises worldwide and 45 industry sectors. HOOV continually expands and updates its database of company and industry information as well as offers its branded search and sort tools, such as Lead Finder and StockScreener, to make information more useful to businesspeople. HOOV also provides information on initial public offerings through IPO Central, feature stories, news, career information, personal finance information, SEC documents, management biographical information, brokerage reports and credit reports. For the quarter ended 6/30/99, the Company's Web site attracted about 1.9 million visitors who accounted for 35.0 million page views (the total number of pages accessed on HOOV's Web site).

ANNUAL FINANCIAL DATA

	3/31/99	3/31/98	3/31/97
Earnings Per Share	d0.42	d0.39	d0.27
Cash Flow Per Share	d0.26	d0.33	d0.24
Tang. Book Val. Per Share	0.97	0.79	...
INCOME STATEMENT (IN THOUSANDS):			
Total Revenues	9,229	5,182	3,360
Costs & Expenses	10,740	6,779	4,142
Depreciation & Amort.	865	273	90
Operating Income	d2,376	d1,870	d873
Net Interest Inc./(Exp.)	121	83	d71
Income Before Income Taxes	d2,255	d1,788	d944
Net Income	d2,255	d1,788	d944
Cash Flow	d1,390	d1,515	d854
Average Shs. Outstg.	5,314	4,569	3,527
BALANCE SHEET (IN THOUSANDS):			
Cash & Cash Equivalents	7,814	3,860	...
Total Current Assets	8,853	5,031	...
Net Property	1,097	724	...
Total Assets	10,076	5,772	...
Total Current Liabilities	3,148	1,604	...
Long-Term Obligations	168	172	...
Net Stockholders' Equity	6,760	3,995	...
Net Working Capital	5,705	3,427	...
Year-end Shs. Outstg.	6,941	5,071	4,064
STATISTICAL RECORD:			
Debt/Total Assets %	1.7	3.0	...
Statistics are as originally reported.			

OFFICERS:
P. J. Spain, Chmn., Pres., C.E.O.
L. Atchison, Sr. V.P., Fin., C.F.O.
C. G. Shepard, Exec. V.P., C.O.O.

PRINCIPAL OFFICE: 1033 La Posada Drive #250, Austin, TX 78752

TELEPHONE NUMBER: (512) 374-4500
WEB: www.hoovers.com

NO. OF EMPLOYEES: 162

SHAREHOLDERS: N/A

ANNUAL MEETING: N/A

INCORPORATED: N/A

INSTITUTIONAL HOLDINGS:
No. of Institutions: N/A
Shares Held: N/A
% Held: N/A

INDUSTRY: Business services, nec (SIC: 7389)

TRANSFER AGENT(S): Continental Stock Transfer & Trust Company, New York, NY

IDT CORPORATION

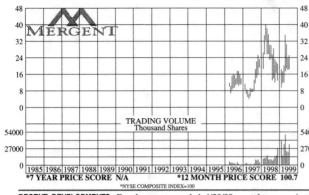

INTERIM EARNINGS (Per Share):

Qtr.	Oct.	Jan.	Apr.	July
1995-96	----	---d0.85---		
1996-97	----	---d0.18---		
1997-98	----	---d0.22---		
1998-99	0.15	0.06	0.06	...

INTERIM DIVIDENDS (Per Share):

Amt.	Decl.	Ex.	Rec.	Pay.
	No dividends paid.			

TRADING VOLUME
Thousand Shares

1985 1986 1987 1988 1989 1990 1991 1992 1993 1994 1995 1996 1997 1998 1999

*7 YEAR PRICE SCORE N/A   ***12 MONTH PRICE SCORE 100.7**

*NYSE COMPOSITE INDEX=100

CAPITALIZATION (7/31/98):

	($000)	(%)
Long-Term Debt	101,834	28.6
Capital Lease Obligations..	11,232	3.2
Minority Interest	3,896	1.1
Common & Surplus	238,748	67.1
Total	355,710	100.0

RECENT DEVELOPMENTS: For the quarter ended 4/30/99, net income fell 57.5% to $2.1 million from $4.8 million in the 1998. Earnings were hampered by the inclusion of $2.1 million in income taxes for the 1999 period, whereas IDTC had no cash tax liability in the prior-year period. Profits were also restricted by a 4.5 percentage point increase in total costs and expenses as a percentage of revenues to 97.5% from 94.8% in 1998. Revenues more than doubled to $191.8 million from $87.1 million a year earlier. This increase was attributed to a 126.7% surge in revenues in the telecommunications business to $179.2 million. The carrier business reported a 69.9% leap in revenues to $75.4 million. IDTC's retail division posted a record $98.8 million in revenues. Internet revenues declined 19.2% to $4.2 million from $5.2 million in the year-earlier quarter. The Company recently expanded its Internet division to offer a more diverse range of services. In addition, IDTC recently launched Nuestra Voz, the nation's first pre-paid bilingual Internet service.

BUSINESS

IDT CORPORATION is a multi-national carrier that provides its wholesale and retail customers with integrated, international and domestic long distance telecommunications services, Internet access and, through its NET2PHONE products and services, Internet telephony services. The Company delivers these services over a high-quality network consisting of 60 switches in the U.S. and Europe and owned and leased capacity on 16 undersea fiber optic cables. In addition, the Company obtains additional transmission capacity from other carriers.

ANNUAL FINANCIAL DATA

	7/31/98	7/31/97	7/31/96	7/31/95	7/31/94	7/31/93
Earnings Per Share	②d0.22	d0.18	①d0.85	d0.13	d0.02	0.02
Cash Flow Per Share	0.18	0.05	d0.78	d0.11	d0.01	0.02
Tang. Book Val. Per Share	7.20	1.10	1.29	0.06	0.13	...
INCOME STATEMENT (IN THOUSANDS):						
Total Revenues	335,373	135,187	57,694	11,664	3,169	1,675
Costs & Expenses	327,835	133,759	72,237	13,535	3,392	1,292
Depreciation & Amort.	11,284	4,873	1,212	304	106	79
Operating Income	d3,746	d3,445	d15,755	d2,175	d329	305
Net Interest Inc./(Exp.)	d396	d427	345	15	23	d18
Income Before Income Taxes	d4,038	d3,837	d15,410	d2,145	d298	302
Income Taxes	cr1,671	...	...	...	...	...
Equity Earnings/Minority Int.	d3,896	...	...	...	...	...
Net Income	②d6,263	d3,837	①d15,410	d2,145	d298	302
Cash Flow	5,021	1,036	d14,198	d1,841	d193	381
Average Shs. Outstg.	28,571	21,153	18,180	16,569	16,569	16,569
BALANCE SHEET (IN THOUSANDS):						
Cash & Cash Equivalents	175,592	7,674	14,894	232	1,052	...
Total Current Assets	227,867	29,017	30,501	2,402	2,022	...
Net Property	75,332	25,726	12,453	1,770	748	...
Total Assets	417,196	58,537	43,797	4,197	2,795	...
Total Current Liabilities	61,487	24,131	16,955	3,286	733	...
Long-Term Obligations	113,066	9,147	...	...	...	...
Net Stockholders' Equity	238,748	25,259	26,843	911	2,062	...
Net Working Capital	166,381	4,887	13,547	d884	1,289	...
Year-end Shs. Outstg.	22,849	21,812	20,841	15,666	15,666	...
STATISTICAL RECORD:						
Operating Profit Margin %	...	...	...	...	...	18.2
Net Profit Margin %	...	...	...	...	...	18.1
Debt/Total Assets %	27.1	15.6	...	...	...	...
Price Range	40¼-11⅞	25¼-4	17½-6¾	...	...	...

Statistics are as originally reported. ① Excl. extraord. loss on retire. of debt of $234,000. ② Excl. extraord. loss on retire. of debt of $132,000, but incl. non-recurr. chrgs. of $25.0 mill. related to acquired research and development.

OFFICERS:
H. S. Jonas, Chmn., C.E.O.
J. Courter, Vice-Chmn., Pres.
S. R. Brown, C.F.O.
J. J. Mason, Sec.

PRINCIPAL OFFICE: 190 Main Street, Hackensack, NJ 07601

TELEPHONE NUMBER: (201) 928-1000
WEB: www.idt.net
NO. OF EMPLOYEES: 712
SHAREHOLDERS: 345
ANNUAL MEETING: In Dec.
INCORPORATED: NY, Aug., 1990; reincorp., DE, Dec., 1995

INSTITUTIONAL HOLDINGS:
No. of Institutions: 49
Shares Held: 4,846,478
% Held: 20.7
INDUSTRY: Computer integrated systems design (SIC: 7373)
TRANSFER AGENT(S): American Stock Transfer & Trust Company, New York, NY

IMALL, INC.

YIELD ...
P/E RATIO ...

INTERIM EARNINGS (Per Share):

Qtr.	Mar.	June	Sept.	Dec.
1996	------------------ 0.01 -----------------			
1997	d0.01	d0.01	d0.02	d0.60
1998	d0.22	d0.39	d0.34	d0.65
1999	d0.28	d0.25	...	...

INTERIM DIVIDENDS (Per Share):

Amt.	Decl.	Ex.	Rec.	Pay.
	No dividends paid.			

CAPITALIZATION (12/31/98):

	($000)	(%)
Preferred Stock.................	16,412	153.2
Common & Surplus	d5,697	-53.2
Total	10,714	100.0

RECENT DEVELOPMENTS: For the quarter ended 6/30/99, the Company reported a net loss of $4.4 million compared with a net loss from continuing operations of $2.3 million in the corresponding quarter a year earlier. Revenue more than tripled to $801,600 from $265,600 in the previous-year quarter. On July 13, 1999, the Company and Excite@Home entered into an agreement for the acquisition of IMAL in a transaction valued at approximately $425 million. Under the agreement, shareholders of the Company's stock will receive 0.46 shares of Excite@Home series A common stock for each share of IMAL common stock held. The transaction is subject to regulatory approvals and is expected to close in the fourth quarter of 1999. Upon completion, the Company will operate as a subsidiary of Excite@Home reporting to its @Work division.

BUSINESS

IMALL, INC. provides electronic commerce services and solutions to small and medium size businesses. The Company's integrated e-commerce solution allows businesses to build Web sites, automatically add electronic commerce services (such as electronic catalogues, product searching, shopping cart services, sales tax and shipping calculations, and sales tracking information), acquire a merchant account on-line within hours and securely process all major credit cards in real time. On 3/8/99, the Company acquired all of the outstanding common shares of Pure Payments, Inc.

ANNUAL FINANCIAL DATA

	12/31/98	12/31/97	12/31/96
Earnings Per Share	d1.61	d0.63	...
Cash Flow Per Share	d1.31	d0.55	0.05
Tang. Book Val. Per Share	...	...	0.07
INCOME STATEMENT (IN THOUSANDS):			
Total Revenues	1,596	16,777	16,047
Costs & Expenses	12,705	21,063	15,768
Depreciation & Amort.	634	496	306
Operating Income	d11,743	d4,783	d27
Net Interest Inc./(Exp.)	575	d77	d3
Income Before Income Taxes	d11,086	d4,720	103
Income Taxes	...	cr17	38
Net Income	d11,086	d4,703	65
Cash Flow	d10,452	d4,207	371
Average Shs. Outstg.	8,008	7,680	7,253
BALANCE SHEET (IN THOUSANDS):			
Cash & Cash Equivalents	11,181	5,537	40
Total Current Assets	12,015	16,165	967
Net Property	2,085	610	1,032
Total Assets	14,502	17,056	2,343
Total Current Liabilities	3,788	2,691	1,598
Long-Term Obligations	...	11	32
Net Stockholders' Equity	10,714	14,354	714
Net Working Capital	8,227	13,474	d630
Year-end Shs. Outstg.	10,636	7,652	7,411
STATISTICAL RECORD:			
Net Profit Margin %	...	...	0.4
Return on Equity %	...	...	9.1
Return on Assets %	...	...	2.8
Debt/Total Assets %	...	0.1	1.3
Price Range	32³⁄₄-4	36-3¹⁄₄	360-14¹⁄₂

Statistics are as originally reported.

OFFICERS:
R. Rosenblatt, C.E.O.
A. P. Mazarella, V.P., C.F.O.

PRINCIPAL OFFICE: 233 Wilshire Boulevard, Suite 820, Santa Monica, CA 90401

TELEPHONE NUMBER: (310) 309-4000
WEB: www.imall.com

NO. OF EMPLOYEES: 65

SHAREHOLDERS: 575 (approx.)

ANNUAL MEETING: In Feb.

INCORPORATED: UT, Feb., 1984; reincorp., NV, Jan., 1996

INSTITUTIONAL HOLDINGS:
No. of Institutions: 17
Shares Held: 3,201,921
% Held: 18.1

INDUSTRY: Computer related services, nec (SIC: 7379)

TRANSFER AGENT(S): American Stock Transfer and Trust Co., New York, NY

INFONAUTICS, INC.

YIELD ...
P/E RATIO ...

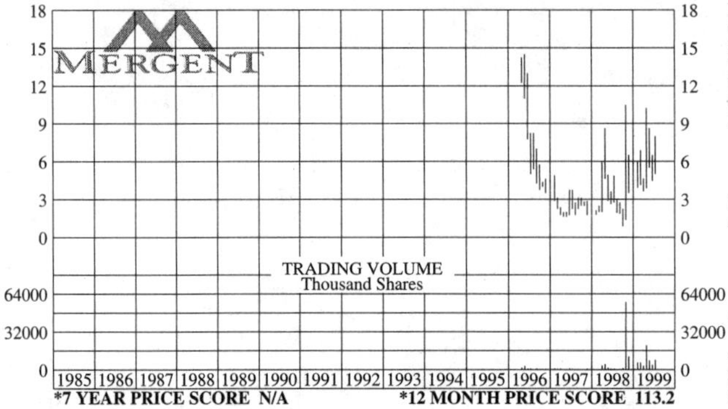

TRADING VOLUME
Thousand Shares

| 1985 | 1986 | 1987 | 1988 | 1989 | 1990 | 1991 | 1992 | 1993 | 1994 | 1995 | 1996 | 1997 | 1998 | 1999 |

*7 YEAR PRICE SCORE N/A　　　　***12 MONTH PRICE SCORE 113.2**

*NYSE COMPOSITE INDEX=100

INTERIM EARNINGS (Per Share):

Qtr.	Mar.	June	Sept.	Dec.
1995	d0.17	d0.23	d0.34	d0.49
1996	d0.50	d0.31	d0.36	d0.48
1997	d0.56	d0.44	d0.41	d0.42
1998	d0.49	d0.50	d0.44	d0.34
1999	d0.25	d0.20	...	...

INTERIM DIVIDENDS (Per Share):

Amt.	Decl.	Ex.	Rec.	Pay.
	No dividends paid.			

CAPITALIZATION (12/31/98):

	($000)	(%)
Capital Lease Obligations..	47	...
Preferred Stock..............	258	...
Common & Surplus	d3,557	...
Total	d-3,251	100.0

RECENT DEVELOPMENTS: For the quarter ended 6/30/99, INFO reported a net loss of $2.4 million compared with a net loss of $4.8 million in 1998. Total revenues advanced 66.9% to $6.0 million from $3.6 million in the prior year. Loss from operations was $1.9 million versus $4.8 million a year earlier. Sales bookings, which represent non-cancelable customer commitments that convert to revenue over the life of the contract, jumped 46.6% to $8.5 million from $5.8 million the year before. INFO's deferred revenue and backlog increased 20.0% over the first quarter to $15.5 million. On 7/8/99, INFO and Bell & Howell Company announced that they have signed a definitive agreement to create a new, as-yet-to-be-named company, which will combine both firms' K-12 reference businesses. The Company will contribute its school and ELECTRIC LIBRARY® business and will receive 27.0% of the new company. In connection with the transaction, INFO will receive $22.0 million in cash.

BUSINESS

INFONAUTICS, INC. is an Internet information company that provides content-rich research and reference services to schools, libraries, individuals and businesses. The Company's Web properties include Company SLEUTH™, ELECTRIC LIBRARY®, JOB SLEUTH™, SPORTS SLEUTH™, ENCYCLOPEDIA.COM™ and RESEARCHPAPER.COM™. Company SLEUTH offers free, legal information about publicly-traded companies. ELECTRIC LIBRARY is a paid subscription site that offers electronic reference products for schools and libraries, serving more than 17,000 institutions in all 50 states. JOB SLEUTH is a free service that searches the Internet's top job sites and databases for opportunies that match its users' profiles. SPORTS SLEUTH offers free, personalized sports news information. ENCYCLOPEDIA.COM is a basic, easy-to-use research tool for anyone on the Web. RESEARCHPAPER.COM provides high school and college students with assistance in researching and writing term papers.

ANNUAL FINANCIAL DATA

	12/31/98	12/31/97	12/31/96	12/31/95	12/31/94	12/31/93
Earnings Per Share	d1.77	d1.83	d1.65	d1.23	d0.72	d0.16
Cash Flow Per Share	d1.61	d1.70	d1.58	d1.19	d0.68	d0.15
Tang. Book Val. Per Share	...	1.10	2.92	...	0.01	...
INCOME STATEMENT (IN THOUSANDS):						
Total Revenues	14,925	6,832	1,442	448	...	...
Costs & Expenses	30,902	23,973	15,813	7,696	3,415	491
Depreciation & Amort.	1,625	1,221	613	247	175	34
Operating Income	d17,602	d18,363	d14,984	d7,495	d3,590	d525
Net Interest Inc./(Exp.)	154	1,004	1,198	14	d110	d31
Income Before Income Taxes	d17,448	d17,359	d13,786	d7,481	d3,699	d555
Net Income	d17,448	d17,359	d13,786	d7,481	d3,699	d555
Cash Flow	d15,823	d16,138	d13,173	d7,234	d3,524	d522
Average Shs. Outstg.	9,831	9,492	8,348	6,062	5,169	3,428
BALANCE SHEET (IN THOUSANDS):						
Cash & Cash Equivalents	3,268	12,397	27,379	962	718	...
Total Current Assets	7,352	15,093	28,381	1,430	775	...
Net Property	2,573	3,020	1,701	816	373	...
Total Assets	10,192	18,794	30,227	2,532	1,254	...
Total Current Liabilities	12,913	7,930	2,540	2,943	999	...
Long-Term Obligations	47	404	...	138	204	...
Net Stockholders' Equity	d3,298	10,460	27,688	d549	51	...
Net Working Capital	d5,561	7,163	25,841	d1,514	d224	...
Year-end Shs. Outstg.	11,623	9,492	9,489	6,036	3,963	...
STATISTICAL RECORD:						
Debt/Total Assets %	0.5	2.2	...	5.5	16.3	...
Price Range	10½-0⅞	4⅞-1⅝	14½-3½	...	...	...

Statistics are as originally reported.

OFFICERS:
D. V. Morris, Pres., C.E.O.
F. F. O'Brien, Acting C.F.O.
J. M. Kopelman, Exec. V.P., Sec.
G. J. Lewis Jr., V.P., Couns., Asst. Sec.

PRINCIPAL OFFICE: 900 West Valley Road, Suite 400, Wayne, PA 19087

TELEPHONE NUMBER: (610) 971-8840
FAX: (610) 971-8859
WEB: www.infonautics.com
NO. OF EMPLOYEES: 164 full-time; 11 part-time
SHAREHOLDERS: 197 (approximately); 6,823 (beneficial)
ANNUAL MEETING: In May
INCORPORATED: PA, Nov., 1992

INSTITUTIONAL HOLDINGS:
No. of Institutions: 9
Shares Held: 819,064
% Held: 8.6

INDUSTRY: Data processing and preparation (SIC: 7374)

TRANSFER AGENT(S): American Stock Transfer & Trust Company, New York, NY

NASDAQ SYMBOL SEEK
Rec. Pr. 38¹/₁₆ (7/31/99)

INFOSEEK CORP.

YIELD ...
P/E RATIO ...

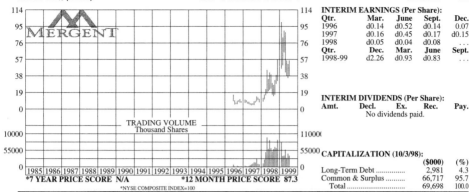

INTERIM EARNINGS (Per Share):

Qtr.	Mar.	June	Sept.	Dec.
1996	d0.14	d0.52	d0.14	0.07
1997	d0.16	d0.45	d0.17	d0.15
1998	d0.05	d0.04	d0.08	...

Qtr.	Dec.	Mar.	June	Sept.
1998-99	d2.26	d0.93	d0.83	...

INTERIM DIVIDENDS (Per Share):

Amt.	Decl.	Ex.	Rec.	Pay.
No dividends paid.				

*7 YEAR PRICE SCORE N/A *12 MONTH PRICE SCORE 87.3
*NYSE COMPOSITE INDEX=100

TRADING VOLUME
Thousand Shares

CAPITALIZATION (10/3/98):

	($000)	(%)
Long-Term Debt	2,981	4.3
Common & Surplus	66,717	95.7
Total	69,698	100.0

RECENT DEVELOPMENTS: On 7/12/99, The Walt Disney Company reached an agreement with SEEK to combine its Buena Vista Internet Group with SEEK by the end of the calendar year, creating a single Internet business called go.com. A new common stock, which is expected to be traded on the New York Stock Exchange under the symbol GO, will be issued. Shareholders of Infoseek will receive 1.15 shares of the new stock for each share held. For the quarter ended 7/3/99, the Company reported a net loss of $51.3 million compared with a loss of $1.3 million in the corresponding quarter of the previous year. Earnings for the 1999 period included costs of $29.0 million related to the amortization of goodwill, and a loss of $2.6 million from joint ventures. Total revenues more than doubled to $36.1 million from $17.1 million a year earlier. Advertising revenues jumped to $33.2 million from $15.3 million. Software licensing revenues improved 63.2% to $2.9 million from $1.8 million a year earlier.

BUSINESS

INFOSEEK CORP. is a provider of Internet services and software products. The Company produces GO network and the Infoseek Service, comprehensive Internet gateways that combine branded content from media leaders, search and navigation with directories of relevant information sources and content sites, and community applications for communicating shared interests such as chat and instant messaging, and for facilitating the purchase of related goods and services. Additionally, the Company produces other Internet sites, including ABCNEWS.com and ESPN.com in partnership with Disney affiliates. SEEK also sells Ultraseek Server, an Internet and intranet software search product. The services offer users six principal means of obtaining information: the GO Network and Infoseek Service home pages, centers, Infoseek Search, Web page directories, communities and commerce. The Company derives a substantial majority of its revenues from the sale of advertisements.

REVENUES

(10/03/1998)	($000)	(%)
Advertising & Other..	45,044	88.8
Software Licensing....	5,671	11.2
Total	50,715	100.0

ANNUAL FINANCIAL DATA

	① 10/3/98	12/31/97	12/31/96	12/31/95	12/31/94	12/31/93
Earnings Per Share	d0.19	② d0.93	d0.73	d0.13	...	...
Cash Flow Per Share	d0.01	d0.72	d0.57	d0.11	...	...
Tang. Book Val. Per Share	2.12	1.00	1.91	...	...	...
INCOME STATEMENT (IN THOUSANDS):						
Total Revenues	50,715	34,603	15,095	1,032	...	...
Costs & Expenses	52,909	54,926	28,872	3,924	1,410	27
Depreciation & Amort.	5,499	5,620	3,504	502	110	...
Operating Income	d7,693	d25,943	d17,281	d3,393	d1,520	d27
Net Interest Inc./(Exp.)	1,999	1,320	1,343	97	10	...
Income Before Income Taxes	d5,694	d24,623	d15,938	d3,296	d1,510	d27
Net Income	d5,694	② d24,623	d15,938	d3,296	d1,510	d27
Cash Flow	d195	d19,003	d12,434	d2,794	d1,400	d27
Average Shs. Outstg.	30,512	26,337	21,737	25,863	...	...
BALANCE SHEET (IN THOUSANDS):						
Cash & Cash Equivalents	51,868	31,334	46,653	1,626	568	...
Total Current Assets	80,146	38,878	49,452	2,235	587	...
Net Property	15,370	10,283	7,587	2,813	272	...
Total Assets	101,656	51,154	58,332	5,123	859	...
Total Current Liabilities	31,958	19,557	7,455	2,143	129	...
Long-Term Obligations	2,981	4,329	1,757	688	...	...
Net Stockholders' Equity	66,717	27,268	48,985	2,142	520	...
Net Working Capital	48,188	19,321	41,997	92	458	...
Year-end Shs. Outstg.	31,508	27,244	25,691	4,000	3,783	...
STATISTICAL RECORD:						
Debt/Total Assets %	2.9	8.5	3.0	13.4	...	...
Price Range	56¹³/₁₆-8⁷/₁₆	14½-4³/₈	16½-5¼	...	...	...

Statistics are as originally reported. ① For 9 mos. due to fiscal year-end change. ② Incl. non-recurr. chrg. $7.3 mill.

OFFICERS:
S. T. Kirsch, Chmn.
H. Motro, Pres. & C.E.O.
R. Canessa, C.F.O. & V.P.
A. E. Newton, V.P., Gen. Couns. & Sec.

PRINCIPAL OFFICE: 1399 Moffet Park Dr., Sunnyvale, CA 94089

TELEPHONE NUMBER: (408) 543-6000
FAX: (408) 567-1889
WEB: www.infoseek.com
NO. OF EMPLOYEES: 319
SHAREHOLDERS: 758 (approx.)
ANNUAL MEETING: In May
INCORPORATED: CA, Aug., 1993; reincorp., DE, Nov., 1998

INSTITUTIONAL HOLDINGS:
No. of Institutions: 113
Shares Held: 13,357,792
% Held: 21.6

INDUSTRY: Prepackaged software (SIC: 7372)

TRANSFER AGENT(S): First National Bank of Boston, Boston, MA

INFOSPACE.COM, INC.

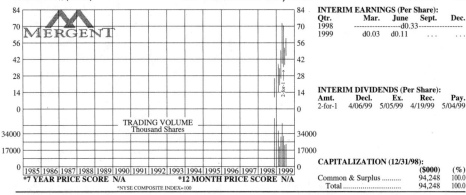

INTERIM EARNINGS (Per Share):

Qtr.	Mar.	June	Sept.	Dec.
1998		------------------d0.33----------------		
1999	d0.03	d0.11	...	...

INTERIM DIVIDENDS (Per Share):

Amt.	Decl.	Ex.	Rec.	Pay.
2-for-1	4/06/99	5/05/99	4/19/99	5/04/99

TRADING VOLUME
Thousand Shares

*7 YEAR PRICE SCORE N/A *12 MONTH PRICE SCORE N/A
*NYSE COMPOSITE INDEX=100

CAPITALIZATION (12/31/98):

	($000)	(%)
Common & Surplus	94,248	100.0
Total	94,248	100.0

RECENT DEVELOPMENTS: For the quarter ended 6/30/99, the Company reported a net loss of $5.0 million compared with a loss of $2.6 million in the corresponding quarter of the previous year. Earnings in the 1999 and 1998 quarters included acquisition related expenses and other non-recurring charges totaling $5.4 million and $3.1 million, respectively. Revenue soared to $6.7 million from $1.8 million in the prior-year period. Gross profit jumped to $5.6 million versus $1.6 million in the prior-year period. Operating loss fell to $8.2 million from a loss of $2.7 million a year ago, as sales and marketing expenses were $6.3 million versus $505,802 and general and administrative expenses more than tripled to $1.7 million. During the quarter, INSP signed 47 advertising agreements and 108 new affiliate agreements. INSP launched ActivePromotion™, allowing e-retailers to promote items though the Company's Internet channels. On 7/1/99, INSP acquired real-time communications technology from Active Voice for $18.0 million.

BUSINESS

INFOSPACE.COM, INC. is a provider of content services for syndication to a broad network of affiliates, including existing and emerging Internet portals, destination sites and suppliers of PCs and other Internet access devices, such as cellular phones, pagers, screen phones, television set-top boxes, on-line kiosks and personal digital assistants. The Company's affiliate network consists of more than 1,800 Web sites and Internet appliances. The foundation of the Company's content services is its nationwide yellow pages and white pages directory information. The Company integrates this directory information with other value-added content to create "The Ultimate Guide" to find people, places and things.

REVENUES

(12/31/98)	($000)	(%)
Advertising	7,322	77.8
Promotions	1,621	17.2
Other revenue	472	5.0
Total	9,415	100.0

ANNUAL FINANCIAL DATA

	12/31/98	12/31/97	12/31/96
Earnings Per Share	① d0.33	d0.02	d0.02
Cash Flow Per Share	d0.24	d0.01	d0.02
Tang. Book Val. Per Share	4.03	0.04	0.05

INCOME STATEMENT (IN THOUSANDS):

Total Revenues	9,414	1,685	199
Costs & Expenses	16,266	1,911	577
Depreciation & Amort.	2,492	224	24
Operating Income	d9,343	d450	d402
Income Before Income Taxes	d8,931	d429	d381
Equity Earnings/Minority Int.	d125	...	...
Net Income	① d9,056	d429	d381
Cash Flow	d6,565	d204	d357
Average Shs. Outstg.	27,121	21,996	18,560

BALANCE SHEET (IN THOUSANDS):

Cash & Cash Equivalents	86,750	324	690
Total Current Assets	93,790	913	876
Net Property	1,162	216	196
Total Assets	102,258	1,398	1,072
Total Current Liabilities	8,010	370	51
Net Stockholders' Equity	94,248	1,028	1,020
Net Working Capital	85,780	543	825
Year-end Shs. Outstg.	22,061	21,142	21,891

STATISTICAL RECORD:

Price Range	26-9¾	...	...

Statistics are as originally reported. Adj. for stk split: 2-for-1, 5/5/99 ① Incl. net non-recurr. chrg. $7.3 mill.

OFFICERS:
N. Jain, Chmn., C.E.O.
B. D. Strom, Pres., C.O.O.
D. A. Bevis, V.P., C.F.O.
E. B. Alben, V.P., Legal, Business Affairs, Sec.

PRINCIPAL OFFICE: 15375 N.E. 90th Street, Redmond, WA 98052

TELEPHONE NUMBER: (425) 882-1602
WEB: www.infospace.com

NO. OF EMPLOYEES: 76

SHAREHOLDERS: 145 (approx.)

ANNUAL MEETING: In May

INCORPORATED: WA, Mar., 1996; reincorp., DE, Apr., 1996

INSTITUTIONAL HOLDINGS:
No. of Institutions: 85
Shares Held: 14,019,172
% Held: 29.7

INDUSTRY: Data processing and preparation (SIC: 7374)

TRANSFER AGENT(S): ChaseMellon Shareholder Services, Seattle, Washington.

INKTOMI CORPORATION

YIELD ...
P/E RATIO ...

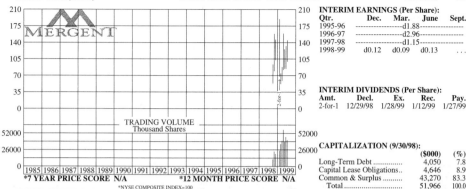

INTERIM EARNINGS (Per Share):

Qtr.	Dec.	Mar.	June	Sept.
1995-96		d1.88		
1996-97		d2.96		
1997-98		d1.15		
1998-99	d0.12	d0.09	d0.13	...

INTERIM DIVIDENDS (Per Share):

Amt.	Decl.	Ex.	Rec.	Pay.
2-for-1	12/29/98	1/28/99	1/12/99	1/27/99

TRADING VOLUME
Thousand Shares

| 1985 | 1986 | 1987 | 1988 | 1989 | 1990 | 1991 | 1992 | 1993 | 1994 | 1995 | 1996 | 1997 | 1998 | 1999 |

*7 YEAR PRICE SCORE N/A   *12 MONTH PRICE SCORE N/A

*NYSE COMPOSITE INDEX=100

CAPITALIZATION (9/30/98):

	($000)	(%)
Long-Term Debt	4,050	7.8
Capital Lease Obligations..	4,646	8.9
Common & Surplus	43,270	83.3
Total	51,966	100.0

RECENT DEVELOPMENTS: For the quarter ended 6/30/99, the Company reported a net loss of $6.3 million, which was unchanged from the corresponding quarter of 1998. The 1999 results included a pre-tax charge of $1.1 million related to the acquisition of Impulse! Buy Network. Total revenues more than tripled to $19.6 million from $6.3 million in 1998. Network products revenues nearly quadrupled to $11.8 million from $3.1 million in the prior year. Portal services revenues more than doubled to $7.8 million from $3.2 million in 1998. The top line benefited from an alliance with America Online for INKT's new search engine as well as the introduction of new scientific innovations. On 7/13/99, INKT announced a strategic agreement with British Telecommunications plc (BT) to integrate the Inktomi traffic server network cache platform into BT's next-generation Internet services. Combining INKT's infrastructure software for network and portal services with BT's network and presence in Europe will accelerate the build-out of Internet Services for the European Internet.

BUSINESS

INKTOMI CORPORATION develops and markets scalable software applications designed to significantly enhance the performance and intelligence of large-scale networks. Inktomi has pioneered the commercial use of parallel processing-based coupled cluster technology, a software architecture that provides true scalability, high-system availability and fault tolerance, and superior price/performance compared with traditional mainframe or symmetric multi-processing based systems. This architecture enables multiple workstations collaborating via high-speed connections to function as one extremely powerful computer. INKT's two areas of business are portal services, comprised of the search, directory and shopping engines, and network products, consisting of the Trafffic Server network cache and associated value-added services. INKT has offices in North America, Europe and Asia. In April 1999, INKT acquired Impulse! Buy Network, Inc., a developer of on-line merchandising software, to supplement functionality of its shopping engine.

ANNUAL FINANCIAL DATA

	9/30/98	9/30/97	9/30/96
Earnings Per Share	① d1.15	d2.96	d1.88
Cash Flow Per Share	d0.96	d2.49	d1.70
Tang. Book Val. Per Share	1.85	0.87	...
INCOME STATEMENT (IN THOUSANDS):			
Total Revenues	20,426	5,785	530
Costs & Expenses	39,469	12,867	3,625
Depreciation & Amort.	3,739	1,385	336
Operating Income	d22,782	d8,466	d3,431
Net Interest Inc./(Exp.)	427	d194	d103
Income Before Income Taxes	d22,355	d8,661	d3,534
Income Taxes	1	2	1
Net Income	① d22,355	d8,662	d3,534
Cash Flow	d18,616	d7,278	d3,198
Average Shs. Outstg.	19,360	2,927	1,884
BALANCE SHEET (IN THOUSANDS):			
Cash & Cash Equivalents	47,436	6,324	416
Total Current Assets	53,068	7,316	581
Net Property	17,362	6,808	1,891
Total Assets	70,641	14,317	2,521
Total Current Liabilities	18,675	5,239	4,180
Long-Term Obligations	8,696	5,029	...
Net Stockholders' Equity	43,270	4,049	d1,659
Net Working Capital	34,393	2,077	d3,599
Year-end Shs. Outstg.	23,388	4,632	2,467
STATISTICAL RECORD:			
Debt/Total Assets %	12.3	35.1	...
Price Range	158½-53⅛	...	...

Statistics are as originally reported. Adjusted for 2-for-1 stock split 1/27/99. ① Incl. pre-tax acquisition-related exps. of $1.0 mill. ② Incl. pre-tax acquisition-related expenses of $1.1 million.

OFFICERS:
D. C. Peterschmidt, Chmn., Pres., C.E.O.
J. M. Kennelly, C.F.O., Sec., V.P., Fin.
T. Stevens, Gen. Couns., Asst. Sec., V.P., Corp. & Legal Affairs

PRINCIPAL OFFICE: 1900 South Norfolk Street, San Mateo, CA 94403

TELEPHONE NUMBER: (650) 653-2800
WEB: www.inktomi.com
NO. OF EMPLOYEES: 185
SHAREHOLDERS: 811
ANNUAL MEETING: In March
INCORPORATED: CA, Feb., 1996; reincorp., DE, Feb., 1998

INSTITUTIONAL HOLDINGS:
No. of Institutions: 132
Shares Held: 18,998,992
% Held: 38.9
INDUSTRY: Computer integrated systems design (SIC: 7373)
TRANSFER AGENT(S): Norwest Shareowner Services, South St. Paul, MN.

INTEL CORPORATION

YIELD 0.2%
P/E RATIO 31.9

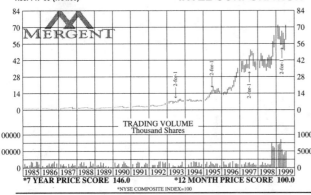

*7 YEAR PRICE SCORE 146.0   *12 MONTH PRICE SCORE 100.0

*NYSE COMPOSITE INDEX=100

INTERIM EARNINGS (Per Share):

Qtr.	Mar.	June	Sept.	Dec.
1996	0.26	0.30	0.37	0.54
1997	0.55	0.46	0.44	0.49
1998	0.36	0.33	0.45	0.60
1999	0.60	0.51	...	...

INTERIM DIVIDENDS (Per Share):

Amt.	Decl.	Ex.	Rec.	Pay.
0.04Q	9/16/98	11/04/98	11/07/98	12/01/98
0.04Q	1/27/99	2/03/99	2/07/99	3/01/99
2-for-1	1/28/99	4/12/99	3/23/99	4/11/99
0.03Q	1/28/99	5/05/99	5/07/99	6/01/99
0.03Q	7/21/99	8/04/99	8/07/99	9/01/99

Indicated div.: $0.12

CAPITALIZATION (12/26/98):

	($000)	(%)
Long-Term Debt	702,000	2.8
Deferred Income Tax	1,387,000	5.4
Common & Surplus	23,377,000	91.8
Total	25,466,000	100.0

RECENT DEVELOPMENTS: For the three months ended 6/26/99, net income surged 49.2% to $1.75 billion from $1.17 billion in the corresponding period of the previous year. Net revenues advanced 13.8% to $6.75 billion versus $5.93 billion in the prior-year quarter. Net revenues for the Intel Architecture Business Group rose 13.0% compared with the prior year, due to higher unit volumes of microprocessors and a shift in mix toward processors based on the P6 microarchitecture. On 8/10/99, INTC completed

its acquisition of Level One Communications, Inc., which provides silicon connectivity solutions for high-speed telecom and networking applications, in a stock-for-stock merger agreement valued at $2.20 billion. On 7/12/99, INTC acquired Dialogic Corporation, which designs, manufactures and markets computer hardware and software enabling technology for computer telephony systems, for $830.0 million.

BUSINESS

INTEL CORPORATION and its subsidiaries are engaged primarily in the business of designing, developing, manufacturing and marketing microcomputer components and related products at various levels of integration. In addition, the Company is building a global network of data centers designed to host Web content and services such as e-commerce. INTC's major products include: microprocessors, including the Pentium®, and related board-level products, chipsets, embedded processors and microcontrollers, flash memory chips, network and communications products and conferencing products.

REVENUES

(12/26/98)	($000)	(%)
United States	11,663,000	44.4
Europe	7,452,000	28.4
Asia Pacific	5,309,000	20.2
Japan........................	1,849,000	7.0
Total	26,273,000	100.0

ANNUAL FINANCIAL DATA

	12/26/98	12/27/97	12/28/96	12/30/95	12/31/94	12/25/93	12/26/92
Earnings Per Share	☐ 1.73	1.93	1.45	1.01	0.66	0.65	0.31
Cash Flow Per Share	2.52	2.55	1.98	1.40	0.95	0.86	0.47
Tang. Book Val. Per Share	7.05	5.93	5.14	3.70	2.80	2.24	1.62
Dividends Per Share	0.07	0.06	0.04	0.04	0.03	0.03	0.01
Dividend Payout %	3.8	2.8	3.1	3.5	4.3	3.8	2.0
INCOME STATEMENT (IN MILLIONS):							
Total Revenues	26,273.0	25,070.0	20,847.0	16,202.0	11,521.0	8,782.0	5,844.0
Costs & Expenses	15,087.0	12,991.0	11,406.0	9,571.0	7,087.0	4,656.0	3,820.0
Depreciation & Amort.	2,807.0	2,192.0	1,888.0	1,379.0	1,047.0	734.0	534.0
Operating Income	8,379.0	9,887.0	7,553.0	5,252.0	3,387.0	3,392.0	1,490.0
Net Interest Inc./(Exp.)	d34.0	d27.0	339.0	243.0	178.0	d50.0	d55.0
Income Before Income Taxes	9,137.0	10,659.0	7,934.0	5,638.0	3,603.0	3,530.0	1,569.0
Income Taxes	3,069.0	3,714.0	2,777.0	2,072.0	1,315.0	1,235.0	502.0
Net Income	☐ 6,068.0	6,945.0	5,157.0	3,566.0	2,288.0	2,295.0	1,066.0
Cash Flow	8,875.0	9,137.0	7,045.0	4,945.0	3,335.0	3,029.0	1,600.0
Average Shs. Outstg. (000)	3,517,000	3,590,000	3,552,000	3,536,000	3,496,000	3,528,000	3,432,000
BALANCE SHEET (IN MILLIONS):							
Cash & Cash Equivalents	7,310.0	9,732.0	7,907.0	2,458.0	2,410.0	3,136.0	2,835.0
Total Current Assets	13,475.0	15,867.0	13,684.0	8,097.0	6,167.0	5,802.0	4,690.0
Net Property	11,609.0	10,666.0	8,487.0	7,471.0	5,367.0	3,996.0	2,815.0
Total Assets	31,471.0	28,880.0	23,735.0	17,504.0	13,816.0	11,344.0	8,087.0
Total Current Liabilities	5,804.0	6,020.0	4,863.0	3,619.0	3,024.0	2,433.0	1,842.0
Long-Term Obligations	702.0	448.0	728.0	400.0	392.0	426.0	249.0
Net Stockholders' Equity	23,377.0	19,295.0	16,872.0	12,140.0	9,267.0	7,500.0	5,444.0
Net Working Capital	7,671.0	9,847.0	8,821.0	4,478.0	3,143.0	3,369.0	2,848.0
Year-end Shs. Outstg. (000)	3,315,000	3,256,000	3,284,000	3,284,000	3,308,000	3,344,000	3,352,000
STATISTICAL RECORD:							
Operating Profit Margin %	31.9	39.4	36.2	32.4	29.4	38.6	25.5
Net Profit Margin %	23.1	27.7	24.7	22.0	19.9	26.1	18.2
Return on Equity %	26.0	36.0	30.6	29.4	24.7	30.6	19.6
Return on Assets %	19.3	24.0	21.7	20.4	16.6	20.2	13.2
Debt/Total Assets %	2.2	1.6	3.1	2.3	2.8	3.8	3.1
Price Range	63⅛-32¹³⁄₁₆	51-31⁷⁄₁₆	35⅜-12⁷⁄₁₆	19⅝-7⅞	9³⁄₁₆-7	9⁵⁄₁₆-5⅜	5¾-2¹⁵⁄₁₆
P/E Ratio	36.5-19.0	26.4-16.3	24.4-8.6	19.4-7.8	14.0-10.7	14.3-8.2	18.4-9.3
Average Yield %	0.1	0.1	0.2	0.3	0.3	0.3	0.1

Statistics are as originally reported. Adj. for stk. splits: 2-for-1, 4/99; 2-for-1, 7/31/97; 2-for-1, 6/16/95; 2-for-1, 6/6/93 ☐ Incl. non-recurr. chrg. of $165.0 million.

OFFICERS:
A. S. Grove, Chmn.
C. R. Barrett, Pres., C.E.O., C.O.O.
A. D. Bryant, Sr. V.P., C.F.O., C.A.O.
F. T. Dunlap, Jr., V.P., Sec., Couns.

PRINCIPAL OFFICE: 2200 Mission College Blvd., Santa Clara, CA 95052-8119

TELEPHONE NUMBER: (408) 765-8080
FAX: (408) 765-2633
WEB: www.intel.com
NO. OF EMPLOYEES: 64,500 (approx.)
SHAREHOLDERS: 216,000
ANNUAL MEETING: In May
INCORPORATED: CA, Jul., 1968; reincorp., DE, May, 1989

INTELLIGENT LIFE CORPORATION

YIELD ...
P/E RATIO ...

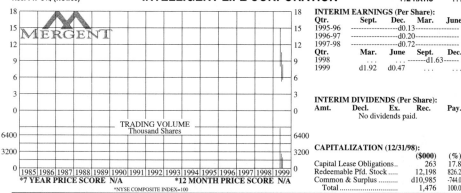

*7 YEAR PRICE SCORE N/A   *12 MONTH PRICE SCORE N/A
*NYSE COMPOSITE INDEX=100

INTERIM EARNINGS (Per Share):

Qtr.	Sept.	Dec.	Mar.	June
1995-96			d0.13	
1996-97			d0.20	
1997-98			d0.72	

Qtr.	Mar.	June	Sept.	Dec.
1998	...	...	d1.63	
1999	d1.92	d0.47	...	...

INTERIM DIVIDENDS (Per Share):

Amt.	Decl.	Ex.	Rec.	Pay.
	No dividends paid.			

CAPITALIZATION (12/31/98):

	($000)	(%)
Capital Lease Obligations..	263	17.8
Redeemable Pfd. Stock	12,198	826.2
Common & Surplus	d10,985	-744.0
Total	1,476	100.0

RECENT DEVELOPMENTS:

For the second quarter ended 6/30/99, the Company reported a net loss of $3.9 million compared with a net loss of $1.2 million in the corresponding prior-year period. Total revenue jumped to $2.8 million from $1.2 million in the previous year. The increase in total revenue resulted primarily from an increase in on-line publishing revenues. On-line publishing revenues surged to $1.9 million from $445,359 a year earlier due to increasing advertising revenues, adding partners, and enhancing the content of ILIF's on-line publications. Print publishing and licensing revenue jumped 17.0% to $886,104 from $757,322 in the second quarter of 1998. On 7/27/99, the Company debuted its weekly TV consumer money report, Cost of Life, along with the launch of its new broadcasting division, which will create a variety of television and radio products for national syndication and broadband distribution and be utilized as an independent news resource for TV station decision-makers.

BUSINESS

INTELLIGENT LIFE CORPORATION publishes personal finance content on the Internet through its principal Web site, bankrate.com, and through arrangements with more than 70 Web site operators. Information includes data regarding mortgage and home equity loans, credit cards, automobile loans, checking accounts, ATM fees and yields on savings instruments. ILIF's Web sites include bankrate.com, which provides editorial and research information on banking and credit products; bankrate.com en Espanol, which provides the same information and many of the services of bankrate.com in Spanish; the Whiz.com, which provides personal financial content that is easy to understand and entertaining; Consejero.com, which provides personal finance information in Spanish and serves as a consumer guide to understanding local and international financial issues and CPNet.com, an on-line network of college newspaper Web sites. ILIF's print publications consist of three newsletters and the Consumer Mortgage Guide, and advertisement for newspapers consisting of product and rate information in tabular form from local mortgage companies.

ANNUAL FINANCIAL DATA

	⌷ 12/31/98	6/30/98	6/30/97	6/30/96
Earnings Per Share	d1.63	d0.72	d0.20	d0.13
Cash Flow Per Share	d1.60	d0.71	d0.19	d0.11
INCOME STATEMENT (IN THOUSANDS):				
Total Revenues	3,469	3,841	2,543	1,628
Costs & Expenses	5,658	6,603	3,348	2,149
Depreciation & Amort.	98	67	74	98
Operating Income	d2,287	d2,829	d879	d619
Net Interest Inc./(Exp.)	192	46	d76	d54
Income Before Income Taxes	d2,095	d2,782	d956	d672
Net Income	d2,095	d2,782	d956	d672
Cash Flow	d6,435	d2,716	d882	d575
Average Shs. Outstg.	4,019	3,846	4,744	5,000
BALANCE SHEET (IN THOUSANDS):				
Cash & Cash Equivalents	1,633	910	1,763	...
Total Current Assets	2,281	1,261	2,044	...
Net Property	814	505	142	...
Total Assets	3,099	1,768	2,193	...
Total Current Liabilities	1,623	1,097	1,157	...
Long-Term Obligations	263	14	...	...
Net Stockholders' Equity	d10,985	657	1,035	...
Net Working Capital	658	164	887	...
Year-end Shs. Outstg.	4,053	3,846	3,846	...
STATISTICAL RECORD:				
Debt/Total Assets %	8.5	0.8	...	...

Statistics are as originally reported. ⌷ For six months due to fiscal year end change from June to December.

OFFICERS:
W. P. Anderson III, Pres., C.E.O.
P. W. Minford, Sr. V.P., C.F.O.

PRINCIPAL OFFICE: 11811 U.S. Highway One, Suite 101, North Palm Beach, FL 33408

TELEPHONE NUMBER: (561) 630-1200
WEB: www.bankrate.com

NO. OF EMPLOYEES: 164

SHAREHOLDERS: 2,128 (approx.)

ANNUAL MEETING: N/A

INCORPORATED: FL

INSTITUTIONAL HOLDINGS:
No. of Institutions: 1
Shares Held: 75,000
% Held: 0.6

INDUSTRY: Information retrieval services (SIC: 7375)

TRANSFER AGENT(S): SunTrust Bank, Inc., Atlanta, GA

INTERNATIONAL BUSINESS MACHINES CORP.

YIELD 0.4%
P/E RATIO 30.8

*7 YEAR PRICE SCORE 158.0   *12 MONTH PRICE SCORE 127.1
*NYSE COMPOSITE INDEX=100

TRADING VOLUME
Thousand Shares

INTERIM EARNINGS (Per Share):

Qtr.	Mar.	June	Sept.	Dec.
1995	0.53	0.75	d0.24	0.78
1996	0.36	0.63	0.62	0.99
1997	0.60	0.73	0.69	1.06
1998	0.53	0.75	0.78	1.24
1999	0.78	1.28	...	...

INTERIM DIVIDENDS (Per Share):

Amt.	Decl.	Ex.	Rec.	Pay.
0.22Q	10/27/98	11/06/98	11/10/98	12/10/98
0.22Q	1/26/99	2/08/99	2/10/99	3/10/99
0.24Q	4/27/99	5/06/99	5/10/99	6/10/99
2-for-1	1/26/99	5/27/99	5/10/99	5/26/99
0.12Q	7/27/99	8/06/99	8/10/99	9/10/99

Indicated div.: $0.48 (Div. Reinv. Plan)

CAPITALIZATION (12/31/98):

	($000)	(%)
Long-Term Debt	15,508,000	42.5
Deferred Income Tax	1,514,000	4.2
Preferred Stock	247,000	0.7
Common & Surplus	19,186,000	52.6
Total	36,455,000	100.0

RECENT DEVELOPMENTS: For the quarter ended 6/30/99, net income soared 64.7% to $2.39 billion versus $1.45 billion in 1998. Results for 1999 included a net gain of $687.0 million related to the sale of the IBM Global Network, charges related to the microelectronics and storage businesses, and an accounting charge. Total revenues were $21.91 billion, up 16.4% from $18.82 billion in the previous year. Revenues reflected strong performances in the services business and hardware unit, despite pricing pressures in some areas of IBM's technology division. Operating income nearly doubled to $4.09 billion versus $2.11 billion a year ago. IBM has purchased a $45.0 million stake in Internet Capital, a provider of capital and consulting for e-business companies. This investment expands IBM's Internet-related services to e-businesses. Also, IBM formed a strategic relationship with i2 Technologies to provide combined integrated solutions to customers as they transform into e-businesses.

BUSINESS

INTERNATIONAL BUSINESS MACHINES CORP. offers customers information technology services, software, systems, products, and financing. Products and services include servers, personal systems, storage and other peripherals, OEM hardware, services, software, maintenance, and financing. Going forward, the Company will heavily invest in e-business commerce in order to increase potential market share and revenue in the growing area of Internet-related services and businesses. Revenues for 1998 were derived: hardware sales, 42%; services, 29%; software, 17%; maintenance, 7%; and rentals and financing, 5%.

ANNUAL FINANCIAL DATA

	12/31/98	12/31/97	12/31/96 ③	12/31/95	12/31/94	12/31/93	12/31/92
Earnings Per Share	3.29	3.01	④2.56	②1.81	1.26	d3.50	①d3.01
Cash Flow Per Share	5.89	5.48	4.93	4.27	3.95	d0.60	d0.27
Tang. Book Val. Per Share	10.04	9.68	9.81	9.01	8.24	6.43	10.29
Dividends Per Share	0.43	0.39	0.33	0.25	0.25	0.40	1.21
Dividend Payout %	13.1	12.9	12.7	13.8	19.9	...	...

INCOME STATEMENT (IN MILLIONS):

	12/31/98	12/31/97	12/31/96	12/31/95	12/31/94	12/31/93	12/31/92
Total Revenues	81,667.0	78,508.0	75,947.0	71,940.0	64,052.0	62,716.0	64,523.0
Costs & Expenses	67,511.0	64,409.0	62,339.0	58,747.0	52,752.0	64,692.0	66,503.0
Depreciation & Amort.	4,992.0	5,001.0	5,012.0	5,602.0	6,295.0	6,661.0	6,259.0
Operating Income	9,164.0	9,098.0	8,596.0	7,591.0	5,005.0	d8,637.0	d8,239.0
Net Interest Inc./(Exp.)	d713.0	d728.0	d716.0	d725.0	d1,227.0	d1,273.0	d1,360.0
Income Before Income Taxes	9,040.0	9,027.0	8,587.0	7,813.0	5,155.0	d8,797.0	d9,026.0
Income Taxes	2,712.0	2,934.0	3,158.0	3,635.0	2,134.0	cr810.0	cr2,161.0
Net Income	6,328.0	6,093.0	④5,429.0	②4,178.0	3,021.0	d7,987.0	①d6,865.0
Cash Flow	11,300.0	11,074.0	10,421.0	9,718.0	9,232.0	d1,373.0	d606.0
Average Shs. Outstg. (000)	1,920,000	2,022,000	2,112,000	2,276,000	2,340,000	2,292,000	2,284,000

BALANCE SHEET (IN MILLIONS):

	12/31/98	12/31/97	12/31/96	12/31/95	12/31/94	12/31/93	12/31/92
Cash & Cash Equivalents	5,768.0	7,553.0	8,137.0	7,701.0	10,554.0	7,133.0	5,649.0
Total Current Assets	42,360.0	40,418.0	40,695.0	40,691.0	41,338.0	39,202.0	39,692.0
Net Property	19,631.0	18,347.0	17,407.0	16,579.0	16,664.0	17,521.0	21,595.0
Total Assets	86,100.0	81,499.0	81,132.0	80,292.0	81,091.0	81,113.0	86,705.0
Total Current Liabilities	36,827.0	33,507.0	34,000.0	31,648.0	29,226.0	33,150.0	36,737.0
Long-Term Obligations	15,508.0	13,696.0	9,872.0	10,060.0	12,548.0	15,245.0	12,853.0
Net Stockholders' Equity	19,433.0	19,816.0	21,628.0	22,423.0	23,413.0	19,738.0	27,624.0
Net Working Capital	5,533.0	6,911.0	6,695.0	9,043.0	12,112.0	6,052.0	2,955.0
Year-end Shs. Outstg. (000)	1,852,000	1,936,000	2,032,000	2,192,000	2,352,000	2,324,000	2,284,000

STATISTICAL RECORD:

	12/31/98	12/31/97	12/31/96	12/31/95	12/31/94	12/31/93	12/31/92
Operating Profit Margin %	11.2	11.6	11.3	10.6	7.8	...	...
Net Profit Margin %	7.7	7.8	7.1	5.8	4.7	...	...
Return on Equity %	32.6	30.7	25.1	18.6	12.9	...	...
Return on Assets %	7.3	7.5	6.7	5.2	3.7	...	...
Debt/Total Assets %	18.0	16.8	12.2	12.5	15.5	18.8	14.8
Price Range	94-47¹³/₁₆	56¾-31¹³/₁₆	41½-20¹³/₁₆	28¹¹/₁₆-17⁹/₁₆	19¹/₈-12⁷/₈	14-10³/₁₆	25¹/₈-12³/₁₆
P/E Ratio	28.9-14.6	18.9-10.6	16.2-8.1	15.8-9.7	15.2-10.2	...	...
Average Yield %	0.6	0.9	1.0	1.1	1.6	3.1	6.5

Statistics are as originally reported. Adj. for 2-for-1 split, 5/99 & 5/97. ① Incl. $11.60 bill. pre-tax restr. chg. & excl. cr$1.90 bill. acct. ② Incl. $488.0 mill. pre-tax chg. & $1.84 bill. chg. rel. to acq. of Lotus Develop. ③ Incl. Lotus Develop., acq. 7/95. ④ Incl. $435.0 mill. one-time chg.

OFFICERS:
L. V. Gerstner Jr., Chmn., C.E.O.
D. L. Maine, Sr. V.P., C.F.O.
J. D. Serkes, V.P., Treas.
W. Berman, Treas.

INVESTOR CONTACT: IBM Investor Relations, (800) 426-4968

PRINCIPAL OFFICE: 1 New Orchard Road, Armonk, NY 10504

TELEPHONE NUMBER: (914) 499-1900
FAX: (914) 765-4190
WEB: www.ibm.com

NO. OF EMPLOYEES: 291,067

SHAREHOLDERS: 618,962

ANNUAL MEETING: In Apr.

INCORPORATED: NY, Jun., 1911

INSTITUTIONAL HOLDINGS:
No. of Institutions: 1,100
Shares Held: 934,826,804
% Held: 51.5

INDUSTRY: Electronic computers (SIC: 3571)

TRANSFER AGENT(S): First Chicago Trust Company of New York, Jersey City, NJ.

INTERNET AMERICA, INC.

YIELD ...
P/E RATIO ...

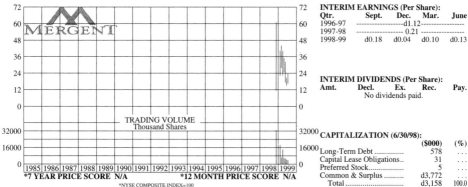

TRADING VOLUME
Thousand Shares

| | 1985 | 1986 | 1987 | 1988 | 1989 | 1990 | 1991 | 1992 | 1993 | 1994 | 1995 | 1996 | 1997 | 1998 | 1999 |

*7 YEAR PRICE SCORE N/A   *12 MONTH PRICE SCORE N/A

*NYSE COMPOSITE INDEX=100

INTERIM EARNINGS (Per Share):

Qtr.	Sept.	Dec.	Mar.	June
1996-97	----------	d1.12	----------	
1997-98	----------	0.21	----------	
1998-99	d0.18	d0.04	d0.10	d0.13

INTERIM DIVIDENDS (Per Share):

Amt.	Decl.	Ex.	Rec.	Pay.
	No dividends paid.			

CAPITALIZATION (6/30/98):

	($000)	(%)
Long-Term Debt	578	...
Capital Lease Obligations..	31	...
Preferred Stock................	5	...
Common & Surplus	d3,772	...
Total	d3,158	100.0

RECENT DEVELOPMENTS: For the year ended 6/30/99, the Company reported a net loss of $2.5 million versus a net loss of $646,000 in the previous fiscal year. The bottom line was pressured by a significant increase in sales and marketing expenses. Total revenues advanced 28.7% to $18.1 million from $14.1 million the year before. Strong internal growth coupled with the acquisition of Cyber-Ramp, a Dallas-based Internet Service Provider, CompuNet, also a Dallas-based Internet Service Provider, and NeoSoft, a Houston-based Internet Service Provider, fueled the growth in revenues as well as the 62.3% increase in subscriber count to 100,000 members. Results were restated to reflect the previously-mentioned acquisitions, which were accounted for under the pooling-of-interest method. Separately, the Company announced that it has acquired the subscribers of INTX-NET (www.intx.net), a San Antonio-based Internet service provider. Terms of the transaction were not disclosed.

BUSINESS

INTERNET AMERICA, INC. is an Internet Service Provider with approximately 100,000 subscribers as of 6/30/99. Internet America offers a wide array of Internet services tailored to meet the needs of individual consumers, including EXPRESSLANE DSL, dial-up Internet access, multiple e-mail addresses, World Wide Web access, Internet Relay Chat, Usenet News, and personal Web sites. Internet America also provides a full range of services to business customers, including dedicated high-speed access, Web hosting, server co-location and domain name registration.

ANNUAL FINANCIAL DATA

	6/30/98	6/30/97
Earnings Per Share	0.21	d1.12
Cash Flow Per Share	0.52	d0.65
INCOME STATEMENT (IN THOUSANDS):		
Total Revenues	10,643	9,471
Costs & Expenses	7,568	11,195
Depreciation & Amort.	1,474	1,618
Operating Income	1,601	d3,343
Net Interest Inc./(Exp.)	d571	d481
Income Before Income Taxes	1,030	d3,824
Income Taxes	24	...
Net Income	1,006	d3,824
Cash Flow	2,480	d2,205
Average Shs. Outstg.	4,783	3,418
BALANCE SHEET (IN THOUSANDS):		
Cash & Cash Equivalents	565	...
Total Current Assets	924	278
Net Property	1,625	2,511
Total Assets	3,150	3,114
Total Current Liabilities	6,308	7,111
Long-Term Obligations	609	684
Net Stockholders' Equity	d3,767	d4,681
Net Working Capital	d5,385	d6,834
Year-end Shs. Outstg.	3,532	3,532
STATISTICAL RECORD:		
Operating Profit Margin %	15.0	...
Net Profit Margin %	9.5	...
Return on Assets %	31.9	...
Debt/Total Assets %	19.3	22.0
Price Range	61-11½	...
P/E Ratio	290.3-54.7	...

Statistics are as originally reported.

OFFICERS:
W. O. Hunt, Chmn.
M. T. Maples, Pres., C.E.O.
J. T. Chaney, V.P., C.F.O., Sec., Treas.
D. L. Davis, Exec. V.P., C.O.O.

PRINCIPAL OFFICE: One Dallas Centre, 350 N. St. Paul, Suite 3000, Dallas, TX 75201

TELEPHONE NUMBER: (214) 861-2500
WEB: www.airmail.net

NO. OF EMPLOYEES: 90 (approx.)

SHAREHOLDERS: 34

ANNUAL MEETING: N/A

INCORPORATED: AZ, Dec., 1994; reincorp., TX, July, 1995

INSTITUTIONAL HOLDINGS:
No. of Institutions: 13
Shares Held: 199,360
% Held: 3.2

INDUSTRY: Prepackaged software (SIC: 7372)

TRANSFER AGENT(S): ChaseMellon Shareholder Services, Ridgefield Park, NJ

INTERNET FINANCIAL SERVICES INC.

YIELD ...
P/E RATIO ...

*7 YEAR PRICE SCORE N/A *12 MONTH PRICE SCORE N/A
*NYSE COMPOSITE INDEX=100

INTERIM EARNINGS (Per Share):

Qtr.	Dec.	Mar.	June	Sept.
1998-99	...	0.02	0.04	...

INTERIM DIVIDENDS (Per Share):

Amt.	Decl.	Ex.	Rec.	Pay.
	No dividends paid.			

CAPITALIZATION (9/30/98):

	($000)	(%)
Long-Term Debt	780	30.8
Common & Surplus	1,754	69.2
Total	2,534	100.0

RECENT DEVELOPMENTS: For the third quarter ended 6/30/99, net income was $313,292 before an extraordinary loss on the early extinguishment of debt. This compares with a net loss of $71,981 in the corresponding quarter the year before. Total revenues increased 156.0% to $6.5 million from $2.5 million in the comparable quarter a year earlier. Commissions revenue more than doubled to $5.1 million from $2.2 million in the equivalent 1998 quarter. Data service revenue jumped 159.2% to $485,037, while principal transaction revenue climbed to $692,112 from $187,644. Total transactions amounted to 210,479, up 317.3% versus the comparable 1998 quarter, and up 47.1% compared with the second quarter of fiscal 1999. The Company has experienced high rankings in on-line brokerage surveys and an increase in its Web traffic by 500.0% from the previous quarter, primarily due to an extensive Internet marketing campaign launched during the quarter.

BUSINESS

INTERNET FINANCIAL SER-VICES INC. provides real-time on-line financial brokerage services and information about the securities markets through its trading systems, UltimateTrader™ and WatleyTrader™. The Company also operates a third market institutional sales desk which specializes in executing and facilitating large-block transactions, which are specifically provided for clients who require that their transactions remain anonymous.

ANNUAL FINANCIAL DATA

	9/30/98	9/30/97
Earnings Per Share	d0.12	d0.30
Cash Flow Per Share	d0.01	d0.24
Tang. Book Val. Per Share	0.34	0.21
INCOME STATEMENT (IN THOUSANDS):		
Total Revenues	9,119	4,533
Costs & Expenses	9,149	5,369
Depreciation & Amort.	589	220
Operating Income	d620	d1,057
Income Before Income Taxes	d620	d1,057
Income Taxes	13	3
Net Income	d632	d1,060
Cash Flow	d43	d840
Average Shs. Outstg.	5,171	3,509
BALANCE SHEET (IN THOUSANDS):		
Cash & Cash Equivalents	1,075	840
Total Current Assets	1,607	1,133
Net Property	3,651	1,010
Total Assets	5,539	2,387
Total Current Liabilities	2,201	802
Long-Term Obligations	780	530
Net Stockholders' Equity	1,754	1,055
Net Working Capital	d594	331
Year-end Shs. Outstg.	5,138	5,050
STATISTICAL RECORD:		
Debt/Total Assets %	14.1	22.2
Statistics are as originally reported.		

OFFICERS:
S. Malin, Chmn. & C.E.O.
H. Simpson, Pres. & C.O.O.

INVESTOR CONTACT: William Arnold, (212) 422-1664

PRINCIPAL OFFICE: 40 Wall Street, New York, NY 10005

TELEPHONE NUMBER: (212) 422-1664
FAX: (212) 634-9924
WEB: www.abwatley.com.

NO. OF EMPLOYEES: 59

SHAREHOLDERS: 66

ANNUAL MEETING: N/A

INCORPORATED: DE, May, 1996

INSTITUTIONAL HOLDINGS:
No. of Institutions: N/A
Shares Held: N/A
% Held: N/A

INDUSTRY: Security brokers and dealers (SIC: 6211)

TRANSFER AGENT(S): American Stock Transfer & Trust Company, New York, NY

INTERVU INC.

YIELD ...
P/E RATIO ...

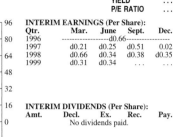

*7 YEAR PRICE SCORE N/A   *12 MONTH PRICE SCORE 138.9

*NYSE COMPOSITE INDEX=100

INTERIM EARNINGS (Per Share):

Qtr.	Mar.	June	Sept.	Dec.
1996	------------------d0.66-----------------			
1997	d0.21	d0.25	d0.51	0.02
1998	d0.66	d0.34	d0.38	d0.35
1999	d0.31	d0.34	...	...

INTERIM DIVIDENDS (Per Share):

Amt.	Decl.	Ex.	Rec.	Pay.
No dividends paid.				

CAPITALIZATION (12/31/98):

	($000)	(%)
Preferred Stock.................	1	0.0
Common & Surplus	27,312	100.0
Total	27,313	100.0

RECENT DEVELOPMENTS: For the quarter ended 6/30/99, the Company reported a net loss of $4.0 million compared with a net loss of $3.1 million in the corresponding period of the prior year. Results for the 1998 quarter included charges associated with the NBC Strategic Alliance Agreement of $500,000. Net revenue advanced to a record $1.7 million from $283,000 a year earlier. During the quarter, ITVU added CNET, Quokka Sports, Tunes.com and NBC6 to its entertainment customer base. Separately, the Company announced an agreement to make 1.2 million 30-second promotional music clips from over 100,000 CDs available to on-line music retailers. The clips will enable customers to sample the music before purchasing it. Meanwhile, ITVU signed several new Internet conferencing customers, including CCBN.com, InvestorBroadcast Network, c-call, and PRNewswire.

BUSINESS

INTERVU INC. provides Web site owners and information publishers with services for the delivery of live and on-demand video and audio content over the Internet. The Company's services automate the publishing, distribution and programming of video and audio content. The Company uses a scalable, patent-pending distribution network comprised of servers strategically located in major Internet hosting centers. The Company's customers use its video and audio distribution services to transmit entertainment, sports, news, business to business, advertising and distance learning content. The Company's current customers include CNET, CNN, House of Blues, Intel, Microsoft, AOL, MovieFone, MSNBC, Music Choice, NBC, OnRadio.com, RadioWave.com, Saatchi & Saatchi, and Turner Broadcasting.

ANNUAL FINANCIAL DATA

	12/31/98	12/31/97	12/31/96	12/31/95
Earnings Per Share	⊡ d1.73	⊡ d0.95	d0.66	...
Cash Flow Per Share	d1.66	d0.87	d0.64	...
Tang. Book Val. Per Share	2.51	2.30	0.65	0.05
INCOME STATEMENT (IN THOUSANDS):				
Total Revenues	1,712	144	...	...
Costs & Expenses	17,992	5,167	2,253	48
Depreciation & Amort.	676	434	77	1
Operating Income	d16,956	d5,458	d2,331	d49
Net Interest Inc./(Exp.)	1,246	192	52	3
Income Before Income Taxes	d15,710	d5,265	d2,278	d46
Net Income	⊡ d15,710	⊡ d5,265	d2,278	d46
Cash Flow	d15,034	d4,831	d2,201	d45
Average Shs. Outstg.	9,074	5,571	3,441	...
BALANCE SHEET (IN THOUSANDS):				
Cash & Cash Equivalents	9,346	21,380	2,508	509
Total Current Assets	27,850	21,538	2,518	509
Net Property	2,469	585	252	13
Total Assets	30,364	22,130	2,776	521
Total Current Liabilities	3,051	591	153	...
Long-Term Obligations	...	8	27	411
Net Stockholders' Equity	27,313	21,532	2,597	110
Net Working Capital	24,799	20,947	2,365	509
Year-end Shs. Outstg.	10,894	9,377	4,007	2,398
STATISTICAL RECORD:				
Debt/Total Assets %	...	...	1.0	78.9
Price Range	32⅜-5⅛	10¼-8½	...	...

Statistics are as originally reported. ⊡ Incl. expenses from the Strategic Alliance Agreement of $4.6 mill., 1998; $750,000, 1997.

OFFICERS:
H. E. Gruber, Chmn., C.E.O.
J. W. Grimes, Vice-Chmn.
K. Ruggiero, V.P., C.F.O.
E. L. Huguez, V.P., C.O.O.

PRINCIPAL OFFICE: 6815 Flanders Drive, San Diego, CA 92121

TELEPHONE NUMBER: (619) 623-8400
WEB: www.intervu.net

NO. OF EMPLOYEES: 120

SHAREHOLDERS: 124

ANNUAL MEETING: In May

INCORPORATED: DE, Aug., 1995

INSTITUTIONAL HOLDINGS:
No. of Institutions: 34
Shares Held: 1,736,610
% Held: 16.0

INDUSTRY: Computer programming services (SIC: 7371)

TRANSFER AGENT(S): Norwest Bank Minnesota N.A., St. Paul, MN

INTRAWARE INC.

YIELD ...
P/E RATIO ...

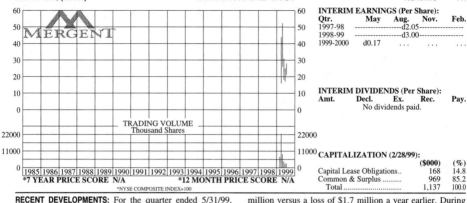

*7 YEAR PRICE SCORE N/A   *12 MONTH PRICE SCORE N/A

*NYSE COMPOSITE INDEX=100

TRADING VOLUME
Thousand Shares

| 1985 | 1986 | 1987 | 1988 | 1989 | 1990 | 1991 | 1992 | 1993 | 1994 | 1995 | 1996 | 1997 | 1998 | 1999 |

INTERIM EARNINGS (Per Share):

Qtr.	May	Aug.	Nov.	Feb.
1997-98		d2.05		
1998-99		d3.00		
1999-2000	d0.17	...	...	...

INTERIM DIVIDENDS (Per Share):

Amt.	Decl.	Ex.	Rec.	Pay.
	No dividends paid.			

CAPITALIZATION (2/28/99):

	($000)	(%)
Capital Lease Obligations..	168	14.8
Common & Surplus	969	85.2
Total	1,137	100.0

RECENT DEVELOPMENTS: For the quarter ended 5/31/99, the Company reported a net loss of $3.8 million compared with a loss of $1.7 million in the corresponding quarter of the previous year. Net revenue soared to $16.5 million from $5.0 the year before. Software product sales jumped to $14.0 million from $5.0 million, while on-line services revenue totaled $2.5 million versus $16,000 in 1998. Gross profit more than tripled to $3.7 million from $1.0 million in the previous year's quarter. Operating loss totaled $4.5 million versus a loss of $1.7 million a year earlier. During the quarter, the Company's membership base increased to over 120,000 customers. Extensive infrastructure investments have improved data transfer performance by more than 50%. Additionally, ITRA upgraded several of its services, and gained new strategic relationships with PeopleSoft and the Sun-Netscape Alliance. In July, ITRA launched UpdateWatch, a service providing ongoing proactive notification on individual product upgrades.

BUSINESS

INTRAWARE INC. is a provider of business-to-business e-commerce-based services for the corporate IT community. The Company provides software through its on-line purchasing service, Intraware.shop. This service includes a selection of business software, as well as provides vendors with a forum to market and sell to this targeted audience. The IT Knowledge Center is a destination Web site for people in need of technical information. The services include: Compariscope, an objective Internet-based software evaluation tool; Radarscope, a destination for IT professionals who need quick information about business products; The Intranet Library, a data base of product information and FAQ's; Ask James, an on-line advice service; IT Book Center, providing feature technical articles and book reviews; and IT Training Center, providing on-line classes and computer- and Internet-based training courses. The Company also provides SubscribNet, a service that sends out proactive notification on all software releases, patches, and enhancements.

REVENUES

(02/28/1999)	($000)	(%)
Software product sales	34,741	90.4
Online Services	3,676	9.6
Total	38,417	100.0

ANNUAL FINANCIAL DATA

	2/28/99	2/28/98	2/28/97
Earnings Per Share	d3.00	d2.05	d1.36
Cash Flow Per Share	d2.48	d1.88	d1.30
Tang. Book Val. Per Share	0.04	0.14	0.11
INCOME STATEMENT (IN THOUSANDS):			
Total Revenues	38,417	10,387	6
Costs & Expenses	48,352	14,017	916
Depreciation & Amort.	2,111	337	42
Operating Income	d12,046	d3,967	d952
Net Interest Inc./(Exp.)	d198	d103	d12
Income Before Income Taxes	d12,033	d4,049	d944
Net Income	d12,033	d4,049	d944
Cash Flow	d9,922	d3,712	d902
Average Shs. Outstg.	4,007	1,972	694
BALANCE SHEET (IN THOUSANDS):			
Cash & Cash Equivalents	1,792	612	303
Total Current Assets	32,692	14,289	341
Net Property	1,962	1,078	662
Total Assets	35,006	15,384	1,026
Total Current Liabilities	33,869	14,509	255
Long-Term Obligations	168	105	189
Net Stockholders' Equity	969	770	582
Net Working Capital	d1,177	d220	86
Year-end Shs. Outstg.	23,756	5,376	5,250
STATISTICAL RECORD:			
Debt/Total Assets %	0.5	0.7	18.4
Statistics are as originally reported.			

OFFICERS:
M. B. Hoffman, Chmn.
C. G. Davis Jr., Vice-Chmn.
P. H. Jackson, Pres., C.E.O.
D. M. Freed, Exec. V.P., C.F.O.

PRINCIPAL OFFICE: 25 Orinda Way, Suite 101, Orinda, CA 94563

TELEPHONE NUMBER: (925) 253-4500
FAX: (925) 253-4584
WEB: www.intraware.com

NO. OF EMPLOYEES: 169

SHAREHOLDERS: 210 (approx.)

ANNUAL MEETING: In August

INCORPORATED: DE, Aug., 1996

INSTITUTIONAL HOLDINGS:
No. of Institutions: 34
Shares Held: 1,986,620
% Held: 8.3

INDUSTRY: Communication services, nec (SIC: 4899)

TRANSFER AGENT(S): Harris Trust Company of California, Chicago, IL

INTUIT INC.

YIELD ...
P/E RATIO 81.0

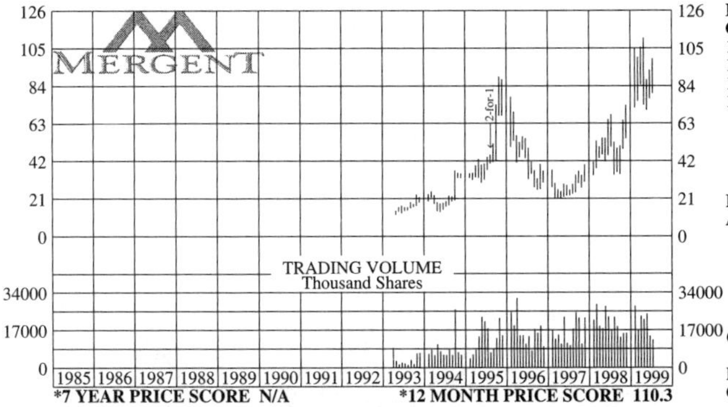

MERGENT

TRADING VOLUME
Thousand Shares

| | 1985 | 1986 | 1987 | 1988 | 1989 | 1990 | 1991 | 1992 | 1993 | 1994 | 1995 | 1996 | 1997 | 1998 | 1999 |

*7 YEAR PRICE SCORE N/A   ***12 MONTH PRICE SCORE 110.3**
*NYSE COMPOSITE INDEX=100

INTERIM EARNINGS (Per Share):

Qtr.	Oct.	Jan.	Apr.	July
1995-96	d0.42	0.46	d0.01	d0.48
1996-97	d0.61	0.94	0.01	d0.42
1997-98	d0.27	0.85	d0.05	d0.70
1998-99	d0.83	1.42	1.12	...

INTERIM DIVIDENDS (Per Share):

Amt.	Decl.	Ex.	Rec.	Pay.
	No dividends paid.			

CAPITALIZATION (7/31/98):

	($000)	(%)
Long-Term Debt	35,566	3.2
Common & Surplus	1,088,361	96.8
Total	1,123,927	100.0

RECENT DEVELOPMENTS: For the quarter ended 4/30/99, the Company reported net income of $72.6 million, which included gains from the sale of marketable securities totaling $58.6 million, compared with a net loss of $2.2 million in the prior year. The 1998 quarter included a non-recurring marketing charge of $16.2 million. Net revenue jumped 68.8% to $239.7 million from $142.0 million the year before. Revenue associated with professional tax software sales by Lacerte, which was acquired in June 1998, was included in the 1999 results and not in the 1998 quarter. Revenue and net income benefited from the launch of QuickBooks 99 in January and strong growth in personal tax products and Internet e-finance services, along with new business from the Lacerte acquisition. Internet commerce contributed 20.0% of total revenue in the recent quarter, more than 2.5 times the revenue in the previous year. INTU reported income from operations of $45.7 million compared with a loss of $7.3 million in 1998.

BUSINESS

INTUIT INC. develops, sells and supports small business accounting, tax preparation and consumer finance desktop software products, financial supplies (such as computer checks, envelopes and invoices), and Internet products and services for individuals and small businesses. The Company's products and services are designed to automate commonly performed financial tasks and to simplify the way individuals and small businesses manage their finances. The Company sells its products throughout North America and in many international markets. Sales are made through retail distribution channels, traditional direct sales to customers and via the Internet. Intuit, Quicken, QuickBooks and Turbo Tax, among others, are registered trademarks and/or registered service marks of the Company. Quicken.com and QuickenMortgage are trademarks and/or service marks of the Company or one of its subsidiaries.

ANNUAL FINANCIAL DATA

	7/31/98	7/31/97	7/31/96	7/31/95	③ 7/31/94	9/30/93	9/30/92
Earnings Per Share	① d0.24	①② d0.06	①② d0.32	① d1.11	① d5.21	0.37	0.25
Cash Flow Per Share	0.83	1.17	1.20	0.46	d3.95	0.53	0.34
Tang. Book Val. Per Share	12.08	7.85	5.84	4.71	2.26	2.20	0.32
INCOME STATEMENT (IN THOUSANDS):							
Total Revenues	592,736	598,925	538,608	395,729	194,126	121,372	83,793
Costs & Expenses	576,080	540,298	476,029	397,946	328,300	104,561	74,166
Depreciation & Amort.	53,238	58,667	68,355	64,011	42,884	3,580	1,773
Operating Income	d36,582	d40	d5,776	d66,228	d177,058	13,231	7,854
Net Interest Inc./(Exp.)	...	...	...	d232	d10	d100	d66
Income Before Income Taxes	d19,823	9,809	1,870	d21,122	d174,561	13,755	8,142
Income Taxes	cr7,666	12,741	16,225	24,241	1,752	5,344	2,866
Net Income	① d12,157	①② d2,932	①② d14,355	① d45,363	① d176,313	8,411	5,276
Cash Flow	41,081	55,735	54,000	18,648	d133,429	11,991	7,049
Average Shs. Outstg.	49,676	47,448	45,149	40,762	33,804	22,700	21,016
BALANCE SHEET (IN THOUSANDS):							
Cash & Cash Equivalents	882,117	395,899	198,018	191,375	83,886	39,540	9,030
Total Current Assets	980,125	454,777	280,413	259,381	119,942	75,511	22,516
Net Property	69,413	83,404	95,611	48,849	24,196	7,422	5,593
Total Assets	1,498,596	663,676	418,020	384,202	244,582	83,281	29,634
Total Current Liabilities	374,669	211,582	110,689	98,083	50,816	34,037	12,127
Long-Term Obligations	35,566	36,444	5,583	4,426	...	...	162
Net Stockholders' Equity	1,088,361	415,061	299,235	281,186	185,823	49,244	17,345
Net Working Capital	605,456	243,195	169,724	161,298	69,126	41,474	10,389
Year-end Shs. Outstg.	59,320	46,942	45,807	43,867	38,472	22,410	12,928
STATISTICAL RECORD:							
Operating Profit Margin %	...	...	...	...	...	10.9	9.4
Net Profit Margin %	...	...	...	...	...	6.9	6.3
Return on Equity %	...	...	...	...	...	17.1	30.4
Return on Assets %	...	...	...	...	...	10.1	17.8
Debt/Total Assets %	2.4	5.5	1.3	1.2	...	...	0.5
Price Range	73⅜-33⅞	40-20⅞	78-25⅞	89¼-29¾	36⅝-13½	23¼-12	...
P/E Ratio	...	...	...	...	...	62.8-32.4	...

Statistics are as originally reported. Adj. for stk. split: 2-for-1, 8/21/95 ① Incl. non-recurr. chrg. 7/31/98: $49.5 mill.; 7/31/97: $21.4 mill.; 7/31/96: $8.0 mill.; 7/31/95: $95.4 mill.; 7/31/94: $172.3 mill. ② Bef. disc. oper. gain 7/31/97: $71.2 mill. ($1.50/sh.); loss 7/31/96: $6.3 mill. ($0.14/sh.) ③ For 10 months due to fiscal year-end change.

OFFICERS:
W. V. Campbell, Chmn.
W. H. Harris Jr., Pres., C.E.O.
G. J. Santora, Sr. V.P., C.F.O., C.A.O.
L. Fellows, Treas.

PRINCIPAL OFFICE: 2535 Garcia Avenue, Mountain View, CA 94043

TELEPHONE NUMBER: (650) 944-6000
FAX: (650) 944-3060
WEB: www.intuit.com
NO. OF EMPLOYEES: 2,860
SHAREHOLDERS: 800 holders of record, 56,000 beneficial holders
ANNUAL MEETING: In Jan.
INCORPORATED: CA, Mar., 1983; reincorp., DE, Mar., 1983

INSTITUTIONAL HOLDINGS:
No. of Institutions: 229
Shares Held: 48,907,217
% Held: 80.0

INDUSTRY: Prepackaged software (SIC: 7372)

TRANSFER AGENT(S): American Stock Transfer & Trust Company, New York, NY.

ISS GROUP, INC.

YIELD ...
P/E RATIO 725.0

INTERIM EARNINGS (Per Share):

Qtr.	Mar.	June	Sept.	Dec.
1996	------------------d0.07------------------			
1997	d0.03	d0.04	d0.07	d0.12
1998	d0.10	d0.03	d0.02	d0.03
1999	0.04	0.04	...	

INTERIM DIVIDENDS (Per Share):

Amt.	Decl.	Ex.	Rec.	Pay.
2-for-1	4/01/99	5/20/99	5/05/99	5/19/99

CAPITALIZATION (12/31/98):

	($000)	(%)
Common & Surplus	66,315	100.0
Total	66,315	100.0

RECENT DEVELOPMENTS: For the quarter ended 6/30/99, net income jumped to $1.7 million compared with a net loss of $1.1 million in the corresponding quarter of 1998. Revenues soared to $16.9 million from $7.3 million in the previous year. Revenues reflected strong demand for the Company's SAFEsuite® security management solutions. Operating income was $238,000 compared with an operating loss of $1.9 million the year before. The Company's

SAFEsuite® products will be deployed into Microsoft's global network to help measure and manage Microsoft's security risk enterprise-wide. Meanwhile, ISSX opened a research and software development center in the U.K. The center will provide sales, marketing, and technical support facilities, as well as operate as a base for the Company's European offices. The Company has also opened three new offices in Latin America.

BUSINESS

ISS GROUP, INC. is a provider of network security monitoring, detection and response solutions that protect the security and integrity of enterprise information systems. The Company also provides security solutions designed to enhance the security performance of existing systems by such safeguards as firewalls, authentication and encryption. ISSX's products use the Adaptive Network Security approach, which includes continuous security monitoring, detection and response to develop and enforce an active network security policy. The Company's solutions are licensed to over 3,000 organizations worldwide, including firms in the Global 2000, U.S. and international government agencies, and major universities. The Company's SAFEsuite® solutions strengthen the security of existing systems and improve the security posture for global organizations. Revenues in 1998 were derived: perpetual licenses, 72.2%; subscriptions, 20.6%; and professional services, 7.2%.

ANNUAL FINANCIAL DATA

	12/31/98	12/31/97	12/31/96	12/31/95
Earnings Per Share	☐ d0.14	d0.25	d0.07	d0.01
Cash Flow Per Share	d0.06	d0.23	d0.07	d0.01
Tang. Book Val. Per Share	1.69	...	...	...
INCOME STATEMENT (IN THOUSANDS):				
Total Revenues	35,929	13,467	4,462	257
Costs & Expenses	40,131	17,280	5,601	393
Depreciation & Amort.	2,204	334	66	4
Operating Income	d6,406	d4,147	d1,205	d140
Net Interest Inc./(Exp.)	2,366	228	74	...
Income Before Income Taxes	d4,040	d3,919	d1,131	d140
Income Taxes	62	...	...	...
Net Income	☐ d4,102	d3,919	d1,131	d140
Cash Flow	d1,898	d3,585	d1,065	d136
Average Shs. Outstg.	29,766	15,814	15,832	10,002
BALANCE SHEET (IN THOUSANDS):				
Cash & Cash Equivalents	52,632	3,929	2,007	6
Total Current Assets	65,961	8,248	4,084	...
Net Property	4,017	1,569	273	...
Total Assets	78,021	9,866	4,380	176
Total Current Liabilities	11,572	5,976	1,786	...
Long-Term Obligations	...	70	140	...
Net Stockholders' Equity	66,315	d5,058	d1,160	d7
Net Working Capital	54,389	2,272	2,298	6
Year-end Shs. Outstg.	34,584	15,842	15,804	...
STATISTICAL RECORD:				
Debt/Total Assets %	...	0.7	3.2	...
Price Range	15⅛-4¼	...	...	...

Statistics are as originally reported. Adj. for 2-for-1 split, 5/99. ☐ Incl. $802,000 charge for in-process R&D rel. to acqs. of March Info. Systems & DbSecure Technology.

OFFICERS:
T. E. Noonan, Chmn., Pres., C.E.O.
R. Macchia, V.P., C.F.O.
C. W. Klaus, C.T.O., Sec.

PRINCIPAL OFFICE: 6600 Peachtree-Dunwoody Rd., 300 Embassy Row, Suite 500, Atlanta, GA 30328

TELEPHONE NUMBER: (678) 443-6000
FAX: (678) 443-6476
WEB: www.iss.net

NO. OF EMPLOYEES: 328 (avg.)

SHAREHOLDERS: 237

ANNUAL MEETING: In May

INCORPORATED: DE, Dec., 1997

INSTITUTIONAL HOLDINGS:
No. of Institutions: 69
Shares Held: 21,957,291
% Held: 59.4

INDUSTRY: Prepackaged software (SIC: 7372)

TRANSFER AGENT(S): SunTrust Bank, Atlanta, GA.

ITURF INC.

YIELD ...
P/E RATIO ...

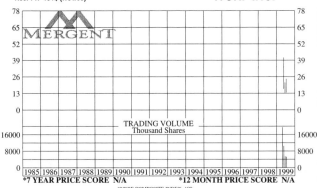

INTERIM EARNINGS (Per Share):

Qtr.	Apr.	July	Oct.	Jan.
1997-98	-------------------- 0.03 --------------------			
1998-99	-------------------- 0.03 --------------------			
1999-00	0.01	...	...	...

INTERIM DIVIDENDS (Per Share):

Amt.	Decl.	Ex.	Rec.	Pay.
	No dividends paid.			

TRADING VOLUME
Thousand Shares

CAPITALIZATION (1/31/99):

	($000)	(%)
Common & Surplus	380	100.0
Total	380	100.0

*7 YEAR PRICE SCORE N/A   *12 MONTH PRICE SCORE N/A

*NYSE COMPOSITE INDEX=100

RECENT DEVELOPMENTS: For the thirteen weeks ended 5/1/99, the Company reported a net loss of $197,000 compared with a net loss of $53,000 in the corresponding period of 1998. Net revenues surged to $2.6 million from $69,000 in the prior year. Results were favorably affected by increased traffic to the Company's e-commerce and community websites. Gross profit rocketed to $1.3 million from $34,000 a year earlier. Going forward, the Company should continue to benefit from its aggressive growth initiatives, customer acquisition programs, and strategic alli-

ances. Meanwhile, a strategic alliance with America Online should provide the Company with a key opportunity to reach the largest audience in cyberspace. The agreement not only provides TURF with significant customer acquisition opportunities, but also serves as a brand building vehicle. Separately, the Company entered into a partnership and marketing agreement with RocketCash Corporation. This agreement should enhance the Company's efforts to drive teens to iTurf's Web sites.

BUSINESS

ITURF INC., a subsidiary of dELiA*s Inc., is a provider of Internet community, content and commerce services focused primarily on Generation Y (people in the age range of 20 to 29). iTurf is an on-line destination, or network of websites, offering interactive magazines, proprietary content, chat rooms, posting boards, personal homepages, e-mail, and on-line shopping consisting of a wide range of apparel, footwear, athletic gear and home furnishings.

QUARTERLY DATA

(01/31/99)($000)	Rev	Inc
1st Quarter	69	(53)
2nd Quarter	760	(24)
3rd Quarter	1,064	99
4th Quarter................	2,121	403

ANNUAL FINANCIAL DATA

	1/31/99	1/31/98	1/31/97
Earnings Per Share	0.03	0.03	Nil
Cash Flow Per Share	0.04	...	...
Tang. Book Val. Per Share	0.01	...	...

INCOME STATEMENT (IN THOUSANDS):

Total Revenues	4,014	134	13
Costs & Expenses	3,076	177	20
Depreciation & Amort.	117	6	...
Operating Income	821	d49	d7
Net Interest Inc./(Exp.)	d41	d20	...
Income Before Income Taxes	780	d69	d7
Income Taxes	355	cr29	cr3
Net Income	425	d40	d4
Cash Flow	542	d34	d4
Average Shs. Outstg.	12,518	12,500	12,500

BALANCE SHEET (IN THOUSANDS):

Cash & Cash Equivalents	375	31	...
Total Current Assets	375	31	...
Net Property	414	95	...
Total Assets	1,216	467	...
Total Current Liabilities	836	512	...
Net Stockholders' Equity	380	d45	...
Net Working Capital	d461	d481	...
Year-end Shs. Outstg.	12,500	12,500	12,500

STATISTICAL RECORD:

Operating Profit Margin %	20.5	...	...
Net Profit Margin %	10.6	...	...
Return on Equity %	111.8	...	...
Return on Assets %	35.0	...	...
Statistics are as originally reported.			

OFFICERS:
S. I. Kahn, Chmn., Pres., C.E.O.
D. Goldstein, C.F.O., Treas.
A. S. Navarro, C.O.O.

PRINCIPAL OFFICE: 435 Hudson St., New York, NY 10014

TELEPHONE NUMBER: (212) 741-7785
WEB: www.iturf.com

NO. OF EMPLOYEES: 40 (avg.)

SHAREHOLDERS: N/A

ANNUAL MEETING: N/A

INCORPORATED: DE, Aug., 1997

INSTITUTIONAL HOLDINGS:
No. of Institutions: 1
Shares Held: 15,400
% Held: 0.3

INDUSTRY: Information retrieval services (SIC: 7375)

TRANSFER AGENT(S): The Bank of New York, New York, NY.

IVILLAGE INC.

YIELD ...
P/E RATIO ...

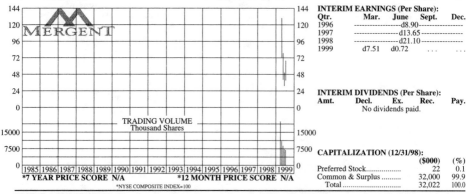

*7 YEAR PRICE SCORE N/A   *12 MONTH PRICE SCORE N/A

*NYSE COMPOSITE INDEX=100

INTERIM EARNINGS (Per Share):

Qtr.	Mar.	June	Sept.	Dec.
1996		d8.90		
1997		d13.65		
1998		d21.10		
1999	d7.51	d0.72	...	...

INTERIM DIVIDENDS (Per Share):

Amt.	Decl.	Ex.	Rec.	Pay.
	No dividends paid.			

CAPITALIZATION (12/31/98):

	($000)	(%)
Preferred Stock..................	22	0.1
Common & Surplus	32,000	99.9
Total	32,022	100.0

RECENT DEVELOPMENTS: For the three months ended 6/30/99, the Company reported a net loss of $17.1 million compared with a net loss of $11.8 million in the corresponding period of the prior year. Total revenues more than tripled to $8.1 million from $2.6 million in the previous-year quarter. Advertising, sponsorship and other revenues nearly tripled to $6.0 million from $2.1 the year before. Commerce revenues were $2.1 million versus $520,000 in the 1998 period. Revenue growth was fueled by an increase in membership to approximately 2.1 million users from 363,000 users in prior-year period. The Company has also invested $28.5 million in a marketing campaign that will consist primarily of broadcast and print advertisements. This campaign is expected to begin during the last week of the third quarter of 1999 and run through the fourth quarter of 1999 and into the first quarter of 2000.

BUSINESS

IVILLAGE INC. is an on-line network of sites tailored to the interests and needs of women aged 25 through 49. The Company provides advertisers and merchants with targeted access to women using the Web. iVillage.com consists of 14 channels organized by subject matter. The channels cover leading topics of interest to women on-line, such as family, health, work, money, food, relationships, shopping, travel, pets and astrology. The Company facilitates channel usage by providing common features and functionality within each channel, including experts, chats, message boards and services.

ANNUAL FINANCIAL DATA

	12/31/98	12/31/97	12/31/96
Earnings Per Share	d21.10	d13.65	d8.90
Cash Flow Per Share	d18.36	d11.80	d8.80
Tang. Book Val. Per Share	13.00	2.70	...
INCOME STATEMENT (IN THOUSANDS):			
Total Revenues	15,012	6,019	732
Costs & Expenses	53,656	24,218	10,334
Depreciation & Amort.	5,683	2,886	109
Operating Income	d44,328	d21,085	d9,711
Net Interest Inc./(Exp.)	591	d216	28
Income Before Income Taxes	d43,654	d21,301	d9,683
Net Income	d43,654	d21,301	d9,683
Cash Flow	d37,971	d18,415	d9,574
Average Shs. Outstg.	2,068	1,561	1,087
BALANCE SHEET (IN THOUSANDS):			
Cash & Cash Equivalents	30,825	4,335	...
Total Current Assets	34,688	6,688	...
Net Property	7,380	3,803	...
Total Assets	46,791	16,236	...
Total Current Liabilities	14,769	5,575	...
Long-Term Obligations	...	139	...
Net Stockholders' Equity	32,022	10,522	...
Net Working Capital	19,919	1,114	...
Year-end Shs. Outstg.	2,113	1,820	1,150
STATISTICAL RECORD:			
Debt/Total Assets %	...	0.9	...

Statistics are as originally reported.

REVENUES

12/31/1998	($000)	(%)
New Media	12,451	82.9
Commerce	2,561	17.1
Total	15,012	100.0

OFFICERS:
C. Carpenter, Co-Chmn., C.E.O.
N. Evans, Co-Chmn., Editor-in-Chief
C. T. Monaghan, C.F.O.
S. A. Elkes, V.P., Business Affairs, Asst. Sec.

PRINCIPAL OFFICE: 170 Fifth Avenue, New York, NY 10010

TELEPHONE NUMBER: (212) 604-0963
WEB: www.ivillage.com

NO. OF EMPLOYEES: 200

SHAREHOLDERS: 75

ANNUAL MEETING: N/A

INCORPORATED: DE, Jun., 1995

INSTITUTIONAL HOLDINGS:
No. of Institutions: 37
Shares Held: 1,504,798
% Held: 6.3

INDUSTRY: Computer integrated systems design (SIC: 7373)

TRANSFER AGENT(S): Continental Stock Transfer & Trust Company, New York, NY

IXL ENTERPRISES, INC.

YIELD ...
P/E RATIO ...

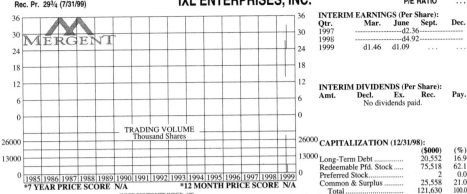

*7 YEAR PRICE SCORE N/A   *12 MONTH PRICE SCORE N/A
*NYSE COMPOSITE INDEX=100

INTERIM EARNINGS (Per Share):

Qtr.	Mar.	June	Sept.	Dec.
1997	------------------d2.36------------------			
1998	------------------d4.92------------------			
1999	d1.46	d1.09	...	...

INTERIM DIVIDENDS (Per Share):

Amt.	Decl.	Ex.	Rec.	Pay.
	No dividends paid.			

CAPITALIZATION (12/31/98):

	($000)	(%)
Long-Term Debt	20,552	16.9
Redeemable Pfd. Stock	75,518	62.1
Preferred Stock.................	2	0.0
Common & Surplus	25,558	21.0
Total.............................	121,630	100.0

RECENT DEVELOPMENTS: For the three months ended 6/30/99, the Company reported a net loss of $16.4 million compared with a net loss of $10.7 million the corresponding period of the previous year. Revenues surged to $45.9 million versus $10.5 million the year before. The increase in revenues was attributed to a series of acquisitions as well as an aggressive hiring initiative that expanded the client base and headcount. Revenue growth was also due to an increase in the number and size of client engagements and the development and growth of industry practice groups. On 8/18/99, the Company announced the expansion of its international presence into Tokyo, Japan. With this addition, the Company's worldwide presence has grown to 20 offices in five countries, including London, Madrid and Hamburg.

BUSINESS

IXL ENTERPRISES, INC. is an Internet services company that provides Internet strategy consulting and Internet-based tools for Fortune 1000 companies and other corporate users of information technology. The Company aims to help businesses identify how the Internet can be used to their competitive advantage through the design, development and deployment of Internet applications and tools. The Company's service offerings include Internet strategy consulting, e-commerce systems and services, business information management systems, interactive learning environments, digital media services, traditional Web site development, customized hosting, proprietary sales presentation sytems, and Web publishing technology.

ANNUAL FINANCIAL DATA

	12/31/98	12/31/97	12/31/96
Earnings Per Share	d4.92	d2.36	d0.37
Cash Flow Per Share	d3.58	d1.35	d0.04
Tang. Book Val. Per Share	...	0.45	...
INCOME STATEMENT (IN THOUSANDS):			
Total Revenues	64,767	18,986	5,379
Costs & Expenses	96,138	29,180	5,636
Depreciation & Amort.	15,807	6,599	1,300
Operating Income	d47,178	d16,793	d1,557
Net Interest Inc./(Exp.)	d20	d102	2
Income Before Income Taxes	d48,866	d18,222	d1,756
Income Taxes	...	cr2,782	cr302
Net Income	d48,866	d15,440	d1,454
Cash Flow	d42,158	d8,841	d154
Average Shs. Outstg.	11,777	6,540	3,972
BALANCE SHEET (IN THOUSANDS):			
Cash & Cash Equivalents	19,259	23,038	...
Total Current Assets	48,440	28,771	...
Net Property	27,975	9,178	...
Total Assets	142,951	57,612	...
Total Current Liabilities	21,321	4,892	...
Long-Term Obligations	20,552	840	...
Net Stockholders' Equity	25,560	21,950	...
Net Working Capital	27,119	23,879	...
Year-end Shs. Outstg.	16,082	8,230	...
STATISTICAL RECORD:			
Debt/Total Assets %	14.4	1.5	...
Statistics are as originally reported.			

OFFICERS:
U. B. Ellis Jr., Chmn., C.E.O.
K. M. Wall, Vice-Chmn.
W. Boylston, C.F.O.
W. C. Nussey, Pres., C.O.O.

PRINCIPAL OFFICE: 1888 Emery St. NW, Atlanta, GA 30318

TELEPHONE NUMBER: (800) 573-5544
FAX: (404) 237-3801
WEB: www.iXL.com.

NO. OF EMPLOYEES: 1,565 (approx.)

SHAREHOLDERS: 276

ANNUAL MEETING: N/A

INCORPORATED: DE, Mar., 1996

INSTITUTIONAL HOLDINGS:
No. of Institutions: 3
Shares Held: 47,900
% Held: 0.1

INDUSTRY: Computer integrated systems design (SIC: 7373)

TRANSFER AGENT(S): SunTrust Bank, Atlanta, GA

JUNO ONLINE SERVICES, INC.

YIELD ...
P/E RATIO ...

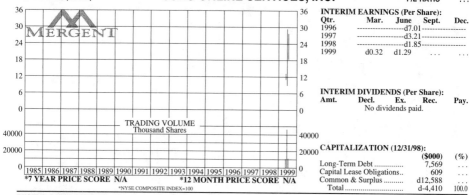

INTERIM EARNINGS (Per Share):

Qtr.	Mar.	June	Sept.	Dec.
1996			d7.01	
1997			d3.21	
1998			d1.85	
1999	d0.32	d1.29	...	...

INTERIM DIVIDENDS (Per Share):

Amt.	Decl.	Ex.	Rec.	Pay.
		No dividends paid.		

CAPITALIZATION (12/31/98):

	($000)	(%)
Long-Term Debt	7,569	...
Capital Lease Obligations..	609	...
Common & Surplus	d12,588	...
Total	d-4,410	100.0

RECENT DEVELOPMENTS: For the quarter ended 6/30/99, JWEB reported a net loss of $17.3 million versus a net loss of $6.9 million in the equivalent period of 1998. Results included subscriber acquisition costs of $13.9 million in 1999 and $427,000 in 1998. Total revenues more than doubled to $11.1 million from $4.3 million in the prior year. Revenues from billing services rocketed to $7.1 million from $709,000 in 1998, while revenues from advertising and transaction fees leapt 75.5% to $2.7 million. Sepa-

rately, an agreement between JWEB and Covad Communications that will make it possible for Juno to deliver high-speed Internet access nationwide should contribute to results. Juno users will have broadband access to, among other services, high-bandwidth multimedia content such as streaming video and audio over the Internet. Juno plans to launch JUNO EXPRESS, the Company's broadband service, in a pilot program later this year, with wider release planned for 2000.

BUSINESS

JUNO ONLINE SERVICES, INC. is a provider of Internet-related services to millions of computer users throughout the United States. The Company offers several levels of service, ranging from basic dial-up Internet e-mail, which is provided to the end-user for free, to full, competitively priced access to the World Wide Web. Juno's revenues are derived primarily from subscription fees charged for certain billable services, the sale of advertising, and direct sale of products to Juno subscribers. Since the launch of Juno's basic e-mail service in 1996, more than 7.2 million Juno accounts have been created.

ANNUAL FINANCIAL DATA

	12/31/98	12/31/97	12/31/96
Earnings Per Share	d1.85	d3.21	d7.01
Cash Flow Per Share	d1.70	d3.17	d7.01
INCOME STATEMENT (IN THOUSANDS):			
Total Revenues	21,694	9,091	136
Costs & Expenses	50,735	42,668	23,266
Depreciation & Amort.	2,629	405	...
Operating Income	d31,670	d33,982	d23,130
Net Interest Inc./(Exp.)	44	243	128
Income Before Income Taxes	d31,626	d33,739	d23,002
Net Income	d31,626	d33,739	d23,002
Cash Flow	d28,997	d33,334	d23,002
Average Shs. Outstg.	17,091	10,500	3,281
BALANCE SHEET (IN THOUSANDS):			
Cash & Cash Equivalents	8,152	13,770	...
Total Current Assets	10,435	16,080	...
Net Property	4,086	3,966	...
Total Assets	14,703	20,133	...
Total Current Liabilities	18,778	9,153	...
Long-Term Obligations	8,178	270	...
Net Stockholders' Equity	d12,588	10,504	...
Net Working Capital	d8,343	6,927	...
STATISTICAL RECORD:			
Debt/Total Assets %	55.6	1.3	...
Statistics are as originally reported.			

REVENUES

(12/31/1998)	($000)	(%)
Billable Services	6,645	30.6
Advertising & Transaction	6,454	29.8
Direct Product Sales	8,595	39.6
Total	21,694	100.0

OFFICERS:
D. E. Shaw, Chmn.
C. E. Ardai, Pres., C.E.O.
R. M. Eaton Jr., C.F.O., Treas.
R. D. Buchband, Sr. V.P., Gen. Couns.

PRINCIPAL OFFICE: 1540 Broadway, New York, NY 10036

TELEPHONE NUMBER: (212) 597-9000
WEB: www.juno.com

NO. OF EMPLOYEES: 147

SHAREHOLDERS: N/A

ANNUAL MEETING: N/A

INCORPORATED: DE, July, 1996

INSTITUTIONAL HOLDINGS:
No. of Institutions: 3
Shares Held: 56,220
% Held: 0.0

INDUSTRY: Business services, nec (SIC: 7389)

TRANSFER AGENT(S): Continental Stock Transfer & Trust Company, New York, NY

LAUNCH MEDIA, INC.

YIELD ...
P/E RATIO ...

7 YEAR PRICE SCORE N/A   **12 MONTH PRICE SCORE N/A**

*NYSE COMPOSITE INDEX=100

TRADING VOLUME
Thousand Shares

1985 1986 1987 1988 1989 1990 1991 1992 1993 1994 1995 1996 1997 1998 1999

INTERIM EARNINGS (Per Share):

Qtr.	Mar.	June	Sept.	Dec.
1996			d5.37	
1997			d7.89	
1998			d16.36	
1999	d4.32	d0.87	...	...

INTERIM DIVIDENDS (Per Share):

Amt.	Decl.	Ex.	Rec.	Pay.
	No dividends paid.			

CAPITALIZATION (12/31/98):

	($000)	(%)
Long-Term Debt	201	2.1
Capital Lease Obligations..	438	4.6
Redeemable Pfd. Stock	36,707	385.6
Common & Surplus	d27,826	-292.3
Total	9,519	100.0

RECENT DEVELOPMENTS: For the quarter ended 6/30/99, the Company reported a net loss of $8.7 million compared with a loss of $3.8 million in the equivalent 1998 quarter. Net revenues were $3.5 million versus $1.1 million a year earlier. The registered user base of LAUN increased 55% to 1.7 million as of 6/30/99 from 1.1 million at 3/31/99. In July, LAUN and RealNetworks®, a media delivery service for the Internet, jointly announced that they have entered into a multi-level agreement. LAUNCH.com will use RealNetworks' streaming media technology to stream LAUN's music video content. In addition, LAUN is debuting its first-ever streaming media music video channel available on the REALPLAYER® G2. Consumers who express a preference for music content when downloading the REALPLAYER G2 will receive the LAUN RealChannel automatically. Separately, LAUN signed a content distribution agreement with Yahoo! Inc. whereby Yahoo! users can access LAUN's music news, album reviews, concert reviews, music videos and music features on co-branded pages with links to LAUNCH.com.

BUSINESS

LAUNCH MEDIA, INC. is a digital media company that provides an Internet destination for discovering new music. Using the inherent advantages of digital media, LAUN offers a music experience for consumers and provides a marketing platform for record labels, artists, advertisers and merchants. The Company delivers its content on the Internet at www.launch.com and on the monthly Launch on CD-ROM.

REVENUES

12/31/1998	($000)	(%)
Advertising...............	3,038	60.6
Subscription..............	1,463	29.2
Merchandise & Other	513	10.2
Total	5,014	100.0

ANNUAL FINANCIAL DATA

	12/31/98	12/31/97	12/31/96
Earnings Per Share	d16.36	d7.89	d5.37
Cash Flow Per Share	d15.81	d7.74	d5.25
INCOME STATEMENT (IN THOUSANDS):			
Total Revenues	5,014	3,137	1,375
Costs & Expenses	18,304	9,669	5,913
Depreciation & Amort.	514	144	115
Operating Income	d13,804	d6,675	d4,653
Net Interest Inc./(Exp.)	389	d14	167
Income Before Income Taxes	d13,415	d6,689	d4,486
Income Taxes	4	3	3
Net Income	d13,419	d6,692	d4,488
Cash Flow	d14,756	d7,156	d4,829
Average Shs. Outstg.	934	925	920
BALANCE SHEET (IN THOUSANDS):			
Cash & Cash Equivalents	6,728	644	...
Total Current Assets	8,011	1,110	...
Net Property	2,587	656	...
Total Assets	13,164	1,790	...
Total Current Liabilities	3,645	4,834	...
Long-Term Obligations	639	77	...
Net Stockholders' Equity	d27,826	d14,186	...
Net Working Capital	4,366	d3,724	...
Year-end Shs. Outstg.	934	933	...
STATISTICAL RECORD:			
Debt/Total Assets %	4.9	4.3	...
Statistics are as originally reported.			

OFFICERS:
D. B. Goldberg, Chmn., C.E.O.
R. D. Roback, Pres.
J. M. Mickeal, C.F.O., Sec.

PRINCIPAL OFFICE: 2700 Pennsylvania Avenue, Santa Monica, CA 90404

TELEPHONE NUMBER: (310) 526-4300
WEB: www.launch.com

NO. OF EMPLOYEES: 73

SHAREHOLDERS: N/A

ANNUAL MEETING: N/A

INCORPORATED: DE, Feb., 1994

INSTITUTIONAL HOLDINGS:
No. of Institutions: 4
Shares Held: 535,305
% Held: 4.2

INDUSTRY: Communication services, nec (SIC: 4899)

TRANSFER AGENT(S): U.S. Stock Transfer Corporation, Glendale, CA

LITRONIC INC.

YIELD ...
P/E RATIO ...

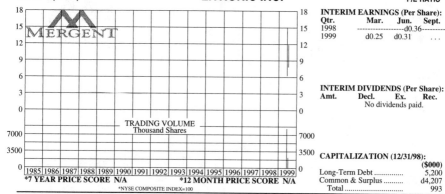

*7 YEAR PRICE SCORE N/A   *12 MONTH PRICE SCORE N/A

*NYSE COMPOSITE INDEX=100

INTERIM EARNINGS (Per Share):

Qtr.	Mar.	Jun.	Sept.	Dec.
1998	----------------d0.36----------------			
1999	d0.25	d0.31	...	...

INTERIM DIVIDENDS (Per Share):

Amt.	Decl.	Ex.	Rec.	Pay.
	No dividends paid.			

CAPITALIZATION (12/31/98):

	($000)	(%)
Long-Term Debt	5,200	523.7
Common & Surplus	d4,207	-423.7
Total	993	100.0

RECENT DEVELOPMENTS: For the quarter ended 6/30/99, the Company reported a net loss of $1.5 million versus a net loss of $160,000 in the corresponding quarter the year before. Total revenue jumped 80.2% to $2.7 million compared with $1.5 million in the prior-year quarter. Product revenue more than doubled to $2.3 milion from $1.0 million in the year-earlier quarter. License and service revenue was $96,000 compared with $518,000, a decrease of 81.5%. Research and development revenue totaled $326,000. Operating loss fell to $1.7 million from a loss of $48,000 a year ago. On 7/12/99, LTNX acquired Pulsar Data Systems, which extends the Company's capabilities in providing integrated, large-scale network and data security solutions for commercial and government organizations. Separately, LTNX has formed a strategic partnership with Datacard Worldwide to offer a more broad-based data security solution using LTNX's ProFile Manager™ and Net Sign™.

BUSINESS

LITRONIC INC. provides Internet data security services and develops and markets software and microprocessor-based products needed to secure electronic commerce business transactions and communications over the Internet and other communications networks based on Internet protocols. LTNX's primary data security products use an advanced form of computer security technology referred to as public key infrastructure which is the standard technology for securing Internet-based commerce and communications. The Company's Internet security products can be used with Web browsers, including Netscape Communicator and Microsoft Internet Explorer, to facilitate secure electronic commerce transactions and other data communications, such as secure e-mail. In July 1999, LTNX acquired Pulsar Data Systems, a network integration solutions company.

REVENUES

(12/31/1998)	($000)	(%)
Product Revenue	5,214	78.4
License & Service Revenue	1,041	15.6
Research & Development	398	6.0
Total	6,653	100.0

ANNUAL FINANCIAL DATA

	12/31/98	12/31/97	12/31/96
Earnings Per Share	d0.36	⊡ 0.41	⊡ 0.49
Cash Flow Per Share	d0.31	0.44	0.50
INCOME STATEMENT (IN THOUSANDS):			
Total Revenues	6,653	10,166	9,396
Costs & Expenses	7,533	8,384	7,395
Depreciation & Amort.	203	129	61
Operating Income	d1,083	1,653	1,940
Net Interest Inc./(Exp.)	d418	d42	d19
Income Before Income Taxes	d1,501	1,611	1,921
Income Taxes	cr95	22	29
Net Income	d1,406	⊡ 1,589	⊡ 1,892
Cash Flow	d1,203	1,718	1,953
Average Shs. Outstg.	3,871	3,871	3,871
BALANCE SHEET (IN THOUSANDS):			
Cash & Cash Equivalents	898	490	...
Total Current Assets	2,556	2,027	...
Net Property	235	320	...
Total Assets	2,791	2,347	...
Total Current Liabilities	1,798	1,642	...
Long-Term Obligations	5,200	606	...
Net Stockholders' Equity	d4,207	d2,801	...
Net Working Capital	758	385	...
Year-end Shs. Outstg.	3,871	3,871	...
STATISTICAL RECORD:			
Operating Profit Margin %	...	16.3	20.6
Net Profit Margin %	...	15.6	20.1
Return on Assets %	...	67.7	...
Debt/Total Assets %	186.3	25.8	...

Statistics are as originally reported. ⊡ Bef. disc. oper. gain $13.7 mill., 12/31/97; loss $986,000, 12/31/96.

OFFICERS:
K. Shah, Chmn., C.E.O.
W. W. Davis Sr., Pres., C.O.O.
T. W. Seykora, C.F.O.

PRINCIPAL OFFICE: 2030 Main Street, Suite 1250, Irvine, CA 92614

TELEPHONE NUMBER: (949) 851-1085
WEB: www.litronic.com

NO. OF EMPLOYEES: 65 full-time; 5 part-time

SHAREHOLDERS: 7

ANNUAL MEETING: N/A

INCORPORATED: DE, 1997

INSTITUTIONAL HOLDINGS:
No. of Institutions: N/A
Shares Held: N/A
% Held: N/A

INDUSTRY: Computer peripheral equipment, nec (SIC: 3577)

TRANSFER AGENT(S): American Stock Transfer Company, New York, NY

NASDAQ SYMBOL LOAX
Rec. Pr. 15⅞ (7/31/99)

LOG ON AMERICA, INC.

YIELD ...
P/E RATIO ...

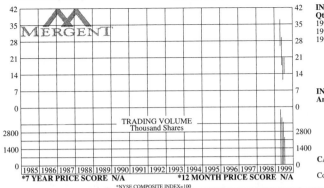

*7 YEAR PRICE SCORE N/A   *12 MONTH PRICE SCORE N/A
*NYSE COMPOSITE INDEX=100

INTERIM EARNINGS (Per Share):

Qtr.	Mar.	June	Sept.	Dec.
1997	------------------d0.12-----------------			
1998	------------------d0.11-----------------			
1999	d0.04	d0.07	...	...

INTERIM DIVIDENDS (Per Share):

Amt.	Decl.	Ex.	Rec.	Pay.
	No dividends paid.			

CAPITALIZATION (12/31/98):

	($000)	(%)
Common & Surplus	656	100.0
Total	656	100.0

RECENT DEVELOPMENTS: For the quarter ended 6/30/99, the Company reported a net loss of $458,941 compared with a net loss of $34,648 in 1998. Results were restricted by a significant increase in general and administrarive expenses. Total revenues advanced 38.6% to $245,267 versus $176,973 in the prior year. Revenue growth was attributed to an increase in sales efforts, services offered, and an aggressive marketing campaign in the Company's local market, Rhode Island. Operating loss amounted to $604,207 in 1999 compared with a loss of $34,648 in the prior year. On 8/4/99, the Company completed the acquisition of cyberTours, Inc., an Internet service provider in northern New England, for 506,667 shares of the Company's common stock, or $7.6 million. The acquisition of cyberTours brings over 22,000 customers under the Log On America brand and will enable the Company to cross-sell high-speed digital service line Internet access and other telecommunications services throughout the region.

BUSINESS

LOG ON AMERICA, INC. is a northeast regional information/Internet service provider. The Company provides business and home Internet users with dial-up access to the Internet via a personal computer and a modem or dedicated line. A large part of the Company's current operations is providing dedicated access lines for commercial accounts. The Company is also a local exchange carrier in the states of Rhode Island and Massachusetts. As a local exchange carrier, the Company provides a full range of local telecommunications services to its customers. These services include Internet, voice, data and cable programming. LOAX clients include residential users, Internet services providers, wireless carriers and business, government and institutional end users.

ANNUAL FINANCIAL DATA

	12/31/98	12/31/97
Earnings Per Share	d0.11	d0.12
Cash Flow Per Share	d0.09	d0.09
Tang. Book Val. Per Share	0.09	...
INCOME STATEMENT (IN THOUSANDS):		
Total Revenues	760	352
Costs & Expenses	1,100	558
Depreciation & Amort.	80	71
Operating Income	d420	d278
Net Interest Inc./(Exp.)	d2	d2
Income Before Income Taxes	d422	d280
Net Income	d422	d280
Cash Flow	d343	d209
Average Shs. Outstg.	3,853	2,435
BALANCE SHEET (IN THOUSANDS):		
Cash & Cash Equivalents	630	...
Total Current Assets	729	...
Net Property	72	...
Total Assets	1,137	...
Total Current Liabilities	481	...
Net Stockholders' Equity	656	...
Net Working Capital	248	...
Year-end Shs. Outstg.	4,611	...

Statistics are as originally reported.

OFFICERS:
D. R. Paolo, Chmn., Pres., C.E.O.
K. M. Cornell, C.F.O.
R. Paolo, V.P., Admin., Sec., Treas.

PRINCIPAL OFFICE: 3 Regency Plaza, Providence, RI 02903

TELEPHONE NUMBER: (401) 453-6100
FAX: (401) 459-6222
WEB: www.loa.com

NO. OF EMPLOYEES: 9 full-time; 4 part-time

SHAREHOLDERS: 64

ANNUAL MEETING: N/A

INCORPORATED: RI, 1992; reincorp., DE, July, 1997

INSTITUTIONAL HOLDINGS:
No. of Institutions: 1
Shares Held: 87,000
% Held: 1.2

INDUSTRY: Data processing and preparation (SIC: 7374)

TRANSFER AGENT(S): Continental Stock Transfer & Trust Company, New York, NY

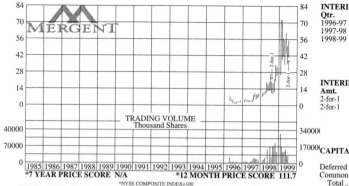

LYCOS, INC.

YIELD ...
P/E RATIO ...

INTERIM EARNINGS (Per Share):

Qtr.	Oct.	Jan.	Apr.	July
1996-97	d0.05	d0.04	d0.03	d0.01
1997-98	Nil	Nil	d1.48	d0.08
1998-99	0.18	d0.11	d0.31	...

INTERIM DIVIDENDS (Per Share):

Amt.	Decl.	Ex.	Rec.	Pay.
2-for-1	7/06/98	8/26/98	8/14/98	8/25/98
2-for-1	5/18/99	7/27/99	7/16/99	7/26/99

TRADING VOLUME
Thousand Shares

*7 YEAR PRICE SCORE N/A ***12 MONTH PRICE SCORE 111.7**
*NYSE COMPOSITE INDEX=100

CAPITALIZATION (7/31/98):

	($000)	(%)
Deferred Income Tax	37	0.0
Common & Surplus	168,687	100.0
Total	168,723	100.0

RECENT DEVELOPMENTS: On 7/1/99, the Company completed its acquisition of Wired Digital, Inc., an on-line media company, in a stock transaction valued at $285.0 million. Wired Digital is the producer of search engine HotBot (www.hotbot.com), and premium content sites Wired News, HotWired, Webmonkey and Suck.com. For the quarter ended 4/30/99, the Company reported a net loss of $13.3 million compared with a net loss of $22.1 million in the corresponding prior-year period. Total revenues more than doubled to $35.1 million from $15.1 million a year earlier. Advertising revenues increased to $23.6 million from $11.7 million in the comparable 1998 period. E-commerce, license and other revenues were $11.5 million versus $3.4 million the year before. Gross profit as a percentage of sales was 79.6% versus 68.6% in the prior-year quarter. On 5/12/99, the Company and USA Networks Inc. terminated the merger agreement between USA Networks and Ticketmaster Online-CitySearch, Inc.

BUSINESS

LYCOS, INC. is a Web media company and owner of the "Lycos Network," a unified set of Web sites that offer a variety of services, including Web navigation resources, homepage building and other Web community services, and a comprehensive shopping center. The Lycos Network is composed of premium sites: Lycos.com, Tripod, WhoWhere, Angelfire, MailCity, HotBot, Hot Wired, Wired News, Webmonkey, Suck.com and MyTime.com. Lycos.com, "Your Personal Internet Guide," is dedicated to helping individual users locate, retrieve and manage information tailored to their personal interests. LCOS is a global Internet concern with a major presence throughout the U.S., Europe and Asia.

ANNUAL FINANCIAL DATA

	7/31/98	7/31/97	7/31/96	7/31/95
Earnings Per Share	d1.56	d0.12	d0.10	Nil
Cash Flow Per Share	d1.51	d0.09	d0.09	...
Tang. Book Val. Per Share	2.07	0.66	0.80	0.03
INCOME STATEMENT (IN THOUSANDS):				
Total Revenues	56,060	22,273	5,257	5
Costs & Expenses	152,325	29,612	10,183	97
Depreciation & Amort.	3,703	1,411	877	14
Operating Income	d99,968	d8,750	d5,802	d105
Net Interest Inc./(Exp.)	3,052	2,130	714	...
Income Before Income Taxes	d96,917	d6,619	d5,088	d105
Net Income	d96,917	d6,619	d5,088	d105
Cash Flow	d93,213	d5,208	d4,211	d92
Average Shs. Outstg.	61,866	55,179	47,970	44,051
BALANCE SHEET (IN THOUSANDS):				
Cash & Cash Equivalents	153,728	40,766	44,142	446
Total Current Assets	200,797	60,745	49,450	451
Net Property	3,960	2,398	1,406	78
Total Assets	248,758	65,419	53,661	1,317
Total Current Liabilities	53,875	22,615	9,476	122
Net Stockholders' Equity	168,687	37,647	44,106	1,145
Net Working Capital	146,922	38,129	39,974	329
Year-end Shs. Outstg.	76,566	55,186	55,172	40,000
STATISTICAL RECORD:				
Price Range	34³/₈-7¹/₂	10¹/₂-2⁵/₈	7⁵/₁₆-1⁷/₁₆	...

Statistics are as originally reported. Adjusted for 2-for-1 stock split, 8/98 & 7/99.

REVENUES

(07/31/1998)	($000)	(%)
Advertising	41,768	74.5
Electr commerce, License	14,292	25.5
Total	56,060	100.0

OFFICERS:
R. J. Davis, Pres., C.E.O.
E. M. Philip, C.O.O., C.F.O., Sec.

INVESTOR CONTACT: Investor Relations,
(781) 370-2875

PRINCIPAL OFFICE: 400-2 Totten Pond Road, Waltham, MA 02154-2000

TELEPHONE NUMBER: (781) 370-2700
FAX: (781) 370-2600
WEB: www.lycos.com

NO. OF EMPLOYEES: 456

SHAREHOLDERS: 776 (approx.)

ANNUAL MEETING: In Dec.

INCORPORATED: DE, June, 1995

INSTITUTIONAL HOLDINGS:
No. of Institutions: 134
Shares Held: 26,965,966(Adj.)
% Held: 30.9

INDUSTRY: Business services, nec (SIC: 7389)

TRANSFER AGENT(S): Boston EquiServe, Canton, MA

NASDAQ SYMBOL MACR
Rec. Pr. 34 7/8 (7/31/99)

MACROMEDIA, INC.

YIELD ...
P/E RATIO 65.8

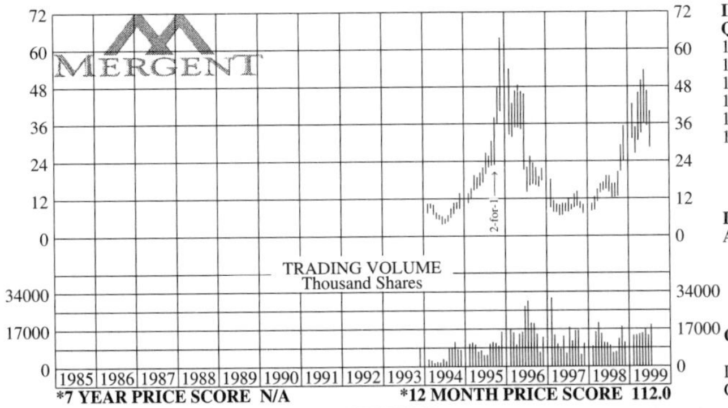

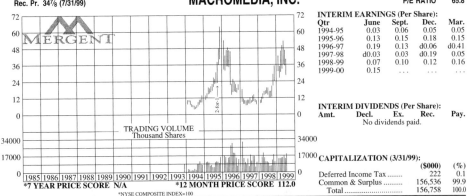

*7 YEAR PRICE SCORE N/A *12 MONTH PRICE SCORE 112.0

*NYSE COMPOSITE INDEX=100

INTERIM EARNINGS (Per Share):

Qtr	June	Sept.	Dec.	Mar.
1994-95	0.03	0.06	0.05	0.05
1995-96	0.13	0.15	0.18	0.15
1996-97	0.19	0.13	d0.06	d0.41
1997-98	d0.03	0.03	d0.19	0.05
1998-99	0.07	0.10	0.12	0.16
1999-00	0.15	...	...	...

INTERIM DIVIDENDS (Per Share):

Amt.	Decl.	Ex.	Rec.	Pay.

No dividends paid.

CAPITALIZATION (3/31/99):

	($000)	(%)
Deferred Income Tax	222	0.1
Common & Surplus	156,536	99.9
Total	156,758	100.0

RECENT DEVELOPMENTS: On 7/12/99, MACR signed a definitive agreement to acquire Elemental Software, a developer of Web application software, for $24.0 million in stock. For the three months ended 6/30/99, net income totaled $7.2 million compared with $3.0 million in the previous year. Revenues jumped 51.3% to $48.9 million from $32.3 million a year earlier. Strong demand for the Company's Web Publishing products, including DREAMWEAVER™, FLASH™ and FIREWORKS®, helped fuel revenue growth. In addition, the Company reported a record number of Flash and Shockwave player downloads during the quarter. Gross profit advanced 50.4% to $43.9 million from $29.2 million the year before. Operating income was $8.5 million compared with $3.0 million the prior year.

BUSINESS

MACROMEDIA, INC. is a provider of software tools, servers, and services for Web publishing, multimedia, graphics, and computer-based learning. The Company's Web Publishing software products, including DIRECTOR®, DREAMWEAVER™, FIREWORKS®, FLASH™, FREEHAND®, GENERATOR™, and SHOCKWAVE™, help create interactive Web experiences for e-commerce, entertainment, news, and information. The Company's Web Learning tools help large companies and educational institutions author, deliver, and manage learning programs over corporate intranets and the Internet. The Company sells its products worldwide through a variety of distribution channels, including traditional software distributors, mail order, educational distributors, value-added resellers, original equipment manufacturers, hardware and software superstores, retail dealers, and direct sales.

REVENUES

(3/31/99)	($000)	(%)
Web Publishing	123,772	82.6
Learning	15,884	10.6
Other	10,230	6.8
Total	149,886	100.0

ANNUAL FINANCIAL DATA

	3/31/99	3/31/98	3/31/97	3/31/96	3/31/95	3/31/94	3/31/93
Earnings Per Share	**0.44**	**[1] d0.16**	**[1] d0.16**	**[1] 0.59**	**[1] 0.19**	**[1] 0.15**	**[1] d0.01**
Cash Flow Per Share	**0.62**	**0.04**	**0.05**	**0.69**	**0.25**	**0.19**	**0.07**
Tang. Book Val. Per Share	**3.87**	**3.35**	**3.50**	**3.66**	**1.28**	**1.37**	**0.19**
INCOME STATEMENT (IN THOUSANDS):							
Total Revenues	149,886	113,086	107,365	116,691	55,892	30,132	25,261
Costs & Expenses	119,369	115,452	113,605	84,998	46,565	25,780	23,865
Depreciation & Amort.	8,144	7,728	7,766	4,013	2,110	1,102	1,476
Operating Income	22,373	d10,094	d14,006	27,680	7,217	3,250	d80
Net Interest Inc./(Exp.)	4,961	4,687	5,353	4,307	1,135	136	d68
Income Before Income Taxes	27,394	d5,358	d9,397	31,781	7,593	3,305	d234
Income Taxes	7,610	828	cr3,477	8,779	1,055	185	1
Net Income	19,784	[1] d6,186	[1] d5,920	[1] 23,002	[1] 6,538	[1] 3,120	[1] d235
Cash Flow	27,928	1,542	1,846	27,015	8,648	4,222	1,241
Average Shs. Outstg.	45,360	38,114	37,488	39,044	34,414	21,690	16,996
BALANCE SHEET (IN THOUSANDS):							
Cash & Cash Equivalents	108,802	86,131	102,451	116,662	33,981	26,468	1,024
Total Current Assets	142,545	106,937	117,592	140,946	45,886	32,605	6,712
Net Property	41,148	38,900	34,150	12,219	5,809	2,418	2,344
Total Assets	194,557	154,184	156,897	155,122	52,430	35,744	9,896
Total Current Liabilities	37,724	25,150	24,981	21,941	12,613	5,809	7,321
Long-Term Obligations	...	...	...	...	...	...	24
Net Stockholders' Equity	156,536	128,465	131,916	133,181	39,681	29,768	2,343
Net Working Capital	104,821	81,787	92,611	119,005	33,273	26,796	d609
Year-end Shs. Outstg.	40,481	38,298	37,743	36,413	31,000	21,256	8,294
STATISTICAL RECORD:							
Operating Profit Margin %	14.9	...	...	23.7	12.9	10.8	...
Net Profit Margin %	13.2	...	...	19.7	11.7	10.4	...
Return on Equity %	12.6	...	...	17.3	16.5	10.5	...
Return on Assets %	10.2	...	...	14.8	12.5	8.7	...
Debt/Total Assets %	...	...	...	...	...	...	0.2
Price Range	35 1/4-7 7/8	18 1/4-6 1/2	53 3/4-14 1/8	63 3/4-10 9/16	13 7/8-3 3/4	...	...
P/E Ratio	80.1-18.0	...	...	108.0-17.9	73.0-19.7	...	...

Statistics are as originally reported. Adj. for 2-for-1 stk. split, 10/13/95. [1] Incl. non-recurr. $7.7 mill. chrg., 1998; $350,000 chrg., 1997; $2.5 mill. chrg., 1996; $3.0 mill. chrg., 1995; $476,000 cr., 1994; $251,000 chrg., 1993; & $4.4 mill. chrg., 1992.

OFFICERS:
R. K. Burgess, Chmn., Pres., C.E.O.
E. A. Nelson, Sr. V.P., C.F.O., Sec.
B. Allum, Sr. V.P.
J. Dunn, Sr. V.P.

INVESTOR CONTACT: Kimberly Leo, (415) 252-2000

PRINCIPAL OFFICE: 600 Townsend Street, San Francisco, CA 94103

TELEPHONE NUMBER: (415) 252-2000
FAX: (415) 626-0554
WEB: www.macromedia.com

NO. OF EMPLOYEES: 553

SHAREHOLDERS: 351

ANNUAL MEETING: In Jul.

INCORPORATED: DE, Feb., 1992

INSTITUTIONAL HOLDINGS:
No. of Institutions: 143
Shares Held: 30,219,155
% Held: 73.6

INDUSTRY: Prepackaged software (SIC: 7372)

TRANSFER AGENT(S): ChaseMellon Shareholder Services, San Francisco, CA

MAIL.COM, INC.

YIELD ...
P/E RATIO ...

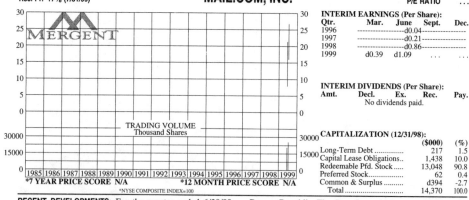

7 YEAR PRICE SCORE N/A **12 MONTH PRICE SCORE N/A**
*NYSE COMPOSITE INDEX=100

INTERIM EARNINGS (Per Share):

Qtr.	Mar.	June	Sept.	Dec.
1996	------------------d0.04------------------			
1997	------------------d0.21------------------			
1998	------------------d0.86------------------			
1999	d0.39	d1.09	...	...

INTERIM DIVIDENDS (Per Share):

Amt.	Decl.	Ex.	Rec.	Pay.
	No dividends paid.			

CAPITALIZATION (12/31/98):

	($000)	(%)
Long-Term Debt	217	1.5
Capital Lease Obligations	1,438	10.0
Redeemable Pfd. Stock	13,048	90.8
Preferred Stock	62	0.4
Common & Surplus	d394	-2.7
Total	14,370	100.0

RECENT DEVELOPMENTS: For the quarter ended 6/30/99, the Company reported a net loss of $8.0 million compared with a net loss of $1.3 million in the corresponding period of the prior year. Revenues advanced to $2.1 million from $139,000 a year earlier. Loss from operations totaled $7.9 million versus a loss from operations of $1.7 million the year before. As of 6/30/99, MAIL had 6.3 million e-mailboxes under management. During the quarter, the Company added 27 new advertisers to its ad network, including Banana Republic, The Gap, General Motors and Microsoft. On 7/19/99, MAIL acquired an approximately 19% equity interest in 3Cube, inc., a supplier of on-line communications and office productivity servics. In addition, the Company acquired eOrganizer, an on-line calendar company. These acquisitions enable MAIL to offer advanced e-mail messaging services to both its consumer and corporate customers.

BUSINESS

MAIL.COM, INC. is a global provider of e-mail and advanced messaging services to high-traffic Web sites, Internet Service Providers, corporations and direct to consumers. The Company provides Internet messaging outsourcing for brand name organizations such as AT&T, NBC, Time Warner, CBS SportsLine, Prodigy, GTE, Standard & Poor's, Snap.com and CNET. The Company generates revenues from advertising, subscription services and outsourcing.

ANNUAL FINANCIAL DATA

	12/31/98	12/31/97	12/31/96
Earnings Per Share	① d0.86	d0.21	d0.04
Cash Flow Per Share	d0.78	d0.19	d0.04
Tang. Book Val. Per Share	...	0.04	...
INCOME STATEMENT (IN THOUSANDS):			
Total Revenues	1,495	173	19
Costs & Expenses	13,451	2,882	527
Depreciation & Amort.	1,175	289	41
Operating Income	d13,131	d2,997	d550
Net Interest Inc./(Exp.)	168	1	5
Income Before Income Taxes	d12,525	d2,996	d545
Net Income	① d12,525	d2,996	d545
Cash Flow	d11,350	d2,707	d504
Average Shs. Outstg.	14,608	14,098	13,725
BALANCE SHEET (IN THOUSANDS):			
Cash & Cash Equivalents	8,414	910	...
Total Current Assets	9,970	946	...
Net Property	4,341	928	...
Total Assets	20,344	2,646	...
Total Current Liabilities	4,894	1,137	...
Long-Term Obligations	1,655	719	...
Net Stockholders' Equity	d333	567	...
Net Working Capital	5,076	d191	...
Year-end Shs. Outstg.	15,931	14,098	...
STATISTICAL RECORD:			
Debt/Total Assets %	8.1	27.2	...

Statistics are as originally reported. ① Incl. gain on the sale of investment of $438,000.

OFFICERS:
G. Gorman, Chmn., C.E.O.
G. Millin, Pres.
D. McClister, Exec. V.P., C.F.O.
D. Ambrosia, Exec. V.P., Gen. Couns.

PRINCIPAL OFFICE: 11 Broadway, New York, NY 10004

TELEPHONE NUMBER: (212) 425-4200
WEB: www.mail.com

NO. OF EMPLOYEES: 125

SHAREHOLDERS: N/A

ANNUAL MEETING: N/A

INCORPORATED: DE, Aug., 1994

INSTITUTIONAL HOLDINGS:
No. of Institutions: N/A
Shares Held: N/A
% Held: N/A

INDUSTRY: Computer integrated systems design (SIC: 7373)

TRANSFER AGENT(S): Continental Stock Transfer & Trust Company, New York, NY

MAPQUEST.COM, INC.

YIELD ...
P/E RATIO ...

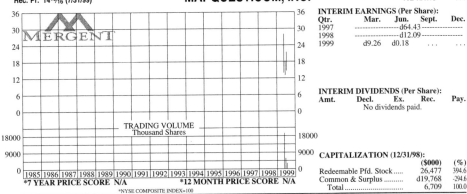

*7 YEAR PRICE SCORE N/A   *12 MONTH PRICE SCORE N/A

*NYSE COMPOSITE INDEX=100

1985|1986|1987|1988|1989|1990|1991|1992|1993|1994|1995|1996|1997|1998|1999

INTERIM EARNINGS (Per Share):

Qtr.	Mar.	Jun.	Sept.	Dec.
1997	---------------- d64.43 ----------------			
1998	---------------- d12.09 ----------------			
1999	d9.26	d0.18	...	...

INTERIM DIVIDENDS (Per Share):

Amt.	Decl.	Ex.	Rec.	Pay.
	No dividends paid.			

CAPITALIZATION (12/31/98):

	($000)	(%)
Redeemable Pfd. Stock	26,477	394.6
Common & Surplus	d19,768	-294.6
Total	6,709	100.0

RECENT DEVELOPMENTS: For the quarter ended 6/30/99, the Company reported a net loss of $3.7 million compared with a net loss of $619,000 a year earlier. Total revenues improved 17.2% to $7.4 million from $6.3 million in the prior-year quarter. Business and consumer revenues more than doubled to $4.0 million versus $1.6 million in the previous year. Digital mapping revenues declined 27.5% to $3.4 million compared with $4.7 million a year earlier. Overall Internet revenues have more than doubled due to significantly higher advertising and licensing. Gross profit as a percentage of revenues was 34.9% versus 27.0% in the a year-ago quarter. MQST and Kingswood Ltd. have entered into an agreement for the Company to supply on-line mapping and driving direction solutions for Kingswood's UK customers. This agreement will expand MQST's presence in the UK market. Also, the Company and NextCard® have entered into an exclusive marketing agreement valued at $4.5 million.

BUSINESS

MAPQUEST.COM, INC. is a provider of mapping and destination information. The Company provides comprehensive on-line mapping solutions to businesses, and customized maps, destination information and driving directions to consumers. The Company also provides traditional and digital mapping products and services to the educational, reference, directory, travel and governmental markets. In addition, the Company offers the underlying mapping and driving directions technology and components to a variety of vertical industries, such as corporate travel, hotels, real estate and retailers.

ANNUAL FINANCIAL DATA

	12/31/98	12/31/97	12/31/96
Earnings Per Share	d12.09	d64.43	d8.84
Cash Flow Per Share	d8.59	d60.36	d6.10
INCOME STATEMENT (IN THOUSANDS):			
Total Revenues	24,717	21,416	19,577
Costs & Expenses	27,064	28,571	20,737
Depreciation & Amort.	1,105	847	559
Operating Income	d3,453	d8,002	d1,719
Net Interest Inc./(Exp.)	54	136	199
Income Before Income Taxes	d3,155	d7,599	d1,276
Net Income	d3,155	d7,599	d1,276
Cash Flow	d2,717	d12,586	d1,243
Average Shs. Outstg.	316	208	204
BALANCE SHEET (IN THOUSANDS):			
Cash & Cash Equivalents	564	2,482	...
Total Current Assets	9,333	11,159	...
Net Property	1,844	1,830	...
Total Assets	11,450	13,221	...
Total Current Liabilities	5,032	3,699	...
Long-Term Obligations	...	48	...
Net Stockholders' Equity	d19,768	d16,237	...
Net Working Capital	4,301	7,460	...
Year-end Shs. Outstg.	336	216	...
STATISTICAL RECORD:			
Debt/Total Assets %	...	0.4	...

Statistics are as originally reported.

REVENUES

(12/31/1998)	($000)	(%)
Business	6,536	26.4
Consumer	1,376	5.6
Digital Mapping	16,805	68.0
Total	24,717	100.0

OFFICERS:
M. Mulligan, Chmn., C.E.O.
J. Thomas, C.O.O., C.F.O., Treas., Sec.
R. Binford, Corp. Contr.

PRINCIPAL OFFICE: 3710 Hempland Road, Mountville, PA 17554

TELEPHONE NUMBER: (717) 285-8500
WEB: www.mapquest.com.

NO. OF EMPLOYEES: 222

SHAREHOLDERS: N/A

ANNUAL MEETING: N/A

INCORPORATED: DE, 1967

INSTITUTIONAL HOLDINGS:
No. of Institutions: 2
Shares Held: 24,200
% Held: 0.1

INDUSTRY: Data processing and preparation (SIC: 7374)

TRANSFER AGENT(S): American Securities Transfer & Trust Company, Denver, CO

MARIMBA, INC.

YIELD ...
P/E RATIO ...

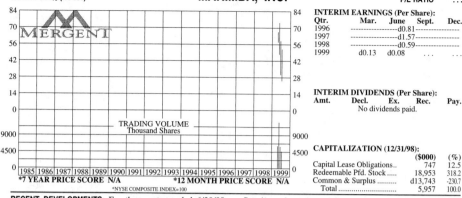

*7 YEAR PRICE SCORE N/A   *12 MONTH PRICE SCORE N/A

*NYSE COMPOSITE INDEX=100

INTERIM EARNINGS (Per Share):

Qtr.	Mar.	June	Sept.	Dec.
1996		d0.81		
1997		d1.57		
1998		d0.59		
1999	d0.13	d0.08	...	...

INTERIM DIVIDENDS (Per Share):

Amt.	Decl.	Ex.	Rec.	Pay.
	No dividends paid.			

CAPITALIZATION (12/31/98):

	($000)	(%)
Capital Lease Obligations..	747	12.5
Redeemable Pfd. Stock	18,953	318.2
Common & Surplus	d13,743	-230.7
Total	5,957	100.0

RECENT DEVELOPMENTS: For the quarter ended 6/30/99, the Company reported a net loss of $1.5 million compared with a net loss of $1.2 million in the equivalent 1998 quarter. Revenues were $6.9 million, up 87.1% from $3.7 million a year earlier. License revenue was $4.9 million, up 56.2% from $3.2 million a year earlier. During the quarter, the Company launched DocService™, a new application for automating targeted document delivery across corporate intranets, extranets and the Internet. DocService™ is the first in a planned portfolio of products delivering out-of-the-box Internet Service Management solutions. Separately, the Company was awarded its first U.S. patent (with five additional patents pending), covering the processes for efficient software and data distribution employed in the Castanet product family. Also during the quarter, the Company released Castanet 4.0.1, with 128-bit SSL encryption, HP-UX and IBM AIX support, a Japanese language version and other significant enhancements.

BUSINESS

MARIMBA, INC. is a provider of Internet-based software management solutions designed to enable companies to expand their market reach, streamline business processes and strengthen relationships with customers, business partners and employees. Marimba's Castanet product family provides an infrastructure by which enterprises can distribute, update and manage applications and related data over corporate intranets, extranets and the Internet. The Company's customer base spans multiple industries, including financial services, insurance, retail, manufacturing and telecommunications.

ANNUAL FINANCIAL DATA

	12/31/98	12/31/97	12/31/96
Earnings Per Share	d0.59	d1.57	d0.81
Cash Flow Per Share	d0.47	d1.50	d0.80
INCOME STATEMENT (IN THOUSANDS):			
Total Revenues	17,085	5,563	...
Costs & Expenses	22,028	13,129	1,289
Depreciation & Amort.	1,185	336	21
Operating Income	d6,128	d7,902	d1,310
Net Interest Inc./(Exp.)	488	338	65
Income Before Income Taxes	d5,640	d7,564	d1,245
Income Taxes	41	154	...
Net Income	d5,681	d7,718	d1,245
Cash Flow	d4,496	d7,382	d1,224
Average Shs. Outstg.	9,606	4,912	1,528
BALANCE SHEET (IN THOUSANDS):			
Cash & Cash Equivalents	7,825	14,402	...
Total Current Assets	11,817	19,241	...
Net Property	2,747	2,401	...
Total Assets	14,862	21,898	...
Total Current Liabilities	8,905	11,205	...
Long-Term Obligations	747	211	...
Net Stockholders' Equity	d13,743	d8,471	...
Net Working Capital	2,912	8,036	...
Year-end Shs. Outstg.	13,053	13,067	10,000
STATISTICAL RECORD:			
Debt/Total Assets %	5.0	1.0	...

Statistics are as originally reported.

QUARTERLY DATA

(12/31/98) ($000)	Rev	Inc
1st Quarter	3,010	(1,389)
2nd Quarter	3,681	(1,156)
3rd Quarter	4,733	(1,496)
4th Quarter	5,661	(1,640)

OFFICERS:
K. K. Polese, Pres., C.E.O.
S. P. Williams, Exec. V.P., C.O.O.
F. M. Gerson, V.P. Fin., C.F.O.

PRINCIPAL OFFICE: 440 Clyde Avenue, Mountain View, CA 94043

TELEPHONE NUMBER: (650) 930-5282
FAX: (650) 930-5600
WEB: www.marimba.com

NO. OF EMPLOYEES: 162 (avg.)

SHAREHOLDERS: 187 (approx.)

ANNUAL MEETING: N/A

INCORPORATED: DE, Feb., 1996

INSTITUTIONAL HOLDINGS:
No. of Institutions: 9
Shares Held: 424,535
% Held: 1.8

INDUSTRY: Prepackaged software (SIC: 7372)

TRANSFER AGENT(S): U.S. Stock Transfer Corporation, Glendale, CA

MARKETWATCH.COM INC.

YIELD ...
P/E RATIO ...

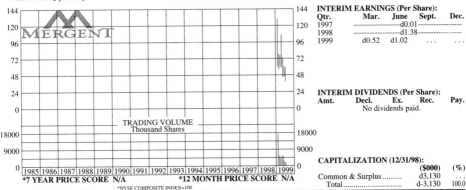

INTERIM EARNINGS (Per Share):

Qtr.	Mar.	June	Sept.	Dec.
1997	----------------d0.01----------------			
1998	----------------d1.38----------------			
1999	d0.52	d1.02	...	...

INTERIM DIVIDENDS (Per Share):

Amt.	Decl.	Ex.	Rec.	Pay.
	No dividends paid.			

CAPITALIZATION (12/31/98):

	($000)	(%)
Common & Surplus	d3,130	...
Total	d-3,130	100.0

RECENT DEVELOPMENTS: For the second quarter ended 6/30/99, the Company reported a net loss of $12.8 million compared with a loss of $2.8 million in the corresponding quarter the year before. Results for the 1999 quarter included approximately $8.0 million in non-cash charges for network advertising and promotion provided by CBS to the Company and amortization of goodwill and other intangible assets resulting from the June 1999 acquisition of BigCharts Inc. Total net revenues more than tripled to $4.8 million from $1.5 million in the comparable quarter a year earlier. Exclusive of BigCharts, the Company's Web sites served 287.0 million page views in the first quarter, an increase of 156.0%, while the average number of unique visitors to the Company's Web sites increased 217.0% to 3.8 million compared with the equivalent 1998 quarter.

BUSINESS

MARKETWATCH.COM INC. is a Web-based provider of real-time business news, financial programing, and analytic tools. As of 6/30/99, CBS Broadcasting Inc. and Data Broadcasting Corporation each owned approximately 32.7% of the Company's outstanding common stock. The Company's Web site serves approximately 2.0 million pages of news each business day to approximately 250,000 people. Throughout the trading day, investors are provided with headlines, stories, analysis, and Special Reports, which give investors late-breaking market coverage. The editorial team contributes financial and economic reports to national CBS radio news feeds, CBS EVENING NEWS WITH DAN RATHER, and CBS News' THIS MORNING. The site also offers investors the ability to create personal portfolios, market and company research, charting services, mutual and money market fund data, direct-brokerage access, and reliable delayed quotes. The Company also offers two pay sites. CBS MarketWatch RT is a paysite that offers real-time snapshot quotes and deeper historical and fundamental data and research tools. CBS MarketWatch LIVE is a paysite that provides users with a virtual trading desk on their computers. On 6/10/99, the Company completed the acquisition of BigCharts Inc.

ANNUAL FINANCIAL DATA

	12/31/98	⬚ 12/31/97
Earnings Per Share	d1.38	d0.01
Cash Flow Per Share	d1.33	d0.01
Tang. Book Val. Per Share	...	0.02
INCOME STATEMENT (IN THOUSANDS):		
Total Revenues	7,027	630
Costs & Expenses	18,811	711
Depreciation & Amort.	470	...
Operating Income	d12,254	d81
Net Interest Inc./(Exp.)	d159	...
Income Before Income Taxes	d12,413	d81
Net Income	d12,413	d81
Cash Flow	d11,943	d81
Average Shs. Outstg.	9,000	9,000
BALANCE SHEET (IN THOUSANDS):		
Cash & Cash Equivalents	140	...
Total Current Assets	1,728	224
Net Property	932	13
Total Assets	4,487	237
Total Current Liabilities	7,617	85
Net Stockholders' Equity	d3,130	152
Net Working Capital	d5,889	139
Year-end Shs. Outstg.	9,000	9,000

Statistics are as originally reported. ⬚ From 10/29/97 (Commencement of operations)

OFFICERS:
L. S. Kramer, Pres. & C.E.O.
J. P. Bardwick, C.F.O.
J. Brichler, Controller

TELEPHONE NUMBER: (415) 733-0500
FAX: (415) 392-1972
WEB: cbs.marketwatch.com

NO. OF EMPLOYEES: 65

SHAREHOLDERS: 148

ANNUAL MEETING: In May

PRINCIPAL OFFICE: 825 Battery Street, San Francisco, CA 94111

INCORPORATED: DE, Jan., 1999

INSTITUTIONAL HOLDINGS:
No. of Institutions: 41
Shares Held: 1,071,196
% Held: 8.8

INDUSTRY: Data processing and preparation (SIC: 7374)

TRANSFER AGENT(S): ChaseMellon Shareholder Services, L.L.C., Ridgefield Park, NJ

NASDAQ SYMBOL WCOM
Rec. Pr. 82½ (7/31/99)

MCI WORLDCOM, INC.

YIELD ...
P/E RATIO ...

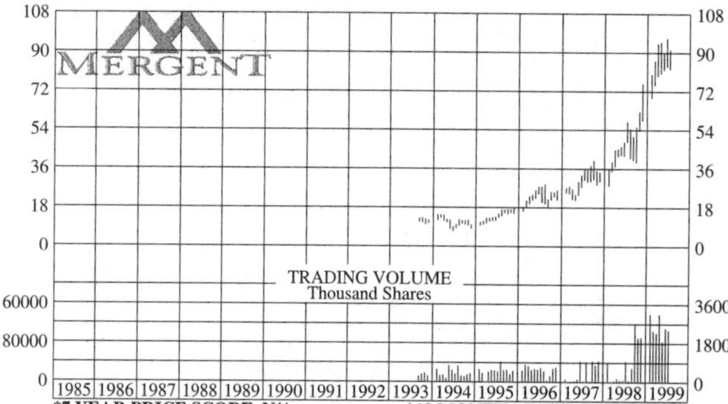
MERGENT
108
90
72
54
36
18
0
TRADING VOLUME
Thousand Shares
60000
80000
0
36000
18000
1985 1986 1987 1988 1989 1990 1991 1992 1993 1994 1995 1996 1997 1998 1999

*7 YEAR PRICE SCORE N/A   *12 MONTH PRICE SCORE 113.0

*NYSE COMPOSITE INDEX=100

INTERIM EARNINGS (Per Share):

Qtr.	Mar.	June	Sept.	Dec.
1996	0.22	d0.62	0.27	d5.22
1997	0.05	0.08	0.12	0.15
1998	d0.28	0.21	d2.44	0.23
1999	0.37	0.45	...	...

INTERIM DIVIDENDS (Per Share):

Amt.	Decl.	Ex.	Rec.	Pay.

No dividends paid.

CAPITALIZATION (12/31/98):

	($000)	(%)
Long-Term Debt	16,083,000	23.5
Deferred Income Tax	2,960,000	4.3
Minority Interest	3,676,000	5.4
Redeemable Pfd. Stock	798,000	1.2
Common & Surplus	45,003,000	65.7
Total	68,520,000	100.0

RECENT DEVELOPMENTS: For the quarter ended 6/30/99, net income soared to $879.0 million compared with $227.0 million in the corresponding quarter the year before. Total revenues grew to $8.94 billion from $2.58 billion in the comparable quarter a year earlier. The increase in total revenue was due to the MCI acquisition and Embratel transaction combined with internal growth. Results included MCI and Embratel operations from September 1998 and CompuServe Network Services and ANS Communications, Inc. from February 1999. Voice segment revenues grew to $5.09 billion from $1.21 billion in the previous year. Data segment revenues jumped to $1.79 billion versus $536.0 million in 1998. Internet revenues grew 59.2% to $836.0 million compared with $525.0 million, while international services revenue climbed to $1.11 billion from $270.0 million the year before. On 5/28/99, the Company agreed to acquire SkyTel Communications, Inc. The transaction is expected to be completed in the Fall of 1999.

BUSINESS

MCI WORLDCOM, INC. is a global business telecommunications company that provides facilities-based and fully-integrated local, long distance, international and Internet services and operates in more than 65 countries. UUNET (www.uu.net), WCOM's Internet services division, provides Internet communications services including Internet access, Web hosting, remote access, and other value-added services to business customers worldwide. UUNET offers services to more than 70,000 businesses and owns and operates a global network in thousands of cities throughout North America, Europe, and Asia Pacific. On 8/4/98, WCOM acquired a 51.8% voting interest and a 19.3% economic interest in Embratel Participacoes S.A., Brazil's only facilities-based national communications provider. On 9/15/98, WCOM acquired MCI Communications Corp., an advanced digital network provider. In October 1998, WCOM changed its name to MCI WorldCom, Inc. On 4/22/99, WCOM completed the sale of MCI Systemhouse to EDS.

ANNUAL FINANCIAL DATA

	12/31/98	12/31/97	12/31/96	12/31/95	12/31/94	12/31/93	12/31/92
Earnings Per Share	**[3] d2.02**	**0.40**	**[1] [2] d5.50**	**0.65**	**d0.47**	**0.43**	**[2] d0.01**
Cash Flow Per Share	**d0.28**	**1.33**	**d4.74**	**1.41**	**0.04**	**0.93**	**0.26**
Tang. Book Val. Per Share	...	...	**0.01**	...	...	...	...
INCOME STATEMENT (IN MILLIONS):							
Total Revenues	17,678.0	7,351.4	4,485.1	3,639.9	2,220.8	1,144.7	800.8
Costs & Expenses	16,453.0	5,332.0	6,025.9	2,652.6	1,987.2	866.6	715.8
Depreciation & Amort.	2,200.0	920.7	303.3	311.3	163.8	79.9	53.9
Operating Income	d975.0	1,098.6	d1,844.1	676.0	69.7	198.2	31.1
Net Interest Inc./(Exp.)	d637.0	d319.7	d221.8	d249.1	d47.3	d27.0	d23.8
Income Before Income Taxes	d1,571.0	799.3	d2,059.4	438.8	d48.3	175.5	8.2
Income Taxes	876.0	415.6	129.5	171.1	73.8	71.3	8.4
Equity Earnings/Minority Int.	d93.0	...	...	...	...	...	...
Net Income	[3] d2,540.0	383.7	[1] [2] d2,188.9	267.7	d122.2	104.2	[2] d0.2
Cash Flow	d353.0	1,277.9	d1,886.5	545.7	13.9	173.7	51.6
Average Shs. Outstg. (000)	1,274,000	959,816	397,890	386,898	315,610	186,944	194,836
BALANCE SHEET (IN MILLIONS):							
Cash & Cash Equivalents	1,710.0	67.7	995.2	41.7	20.3	6.2	4.1
Total Current Assets	10,639.0	1,682.6	2,296.1	654.8	589.4	322.0	178.2
Net Property	24,307.0	5,993.0	3,897.1	1,569.3	626.7	344.3	213.1
Total Assets	86,401.0	22,389.6	19,862.0	6,634.6	3,430.2	2,514.5	869.6
Total Current Liabilities	16,029.0	2,047.9	1,910.0	1,978.8	710.7	309.0	164.1
Long-Term Obligations	16,083.0	6,527.2	4,803.6	2,278.4	788.0	526.0	333.7
Net Stockholders' Equity	45,003.0	13,509.9	12,960.0	2,187.3	1,827.2	1,621.7	343.0
Net Working Capital	d5,390.0	d365.2	386.1	d1,324.0	d121.2	13.0	14.1
Year-end Shs. Outstg. (000)	1,840,280	909,201	885,080	386,486	319,286	238,510	199,040
STATISTICAL RECORD:							
Operating Profit Margin %	...	14.9	...	18.6	3.1	17.3	3.9
Net Profit Margin %	...	5.2	...	7.4	...	9.1	...
Return on Equity %	...	2.8	...	12.2	...	6.4	...
Return on Assets %	...	1.7	...	4.0	...	4.1	...
Debt/Total Assets %	18.6	29.2	24.2	34.3	23.0	20.9	38.4
Price Range	75¾-28	39⅞-21¼	28⅞-16¼	17 15/16-9 9/16	14¾-7	13 3/16-10 1/16	...
P/E Ratio	...	99.7-53.1	...	27.6-14.7	...	31.0-23.7	...

Statistics are as originally reported. Adj. for stk. splits: 2-for-1, 7/3/96; 2-for-1, 1/7/94; 3-for-2, 1/15/93; 3-for-2, 6/26/91 [1] Incl. non-recurr. chrg. $2.74 bill. [2] Bef. extraord. chrg. 12/31/96: $24.4 mill. ($0.06/sh.); 12/31/92: $5.8 mill. ($0.03/sh.) [3] Incl. $3.73 bill. in-process R&D and other chgs.

OFFICERS:
J. W. Sidgmore, Vice-Chmn. & C.O.O.
B. J. Ebbers, Pres. & C.E.O.
S. D. Sullivan, C.F.O. & Sec.

INVESTOR CONTACT: MCI WorldCom Investor Relations, (601) 460-8608

PRINCIPAL OFFICE: 515 E. Amite St. Jackson, MS 39201-2702

TELEPHONE NUMBER: (601) 360-8600
FAX: (601) 974-8350
WEB: www.wcom.com
NO. OF EMPLOYEES: 77,000 (approx.)
SHAREHOLDERS: 58,662
ANNUAL MEETING: In May
INCORPORATED: DE, 1972; reincorp., GA, 1993

INSTITUTIONAL HOLDINGS:
No. of Institutions: 942
Shares Held: 1,236,128,804
% Held: 66.4

INDUSTRY: Telephone communications, exc. radio (SIC: 4813)

TRANSFER AGENT(S): The Bank of New York, New York, NY

MEDIA METRIX, INC.

YIELD ...
P/E RATIO ...

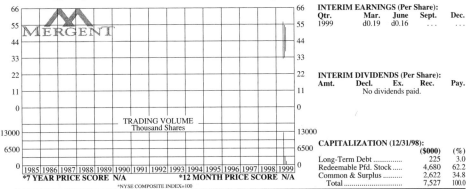

INTERIM EARNINGS (Per Share):

Qtr.	Mar.	June	Sept.	Dec.
1999	d0.19	d0.16	...	...

INTERIM DIVIDENDS (Per Share):

Amt.	Decl.	Ex.	Rec.	Pay.
	No dividends paid.			

CAPITALIZATION (12/31/98):

	($000)	(%)
Long-Term Debt	225	3.0
Redeemable Pfd. Stock	4,680	62.2
Common & Surplus	2,622	34.8
Total	7,527	100.0

RECENT DEVELOPMENTS: On 5/7/99, MMXI commenced an initial public offering of 3.3 million shares of its common stock at a price of $17.00 per share. The IPO resulted in net proceeds of approximately $49.4 million. For the three months ended 6/30/99, the Company reported a net loss of $2.6 million compared with a loss of $835,884 a year earlier. Results for the recent quarter were negatively affected by a one-time charge of $748,505 stemming from the November 1998 acquisition of RelevantKnowledge.

Revenues more than tripled to $4.3 million from $1.3 million in the previous year. Revenue growth was fueled by the successful integration of RelevantKnowledge coupled with growing demand for the Company's Internet and Digital Media measurement services. Gross profit jumped to $2.1 million from $543,946 a year ago. However, loss from operations grew to $2.9 million from $839,167 the prior year, reflecting higher costs associated with the development of new products and services.

BUSINESS

MEDIA METRIX, INC. provides Internet audience measurement products and services to financial services companies, Internet advertisers and advertising agencies, new and traditional media companies, e-commerce marketers and technology companies. The Company measures usage of the entire Internet, including its largest segments, the World Wide Web and proprietary on-line services. The Company collects data by measuring Internet usage from a representative sample, or panel, of personal computer users with MMXI's proprietary tracking technology. The Company maintains a large panel of Internet users reporting Internet usage at work and at home, as well as the usage of proprietary on-line services. The Company's customers include Amazon.com, America Online, Beyond.com, Buena Vista/Disney, eBay, Everen Securities, Fidelity, IBM, Infoseek, Interpublic Group, Microsoft, Omnicom, Time Warner, Xoom.com and Yahoo!.

ANNUAL FINANCIAL DATA

	12/31/98	12/31/97	12/31/96
Earnings Per Share	d0.98	d0.75	d0.52
Cash Flow Per Share	d0.86	d0.74	d0.52
INCOME STATEMENT (IN THOUSANDS):			
Total Revenues	6,330	3,188	1,033
Costs & Expenses	12,641	7,848	4,408
Depreciation & Amort.	914	18	...
Operating Income	d7,224	d4,679	d3,376
Net Interest Inc./(Exp.)	65	95	...
Net Income	d7,159	d4,584	d3,376
Cash Flow	d6,559	d4,856	d3,376
Average Shs. Outstg.	7,619	6,523	6,523
BALANCE SHEET (IN THOUSANDS):			
Cash & Cash Equivalents	8,012	1,869	...
Total Current Assets	9,590	2,648	...
Net Property	650	117	...
Total Assets	16,060	2,787	...
Total Current Liabilities	8,533	2,695	...
Long-Term Obligations	225	...	...
Net Stockholders' Equity	2,622	d8,274	...
Net Working Capital	1,057	d47	...
Year-end Shs. Outstg.	13,099	6,523	...
STATISTICAL RECORD:			
Debt/Total Assets %	1.4	...	...
Statistics are as originally reported.			

QUARTERLY DATA

(12/31/98)($000)	Rev	Inc
1st Quarter..................	1,160	(852)
2nd Quarter.................	1,345	(835)
3rd Quarter	1,493	(956)
4th Quarter.................	2,333	(4,515)

OFFICERS:
T. Johnson, Chmn., C.E.O.
J. C. Levy, Vice-Chmn.
M. A. Packo, Pres., C.O.O.
T. A. Lynch, C.F.O., Sec., Treas.

PRINCIPAL OFFICE: 35 East 21st Street, New York, NY 10010

TELEPHONE NUMBER: (212) 460-7980
WEB: www.mediametrix.com

NO. OF EMPLOYEES: 95

SHAREHOLDERS: 128

ANNUAL MEETING: N/A

INCORPORATED: DE, Mar., 1997

INSTITUTIONAL HOLDINGS:
No. of Institutions: 5
Shares Held: 654,700
% Held: N/A

INDUSTRY: Computer related services, nec (SIC: 7379)

TRANSFER AGENT(S): Continental Stock Transfer and Trust Company, New York, NY

NASDAQ SYMBOL MRNT
Rec. Pr. 22½ (7/31/99)

MERANT PLC

YIELD ...
P/E RATIO ...

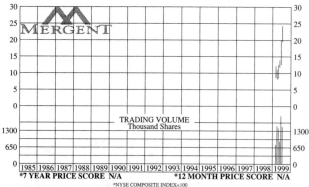

1985 1986 1987 1988 1989 1990 1991 1992 1993 1994 1995 1996 1997 1998 1999
*7 YEAR PRICE SCORE N/A   *12 MONTH PRICE SCORE N/A
*NYSE COMPOSITE INDEX=100

INTERIM EARNINGS (Per Share):

Qtr.	Apr.	July	Oct.	Jan.
1996-97	---------------- d0.77 ----------------			
1997-98	---------------- 1.11 ----------------			

Qtr.	July	Oct.	Jan.	Apr.
1997-98				0.30
1998-99	0.30	d1.45	0.20	0.05

INTERIM DIVIDENDS (Per Share):

Amt.	Decl.	Ex.	Rec.	Pay.
		No dividends paid.		

CAPITALIZATION (1/31/98):

	($000)	(%)
Deferred Income Tax	10,466	8.3
Common & Surplus	115,802	91.7
Total	126,268	100.0

RECENT DEVELOPMENTS: For the year ended 4/30/99, the Company reported a net loss of $28.5 million compared with net income of $23.1 million in 1998. Results included pre-tax one-times charges of $50.0 million in 1999 and $17.5 million in 1998. Total revenues slipped 1.3% to $374.2 million from $379.0 million a year earlier. This reflected an 8.6% reduction in product revenues to $193.1 million. However, maintenance revenue grew 11.9% to $98.9 million and service revenue rose 3.4% to $82.2 mil-lion. Gross profit declined 4.5% to $267.3 million from $280.0 million a year earlier. Loss from operations amounted to $33.1 million versus income from operations of $30.6 million in 1998. MERANT expects to realize cost savings of more than $10.0 million in fiscal 2000 as a result of the successful integration of Micro Focus Italia, s.r.l. and INTERSOLV, Inc. into the Company's operations. Beginning in the second quarter of fiscal 2000, the Company expects revenues and profit growth to accelerate.

BUSINESS

MERANT PLC (formerly Micro Focus Group) is a supplier of enterprise application development tools. The Company provides products and services to help customers accelerate the development, delivery and integration of applications in multi-platform computing environments. The Company enables organizations to transform their enterprise applications for the changing technology and business requirements of the e-business environment as well as manage the application development process. The Company also provides integrated data connectivity across the enterprise, from the mainframe to the Internet. Merant's U.S. subsidiary, Intersolv, provides tools for the entire application enablement process. The Company has operations in the U.K., the U.S., Japan, Germany, France, Spain, the Netherlands, Italy, and Australia. The Company has approximately 500 technology partners and more than five million licenses at over 35,000 customer sites.

ANNUAL FINANCIAL DATA

	1/31/98	1/31/97	1/31/96	1/31/95	1/31/94	1/31/93	1/31/92
Earnings Per Share	1.11	d0.77	d3.28	2.54	7.81	8.27	7.71
Cash Flow Per Share	5.54	d3.85	d3.22	2.54	7.81	8.27	7.71
Tang. Book Val. Per Share	30.08	24.57	25.98	29.38	30.47	24.87	16.85
INCOME STATEMENT (IN THOUSANDS):							
Total Revenues	158,474	117,089	116,157	142,827	125,604	101,773	99,681
Costs & Expenses	137,670	129,116	129,139	130,859	95,670	70,892	70,945
Operating Income	20,804	d12,028	d12,981	11,968	29,934	30,881	28,736
Net Interest Inc./(Exp.)	4,053	2,722	3,145	3,391	2,667	2,579	2,787
Income Before Income Taxes	24,857	d9,306	d9,836	13,861	32,600	33,460	32,376
Income Taxes	7,826	2,358	cr108	6,567	10,508	10,757	11,449
Equity Earnings/Minority Int.	...	...	...	...	...	...	30
Net Income	17,031	d11,664	d9,728	7,294	22,092	22,703	20,957
Cash Flow	17,031	d11,664	d9,728	7,294	22,092	22,703	20,957
Average Shs. Outstg.	3,075	3,031	3,020	2,867	2,828	2,746	2,719
BALANCE SHEET (IN THOUSANDS):							
Cash & Cash Equivalents	84,155	71,649	58,594	88,703	86,207	79,535	55,176
Total Current Assets	135,104	95,218	81,908	116,386	116,450	105,725	74,392
Net Property	38,938	32,910	37,452	35,708	22,340	16,861	14,525
Total Assets	202,268	160,527	154,679	183,447	164,664	143,474	108,676
Total Current Liabilities	75,979	46,902	40,853	58,302	43,514	43,759	33,052
Net Stockholders' Equity	115,802	97,921	105,526	115,768	112,507	89,455	65,901
Net Working Capital	59,125	48,316	41,055	58,084	72,936	61,966	41,340
Year-end Shs. Outstg.	3,177	3,034	3,029	2,873	2,843	2,757	2,738
STATISTICAL RECORD:							
Operating Profit Margin %	13.1	...	...	8.4	23.8	30.3	28.8
Net Profit Margin %	10.7	...	...	5.1	17.6	22.3	21.0
Return on Equity %	14.7	...	...	6.3	19.6	25.4	31.8
Return on Assets %	8.4	...	...	4.0	13.4	15.8	19.3

Statistics are as originally reported. On 11/30/98, the Company changed its fiscal year end to April 30 from Jan. 31. All figures are in U.S. dollars unless otherwise noted. Exchange rates are as follows: $1=£1.6335, 1/31/98; £1.6020, 1/31/97; £1.5035, 1/31/96; £1.5890, 1/31/95; £1.4981, 1/31/94; £1.5022, 1/31/93; £1.7842, 1/31/92. All share and per share amounts are per ADRs. One ADR is equal to five Ordinary shares.

OFFICERS:
G. Greenfield, Pres., C.E.O.
K. A. Sexton, Sr. V.P., C.F.O.

PRINCIPAL OFFICE: 22-30 Old Bath Road, Newbury, Berkshire, United Kingdom

TELEPHONE NUMBER: 011 44 1 635 32 646
FAX: 011 44 1 635 33 966
WEB: www.merant.com
NO. OF EMPLOYEES: 719 (avg.)
SHAREHOLDERS: N/A
ANNUAL MEETING: In June
INCORPORATED: GBR, Mar., 1983

INSTITUTIONAL HOLDINGS:
No. of Institutions: 28
Shares Held: 492,847 (Adj.)
% Held: 3.1

INDUSTRY: Electronic computers (SIC: 3571)

DEPOSITARY BANKS(S): The Bank of New York, New York, NY

METRICOM, INC.

INTERIM EARNINGS (Per Share):

Qtr.	Mar.	June	Sept.	Dec.
1995	----------------d1.79----------------			
1996	d0.54	d0.63	d0.80	d0.96
1997	d1.03	d1.17	d0.94	d1.21
1998	d0.69	d0.71	d1.13	d2.04
1999	d0.80	d0.86	...	...

INTERIM DIVIDENDS (Per Share):

Amt.	Decl.	Ex.	Rec.	Pay.
No dividends paid.				

7 YEAR PRICE SCORE 49.4   **12 MONTH PRICE SCORE 243.9**

*NYSE COMPOSITE INDEX=100

CAPITALIZATION (12/31/98):

	($000)	(%)
Long-Term Debt	55,098	305.7
Minority Interest	5,184	28.8
Common & Surplus	d42,259	-234.5
Total	18,023	100.0

RECENT DEVELOPMENTS: For the quarter ended 6/30/99, the Company reported a net loss of $16.6 million compared with net loss of $13.2 million in the comparable 1998 quarter. Total revenues jumped 6.9% to $4.7 million from $4.4 million in the prior-year period. Service revenues declined 3.6% to $2.2 million compared with $2.3 million the year before. Product revenues grew 18.4% to $2.5 million from $2.1 million in the prior-year quarter. On 6/21/99, the Company announced that it received $600.0 million in investments from Vulcan Ventures, Inc. and MCI WorldCom, to fund the national rollout of its Ricochet 128 kbps mobile data service, which is scheduled to be commercially available by mid-2000. Terms of the investments allow for MCI WorldCom and Vulcan to purchase 60.0 million convertible preferred shares of MCOM at $10.00 per share. Upon consummation and conversion of the preferred shares to common stock, Vulcan and MCI WorldCom will own 49.0% and 38.0% of the Company, respectively. The remaining 13.0% ownership will be held by other public shareholders.

BUSINESS

METRICOM, INC. is a provider of wireless data communications technologies. The Company designs, develops and markets wireless network products and services that provide data communications, which can be used in a broad range of personal computer and industrial applications. The Company's primary service, Ricochet, provides users of portable and desktop computers and hand-held computing devices with wireless access to the Internet, private intranets, local area networks, e-mail and on-line services. Ricochet service is available in San Francisco, Seattle, Washington D.C. and New York.

ANNUAL FINANCIAL DATA

	12/31/98	12/31/97	12/31/96	12/31/95	12/31/94	12/31/93	12/31/92
Earnings Per Share	d4.63	d4.35	d2.93	d1.79	d0.96	d0.74	d0.61
Cash Flow Per Share	d4.12	d3.74	d2.63	d1.65	d0.91	d0.69	d0.56
Tang. Book Val. Per Share	...	...	3.19	6.05	7.82	3.11	1.97
INCOME STATEMENT (IN THOUSANDS):							
Total Revenues	15,859	13,439	7,154	5,784	21,564	10,057	6,405
Costs & Expenses	88,794	62,070	44,371	31,766	35,979	16,197	10,910
Depreciation & Amort.	9,205	8,366	4,135	1,902	634	419	356
Operating Income	d82,140	d56,997	d41,352	d27,884	d15,049	d6,559	d4,861
Net Interest Inc./(Exp.)	d2,024	d2,331	2,007	4,363	3,300	410	394
Income Before Income Taxes	d84,164	d59,328	d39,345	d23,521	d11,749	d6,149	d4,451
Income Taxes	...	...	...	...	...	...	2
Net Income	d84,164	d59,328	d39,345	d23,521	d11,749	d6,149	d4,453
Cash Flow	d74,959	d50,962	d35,210	d21,619	d11,115	d5,730	d4,097
Average Shs. Outstg.	18,195	13,641	13,413	13,140	12,202	8,353	7,286
BALANCE SHEET (IN THOUSANDS):							
Cash & Cash Equivalents	19,141	14,174	62,071	45,291	69,252	25,020	11,888
Total Current Assets	25,159	20,587	68,056	51,863	76,559	31,465	16,140
Net Property	5,555	25,875	26,776	14,923	8,404	858	882
Total Assets	34,466	51,103	101,799	86,076	105,534	32,483	17,472
Total Current Liabilities	15,763	13,607	10,318	5,092	3,547	2,920	1,514
Long-Term Obligations	55,098	45,000	45,000	...	...	392	219
Net Stockholders' Equity	d42,259	d13,817	43,306	80,374	101,516	29,171	15,739
Net Working Capital	9,396	6,980	57,738	46,771	73,012	28,545	14,626
Year-end Shs. Outstg.	18,793	13,819	13,555	13,291	12,979	9,389	7,974
STATISTICAL RECORD:							
Debt/Total Assets %	159.9	88.1	44.2	...	...	1.2	1.3
Price Range	13¼-3	18⅜-4⅜	19¾-9¼	25¾-10¼	34-11½	28¾-5⅜	7¾-3¾

Statistics are as originally reported.

REVENUES

(12/31/98)	($000)	(%)
Service Revenues	8,419	53.1
Product Revenues	7,440	46.9
Total	15,859	100.0

OFFICERS:
R. S. Cline, Chmn.
T. A. Dreisbach, Pres., C.E.O.
D. W. Marquart, Sr. V.P., Gen. Couns.
J. Wall, C.F.O.

PRINCIPAL OFFICE: 980 University Avenue, Los Gatos, CA 95032-2375

TELEPHONE NUMBER: (408) 399-8200
FAX: (408) 354-1024
WEB: www.metricom.com
NO. OF EMPLOYEES: 310 (avg.)
SHAREHOLDERS: 430 (approx.)
ANNUAL MEETING: In Jun.
INCORPORATED: CA, Dec., 1985; reincorp., DE, May, 1992

INSTITUTIONAL HOLDINGS:
No. of Institutions: 19
Shares Held: 1,121,841
% Held: 5.9
INDUSTRY: Radio & TV communications equipment (SIC: 3663)
TRANSFER AGENT(S): Boston EquiServe, Boston, MA

NASDAQ SYMBOL MWHS
Rec. Pr. 14⅛ (7/31/99)

MICRO WAREHOUSE, INC.

YIELD ...
P/E RATIO 10.2

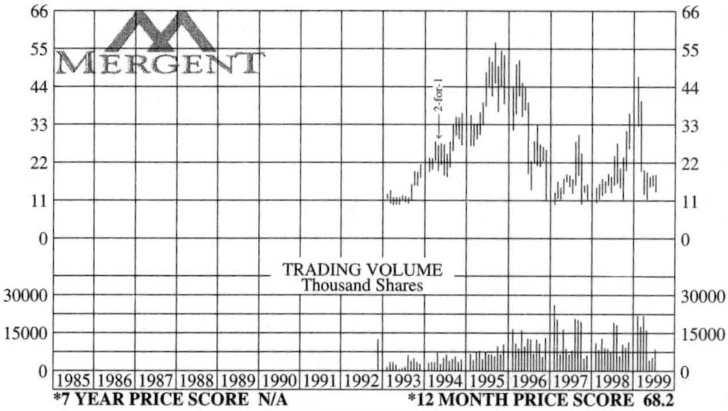

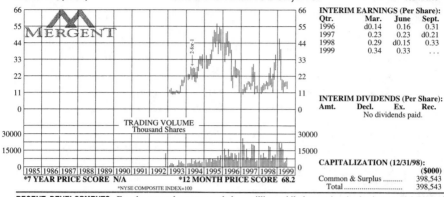

***7 YEAR PRICE SCORE N/A** ***12 MONTH PRICE SCORE 68.2**

*NYSE COMPOSITE INDEX=100

INTERIM EARNINGS (Per Share):

Qtr.	Mar.	June	Sept.	Dec.
1996	d0.14	0.16	0.31	0.17
1997	0.23	0.23	d0.21	d1.30
1998	0.29	d0.15	0.33	0.38
1999	0.34	0.33	...	...

INTERIM DIVIDENDS (Per Share):

Amt.	Decl.	Ex.	Rec.	Pay.
No dividends paid.				

CAPITALIZATION (12/31/98):

	($000)	(%)
Common & Surplus	398,543	100.0
Total	398,543	100.0

RECENT DEVELOPMENTS: For the second quarter ended 6/30/99, net income amounted to $12.0 million. This compares with a net loss of $5.0 million in the corresponding prior-year quarter. Results for the 1998 quarter included a $15.8 million after-tax charge associated with the settlement of litigation. Net sales increased 10.4% to $575.5 million from $521.5 million in the comparable quarter a year earlier. Domestic sales increased 11.0% to $420.8 million, while international sales increased 8.7% to $154.7 million. Internet-related sales increased 71.0% to $70.8 million versus $41.4 million in the equivalent 1998 quarter. Gross profit as a percentage of net sales decreased to 15.7% from 16.2% a year earlier. The lower gross margin was primarily due to a decline in gross margins for CPUs, memory, networking products, and software.

BUSINESS

MICRO WAREHOUSE, INC. is a specialty catalog and on-line retailer and direct marketer of microcomputer software and hardware products for users of Macintosh and IBM-compatible personal computers. Through its catalogs, the Company markets more than 20,000 products in 15 countries. MWHS also has a telemarketing sales force that focuses on commercial, educational and governmental accounts. The Company operates a full-service internet shopping site at www.warehouse.com, a live auction site at www.webauction.com, and discount computer retailer at www.Computersbynet.com.

GEOGRAPHIC DATA

(12/31/98)	REV (%)	INC (%)
United States	72.2	91.7
International	27.8	8.3
Total	100.0	100.0

ANNUAL FINANCIAL DATA

	12/31/98	12/31/97	12/31/96	12/31/95	12/31/94	12/31/93	12/31/92
Earnings Per Share	**0.85**	**d1.06**	**1 0.49**	**1.48**	**1.01**	**0.64**	**2 0.39**
Cash Flow Per Share	**1.28**	**d0.60**	**0.84**	**1.74**	**1.21**	**0.74**	**0.12**
Tang. Book Val. Per Share	**10.00**	**8.75**	**9.25**	**9.55**	**7.30**	**3.82**	**2.65**
INCOME STATEMENT (IN MILLIONS):							
Total Revenues	2,220.0	2,125.7	1,916.2	1,308.0	776.4	450.4	269.6
Costs & Expenses	2,152.5	2,152.0	1,870.8	1,226.0	725.7	422.4	262.9
Depreciation & Amort.	15.0	16.2	12.3	8.1	5.3	2.5	1.9
Operating Income	52.5	d42.5	33.1	74.0	45.4	25.5	4.8
Net Interest Inc./(Exp.)	9.1	4.6	3.5	1.9	1.6	0.5	d1.3
Income Before Income Taxes	61.6	d37.8	36.6	75.8	46.9	26.0	3.5
Income Taxes	31.4	cr1.1	19.7	30.7	18.9	11.0	3.3
Net Income	30.2	d36.7	1 16.9	45.1	28.0	15.0	0.2
Cash Flow	45.2	d20.5	29.2	53.2	33.3	17.5	2.2
Average Shs. Outstg. (000)	35,349	34,475	34,793	30,567	27,618	23,532	17,854
BALANCE SHEET (IN MILLIONS):							
Cash & Cash Equivalents	188.6	78.9	52.3	91.7	74.5	30.6	18.6
Total Current Assets	580.1	533.0	494.8	345.1	248.8	128.5	70.6
Net Property	37.0	32.4	29.7	24.6	19.7	9.3	6.0
Total Assets	666.5	619.3	607.8	416.1	294.1	141.2	77.1
Total Current Liabilities	268.0	270.5	223.3	75.7	53.8	44.1	15.9
Long-Term Obligations	...	0.1	0.4	0.4	0.6	...	1.4
Net Stockholders' Equity	398.5	348.8	384.2	340.0	239.6	97.2	59.8
Net Working Capital	312.1	262.5	271.5	269.4	195.0	84.4	54.7
Year-end Shs. Outstg. (000)	35,413	34,639	34,359	30,929	29,534	24,862	22,556
STATISTICAL RECORD:							
Operating Profit Margin %	2.4	...	1.7	5.7	5.8	5.7	1.8
Net Profit Margin %	1.4	...	0.9	3.4	3.6	3.3	0.1
Return on Equity %	7.6	...	4.4	13.3	11.7	15.4	0.4
Return on Assets %	4.5	...	2.8	10.8	9.5	10.6	0.3
Debt/Total Assets %	...	...	0.1	0.1	0.2	...	1.8
Price Range	36⅜-10¼	30-9¾	51¾-10¾	56⅞-26¾	36¼-17¾	21⅜-9⅝	...
P/E Ratio	42.8-12.1	...	105.6-21.9	38.4-18.1	35.9-17.6	33.7-15.2	...

Statistics are as originally reported. Adj. for stk. splits: 2-for-1, 4/15/94 1 Bef. extraord. chrg. $1.6 mill. 2 Pro forma

OFFICERS:
P. Godfrey, Chmn., Pres. & C.E.O.
W. P. Garten, Exec. V.P. & C.F.O.
B. L. Lev, V.P., Couns. & Sec.
M. Seiler, Exec. V.P. & C.O.O.

INVESTOR CONTACT: Melinda LeVino, (203) 899-4672

PRINCIPAL OFFICE: 535 Connecticut Avenue, Norwalk, CT 06854

TELEPHONE NUMBER: (203) 899-4000
FAX: (203) 853-6164
WEB: www.warehouse.com

NO. OF EMPLOYEES: 3,595

SHAREHOLDERS: 182 (approx.)

ANNUAL MEETING: In June

INCORPORATED: CT, 1987; reincorp., DE, Oct., 1992

INSTITUTIONAL HOLDINGS:
No. of Institutions: 107
Shares Held: 26,421,671
% Held: 73.8

INDUSTRY: Catalog and mail-order houses (SIC: 5961)

TRANSFER AGENT(S): Boston EquiServe, JV, Canton, MA

MICROSOFT CORPORATION

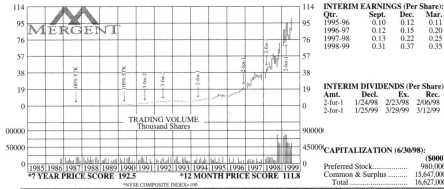

INTERIM EARNINGS (Per Share):

Qtr.	Sept.	Dec.	Mar.	June
1995-96	0.10	0.12	0.11	0.11
1996-97	0.12	0.15	0.20	0.20
1997-98	0.13	0.22	0.25	0.25
1998-99	0.31	0.37	0.35	0.40

INTERIM DIVIDENDS (Per Share):

Amt.	Decl.	Ex.	Rec.	Pay.
2-for-1	1/24/98	2/23/98	2/06/98	2/20/98
2-for-1	1/25/99	3/29/99	3/12/99	3/26/99

TRADING VOLUME
Thousand Shares

CAPITALIZATION (6/30/98):

	($000)	(%)
Preferred Stock.................	980,000	5.9
Common & Surplus	15,647,000	94.1
Total	16,627,000	100.0

*7 YEAR PRICE SCORE 192.5   *12 MONTH PRICE SCORE 111.8
*NYSE COMPOSITE INDEX=100

RECENT DEVELOPMENTS: For the fiscal year ended 6/30/99, net income increased 73.4% to $7.79 billion compared with $4.49 billion in the previous year. Revenues amounted to $19.75 billion, up 29.4% from $15.26 billion a year earlier. Revenue growth reflected continued strong demand for Microsoft Windows® and Office®. In addition, newer products such as Office 2000 Premium® and WindowsNT® continue to gain acceptance. Software license volume increases have been the principal factor in Microsoft's revenue growth. Windows platforms product revenue grew 35.4% to $8.50 billion, while productivity applications and developer product revenues grew 25.2% to $8.12 billion the year before. The Company's legal battle with the U.S. Government continues, as the Company is accused of using anti-competitive practices associated with tying its Internet web browser to its Windows operating system.

BUSINESS

MICROSOFT CORPORATION is engaged in the development, manufacture, marketing, licensing and support of a wide range of software products, including operating systems for personal computers, office machines and personal information devices; applications programs; and languages; as well as personal computer books, hardware, and multimedia products. MSFT's primary operating systems for PCs are: the Microsoft Windows®, Windows® 95 and Windows® 98 operating systems, the Microsoft Windows® NT® Workstation, and the Microsoft MS-DOS® operating system. Software titles include Microsoft Word, a word processing application; Microsoft Excel®, MSFT's spreadsheet application; Microsoft PowerPoint®, a graphics presentation program; Microsoft Money, a financial organization program; MSN™ Personal Home Pages; MSN Mobile; and MSN Health. The Company also offers Microsoft Internet Explorer, its Internet browser software for access to the World Wide Web.

ANNUAL FINANCIAL DATA

	6/30/98	6/30/97	6/30/96	6/30/95	6/30/94	6/30/93	6/30/92
Earnings Per Share	0.84	0.66	0.43	0.29	0.24	0.20	0.15
Cash Flow Per Share	1.13	0.76	0.52	0.34	0.28	0.23	0.17
Tang. Book Val. Per Share	3.17	2.03	1.45	1.13	0.96	0.72	0.50
INCOME STATEMENT (IN MILLIONS):							
Total Revenues	14,484.0	11,358.0	8,671.0	5,937.0	4,649.0	3,753.0	2,758.7
Costs & Expenses	7,046.0	5,671.0	5,113.0	3,630.0	2,686.0	2,276.0	1,650.4
Depreciation & Amort.	1,024.0	557.0	480.0	269.0	237.0	151.0	112.3
Operating Income	6,414.0	5,130.0	3,078.0	2,038.0	1,726.0	1,326.0	996.0
Net Interest Inc./(Exp.)	703.0	443.0	320.0	191.0	102.0	82.0	55.9
Income Before Income Taxes	7,117.0	5,314.0	3,379.0	2,167.0	1,722.0	1,401.0	1,041.3
Income Taxes	2,627.0	1,860.0	1,184.0	714.0	576.0	448.0	333.2
Net Income	4,490.0	3,454.0	2,195.0	1,453.0	1,146.0	953.0	708.1
Cash Flow	5,486.0	3,996.0	2,675.0	1,722.0	1,383.0	1,104.0	820.4
Average Shs. Outstg. (000)	4,864,000	5,248,000	5,124,000	5,016,000	4,880,000	4,848,000	4,707,488
BALANCE SHEET (IN MILLIONS):							
Cash & Cash Equivalents	13,927.0	8,966.0	6,940.0	4,750.0	3,614.0	2,290.0	1,344.9
Total Current Assets	15,889.0	10,373.0	7,839.0	5,620.0	4,312.0	2,850.0	1,769.7
Net Property	1,505.0	1,465.0	1,326.0	1,192.0	930.0	867.0	766.6
Total Assets	22,357.0	14,387.0	10,093.0	7,210.0	5,363.0	3,805.0	2,639.9
Total Current Liabilities	5,730.0	3,610.0	2,425.0	1,347.0	913.0	563.0	446.9
Net Stockholders' Equity	16,627.0	10,777.0	6,908.0	5,333.0	4,450.0	3,242.0	2,193.0
Net Working Capital	10,159.0	6,763.0	5,414.0	4,273.0	3,399.0	2,287.0	1,322.8
Year-end Shs. Outstg. (000)	4,940,000	4,816,000	4,776,000	4,704,000	4,648,000	4,512,000	4,354,224
STATISTICAL RECORD:							
Operating Profit Margin %	44.3	45.2	35.5	34.3	37.1	35.3	36.1
Net Profit Margin %	31.0	30.4	25.3	24.5	24.7	25.4	25.7
Return on Equity %	27.0	32.0	31.8	27.2	25.8	29.4	32.3
Return on Assets %	20.1	24.0	21.7	20.2	21.4	25.0	26.8
Price Range	72-31⅛	37¹¹/₁₆-20³/₁₆	21⁹/₁₆-9	13¹¹/₁₆-7⁵/₁₆	8¹/₈-4⁷/₈	6¹/₈-4³/₈	5¹⁵/₁₆-4¹/₈
P/E Ratio	86.2-37.2	57.4-30.7	50.4-23.4	47.1-25.1	34.6-20.7	31.1-22.3	39.3-27.2

Statistics are as originally reported. Adj. for stk. splits: 2-for-1, 3/99; 2/98; 12/96; 5/94; 3-for-2, 6/92

OFFICERS:
W. H. Gates, Chmn. & C.E.O.
S. A. Ballmar, Pres.
R. J. Herbold, Exec. V.P. & C.O.O.

INVESTOR CONTACT: Investor Relations Department, (800) 285-7772

PRINCIPAL OFFICE: One Microsoft Way, Redmond, WA 98052-6399

TELEPHONE NUMBER: (425) 882-8080
FAX: (425) 936-7329
WEB: www.microsoft.com

NO. OF EMPLOYEES: 22,232

SHAREHOLDERS: 70,491

ANNUAL MEETING: In Nov.

INCORPORATED: WA, Jun., 1981

INSTITUTIONAL HOLDINGS:
No. of Institutions: 1,113
Shares Held: 1,919,711,067
% Held: 37.6

INDUSTRY: Prepackaged software (SIC: 7372)

TRANSFER AGENT(S): ChaseMellon Shareholder Services, Ridgefield Park, NJ.

MINDSPRING ENTERPRISES, INC.

YIELD ...
P/E RATIO N.M.

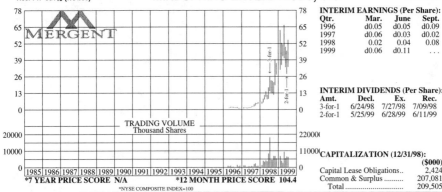

INTERIM EARNINGS (Per Share):

Qtr.	Mar.	June	Sept.	Dec.
1996	d0.05	d0.05	d0.09	d0.06
1997	d0.06	d0.03	d0.02	0.01
1998	0.02	0.04	0.08	0.07
1999	d0.06	d0.11	...	...

INTERIM DIVIDENDS (Per Share):

Amt.	Decl.	Ex.	Rec.	Pay.
3-for-1	6/24/98	7/27/98	7/09/98	7/24/98
2-for-1	5/25/99	6/28/99	6/11/99	6/25/99

TRADING VOLUME
Thousand Shares

*7 YEAR PRICE SCORE N/A ***12 MONTH PRICE SCORE 104.4**
*NYSE COMPOSITE INDEX=100

CAPITALIZATION (12/31/98):

	($000)	(%)
Capital Lease Obligations..	2,424	1.2
Common & Surplus	207,081	98.8
Total	209,505	100.0

RECENT DEVELOPMENTS: For the three months ended 6/30/99, net loss totaled $7.1 million compared with net income of $2.0 million in the corresponding quarter a year earlier. Results in the recent period were negatively affected by acquired customer base amortization of $23.7 million, largely stemming from MSPG's 2/17/99 acquisition of Netcom On-Line Communication Services, Inc.

Total revenues more than tripled to $85.7 million from $25.1 million the previous year. Gross margin was $56.5 million versus $17.5 million a year ago. However, as a percentage of total revenues, gross margin slipped to 66.0% compared with 69.7% the year before. MSPG's customer base increased 67% from the first quarter of 1999 as the Company surpassed the 1.0 million customer mark.

BUSINESS

MINDSPRING ENTERPRISES, INC. is an Internet service provider with approximately 1.2 million subscribers nationwide, of which most are individuals and small businesses. The Company offers local Internet access to subscribers in most major U.S. metropolitan areas through Company-owned points of presence (POPs), a third-party network provider's POP or a combination of the two. The Company's MindSpring Biz division provides Internet access and Web-based tools, including Web hosting services, domain name registration and Web page design, to small- and medium-sized businesses.

REVENUES

(12/31/98)	($000)	(%)
Access........................	95,852	83.6
Business Services	14,735	12.9
Subscriber Start-Up		
Fees.......................	4,086	3.5
Total	114,673	100.0

ANNUAL FINANCIAL DATA

	12/31/98	12/31/97	12/31/96	12/31/95	12/31/94
Earnings Per Share	0.21	d0.09	d0.24	d0.10	...
Cash Flow Per Share	0.51	0.10	d0.14	d0.09	...
Tang. Book Val. Per Share	3.05	0.31	0.33	...	...
INCOME STATEMENT (IN THOUSANDS):					
Total Revenues	114,673	52,557	18,132	2,227	103
Costs & Expenses	91,660	47,606	22,369	3,196	173
Depreciation & Amort.	15,227	8,695	3,285	265	5
Operating Income	7,786	d3,745	d7,522	d1,234	d75
Net Interest Inc./(Exp.)	1,214	d338	d90	d725	...
Income Before Income Taxes	9,000	d4,083	d7,612	d1,959	d75
Income Taxes	cr1,544	...	...	...	...
Net Income	10,544	d4,083	d7,612	d1,959	d75
Cash Flow	25,771	4,612	d4,327	d1,694	d70
Average Shs. Outstg.	50,862	45,085	31,516	19,052	...
BALANCE SHEET (IN THOUSANDS):					
Cash & Cash Equivalents	167,743	9,386	9,653	425	585
Total Current Assets	175,200	12,431	12,620	1,263	599
Net Property	35,841	23,638	11,583	3,539	101
Total Assets	247,599	44,286	35,232	4,845	722
Total Current Liabilities	38,094	17,782	7,100	4,363	52
Long-Term Obligations	2,424	5,090	2,725	...	...
Net Stockholders' Equity	207,081	21,414	25,407	482	670
Net Working Capital	137,106	d5,351	5,520	d3,099	548
Year-end Shs. Outstg.	56,568	45,207	44,863	7,604	7,604
STATISTICAL RECORD:					
Operating Profit Margin %	6.8	...	...	...	...
Net Profit Margin %	9.2	...	...	...	...
Return on Equity %	5.1	...	...	...	...
Return on Assets %	4.3	...	...	...	...
Debt/Total Assets %	1.0	11.5	7.7	...	...
Price Range	39½-4⅝	5¾-1⁵/₁₆	2³/₁₆-⅞	...	...
P/E Ratio	192.6-22.4	...	...	...	...

Statistics are as originally reported. Adj. for 2-for-1 stk. split, 6/99; 3-for-1 stk. split, 7/98.

OFFICERS:
C. M. Brewer, Chmn., C.E.O.
M. S. McQuary, Pres., C.O.O.
J. M. Reising, Exec. V.P., C.F.O.
S. R. DeSimone, Jr., Exec. V.P., Gen. Couns.

PRINCIPAL OFFICE: 1430 W. Peachtree, Suite 400, Atlanta, GA 30309

TELEPHONE NUMBER: (404) 815-0770
FAX: (404) 815-8805
WEB: www.mindspring.com

NO. OF EMPLOYEES: 1,600 (avg.)

SHAREHOLDERS: 741

ANNUAL MEETING: In May

INCORPORATED: GA, Feb., 1994; reincorp., DE, Dec., 1995

INSTITUTIONAL HOLDINGS:
No. of Institutions: 117
Shares Held: 21,253,860 (Adj.)
% Held: 38.2

INDUSTRY: Prepackaged software (SIC: 7372)

TRANSFER AGENT(S): American Stock Transfer and Trust Company, New York, NY

MODEM MEDIA . POPPE TYSON, INC.

YIELD ...
P/E RATIO ...

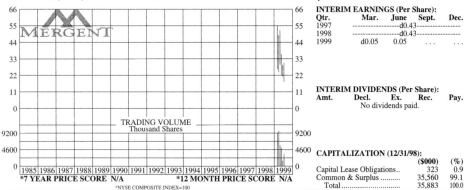

INTERIM EARNINGS (Per Share):

Qtr.	Mar.	June	Sept.	Dec.
1997	------------------d0.43------------------			
1998	------------------d0.43------------------			
1999	d0.05	0.05	...	...

INTERIM DIVIDENDS (Per Share):

Amt.	Decl.	Ex.	Rec.	Pay.
	No dividends paid.			

CAPITALIZATION (12/31/98):

	($000)	(%)
Capital Lease Obligations..	323	0.9
Common & Surplus	35,560	99.1
Total	35,883	100.0

*7 YEAR PRICE SCORE N/A   *12 MONTH PRICE SCORE N/A

*NYSE COMPOSITE INDEX=100

RECENT DEVELOPMENTS: For the quarter ended 6/30/99, net income totaled $581,000 compared with a net loss of $768,000 in the corresponding quarter of the previous year. Revenue jumped 53.5% to $16.0 million from $10.5 million the year before. The increase in revenue primarily resulted from increased services as well as the addition of new clients. Operating income advanced to $1.3 million versus a loss of $817,000 in the prior-year period. During the quarter, the Company had average annualized revenue of $5.0 million for each of its top 10 clients. In August, MMPT announced a contract with General Electric Company. Under the contract, MMPT will provide Internet and intranet planning and development services to GE Corporate and its business unit for more than $11.0 million in revenues through September, 2000.

BUSINESS

MODEM MEDIA . POPPE TYSON, INC. is an Internet marketing company that attracts, acquires and retains customers for global clients. The Company offers its clients a wide range of digital interactive marketing services such as strategic consulting and research, Web site design, electronic commerce and electronic customer communication services, interactive advertising and data collection and analysis. The Company's marketing programs are designed to enable its clients to target narrowly-defined market segments, provide their customers with detailed product and service information, sell products and services, provide post-sale customer support electronically, and promote consumer interest in their entire product lines. Customers have inculded 3M, Citibank, Delta Airlines, IBM, E*Trade, JCPenny, and Sony Computer Entertainment.

ANNUAL FINANCIAL DATA

	12/31/98	12/31/97	12/31/96	12/31/95
Earnings Per Share	d0.43	d0.43	d35.10	...
Cash Flow Per Share	0.06	d0.03	d34.35	...
Tang. Book Val. Per Share	0.30	0.55	...	...
INCOME STATEMENT (IN THOUSANDS):				
Total Revenues	42,544	25,497	2,093	438
Costs & Expenses	42,264	25,923	3,328	2,285
Depreciation & Amort.	3,614	2,855	15	4
Operating Income	d3,334	d3,281	d1,250	d1,851
Net Interest Inc./(Exp.)	29	d76	...	...
Income Before Income Taxes	d3,305	d3,357	d1,250	d1,851
Income Taxes	cr102	cr248	cr548	cr873
Net Income	d3,203	d3,109	d702	d978
Cash Flow	411	d254	d687	d974
Average Shs. Outstg.	7,465	7,260	20	...
BALANCE SHEET (IN THOUSANDS):				
Cash & Cash Equivalents	7,824	7,056	2,726	...
Total Current Assets	29,467	16,816	10,709	...
Net Property	6,826	2,825	1,827	...
Total Assets	71,286	59,024	54,022	...
Total Current Liabilities	35,384	13,547	7,281	...
Long-Term Obligations	323	9,818	6,193	...
Net Stockholders' Equity	35,560	35,618	40,493	...
Net Working Capital	d5,917	3,269	3,428	...
Year-end Shs. Outstg.	8,073	7,263	...	...
STATISTICAL RECORD:				
Debt/Total Assets %	0.5	16.6	11.5	...
Statistics are as originally reported.				

GEOGRAPHIC DATA

	REV	INC
(12/31/98)	(%)	(%)
Domestic....................	87.8	(75.2)
International	12.2	(24.8)
Total	100.0	100.0

OFFICERS:
G. M. O'Connell, C.E.O.
R. C. Allen II, Pres.
S. C. Roberts, C.F.O.

TELEPHONE NUMBER: (203) 299-7000
WEB: www.modemmedia.com

NO. OF EMPLOYEES: 400 (approx.)

SHAREHOLDERS: N/A

ANNUAL MEETING: N/A

PRINCIPAL OFFICE: 230 East Avenue, Norwalk, CT 06855

INCORPORATED: 1996

INSTITUTIONAL HOLDINGS:
No. of Institutions: 29
Shares Held: 1,509,262
% Held: 27.7

INDUSTRY: Business services, nec (SIC: 7389)

TRANSFER AGENT(S): First Chicago Trust Company of New York, New York, NY

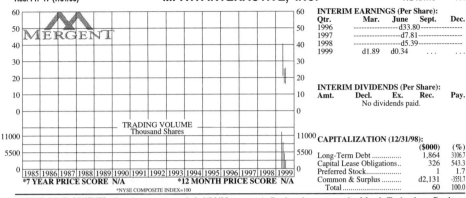

NASDAQ SYMBOL MPTH
Rec. Pr. 17 (7/31/99)

MPATH INTERACTIVE, INC.

YIELD ...
P/E RATIO ...

INTERIM EARNINGS (Per Share):

Qtr.	Mar.	June	Sept.	Dec.
1996	----------------d33.80----------------			
1997	----------------d7.81----------------			
1998	----------------d5.39----------------			
1999	d1.89	d0.34	...	...

TRADING VOLUME
Thousand Shares

*7 YEAR PRICE SCORE N/A   *12 MONTH PRICE SCORE N/A
*NYSE COMPOSITE INDEX=100

INTERIM DIVIDENDS (Per Share):

Amt.	Decl.	Ex.	Rec.	Pay.
	No dividends paid.			

CAPITALIZATION (12/31/98):

	($000)	(%)
Long-Term Debt	1,864	3106.7
Capital Lease Obligations..	326	543.3
Preferred Stock.................	1	1.7
Common & Surplus	d2,131	-3551.7
Total	60	100.0

RECENT DEVELOPMENTS: For the quarter ended 6/30/99, the Company reported a net loss of $5.2 million compared with a net loss of $3.2 million in the equivalent 1998 quarter. Revenues more than doubled to $3.2 million in 1999 from $1.5 million a year earlier. The improvement in revenues was primarily attributed to MPTH's live communities. The live communities unit benefited from a 27.3% increase in registered users to 4.2 million and average monthly user minutes of just over 200 million per month (with a forecast for July of close to 250 million user minutes). During the quarter, the Mpath Technology Products business unit signed several new deals for its technology products. MPTH unveiled a program for commercial partners on HearMe.com, adding six new Web site partners by the end of the quarter, including E! Online and Bolt. In early July, HearMe.com introduced a second voice chat affiliate program, targeting non-commercial and small commercial sites. The program, called my VoiceChat™, allows any web site to add live voice chat for free.

BUSINESS

MPATH INTERACTIVE, INC. develops, licenses and operates technologies that enable Internet sites to create and manage live communities characterized by real-time interaction among multiple simultaneous users. The Company operates its own live communities, Mplayer.com and HearMe.com. Mplayer.com is a premier live entertainment service on the Internet that consists of three active communities built around common interests and offers 100 on-line multiparticipant games. HearMe.com is comprised of seven live communities, making live audio interaction available to people whose interests extend beyond entertainment. Through Mpath Technology Products, the Company leverages its proprietary technology by providing third party site operators with software products and services for building live communities.

ANNUAL FINANCIAL DATA

	12/31/98	12/31/97	12/31/96
Earnings Per Share	d5.39	d7.81	d33.80
Cash Flow Per Share	d4.95	d7.29	d33.26
Tang. Book Val. Per Share	...	2.76	...
INCOME STATEMENT (IN THOUSANDS):			
Total Revenues	8,027	2,727	124
Costs & Expenses	18,889	15,388	25,057
Depreciation & Amort.	976	899	402
Operating Income	d11,838	d13,560	d25,335
Net Interest Inc./(Exp.)	d111	d93	291
Income Before Income Taxes	d11,949	d13,653	d25,044
Income Taxes	2	1	1
Net Income	d11,951	d13,654	d25,045
Cash Flow	d10,975	d12,755	d24,643
Average Shs. Outstg.	2,217	1,749	741
BALANCE SHEET (IN THOUSANDS):			
Cash & Cash Equivalents	1,114	9,132	...
Total Current Assets	4,050	10,147	...
Net Property	1,878	1,974	...
Total Assets	6,177	12,356	...
Total Current Liabilities	6,117	2,567	...
Long-Term Obligations	2,190	2,648	...
Net Stockholders' Equity	d2,130	7,141	...
Net Working Capital	d2,067	7,580	...
Year-end Shs. Outstg.	3,835	2,584	...
STATISTICAL RECORD:			
Debt/Total Assets %	35.5	21.4	...
Statistics are as originally reported.			

OFFICERS:
P. Matteucci, Pres., C.E.O.
L. Palmor, C.F.O.
L. Heublein, C.O.O.

PRINCIPAL OFFICE: 665 Clyde Avenue, Mountain View, CA 94043

TELEPHONE NUMBER: (650) 429-3900
WEB: www.mpath.com
NO. OF EMPLOYEES: 111
SHAREHOLDERS: 207
ANNUAL MEETING: N/A
INCORPORATED: DE, Jan., 1995

INSTITUTIONAL HOLDINGS:
No. of Institutions: 3
Shares Held: 271,400
% Held: 1.3
INDUSTRY: Computer programming services (SIC: 7371)
TRANSFER AGENT(S): BankBoston, N.A., Canton, MA

MULTEX.COM, INC.

YIELD ...
P/E RATIO ...

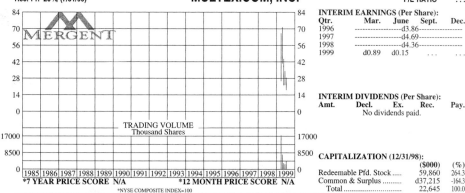

INTERIM EARNINGS (Per Share):

Qtr.	Mar.	June	Sept.	Dec.
1996	------------------d3.86-----------------			
1997	------------------d4.69-----------------			
1998	------------------d4.36-----------------			
1999	d0.89	d0.15	...	...

INTERIM DIVIDENDS (Per Share):

Amt.	Decl.	Ex.	Rec.	Pay.
	No dividends paid.			

CAPITALIZATION (12/31/98):

	($000)	(%)
Redeemable Pfd. Stock	59,860	264.3
Common & Surplus	d37,215	-164.3
Total	22,645	100.0

RECENT DEVELOPMENTS: For the quarter ended 6/30/99, the Company reported a net loss of $3.3 million compared with a net loss of $1.8 million in the corresponding period of the prior year. Earnings were negatively affected by a 103.5% increase in total operating expenses. Revenues almost doubled to $6.1 million from $3.1 million in the prior-year period. The improvement in revenues was a result of an 82.0% increase in the number of registered users, reflecting increased demand for MLTX products by investment professionals and individuals. Gross profit almost doubled to $4.6 million from $2.4 million the year before. The Company has agreed to acquire Market Guide, an Internet provider of value-added financial content for both individual investors and institutional investors, for approximately 5.6 million shares of stock. The acquisition is expected to be completed in the Fall of 1999.

BUSINESS

MULTEX.COM, INC. provides on-line investment research and information services designed to meet the needs of individual and institutional investors, including investment banks, brokerage firms and corporations. The Company's products and services provide research delivery, graphically rich original text formats, e-mail alerts, security and document entitlement features, and advanced searching and filtering applications. MLTX's services enable on-line access to over 1.3 million research reports and other investment information on over 20,000 companies published by more than 500 investment banks, brokerage firms and third-party research providers worldwide. The Company's services are used by more than 1.0 million customers.

ANNUAL FINANCIAL DATA

	12/31/98	12/31/97	12/31/96
Earnings Per Share	d4.36	d4.69	d3.86
Cash Flow Per Share	d3.70	d4.03	d3.31
INCOME STATEMENT (IN THOUSANDS):			
Total Revenues	13,182	6,014	2,647
Costs & Expenses	20,063	12,742	7,990
Depreciation & Amort.	2,019	1,434	1,126
Operating Income	d8,901	d8,162	d6,470
Net Interest Inc./(Exp.)	d126	125	60
Income Before Income Taxes	d9,743	d8,037	d6,410
Net Income	d9,743	d8,037	d6,410
Cash Flow	d10,528	d8,784	d6,686
Average Shs. Outstg.	2,847	2,179	2,022
BALANCE SHEET (IN THOUSANDS):			
Cash & Cash Equivalents	22,332	10,197	...
Total Current Assets	25,001	12,270	...
Net Property	2,843	2,161	...
Total Assets	27,968	14,733	...
Total Current Liabilities	5,264	4,249	...
Net Stockholders' Equity	d37,215	d26,750	...
Net Working Capital	19,736	8,021	...
Year-end Shs. Outstg.	3,251	2,445	2,069

Statistics are as originally reported.

QUARTERLY DATA

(12/31/1998)($000)	Rev	Inc
1st Quarter	2,714	(1,659)
2nd Quarter	3,115	(1,807)
3rd Quarter	3,492	(2,751)
4th Quarter	3,861	(3,526)

OFFICERS:
I. Karaev, Chmn., C.E.O.
J. M. Tousignant, Pres.
P. Callaghan, C.F.O.

PRINCIPAL OFFICE: 33 Maiden Lane, 5th Floor, New York, NY 10038

TELEPHONE NUMBER: (212) 859-9800
FAX: (212) 859-9810
WEB: www.multex.com

NO. OF EMPLOYEES: 149 (avg.)

SHAREHOLDERS: 89

ANNUAL MEETING: N/A

INCORPORATED: DE, Apr., 1993

INSTITUTIONAL HOLDINGS:
No. of Institutions: 27
Shares Held: 3,047,240
% Held: 14.0

INDUSTRY: Data processing and preparation (SIC: 7374)

TRANSFER AGENT(S): American Stock Transfer and Trust Company, New York, NY

NAVIDEC, INC.

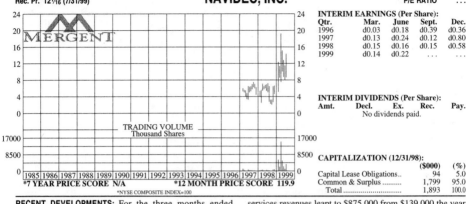

TRADING VOLUME
Thousand Shares

| 1985 | 1986 | 1987 | 1988 | 1989 | 1990 | 1991 | 1992 | 1993 | 1994 | 1995 | 1996 | 1997 | 1998 | 1999 |

7 YEAR PRICE SCORE N/A   *12 MONTH PRICE SCORE 119.9*
*NYSE COMPOSITE INDEX=100

YIELD ...
P/E RATIO ...

INTERIM EARNINGS (Per Share):

Qtr.	Mar.	June	Sept.	Dec.
1996	d0.03	d0.18	d0.39	d0.36
1997	d0.13	d0.24	d0.12	d0.80
1998	d0.15	d0.16	d0.15	d0.58
1999	d0.14	d0.22	...	...

INTERIM DIVIDENDS (Per Share):

Amt.	Decl.	Ex.	Rec.	Pay.
No dividends paid.				

CAPITALIZATION (12/31/98):

	($000)	(%)
Capital Lease Obligations..	94	5.0
Common & Surplus	1,799	95.0
Total	1,893	100.0

RECENT DEVELOPMENTS: For the three months ended 6/30/99, the Company reported a net loss of $1.6 million compared with a net loss of $558,000 in the corresponding period of the prior year. Total revenues soared to $3.8 million from $1.8 million the year before. Gross profit as a percentage of total revenues advanced to 40.5% of revenues versus 30.1% of revenues in the comparable 1998 period. Internet services revenues advanced to $2.5 million from $1.0 million in the previous year. On-line automotive services revenues leapt to $875,000 from $139,000 the year before, while revenues from the product distribution division fell 39.6% to $391,000 from $647,000 in the prior-year period. On 7/25/99, WFC Holdings Corporation, a subsidiary of Wells Fargo & Company, committed to making a strategic investment of $25.0 million in the Company to help expand NVDC's business of consulting, building and managing e-business tools.

BUSINESS

NAVIDEC, INC. develops component-based open systems tools that provide on-line tools for the automotive industry. The Company also serves as a distributor of various high technology and other products through traditional and electronic channels. NVDC is organized into three business groups: DriveOff.com Inc., which is comprised of 14 automotive shopping Web sites; Net Solutions Group, which helps customers apply Internet-based technology to achieve specific business objectives; and Products Group, which sells high tech products from temperature sensing technology to color printers and supplies.

ANNUAL FINANCIAL DATA

	12/31/98	12/31/97	12/31/96	12/31/95	12/31/94
Earnings Per Share	d1.10	d1.47	d0.73	d0.02	...
Cash Flow Per Share	d0.95	d1.16	d0.64	0.01	...
Tang. Book Val. Per Share	0.25	0.43	...	...	...
INCOME STATEMENT (IN THOUSANDS):					
Total Revenues	8,555	6,008	5,470	4,121	1,831
Costs & Expenses	11,582	7,721	6,511	4,090	1,862
Depreciation & Amort.	522	865	173	34	6
Operating Income	d3,549	d2,578	d1,214	d3	d37
Net Interest Inc./(Exp.)	d414	d236	d204	d30	d18
Income Before Income Taxes	d3,933	d4,107	d1,415	d23	d23
Net Income	d3,933	d4,107	d1,415	d23	d23
Cash Flow	d3,411	d3,242	d1,242	10	d17
Average Shs. Outstg.	3,578	2,800	1,948	1,352	...
BALANCE SHEET (IN THOUSANDS):					
Cash & Cash Equivalents	991	369	231	...	...
Total Current Assets	3,658	1,917	600	882	...
Net Property	981	713	464	38	...
Total Assets	5,265	3,099	2,257	920	...
Total Current Liabilities	3,372	1,239	1,311	975	...
Long-Term Obligations	94	310	1,657	...	...
Net Stockholders' Equity	1,799	1,550	d710	d55	...
Net Working Capital	286	678	d711	d92	...
Year-end Shs. Outstg.	4,709	3,201	2,805	217	...
STATISTICAL RECORD:					
Debt/Total Assets %	1.8	10.0	73.4	...	...
Price Range	7¹⁄₄-2¹⁄₁₆	7¹⁄₂-3¹⁄₄	...	...	...

Statistics are as originally reported.

OFFICERS:
R. Armijo, Pres., C.E.O.
P. R. Mawhinney, C.F.O., Treas.
K. P. Bero, C.O.O.

PRINCIPAL OFFICE: 14 Iverness Dr., Suite F-116, Englewood, CO 80112

TELEPHONE NUMBER: (303) 790-7565
FAX: (303) 790-8845
WEB: www.navidec.com

NO. OF EMPLOYEES: 75

SHAREHOLDERS: 900 (approx)

ANNUAL MEETING: In June

INCORPORATED: CO, Jul., 1993

INSTITUTIONAL HOLDINGS:
No. of Institutions: 6
Shares Held: 100,800
% Held: 1.4

INDUSTRY: Computer integrated systems design (SIC: 7373)

TRANSFER AGENT(S): American Securities Transfer & Trust, Inc., New York, NY

NEON SYSTEMS, INC.

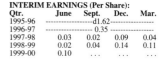

YIELD ...
P/E RATIO 84.3

INTERIM EARNINGS (Per Share):

Qtr.	June	Sept.	Dec.	Mar.
1995-96			d1.62	
1996-97		0.35		
1997-98	0.03	0.02	0.09	0.04
1998-99	0.02	0.04	0.14	0.11
1999-00	0.10	...	...	...

INTERIM DIVIDENDS (Per Share):

Amt.	Decl.	Ex.	Rec.	Pay.
		No dividends paid.		

TRADING VOLUME
Thousand Shares

*7 YEAR PRICE SCORE N/A   *12 MONTH PRICE SCORE N/A
*NYSE COMPOSITE INDEX=100

CAPITALIZATION (3/31/99):

	($000)	(%)
Common & Surplus	45,830	100.0
Total	45,830	100.0

RECENT DEVELOPMENTS: For the quarter ended 6/30/99, net income rocketed to $1.1 million from $145,000 in the corresponding period of 1998. Earnings were positively affected by a 6.7 percentage point reduction in total operating expenses as a percentage of total revenues to 74.0% from 80.7% a year earlier. Total revenues advanced 58.1% to $6.1 million from $3.8 million in the prior year. License revenues increased 52.2% to $4.5 million, while maintenance revenues leapt 76.7% to $1.6 million. Gross profit improved 69.6% to $5.7 million from $3.4 million a year earlier. Operating income amounted to $1.2 million versus $265,000 in 1998. Results should be positively affected by the introduction of SPEED LOAD™ version 2.2 and SPEED UNLOAD™ version 2.2. These new releases are designed to benefit information management systems data centers by reducing central processing unit and input/output overhead, along with associated costs.

BUSINESS

NEON SYSTEMS, INC. develops, markets and supports enterprise access and integration software. NEON's primary product family, SHADOW, provides access to, and connectivity between, enterprise data, transactions and applications. SHADOW products enable the deployment of new applications and the extension of legacy applications across a variety of computing environments, including the Internet and client/server and mainframe systems. SHADOW DIRECT enables client/server applications to access and integrate with mainframe data and applications. SHADOW WEB SERVER enables Web browsers to access and integrate with mainframe data and applications. SHADOW ENTERPRISE DIRECT provides access and integration between client/server systems.

REVENUES

(03/31/1999)	($000)	(%)
License	15,420	77.0
Maintenance	4,596	23.0
Total	20,016	100.0

ANNUAL FINANCIAL DATA

	3/31/99	3/31/98	3/31/97	3/31/96
Earnings Per Share	0.30	0.19	0.35	d1.62
Cash Flow Per Share	0.32	0.19	0.39	d1.55
Tang. Book Val. Per Share	5.18	...	...	...
INCOME STATEMENT (IN THOUSANDS):				
Total Revenues	20,016	12,203	7,186	2,466
Costs & Expenses	16,371	10,615	6,222	2,967
Depreciation & Amort.	199	144	73	31
Operating Income	3,447	1,443	891	d532
Net Interest Inc./(Exp.)	131	d21	d68	d66
Income Before Income Taxes	3,632	1,471	823	d598
Income Taxes	1,380	310	7	...
Net Income	2,252	1,161	816	d598
Cash Flow	2,375	1,205	810	d647
Average Shs. Outstg.	7,517	6,268	2,094	417
BALANCE SHEET (IN THOUSANDS):				
Cash & Cash Equivalents	45,400	2,804	1,705	...
Total Current Assets	52,100	5,895	2,773	...
Net Property	487	452	320	...
Total Assets	52,635	6,352	3,093	...
Total Current Liabilities	6,805	4,923	1,897	...
Long-Term Obligations	...	...	1,049	...
Net Stockholders' Equity	45,830	d234	d1,416	...
Net Working Capital	45,295	973	876	...
Year-end Shs. Outstg.	8,848	2,536	2,260	...
STATISTICAL RECORD:				
Operating Profit Margin %	17.2	11.8	12.4	...
Net Profit Margin %	11.3	9.5	11.4	...
Return on Equity %	4.9	...	...	...
Return on Assets %	4.3	18.3	26.4	...
Debt/Total Assets %	...	...	33.9	...

Statistics are as originally reported.

OFFICERS:
J. J. Moores, Chmn.
J. Backer, Pres., C.E.O.
J. S. Reiland, C.F.O.

PRINCIPAL OFFICE: 14100 Southwest Freeway, Suite 500, Sugar Land, TX 77478

TELEPHONE NUMBER: (281) 491-4200
WEB: www.neonsys.com

NO. OF EMPLOYEES: 90

SHAREHOLDERS: 113

ANNUAL MEETING: N/A

INCORPORATED: May, 1993

INSTITUTIONAL HOLDINGS:
No. of Institutions: 43
Shares Held: 2,472,749
% Held: 29.3

INDUSTRY: Prepackaged software (SIC: 7372)

TRANSFER AGENT(S): ChaseMellon Shareholder Services, L.L.C., Dallas, Tex.

NET.B@NK, INC.

YIELD ...
P/E RATIO 179.2

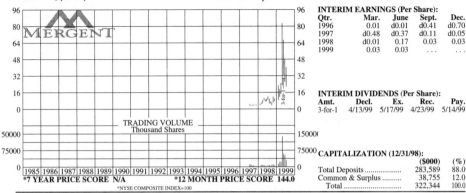

INTERIM EARNINGS (Per Share):

Qtr.	Mar.	June	Sept.	Dec.
1996	0.01	d0.01	d0.41	d0.70
1997	d0.48	d0.37	d0.11	d0.05
1998	d0.01	0.17	0.03	0.03
1999	0.03	0.03	...	...

INTERIM DIVIDENDS (Per Share):

Amt.	Decl.	Ex.	Rec.	Pay.
3-for-1	4/13/99	5/17/99	4/23/99	5/14/99

TRADING VOLUME
Thousand Shares

1985 1986 1987 1988 1989 1990 1991 1992 1993 1994 1995 1996 1997 1998 1999
*7 YEAR PRICE SCORE N/A   *12 MONTH PRICE SCORE 144.0
*NYSE COMPOSITE INDEX=100

CAPITALIZATION (12/31/98):

	($000)	(%)
Total Deposits	283,589	88.0
Common & Surplus	38,755	12.0
Total	322,344	100.0

RECENT DEVELOPMENTS: For the three months ended 6/30/99, net income was $768,000 compared with $3.3 million in the corresponding period of the prior year. The results from 1998 included a one-time tax benefit of $3.0 million. Interest income more than doubled to $10.4 million from $4.3 million in the prior-year period. Fueling the improvement in interest income was strong growth in customer accounts, which have more than doubled since 12/31/98. Non-interest income was $232,000 versus $104,000 in the corresponding quarter a year earlier. Recently, the Company announced plans to offer consumer loans, including home equity and automobile loans, beginning in the third quarter of 1999. Also, NTBK intends to develop additional products and services such as insurance products, electronic bill presentment and electronic document and image storage in a virtual safe deposit box.

BUSINESS

NET.B@NK, INC. is a federally-insured bank operating exclusively on the Internet. The Company's mission is to profitably provide a broad range of banking and financial services to the growing number of Internet users. NTBK offers products and services that are typical of traditional banks, including checking and money market accounts, certificates of deposit, electronic bill payment, debit cards, credit cards, mortgage loans, business equipment leases and securities brokerage services. At 12/31/98, customer accounts totaled 17,408 and total deposits amounted to $283.6 million.

LOAN DISTRIBUTION

12/31/98	($000)	(%)
Residential		
Mortgages	144,361	51.5
Construction	27,997	9.9
Commercial	8,556	3.1
Home Equity Lines....	89,054	31.8
Auto..........................	7,804	2.8
Personal & Other	2,656	0.9
Total	280,428	100.0

ANNUAL FINANCIAL DATA

	12/31/98	12/31/97	⬚ 12/31/96
Earnings Per Share	0.23	d0.55	d1.44
Tang. Book Val. Per Share	2.10	1.85	0.67
INCOME STATEMENT (IN THOUSANDS):			
Total Interest Income	18,088	2,223	8
Total Interest Expense	11,424	1,260	...
Net Interest Income	6,664	963	8
Provision for Loan Losses	20	472	...
Non-Interest Income	683	63	60
Non-Interest Expense	5,187	6,132	3,907
Income Before Taxes	2,139	d5,577	d3,839
Net Income	4,464	d5,577	d3,839
Average Shs. Outstg.	19,152	10,062	2,658
BALANCE SHEET (IN THOUSANDS):			
Securities Avail. for Sale	61,465	18,279	...
Total Loans & Leases	280,428	44,480	...
Allowance for Credit Losses	3,472	...	...
Net Loans & Leases	276,955	44,480	...
Total Assets	388,437	93,220	1,246
Total Deposits	283,589	58,727	...
Total Liabilities	349,682	59,102	1,633
Net Stockholders' Equity	38,755	34,117	d386
Year-end Shs. Outstg.	18,471	18,437	3,748
STATISTICAL RECORD:			
Return on Equity %	11.5	...	...
Return on Assets %	1.1	...	...
Equity/Assets %	10.0	36.6	...
Non-Int. Exp./Tot. Inc. %	70.6	597.6	...
Price Range	12⅛-3⁹⁄₁₆	4⁷⁄₁₆-2⁷⁄₈	...
P/E Ratio	52.7-15.5	...	...

Statistics are as originally reported. Adj. for stk. split: 3-for-1, 5/99 ⬚ Period from 2/20/96 to 12/31/96

OFFICERS:
T. S. Johnson, Chmn.
D. R. Grimes, Vice-Chmn., C.E.O.
D. S. Shapleigh Jr., Pres., C.O.O.
R. E. Bowers, C.F.O.

INVESTOR CONTACT: Eve McDowell, Media and Public Relations, (770) 343-6006

PRINCIPAL OFFICE: 950 North Point Pkwy., Ste. 350, Alpharetta, GA 30005

TELEPHONE NUMBER: (770) 343-6006
FAX: (770) 396-7870
WEB: www.netbank.com

NO. OF EMPLOYEES: 25 (avg.)

SHAREHOLDERS: 90 (of record)

ANNUAL MEETING: In Apr.

INCORPORATED: GA, Feb., 1996

INSTITUTIONAL HOLDINGS:
No. of Institutions: 45
Shares Held: 10,801,461
% Held: 37.5

INDUSTRY: Savings institutions, except federal (SIC: 6036)

TRANSFER AGENT(S): SunTrust Bank, N.A., Atlanta, Georgia.

NETGRAVITY, INC.

YIELD ...
P/E RATIO ...

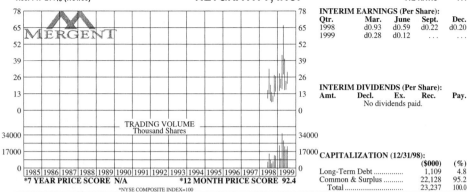

*7 YEAR PRICE SCORE N/A   ***12 MONTH PRICE SCORE 92.4**
NYSE COMPOSITE INDEX=100

INTERIM EARNINGS (Per Share):

Qtr.	Mar.	June	Sept.	Dec.
1998	d0.93	d0.59	d0.22	d0.20
1999	d0.28	d0.12	...	...

INTERIM DIVIDENDS (Per Share):

Amt.	Decl.	Ex.	Rec.	Pay.
	No dividends paid.			

CAPITALIZATION (12/31/98):

	($000)	(%)
Long-Term Debt	1,109	4.8
Common & Surplus	22,128	95.2
Total	23,237	100.0

RECENT DEVELOPMENTS: On 7/13/99, the Company signed an agreement to be acquired by DoubleClick Inc. Under the terms of the agreement, DoubleClick will exchange 0.28 shares of its common stock for each share of NETG common stock outstanding. The transaction is expected to be completed early in the fourth quarter of 1999. For the three months ended 6/30/99, the Company reported a net loss of $2.1 million compared with a loss of $3.0 million a year earlier. Revenues more than doubled to $5.6 million from $2.3 million the previous year. Gross profit jumped to $3.1 million, or 54.1% of revenues, from $1.2 million, or 52.3% of revenues, the year before. Loss from operations was $3.5 million compared with a loss of $3.0 million the prior year.

BUSINESS

NETGRAVITY, INC. develops and produces on-line advertising management and direct marketing software for e-commerce merchants, advertising agencies, and content publishers. The Company's core product, AdServer, manages the process of placing advertisements, promotions and other offers on Web pages. The Company also offers a transaction-based data service that gives its customers access to a database of anonymous consumer profiles for use in targeting on-line advertisements, promotions and other offers.

REVENUES

(12/31/98)	($000)	(%)
Software Licenses	4,115	35.6
Software Upgrades	2,394	20.7
Consulting &		
Support	4,637	40.1
Transactional		
Services	411	3.6
Total	11,557	100.0

ANNUAL FINANCIAL DATA

	12/31/98	12/31/97	12/31/96
Earnings Per Share	d1.28	d2.46	d2.19
Cash Flow Per Share	d0.99	d2.22	d2.11
Tang. Book Val. Per Share	1.63	0.71	...
INCOME STATEMENT (IN THOUSANDS):			
Total Revenues	11,557	6,358	1,939
Costs & Expenses	20,813	12,575	6,448
Depreciation & Amort.	2,577	655	172
Operating Income	d11,833	d6,872	d4,681
Net Income	d11,293	d6,882	d4,627
Cash Flow	d8,716	d6,227	d4,455
Average Shs. Outstg.	8,823	2,799	2,111
BALANCE SHEET (IN THOUSANDS):			
Cash & Cash Equivalents	10,236	5,637	1,020
Total Current Assets	27,888	8,531	2,420
Net Property	3,473	1,356	695
Total Assets	33,420	9,887	3,159
Total Current Liabilities	10,183	6,309	2,641
Long-Term Obligations	1,109	727	682
Net Stockholders' Equity	22,128	2,851	d164
Net Working Capital	17,705	2,222	d221
Year-end Shs. Outstg.	13,590	3,979	4,235
STATISTICAL RECORD:			
Debt/Total Assets %	3.3	7.4	21.6
Price Range	32½-6⁵/₁₆	...	...

Statistics are as originally reported.

OFFICERS:
J. W. Danner, Chmn.
E. W. Spivey, Pres., C.E.O.
S. E. Recht, C.F.O., Sec.

INVESTOR CONTACT: Steve Recht, C.F.O. & Sec., (650) 425-6000

PRINCIPAL OFFICE: 1900 South Norfolk Street, Suite 150, San Mateo, CA 94403-1151

TELEPHONE NUMBER: (650) 425-6000
FAX: (650) 425-6060
WEB: www.netgravity.com

NO. OF EMPLOYEES: 125 (avg.)

SHAREHOLDERS: 191 (approx.)

ANNUAL MEETING: In May

INCORPORATED: DE, Sep., 1995

INSTITUTIONAL HOLDINGS:
No. of Institutions: 64
Shares Held: 7,813,375
% Held: 56.7

INDUSTRY: Prepackaged software (SIC: 7372)

TRANSFER AGENT(S): ChaseMellon Shareholder Services, Ridgefield Park, NJ

NETSPEAK CORPORATION

YIELD ...
P/E RATIO ...

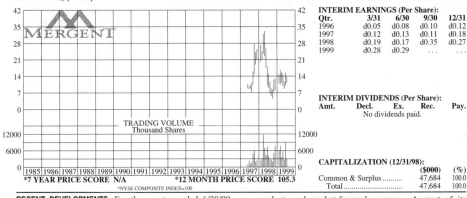

INTERIM EARNINGS (Per Share):

Qtr.	3/31	6/30	9/30	12/31
1996	d0.05	d0.08	d0.10	d0.12
1997	d0.12	d0.13	d0.11	d0.18
1998	d0.19	d0.17	d0.35	d0.27
1999	d0.28	d0.29	...	...

INTERIM DIVIDENDS (Per Share):

Amt.	Decl.	Ex.	Rec.	Pay.
		No dividends paid.		

*7 YEAR PRICE SCORE N/A   *12 MONTH PRICE SCORE 105.3

*NYSE COMPOSITE INDEX=100

CAPITALIZATION (12/31/98):

	($000)	(%)
Common & Surplus	47,684	100.0
Total	47,684	100.0

RECENT DEVELOPMENTS: For the quarter ended 6/30/99, the Company reported a net loss of $3.7 million compared with a net loss of $2.1 million in the equivalent 1998 quarter. Net revenues declined 65.1% to $1.0 million compared with $2.9 million in the corresponding 1998 period. Net revenues were generated primarily from sales of NSPK's voice over Internet Protocol (IP) call management software applications and gateway systems. The Company embarked upon its transition from a technology-focused to a product- and market-focused company. As part of its transition, in April 1999, the Company introduced its Solution Suite product line, which offers service providers the ability to deploy revenue-generating voice and fax over IP services. In June, NSPK introduced its newest technology, Internet Call Waiting™ with "Class," which enables Internet users to use a single phone line for both voice calls and Internet access.

BUSINESS

NETSPEAK CORPORATION develops, markets, licenses and supports a suite of intelligent software modules which provide business solutions for concurrent, real-time interactive voice, video and data communications over packetized data networks such as the Internet, local-area networks and wide-area networks. NSPK's products are designed to help organizations build new voice and video-enabled communications networks or to add these communications capabilities to their existing enterprise. NSPK's solutions integrate a variety of features and functions commonly found in traditional voice transmission networks into packetized data networks. NSPK's product lines consist of call management software, gateway systems and software based client telephones.

ANNUAL FINANCIAL DATA

	12/31/98	12/31/97	12/31/96	① 12/31/95
Earnings Per Share	② d0.98	d0.54	d0.35	Nil
Cash Flow Per Share	d0.86	d0.48	d0.33	...
Tang. Book Val. Per Share	3.74	2.00	0.74	0.08
INCOME STATEMENT (IN THOUSANDS):				
Total Revenues	7,719	5,353	867	...
Costs & Expenses	20,340	10,368	3,664	642
Depreciation & Amort.	1,524	609	198	...
Operating Income	d14,145	d5,624	d2,995	d642
Income Before Income Taxes	d12,028	d4,871	d2,823	d642
Income Taxes	35	209	43	...
Net Income	② d12,063	d5,080	d2,866	d642
Cash Flow	d10,539	d4,471	d2,668	d642
Average Shs. Outstg.	12,282	9,396	8,198	...
BALANCE SHEET (IN THOUSANDS):				
Cash & Cash Equivalents	44,922	19,054	6,295	483
Total Current Assets	47,118	20,506	6,903	499
Net Property	3,614	2,178	1,050	31
Total Assets	51,725	23,201	8,278	556
Total Current Liabilities	4,041	2,093	2,599	108
Net Stockholders' Equity	47,684	21,108	5,679	448
Net Working Capital	43,077	18,413	4,304	391
Year-end Shs. Outstg.	12,751	10,555	7,699	5,450
STATISTICAL RECORD:				
Price Range	33¹/₈-4⁷/₁₆	27³/₄-7³/₁₆	...	...

Statistics are as originally reported. ① From 12/8/95 to 12/31/95. ② Incl. non-recurr. chrg. $383,000.

OFFICERS:
S. R. Cohen, Chmn., C.E.O.
R. Kennedy, Vice-Chmn.
M. R. Rich, Pres., C.O.O.
J. W. Staten, C.F.O.

PRINCIPAL OFFICE: 902 Clint Moore Road, Suite 104, Boca Raton, FL 33487

TELEPHONE NUMBER: (561) 998-8700
FAX: (561) 997-2401
WEB: www.netspeak.com

NO. OF EMPLOYEES: 124

SHAREHOLDERS: 115 2500 beneficial holders

ANNUAL MEETING: N/A
INCORPORATED: FL, Dec., 1995

INSTITUTIONAL HOLDINGS:
No. of Institutions: 13
Shares Held: 555,696
% Held: 4.3

INDUSTRY: Computer integrated systems design (SIC: 7373)

TRANSFER AGENT(S): American Stock Transfer & Trust Company, New York, NY

NETWORK COMPUTING DEVICES, INC.

YIELD ...
P/E RATIO ...

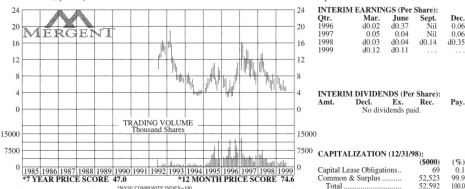

*7 YEAR PRICE SCORE 47.0   ***12 MONTH PRICE SCORE 74.6**
*NYSE COMPOSITE INDEX=100

INTERIM EARNINGS (Per Share):

Qtr.	Mar.	June	Sept.	Dec.
1996	d0.02	d0.37	Nil	0.06
1997	0.05	0.04	Nil	0.06
1998	d0.03	d0.04	d0.14	d0.35
1999	d0.12	d0.11	...	...

INTERIM DIVIDENDS (Per Share):

Amt.	Decl.	Ex.	Rec.	Pay.
		No dividends paid.		

CAPITALIZATION (12/31/98):

	($000)	(%)
Capital Lease Obligations..	69	0.1
Common & Surplus	52,523	99.9
Total	52,592	100.0

RECENT DEVELOPMENTS: For the second quarter ended 6/30/99, the Company reported a net loss of $1.8 million compared with a net loss of $733,000 in the corresponding period of the prior year. Total net revenues increased 23.0% to $27.9 million from $22.7 million a year earlier. The improved results reflected strong growth in sales of the Company's new Windows-based terminals products, such as its NCD ThinSTAR systems and NCD ThinPATH software products. Operating loss amounted to $1.9 million versus an operating loss of $3.5 million in the previous year. The Company is on its way toward replacing declining revenue from low-margin OEM shipments to IBM and sales of third-party software with sales of the Company's new, higher-margin products. Going forward, results should benefit from growing acceptance of the Company's systems and software products in the thin client marketplace.

BUSINESS

NETWORK COMPUTING DEVICES, INC. provides thin client hardware and software that delivers access to all of the information on enterprise intranets and the Internet from thin client, UNIX and PC desktops. The Company's product line includes the NCD ThinSTAR line of Windows-based terminals, optimized to access Microsoft's Windows NT Server 4.0, Terminal Server Edition, the NCD EXPLORA thin clients and the NCD NC400 network computers, acquired in the acquisition of Tektronix Inc. Network Displays business unit in December 1998. On the software side, NCDI's products are the NCD ThinPATH family of client and server software, developed to enhance the connectivity, management and features of the NCD thin clients as well as PCs in accessing information and applications on Terminal Server. Since introducing its first product in 1989, NCDI has installed over 1.0 million thin clients worldwide. Thin clients are units with limited processing capabilities, connected with servers via networks.

ANNUAL FINANCIAL DATA

	12/31/98	12/31/97	12/31/96	12/31/95	12/31/94	12/31/93	12/31/92
Earnings Per Share	[1] d0.56	[2] 0.15	[3] d0.32	[4] d0.25	[5] d0.68	[6] 0.55	[7] 0.43
Cash Flow Per Share	d0.37	0.33	d0.04	0.04	d0.41	0.79	0.65
Tang. Book Val. Per Share	3.27	3.72	3.96	4.22	4.60	5.08	4.43
INCOME STATEMENT (IN THOUSANDS):							
Total Revenues	105,596	133,400	120,608	139,328	160,871	144,265	120,345
Costs & Expenses	116,020	128,377	133,290	142,480	172,044	127,687	107,242
Depreciation & Amort.	3,022	3,287	4,559	4,505	4,334	3,653	3,151
Operating Income	d13,446	1,736	d17,241	d7,657	d15,507	12,925	9,952
Net Interest Inc./(Exp.)	1,595	1,895	1,588	1,359	908	854	1,084
Income Before Income Taxes	d9,761	3,831	d8,721	d6,205	d7,285	13,758	10,617
Income Taxes	cr658	1,150	cr3,489	cr2,176	3,558	5,090	4,509
Net Income	[1] d9,103	[2] 2,681	[3] d5,232	[4] d4,029	[5] d10,843	[6] 8,668	[7] 6,108
Cash Flow	d6,081	5,968	d673	476	d6,509	12,321	9,259
Average Shs. Outstg.	16,393	18,313	16,579	15,832	15,908	15,587	14,185
BALANCE SHEET (IN THOUSANDS):							
Cash & Cash Equivalents	21,359	31,480	35,671	36,150	31,220	35,632	43,535
Total Current Assets	63,651	79,646	78,935	86,002	90,445	83,123	83,830
Net Property	3,850	4,424	4,895	6,749	6,052	5,781	4,952
Total Assets	75,146	86,514	85,693	97,537	101,029	94,169	91,139
Total Current Liabilities	22,554	25,835	17,954	28,532	27,643	15,642	24,094
Long-Term Obligations	69	160	314	991	1,497	1,990	1,916
Net Stockholders' Equity	52,523	60,519	67,425	68,014	71,889	76,537	65,129
Net Working Capital	41,097	53,811	60,981	57,470	62,802	67,481	59,736
Year-end Shs. Outstg.	16,049	16,284	17,037	16,119	15,637	15,052	14,700
STATISTICAL RECORD:							
Operating Profit Margin %	...	1.3	...	...	...	9.0	8.3
Net Profit Margin %	...	2.0	...	...	...	6.0	5.1
Return on Equity %	...	4.4	...	...	...	11.3	9.4
Return on Assets %	...	3.1	...	...	...	9.2	6.7
Debt/Total Assets %	0.1	0.2	0.4	1.0	1.5	2.1	2.1
Price Range	13³⁄₄-4³⁄₈	16¹⁄₄-5⁷⁄₈	11¹⁄₄-2⁷⁄₈	11¹⁄₈-3⁷⁄₈	8³⁄₄-3¹⁄₄	19-6¹⁄₄	16³⁄₄-9⁵⁄₈
P/E Ratio	...	108.3-39.1	...	...	...	34.5-11.4	38.9-22.4

Statistics are as originally reported. [1] Incl. non-recurr. chrg. $2.4 mill. [2] Incl. non-recurr. chrg. $147,000 [3] Incl. non-recurr. credit $48,000 [4] Incl. non-recurr. chrg. $4.8 mill. [5] Incl. non-recurr. chrg. $17.5 mill. [6] Bef. acctg. change credit $573,000 [7] Incl. non-recurr. chrg. $3.6 mill.

OFFICERS:
P. Preuss, Chmn.
R. G. Gilbertson, Pres. & C.E.O.
R. G. Morin, Exec. V.P. & C.F.O.

INVESTOR CONTACT: Rudy G. Morin, Exec. V.P. & C.F.O., (650) 919-2734

PRINCIPAL OFFICE: 350 N. Bernardo Avenue, Mountain View, CA 94043

TELEPHONE NUMBER: (650) 694-0650
FAX: (650) 961-7711
WEB: www.ncd.com

NO. OF EMPLOYEES: 340

SHAREHOLDERS: 209 (approx.)

ANNUAL MEETING: In May

INCORPORATED: CA, Feb., 1988; reincorp., DE, Oct., 1998

INSTITUTIONAL HOLDINGS:
No. of Institutions: 22
Shares Held: 4,044,365
% Held: 25.2

INDUSTRY: Computer terminals (SIC: 3575)

TRANSFER AGENT(S): ChaseMellon Shareholder Services, L.L.C., Ridgefield Park, NJ

NETWORK SOLUTIONS, INC.

YIELD ...
P/E RATIO 122.1

7 YEAR PRICE SCORE N/A   **12 MONTH PRICE SCORE 102.2**
*NYSE COMPOSITE INDEX=100

INTERIM EARNINGS (Per Share):

Qtr.	Mar.	June	Sept.	Dec.
1997	0.02	0.03	0.05	0.05
1998	0.07	0.08	0.09	0.11
1999	0.14	0.17	...	...

INTERIM DIVIDENDS (Per Share):

Amt.	Decl.	Ex.	Rec.	Pay.
2-for-1	1/04/99	3/24/99	2/26/99	3/23/99

CAPITALIZATION (12/31/98):

	($000)	(%)
Capital Lease Obligations..	247	0.3
Common & Surplus	75,130	99.7
Total	75,377	100.0

RECENT DEVELOPMENTS: For the three months ended 6/30/99, net income more than doubled to $5.8 million from $2.5 million in the corresponding quarter of the prior year. Net revenue jumped to $47.5 million from $20.5 million the previous year. The increase in net revenue was attributed to an increase in the number of domain name registrations. Gross profit was $29.8 million, or 62.7% of net revenue, compared with $11.7 million, or 57.1% of net

revenue, the prior year. During the second quarter, the Company registered a record 1.2 million net new Internet domain names compared with 443,000 in the same quarter a year earlier. Growth in net registration was driven by the widespread use and adoption by businesses of the Internet and Intranets. The number of net new international registrations in .com, .net and .org totaled 368,000, up sharply versus 128,000 the year before.

BUSINESS

NETWORK SOLUTIONS, INC. is an Internet domain name registration service provider. The Company registers Web addresses ending in .com, .net, .org and .edu. Domain names are used to identify a unique site or presence on the Internet from which to communicate and conduct commerce. As registry and registrar for these domains, the Company registers new domain names and is responsible for the maintenance of the master file of domain names through daily updates to the Internet. The Company also provides Internet Technology Services, focusing on network engineering, network and systems security and network management solutions.

QUARTERLY DATA

12/31/98($000)	Rev	Inc
1st Quarter................	16,492	2,049
2nd Quarter..............	20,476	2,463
3rd Quarter	25,427	3,005
4th Quarter................	31,257	3,718

ANNUAL FINANCIAL DATA

	12/31/98	12/31/97	12/31/96	12/31/95
Earnings Per Share	0.34	0.16	d0.06	...
Cash Flow Per Share	0.45	0.25	d0.01	...
Tang. Book Val. Per Share	2.26	1.48	...	...
INCOME STATEMENT (IN THOUSANDS):				
Total Revenues	93,652	45,326	18,862	5,309
Costs & Expenses	76,741	37,287	20,209	6,169
Depreciation & Amort.	3,754	2,432	1,417	765
Operating Income	13,157	5,607	d2,764	d1,625
Net Interest Inc./(Exp.)	6,303	2,211	496	d52
Income Before Income Taxes	19,344	7,702	d2,268	d1,677
Income Taxes	8,109	3,471	cr643	cr287
Net Income	11,235	4,231	d1,625	① d1,390
Cash Flow	14,989	6,663	d208	d625
Average Shs. Outstg.	33,397	26,966	26,974	...
BALANCE SHEET (IN THOUSANDS):				
Cash & Cash Equivalents	131,670	81,346	15,540	5
Total Current Assets	198,807	134,169	56,603	6,774
Net Property	16,005	6,146	2,266	1,067
Total Assets	243,867	149,620	66,118	11,748
Total Current Liabilities	133,016	83,222	55,241	7,333
Long-Term Obligations	247	1,081	...	...
Net Stockholders' Equity	75,130	47,655	1,437	3,062
Net Working Capital	65,791	50,947	1,362	d559
Year-end Shs. Outstg.	32,990	31,440	25,000	25,000
STATISTICAL RECORD:				
Operating Profit Margin %	14.0	12.4	...	...
Net Profit Margin %	12.0	9.3	...	...
Return on Equity %	15.0	8.9	...	...
Return on Assets %	4.6	2.8	...	...
Debt/Total Assets %	0.1	0.7	...	...
Price Range	86⅛-6¼	13⅜-5⅞	...	...
P/E Ratio	253.2-18.4	86.2-37.9	...	...

Statistics are as originally reported. Adj. for 2-for-1 stk. split, 3/23/99. ① Bef. disc. oper. loss $28,000

OFFICERS:
M. A. Daniels, Chmn., Acting C.E.O.
R. J. Korzeniewski, C.F.O., Acting C.O.O.
J. W. Emery, Sr. V.P., Gen. Couns., Sec.
M. G. Voslow, V.P.-Fin., Treas.

PRINCIPAL OFFICE: 505 Huntmar Park Dr., Herndon, VA 20170

TELEPHONE NUMBER: (703) 742-0400
WEB: www.netsol.com
NO. OF EMPLOYEES: 385 (approx.)
SHAREHOLDERS: 105
ANNUAL MEETING: In May
INCORPORATED: DC, 1979; reincorp., DE, Nov., 1996

INSTITUTIONAL HOLDINGS:
No. of Institutions: 90
Shares Held: 12,275,306
% Held: 38.1

INDUSTRY: Prepackaged software (SIC: 7372)

TRANSFER AGENT(S): ChaseMellon Shareholder Services, Ridgefield Park, NJ

NETWORK-1 SECURITY SOLUTIONS, INC.

YIELD ...
P/E RATIO ...

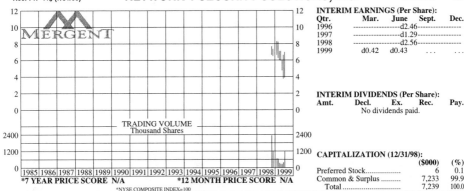

*7 YEAR PRICE SCORE N/A   *12 MONTH PRICE SCORE N/A
*NYSE COMPOSITE INDEX=100

TRADING VOLUME
Thousand Shares

INTERIM EARNINGS (Per Share):

Qtr.	Mar.	June	Sept.	Dec.
1996	------------------d2.46------------------			
1997	------------------d1.29------------------			
1998	------------------d2.56------------------			
1999	d0.42	d0.43	...	...

INTERIM DIVIDENDS (Per Share):

Amt.	Decl.	Ex.	Rec.	Pay.
No dividends paid.				

CAPITALIZATION (12/31/98):

	($000)	(%)
Preferred Stock...............	6	0.1
Common & Surplus	7,233	99.9
Total	7,239	100.0

RECENT DEVELOPMENTS: For the quarter ended 6/30/99, NSSI incurred a net loss of $1.9 million compared with a net loss of $1.3 million in the corresponding period of the prior year. Revenues fell 7.6% to $520,000 from $563,000 a year earlier. With the release on 8/16/99 of its CYBERWALLPLUS-SV 5.1™ product for Windows NT servers, with enhanced performance for on-line environments, NSSI announced the availability of a firewall security architecture for Web sites and on-line service providers aimed at resetting current thinking among corporations' IT executives. On 7/7/99, the Company announced a strategic relationship with Microsoft Corporation to promote NSSI's intrusion detection and prevention and network access control product and security services through Microsoft's Security Partners Program.

BUSINESS

NETWORK-1 SECURITY SOLUTIONS, INC. develops, markets, licenses and supports a family of network security software products designed to provide comprehensive security to computer networks, including Internet-based systems and internal networks and computing resources. The Company's CYBERWALLPLUS™ family of security software products enables an organization to protect its computer networks from internal and external attacks and to secure organizational communications over such internal networks and the Internet. The Company also offers its customers a full range of consulting services in network security and network design and support in order to build, maintain and enhance customer relationships and increase the demand for its software products.

ANNUAL FINANCIAL DATA

	12/31/98	12/31/97	12/31/96
Earnings Per Share	① d2.56	d1.29	d2.46
Cash Flow Per Share	d1.79	d0.76	d2.10
Tang. Book Val. Per Share	1.66	...	0.69
INCOME STATEMENT (IN THOUSANDS):			
Total Revenues	1,831	2,369	1,027
Costs & Expenses	4,727	3,225	4,592
Depreciation & Amort.	1,727	981	674
Operating Income	d4,623	d1,837	d4,239
Net Interest Inc./(Exp.)	d1,154	d553	d260
Income Before Income Taxes	d5,777	d2,390	d4,499
Net Income	① d5,777	d2,390	d4,499
Cash Flow	d4,050	d1,409	d3,825
Average Shs. Outstg.	2,258	1,855	1,825
BALANCE SHEET (IN THOUSANDS):			
Cash & Cash Equivalents	6,423	60	217
Total Current Assets	6,791	525	438
Net Property	415	400	518
Total Assets	8,168	2,404	1,878
Total Current Liabilities	929	1,186	479
Long-Term Obligations	...	1,234	8
Net Stockholders' Equity	7,239	d75	1,391
Net Working Capital	5,862	d661	d41
Year-end Shs. Outstg.	4,367	1,706	2,005
STATISTICAL RECORD:			
Debt/Total Assets %	...	51.3	0.4
Price Range	7¹¹⁄₁₆-6½	...	...

Statistics are as originally reported. ① Includes write-off of in-process research & development of $469,000.

OFFICERS:
C. M. Horowitz, Chmn.
A. A. Fogel, Pres., C.E.O.
M. P. Fish, C.F.O.
R. M. Russo, Sec., V.P., Business Devel.

PRINCIPAL OFFICE: 1601 Trapelo Road, Reservoir Place, Waltham, MA 02451

TELEPHONE NUMBER: (781) 522-3400
WEB: www.network-1.com

NO. OF EMPLOYEES: 36

SHAREHOLDERS: 79

ANNUAL MEETING: N/A

INCORPORATED: DE, Jul., 1990

INSTITUTIONAL HOLDINGS:
No. of Institutions: 1
Shares Held: 5,000
% Held: 0.1

INDUSTRY: Prepackaged software (SIC: 7372)

TRANSFER AGENT(S): American Stock Transfer & Trust Company, New York, NY

NASDAQ SYMBOL NETA
Rec. Pr. 17½ (7/31/99)

NETWORKS ASSOCIATES, INC.

YIELD ...
P/E RATIO ...

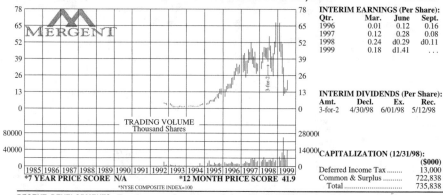

TRADING VOLUME
Thousand Shares

*7 YEAR PRICE SCORE N/A   *12 MONTH PRICE SCORE 41.9
*NYSE COMPOSITE INDEX=100

INTERIM EARNINGS (Per Share):

Qtr.	Mar.	June	Sept.	Dec.
1996	0.01	0.12	0.16	0.19
1997	0.12	0.28	0.08	d0.77
1998	0.24	d0.29	d0.11	0.40
1999	0.18	d1.41	...	...

INTERIM DIVIDENDS (Per Share):

Amt.	Decl.	Ex.	Rec.	Pay.
3-for-2	4/30/98	6/01/98	5/12/98	5/29/98

CAPITALIZATION (12/31/98):

	($000)	(%)
Deferred Income Tax	13,000	1.8
Common & Surplus	722,838	98.2
Total	735,838	100.0

RECENT DEVELOPMENTS: For the second quarter ended 6/30/99, the Company reported a net loss of $195.8 million compared with a net loss of $38.5 million in the corresponding prior-year quarter. Earnings for 1999 and 1998 included charges of $13.7 million and $83.3 million, respectively, related to the amortization of intangibles, a stock compensation charge and acquisition-related costs. Net revenues plummeted to $25.2 million from $249.3 mil-

lion in 1998. During the quarter, the Company and Cisco Systems announced that NETA will become a charter member of Cisco's newly introduced Virtual Private Network client interoperability program. Under the program, NETA's PGP VPN client software for Windows and Macintosh will be certified to seamlessly interoperate with Cisco's comprehensive family of VPN-optimized routers and firewalls.

BUSINESS

NETWORKS ASSOCIATES, INC. (formerly McAfee Associates, Inc.) is a supplier of enterprise network security and management tools. The Company's product offering includes four individual software suites, Total Virus Defense, Total Network Security, Total Network Visibility and Total Service Desk, which can be centrally managed from within NETA's Net-Tools unified management environment. Many of NETA's network security and management products are available as stand-alone products or as part of smaller product suites. Electronic software distribution is one of the principal means by which NETA distributes its software products. NETA generally licenses its products to corporate customers, its primary customer base, under either a one-year or a two-year product license. NETA also offers a full range of consumer-oriented security and management software products to retail customers, both through traditional retail stores and via the Internet. The Company was formed through the 12/1/97 merger of McAfee Associates and Network General.

ANNUAL FINANCIAL DATA

	12/31/98	12/31/97	12/31/96	12/31/95	12/31/94	12/31/93	12/31/92
Earnings Per Share	② 0.26	② d0.27	② 0.49	② 0.20	② 0.03	0.14	① 0.13
Cash Flow Per Share	0.81	d0.03	0.56	0.24	0.05	0.14	0.22
Tang. Book Val. Per Share	5.27	3.43	2.03	0.87	0.38	0.36	0.21
INCOME STATEMENT (IN THOUSANDS):							
Total Revenues	990,045	612,193	181,126	90,065	32,900	17,911	13,683
Costs & Expenses	794,744	568,536	107,897	62,809	30,018	6,197	3,168
Depreciation & Amort.	75,335	25,436	5,960	2,998	1,198	165	61
Operating Income	119,966	18,221	67,269	24,258	1,684	11,549	10,454
Net Interest Inc./(Exp.)	d15,246	...	...	...	631	645	d4,374
Income Before Income Taxes	138,167	32,964	70,730	25,971	2,315	12,194	6,080
Income Taxes	101,729	61,320	31,713	11,055	928	4,890	cr5,012
Net Income	② 36,438	② d28,356	② 39,017	② 14,916	② 1,387	7,304	11,092
Cash Flow	111,773	d2,920	44,977	17,914	2,585	7,469	11,153
Average Shs. Outstg.	138,609	103,122	79,811	74,048	55,734	53,919	49,929
BALANCE SHEET (IN THOUSANDS):							
Cash & Cash Equivalents	517,414	247,376	126,731	55,357	26,545	27,695	18,935
Total Current Assets	903,618	430,272	163,948	90,685	45,178	37,258	26,594
Net Property	54,489	28,570	7,486	3,399	1,201	549	224
Total Assets	1,536,721	601,931	194,485	104,020	56,398	39,074	28,512
Total Current Liabilities	366,562	228,986	41,295	35,853	24,720	15,696	14,072
Net Stockholders' Equity	722,838	359,759	149,527	63,542	23,015	18,363	10,333
Net Working Capital	537,056	201,286	122,653	54,832	20,458	21,562	12,522
Year-end Shs. Outstg.	137,124	104,882	72,993	69,195	52,542	50,400	49,794
STATISTICAL RECORD:							
Operating Profit Margin %	12.1	3.0	37.1	26.9	5.1	64.5	76.4
Net Profit Margin %	3.7	...	21.5	16.6	4.2	40.8	81.1
Return on Equity %	5.0	...	26.1	23.5	6.0	39.8	107.3
Return on Assets %	2.4	...	20.1	14.3	2.5	18.7	38.9
Price Range	67¹¹/₁₆-25½	52⁵/₁₆-24⁵/₁₆	35¼-9¼	15¹¹/₁₆-2⁵/₁₆	4-1⁵/₁₆	4-0⁷/₈	4⁹/₁₆-2⁹/₁₆
P/E Ratio	260.2-98.0	...	72.3-19.0	78.3-14.8	159.4-51.2	29.4-6.5	36.1-20.2

Statistics are as originally reported. Adj. for stk. splits: 3-for-2, 5/29/98; 3-for-2, 10/17/96; 3-for-2, 5/16/96 ① Pro forma ② Incl. non-recurr. chgs. $135.6 mill., 12/98; $175.8 mill., 12/97; $11.2 mill., 12/96; $12.8 mill., 12/95; $12.8 mill., 12/94

REVENUES

(12/31/98)	($000)	(%)
Product	831,363	84.0
Services and Support	158,682	16.0
Total	990,045	100.0

OFFICERS:
W. L. Larson, Chmn. & C.E.O.
P. K. Goyal, Treas., Sec. & V.P.

PRINCIPAL OFFICE: 3965 Freedom Circle, Santa Clara, CA 95054

TELEPHONE NUMBER: (408) 988-3832
FAX: (408) 970-9727
WEB: www.nai.com

NO. OF EMPLOYEES: 2,700 (approx.)

SHAREHOLDERS: 1,391

ANNUAL MEETING: In June

INCORPORATED: DE, Aug., 1992

INSTITUTIONAL HOLDINGS:
No. of Institutions: 273
Shares Held: 98,215,092
% Held: 71.1

INDUSTRY: Prepackaged software (SIC 7372)

TRANSFER AGENT(S): ChaseMellon Shareholder Services, L.L.C., Ridgefield Park, NJ

NEWSEDGE CORP.

YIELD ...
P/E RATIO ...

TRADING VOLUME
Thousand Shares

| | | | | | | | | | | | | | | |
|1985|1986|1987|1988|1989|1990|1991|1992|1993|1994|1995|1996|1997|1998|1999|

*7 YEAR PRICE SCORE N/A   ***12 MONTH PRICE SCORE 86.4**
*NYSE COMPOSITE INDEX=100

INTERIM EARNINGS (Per Share):

Qtr.	Mar.	June	Sept.	Dec.
1994	----------------d0.06----------------			
1995	---------------- 0.43 -----------------			
1996	---------------- 0.52 -----------------			
1997	0.10	0.07	0.06	0.08
1998	d0.82	d0.09	d0.05	d0.05
1999	d0.18	d0.15	...	...

INTERIM DIVIDENDS (Per Share):

Amt.	Decl.	Ex.	Rec.	Pay.
	No dividends paid.			

CAPITALIZATION (12/31/98):

	($000)	(%)
Long-Term Debt	303	1.5
Common & Surplus	19,249	98.5
Total	19,552	100.0

RECENT DEVELOPMENTS: For the quarter ending 6/30/99, NEWZ reported a net loss of $2.6 million versus a loss of $1.5 million in 1998. Total revenues rose 1.9% to $19.6 million from $19.2 million in the previous year. Operating loss was $3.0 million versus a loss of $2.1 million a year ago. Results reflected NEWZ's goals of cutting losses in half and ongoing efforts to increase market share in the Enterprise division. NEWZ completed the formation of NewsPage.com, Inc. as a wholly-owned subsidiary in July

1999. NEWZ plans to heavily invest in growing News-Page.com through advertising, sponsorship and e-commerce. In conjunction with the subsidiary announcement, NewsPage.com is now totally free to its users. Meanwhile, NewsEdge Insight™ will become the global news provider for SmithKline Beecham, a pharmaceutical company. NewsEdge Insight™ provides briefings from over 1,500 NewsEdge Review™ subjects with real-time news wires and cover-to-cover publication sources.

BUSINESS

NEWSEDGE CORPORATION is an independent provider of global news for business. NEWZ aggregates news and information from over 2,000 sources published by over one hundred global content providers. NEWZ operates through two lines of business: the Enterprise segment and the NewsPage segment. The Enterprise segment sells services directly to large organizations and delivers information to users within the organization through corporate intranets or local area networks. The NewsPage segment operates NewsPage.com, a Web site that customize, business-oriented news and information. This service is supported through strategic alliances with other Web sites and targets advertising and electronic commerce. NewsPage.com, Inc. was launched as a subsidiary in July 1999. Revenues in 1998 were derived: Enterprise, 84.7%; NewsPage, 8.0%; and other, 7.3%.

ANNUAL FINANCIAL DATA

	12/31/98	12/31/97	12/31/96	12/31/95	12/31/94	12/31/93	12/31/92
Earnings Per Share	① d1.00	① 0.31	0.52	0.43	d0.06	...	...
Cash Flow Per Share	d0.67	0.48	0.62	0.50	d0.02	...	...
Tang. Book Val. Per Share	1.12	3.90	3.48	2.89	...	...	...
INCOME STATEMENT (IN THOUSANDS):							
Total Revenues	79,532	42,182	33,779	23,186	14,358	7,660	4,207
Costs & Expenses	93,195	38,808	29,578	21,264	14,434	8,760	5,497
Depreciation & Amort.	5,707	1,524	898	499	307	196	135
Operating Income	d19,370	1,850	3,303	1,423	d384	d1,295	d1,425
Net Interest Inc./(Exp.)	...	2,140	1,896	897	97	34	d9
Income Before Income Taxes	d17,062	3,990	5,199	2,320	d287	d1,262	d1,434
Income Taxes	166	1,297	614	183	...	...	...
Net Income	① d17,228	① 2,693	4,585	2,137	d287	d1,262	d1,434
Cash Flow	d11,521	4,217	5,483	3,767	d115	d1,066	d1,299
Average Shs. Outstg.	17,194	8,742	8,778	7,519	6,670	...	...
BALANCE SHEET (IN THOUSANDS):							
Cash & Cash Equivalents	41,590	43,157	28,855	32,418	4,073	2,209	...
Total Current Assets	59,739	54,678	35,617	36,766	7,076	4,177	...
Net Property	9,138	5,732	4,640	1,991	1,088	665	...
Total Assets	69,154	60,584	48,327	38,879	8,220	4,875	...
Total Current Liabilities	49,445	26,638	18,115	14,188	11,740	6,144	...
Long-Term Obligations	303	6	38	53	62	...	...
Net Stockholders' Equity	19,249	33,901	29,985	24,605	d6,077	d5,464	...
Net Working Capital	10,294	28,040	17,502	22,578	d4,664	d1,967	...
Year-end Shs. Outstg.	17,155	8,691	8,626	8,511	2,642	2,401	...
STATISTICAL RECORD:							
Operating Profit Margin %	...	4.4	9.8	6.1	...	...	...
Net Profit Margin %	...	6.4	13.6	9.2	...	...	...
Return on Equity %	...	7.9	15.3	8.7	...	...	...
Return on Assets %	...	4.4	9.5	5.5	...	...	...
Debt/Total Assets %	0.4	...	0.1	0.1	0.8	...	...
Price Range	19¾-3⅝	20-5	40¾-17¼	38-21	...	...	...
P/E Ratio	...	64.5-16.1	78.4-33.2	88.4-48.8	...	...	...

Statistics are as originally reported. ① Incl. $11.1 mill. chg. for merger, disposition & other chgs, 1998; $5.1 mill., 1997.

OFFICERS:
D. L. McLagan, Chmn., C.E.O.
M. E. Kolowich, Vice-Chmn.
C. Pollan, Pres., C.O.O.
R. Benanto, C.F.O., V.P.

INVESTOR CONTACT: Mark J. Solitro, (781) 229-3050

PRINCIPAL OFFICE: 80 Blanchard Road, Burlington, MA 01803

TELEPHONE NUMBER: (781) 229-3000
FAX: (781) 229-3030
WEB: www.newsedge.com

NO. OF EMPLOYEES: 412

SHAREHOLDERS: 203 (approx.)

ANNUAL MEETING: In Jun.

INCORPORATED: DE, Jul., 1988

INSTITUTIONAL HOLDINGS:
No. of Institutions: 29
Shares Held: 6,289,714
% Held: 36.3

INDUSTRY: Computer related services, nec (SIC: 7379)

TRANSFER AGENT(S): BankBoston, c/o Boston EquiServe, Boston MA.

NEXTCARD, INC.

YIELD ...
P/E RATIO ...

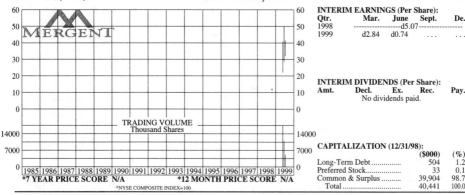

7 YEAR PRICE SCORE N/A **12 MONTH PRICE SCORE N/A**
*NYSE COMPOSITE INDEX=100

INTERIM EARNINGS (Per Share):

Qtr.	Mar.	June	Sept.	De.
1998	----------------d5.07----------------			
1999	d2.84	d0.74	...	...

INTERIM DIVIDENDS (Per Share):

Amt.	Decl.	Ex.	Rec.	Pay.
	No dividends paid.			

CAPITALIZATION (12/31/98):

	($000)	(%)
Long-Term Debt	504	1.2
Preferred Stock.................	33	0.1
Common & Surplus	39,904	98.7
Total	40,441	100.0

RECENT DEVELOPMENTS: For the three months ended 6/30/99, the Company reported a net loss of $18.7 million compared with a net loss of $3.1 million in the corresponding period of the previous year. Total interest income surged to $3.0 million from $79,000 the year before. Interest income from cash and investments jumped to $905,000 versus $79,000, while the Company reported interest income from credit card loans of $2.1 million. Total noninterest income leapt to $613,000 compared with $133,000

in the comparable 1998 quarter. On 8/16/99, the Company entered into a definitive agreement to acquire Textron National Bank (TNB), a subsidiary of Textron Financial Corp. Upon completion of the transaction, TNB will change its name to NextBank, National Association. This transaction should allow the Company to further diversify its funding sources. NXCD also announced co-branding relationships with Dilbert, PlanetOne and BabyCenter.com, The Knot, ACMEPet.com, chipset.com, and Kodak.

BUSINESS

NEXTCARD, INC. is an Internet-based provider of consumer credit. The Company was the first to offer an on-line approval system for a Visa® card and to provide interactive, customized offers for credit card applicants. The Company combines consumer credit, an exclusive Internet focus and a direct marketing technique with the aim of attracting profitable customer segments on the Internet. The product, the NextCard® Visa, is marketed to consumers exclusively through www.nextcard.com. The Company offers credit card customers customization, shopping enhancements and on-line customer service. The NextCard Visa can be used for both on-line and off-line purchases. The Company has also developed the NextCard e-wallet for one-click shopping and customized digital coupons.

ANNUAL FINANCIAL DATA

	12/31/98	12/31/97
Earnings Per Share	d5.07	d1.08
Cash Flow Per Share	d4.43	d1.07
Tang. Book Val. Per Share	8.09	0.57
INCOME STATEMENT (IN THOUSANDS):		
Total Revenues	1,199	93
Costs & Expenses	15,210	1,962
Depreciation & Amort.	2,051	16
Operating Income	d16,062	d1,885
Income Before Income Taxes	d16,062	d1,885
Income Taxes	2	2
Net Income	d16,064	d1,886
Cash Flow	d14,013	d1,871
Average Shs. Outstg.	3,166	1,747
BALANCE SHEET (IN THOUSANDS):		
Cash & Cash Equivalents	40,134	2,840
Total Current Assets	43,200	3,340
Net Property	2,103	293
Total Assets	45,542	3,688
Total Current Liabilities	5,102	901
Long-Term Obligations	504	...
Net Stockholders' Equity	39,937	2,787
Net Working Capital	38,098	2,439
Year-end Shs. Outstg.	4,932	4,895
STATISTICAL RECORD:		
Debt/Total Assets %	1.1	...
Statistics are as originally reported.		

OFFICERS:
J. R. Lent, Chmn., Pres., C.E.O.
J. V. Hashman, C.F.O.
R. Linderman, Gen. Couns., Sec.
T. J. Coltrell, C.O.O.
INVESTOR CONTACT: Susan Weinstein, V.P., (415) 369-5633
PRINCIPAL OFFICE: 595 Market Street, Suite 1800, San Francisco, CA 94105

TELEPHONE NUMBER: (415) 836-9700
FAX: (415) 836-9790
WEB: www.nextcard.com
NO. OF EMPLOYEES: 135
SHAREHOLDERS: 64
ANNUAL MEETING: N/A
INCORPORATED: CA, Jun., 1996; reincorp., DE, Apr., 1999

INSTITUTIONAL HOLDINGS:
No. of Institutions: 2
Shares Held: 111,500
% Held: 0.3
INDUSTRY: Personal credit institutions (SIC: 6141)
TRANSFER AGENT(S): BankBoston, N.A. EquiServe L.P., Canton, MA

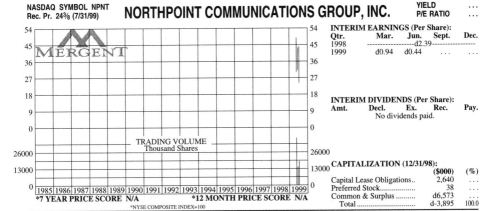

NASDAQ SYMBOL NPNT
Rec. Pr. 24⅜ (7/31/99)

NORTHPOINT COMMUNICATIONS GROUP, INC.

YIELD ...
P/E RATIO ...

*7 YEAR PRICE SCORE N/A   *12 MONTH PRICE SCORE N/A

*NYSE COMPOSITE INDEX=100

INTERIM EARNINGS (Per Share):

Qtr.	Mar.	Jun.	Sept.	Dec.
1998	------------------d2.39----------------			
1999	d0.94	d0.44	...	...

INTERIM DIVIDENDS (Per Share):

Amt.	Decl.	Ex.	Rec.	Pay.
	No dividends paid.			

CAPITALIZATION (12/31/98):

	($000)	(%)
Capital Lease Obligations..	2,640	...
Preferred Stock.................	38	...
Common & Surplus	d6,573	...
Total	d-3,895	100.0

RECENT DEVELOPMENTS: For the quarter ended 6/30/99, the Company reported a net loss of $37.9 million compared with a net loss of $3.3 million in the corresponding quarter the year before. Earnings were negatively affected by higher operating expenses. Operating expenses increased to $35.7 million compared with $3.4 million in the prior-year quarter. Revenues jumped to $2.5 million from $128,000 in the comparable quarter a year ago. Loss from operations was $33.2 million, up from $3.2 million in the previous year. During the quarter, the Company entered into several strategic partnerships creating additional distribution channels for the Company's DSL service. The Company expects to expand its DSL service to 28 markets, or 61 metropolitan statistical areas by the end of 1999. Upon completion, NPNT's DSL network will pass 4.0 million businesses and 30.0 million homes.

BUSINESS

NORTHPOINT COMMUNICA-TIONS GROUP, Inc. is a national provider of high speed, local data network services. The Company's networks use digital subscriber line, or DSL, technology to enable data transport over telephone company copper lines at speeds up to 25 times faster than common dial-up modems. The Company markets its network and data transport services to Internet service providers, long-distance and local telephone companies and data service providers. The Company currently operates DSL-based local networks in 24 major markets, representing 37 metropolitan statistical areas in the United States.

ANNUAL FINANCIAL DATA

	12/31/98	① 12/31/97
Earnings Per Share	d1.18	d0.07
Cash Flow Per Share	d0.94	d0.06
Tang. Book Val. Per Share	...	0.41
INCOME STATEMENT (IN THOUSANDS):		
Total Revenues	931	...
Costs & Expenses	20,244	1,429
Depreciation & Amort.	6,048	201
Operating Income	d25,362	d1,630
Net Interest Inc./(Exp.)	d3,485	190
Income Before Income Taxes	d28,847	d1,440
Net Income	d28,847	d1,440
Cash Flow	d22,799	d1,239
Average Shs. Outstg.	24,379	21,734
BALANCE SHEET (IN THOUSANDS):		
Cash & Cash Equivalents	10,956	9,448
Total Current Assets	14,128	9,507
Net Property	46,078	1,776
Total Assets	60,502	11,356
Total Current Liabilities	64,396	514
Long-Term Obligations	2,640	867
Net Stockholders' Equity	d6,534	9,975
Net Working Capital	d50,268	8,993
Year-end Shs. Outstg.	24,593	24,345
STATISTICAL RECORD:		
Debt/Total Assets %	4.4	7.6

Statistics are as originally reported. ① From May 16, 1997 (commencement of operations)

OFFICERS:
M. W. Malaga, Chmn., C.E.O.
E. A. Fetter, Pres., C.O.O.
H. P. Huff, V.P., Fin., C.F.O.
S. J. Gorosh, V.P., Gen. Couns., Sec.

PRINCIPAL OFFICE: 222 Sutter Street, San Francisco, CA 94108

TELEPHONE NUMBER: (415) 403-4003
WEB: www.northpointcom.com.

NO. OF EMPLOYEES: 506

SHAREHOLDERS: 67

ANNUAL MEETING: N/A

INCORPORATED: DE, 1997

INSTITUTIONAL HOLDINGS:
No. of Institutions: 7
Shares Held: 541,785
% Held: 0.4

INDUSTRY: Telephone communications, exc. radio (SIC: 4813)

TRANSFER AGENT(S): ChaseMellon Shareholder Services, L.L.C., San Francisco, CA

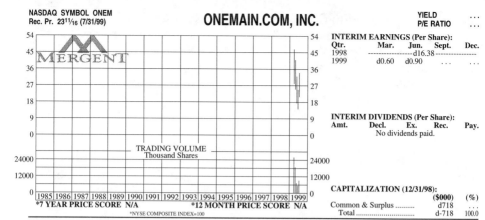

ONEMAIN.COM, INC.

YIELD ...
P/E RATIO ...

INTERIM EARNINGS (Per Share):

Qtr.	Mar.	Jun.	Sept.	Dec.
1998	----------------d16.38----------------			
1999	d0.60	d0.90	...	...

TRADING VOLUME
Thousand Shares

*7 YEAR PRICE SCORE N/A   *12 MONTH PRICE SCORE N/A
*NYSE COMPOSITE INDEX=100

INTERIM DIVIDENDS (Per Share):

Amt.	Decl.	Ex.	Rec.	Pay.
	No dividends paid.			

CAPITALIZATION (12/31/98):

	($000)	(%)
Common & Surplus	d718	...
Total	d-718	100.0

RECENT DEVELOPMENTS: For the quarter ended 6/30/99, the Company reported a net loss of $19.7 million compared with a net loss of $18.1 million in the corresponding quarter the year before. Total revenues jumped 74.2% to $23.0 million from $13.2 million in the prior-year quarter. Access revenues improved 77.2% to $21.5 million versus $12.1 million in the year-earlier quarter. Other revenues were $1.5 million, an increase of 41.6% from $1.1 million in the second quarter of 1998. Gross margin as a percentage of total revenues was 60.2% compared with 59.0% in the 1998 quarter. In July 1999, ONEM acquired The Internet Ramp, an Internet service provider serving the State of Michigan. Separately, ONEM entered into an agreement with Kenan Systems, a wholly-owned subsidiary of Lucent Technologies, to help deliver a single, fully-integrated billing system for its growing customer base. ONEM expects to complete its integration strategy by the middle of 2000 and plans to have more than 200,000 customers under one billing system by the end of 1999.

BUSINESS

ONEMAIN.COM, INC. provides Internet access and related services throughout the United States to individuals and businesses located predominantly in communities outside large metropolitan areas. As of 6/30/99, the Company had approximately 472,000 subscribers and is one of the largest independent Internet service providers.

ANNUAL FINANCIAL DATA

	▯ 12/31/98
Earnings Per Share	**d16.38**
Cash Flow Per Share	**d0.16**
INCOME STATEMENT (IN THOUSANDS):	
Costs & Expenses	761
Operating Income	d761
Net Interest Inc./(Exp.)	d4
Income Before Income Taxes	d765
Net Income	d765
Cash Flow	d765
Average Shs. Outstg.	4,668
BALANCE SHEET (IN THOUSANDS):	
Cash & Cash Equivalents	172
Total Current Assets	6,330
Total Assets	6,330
Total Current Liabilities	7,049
Net Stockholders' Equity	d718
Net Working Capital	d718
Year-end Shs. Outstg.	4,783
STATISTICAL RECORD:	

Statistics are as originally reported. ▯ For the period 8/19/98 (inception) to 12/31/98.

OFFICERS:
S. E. Smith, Chmn., Pres., C.E.O.
A. H. Lefever, Vice-Chmn.
D. K. Shay, Exec. V.P., C.F.O.
M. C. Crabtree, C.O.O.

PRINCIPAL OFFICE: 8150 Leesburg Pike, 6th Floor, Vienna, VA 22182

TELEPHONE NUMBER: (703) 883-8262
WEB: www.onemain.com.
NO. OF EMPLOYEES: 652 full-time (approx.); 91 part-time (approx.)
SHAREHOLDERS: 303
ANNUAL MEETING: N/A
INCORPORATED: DE, Aug., 1998

INSTITUTIONAL HOLDINGS:
No. of Institutions: 38
Shares Held: 2,494,556
% Held: 11.6
INDUSTRY: Computer related services, nec (SIC: 7379)
TRANSFER AGENT(S): American Stock Transfer & Trust Company.

ONESOURCE INFORMATION SERVICES, INC.

YIELD ...
P/E RATIO ...

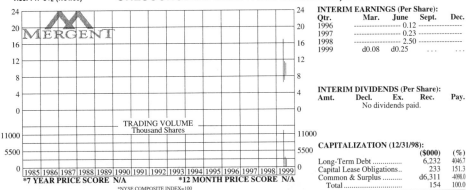

INTERIM EARNINGS (Per Share):

Qtr.	Mar.	June	Sept.	Dec.
1996	------------------	0.12	------------------	
1997	------------------	0.23	------------------	
1998	------------------	2.50	------------------	
1999	d0.08	d0.25	...	...

INTERIM DIVIDENDS (Per Share):

Amt.	Decl.	Ex.	Rec.	Pay.
		No dividends paid.		

CAPITALIZATION (12/31/98):

	($000)	(%)
Long-Term Debt	6,232	4046.7
Capital Lease Obligations..	233	151.3
Common & Surplus	d6,311	-4098.0
Total	154	100.0

7 YEAR PRICE SCORE N/A   **12 MONTH PRICE SCORE N/A**

*NYSE COMPOSITE INDEX=100

RECENT DEVELOPMENTS: For the quarter ended 6/30/99, the Company reported a net loss of $2.2 million compared with net income of $11.1 million in the corresponding quarter of the previous year. Earnings in 1998 included a $12.8 million gain related to the sale of the Company's CD-Insurance division. Total revenues increased 4.8% to $8.4 million from $7.7 million a year ago. Web-based product revenue more than doubled to $7.5 million from $3.4 million the year before. CD-ROM revenues dropped to $867,000 from $4.3 million in 1998, reflecting a change in the Company's focus towards Web-based products. Gross profit advanced 12.4% to $4.7 million versus $4.2 million in the prior-year period. ONES incurred an operating loss of $2.5 million compared with a loss of $1.3 million in the previous year. During the quarter, the Company introduced its US Company Browser, which delivers news, profiles and financial information on over 250,000 public and private companies.

BUSINESS

ONESOURCE INFORMATION SERVICES, INC. provides Web-based business and financial information to professionals who need quick access to corporate, industry and market intelligence. The Company uses a Web-based Business Browser which integrates up-to-date business and financial information on over one million public and private companies from more than 25 information providers drawing upon over 2,500 sources of content. These sources include both textual information, such as news, trade press, SEC filings, executive biographies and analyst reports, and numeric information, such as company financial results, stock quotes and industry statistics.

ANNUAL FINANCIAL DATA

	12/31/98	12/31/97	12/31/96
Earnings Per Share	2.50	0.23	0.12
Cash Flow Per Share	0.71	d0.05	0.07
INCOME STATEMENT (IN THOUSANDS):			
Total Revenues	30,428	30,384	30,434
Costs & Expenses	33,753	29,870	29,249
Depreciation & Amort.	1,639	1,918	2,778
Operating Income	d4,964	d1,404	d1,593
Net Interest Inc./(Exp.)	d595	d930	d733
Income Before Income Taxes	7,238	d1,833	d1,933
Income Taxes	250	...	...
Net Income	6,988	d1,833	d1,933
Cash Flow	7,260	d329	510
Average Shs. Outstg.	10,280	7,263	7,206
BALANCE SHEET (IN THOUSANDS):			
Cash & Cash Equivalents	8,665	341	...
Total Current Assets	25,374	14,404	...
Net Property	1,770	1,826	...
Total Assets	27,646	16,644	...
Total Current Liabilities	27,492	24,196	...
Long-Term Obligations	6,465	6,061	...
Net Stockholders' Equity	d6,311	d13,613	...
Net Working Capital	d2,118	d9,792	...
Year-end Shs. Outstg.	7,383	7,300	...
STATISTICAL RECORD:			
Net Profit Margin %	23.0	...	...
Return on Assets %	25.3	...	...
Debt/Total Assets %	23.4	36.4	...

Statistics are as originally reported.

REVENUES

(12/31/1998)	($000)	(%)
Web-based Product ...	16,058	52.8
CD Rom Product	14,370	47.2
Total	30,428	100.0

OFFICERS:
M. Kahn, Chmn.
D. J. Schimmel, Pres., C.E.O.

PRINCIPAL OFFICE: 300 Baker Avenue, Concord, MA 01742

TELEPHONE NUMBER: (978) 318-4300
FAX: (978) 318-4690
WEB: www.onesource.com
NO. OF EMPLOYEES: 168
SHAREHOLDERS: 57
ANNUAL MEETING: N/A
INCORPORATED: DE, Jul., 1993

INSTITUTIONAL HOLDINGS:
No. of Institutions: 5
Shares Held: 192,500
% Held: 1.9

INDUSTRY: Data processing and preparation (SIC: 7374)

TRANSFER AGENT(S): American Stock Transfer & Trust Company, New York, NY

ONSALE, INC.

YIELD ...
P/E RATIO ...

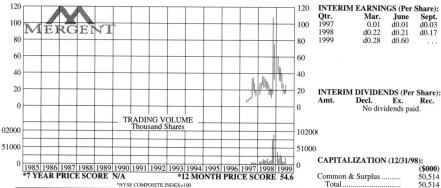

INTERIM EARNINGS (Per Share):

Qtr.	Mar.	June	Sept.	Dec.
1997	0.01	d0.01	d0.03	d0.09
1998	d0.22	d0.21	d0.17	d0.16
1999	d0.28	d0.60	...	...

INTERIM DIVIDENDS (Per Share):

Amt.	Decl.	Ex.	Rec.	Pay.
	No dividends paid.			

*7 YEAR PRICE SCORE N/A   *12 MONTH PRICE SCORE 54.6

*NYSE COMPOSITE INDEX=100

CAPITALIZATION (12/31/98):

	($000)	(%)
Common & Surplus	50,514	100.0
Total	50,514	100.0

RECENT DEVELOPMENTS: On 7/14/99, the Company signed a definitive agreement with Egghead.com, Inc., under which ONSL will exchange 0.565 shares of its common stock for each share of Egghead.com outstanding. After completion, current Egghead.com shareholders will own approximately 47.0% of the combined company. For the quarter ended 6/30/99, ONSL reported a net loss of $11.8 million compared with a loss of $4.0 million a year earlier. Total revenue advanced 60.2% to $81.4 million from $50.8 million in the previous year. Revenues benefited from the Company's aggressive marketing initiatives and a larger customer base. Merchandise revenue jumped 56.9% to $78.7 million from $50.1 million the prior year, while commission and other revenue totaled $2.7 million versus $658,000 a year ago. Gross profit slid 59.8% to $2.4 million from $6.0 million the year before. Loss from operations totaled $12.0 million versus a loss of $4.8 million in 1998.

BUSINESS

ONSALE, INC. is an Internet retailer that operates two on-line "stores," Onsale atAuction™ and Onsale atCost™. Through Onsale atAuction, the Company provides its customers the opportunity to bid on a range of excess and closeout computer products, consumer electronics, sports and fitness equipment, and vacation packages. Onsale atCost offers computer equipment at wholesale prices directly to businesses and consumers.

REVENUES

(12/31/98)	($000)	(%)
Merchandise	204,124	98.3
Commission...............	3,627	1.7
Total	207,751	100.0

ANNUAL FINANCIAL DATA

	12/31/98	12/31/97	12/31/96	12/31/95
Earnings Per Share	d0.77	0.16	0.02	d0.04
Cash Flow Per Share	d0.69	0.12	0.03	d0.04
Tang. Book Val. Per Share	2.62	3.34	0.19	...
INCOME STATEMENT (IN THOUSANDS):				
Total Revenues	207,751	88,981	14,269	140
Costs & Expenses	223,442	91,736	13,844	570
Depreciation & Amort.	1,521	616	58	10
Operating Income	d17,212	d3,371	367	d440
Income Before Income Taxes	d14,666	d2,472	404	d440
Income Taxes	...	...	43	...
Equity Earnings/Minority Int.	d200	...	...	...
Net Income	d14,666	d2,472	361	d440
Cash Flow	d13,145	d1,856	419	d430
Average Shs. Outstg.	18,953	15,742	15,326	12,015
BALANCE SHEET (IN THOUSANDS):				
Cash & Cash Equivalents	46,704	56,566	2,729	20
Total Current Assets	63,216	65,453	5,083	43
Net Property	4,024	1,535	578	30
Total Assets	69,426	67,143	5,680	73
Total Current Liabilities	16,896	4,874	3,352	492
Net Stockholders' Equity	50,514	62,269	2,328	d419
Net Working Capital	46,320	60,579	1,731	d449
Year-end Shs. Outstg.	19,315	18,642	12,179	12,043
STATISTICAL RECORD:				
Operating Profit Margin %	...	...	2.6	...
Net Profit Margin %	...	...	2.5	...
Return on Equity %	...	...	15.5	...
Return on Assets %	...	...	6.4	...
Price Range	108-10⅝	35¼-4¾	...	...

Statistics are as originally reported.

OFFICERS:
S. J. Kaplan, Pres., C.E.O.
J. Labbett, C.F.O., Sr. V.P.
J. F. Sheahan, C.O.O., Sr. V.P.

INVESTOR CONTACT: Brian K. Fawkes, (650) 470-2713

PRINCIPAL OFFICE: 1350 Willow Road, Suite 100, Menlo Park, CA 94025

TELEPHONE NUMBER: (650) 470-2400
FAX: (650) 473-6990
WEB: www.onsale.com
NO. OF EMPLOYEES: 200
SHAREHOLDERS: 172
ANNUAL MEETING: In May
INCORPORATED: CA, Jul., 1994; reincorp., DE, Mar., 1997

INSTITUTIONAL HOLDINGS:
No. of Institutions: 48
Shares Held: 2,357,313
% Held: 12.3

INDUSTRY: Catalog and mail-order houses (SIC: 5961)

TRANSFER AGENT(S): Boston EquiServe, Boston, MA

OPEN MARKET, INC.

YIELD ...
P/E RATIO ...

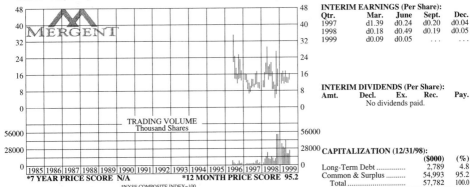

INTERIM EARNINGS (Per Share):

Qtr.	Mar.	June	Sept.	Dec.
1997	d1.39	d0.24	d0.20	d0.04
1998	d0.18	d0.49	d0.19	d0.05
1999	d0.09	d0.05	...	...

INTERIM DIVIDENDS (Per Share):

Amt.	Decl.	Ex.	Rec.	Pay.
	No dividends paid.			

CAPITALIZATION (12/31/98):

	($000)	(%)
Long-Term Debt	2,789	4.8
Common & Surplus	54,993	95.2
Total	57,782	100.0

*7 YEAR PRICE SCORE N/A   *12 MONTH PRICE SCORE 95.2

*NYSE COMPOSITE INDEX=100

RECENT DEVELOPMENTS: For the quarter ended 6/30/99, the Company reported a net loss of $1.9 million compared with a net loss of $11.1 million in the equivalent 1998 quarter. Total revenues advanced 12.2% to $18.6 million compared with $16.5 million in the corresponding 1998 period. Results for 1998 have been restated. Internet commerce-related revenues for the quarter were $15.6 million, up 32.2% from $11.8 million in 1998. On 7/14/99, OMKT agreed to acquire FutureTense®, Inc., a provider of Internet content management software, for approximately $125.0 million. On 7/20/99, OMKT partnered with SpeechWorks International, Inc., a provider of conversational speech recognition technology and products for over-the-telephone applications, to sell commerce services coupling Transact™ with SpeechSite™, to provide customers with a single speech activated system that gives customers the ability to conduct commerce, even if they do not have access to a computer.

BUSINESS

OPEN MARKET, INC. develops, markets, licenses and supports a family of application software products that allow its customers to engage in business-to-business and business-to-consumer Internet commerce, information commerce and commercial publishing. OMKT's software includes a wide spectrum of functionality required to effectively conduct business on the Internet, allowing companies to attract customers to their Web sites, interest them in acting upon an offer, complete a transaction and service them once a transaction has been completed. The Company's software products include Transact, LiveCommerce, ShopSite and the Folio Product Suite.

REVENUES

(12/31/1998)	($000)	(%)
Product Revenues	42,245	68.0
Service Revenues	19,900	32.0
Total	62,145	100.0

ANNUAL FINANCIAL DATA

	12/31/98	12/31/97	12/31/96	12/31/95	12/31/94
Earnings Per Share	[1] d0.91	[1] d1.87	d0.96	d0.53	...
Cash Flow Per Share	d0.68	d1.71	d0.90	d0.50	...
Tang. Book Val. Per Share	1.23	1.15	2.53	...	...
INCOME STATEMENT (IN THOUSANDS):					
Total Revenues	62,145	61,260	22,501	1,806	...
Costs & Expenses	84,491	115,366	49,898	15,026	1,243
Depreciation & Amort.	7,792	5,148	1,723	808	37
Operating Income	d30,138	d59,254	d29,120	d14,028	d1,280
Net Interest Inc./(Exp.)	276	2,050	2,963	156	30
Income Before Income Taxes	d30,147	d57,422	d26,150	d13,872	d1,250
Income Taxes	325	584	360	...	...
Net Income	[1] d30,472	[1] d58,006	d26,510	d13,872	d1,250
Cash Flow	d22,680	d52,858	d24,787	d13,064	d1,213
Average Shs. Outstg.	33,483	30,994	27,587	26,385	...
BALANCE SHEET (IN THOUSANDS):					
Cash & Cash Equivalents	34,879	30,638	72,033	3,712	636
Total Current Assets	65,021	56,156	80,127	5,487	658
Net Property	15,428	15,157	5,200	2,357	301
Total Assets	94,958	80,874	85,802	7,947	959
Total Current Liabilities	37,176	37,316	13,307	11,270	197
Long-Term Obligations	2,789	99	128	659	195
Net Stockholders' Equity	54,993	43,459	72,367	d15,187	d1,283
Net Working Capital	27,845	18,840	66,820	d5,783	461
Year-end Shs. Outstg.	35,291	30,971	28,565	9,390	9,336
STATISTICAL RECORD:					
Debt/Total Assets %	2.9	0.1	0.1	8.3	20.3
Price Range	29⅛-4¼	17⅜-6½	42¼-11½	...	...

Statistics are as originally reported. [1] Incl. non-recurr. chrg. $7.7 mill., 12/98; $34.3 mill., 12/97.

OFFICERS:
S. Ghosh, Chmn.
D. K. Gifford, Vice-Chmn.
G. B. Eichhorn, Pres., C.E.O.
B. J. Savage, C.F.O., V.P.

PRINCIPAL OFFICE: One Wayside Rd., Burlington, MA 01803

TELEPHONE NUMBER: (781) 359-3000
WEB: www.openmarket.com

NO. OF EMPLOYEES: 398

SHAREHOLDERS: 418

ANNUAL MEETING: In May

INCORPORATED: DE, Dec., 1993

INSTITUTIONAL HOLDINGS:
No. of Institutions: 51
Shares Held: 5,853,158
% Held: 16.3

INDUSTRY: Prepackaged software (SIC: 7372)

TRANSFER AGENT(S): The First National Bank of Boston, Boston, MA

OPEN TEXT CORPORATION

YIELD ...
P/E RATIO 27.7

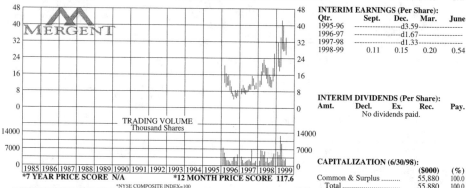

*7 YEAR PRICE SCORE N/A   *12 MONTH PRICE SCORE 117.6
*NYSE COMPOSITE INDEX=100

INTERIM EARNINGS (Per Share):

Qtr.	Sept.	Dec.	Mar.	June
1995-96		d3.59		
1996-97		d1.67		
1997-98		d1.33		
1998-99	0.11	0.15	0.20	0.54

INTERIM DIVIDENDS (Per Share):

Amt.	Decl.	Ex.	Rec.	Pay.
	No dividends paid.			

CAPITALIZATION (6/30/98):

	($000)	(%)
Common & Surplus	55,880	100.0
Total	55,880	100.0

RECENT DEVELOPMENTS: For the year ended 6/30/99, the Company reported net income of $20.2 million compared with a net loss of $6.3 million in the previous fiscal year. Results included gains of $8.6 million in 1998-99 and $1.0 million in 1997-98 from income tax recovery. Results also included pre-tax charges of $3.4 million in the recent year and $8.0 million in the previous year for acquired in-process research and development. Total revenues more than doubled to $92.5 million from $45.3 million a year earlier.

License revenues leapt 81.0% to $53.7 million, while service revenues rocketed 148.3% to $38.9 million. Gross profit more than doubled to $72.7 million from $36.2 million in 1998. On 7/26/99, the Company entered into an agreement to acquire Microstar Software Ltd. of Ottawa, Ontario for $2.10 per share payable in cash. Microstar, which had revenues of $6.2 million for its last fiscal year ended 1/31/99, provides structured information management tools comprised of technology and services.

BUSINESS

OPEN TEXT CORPORATION markets, develops, licenses and supports management application software for use in intranets, extranets and the Internet. The software enables users to find electronically stored information, do group calendaring and scheduling and distribute the resulting work product. As of 3/31/99, OTEX had a worldwide installed base of 3.0 million users in 3,600 corporations. The Company's core product, LIVELINK®, is an off-the-shelf, enterprise scalable, collaborative application for companies that want to leverage their information and resources through their intranets. LIVELINK provides a powerful collaborative environment, enabling project teams to form, and to capture, share, and reuse corporate knowledge to achieve the organization's mission and objectives.

ANNUAL FINANCIAL DATA

	6/30/98	6/30/97	② 6/30/96	① 6/30/95	① 6/30/94
Earnings Per Share	③ d1.33	③ d1.67	③ d3.59	d0.34	d0.18
Cash Flow Per Share	d1.19	1.57	d1.03	d0.29	d0.16
Tang. Book Val. Per Share	3.09	2.61	3.42	0.08	0.18
INCOME STATEMENT (IN THOUSANDS):					
Total Revenues	45,300	22,648	9,995	2,480	1,672
Costs & Expenses	69,301	50,977	23,895	3,327	2,201
Depreciation & Amort.	2,374	1,689	30,793	144	65
Operating Income	d26,375	d30,018	d44,693	d992	d595
Net Interest Inc./(Exp.)	1,620	1,796	1,349	108	93
Income Before Income Taxes	d24,475	d28,165	d43,199	d1,100	d688
Income Taxes	cr1,000	...	...	...	...
Net Income	③ d23,475	③ d28,165	③ d43,199	d1,100	d688
Cash Flow	d21,101	d26,476	d12,406	d956	d623
Average Shs. Outstg.	17,680	16,866	12,042	3,242	3,788
BALANCE SHEET (IN THOUSANDS):					
Cash & Cash Equivalents	40,390	31,762	51,139	...	...
Total Current Assets	66,148	42,792	58,758	1,914	1,169
Net Property	8,710	5,054	3,536	548	450
Total Assets	83,388	52,345	66,158	2,601	1,814
Total Current Liabilities	27,508	9,379	9,866	1,927	775
Long-Term Obligations	...	511	742	157	281
Net Stockholders' Equity	55,880	44,953	55,550	516	758
Net Working Capital	38,640	33,413	48,892	d13	394
Year-end Shs. Outstg.	18,087	17,204	16,236	6,124	4,110
STATISTICAL RECORD:					
Debt/Total Assets %	...	1.0	1.1	6.1	15.5
Price Range	26⅜-10	15½-6½	26½-4⅛	...	...

Statistics are as originally reported. ① Financials reported in Canadian dollars. ② During 1996, the Company's functional currency changed from Canadian dollars to U.S. dollars, as a greater part of its operations is denominated in U.S. dollars. ③ Incl. non-recurr. chrg. $25.6 mill., 6/98; $650,000, 6/97; $3.4 mill., 6/96.

OFFICERS:
P. T. Jenkins, C.E.O.
B. Newbold, Pres.
T. J. Hearne, C.F.O.

PRINCIPAL OFFICE: 185 Columbia Street West, Waterloo, Ontario, Canada

TELEPHONE NUMBER: (519) 888-7111
WEB: www.opentext.com

NO. OF EMPLOYEES: 700 (approx.)

SHAREHOLDERS: 3,700 (approx.)

ANNUAL MEETING: In Feb.

INCORPORATED: CAN, June, 1991

INSTITUTIONAL HOLDINGS:
No. of Institutions: 35
Shares Held: 6,160,849
% Held: 29.4

INDUSTRY: Computer integrated systems design (SIC: 7373)

TRANSFER AGENT(S): Montreal Trust Company of Canada, Toronto.

ORACLE CORPORATION

YIELD ...
P/E RATIO 42.8

INTERIM EARNINGS (Per Share):

Qtr.	Aug.	Nov.	Feb.	May
1995-96	0.04	0.09	0.10	0.18
1996-97	0.08	0.12	0.11	0.24
1997-98	0.03	0.13	0.15	0.27
1998-99	0.14	0.19	0.20	0.36

INTERIM DIVIDENDS (Per Share):

Amt.	Decl.	Ex.	Rec.	Pay.
3-for-2	7/14/97	8/18/97	8/01/97	8/15/97
50% STK	2/01/99	3/01/99	2/10/99	2/26/99

CAPITALIZATION (5/31/98):

	($000)	(%)
Long-Term Debt	304,337	9.3
Deferred Income Tax	15,856	0.5
Common & Surplus	2,957,558	90.2
Total	3,277,751	100.0

*7 YEAR PRICE SCORE 121.4   *12 MONTH PRICE SCORE 117.8
*NYSE COMPOSITE INDEX=100

RECENT DEVELOPMENTS: For the fiscal year ended 5/31/99, net income increased 58.3% to $1.29 billion compared with $813.7 million in the corresponding prior-year period. Earnings for 1998 included a charge of $167.1 million related to acquired in-process research and development. Total revenues advanced 23.6% to $8.83 billion from $7.14 billion in the previous year. Licenses and other revenues rose 15.5% to $3.69 billion from $3.19 billion in 1998.

Services revenues increased 30.1% to $5.14 billion from $3.95 billion the year before. Operating income climbed 50.5% to $1.87 billion from $1.24 billion a year earlier. On 6/24/99, the Company acquired Netherlands-based Geodan EDT BV, whose products enable businesses to manage the planning, scheduling and routing of field service engineers. ORCL has created a strategic business unit to develop and market Linux-based software products.

BUSINESS

ORACLE CORPORATION is a supplier of software for information management. The Company's products include the ORACLE™ database, development tools, and Internet-enabled business applications for customer relationship management, manufacturing and supply chain, finance and human resources. ORCL offers its products, along with related consulting, education, and support services, in more than 145 countries around the world. ORACLE8i™, the latest version of the Company's database, has Internet features built directly into the database that are designed to simplify development and deployment of Web-based applications.

ANNUAL FINANCIAL DATA

	5/31/98	5/31/97	5/31/96	5/31/95	5/31/94	5/31/93	5/31/92
Earnings Per Share	① 0.54	0.54	0.40	0.29	0.19	② 0.10	0.04
Cash Flow Per Share	0.76	0.72	0.55	0.39	0.26	0.15	0.09
Tang. Book Val. Per Share	1.96	1.55	1.20	0.76	0.44	0.30	0.24
INCOME STATEMENT (IN MILLIONS):							
Total Revenues	7,143.9	5,684.3	4,223.3	2,966.9	2,001.1	1,502.8	1,178.5
Costs & Expenses	5,571.1	4,156.6	3,098.9	2,169.4	1,476.6	1,206.6	999.1
Depreciation & Amort.	328.6	264.8	219.5	147.8	104.6	79.2	65.8
Operating Income	1,244.2	1,263.0	904.9	649.7	420.0	217.0	113.7
Net Interest Inc./(Exp.)	69.3	40.6	23.6	14.1	11.1	4.8	d12.5
Income Before Income Taxes	1,327.8	1,283.5	919.5	659.0	423.5	218.0	96.1
Income Taxes	514.1	462.1	316.2	217.5	139.7	76.3	34.6
Net Income	① 813.7	821.5	603.3	441.5	283.7	② 141.7	61.5
Cash Flow	1,142.3	1,086.2	822.8	589.3	388.3	220.9	127.3
Average Shs. Outstg. (000)	1,499,588	1,513,942	1,508,981	1,497,146	1,497,155	1,483,070	1,445,537
BALANCE SHEET (IN MILLIONS):							
Cash & Cash Equivalents	1,919.2	1,213.2	840.9	585.8	464.8	357.8	176.5
Total Current Assets	4,323.1	3,271.1	2,284.5	1,617.2	1,075.6	842.3	640.7
Net Property	934.4	868.9	685.8	535.0	378.5	189.2	207.0
Total Assets	5,819.0	4,624.3	3,357.2	2,424.5	1,595.0	1,184.0	955.6
Total Current Liabilities	2,484.2	1,922.1	1,455.0	1,055.1	682.1	551.3	406.0
Long-Term Obligations	304.3	300.8	0.9	81.7	82.8	86.4	95.9
Net Stockholders' Equity	2,957.6	2,369.7	1,870.4	1,211.4	740.6	528.0	435.0
Net Working Capital	1,838.9	1,349.0	829.5	562.0	393.5	291.0	234.7
Year-end Shs. Outstg. (000)	1,460,006	1,466,955	1,475,609	1,462,581	1,449,704	1,440,059	1,416,454
STATISTICAL RECORD:							
Operating Profit Margin %	17.4	22.2	21.4	21.9	21.0	14.4	9.6
Net Profit Margin %	11.4	14.5	14.3	14.9	14.2	9.4	5.2
Return on Equity %	27.5	34.7	32.3	36.4	38.3	26.8	14.1
Return on Assets %	14.0	17.8	18.0	18.2	17.8	12.0	6.4
Debt/Total Assets %	5.2	6.5	...	3.4	5.2	7.3	10.0
Price Range	28¹/₁₆-13¹⁵/₁₆	22¹¹/₁₆-11¹¹/₁₆	14⁷/₁₆-7⅞	9³/₁₆-5³/₁₆	7⁷/₁₆-2⅝	2¹³/₁₆-1³/₁₆	1⅝-0⁹/₁₆
P/E Ratio	52.0-25.8	41.8-21.6	36.1-19.7	31.3-17.7	39.0-13.8	29.7-12.5	38.1-12.6

Statistics are as originally reported. Adj. for stk. splits: 3-for-2, 2/26/99; 3-for-2, 8/15/97; 3-for-2, 4/16/96; 3-for-2, 2/22/95; 2-for-1, 11/9/93 ① Incl. non-recurr. chrg. $167.1 mill. ($0.17/sh.) ② Bef. acctg. change chrg. $43.5 mill. ($0.04/sh.)

OFFICERS:
L.J. Ellison, Chmn. & C.E.O.
R.J. Lane, Pres. & C.O.O.
J.O. Henley, Exec. V.P. & C.F.O.
D. Cooperman, Sr. V.P., Couns. & Sec.

INVESTOR CONTACT: Chris C. Shilakes, Manager of Investor Relations, (650) 506-4184

PRINCIPAL OFFICE: 500 Oracle Parkway, Redwood City, CA 94065

TELEPHONE NUMBER: (650) 506-7000
FAX: (650) 506-7200
WEB: www.oracle.com

NO. OF EMPLOYEES: 36,802

SHAREHOLDERS: 14,368 (approx.)

ANNUAL MEETING: In Oct.

INCORPORATED: DE, Mar., 1987

INSTITUTIONAL HOLDINGS:
No. of Institutions: 570
Shares Held: 647,710,714
% Held: 45.0

INDUSTRY: Prepackaged software (SIC: 7372)

TRANSFER AGENT(S): Harris Trust Company, Chicago, IL

PCORDER.COM, INC.

YIELD ...
P/E RATIO ...

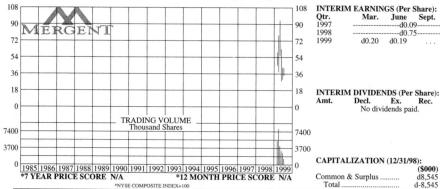

TRADING VOLUME
Thousand Shares

| | | | | | | | | | | | | | | |
|1985|1986|1987|1988|1989|1990|1991|1992|1993|1994|1995|1996|1997|1998|1999|

*7 YEAR PRICE SCORE N/A　　　　***12 MONTH PRICE SCORE N/A**

*NYSE COMPOSITE INDEX=100

INTERIM EARNINGS (Per Share):

Qtr.	Mar.	June	Sept.	Dec.
1997	------------------d0.09----------------			
1998	------------------d0.75----------------			
1999	d0.20	d0.19	...	...

INTERIM DIVIDENDS (Per Share):

Amt.	Decl.	Ex.	Rec.	Pay.
	No dividends paid.			

CAPITALIZATION (12/31/98):

	($000)	(%)
Common & Surplus	d8,545	...
Total	d-8,545	100.0

RECENT DEVELOPMENTS: For the quarter ended 6/30/99, the Company reported a net loss of $2.9 million compared with a net loss of $967,000 in the corresponding period of the previous year. The net loss reflected increased investment in sales and marketing, product development, and general corporate activities. Total revenues jumped 75.4% to $8.9 million from $5.1 million in the prior-year period. During the second quarter, PCOR and Compaq Computer Corporation formed an alliance designed to deliver e-commerce tools to Compaq customers and resellers worldwide. The Company also signed a comprehensive multi-year agreement with Scribona Computer Products AB, a distributor of computers and computer-related products in the Nordic region. This partnership establishes a strong European presence for PCOR and positions the Company for future international expansion.

BUSINESS

PCORDER.COM, INC. is a provider of Internet-based electronic commerce products that enable the computer industry's suppliers, resellers and end users to buy and sell computer products on-line. The Company's products are designed to increase the efficiency and effectiveness of the sales, marketing and distribution of computer products and to enable members of the industry to take advantage of the increasing adoption of e-commerce. PCOR's offerings include software applications and content databases that enable industry participants to buy and sell computer products on-line by increasing the automation of product search, comparison, configuration, pricing, financing, ordering and reseller selection. Furthermore, the Company provides software integration, customization, training and Web hosting services designed to ensure the successful deployment of its products. Current customers include Compaq Computer Corporation, Egghead.com, GE Capital ITS, Hartford, Hewlett-Packard, IBM, Ingram Micro, Inktomi, Nortel Networks, Sarcom, SGI and Tech Data.

ANNUAL FINANCIAL DATA

	12/31/98	12/31/97
Earnings Per Share	**d0.75**	**d0.09**
Cash Flow Per Share	**d0.54**	**d0.05**
INCOME STATEMENT (IN THOUSANDS):		
Total Revenues	21,714	10,589
Costs & Expenses	29,253	10,831
Depreciation & Amort.	2,657	459
Operating Income	d10,196	d701
Net Interest Inc./(Exp.)	172	...
Income Before Income Taxes	d10,024	d701
Income Taxes	cr386	427
Net Income	d9,638	d1,128
Cash Flow	d6,981	d669
Average Shs. Outstg.	12,861	12,800
BALANCE SHEET (IN THOUSANDS):		
Cash & Cash Equivalents	4,726	2,207
Total Current Assets	9,651	4,484
Net Property	1,938	494
Total Assets	12,254	4,978
Total Current Liabilities	18,696	5,973
Net Stockholders' Equity	d8,545	d995
Net Working Capital	d9,045	d1,489
Year-end Shs. Outstg.	12,949	12,800

Statistics are as originally reported.

OFFICERS:
R. A. Cooley, Chmn., C.E.O.
C. C. Jones, Pres., C.O.O.
J. J. Luttenbacher, V.P., C.F.O., Sec.

PRINCIPAL OFFICE: 5000 Plaza on the Lake, Austin, TX 78746

TELEPHONE NUMBER: (512) 684-1100
FAX: (512) 684-1200
WEB: www.pcorder.com

NO. OF EMPLOYEES: 194 full-time; 44 part-time

SHAREHOLDERS: N/A

ANNUAL MEETING: N/A

INCORPORATED: DE, Jul., 1994

INSTITUTIONAL HOLDINGS:
No. of Institutions: 49
Shares Held: 1,448,938
% Held: 52.3

INDUSTRY: Prepackaged software (SIC: 7372)

TRANSFER AGENT(S): American Stock Transfer & Trust Company, New York, NY

NASDAQ SYMBOL PPOD
Rec. Pr. 8⁵/₁₆ (7/31/99)

PEAPOD, INC.

YIELD ...
P/E RATIO ...

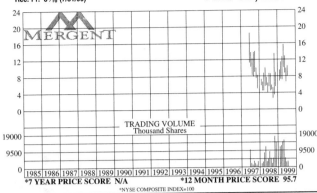

INTERIM EARNINGS (Per Share):

Qtr.	Mar.	June	Sept.	Dec.
1997	d0.23	d0.22	d0.17	d0.25
1998	d0.24	d0.26	d0.30	d0.47
1999	d0.29	d0.28	...	...

INTERIM DIVIDENDS (Per Share):

Amt.	Decl.	Ex.	Rec.	Pay.
	No dividends paid.			

CAPITALIZATION (12/31/98):

	($000)	(%)
Capital Lease Obligations..	395	1.2
Common & Surplus	33,606	98.8
Total	34,001	100.0

RECENT DEVELOPMENTS: For the quarter ended 6/30/99, the Company incurred a net loss of $4.9 million compared with a net loss of $4.5 million in the corresponding period of the previous year. Earnings for the 1999 and 1998 quarters included pre-opening expenses of $360,000 and $41,000, respectively. Net sales declined 2.6% to $17.1 million from $17.5 million in the prior year. Gross profit as a percentage of net sales grew to 24.4% from 22.5% a year earlier. On 7/1/99, PPOD announced that Hershey Foods Corporation began subscribing to CONSUMER DIRECTIONS™, an on-line research service that provides consumer goods companies with information unique to the Internet distribution channel.

BUSINESS

PEAPOD, INC. is an interactive, on-line grocery shopping and delivery company and provider of targeted media and research services. The Company currently provides branded grocery services in eight metropolitan markets in the United States and services approximately 90,000 members. The Company's "Smart Shopping for Busy People®" product is designed to provide consumers with time savings and convenience through a user-friendly, highly functional virtual supermarket, personalized shopping and delivery services, and responsive telephonic and e-mail support. CONSUMER DIRECTIONS™ is an on-line research service designed to provide consumer goods companies with a medium for targeting promotions and advertising at the point of purchase and conducting cost-effective research. Current subscribers include Coca-Cola USA, Colgate-Palmolive Company, Kraft Foods, Inc., Kimberly-Clark Corporation, Nestle U.S.A., Inc., Ralston-Purina Company, and Hershey Foods Corporation.

ANNUAL FINANCIAL DATA

	12/31/98	12/31/97	⚀ 12/31/96	⚀ 12/31/95	⚀ 12/31/94
Earnings Per Share	d1.27	d0.87	...	...	...
Cash Flow Per Share	d1.08	d0.79	...	...	...
Tang. Book Val. Per Share	1.96	3.19	...	...	...
INCOME STATEMENT (IN THOUSANDS):					
Total Revenues	69,265	59,607	29,173	15,943	8,346
Costs & Expenses	90,059	73,322	38,552	22,158	12,373
Depreciation & Amort.	3,264	1,234	651	370	290
Operating Income	d24,058	d14,949	d10,030	d6,584	d4,317
Net Interest Inc./(Exp.)	2,493	1,969	465	d7	d30
Income Before Income Taxes	d21,565	d12,980	d9,566	d6,592	d4,347
Net Income	d21,565	d12,980	d9,566	d6,592	d4,347
Cash Flow	d18,301	d11,746	d8,915	d6,222	d4,057
Average Shs. Outstg.	16,964	14,916	...	...	...
BALANCE SHEET (IN THOUSANDS):					
Cash & Cash Equivalents	20,177	62,877	13,039	2,466	...
Total Current Assets	23,853	64,744	14,212	3,036	...
Net Property	3,905	3,251	2,010	1,294	...
Total Assets	42,971	69,110	16,528	4,531	...
Total Current Liabilities	8,522	12,394	6,857	2,598	...
Long-Term Obligations	395	701	340	374	...
Net Stockholders' Equity	33,606	54,802	8,403	1,413	...
Net Working Capital	15,331	52,350	7,356	438	...
Year-end Shs. Outstg.	17,128	16,851	...	...	...
STATISTICAL RECORD:					
Debt/Total Assets %	0.9	1.0	2.1	8.3	...
Price Range	13½-2¹¹/₁₆	18½-5	...	...	...

Statistics are as originally reported. ⚀ Results prior to 5/31/97 represent the fin. & operating info. of Peapod LP, the predecessor entity to the Company & the Company.

OFFICERS:
A. B. Parkinson, Chmn., Pres., C.E.O.
D. Robinowitz, C.F.O., V.P.

INVESTOR CONTACT: Investor Relations, (847) 583-9400

PRINCIPAL OFFICE: 9933 Woods Dr., Skokie, IL 60077

TELEPHONE NUMBER: (847) 583-9400
WEB: www.peapod.com

NO. OF EMPLOYEES: 240 full-time; 1,125 part-time

SHAREHOLDERS: 269 (approx.)

ANNUAL MEETING: In May

INCORPORATED: DE, Dec., 1996; reincorp., IL,

INSTITUTIONAL HOLDINGS:
No. of Institutions: 30
Shares Held: 3,071,424
% Held: 17.6

INDUSTRY: Business services, nec (SIC) 7389)

TRANSFER AGENT(S): First Chicago Trust Company, Jersey City, NJ.

PHONE.COM INC.

YIELD ...
P/E RATIO ...

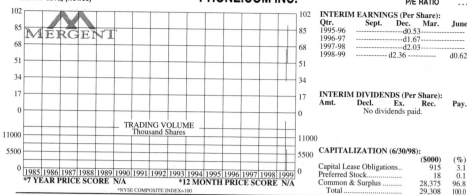

*7 YEAR PRICE SCORE N/A   *12 MONTH PRICE SCORE N/A
*NYSE COMPOSITE INDEX=100

INTERIM EARNINGS (Per Share):

Qtr.	Sept.	Dec.	Mar.	June
1995-96	------------------d0.53------------------			
1996-97	------------------d1.67------------------			
1997-98	------------------d2.03------------------			
1998-99	------------ d2.36 -----------			d0.62

INTERIM DIVIDENDS (Per Share):

Amt.	Decl.	Ex.	Rec.	Pay.
	No dividends paid.			

CAPITALIZATION (6/30/98):

	($000)	(%)
Capital Lease Obligations..	915	3.1
Preferred Stock.................	18	0.1
Common & Surplus	28,375	96.8
Total	29,308	100.0

RECENT DEVELOPMENTS: For the year ended 6/30/99, the Company reported a net loss of $20.8 million compared with a loss of $10.6 million in 1998. Total revenues soared to $13.4 million from $2.2 million in the prior year. Operating loss was $20.5 million compared with a loss of $11.6 million the year before. In June, the Company completed its initial offering of 4.6 million shares and reported net proceeds of about $67.0 million from the sale. Separately, PHCM signed a licensing agreement with 3Com Corporation. Under the agreement, PHCM's wireless application protocol compatible UP.Browser™ will be incorporated in 3Com's Palm Computing® platform. PHCM also introduced the Mobile Management Architecture, an architecture that provides wireless network operators with control over the settings and software of wireless handsets. PHCM has signed several license agreements with major wireless network operators, including Sprint PCS, US West, Bell Mobility in Canada, Cegetel/SFR in France, Omnitel in Italy, and DDI Corporation and IDO Corporation in Japan.

BUSINESS

PHONE.COM INC. is a provider of software that enables the delivery of Internet-based services to mass-market wireless telephones. Clients are able to provide Internet-based services to their wireless subscribers and wireless telephone manufacturers through the use of PHCM's software, including e-mail, news, stocks, weather, travel and sports. Subscribers also have access to network operators' Internet-based telephony services, including over-the-air activation, call management, billing history, pricing, and voice message management. The Company's software platform consists of the UP.Link Server Suite, which is installed on the network operators' systems, and UP.Browser, which is embedded in wireless telephones.

ANNUAL FINANCIAL DATA

	6/30/98	6/30/97	6/30/96
Earnings Per Share	d2.03	d1.67	d0.53
Cash Flow Per Share	d1.89	d1.58	d0.50
Tang. Book Val. Per Share	4.48	1.31	...
INCOME STATEMENT (IN THOUSANDS):			
Total Revenues	2,205	292	...
Costs & Expenses	13,072	8,300	2,558
Depreciation & Amort.	738	447	108
Operating Income	d11,605	d8,455	d2,666
Net Interest Inc./(Exp.)	982	464	196
Income Before Income Taxes	d10,623	d7,991	d2,470
Net Income	d10,623	d7,991	d2,470
Cash Flow	d9,885	d7,544	d2,362
Average Shs. Outstg.	5,221	4,776	4,704
BALANCE SHEET (IN THOUSANDS):			
Cash & Cash Equivalents	33,464	8,014	...
Total Current Assets	36,540	8,268	...
Net Property	1,336	1,226	...
Total Assets	39,144	9,759	...
Total Current Liabilities	9,836	1,634	...
Long-Term Obligations	915	...	...
Net Stockholders' Equity	28,393	8,125	...
Net Working Capital	26,704	6,634	...
Year-end Shs. Outstg.	6,333	6,192	...
STATISTICAL RECORD:			
Debt/Total Assets %	2.3	...	...

Statistics are as originally reported.

OFFICERS:
A. Rossmann, Chmn., C.E.O.
A. Black, V.P., Fin., Admin., C.F.O., Treas.
C. Parrish, Exec. V.P.

PRINCIPAL OFFICE: 800 Chesapeake Dr., Redwood City, CA 94063

TELEPHONE NUMBER: (650) 562-0200
WEB: www.phone.com
NO. OF EMPLOYEES: 157
SHAREHOLDERS: 96 approx.
ANNUAL MEETING: N/A
INCORPORATED: DE, Dec., 1994

INSTITUTIONAL HOLDINGS:
No. of Institutions: 4
Shares Held: 95,735
% Held: 0.3
INDUSTRY: Prepackaged software (SIC: 7372)
TRANSFER AGENT(S): U.S. Stock Transfer Corporation, Glendale, CA.

PILOT NETWORK SERVICES, INC.

YIELD ...
P/E RATIO ...

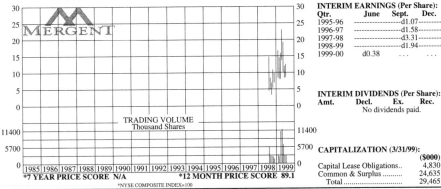

7 YEAR PRICE SCORE N/A   **12 MONTH PRICE SCORE 89.1**

NYSE COMPOSITE INDEX=100

INTERIM EARNINGS (Per Share):

Qtr.	June	Sept.	Dec.	Mar.
1995-96		----------------d1.07----------------		
1996-97		----------------d1.58----------------		
1997-98		----------------d3.31----------------		
1998-99		----------------d1.94----------------		
1999-00	d0.38	...	...	...

INTERIM DIVIDENDS (Per Share):

Amt.	Decl.	Ex.	Rec.	Pay.
		No dividends paid.		

CAPITALIZATION (3/31/99):

	($000)	(%)
Capital Lease Obligations..	4,830	16.4
Common & Surplus	24,635	83.6
Total	29,465	100.0

RECENT DEVELOPMENTS: For the quarter ended 6/30/99, the Company reported a net loss of $5.2 million compared with a net loss of $3.6 million in the corresponding period of 1998. Service revenues jumped 56.3% to $5.8 million from $3.7 million in the prior year. Operating loss amounted to $4.9 million versus $3.4 million the year before. During the quarter, the Company joined the London Internet Exchange Ltd. to provide expanded levels of secure interconnectivity for U.K. customers and for the growing number of U.S. customers extending their secure e-business operations into Europe. The Company signed a total of 87 new service agreements with new and existing customers during the quarter. PILT has signed an agreement with Zantaz.com whereby the Company will protect the data integrity and confidentiality of Zantaz's clients' vital e-business transactions, which include e-mail, on-line financial orders, and money transfers.

BUSINESS

PILOT NETWORK SERVICES, INC. is a provider of secure Internet services that protect corporate networks and Web sites against intruders. Protection against intruders is provided through the PILOT HEURISTIC DEFENSE INFRASTRUCTURE™, which is proactively upgraded and monitored by network security engineers. The PILOT HEURISTIC DEFENSE INFRASTRUCTURE incorporates multilayer filtering, application gateways, and proxied services, with proprietary deterrence and defense techniques. Pilot's services include secure Internet connectivity with 24-hour-a-day, 7-day-a-week security monitoring and reporting; Web, FTP and News hosting services; Secure Telecommuting; authentication and encryption; Web filtering and virus scanning; and corporate partner privacy through Pilot's nationwide security centers.

QUARTERLY DATA

(03/31/99)	Rev ($000)	Inc ($000)
1st Quarter................	3,720	(3,632)
2nd Quarter................	3,770	(5,090)
3rd Quarter	4,480	(4,662)
4th Quarter................	5,552	(4,711)

ANNUAL FINANCIAL DATA

	3/31/99	3/31/98	3/31/97	3/31/96
Earnings Per Share	d1.94	d3.31	d1.58	d1.07
Cash Flow Per Share	0.65	d6.02	d1.93	d1.89
Tang. Book Val. Per Share	1.77	...	...	...
INCOME STATEMENT (IN THOUSANDS):				
Total Revenues	17,522	11,317	6,300	2,525
Costs & Expenses	28,031	15,259	6,192	3,694
Depreciation & Amort.	6,213	1,222	2,438	450
Operating Income	d16,722	d5,164	d2,329	d1,619
Net Interest Inc./(Exp.)	d1,373	d471	d322	d132
Income Before Income Taxes	d18,095	d5,635	d2,652	d1,750
Net Income	d18,095	d5,635	d2,652	d1,750
Cash Flow	6,213	d12,186	d3,822	d3,576
Average Shs. Outstg.	9,568	2,025	1,982	1,889
BALANCE SHEET (IN THOUSANDS):				
Cash & Cash Equivalents	23,012	1,447	3,081	...
Total Current Assets	27,233	2,786	3,927	...
Net Property	14,184	5,994	3,479	...
Total Assets	42,115	8,922	7,439	...
Total Current Liabilities	12,650	5,749	3,291	...
Long-Term Obligations	4,830	3,444	1,946	...
Net Stockholders' Equity	24,635	d12,414	d5,882	...
Net Working Capital	14,583	d2,963	635	...
Year-end Shs. Outstg.	13,913	2,051	2,002	...
STATISTICAL RECORD:				
Debt/Total Assets %	11.5	38.6	26.2	...
Price Range	14¾-3¼	...	...	...

Statistics are as originally reported.

OFFICERS:
M. M. Silvera, Pres., C.E.O.
W. C. Leetham, Sr. V.P., C.F.O., Treas., Sec.

PRINCIPAL OFFICE: 1080 Marina Village Pkwy., Alameda, CA 94501

TELEPHONE NUMBER: (510) 433-7800
WEB: www.pilot.net
NO. OF EMPLOYEES: 149
SHAREHOLDERS: 78 (approx.)
ANNUAL MEETING: In Sep.
INCORPORATED: CA, Aug., 1992; reincorp., DE, Aug., 1998

INSTITUTIONAL HOLDINGS:
No. of Institutions: 17
Shares Held: 1,982,827
% Held: 14.7

INDUSTRY: Prepackaged software (SIC: 7372)

TRANSFER AGENT(S): U.S. Stock Transfer Corporation, Glendale, CA

PORTAL SOFTWARE, INC.

YIELD ...
P/E RATIO ...

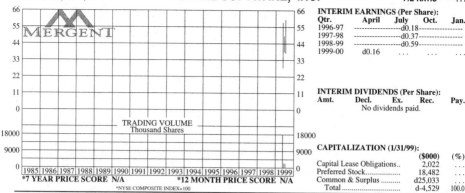

TRADING VOLUME
Thousand Shares

1985|1986|1987|1988|1989|1990|1991|1992|1993|1994|1995|1996|1997|1998|1999
*7 YEAR PRICE SCORE N/A   *12 MONTH PRICE SCORE N/A
*NYSE COMPOSITE INDEX=100

INTERIM EARNINGS (Per Share):

Qtr.	April	July	Oct.	Jan.
1996-97	------------------d0.18------------------			
1997-98	------------------d0.37------------------			
1998-99	------------------d0.59------------------			
1999-00	d0.16	...	...	...

INTERIM DIVIDENDS (Per Share):

Amt.	Decl.	Ex.	Rec.	Pay.
	No dividends paid.			

CAPITALIZATION (1/31/99):

	($000)	(%)
Capital Lease Obligations..	2,022	...
Preferred Stock.................	18,482	...
Common & Surplus	d25,033	...
Total	d-4,529	100.0

RECENT DEVELOPMENTS: For the quarter ended 4/30/99, the Company reported a net loss of $5.5 million compared with a net loss of $2.1 million in the equivalent 1998 quarter. Total revenues were $15.2 million, up from $4.1 million a year earlier. The decline in earnings was primarily attributed to increased investments in product development and sales and marketing efforts worldwide. Meanwhile, revenues were boosted by the Company's software services as well as several strategic alliances and technology partnerships. In July, PRSF announced that Tiscli S.p.a. has implemented PRSF's customer management solution, Infranet FreeServ™, for its new FreeNet service. Infranet FreeServ now supports all customer management functions for the FreeNet service including registration, authentication, authorization and usage tracking. During the quarter, Portal entered into a strategic alliance and marketing agreement with PriceWaterhouseCoopers to deliver, implement and support Portal INFRANET® real-time customer management and billing software.

BUSINESS

PORTAL SOFTWARE, INC. develops, markets and supports real-time, scalable customer management and billing software, or CM&B software, for providers of Internet-based services. Portal's INFRANET® software is designed to help companies meet the complex, mission-critical provisioning, accounting, reporting and marketing needs of providers of Internet-based services.

REVENUES

01/31/1999	($000)	(%)
Lincense Fees	13,536	50.8
Services	13,133	49.2
Total	26,669	100.0

ANNUAL FINANCIAL DATA

	1/31/99	1/31/98	1/31/97
Earnings Per Share	d0.59	d0.37	d0.18
Cash Flow Per Share	d0.48	d0.34	d0.16
INCOME STATEMENT (IN THOUSANDS):			
Total Revenues	26,669	9,416	5,045
Costs & Expenses	40,560	16,277	7,063
Depreciation & Amort.	3,237	525	236
Operating Income	d17,128	d7,386	d2,254
Net Interest Inc./(Exp.)	d416	d240	d40
Income Before Income Taxes	d16,693	d7,587	d2,274
Income Taxes	715	...	...
Net Income	d17,408	d7,587	d2,274
Cash Flow	d14,171	d7,062	d2,038
Average Shs. Outstg.	29,531	20,786	12,432
BALANCE SHEET (IN THOUSANDS):			
Cash & Cash Equivalents	11,809	14,646	...
Total Current Assets	27,723	20,443	...
Net Property	4,417	2,537	...
Total Assets	32,344	23,125	...
Total Current Liabilities	36,873	13,862	...
Long-Term Obligations	2,022	1,500	...
Net Stockholders' Equity	d6,551	7,763	...
Net Working Capital	d9,150	6,581	...
Year-end Shs. Outstg.	39,183	38,172	...
STATISTICAL RECORD:			
Debt/Total Assets %	6.3	6.5	...

Statistics are as originally reported.

OFFICERS:
J. E. Little, Chmn., Pres., C.E.O.
J. L. Acosta, V.P., C.F.O.
M. L. Gaynor, Gen. Couns., Sec.

PRINCIPAL OFFICE: 20883 Stevens Creek Boulevard, Cupertino, CA 95014

TELEPHONE NUMBER: (408) 343-4400
WEB: www.portal.com
NO. OF EMPLOYEES: 303
SHAREHOLDERS: N/A
ANNUAL MEETING: N/A
INCORPORATED: CA, Mar., 1994; reincorp., DE, May, 1999

INSTITUTIONAL HOLDINGS:
No. of Institutions: 2
Shares Held: 173,000
% Held: 0.2
INDUSTRY: Computer programming services (SIC: 7371)
TRANSFER AGENT(S): EquiServe, Canton, MA

PREVIEW TRAVEL, INC.

YIELD ...
P/E RATIO ...

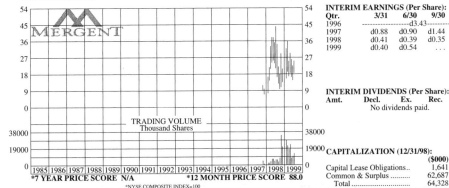

7 YEAR PRICE SCORE N/A   **12 MONTH PRICE SCORE 88.0**

*NYSE COMPOSITE INDEX=100

INTERIM EARNINGS (Per Share):

Qtr.	3/31	6/30	9/30	12/31
1996		d3.43		
1997	d0.88	d0.90	d1.44	d0.32
1998	d0.41	d0.39	d0.35	d0.32
1999	d0.40	d0.54	...	...

INTERIM DIVIDENDS (Per Share):

Amt.	Decl.	Ex.	Rec.	Pay.
		No dividends paid.		

CAPITALIZATION (12/31/98):

	($000)	(%)
Capital Lease Obligations..	1,641	2.6
Common & Surplus	62,687	97.4
Total	64,328	100.0

RECENT DEVELOPMENTS: For the second quarter ended 6/30/99, net loss was $7.4 million compared with a loss from continuing operations of $4.6 million in the corresponding prior-year period. The decrease in bottom-line results for the 1999 quarter was primarily due to higher costs for marketing and sales, technology operations and other general operating expenses. Total revenues more than doubled to $7.3 million from $3.1 million a year earlier.

Revenues benefited from a significant increase in transactions, which rose to 281,000 versus 160,000 in the comparable 1998 period. Gross profit as a percentage of revenues was 67.2% compared with 54.1% the year before. On-line travel gross bookings were $90.0 million, up 81.8% from $49.5 million in the second quarter of 1998. The Company's number of registered voters grew 84.1% to 8.1 million.

BUSINESS

PREVIEW TRAVEL, INC. is a provider of branded on-line travel services for leisure and small business travelers. The Company, through its Web site, offers one-stop travel shopping and reservation services, providing reliable real-time access to schedule, pricing and availability information for over 500 airlines, 25,000 hotels and all major car rental companies. In addition to its reservation and ticket service, the Company offers vacation packages, discounted and promotional fares, travel news and destination content, including content licensed from Fodor's Travel Publications, Inc.

REVENUES

12/31/98	($000)	(%)
Transaction	10,667	76.1
Advertising	3,341	23.9
Total	14,008	100.0

ANNUAL FINANCIAL DATA

	12/31/98	12/31/97	12/31/96	12/31/95	12/31/94
Earnings Per Share	① d2.11	d3.54	d1.60	d1.61	d1.82
Cash Flow Per Share	d1.60	d2.74	d0.93	d0.82	d0.76
Tang. Book Val. Per Share	4.59	3.12	2.59	0.80	...
INCOME STATEMENT (IN THOUSANDS):					
Total Revenues	14,008	13,644	12,374	10,143	9,598
Costs & Expenses	37,051	21,782	15,520	12,415	12,049
Depreciation & Amort.	1,620	2,294	2,355	2,395	3,141
Operating Income	d24,663	d10,432	d5,501	d4,667	d5,592
Net Interest Inc./(Exp.)	2,636	266	d89	d264	d246
Income Before Income Taxes	d22,027	d10,166	d5,590	d4,931	d5,838
Income Taxes	51	2	2	2	cr420
Net Income	① d22,078	d10,168	d5,592	d4,933	d5,418
Cash Flow	d20,458	d7,874	d3,237	d2,538	d2,277
Average Shs. Outstg.	12,796	2,869	3,488	3,085	2,997
BALANCE SHEET (IN THOUSANDS):					
Cash & Cash Equivalents	46,864	28,662	6,016	1,064	...
Total Current Assets	52,428	36,739	7,487	3,471	...
Net Property	4,124	3,644	2,100	1,839	...
Total Assets	72,168	42,785	12,554	9,066	...
Total Current Liabilities	7,226	5,806	7,095	6,932	...
Long-Term Obligations	1,641	1,614	1,048	885	...
Net Stockholders' Equity	62,687	35,365	4,411	1,249	...
Net Working Capital	45,202	30,933	392	d3,461	...
Year-end Shs. Outstg.	13,657	11,337	1,702	1,564	...
STATISTICAL RECORD:					
Debt/Total Assets %	2.3	3.8	8.3	9.8	...
Price Range	44-7½	11¹⁵/₁₆-6⁷/₈	...	...	...

Statistics are as originally reported. ① Bef. loss of $681,000 from disc. ops.

OFFICERS:
J. J. Hornthal, Chmn.
C. E. Clouser, Pres. & C.E.O.
T. W. Cardy, Exec. V.P., C.F.O.
L. R. Stein, Sr. V.P., Gen. Counsel

PRINCIPAL OFFICE: 747 Front St., San Francisco, CA 94111

TELEPHONE NUMBER: (415) 439-1200
FAX: (415) 421-4982
WEB: www.previewtravel.com

NO. OF EMPLOYEES: 224

SHAREHOLDERS: 281

ANNUAL MEETING: In June

INCORPORATED: CA, Mar., 1985; reincorp., DE, Nov., 1997

INSTITUTIONAL HOLDINGS:
No. of Institutions: 47
Shares Held: 3,471,542
% Held: 25.1

INDUSTRY: Travel agencies (SIC: 4724)

TRANSFER AGENT(S): U.S. Stock Transfer Corporation, Glendale, CA.

PRICELINE.COM, INC.

YIELD ...
P/E RATIO ...

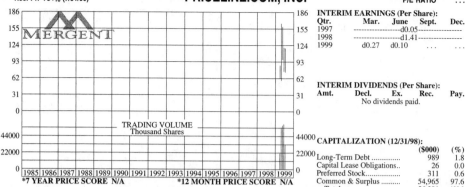

*7 YEAR PRICE SCORE N/A   *12 MONTH PRICE SCORE N/A
*NYSE COMPOSITE INDEX=100

INTERIM EARNINGS (Per Share):

Qtr.	Mar.	June	Sept.	Dec.
1997	------------------d0.05-----------------			
1998	------------------d1.41-----------------			
1999	d0.27	d0.10	...	...

INTERIM DIVIDENDS (Per Share):

Amt.	Decl.	Ex.	Rec.	Pay.
	No dividends paid.			

CAPITALIZATION (12/31/98):

	($000)	(%)
Long-Term Debt	989	1.8
Capital Lease Obligations..	26	0.0
Preferred Stock.................	311	0.6
Common & Surplus	54,965	97.6
Total	56,291	100.0

RECENT DEVELOPMENTS: For the quarter ended 6/30/99, the Company reported a net loss of $14.3 million compared with a net loss of $14.0 million in the corresponding quarter of the previous year. Revenues soared to $111.6 million from $7.0 million the year before. PLCN sold approximately 440,000 airline tickets during the quarter and averaged about 10,000 room nights a week. Approximately 852,000 new customers used the Company's Web site during the quarter. Gross profit jumped to $10.5 million versus a loss of $921,201 in the previous year. The Company recorded an operating loss of $16.2 million versus a loss of $14.1 million a year ago. Operating income was negatively affected by a substantial increase in sales and marketing expenses. During the quarter, the Company received a new patent covering the specific type of airline ticket sold through the Company's travel services unit. In July 1999, Continental Airlines joined the Company's airline ticket service.

BUSINESS

PRICELINE.COM, INC. utilizes an e-commerce demand collection system that enables consumers to use the Internet to purchase a wide range of products and services through a patented Internet pricing system. The Company collects consumer demand, in the form of individual customer offers guaranteed by a credit card, for a particular product or service at a price set by the customer. The Company then either communicates that demand directly to participating sellers or accesses participating sellers' private databases to determine whether the customer's offer can be fulfilled on the basis of the pricing information and rules established by the sellers. PCLN's services expanded from its original airline ticket sales to include the sale of new automobiles in July 1998, hotel room reservations in October 1998, and home mortgages through a third-party mortgage service in January 1999. In addition to home mortgages, the Company's home financing services now include home equity loans and refinancing services.

ANNUAL FINANCIAL DATA

	12/31/98	12/31/97
Earnings Per Share	① d1.41	d0.05
Cash Flow Per Share	d1.39	d0.05
Tang. Book Val. Per Share	0.59	...
INCOME STATEMENT (IN THOUSANDS):		
Total Revenues	35,237	...
Costs & Expenses	146,168	2,301
Depreciation & Amort.	1,860	212
Operating Income	d112,791	d2,513
Net Interest Inc./(Exp.)	548	...
Income Before Income Taxes	d112,242	d2,513
Net Income	① d112,242	d2,513
Cash Flow	d112,566	d2,301
Average Shs. Outstg.	81,231	50,834
BALANCE SHEET (IN THOUSANDS):		
Cash & Cash Equivalents	54,105	16
Total Current Assets	60,204	266
Net Property	5,927	1,180
Total Assets	66,572	1,449
Total Current Liabilities	10,282	2,655
Long-Term Obligations	1,015	51
Net Stockholders' Equity	55,276	d1,257
Net Working Capital	49,922	d2,389
Year-end Shs. Outstg.	93,225	51,670
STATISTICAL RECORD:		
Debt/Total Assets %	1.5	3.5

Statistics are as originally reported. ① Incl. non-recurr. chrg. $58.0 mill.

OFFICERS:
R. S. Braddock, Chmn., C.E.O.
J. S. Walker, Vice-Chmn., Founder
D. H. Schulman, Pres., C.O.O.
P. E. Francis, C.F.O.

PRINCIPAL OFFICE: Five High Ridge Park, Stamford, CT 06905

TELEPHONE NUMBER: (203) 705-3000
FAX: (203) 595-8264
WEB: www.priceline.com
NO. OF EMPLOYEES: 194
SHAREHOLDERS: N/A
ANNUAL MEETING: N/A
INCORPORATED: Jul., 1997

INSTITUTIONAL HOLDINGS:
No. of Institutions: 60
Shares Held: 28,948,625
% Held: 20.3
INDUSTRY: Computer integrated systems design (SIC: 7373)
TRANSFER AGENT(S): ChaseMellon Shareholder Services, L.L.C., Ridgefield Park, NJ

PRODIGY COMMUNICATIONS CORP.

YIELD   ...
P/E RATIO   ...

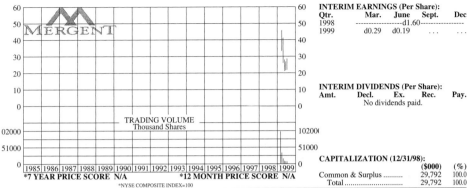

*7 YEAR PRICE SCORE N/A   *12 MONTH PRICE SCORE N/A
*NYSE COMPOSITE INDEX=100

TRADING VOLUME
Thousand Shares

INTERIM EARNINGS (Per Share):

Qtr.	Mar.	June	Sept.	Dec
1998	-------------------d1.60-----------------			
1999	d0.29	d0.19	...	...

INTERIM DIVIDENDS (Per Share):

Amt.	Decl.	Ex.	Rec.	Pay.
	No dividends paid.			

CAPITALIZATION (12/31/98):

	($000)	(%)
Common & Surplus	29,792	100.0
Total	29,792	100.0

RECENT DEVELOPMENTS: For the quarter ended 6/30/99, the Company reported a net loss of $11.4 million compared with a loss of $15.5 million in the corresponding quarter of the previous year. Results for the 1999 period included a $3.3 million gain related to the sale of TCI Music shares. Total revenue increased 9.3% to $37.1 million from $33.9 million in the prior-year period. Internet revenue totaled $30.1 million versus $19.2 million, while Classic revenue decreased to $5.0 million from $12.8 million the year before. The decrease in Classic service revenue was primarily related to the phasing-out of the Classic service later in 1999. Operating income slipped to a loss of $16.6 million versus a loss of $15.4 million a year ago. The number of Internet subscribers managed increased to 796,000, up from 386,000 in 1998. During the quarter, PRGY launched a nationwide bilingual Spanish language service. In July, PRGY completed the acquisition of Cable & Wireless USA's dial-up subscribers.

BUSINESS

PRODIGY COMMUNICATIONS CORP. is a nationwide Internet Service Provider that provides Internet access and related services. The Company utilizes a nationwide network covering over 750 cities in all 50 states, offering approximately 83.0% of the U.S. population access to the Company's services with a local telephone call. The Prodigy Internet service provides subscribers with Internet access, an electronic mailbox enabling subscribers to send and receive text, graphics and multimedia messages, and disk space on the Company's servers to host a personal Web page. PRGY also offers subscribers Company-branded Web content, personalized homepages, customer service and on-line member support, content generated by community members, and access to on-line transactions on the Web.

ANNUAL FINANCIAL DATA

	12/31/98	12/31/97	12/31/96	12/31/95	12/31/94
Earnings Per Share	d1.60	d7.66	d8.76	...	...
Cash Flow Per Share	d1.22	d6.53	d7.71	...	...
INCOME STATEMENT (IN THOUSANDS):					
Total Revenues	136,140	134,192	98,914	12	...
Costs & Expenses	191,283	234,332	166,963	3,061	1,035
Depreciation & Amort.	15,342	19,497	10,910	28	4
Operating Income	d70,485	d119,637	d78,959	d3,077	d1,040
Net Interest Inc./(Exp.)	226	d1,287	2,251	d11	...
Income Before Income Taxes	d65,083	d132,775	d90,802	d3,088	d1,040
Net Income	d65,083	d132,775	d90,802	d3,088	d1,040
Cash Flow	d49,741	d113,278	d79,892	d3,059	d1,035
Average Shs. Outstg.	40,746	17,337	10,361	...	...
BALANCE SHEET (IN THOUSANDS):					
Cash & Cash Equivalents	12,180	12,363	21,275	414	242
Total Current Assets	14,943	17,264	27,217	603	242
Net Property	12,998	18,327	31,257	1,491	53
Total Assets	78,332	93,450	126,568	2,501	370
Total Current Liabilities	48,540	65,769	82,021	862	122
Long-Term Obligations	...	10,000	56,000	1,600	423
Net Stockholders' Equity	29,792	17,681	d11,453	38	d175
Net Working Capital	d33,597	d48,505	d54,804	d259	120
Year-end Shs. Outstg.	45,034	33,804	12,310	...	...
STATISTICAL RECORD:					
Debt/Total Assets %	...	10.7	44.2	64.0	114.2
Statistics are as originally reported.					

REVENUES

12/31/1998	($000)	(%)
Prodigy Internet.........	80,696	62.6
Prodigy Classic..........	48,212	37.4
Total	128,908	100.0

OFFICERS:
S. F. Salameh, Chmn., C.E.O.
A. Sanchez, Vice-Chmn.
D. C. Trachtenberg, Pres., C.O.O.
D. R. Henkel, Exec. V.P., C.F.O.

PRINCIPAL OFFICE: 44 South Broadway, White Plains, NY 10601

TELEPHONE NUMBER: (914) 448-8000
FAX: (914) 448-8083
WEB: www.prodigy.com
NO. OF EMPLOYEES: 313
SHAREHOLDERS: 486
ANNUAL MEETING: N/A
INCORPORATED: DE, Jun., 1996

INSTITUTIONAL HOLDINGS:
No. of Institutions: 42
Shares Held: 2,035,764
% Held: 3.3

INDUSTRY: Information retrieval services
(SIC: 7375)

TRANSFER AGENT(S): American Stock Transfer & Trust Company, New York, NY

PROGRESS SOFTWARE CORP.

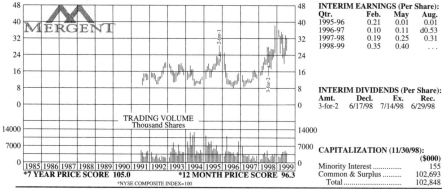

INTERIM EARNINGS (Per Share):

Qtr.	Feb.	May	Aug.	Nov.
1995-96	0.21	0.01	0.01	0.03
1996-97	0.10	0.11	d0.53	0.20
1997-98	0.19	0.25	0.31	0.43
1998-99	0.35	0.40	...	...

INTERIM DIVIDENDS (Per Share):

Amt.	Decl.	Ex.	Rec.	Pay.
3-for-2	6/17/98	7/14/98	6/29/98	7/13/98

TRADING VOLUME
Thousand Shares

| 1985 | 1986 | 1987 | 1988 | 1989 | 1990 | 1991 | 1992 | 1993 | 1994 | 1995 | 1996 | 1997 | 1998 | 1999 |

*7 YEAR PRICE SCORE 105.0   ***12 MONTH PRICE SCORE 96.3**
*NYSE COMPOSITE INDEX=100

CAPITALIZATION (11/30/98):

	($000)	(%)
Minority Interest	155	0.2
Common & Surplus	102,693	99.8
Total	102,848	100.0

RECENT DEVELOPMENTS: For the second quarter ended 5/31/99, net income increased 67.8% to $7.8 million compared with net income of $4.7 million in the prior-year quarter. Total revenue advanced 23.9% to $70.8 million from $57.1 million in the 1998 quarter. Software license revenue grew 16.0% to $32.1 million from $27.7 million a year earlier. Maintenance and services revenue climbed 31.3% to $38.6 million from $29.4 million the year before. Revenues were adversely affected by the stronger U.S. dollar. On 4/20/99, the Company announced it had strengthened its network of international operations by forming a subsidiary in Poland. PRGS already has customers there including Daewoo Motor Co. and Levi Strauss Poland. On 8/9/99, PRGS announced the formation of its Application Service Provider business unit. This unit will provide a combination of technology, professional services and partnerships to the independent software vendor community.

BUSINESS

PROGRESS SOFTWARE CORPORATION is a supplier of application development and database software to professional information systems and services organizations in business, government and industry worldwide. The Company's products include application servers, databases, development tools and application management products for Internet/Web, extranet and intranet applications. The Company's principal product line, PROGRESS®, is an integrated, component-based visual development environment for building and deploying multi-tier, enterprise-class business applications. The PROGRESS® APPTIVITY™ product line enables the development and deployment of distributed, multi-tier Java™ business applications. The Internet Software Quality product line enhances information system availability and performance by monitoring, measuring and managing Internet devices, networks, systems and applications. PRGS develops and supports the PROGRESS® product line directly and through value-added sellers who offer thousands of applications to a wide variety of industries. PRGS markets and supports its products in the United States and in over 20 countries and through independent distributors throughout Europe, Australia, Latin America and Asia.

ANNUAL FINANCIAL DATA

	11/30/98	11/30/97	11/30/96	11/30/95	11/30/94	11/30/93	11/30/92
Earnings Per Share	1.18	d0.09	0.28	0.83	0.75	0.67	0.51
Cash Flow Per Share	1.87	0.62	0.86	1.27	1.07	0.86	0.64
Tang. Book Val. Per Share	5.73	5.19	5.72	5.62	4.62	3.73	2.94
INCOME STATEMENT (IN THOUSANDS):							
Total Revenues	239,890	188,314	176,690	180,135	139,237	111,640	85,050
Costs & Expenses	196,310	177,629	160,682	147,810	113,129	90,350	69,403
Depreciation & Amort.	13,553	12,909	11,547	8,993	6,277	3,823	2,542
Operating Income	30,027	d2,224	4,461	23,332	19,831	17,467	13,105
Net Interest Inc./(Exp.)	4,529	3,743	3,874	3,570	2,259	2,179	2,073
Income Before Income Taxes	33,968	3,132	8,330	26,501	21,967	19,836	15,020
Income Taxes	11,210	4,739	2,833	9,817	7,579	6,943	5,407
Equity Earnings/Minority Int.	d113	556	415	403	...	...	...
Net Income	22,532	d1,607	5,497	16,684	14,388	12,893	9,613
Cash Flow	36,085	11,302	17,044	25,677	20,665	16,716	12,155
Average Shs. Outstg.	19,280	18,168	19,833	20,258	19,317	19,383	19,023
BALANCE SHEET (IN THOUSANDS):							
Cash & Cash Equivalents	113,999	93,485	97,323	92,338	74,286	61,300	54,584
Total Current Assets	173,048	141,777	140,951	144,111	111,390	89,890	71,494
Net Property	22,458	23,183	24,230	24,318	18,393	15,662	8,822
Total Assets	206,708	171,733	173,188	175,736	134,554	107,786	81,415
Total Current Liabilities	103,860	74,017	56,744	58,840	44,522	36,509	27,502
Long-Term Obligations	...	...	85	73	128	161	223
Net Stockholders' Equity	102,693	96,439	113,793	113,481	88,517	69,876	53,234
Net Working Capital	69,188	67,760	84,207	85,271	66,868	53,381	43,992
Year-end Shs. Outstg.	17,091	17,718	18,950	19,359	18,534	18,348	17,853
STATISTICAL RECORD:							
Operating Profit Margin %	12.5	...	2.5	13.0	14.2	15.6	15.4
Net Profit Margin %	9.4	...	3.1	9.3	10.3	11.5	11.3
Return on Equity %	21.9	...	4.8	14.7	16.3	18.5	18.1
Return on Assets %	10.9	...	3.2	9.5	10.7	12.0	11.8
Debt/Total Assets %	...	...	...	...	0.1	0.1	0.3
Price Range	38⅜-14¹¹⁄₁₆	16¹³⁄₁₆-8⁷⁄₁₆	25³⁄₁₆-8¹⁄₁₆	25⁵⁄₁₆-12⁷⁄₁₆	18¹⁵⁄₁₆-9	20¹⁄₁₆-10¾	20½-9¹¹⁄₁₆
P/E Ratio	32.5-11.9	...	89.9-28.9	30.6-15.0	25.3-12.0	30.1-16.1	40.4-19.1

Statistics are as originally reported. Adj. for stk. splits: 3-for-2, 7/13/98; 2-for-1, 11/27/95

OFFICERS:
J. W. Alsop, Pres. & Treas.
N. R. Robertson, V.P. & C.F.O.

PRINCIPAL OFFICE: 14 Oak Park, Bedford, MA 01730

TELEPHONE NUMBER: (781) 280-4000
FAX: (781) 280-4095
WEB: www.progress.com

NO. OF EMPLOYEES: 1,201

SHAREHOLDERS: 4,000 (approx.)

ANNUAL MEETING: In Apr.

INCORPORATED: MA, 1981

INSTITUTIONAL HOLDINGS:
No. of Institutions: 110
Shares Held: 15,503,524
% Held: 88.5

INDUSTRY: Prepackaged software (SIC: 7372)

TRANSFER AGENT(S): EquiServe-Boston, Canton, MA

NASDAQ SYMBOL PXCM
Rec. Pr. 34¾ (7/31/99)

PROXICOM INC.

YIELD ...
P/E RATIO ...

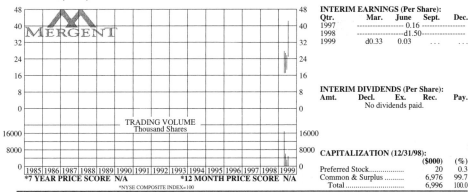

*7 YEAR PRICE SCORE N/A   *12 MONTH PRICE SCORE N/A
*NYSE COMPOSITE INDEX=100

INTERIM EARNINGS (Per Share):

Qtr.	Mar.	June	Sept.	Dec.
1997	---------------- 0.16 ----------------			
1998	------------------d1.50----------------			
1999	d0.33	0.03	...	...

INTERIM DIVIDENDS (Per Share):

Amt.	Decl.	Ex.	Rec.	Pay.
	No dividends paid.			

CAPITALIZATION (12/31/98):

	($000)	(%)
Preferred Stock...............	20	0.3
Common & Surplus	6,976	99.7
Total	6,996	100.0

RECENT DEVELOPMENTS: For the second quarter ended 6/30/99, net income increased to $764,000 compared with $65,000 in the corresponding quarter the year before. Revenues increased 54.4% to $16.2 million from $10.5 million in the comparable quarter a year earlier. Results benefited from increased worldwide demand for the Company's Internet services and growth in new customers. Gross profit as a percentage of revenue decreased to 45.1% versus 45.9% in the equivalent 1998 quarter. During the quarter,

PXCM opened a new office in Rome and expanded offices in Chicago, New York, and Munich. For the six months ended 6/30/99, net income amounted to $616,000 compared with a net loss of $422,000 in the corresponding prior-year period. Results for the 1999 and 1998 periods included acquisition and merger costs of $300,000 and $130,000, respectively. Revenues grew 58.9% to $29.5 million from $18.6 million in 1998.

BUSINESS

PROXICOM INC. is a provider of Internet services to the Global 1000 companies and other organizations. The Company's Internet services include business-to-consumer electronic commerce Internet sites, business-to-business electronic commerce extranets, and company-specific intranets. The Company sells and delivers its services through four industry sectors: energy and telecommunications; financial services; retail and manufacturing; and service industries.

ANNUAL FINANCIAL DATA

	12/31/98	12/31/97	12/31/96
Earnings Per Share	① d1.50	0.16	0.08
Cash Flow Per Share	d1.40	0.21	0.11
Tang. Book Val. Per Share	0.48	0.79	...
INCOME STATEMENT (IN THOUSANDS):			
Total Revenues	42,405	27,356	12,431
Costs & Expenses	62,429	23,595	10,861
Depreciation & Amort.	1,407	818	356
Operating Income	d21,431	2,943	1,214
Income Before Income Taxes	d21,542	3,023	1,269
Income Taxes	cr900	330	185
Net Income	① d20,642	2,693	1,084
Cash Flow	d19,235	3,511	1,440
Average Shs. Outstg.	13,762	16,333	12,993
BALANCE SHEET (IN THOUSANDS):			
Cash & Cash Equivalents	2,760	3,444	...
Total Current Assets	17,461	13,241	...
Net Property	2,858	2,572	...
Total Assets	22,077	16,097	...
Total Current Liabilities	15,081	5,721	...
Net Stockholders' Equity	6,996	10,376	...
Net Working Capital	2,380	7,520	...
Year-end Shs. Outstg.	14,610	13,027	...
STATISTICAL RECORD:			
Operating Profit Margin %	...	10.8	9.8
Net Profit Margin %	...	9.8	8.7
Return on Equity %	...	26.0	...
Return on Assets %	...	16.7	...

Statistics are as originally reported. ① Incl. non-recurr. chrgs. $21.1 mill.

OFFICERS:
R. J. Fernandez, Chmn., Pres. & C.E.O.
K. J. Tarpey, Sr. V.P., C.F.O. & Treas.
C. Capuano, V.P., Gen. Couns. & Sec.

INVESTOR CONTACT: Ken Tarpey, (703) 262-3200

PRINCIPAL OFFICE: 11600 Sunrise Valley Drive, Reston, VA 20191

TELEPHONE NUMBER: (703) 262-3200
FAX: (703) 262-3201
WEB: www.proxicom.com

NO. OF EMPLOYEES: 380

SHAREHOLDERS: 180

ANNUAL MEETING: N/A

INCORPORATED: MA, 1991; reincorp., DE, 1996

INSTITUTIONAL HOLDINGS:
No. of Institutions: 8
Shares Held: 613,630
% Held: 2.4

INDUSTRY: Computer programming services (SIC: 7371)

TRANSFER AGENT(S): Bank of New York, New York, NY

NASDAQ SYMBOL PSIX
Rec. Pr. 51¾ (7/31/99)

PSINET INC.

YIELD ...
P/E RATIO ...

*7 YEAR PRICE SCORE N/A   *12 MONTH PRICE SCORE 138.8

*NYSE COMPOSITE INDEX=100

INTERIM EARNINGS (Per Share):

Qtr.	3/31	6/30	9/30	12/31
1996	----------------d1.40----------------			
1997	d0.23	d0.28	d0.26	d0.36
1998	d0.67	d1.06	d0.93	d2.56
1999	d1.11	d1.00	...	...

INTERIM DIVIDENDS (Per Share):

Amt.	Decl.	Ex.	Rec.	Pay.
	No dividends paid.			

CAPITALIZATION (12/31/98):

	($000)	(%)
Long-Term Debt	1,064,633	112.0
Deferred Income Tax	6,123	0.6
Preferred Stock	28,802	3.0
Common & Surplus	d148,976	-15.7
Total	950,582	100.0

RECENT DEVELOPMENTS: For the quarter ended 6/30/99, net loss was $57.8 million versus a net loss of $53.6 million, including a pre-tax charge of $20.0 million, in the corresponding prior-year period. Total revenues more than doubled to $123.8 million from $53.7 million in the equivalent 1998 quarter. The substantial improvement in revenues was primarily due to continued strong customer growth, as PSIX provided service to over 73,400 customer accounts as of 6/30/99, an increase of 89.7% from the previous year. Loss from operations was $34.2 million versus a loss of $43.9 million in the comparable 1998 quarter due to higher costs for sales and marketing, depreciation and amortization and other general corporate operations. On 7/26/99, the Company acquired Intercomputer and ABAFoRUM, two privately-held Spanish Internet service providers (ISPs). The acquisition positions PSIX as the second largest corporate ISP in Spain, the eleventh largest telecommuications market in the world.

BUSINESS

PSINET INC. is a global Internet data communications carrier focused on the business marketplace. The Company offers a broad set of high-speed corporate connectivity services supporting managed security and guaranteed Internet, intranet, electronic commerce, Web hosting services, and services for other carriers and Internet service providers. PSIX operates an international technologically advanced frame relay and ATM-based, IP-optimized network consisting of more than 600 POPs (one guage used for estimating potential customers) around the world. Its network serves more than 73,000 businesses in primary markets in Argentina, Austria, Belgium, Brazil, Canada, France, Germany, Hong Kong, Italy, Japan, the Republic of Korea, Luxembourg, Mexico, the Netherlands, Spain, Switzerland, the U.S. and the U.K.

ANNUAL FINANCIAL DATA

	12/31/98	12/31/97	12/31/96	12/31/95	12/31/94	12/31/93
Earnings Per Share	⬜ d5.32	d1.14	d1.40	⬜ d1.78	d0.26	...
Cash Flow Per Share	d3.94	d0.43	d0.69	d1.29	d0.11	...
Tang. Book Val. Per Share	...	1.00	1.82	2.95	...	...
INCOME STATEMENT (IN MILLIONS):						
Total Revenues	259.6	121.9	89.8	38.7	15.2	8.7
Costs & Expenses	370.1	143.1	117.8	76.6	16.7	8.8
Depreciation & Amort.	65.8	28.3	28.0	14.8	3.2	1.7
Operating Income	d176.3	d49.6	d56.1	d52.6	d4.7	d1.9
Net Interest Inc./(Exp.)	d37.4	3.5	1.6	d0.3	d0.6	d0.3
Income Before Income Taxes	d262.7	d46.1	d55.3	d53.2	d5.3	d2.2
Income Taxes	cr0.8	cr0.5	cr0.2	...	...	cr0.2
Equity Earnings/Minority Int.	...	...	d0.8	d0.2	...	...
Net Income	⬜ d261.9	d45.6	d55.1	⬜ d53.2	d5.3	d1.9
Cash Flow	d198.8	d17.3	d27.1	d38.4	d2.2	d0.2
Average Shs. Outstg. (000)	49,806	40,306	39,378	29,832	20,395	...
BALANCE SHEET (IN MILLIONS):						
Cash & Cash Equivalents	485.0	54.0	57.3	102.7	3.4	2.9
Total Current Assets	565.3	78.9	82.3	116.4	5.6	5.0
Net Property	389.5	95.6	72.1	51.4	10.5	8.4
Total Assets	1,284.2	186.2	177.1	201.8	17.1	13.8
Total Current Liabilities	289.6	77.6	59.1	32.7	7.1	4.9
Long-Term Obligations	1,064.6	33.8	26.9	24.1	4.4	3.6
Net Stockholders' Equity	d120.2	73.4	89.8	143.2	4.9	5.0
Net Working Capital	275.6	1.3	23.2	83.6	d1.6	0.1
Year-end Shs. Outstg. (000)	52,084	40,478	40,113	37,915	11,203	11,110
STATISTICAL RECORD:						
Debt/Total Assets %	82.9	18.2	15.2	12.0	25.8	25.9
Price Range	25¹¹⁄₁₆-5	13⅜-4¼	22¾-6¾	29-12	...	...

Statistics are as originally reported. ⬜ Incls. one-time chrg. of $70.8 mill., 12/98; chrg. of $9.9 mill., 12/95.

QUARTERLY DATA

(12/31/98)($000)	Rev	Inc
1st Quarter	44,500	(29,100)
2nd Quarter	53,700	(53,600)
3rd Quarter	67,600	(47,300)
4th Quarter	93,900	(131,800)

OFFICERS:
W. L. Schrader, Chmn., C.E.O.
H. S. Wills, Pres., C.O.O.
E. D. Postal, Sr. V.P., C.F.O.
D. N. Kunkel, Exec. V.P., Gen. Couns.

INVESTOR CONTACT: Kelli Harrington, (703) 375-1245

PRINCIPAL OFFICE: 510 Huntmar Park Drive, Herndon, VA 20170

TELEPHONE NUMBER: (703) 904-4100
FAX: (703) 904-8733
WEB: www.psinet.com

NO. OF EMPLOYEES: 1,817 (approx.)

SHAREHOLDERS: 849

ANNUAL MEETING: In May

INCORPORATED: NY, Oct., 1988

INSTITUTIONAL HOLDINGS:
No. of Institutions: 92
Shares Held: 23,331,556
% Held: 36.2

INDUSTRY: Computer integrated systems design (SIC: 7373)

TRANSFER AGENT(S): First Chicago Trust Company, Jersey City, NJ

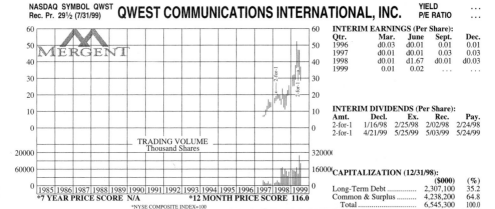

QWEST COMMUNICATIONS INTERNATIONAL, INC.

YIELD ...
P/E RATIO ...

INTERIM EARNINGS (Per Share):

Qtr.	Mar.	June	Sept.	Dec.
1996	d0.03	d0.01	0.01	0.01
1997	d0.01	d0.01	0.03	0.03
1998	d0.01	d1.67	d0.01	d0.03
1999	0.01	0.02	...	...

INTERIM DIVIDENDS (Per Share):

Amt.	Decl.	Ex.	Rec.	Pay.
2-for-1	1/16/98	2/25/98	2/02/98	2/24/98
2-for-1	4/21/99	5/25/99	5/03/99	5/24/99

TRADING VOLUME
Thousand Shares

*7 YEAR PRICE SCORE N/A   *12 MONTH PRICE SCORE 116.0
*NYSE COMPOSITE INDEX=100

CAPITALIZATION (12/31/98):

	($000)	(%)
Long-Term Debt	2,307,100	35.2
Common & Surplus	4,238,200	64.8
Total	6,545,300	100.0

RECENT DEVELOPMENTS: For the second quarter ended 6/30/99, the Company reported net earnings of $18.5 million compared with a net loss of $808.9 million in the corresponding 1998 quarter. Results for 1998 included merger related costs of $812.5 million. Total revenue surged to $873.7 million from $393.7 million in the prior-year quarter. Communications services jumped to $790.4 million from $239.8 million in the previous year. Construc-

tion services declined 45.9% to $83.3 million from $153.9 million a year earlier. On 8/10/99, LMCI Communications announced it will purchase at least $25.0 million worth of advanced network services from QWST, including Qwest Dedicated Internet Access, Qwest ATM Service, Private Line Service and Frame Relay Service. In addition, LMCI will co-locate equipment within Qwest CyberCenters[SM].

BUSINESS

QWEST COMMUNICATIONS INTERNATIONAL, INC. is a facilities-based provider of broadband Internet-based data, voice and image communications for businesses and consumers in North America, Europe and Mexico. The Qwest Macro Capacity® Fiber Network, designed with the newest optical networking, spans more than 18,500 route miles in the United States, with an additional 315-mile network route to be completed by the end of the year. In addition, Qwest and KPN, the Dutch telecommunications company, formed a venture to build and operate a high-capacity European fiber optic, Internet Protocol-based network that has 2,100 miles and will span 8,100 miles when it is completed in 2001. Qwest also has completed a 1,400-mile network in Mexico. In July 1998, the Company agreed to acquire U S West Inc. for approximately $34.8 million in cash and the assumption of $12.00 billion in debt. The deal is expected to close in mid-2000.

REVENUES

12/31/98	($000)	(%)
Communications services	1,554,300	69.3
Construction services	688,400	30.7
Total	2,242,700	100.0

ANNUAL FINANCIAL DATA

	12/31/98	12/31/97	12/31/96	12/31/95	12/31/94
Earnings Per Share	[1] d1.51	0.04	d0.02	d0.07	d0.02
Cash Flow Per Share	d1.15	0.09	0.03	d0.04	d0.01
Tang. Book Val. Per Share	6.11	0.92	0.03	0.08	...
INCOME STATEMENT (IN MILLIONS):					
Total Revenues	2,242.7	696.7	231.0	125.1	70.9
Costs & Expenses	2,794.7	653.0	226.8	151.2	79.1
Depreciation & Amort.	201.7	20.3	16.2	10.0	2.4
Operating Income	d753.7	23.5	d12.0	d36.1	d10.6
Net Interest Inc./(Exp.)	d97.3	d7.2	d4.4	d2.5	...
Income Before Income Taxes	d849.8	23.6	d10.2	d38.5	d10.7
Income Taxes	cr5.8	9.1	cr3.2	cr13.3	cr3.8
Net Income	[1] d844.0	14.5	d7.0	d25.1	d6.9
Cash Flow	d642.3	34.8	9.3	d15.1	d4.5
Average Shs. Outstg. (000)	558,200	388,110	346,000	352,632	352,632
BALANCE SHEET (IN MILLIONS):					
Cash & Cash Equivalents	462.8	379.8	6.9	1.5	...
Total Current Assets	1,439.1	723.9	56.4	52.4	...
Net Property	2,655.4	614.6	186.5	114.7	...
Total Assets	8,067.6	1,398.1	262.6	184.2	...
Total Current Liabilities	1,237.5	315.4	132.1	55.0	...
Long-Term Obligations	2,307.1	630.5	109.3	95.9	...
Net Stockholders' Equity	4,238.2	381.7	9.4	26.5	...
Net Working Capital	201.6	408.5	d75.7	d2.6	...
Year-end Shs. Outstg. (000)	694,000	413,340	346,000	346,000	...
STATISTICAL RECORD:					
Operating Profit Margin %	...	3.4	...	...	...
Net Profit Margin %	...	2.1	...	...	...
Return on Equity %	...	3.8	...	...	...
Return on Assets %	...	1.0	...	...	...
Debt/Total Assets %	28.6	45.1	41.6	52.1	...
Price Range	25¹¹⁄₁₆-11	17¼-6⅝	...	...	...
P/E Ratio	...	490.6-187.9	...	...	...

Statistics are as originally reported. Adj. for stk. split: 2-for-1, 5/24/99 & 2/24/98 [1] Incl. non-recurr. chrg. $846.5 mill.

OFFICERS:
J. P. Nacchio, Co-Chmn. & C.E.O.
A. Mohebbi, Pres. & C.O.O.
R. S. Woodruff, Exec. V.P., C.F.O. & Treas.
J. T. Garrity, Sec.

INVESTOR CONTACT: Investor Relations, (877) 877-7978

PRINCIPAL OFFICE: 555 Seventeenth Street, Denver, CO 80202

TELEPHONE NUMBER: (303) 992-1400
FAX: (303) 291-1724
WEB: www.qwest.com

NO. OF EMPLOYEES: 8,700 (approx.)

SHAREHOLDERS: 4,213

ANNUAL MEETING: In May

INCORPORATED: DE, 1997

INSTITUTIONAL HOLDINGS:
No. of Institutions: 326
Shares Held: 222,782,345
% Held: 31.8

INDUSTRY: Telephone communications, exc. radio (SIC: 4813)

TRANSFER AGENT(S): ChaseMellon Shareholder Services, L.L.C., Ridgefield Park, NJ

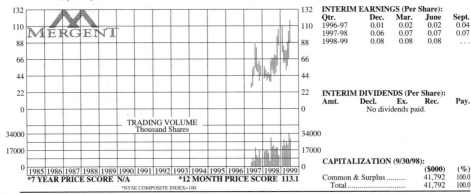

RAMBUS INC.

YIELD ...
P/E RATIO 287.3

INTERIM EARNINGS (Per Share):

Qtr.	Dec.	Mar.	June	Sept.
1996-97	0.01	0.02	0.02	0.04
1997-98	0.06	0.07	0.07	0.07
1998-99	0.08	0.08	0.08	...

INTERIM DIVIDENDS (Per Share):

Amt.	Decl.	Ex.	Rec.	Pay.
		No dividends paid.		

TRADING VOLUME
Thousand Shares

*7 YEAR PRICE SCORE N/A   *12 MONTH PRICE SCORE 113.1

*NYSE COMPOSITE INDEX=100

CAPITALIZATION (9/30/98):

	($000)	(%)
Common & Surplus	41,792	100.0
Total	41,792	100.0

RECENT DEVELOPMENTS: For the third quarter ended 6/30/99, net income increased 18.1% to $2.0 million compared with $1.7 million in the corresponding quarter the year before. Total revenues grew 16.1% to $10.6 million from $9.2 million. Revenues included approximately $500,000 of deferred revenue related to the termination of a contract. Contract revenues jumped 17.2% to $8.8 million from $7.5 million. The majority of the increase in contract revenues was due to accelerated revenue recognition on the balance of deferred revenue in the Texas Instruments DRAM contract. Royalties revenue increased 10.9% to $1.8 million from $1.6 million in the equivalent 1998 quarter. Operating profit as a percentage of total revenues increased to 19.3% versus 18.5% in the prior-year period. As of 6/30/99, the Company had 30 active licensees for the Company's newest generation of products versus 23 licensees a year earlier.

BUSINESS

RAMBUS INC. designs, develops, licenses, and markets high-speed chip-to-chip interface technology to enhance the performance and cost-effectiveness of consumer electronics, computer systems, and other electronic systems. The Company licenses semiconductor companies to manufacture and sell memory and logic integrated circuits incorporating the Company's interface technology and markets its technology to systems companies to encourage them to design the Company's interface technology into their products. Currently, 30 companies, including eight of the world's top 10 semiconductor companies, license the Company's technology. Products incorporating the Company's technology include Compaq's AlphaServer computing systems, IBM's PC 300GL with Pentium II, and Sony's Next Generation PlayStation® System.

ANNUAL FINANCIAL DATA

	9/30/98	9/30/97	9/30/96	9/30/95	9/30/94
Earnings Per Share	0.28	0.09	d0.73	d1.24	d1.29
Cash Flow Per Share	0.39	0.19	d0.53	d0.97	d0.97
Tang. Book Val. Per Share	1.82	1.20	...	...	...
INCOME STATEMENT (IN THOUSANDS):					
Total Revenues	37,864	26,015	11,270	7,364	5,000
Costs & Expenses	27,062	21,991	14,644	11,865	9,527
Depreciation & Amort.	2,835	2,070	1,194	1,552	1,670
Operating Income	7,967	1,954	d4,568	d6,053	d6,197
Net Interest Inc./(Exp.)	d52	d194	d298	d297	d296
Income Before Income Taxes	11,328	3,296	d4,129	d5,731	d6,278
Income Taxes	4,540	1,315	286	1,289	351
Net Income	6,788	1,981	d4,415	d7,020	d6,629
Cash Flow	9,623	4,051	d3,221	d5,468	d4,959
Average Shs. Outstg.	24,376	21,711	6,088	5,665	5,124
BALANCE SHEET (IN THOUSANDS):					
Cash & Cash Equivalents	79,711	71,825	8,554	14,150	...
Total Current Assets	91,793	80,757	10,145	16,196	...
Net Property	3,989	4,338	2,340	1,598	...
Total Assets	97,910	87,878	12,868	18,307	...
Total Current Liabilities	32,175	31,021	15,072	11,763	...
Long-Term Obligations	...	130	544	687	...
Net Stockholders' Equity	41,792	26,661	d12,144	d7,936	...
Net Working Capital	59,618	49,736	d4,927	4,433	...
Year-end Shs. Outstg.	22,926	22,310	5,759	5,561	...
STATISTICAL RECORD:					
Operating Profit Margin %	21.0	7.5	...	...	...
Net Profit Margin %	17.9	7.6	...	...	...
Return on Equity %	16.2	7.4	...	...	...
Return on Assets %	6.9	2.3	...	...	...
Debt/Total Assets %	...	0.1	4.2	3.8	...
Price Range	105⁷/₈-35¹/₂	86³/₄-27³/₄	...	...	...
P/E Ratio	378.0-126.7	962.8-308.0	...	...	...

Statistics are as originally reported.

REVENUES

09/30/1998	($000)	%
Contract	28,727	76.0
Royalties	9,137	24.0
Total	37,864	100.0

OFFICERS:
W. Davidow, Chmn.
G. Tate, Pres. & C.E.O.
G. Harmon, V.P., C.F.O. & Sec.

INVESTOR CONTACT: Denise Allen, Stockholder Relations, (650) 944-7900

PRINCIPAL OFFICE: 2465 Latham Street, Mountain View, CA 94040

TELEPHONE NUMBER: (650) 944-8000
WEB: www.rambus.com

NO. OF EMPLOYEES: 147

SHAREHOLDERS: 508

ANNUAL MEETING: In Jan.

INCORPORATED: CA, Mar., 1990; reincorp., DE, Mar., 1997

INSTITUTIONAL HOLDINGS:
No. of Institutions: 106
Shares Held: 9,437,999
% Held: 40.5

INDUSTRY: Semiconductors and related devices (SIC: 3674)

TRANSFER AGENT(S): Boston EquiServe, Canton, MA

NASDAQ SYMBOL RAMP
Rec. Pr. 18⅞ (7/31/99)

RAMP NETWORKS, INC.

YIELD ...
P/E RATIO ...

TRADING VOLUME
Thousand Shares

| 1985 | 1986 | 1987 | 1988 | 1989 | 1990 | 1991 | 1992 | 1993 | 1994 | 1995 | 1996 | 1997 | 1998 | 1999 |

*7 YEAR PRICE SCORE N/A   *12 MONTH PRICE SCORE N/A
*NYSE COMPOSITE INDEX=100

INTERIM EARNINGS (Per Share):

Qtr.	Mar.	June	Sept.	Dec.
1996	------------------d2.50-----------------			
1997	------------------d3.92-----------------			
1998	------------------d3.50-----------------			
1999	d0.71	d0.45	...	...

INTERIM DIVIDENDS (Per Share):

Amt.	Decl.	Ex.	Rec.	Pay.
	No dividends paid.			

CAPITALIZATION (12/31/98):

	($000)	(%)
Long-Term Debt	546	12.0
Capital Lease Obligations..	40	0.9
Redeemable Pfd. Stock	37,346	817.6
Common & Surplus	d33,364	-730.4
Total	4,568	100.0

RECENT DEVELOPMENTS: For the second quarter ended 6/30/99, the Company recorded a net loss of $2.5 million compared with a net loss of $3.3 million in the corresponding quarter the year before. Total revenues increased 143.7% to $4.5 million from $1.9 million in the comparable quarter a year earlier. Gross margin as a percentage of total revenues increased to 38.5% versus 28.0% in the equivalent 1998 quarter. Operating loss totaled $2.3 million compared with a loss of $3.5 million the year before. During the quarter, the Company completed its initial public offering, launched its DSL and Internet fax products, added over 1,000 new Value Added Resellers bringing the total to 6,000, and opened major accounts with General Motors and PIP Printing.

BUSINESS

RAMP NETWORKS, INC. provides shared Internet access services to small businesses. The Company's WebRamp product family enables users in a small office to share the same Internet connection simultaneously while optimizing each user's access speed. The WebRamp product family provides software-based routing and bridging functionality to deliver Internet-enabled applications and services. These products support existing analog phone lines, along with integrated services digital networks, digital subscriber lines, and cable modems. Connection Optimized Link Technology software allows many users to access the Internet simultaneously through regular phone lines and analog modems at up to three times the access speed of a single analog connection. RAMP's products are sold through North American, European, and Asian based distributors. The Company completed its initial public offering on 6/22/99.

ANNUAL FINANCIAL DATA

	12/31/98	12/31/97	12/31/96
Earnings Per Share	**d3.50**	**d3.92**	**d2.50**
Cash Flow Per Share	**d3.36**	**d3.80**	**d2.42**
INCOME STATEMENT (IN THOUSANDS):			
Total Revenues	9,858	5,587	517
Costs & Expenses	23,200	16,881	6,938
Depreciation & Amort.	502	349	204
Operating Income	d13,844	d11,643	d6,625
Income Before Income Taxes	d13,418	d11,534	d6,322
Net Income	d13,418	d11,534	d6,322
Cash Flow	d12,916	d11,185	d6,118
Average Shs. Outstg.	3,839	2,945	2,528
BALANCE SHEET (IN THOUSANDS):			
Cash & Cash Equivalents	3,764	15,112	...
Total Current Assets	7,402	18,217	...
Net Property	1,299	637	...
Total Assets	8,878	18,854	...
Total Current Liabilities	4,310	2,189	...
Long-Term Obligations	586	240	...
Net Stockholders' Equity	d33,364	d20,219	...
Net Working Capital	3,092	16,028	...
Year-end Shs. Outstg.	4,388	4,135	...
STATISTICAL RECORD:			
Debt/Total Assets %	6.6	1.3	...
Statistics are as originally reported.			

OFFICERS:
A. Sun, Chmn.
M. Veerina, Pres. & C.E.O.
T. Gibson, V.P., C.F.O. & Sec.

INVESTOR CONTACT: Terry Gibson, (408) 588-2436

PRINCIPAL OFFICE: 3100 De La Cruz Boulevard, Santa Clara, CA 95054

TELEPHONE NUMBER: (408) 988-5353
FAX: (408) 988-6363
WEB: www.rampnet.com

NO. OF EMPLOYEES: 103

SHAREHOLDERS: 95 (approx.)

ANNUAL MEETING: N/A

INCORPORATED: CA, Feb., 1994; reincorp., DE, Jun., 1999

INSTITUTIONAL HOLDINGS:
No. of Institutions: 2
Shares Held: 65,000
% Held: 0.3

INDUSTRY: Computer programming services (SIC: 7371)

TRANSFER AGENT(S): Boston EquiServe, LP, Boston, MA

RAZORFISH, INC.

YIELD ...
P/E RATIO ...

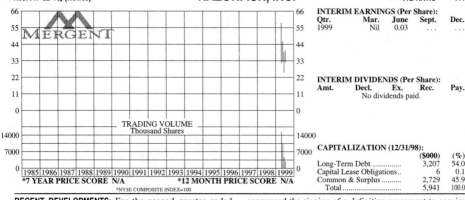

*7 YEAR PRICE SCORE N/A   *12 MONTH PRICE SCORE N/A
*NYSE COMPOSITE INDEX=100

INTERIM EARNINGS (Per Share):

Qtr.	Mar.	June	Sept.	Dec.
1999	Nil	0.03	...	...

INTERIM DIVIDENDS (Per Share):

Amt.	Decl.	Ex.	Rec.	Pay.
		No dividends paid.		

CAPITALIZATION (12/31/98):

	($000)	(%)
Long-Term Debt	3,207	54.0
Capital Lease Obligations..	6	0.1
Common & Surplus	2,729	45.9
Total	5,941	100.0

RECENT DEVELOPMENTS: For the second quarter ended 6/30/99, the Company reported net income of $635,0000 compared with a net loss of $429,000 in the corresponding prior-year period. Revenues surged to $15.1 million from $3.0 million a year earlier. Gross profit as a percentage of revenues grew to 48.8% from 47.2% in the previous year. Income from operations jumped to $1.4 million from a loss of $996,000 the year before. On 8/10/99, the Company announced the signing of a definitive agreement to acquire i-Cube, a provider of electronic business transformation services. Approved by each company's board of directors, the transaction is valued at approximately $67.0 million. Each share of i-Cube will be exchanged for 0.875 shares of RAZF. The Company will combine its Digital Change Management^SM service offering with i-Cube's consulting and integration services.

BUSINESS

RAZORFISH, INC. is an international digital communications services provider. The Company's digital communications services are designed to help its clients increase sales, improve communications and create and enhance business identities. RAZF provides an integrated service offering consisting of strategic consulting, design of information architectures and user-interfaces, and creation and customization of software. The Company primarily uses Internet-based technologies to create digital communications solutions for the World Wide Web. However, the Company's services will increasingly incorporate additional communications technologies, such as wireless, satellite and broadband communications, for use with a variety of digital devices and information appliances, including mobile phones, pagers and personal digital assistants. RAZF currently has offices in New York, San Francisco, Los Angeles, London, Stockholm, Oslo, Helsinki and Hamburg. On 8/10/99, the Company announced the signing of a definitive agreement to acquire i-Cube, a provider of electronic business transformation services.

ANNUAL FINANCIAL DATA

	12/31/98
Earnings Per Shae	Nil
Cash Flow Per Share	0.05

INCOME STATEMENT (IN THOUSANDS):

Total Revenues	13,843
Costs & Expenses	12,706
Depreciation & Amort.	442
Operating Income	695
Net Interest Inc./(Exp.)	d241
Income Before Income Taxes	454
Income Taxes	455
Net Income	d1
Cash Flow	441
Average Shs. Outstg.	9,671

BALANCE SHEET (IN THOUSANDS):

Cash & Cash Equivalents	599
Total Current Assets	5,575
Net Property	1,186
Total Assets	12,085
Total Current Liabilities	6,126
Long-Term Obligations	3,212
Net Stockholders' Equity	2,729
Net Working Capital	d551
Year-end Shs. Outstg.	9,224

STATISTICAL RECORD:

Operating Profit Margin %	5.0
Debt/Total Assets %	26.6

Statistics are as originally reported.

OFFICERS:
P. I. Bystedt, Chmn.
C. M. Kanarick, Vice-Chmn., Sec. & Chief Scientist
J. S. Svensson, Vice-Chmn. & Exec. V.P.
J. A. Dachis, C.E.O., Pres. & Treas.

PRINCIPAL OFFICE: 107 Grand St., 3rd floor, New York, NY 10013

TELEPHONE NUMBER: (212) 966-5960
FAX: (212) 966-6915
WEB: www.razorfish.com

NO. OF EMPLOYEES: 414

SHAREHOLDERS: N/A

ANNUAL MEETING: N/A

INCORPORATED: DE, 1995

INSTITUTIONAL HOLDINGS:
No. of Institutions: 3
Shares Held: 294,170
% Held: 1.2

INDUSTRY: Computer integrated systems design (SIC: 7373)

TRANSFER AGENT(S): Morrison & Foerster LLP, New York, NY

RCN CORPORATION

YIELD ...
P/E RATIO ...

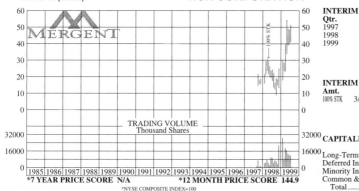

INTERIM EARNINGS (Per Share):

Qtr.	Mar.	Jun.	Sept.	Dec.
1997	------------------d0.89----------------			
1998	d1.21	d0.84	d0.81	d0.50
1999	d1.03	d0.97	...	...

INTERIM DIVIDENDS (Per Share):

Amt.	Decl.	Ex.	Rec.	Pay.
100% STK	3/09/98	4/06/98	3/20/98	4/03/98

CAPITALIZATION (12/31/98):

	($000)	(%)
Long-Term Debt	1,263,036	73.7
Deferred Income Tax	3,281	0.2
Minority Interest	77,116	4.5
Common & Surplus	371,446	21.7
Total	1,714,879	100.0

RECENT DEVELOPMENTS: For the quarter ended 6/30/99, the Company reported a net loss of $63.4 million, before an extraordinary charge of $424,000 for prepayment of debt, compared with a net loss of $67.8 million in the corresponding quarter the year before. Results for the 1999 quarter included a gain of $8.9 million related to the sale of Lancit Media. Total sales rose to $81.3 million from $79.7 million in the previous year. Voice sales declined slightly to $14.7 million versus $14.8 million in the year-earlier quarter. Video sales improved 2.6% to $31.3 million from $30.5 million in the prior-year quarter. Data sales were $28.3 million, an increase of 4.6% from $27.1 million. Other sales dropped 5.4% to $7.0 million compared with $7.4 million in the corresponding prior-year period.

BUSINESS

RCN CORPORATION is a provider of bundled communications services to the residential market, and an Internet service provider with over 500,000 customers. The Company is currently providing local and long-distance telephone, video programming and data services, cable television and its rcn.com Internet services to the densest telecommunications markets in the country, from Boston to Washington, D.C. in the East and San Francisco to San Diego in the West.

QUARTERLY DATA

(12/31/1998)($000)	REV	INC
1st Quarter	40,138	(41,785)
2nd Quarter	49,808	(43,795)
3rd Quarter	58,172	(54,430)
4th Quarter	62,822	(64,791)

ANNUAL FINANCIAL DATA

	12/31/98	12/31/97	12/31/96	12/31/95	12/31/94
Earnings Per Share	d3.35	d0.89	d0.11	Nil	Nil
Cash Flow Per Share	d1.85	0.07	...	...	...
Tang. Book Val. Per Share	3.11	4.73	...	...	...
INCOME STATEMENT (IN THOUSANDS):					
Total Revenues	210,940	127,297	104,910	91,997	59,500
Costs & Expenses	277,829	144,967	79,107	75,003	49,747
Depreciation & Amort.	91,904	53,205	38,881	22,336	9,803
Operating Income	d158,793	d70,875	d13,078	d5,342	d50
Net Interest Inc./(Exp.)	d53,560	d2,778	9,556	12,484	4,878
Income Before Income Taxes	d214,242	d73,522	d4,068	6,838	6,171
Income Taxes	cr4,998	cr20,849	979	1,119	2,340
Equity Earnings/Minority Int.	4,443	3,492	d942	d3,605	d95
Net Income	d204,801	d49,181	d5,989	2,114	3,736
Cash Flow	d112,897	4,024	32,892	24,450	13,539
Average Shs. Outstg.	61,187	54,966	...	...	...
BALANCE SHEET (IN THOUSANDS):					
Cash & Cash Equivalents	1,012,574	638,513	108,674	158,485	...
Total Current Assets	1,092,868	703,232	142,612	191,264	...
Net Property	448,375	200,340	135,828	102,080	...
Total Assets	1,907,615	1,150,992	628,085	649,610	...
Total Current Liabilities	178,069	69,705	57,292	75,307	...
Long-Term Obligations	1,263,036	686,103	143,104	140,802	...
Net Stockholders' Equity	371,446	356,584	390,765	394,069	...
Net Working Capital	914,799	633,527	85,320	115,957	...
Year-end Shs. Outstg.	64,920	54,990	...	...	...
STATISTICAL RECORD:					
Net Profit Margin %	...	...	...	2.3	6.3
Return on Equity %	...	...	...	0.5	...
Return on Assets %	...	...	...	0.3	...
Debt/Total Assets %	66.2	59.6	22.8	21.7	...
Price Range	30⅝-8¾	21⅝-14⅜	...	...	...

Statistics are as originally reported. Adj. for stock split: 100% stk. div., 4/3/98

OFFICERS:
D. C. McCourt, Chmn., C.E.O.
M. J. Mahoney, Pres., C.O.O.
B. C. Godfrey, Exec. V.P., C.F.O.
T. J. Stoklosa, Sr. V.P., Treas.

INVESTOR CONTACT: Valerie C. Haertel, Director of Investor Relations, (609) 734-3816

PRINCIPAL OFFICE: 105 Carnegie Center, Princeton, NJ 08540-6215

TELEPHONE NUMBER: (609) 734-3700
WEB: www.rcn.com

NO. OF EMPLOYEES: 2,150 full-time; 200 part-time

SHAREHOLDERS: 2,834

ANNUAL MEETING: In May

INCORPORATED: DE, 1997

INSTITUTIONAL HOLDINGS:
No. of Institutions: 103
Shares Held: 18,799,431
% Held: 25.0

INDUSTRY: Computer integrated systems design (SIC: 7373)

TRANSFER AGENT(S): First Union National Bank, Charlotte, NC

REALNETWORKS, INC.

YIELD ...
P/E RATIO ...

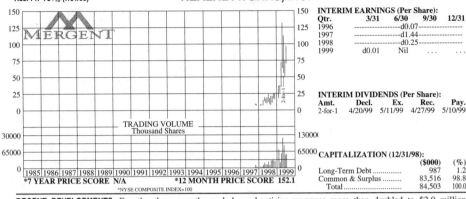

*7 YEAR PRICE SCORE N/A   *12 MONTH PRICE SCORE 152.1
*NYSE COMPOSITE INDEX=100

TRADING VOLUME
Thousand Shares

INTERIM EARNINGS (Per Share):

Qtr.	3/31	6/30	9/30	12/31
1996		d0.07		
1997		d1.44		
1998		d0.25		
1999	d0.01	Nil	...	...

INTERIM DIVIDENDS (Per Share):

Amt.	Decl.	Ex.	Rec.	Pay.
2-for-1	4/20/99	5/11/99	4/27/99	5/10/99

CAPITALIZATION (12/31/98):

	($000)	(%)
Long-Term Debt	987	1.2
Common & Surplus	83,516	98.8
Total	84,503	100.0

RECENT DEVELOPMENTS:

For the three months ended 6/30/99, net loss was $270,000 compared with a net loss of $2.6 million in the corresponding prior-year period. Total net revenues were $28.0 million, up 86.3% from $15.1 million in the equivalent quarter a year earlier. The improvement in revenues was driven by strong growth from all of the Company's business segments. In particular, advertising revenues more than doubled to $2.0 million from $765,000 a year earlier. Revenues from software license fees jumped 87.6% to $20.3 million from $10.8 million the year before, while service revenues increased 64.8% to $5.8 million from $3.5 million in the prior year. Operating loss was $1.6 million versus a loss of $3.8 million in the comparable 1998 period.

BUSINESS

REALNETWORKS, INC., is a provider of branded software products and services that enable the creation and real-time delivery and playback, or "streaming" of audio, video, text, animation and other media content over the Internet and intranets on both a live and on-demand basis. The Company's products and services include: RealSystem G2, a streaming media product that includes the Company's popular RealAudio and RealVideo technology; an electronic commerce Web site from which the Company distributes, sell and promotes streaming media products; services and programming; and a support network of advertising-supported Web sites from which the Company hosts and promotes streaming media content. The Company's customer base consists of businesses and individuals throughout the world. Sales to customers outside of the U.S. accounted for approximately 23.0% of total revenues at 12/31/98. In 3/98, the Company acquired Vivo Software, Inc., a developer of streaming media creation tools.

ANNUAL FINANCIAL DATA

	12/31/98	12/31/97	12/31/96	12/31/95
Earnings Per Share	d0.25	d1.44	d0.07	...
Cash Flow Per Share	d0.18	d1.12	d55.62	...
Tang. Book Val. Per Share	1.20	1.41	...	...
INCOME STATEMENT (IN THOUSANDS):				
Total Revenues	64,839	32,720	14,012	1,812
Costs & Expenses	80,776	43,749	17,330	3,313
Depreciation & Amort.	5,053	2,132	699	93
Operating Income	d20,990	d13,161	d4,017	d1,595
Net Interest Inc./(Exp.)	5,325	2,225	296	94
Income Before Income Taxes	d16,414	d11,169	d3,789	d1,501
Net Income	d16,414	d11,169	d3,789	d1,501
Cash Flow	d11,361	d9,037	d3,090	d1,408
Average Shs. Outstg.	64,646	8,081	56	...
BALANCE SHEET (IN THOUSANDS):				
Cash & Cash Equivalents	89,777	92,028	19,595	6,116
Total Current Assets	97,930	109,859	23,528	6,979
Net Property	6,273	5,143	2,679	594
Total Assets	128,059	116,704	26,468	7,574
Total Current Liabilities	37,723	22,339	6,635	1,031
Long-Term Obligations	987	963	...	...
Net Stockholders' Equity	83,516	77,902	d3,320	d1,111
Net Working Capital	60,207	87,519	16,893	5,948
Year-end Shs. Outstg.	61,976	55,055	1,071	74
STATISTICAL RECORD:				
Debt/Total Assets %	0.8	0.8	...	...
Price Range	24⁷/₈-6³/₄	9¹¹/₁₆-6¹³/₁₆	...	...

Statistics are as originally reported. Adj. for 2-for-1 stk. split, 5/99.

OFFICERS:
R. Glaser, Chmn., C.E.O., Treas.
B. Jacobsen, Pres., C.O.O.
P. Bialek, Sr. V.P., Fin.& Oper., C.F.O.
K. J. MacArthur, V.P., Gen. Couns., Sec.

INVESTOR CONTACT: Investor Relations,
(206) 674-2330

PRINCIPAL OFFICE: 1111 Third Ave., Ste.
2900, Seattle, WA 98101

TELEPHONE NUMBER: (206) 674-2700
FAX: (206) 674-2699
WEB: www.real.com

NO. OF EMPLOYEES: 434

SHAREHOLDERS: 404 (approx.)

ANNUAL MEETING: In May

INCORPORATED: WA, Feb., 1994

INSTITUTIONAL HOLDINGS:
No. of Institutions: 111
Shares Held: 17,430,396
% Held: 24.9

INDUSTRY: Computer programming services
(SIC: 7371)

TRANSFER AGENT(S): ChaseMellon
Shareholder Services, LLC, South
Hackensack, NJ

NASDAQ SYMBOL RTHM
Rec. Pr. 43½ (7/31/99)

RHYTHMS NETCONNECTIONS, INC.

YIELD ...
P/E RATIO ...

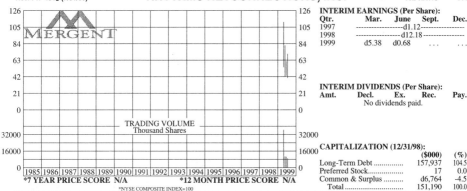

INTERIM EARNINGS (Per Share):

Qtr.	Mar.	June	Sept.	Dec.
1997	---------------d1.12---------------			
1998	---------------d12.18---------------			
1999	d5.38	d0.68	...	...

INTERIM DIVIDENDS (Per Share):

Amt.	Decl.	Ex.	Rec.	Pay.
	No dividends paid.			

*7 YEAR PRICE SCORE N/A   *12 MONTH PRICE SCORE N/A
*NYSE COMPOSITE INDEX=100

CAPITALIZATION (12/31/98):

	($000)	(%)
Long-Term Debt	157,937	104.5
Preferred Stock	17	0.0
Common & Surplus	d6,764	-4.5
Total	151,190	100.0

RECENT DEVELOPMENTS: For the quarter ended 6/30/99, RTHM reported a net loss of $42.9 million compared with a net loss of $6.8 million in the equivalent prior-year period. Earnings for the 1999 period included costs of $1.5 million related to amortized deferred business acquisition costs. Revenue jumped to $1.6 million from $71,000 in the previous year. The increase in revenue was attributed to the Company's continued rapid expansion. RTHM reported a loss from operations of $35.7 million versus $5.1 million a year earlier. The Company added 70 employees to its direct sales force, bringing the total direct sales force to 140 employees. On 8/17/99, the Company extended an agreement with Intermedia Communications that will add the Company's Digital Subscriber Line service to the Intermedia product portfolio in a total of 33 markets.

BUSINESS

RHYTHMS NETCONNECTIONS, INC. is a service provider of high-speed local access networking solutions using DSL technology to businesses. The Company has designed its network to give its customers a high-speed "always on" local connection to the Internet and to private local and wide area networks. Through the Company's packet-based network, multiple users on a single connection are able to simultaneously access the Internet and private networks. Beyond high-speed access, RTHM also offers a growing suite of features and applications that the Company can individually configure to each user's needs. The Company began offering commercial services in San Diego in 4/98, and has subsequently begun service in nine additional markets: San Francisco, San Jose, Oakland/East Bay, Chicago, Los Angeles, Orange County, Boston, Sacramento and New York. RTHM intends to continue its network rollout into an additional 23 markets in 1999 and a further 17 markets by the end of 2000.

ANNUAL FINANCIAL DATA

	12/31/98	12/31/97
Earnings Per Share	d12.18	d1.12
Cash Flow Per Share	d7.10	d1.03
Tang. Book Val. Per Share	...	4.16
INCOME STATEMENT (IN THOUSANDS):		
Total Revenues	528	...
Costs & Expenses	13,783	2,342
Depreciation & Amort.	15,146	193
Operating Income	d28,401	d2,535
Net Interest Inc./(Exp.)	d7,966	113
Income Before Income Taxes	d36,334	d2,422
Net Income	d36,334	d2,422
Cash Flow	d21,188	d2,229
Average Shs. Outstg.	2,984	2,162
BALANCE SHEET (IN THOUSANDS):		
Cash & Cash Equivalents	136,812	10,166
Total Current Assets	139,758	10,261
Net Property	11,510	1,621
Total Assets	171,726	12,241
Total Current Liabilities	13,789	1,453
Long-Term Obligations	157,937	442
Net Stockholders' Equity	d6,747	10,346
Net Working Capital	125,969	8,808
Year-end Shs. Outstg.	7,604	2,482
STATISTICAL RECORD:		
Debt/Total Assets %	92.0	3.6
Statistics are as originally reported.		

OFFICERS:
C. M. Hapka, Pres., C.E.O.
S. C. Chandler, C.F.O.
J. Blumenfeld, V.P., Gen. Couns.

PRINCIPAL OFFICE: 6933 South Revere Parkway, Englewood, CO 80112

TELEPHONE NUMBER: (303) 476-4200
FAX: (303) 476-4201
WEB: www.rhythms.com

NO. OF EMPLOYEES: 400 (avg.)

SHAREHOLDERS: 75

ANNUAL MEETING: N/A

INCORPORATED: DE, Feb., 1997

INSTITUTIONAL HOLDINGS:
No. of Institutions: 9
Shares Held: 1,256,005
% Held: 1.7

INDUSTRY: Communication services, nec (SIC: 4899)

TRANSFER AGENT(S): American Securities Transfer & Trust, Inc., New York, NY

ROGUE WAVE SOFTWARE, INC.

YIELD ...
P/E RATIO 20.4

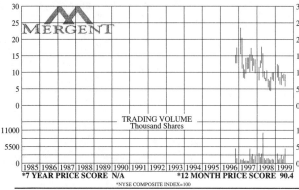

INTERIM EARNINGS (Per Share):

Qtr.	Dec.	Mar.	June	Sept.
1996-97	0.04	0.07	0.09	0.12
1997-98	0.13	d0.03	Nil	0.08
1998-99	0.08	0.10	0.04	...

INTERIM DIVIDENDS (Per Share):

Amt.	Decl.	Ex.	Rec.	Pay.
	No dividends paid.			

TRADING VOLUME
Thousand Shares

*7 YEAR PRICE SCORE N/A   ***12 MONTH PRICE SCORE 90.4**
*NYSE COMPOSITE INDEX=100

CAPITALIZATION (9/30/98):

	($000)	(%)
Common & Surplus	42,905	100.0
Total	42,905	100.0

RECENT DEVELOPMENTS: For the quarter ended 6/30/99, the Company reported net income of $434,000 compared with $13,000 in the corresponding quarter of the previous year. Results in 1999 and 1998 included merger and relocation charges of $384,000 and $580,000, respectively. Revenue climbed 25.9% to $14.0 million from $11.1 million the year before. License revenue rose 11.0% to $8.2 million from 7.4 million, while service and maintenance revenue soared 55.3% to $5.8 million from $3.7 million the year

before. New products and product upgrades contributed to the higher revenues, but were somewhat offset by a longer sales cycle and product learning curve for Nouveau products, lower European sales and the NobleNet merger and integration distractions. In May 1999, the Company introduced the Rogue Wave InterNet Architecture, a component framework for the development and deployment of scalable Internet applications that interoperate throughout different computing platforms.

BUSINESS

ROGUE WAVE SOFTWARE, INC. is a provider of software solutions for creating and managing enterprise systems using object-oriented, component technology. The Company offers software components for building distributed client-server, intranet and Internet applications that scale to the enterprise, honor legacy investments, and are highly customizable. RWAV's products fall into three different product groups: Cross-platform C++ development, Windows-specific development, and Java development. Along with its Professional Services Group, the Company's products are designed to be used individually, with each other, or with other industry standard products. On 3/1/99, the Company acquired NobleNet Inc. for $11.8 million in cash.

REVENUES

(09/30/98)	($000)	(%)
License	28,663	64.5
Service &		
Maintenance	15,776	35.5
Total	44,439	100.0

ANNUAL FINANCIAL DATA

	9/30/98	9/30/97	9/30/96	9/30/95	9/30/94
Earnings Per Share	☐ 0.20	0.32	0.01	0.02	0.14
Cash Flow Per Share	0.50	0.53	0.14	0.12	0.20
Tang. Book Val. Per Share	4.10	4.71	0.18	0.18	...
INCOME STATEMENT (IN THOUSANDS):					
Total Revenues	44,439	30,166	18,845	11,937	7,209
Costs & Expenses	38,980	25,459	18,118	11,228	6,299
Depreciation & Amort.	3,115	1,825	807	514	266
Operating Income	2,344	2,882	d80	195	644
Income Before Income Taxes	3,138	4,257	11	185	648
Income Taxes	961	1,459	cr24	106	80
Net Income	☐ 2,177	2,798	35	79	568
Cash Flow	5,292	4,623	842	593	834
Average Shs. Outstg.	10,670	8,747	6,045	5,009	4,154
BALANCE SHEET (IN THOUSANDS):					
Cash & Cash Equivalents	35,264	35,021	1,714	1,010	...
Total Current Assets	45,759	42,501	7,222	3,466	...
Net Property	4,820	3,934	2,718	889	...
Total Assets	54,527	48,690	10,194	4,758	...
Total Current Liabilities	11,622	8,934	4,540	2,769	...
Long-Term Obligations	...	351	322	230	...
Net Stockholders' Equity	42,905	39,405	668	619	...
Net Working Capital	34,137	33,567	2,682	697	...
Year-end Shs. Outstg.	10,457	8,372	3,655	3,425	...
STATISTICAL RECORD:					
Operating Profit Margin %	5.3	9.6	...	1.6	8.9
Net Profit Margin %	4.9	9.3	0.2	0.7	7.9
Return on Equity %	5.1	7.1	5.2	12.8	...
Return on Assets %	4.0	5.7	0.3	1.7	...
Debt/Total Assets %	...	0.7	3.2	4.8	...
Price Range	17¾-4⅜	23½-8⅛	17½-12¾	...	...
P/E Ratio	88.7-21.9	73.4-25.4	N.M.	...	...

Statistics are as originally reported. ☐ Incl. non-recurr. chrg. $1.8 mill.

OFFICERS:
T. Keffer, Chmn.
M. J. Scally, Pres., C.E.O.
R. M. Holburn Jr., V.P., C.F.O., Sec.

PRINCIPAL OFFICE: 5500 Flatiron Parkway, Boulder, CO 80301

TELEPHONE NUMBER: (303) 473-9118
FAX: (303) 443-7780
WEB: www.roguewave.com
NO. OF EMPLOYEES: 292 (avg.)
SHAREHOLDERS: 124
ANNUAL MEETING: In Jan.
INCORPORATED: OR, Jul., 1991; reincorp., DE, Nov., 1996

INSTITUTIONAL HOLDINGS:
No. of Institutions: 20
Shares Held: 3,457,973
% Held: 33.2

INDUSTRY: Prepackaged software (SIC: 7372)

TRANSFER AGENT(S): ChaseMellon Shareholder Services, Ridgefield Park, NJ.

NASDAQ SYMBOL ROWE
Rec. Pr. 19½ (7/31/99)

ROWECOM INC.

YIELD ...
P/E RATIO ...

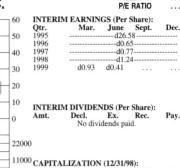

*7 YEAR PRICE SCORE N/A   *12 MONTH PRICE SCORE N/A

*NYSE COMPOSITE INDEX=100

TRADING VOLUME
Thousand Shares

INTERIM EARNINGS (Per Share):

Qtr.	Mar.	June	Sept.	Dec.
1995		d26.58		
1996		d0.65		
1997		d0.77		
1998		d1.24		
1999	d0.93	d0.41	...	...

INTERIM DIVIDENDS (Per Share):

Amt.	Decl.	Ex.	Rec.	Pay.
	No dividends paid.			

CAPITALIZATION (12/31/98):

	($000)	(%)
Redeemable Pfd. Stock	28,423	175.8
Common & Surplus	d12,251	-75.8
Total	16,172	100.0

RECENT DEVELOPMENTS: For the quarter ended 6/30/99, the Company reported a net loss of $4.2 million compared with a loss of $1.8 million in the equivalent quarter of 1998. Results for the second quarter of 1999 included a charge of $204,000 related to the acquisition of Corporate Subscription Services, Inc. The transaction will be amortized over the next three years. Revenues jumped to $2.0 million from $865,000 in the prior-year period. Operating loss was $4.9 million compared with a loss of $1.8 million a year ago. The Company announced a strategic alliance with Concur Technologies, a provider of Web-based employee-facing business applications. Under the agreement, Concur will integrate its EmployeeDesktop application with ROWE's KnowledgeStore. Bayer Corporation, a research-based company with businesses in healthcare, life sciences, and chemicals, will utilize ROWE's Knowledge-Store application as its primary service for the management of its subscriptions.

BUSINESS

ROWECOM INC. is a business-to-business provider of e-commerce services for purchasing and managing the acquisition of magazines, newspapers, journals, books and other knowledge sources. The Company's principal product is the KnowledgeStore, which gives customers access to a large catalog of printed publications on the Internet. ROWE targets knowledge-intense industries, including the financial and professional services, high technology, healthcare, and some academic and non-profit organizations. Services can be purchased via a client's desktop computer and provide businesses a way of managing and controlling purchases of knowledge resources and reducing costs. The Company acquired Corporate Subscription Services, Inc. in June 1999.

ANNUAL FINANCIAL DATA

	12/31/98	12/31/97
Earnings Per Share	d5.49	d2.22
Cash Flow Per Share	d5.35	d2.16
INCOME STATEMENT (IN THOUSANDS):		
Total Revenues	19,053	12,890
Costs & Expenses	26,533	15,991
Depreciation & Amort.	212	79
Operating Income	d7,693	d3,181
Income Before Income Taxes	d7,520	d3,117
Income Taxes	109	136
Net Income	d7,629	d3,254
Cash Flow	d8,180	d3,358
Average Shs. Outstg.	1,528	1,552
BALANCE SHEET (IN THOUSANDS):		
Cash & Cash Equivalents	16,974	1,280
Total Current Assets	19,560	1,763
Net Property	632	235
Total Assets	20,284	2,108
Total Current Liabilities	4,113	1,578
Net Stockholders' Equity	d12,251	d3,768
Net Working Capital	15,447	185
Year-end Shs. Outstg.	1,473	1,544
Statistics are as originally reported.		

OFFICERS:
R. R. Rowe Ph.D., Chmn., Pres., C.E.O.
L. Hernandez Jr., Exec. V.P., C.F.O.
W. Crosby, V.P., C.T.O.

INVESTOR CONTACT: Ilyssa Frey, (617) 588-8251

PRINCIPAL OFFICE: 725 Concord Avenue, Cambridge, MA 02138

TELEPHONE NUMBER: (617) 497-5800
WEB: www.rowe.com

NO. OF EMPLOYEES: 95 full-time; 6 part-time

SHAREHOLDERS: N/A

ANNUAL MEETING: N/A

INCORPORATED: DE, Jan., 1994

INSTITUTIONAL HOLDINGS:
No. of Institutions: 28
Shares Held: 1,241,750
% Held: 12.3

INDUSTRY: Catalog and mail-order houses (SIC: 5961)

TRANSFER AGENT(S): EquiServe, Canton, MA.

NASDAQ SYMBOL SGNT
Rec. Pr. 9¹³⁄₁₆ (7/31/99)

SAGENT TECHNOLOGY, INC.

YIELD ...
P/E RATIO ...

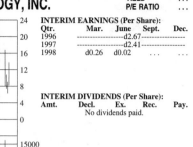

*7 YEAR PRICE SCORE N/A   *12 MONTH PRICE SCORE N/A
*NYSE COMPOSITE INDEX=100

TRADING VOLUME
Thousand Shares

INTERIM EARNINGS (Per Share):

Qtr.	Mar.	June	Sept.	Dec.
1996	------------------d2.67------------------			
1997	------------------d2.41------------------			
1998	d0.26	d0.02	...	...

INTERIM DIVIDENDS (Per Share):

Amt.	Decl.	Ex.	Rec.	Pay.
	No dividends paid.			

CAPITALIZATION (12/31/98):

	($000)	(%)
Capital Lease Obligations..	627	16.7
Preferred Stock.................	12	0.3
Common & Surplus	3,111	83.0
Total	3,750	100.0

RECENT DEVELOPMENTS: For the second quarter ended 6/30/99, the Company recorded a net loss of $598,000 compared with a net loss of $3.4 million in the corresponding quarter the year before. Total revenues more than doubled to $7.5 million from $3.7 million in the comparable quarter a year earlier. License fee revenue increased 135.3% to $5.0 million from $2.1 million, while Services revenue grew 58.7% to $2.5 million from $1.6 million in the equivalent 1998 quarter. Gross profit as a percentage of total revenues jumped to 82.8% versus 61.6% in the prior-year quarter. During the quarter, the Company launched Sagent Solution 4.0, a new, fully-integrated, end-to-end Internet enterprise intelligence system constructed for high performance and scalability on the World Wide Web. On 6/1/99, the Company completed the acquisition of its UK-based distributor.

BUSINESS

SAGENT TECHNOLOGY INC. is a provider of Web-based enterprise intelligence software and services for competitive markets. The Sagent Solution is a comprehensive, single-source software platform for acquiring, organizing, and distributing information to all levels of business users over the Web and throughout the enterprise.

ANNUAL FINANCIAL DATA

	12/31/98	12/31/97	12/31/96
Earnings Per Share	d3.68	d2.41	d2.67
Cash Flow Per Share	d3.29	d2.12	d2.57
Tang. Book Val. Per Share	0.75	0.51	...
INCOME STATEMENT (IN THOUSANDS):			
Total Revenues	17,043	7,078	279
Costs & Expenses	29,282	13,151	7,242
Depreciation & Amort.	1,445	835	268
Operating Income	d13,684	d6,908	d7,231
Net Interest Inc./(Exp.)	d207	d191	d65
Income Before Income Taxes	d13,701	d6,900	d7,039
Net Income	d13,701	d6,900	d7,039
Cash Flow	d12,256	d6,065	d6,771
Average Shs. Outstg.	3,722	2,860	2,637
BALANCE SHEET (IN THOUSANDS):			
Cash & Cash Equivalents	3,813	3,093	...
Total Current Assets	5,636	9,301	...
Net Property	1,396	3,044	...
Total Assets	7,185	13,196	...
Total Current Liabilities	3,435	8,179	...
Long-Term Obligations	627	3,346	...
Net Stockholders' Equity	3,123	1,671	...
Net Working Capital	2,201	1,122	...
Year-end Shs. Outstg.	4,125	3,249	...
STATISTICAL RECORD:			
Debt/Total Assets %	8.7	25.4	...
Statistics are as originally reported.			

OFFICERS:
K. C. Gardner, Pres. & C.E.O.
W. V. Walker, Exec. V.P. & C.F.O.

PRINCIPAL OFFICE: 800 W. El Camino
Real, Suite 300, Mountain View, CA 94040

TELEPHONE NUMBER: (650) 815-3100
FAX: (650) 815-3500
WEB: www.sagent.com

NO. OF EMPLOYEES: 152

SHAREHOLDERS: 144 (approx.)

ANNUAL MEETING: N/A

INCORPORATED: CA, Apr., 1995; reincorp.,
DE, Sep., 1998

INSTITUTIONAL HOLDINGS:
No. of Institutions: 4
Shares Held: 431,950
% Held: 1.7

INDUSTRY: Prepackaged software (SIC: 7372)

TRANSFER AGENT(S): ChaseMellon
Shareholder Services, L.L.C., Ridgefield
Park, NJ

SAPIENT CORP.

YIELD ...
P/E RATIO 102.3

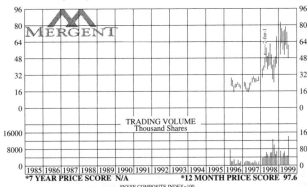

*7 YEAR PRICE SCORE N/A   *12 MONTH PRICE SCORE 97.6

*NYSE COMPOSITE INDEX=100

INTERIM EARNINGS (Per Share):

Qtr.	Mar.	June	Sept.	Dec.
1996	0.06	0.07	0.07	0.09
1997	0.10	0.11	0.12	0.14
1998	0.16	0.18	d0.15	0.30
1999	0.14	0.25	...	...

INTERIM DIVIDENDS (Per Share):

Amt.	Decl.	Ex.	Rec.	Pay.
2-for-1	1/29/98	3/10/98	2/20/98	3/09/98

CAPITALIZATION (12/31/98):

	($000)	(%)
Deferred Income Tax	773	0.5
Common & Surplus	154,381	99.5
Total	155,154	100.0

RECENT DEVELOPMENTS: For the quarter ended 6/30/99, the Company reported net income of $7.7 million compared with $5.3 million in the corresponding quarter of the previous year. Results for the 1999 quarter included non-cash and merger related charges totaling $629,000. Revenues climbed 76.3% to $64.2 million from $36.4 million the year before. Operating expenses soared 82.9% to $52.9 million versus $28.9 million a year ago. Income from operations rose 50.6% to $11.3 million from $7.5 million in 1998. In June 1999, the Company fused its Studio Archetype, Adjacency and EXOR divisions into one corporate brand. The new brand will focus on delivering end-to-end e-services. Additionally, SAPE introduced its One Team™ methodology. This new service allows the Company to work collaboratively with its clients to construct an integrated, multidisciplinary approach to creating e-business and e-services tools.

BUSINESS

SAPIENT CORP. is a provider of e-services consultancy and Internet commerce products and services. The Company aids in the transformation of emerging and evolving businesses into e-businesses. Using a fixed-price model designed to ensure on-budget and on-time delivery, SAPE offers a variety of integrated services to help clients rapidly achieve their critical business objectives. SAPE's services include: implementation and integration of packaged software solutions, custom software development, implementation of enterprise resource planning systems, production support, and business and operational consulting. In December 1997, SAPE acquired EXOR Technologies, Inc., a Dallas-based consulting and systems-integration firm. In August 1998, Sapient acquired Studio Archetype, Inc., a leader in the integration of brand strategy, design and interactive technology. SAPE acquired Adjacency in March 1999. The Company has offices in Cambridge, Massachusetts, London, Sydney, New York, San Francisco, Chicago, Atlanta, Dallas, and Los Angeles.

ANNUAL FINANCIAL DATA

	12/31/98	12/31/97	12/31/96	12/31/95	12/31/94	12/31/93
Earnings Per Share	① 0.49	① 0.47	0.28	0.14	0.06	0.05
Cash Flow Per Share	0.64	0.57	0.33	0.16	0.07	0.05
Tang. Book Val. Per Share	5.34	3.39	2.88	0.30	0.14	...
INCOME STATEMENT (IN THOUSANDS):						
Total Revenues	160,372	90,360	44,580	21,930	9,373	4,888
Costs & Expenses	136,746	69,927	34,013	16,633	7,083	3,179
Depreciation & Amort.	4,224	2,450	1,089	512	223	17
Operating Income	19,402	17,983	9,478	4,784	2,067	1,691
Net Interest Inc./(Exp.)	2,957	2,078	1,091	10	9	...
Income Before Income Taxes	22,359	20,061	10,569	4,794	2,076	1,691
Income Taxes	8,660	7,703	3,998	1,964	851	691
Net Income	① 13,699	① 12,358	6,571	2,830	1,225	1,000
Cash Flow	17,923	14,808	7,660	3,342	1,448	1,018
Average Shs. Outstg.	27,901	26,079	23,444	20,514	20,231	19,584
BALANCE SHEET (IN THOUSANDS):						
Cash & Cash Equivalents	91,260	64,406	59,538	378	2,656	...
Total Current Assets	150,761	91,368	76,239	10,627	5,538	...
Net Property	13,620	6,315	2,257	1,350	776	...
Total Assets	184,912	98,013	78,557	12,086	6,349	...
Total Current Liabilities	28,495	14,983	10,256	6,837	3,890	...
Long-Term Obligations	...	...	755	37	61	...
Net Stockholders' Equity	154,381	81,999	66,250	5,211	2,350	...
Net Working Capital	122,266	76,385	65,983	3,789	1,649	...
Year-end Shs. Outstg.	26,316	24,207	22,986	17,663	17,097	...
STATISTICAL RECORD:						
Operating Profit Margin %	12.1	19.9	21.3	21.8	22.1	34.6
Net Profit Margin %	8.5	13.7	14.7	12.9	13.1	20.5
Return on Equity %	8.9	15.1	9.9	54.3	52.1	...
Return on Assets %	7.4	12.6	8.4	23.4	19.3	...
Debt/Total Assets %	...	...	1.0	0.3	1.0	...
Price Range	69-24¼	30½-15	29⅛-14⅞	...	...	...
P/E Ratio	140.8-49.5	64.9-31.9	104.0-53.1	...	...	...

Statistics are as originally reported. Adj. for stk. split: 2-for-1, 3/9/98. ① Incl. non-recurr. chrg. $11.1 mill, 12/98; $560,000, 12/97

OFFICERS:
J. A. Greenberg, Co-Chmn., Co-C.E.O., Sec.
J. S. Moore, Co-Chmn., Co-C.E.O.
S. D. Johnson, C.F.O., Treas.

PRINCIPAL OFFICE: One Memorial Dr., Cambridge, MA 02142

TELEPHONE NUMBER: (617) 621-0200
FAX: (617) 621-1300
WEB: www.sapient.com

NO. OF EMPLOYEES: 1,450

SHAREHOLDERS: 280 (approx.)

ANNUAL MEETING: In June

INCORPORATED: DE, Sep., 1991

INSTITUTIONAL HOLDINGS:
No. of Institutions: 92
Shares Held: 11,609,491
% Held: 41.7

INDUSTRY: Computer integrated systems design (SIC: 7373)

TRANSFER AGENT(S): American Stock Transfer & Trust Company, New York, NY

SCHWAB (CHARLES) CORPORATION

YIELD 0.1%
P/E RATIO 66.8

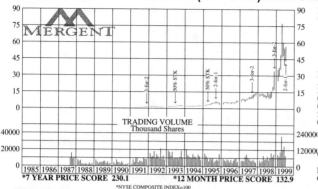

*7 YEAR PRICE SCORE 230.1   *12 MONTH PRICE SCORE 132.9
*NYSE COMPOSITE INDEX=100

INTERIM EARNINGS (Per Share):

Qtr.	Mar.	June	Sept.	Dec.
1996	0.06	0.09	0.07	0.08
1997	0.09	0.08	0.10	0.08
1998	0.09	0.10	0.18	0.13
1999	0.17	0.18	...	...

INTERIM DIVIDENDS (Per Share):

Amt.	Decl.	Ex.	Rec.	Pay.
3-for-2	10/22/98	12/14/98	11/13/98	12/11/98
0.028Q	1/20/99	2/10/99	2/12/99	2/26/99
0.028Q	4/20/99	5/10/99	5/12/99	5/26/99
2-for-1	4/22/99	7/02/99	6/01/99	7/01/99
0.014Q	7/22/99	8/10/99	8/12/99	8/26/99

Indicated div.: $0.06 (Div. Reinv. Plan)

CAPITALIZATION (12/31/98):

	($000)	(%)
Long-Term Debt	351,000	19.7
Common & Surplus	1,428,622	80.3
Total	1,779,622	100.0

RECENT DEVELOPMENTS: For the quarter ended 6/30/99, net income advanced 97.9% to $151.0 million compared with $76.3 million in the corresponding period of the prior year. Total revenues rose 53.9% to $982.1 million from $638.0 million the year before. Commissions revenue grew 55.0% to $464.2 million, while mutual fund service fees improved 31.8% to $179.6 million. Principal transactions revenue jumped to $136.8 million from $59.0 million a

year earlier. Net interest income increased 44.3% to $167.8 million, while other revenue advanced 24.8% to $33.7 million. On 6/2/99, the Company announced an agreement in principle to establish a joint venture with The Tokio Marine and Fire Insurance Co., Ltd. to develop a full-service brokerage operation for Japanese investors. The joint venture will be 50% owned by SCH and will commence in the Fall of 1999.

BUSINESS

THE CHARLES SCHWAB CORPORATION and its subsidiaries provide brokerage and related investment services to 6.2 million active investor accounts, with $592.00 billion in client assets as of 6/99. The Company's principal subsidiary, Charles Schwab & Co. Inc., is a securities broker-dealer and is the United States' largest on-line brokerage firm. Mayer & Schweitzer, Inc., a market-maker in Nasdaq securities, provides trade-execution services to institutional clients and broker-dealers. With a network of 310 branch offices, SCH is represented in 47 states, Puerto Rico, the United Kingdom, the U.S. Virgin Islands, the Caymen Islands and Hong Kong.

REVENUES

(12/31/98)	($000)	(%)
Commissions	1,309,383	47.9
Mutual Fund Service Fees	559,241	20.4
Interest Revenue	475,617	17.4
Principal Transactions	286,754	10.5
Other	105,226	3.8
Total	2,736,221	100.0

ANNUAL FINANCIAL DATA

	12/31/98	12/31/97	12/31/96	12/31/95	12/31/94	12/31/93	12/31/92
Earnings Per Share	0.43	② 0.33	0.29	0.22	0.17	① 0.15	0.10
Cash Flow Per Share	0.59	0.48	0.43	0.30	0.24	0.21	0.15
Tang. Book Val. Per Share	1.72	1.36	1.00	0.70	0.57	0.44	0.27
Dividends Per Share	0.05	0.05	0.04	0.03	0.02	0.01	0.01
Dividend Payout %	12.7	14.1	13.8	14.4	12.1	9.1	10.5
INCOME STATEMENT (IN MILLIONS):							
Total Revenues	2,736.2	2,298.8	1,850.9	1,419.9	1,064.6	965.0	749.5
Costs & Expenses	2,021.2	1,726.8	1,358.5	1,074.0	785.7	714.3	562.8
Depreciation & Amort.	138.5	124.7	98.3	68.8	54.6	44.4	40.5
Operating Income	576.5	447.2	394.1	277.1	224.3	206.3	146.2
Income Before Income Taxes	576.5	447.2	394.1	277.1	224.3	206.3	146.2
Income Taxes	228.1	177.0	160.3	104.5	89.0	81.9	65.0
Net Income	348.5	② 270.3	233.8	172.6	135.3	① 124.4	81.2
Cash Flow	486.9	395.0	332.1	241.4	189.9	168.8	121.7
Average Shs. Outstg. (000)	823,010	817,726	779,727	803,142	788,427	802,575	790,668
BALANCE SHEET (IN MILLIONS):							
Cash & Cash Equivalents	11,398.9	7,571.5	7,869.3	5,855.9	4,587.1	3,956.1	3,714.4
Total Current Assets	21,379.3	15,590.1	13,113.0	9,944.1	7,597.0	6,581.0	5,666.3
Net Property	396.2	342.3	315.4	243.5	129.1	136.4	89.5
Total Assets	22,264.4	16,481.7	13,778.8	10,552.0	7,917.9	6,896.5	5,905.2
Total Current Liabilities	20,484.8	14,975.5	12,640.4	9,673.0	7,279.5	6,332.0	5,494.7
Long-Term Obligations	351.0	361.0	283.8	246.1	171.4	185.3	151.7
Net Stockholders' Equity	1,428.6	1,145.1	854.6	632.9	467.0	379.2	258.8
Net Working Capital	894.6	614.5	472.6	271.2	317.5	249.0	171.5
Year-end Shs. Outstg. (000)	803,766	803,066	787,806	783,144	769,032	769,032	765,117
STATISTICAL RECORD:							
Operating Profit Margin %	21.1	19.5	21.3	19.5	21.1	21.4	19.5
Net Profit Margin %	12.7	11.8	12.6	12.2	12.7	12.9	10.8
Return on Equity %	24.4	23.6	27.4	27.3	29.0	32.8	31.4
Return on Assets %	1.6	1.6	1.7	1.6	1.7	1.8	1.4
Debt/Total Assets %	1.6	2.2	2.1	2.3	2.2	2.7	2.6
Price Range	34¹/₄-9¹/₄	14³/₄-6³/₄	7⁵/₁₆-4	6⁷/₁₆-2⁷/₁₆	2³/₄-1³/₄	2¹³/₁₆-1¹/₄	1⁷/₈-0¹³/₁₆
P/E Ratio	80.6-21.8	44.7-20.5	25.2-13.8	29.9-11.4	16.0-10.3	18.4-7.9	18.0-7.9
Average Yield %	0.2	0.4	0.7	0.7	0.9	0.7	0.8

Statistics are as originally reported. Adj. for 2-for-1 split: 7/99 & 9/95; 3-for-2 split: 12/98, 9/97, 3/95 & 6/93. ① Bef. extra. chg. of $6.7 mill. for early retire. of debt. ② Incl. $23.6 mill. chg. for settlement of market-maker litigation.

OFFICERS:
C. R. Schwab, Chmn., Co-C.E.O.
D. S. Pottruck, Pres., Co-C.E.O.
S. L. Scheid, Exec. V.P., C.F.O.

INVESTOR CONTACT: Christopher V. Dodds, Senior Vice President and Controller, (415) 636-9862

PRINCIPAL OFFICE: 120 Kearny St., San Francisco, CA 94104

TELEPHONE NUMBER: (415) 627-7000
FAX: (415) 627-8894
WEB: www.schwab.com

NO. OF EMPLOYEES: 13,300 (approx.)

SHAREHOLDERS: 7,350

ANNUAL MEETING: In May

INCORPORATED: DE, Nov., 1986

INSTITUTIONAL HOLDINGS:
No. of Institutions: 401
Shares Held: 393,518,298 (Adj.)
% Held: 24.1

INDUSTRY: Security brokers and dealers (SIC: 6211)

TRANSFER AGENT(S): Norwest Bank Minnesota, N.A., St. Paul, MN

SECURE COMPUTING CORPORATION

YIELD ...
P/E RATIO ...

TRADING VOLUME
Thousand Shares

*7 YEAR PRICE SCORE N/A   *12 MONTH PRICE SCORE 26.5
*NYSE COMPOSITE INDEX=100

INTERIM EARNINGS (Per Share):

Qtr.	Mar.	June	Sept.	Dec.
1997	d0.18	d0.08	d0.02	0.01
1998	d0.46	0.06	0.11	0.05
1999	d0.58	d1.11	...	...

INTERIM DIVIDENDS (Per Share):

Amt.	Decl.	Ex.	Rec.	Pay.
No dividends paid.				

CAPITALIZATION (12/31/98):

	($000)	(%)
Common & Surplus	43,053	100.0
Total	43,053	100.0

RECENT DEVELOPMENTS: For the three months ended 6/30/99, net loss was $19.7 million versus net income of $969,000 in the corresponding prior-year period. Results for the current-year quarter were restrained by higher operating expenses, which included significant additional charges of $11.7 million related to product line rationalization, refocusing of the company on enabling e-commerce and streamlining initiatives. Total revenues dropped 62.1% to $5.5 million mainly due to continued delays in closing transactions, lengthening of the sales cycle on enterprise level transactions, and deferral of purchasing decisions by customers due to Year 2000 and related issues. Products and services revenue was down 59.5% to $4.8 million, while Government contracts revenue decreased 73.0% to $747,000. Operating loss slipped to $18.9 million from income of $694,000 in the 1998 quarter.

BUSINESS

SECURE COMPUTING CORPORATION is a provider of complete network security services including spanning firewalls, identification, authentication, authorization, Web productivity, extranet Web access and authorization, and network security services. The Company enables business and government network security through its integrated and interoperable services, core technologies, services and partner programs. The Company's customer base includes Fortune 500 companies, small branch offices, and government agencies.

REVENUES

(12/31/98)	($000)	(%)
Products & services...	51,500	83.8
Goverment contracts .	9,942	16.2
Total	61,442	100.0

ANNUAL FINANCIAL DATA

	12/31/98	12/31/97	12/31/96	12/31/95	12/31/94	12/31/93	12/31/92
Earnings Per Share	② d0.20	② d0.27	② d1.76	d0.60	0.78	① 0.58	...
Cash Flow Per Share	d0.09	d0.07	d1.61	0.02	1.72	1.30	...
Tang. Book Val. Per Share	2.48	1.50	1.67	5.70	...	...	...
INCOME STATEMENT (IN THOUSANDS):							
Total Revenues	61,442	46,976	40,262	20,712	15,230	9,397	5,265
Costs & Expenses	64,517	49,606	64,518	20,848	13,495	8,350	5,122
Depreciation & Amort.	1,858	3,104	2,217	999	706	636	550
Operating Income	d4,933	d5,734	d26,473	d1,135	1,029	411	d406
Net Interest Inc./(Exp.)	...	...	d129	d100	d164	d218	d299
Income Before Income Taxes	d4,459	d5,228	d25,094	d974	991	210	d1,078
Income Taxes	cr1,197	cr977	...	...	cr502	cr502	...
Net Income	② d3,262	② d4,251	② d25,094	d974	1,493	① 712	d1,079
Cash Flow	d1,404	d1,147	d22,877	d82	1,717	898	d836
Average Shs. Outstg.	16,106	15,480	14,222	1,623	1,282	1,039	...
BALANCE SHEET (IN THOUSANDS):							
Cash & Cash Equivalents	20,878	4,880	18,065	32,599	934	325	...
Total Current Assets	45,312	23,429	29,429	37,981	3,997	1,854	...
Net Property	3,794	5,618	5,846	2,450	1,499	1,276	...
Total Assets	54,348	31,054	36,775	41,350	6,590	4,075	...
Total Current Liabilities	11,295	6,254	10,543	3,982	2,073	2,333	...
Long-Term Obligations	...	...	...	...	1,003	1,000	...
Net Stockholders' Equity	43,053	24,800	26,232	37,368	d4,435	d5,444	...
Net Working Capital	34,017	17,175	18,886	33,999	1,924	d479	...
Year-end Shs. Outstg.	16,546	15,763	15,101	6,480	388	327	...
STATISTICAL RECORD:							
Operating Profit Margin %	...	...	...	...	6.8	4.4	...
Net Profit Margin %	...	...	...	...	9.8	7.6	...
Return on Assets %	...	...	...	...	22.7	17.5	...
Debt/Total Assets %	...	...	...	...	15.2	24.5	...
Price Range	22¼-6⅜	14¹³⁄₁₆-4¼	56-7⅝	64½-38	...	...	...

Statistics are as originally reported. ① Bef. acctg. change credit of $349,000 ② Incl. non-recurr. chrgs. $10.0 mill., 12/98; $900,000, 12/97; $13.1 mill., 12/96

OFFICERS:
J. McNulty, Pres., C.E.O., C.O.O.
T. P. McGurran, C.F.O., Sr. V.P., Oper.

PRINCIPAL OFFICE: One Almaden Boulevard, Suite 400, San Jose, CA 95113

TELEPHONE NUMBER: (408) 918-6100
FAX: (408) 628-2701
WEB: www.securecomputing.com

NO. OF EMPLOYEES: 321

SHAREHOLDERS: 463 (of record); 7,220 (approx. beneficial)

ANNUAL MEETING: In May

INCORPORATED: MD, 1989; reincorp., DE, Sep., 1995

INSTITUTIONAL HOLDINGS:
No. of Institutions: 47
Shares Held: 7,298,249
% Held: 41.9

INDUSTRY: Computer programming services (SIC: 7371)

TRANSFER AGENT(S): Norwest Bank, South St. Paul, MN

SECURITY DYNAMICS TECHNOLOGIES, INC.

YIELD ...
P/E RATIO 7.6

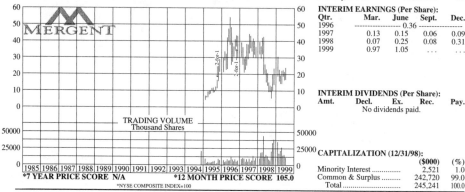

7 YEAR PRICE SCORE N/A   **12 MONTH PRICE SCORE 105.0**
*NYSE COMPOSITE INDEX=100

INTERIM EARNINGS (Per Share):

Qtr.	Mar.	June	Sept.	Dec.
1996	----------	0.36	----------	
1997	0.13	0.15	0.06	0.09
1998	0.07	0.25	0.08	0.31
1999	0.97	1.05	...	...

INTERIM DIVIDENDS (Per Share):

Amt.	Decl.	Ex.	Rec.	Pay.
	No dividends paid.			

CAPITALIZATION (12/31/98):

	($000)	(%)
Minority Interest	2,521	1.0
Common & Surplus	242,720	99.0
Total	245,241	100.0

RECENT DEVELOPMENTS: For the quarter ended 6/30/99, net income was $43.0 million compared with $10.7 million in the equivalent 1998 quarter. Revenues were $51.8 million, up 19.5% from $43.4 million a year earlier. Operating income surged 61.7% to $6.9 million versus $4.2 million in 1998. Net income for 1999 included a gain of $54.8 million from the sale of 500,000 shares of SDTI's common stock holdings in VeriSign, Inc. During the quarter, the Company introduced its new Keon Certificate Server software to the market and geared up the sales, support and marketing organizations to conduct an aggressive sales launch for Keon 5.0 enterprise PKI in the late summer and early fall. During July, SDTI and Tri-Stage™, Inc. announced the immediate availability of a managed, strong, two-factor authentication service for use with remote access services for virtual private networks.

BUSINESS

SECURITY DYNAMICS TECHNOLOGIES, INC. is a provider of enterprise network and data security tools designed to help companies conduct business securely, protect corporate information assets and facilitate business-to-business electronic commerce through the Company's knowledge of authentication management, public key encryption and access control.

ANNUAL FINANCIAL DATA

	12/31/98	12/31/97	12/31/96	12/31/95	12/31/94	12/31/93	12/31/92
Earnings Per Share	① 0.69	① 0.41	① 0.36	0.23	0.13	② 0.10	...
Cash Flow Per Share	0.85	0.52	0.41	0.26	0.15	0.10	...
Tang. Book Val. Per Share	6.00	5.02	3.53	3.52	1.29	...	...
INCOME STATEMENT (IN THOUSANDS):							
Total Revenues	171,334	135,930	76,148	33,804	17,572	12,110	8,900
Costs & Expenses	156,184	112,427	66,490	25,303	13,723	9,394	7,514
Depreciation & Amort.	6,845	4,352	1,793	749	394	180	109
Operating Income	① 8,305	① 19,151	① 7,865	7,752	3,455	2,536	1,277
Net Interest Inc./(Exp.)	...	...	4,932	1,699	105	37	48
Income Before Income Taxes	52,408	29,624	23,843	9,451	3,560	2,573	1,325
Income Taxes	23,571	13,142	10,798	3,639	1,245	900	520
Equity Earnings/Minority Int.	578	d114	...	...	...	...	...
Net Income	① 29,415	① 16,368	① 13,045	5,812	2,315	② 1,673	805
Cash Flow	36,260	20,720	14,838	6,561	2,709	1,853	914
Average Shs. Outstg.	42,497	39,864	36,515	25,364	18,160	18,020	...
BALANCE SHEET (IN THOUSANDS):							
Cash & Cash Equivalents	158,236	163,811	104,832	89,540	25,483	2,827	1,887
Total Current Assets	216,499	206,311	124,935	98,438	31,409	6,572	4,895
Net Property	29,568	17,492	10,108	2,027	987	510	402
Total Assets	280,855	231,672	139,942	101,557	32,589	7,259	5,472
Total Current Liabilities	35,614	29,300	17,302	6,537	3,685	2,383	1,886
Net Stockholders' Equity	242,720	199,273	121,446	95,020	28,857	d3,677	d5,437
Net Working Capital	180,885	177,011	107,633	91,901	27,724	4,189	3,009
Year-end Shs. Outstg.	40,476	39,682	34,390	26,906	22,312	4,764	2,310
STATISTICAL RECORD:							
Operating Profit Margin %	4.8	14.1	10.3	22.9	19.7	20.9	14.3
Net Profit Margin %	17.2	12.0	17.1	17.2	13.2	13.8	9.0
Return on Equity %	12.1	8.2	10.7	6.1	8.0	...	...
Return on Assets %	10.5	7.1	9.3	5.7	7.1	23.0	14.7
Price Range	42¾-5⁷⁄₁₆	44³⁄₈-21	54½-21¼	29¹⁄₈-4⁷⁄₁₆	...	...	...
P/E Ratio	61.9-7.9	108.2-51.2	151.3-59.0	126.6-19.2	...	...	...

Statistics are as originally reported. Adj. for stk. splits: 2-for-1, 10/95 & 11/96 ① Inc. non-recurr. chrg. for merger & integration 1998: $2.6 mill.; 1997: $5.7 mill.; 1996: $6.1 mill. ② Bef. acctg. change credit $564,000

NASDAQ SYMBOL SONE
Rec. Pr. 34⅞ (7/31/99)

SECURITY FIRST TECHNOLOGIES CORP.

YIELD ...
P/E RATIO ...

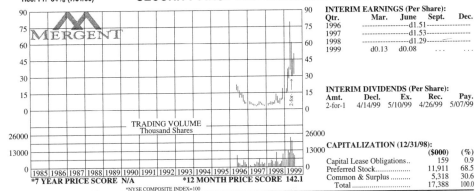

*7 YEAR PRICE SCORE N/A   *12 MONTH PRICE SCORE 142.1
*NYSE COMPOSITE INDEX=100

INTERIM EARNINGS (Per Share):

Qtr.	Mar.	June	Sept.	Dec.
1996			d1.51	
1997			d1.53	
1998			d1.29	
1999	d0.13	d0.08	...	...

INTERIM DIVIDENDS (Per Share):

Amt.	Decl.	Ex.	Rec.	Pay.
2-for-1	4/14/99	5/10/99	4/26/99	5/07/99

CAPITALIZATION (12/31/98):

	($000)	(%)
Capital Lease Obligations..	159	0.9
Preferred Stock..................	11,911	68.5
Common & Surplus	5,318	30.6
Total	17,388	100.0

RECENT DEVELOPMENTS: For the quarter ended 6/30/99, the Company reported a loss from continuing operations of $2.2 million versus a loss from continuing operations of $8.1 million in the comparable period of the prior year. The loss in the current quarter included approximately $250,000 of costs incurred from acquisition related activity. Total revenues more than tripled to $15.7 million from $4.5 million in the year-ago quarter. Gross profit as a percentage of total revenues advanced to 43.1% from 10.4% in the previous year. On 5/17/99, the Company announced plans to acquire Edify Corporation of Santa Clara, CA and FICS Group, N.V., a privately held company based in Brussels, Belgium. Also on 5/17/99, SONE and Intuit Inc. and its affiliates announced that the companies entered into a strategic alliance to deliver on-line personal financial software and services to financial institutions.

BUSINESS

SECURITY FIRST TECHNOLO-GIES CORP., a subsidiary of Security First Network Bank until September 1998, develops integrated brandable Internet applications that enable companies offering financial services to create their own financial manager that integrates banking, investment, loan and credit card accounts at an institution, with content such as news, weather and sports personalized by the end-user. The Company licenses its Virtual Financial Manager software, provides installation and integration services and offers outsourced Internet transaction processing through its data center. The Company has established strategic relationships with Hewlett-Packard, Andersen Consulting, and Broad Vision.

REVENUES

(12/31/98)	($000)	(%)
Software Licenses	4,781	19.8
Professional Services.	16,218	67.1
Data Center................	3,181	13.1
Total	24,180	100.0

ANNUAL FINANCIAL DATA

	12/31/98	12/31/97	12/31/96	12/31/95	12/31/94
Earnings Per Share	d1.29	d1.53	d1.51	d0.08	0.02
Cash Flow Per Share	d0.84	d1.25	d1.39	...	...
Tang. Book Val. Per Share	0.10	0.85	2.13	0.72	1.06
INCOME STATEMENT (IN THOUSANDS):					
Total Revenues	24,180	10,830	1,267	4,641	5,820
Costs & Expenses	43,363	34,617	19,291	6,465	5,145
Depreciation & Amort.	9,958	4,996	1,471	109	48
Operating Income	d29,141	d28,783	d19,495	d1,933	627
Net Interest Inc./(Exp.)	583	1,481	1,672	...	...
Income Before Income Taxes	d28,558	d27,302	d17,823	d1,983	459
Income Taxes	...	...	...	cr503	156
Net Income	d28,558	d27,302	d17,823	d1,480	303
Cash Flow	d18,600	d22,306	d16,352	d1,371	351
Average Shs. Outstg.	22,036	17,846	11,748	...	...
BALANCE SHEET (IN THOUSANDS):					
Cash & Cash Equivalents	18,440	19,951	36,155	15,748	11,495
Total Current Assets	37,270	25,115	37,938	16,016	12,011
Net Property	5,355	5,797	5,190	3,116	1,356
Total Assets	48,293	36,192	45,941	40,519	77,690
Total Current Liabilities	18,871	8,695	6,028	34,812	70,397
Long-Term Obligations	159	...	...	1,282	1,394
Net Stockholders' Equity	17,229	25,140	39,913	3,464	5,075
Net Working Capital	18,399	16,420	31,910	d18,796	d58,386
Year-end Shs. Outstg.	24,526	20,974	16,520	4,800	4,800
STATISTICAL RECORD:					
Operating Profit Margin %	...	...	...	...	10.8
Net Profit Margin %	...	...	...	...	5.2
Return on Equity %	...	...	...	...	6.0
Return on Assets %	...	...	...	...	0.4
Debt/Total Assets %	0.3	...	...	3.2	1.8
Price Range	18⅞-3³/₁₆	7⅛-2⅝	22½-5	...	...

Statistics are as originally reported.

OFFICERS:
M. C. McChesney, Chmn.
J. S. Mahan III, C.E.O., Pres.
R. F. Stockwell, C.F.O., Treas.

INVESTOR CONTACT: Robert F. Stockwell, Exec. V.P. & CFO, (404) 812-6426

PRINCIPAL OFFICE: 3390 Peachtree Road, NE, Suite 1700, Atlanta, GA 30326

TELEPHONE NUMBER: (404) 812-6200
FAX: (404) 812-6727
WEB: www.s1.com

NO. OF EMPLOYEES: 312

SHAREHOLDERS: 375

ANNUAL MEETING: In June

INCORPORATED: KY, 1998

INSTITUTIONAL HOLDINGS:
No. of Institutions: 54
Shares Held: 8,485,288
% Held: 33.4

INDUSTRY: Federal savings institutions
(SIC: 6035)

TRANSFER AGENT(S): American Stock Transfer & Trust Company, New York, NY

SILKNET SOFTWARE, INC.

NASDAQ SYMBOL SILK
Rec. Pr. 32³⁄₁₆ (7/31/99)

YIELD ...
P/E RATIO ...

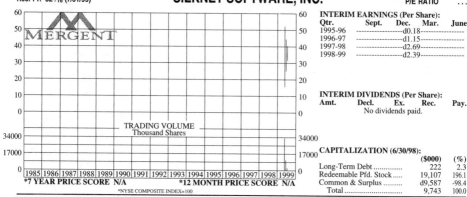

*7 YEAR PRICE SCORE N/A   *12 MONTH PRICE SCORE N/A

*NYSE COMPOSITE INDEX=100

INTERIM EARNINGS (Per Share):

Qtr.	Sept.	Dec.	Mar.	June
1995-96		d0.18		
1996-97		d1.15		
1997-98		d2.69		
1998-99		d2.39		

INTERIM DIVIDENDS (Per Share):

Amt.	Decl.	Ex.	Rec.	Pay.
	No dividends paid.			

CAPITALIZATION (6/30/98):

	($000)	(%)
Long-Term Debt	222	2.3
Redeemable Pfd. Stock	19,107	196.1
Common & Surplus	d9,587	-98.4
Total	9,743	100.0

RECENT DEVELOPMENTS: For the year ended 6/30/99, the Company reported a net loss of $9.4 million compared with a loss of $6.0 million in 1998. Total revenues jumped to $13.9 million from $3.6 million in the prior year. Operating loss was $10.0 million compared with a loss of $6.1 million the year before. Results reflected revenue growth attributed to the industry acceptance of e-commerce models. The Company plans to capitalize on this shift and continue implementing e-business solutions to increase its growing customer base. Separately, ChannelPoint, Inc., an Internet exchange provider for insurance, will integrate Silknet eBusiness System™ and Silknet eService™ in order to create a customer service facility for its users. In addition, KPMG LLP, an accounting, tax and consulting firm, purchased the same SILK products to provide its consultants with a system for easier management of communication channels.

BUSINESS

SILKNET SOFTWARE, INC. provides software that enables companies to offer personalized marketing, sales, electronic commerce and customer support services through a company-tailored Web site interface. SILK's products allow clients to deliver these services to their customers over the Internet through real-time collaboration and self-service, as well as coordinate interactions with customers through a range of communication media, including the Web, e-mail, and telephone. The Company's software can consolidate all of these sources and distribute the information throughout a client's business. The Company's clients include 3Com, Bank of America, Bell Advanced Communications, Cigna, Microsoft, Compaq Computers, and Inacom.

ANNUAL FINANCIAL DATA

	6/30/98	6/30/97	6/30/96
Earnings Per Share	d2.69	d1.15	d0.18
Cash Flow Per Share	d2.53	d1.04	d0.10
INCOME STATEMENT (IN THOUSANDS):			
Total Revenues	3,647	194	266
Costs & Expenses	9,361	2,606	515
Depreciation & Amort.	423	280	210
Operating Income	d6,137	d2,692	d458
Income Before Income Taxes	d6,003	d2,753	d465
Net Income	d6,003	d2,753	d465
Cash Flow	d6,483	d2,662	d255
Average Shs. Outstg.	2,566	2,557	2,551
BALANCE SHEET (IN THOUSANDS):			
Cash & Cash Equivalents	9,045	4,752	...
Total Current Assets	10,858	4,844	...
Net Property	1,217	529	...
Total Assets	12,129	5,402	...
Total Current Liabilities	2,386	689	...
Long-Term Obligations	222	115	...
Net Stockholders' Equity	d9,587	d2,834	...
Net Working Capital	8,472	4,155	...
Year-end Shs. Outstg.	2,628	2,558	...
STATISTICAL RECORD:			
Debt/Total Assets %	1.8	2.1	...

Statistics are as originally reported.

OFFICERS:
J. C. Wood, Chmn., Pres., C.E.O.
P. J. Scannell Jr., C.F.O.
N. K. Donovan, Sr. V.P., C.O.O.
E. Carlson, V.P., C.T.O.

PRINCIPAL OFFICE: 50 Phillippe Cote Street, Manchester, NH 03101

TELEPHONE NUMBER: (603) 625-0070
WEB: www.silknet.com

NO. OF EMPLOYEES: 136

SHAREHOLDERS: 85

ANNUAL MEETING: N/A

INCORPORATED: NH, Mar., 1995; reincorp., DE, Feb., 1999

INSTITUTIONAL HOLDINGS:
No. of Institutions: 2
Shares Held: 9,170
% Held: 0.1

INDUSTRY: Prepackaged software (SIC: 7372)

TRANSFER AGENT(S): American Stock Transfer & Trust Company, New York, NY.

SOFTWARE.COM, INC.

YIELD ...
P/E RATIO ...

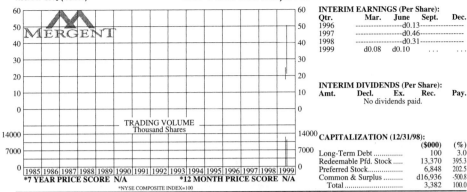

7 YEAR PRICE SCORE N/A **12 MONTH PRICE SCORE N/A**
*NYSE COMPOSITE INDEX=100

INTERIM EARNINGS (Per Share):

Qtr.	Mar.	June	Sept.	Dec.
1996	------------------d0.13------------------			
1997	------------------d0.46------------------			
1998	------------------d0.31------------------			
1999	d0.08	d0.10	...	...

INTERIM DIVIDENDS (Per Share):

Amt.	Decl.	Ex.	Rec.	Pay.
	No dividends paid.			

CAPITALIZATION (12/31/98):

	($000)	(%)
Long-Term Debt	100	3.0
Redeemable Pfd. Stock	13,370	395.3
Preferred Stock..................	6,848	202.5
Common & Surplus	d16,936	-500.8
Total	3,382	100.0

RECENT DEVELOPMENTS: For the three months ended 6/30/99, the Company reported a net loss of $2.9 million compared with a net loss of $1.2 million in the corresponding period of the prior year. Total revenues advanced 47.4% to $9.0 million from $6.1 million in the comparable 1998 quarter. Software licenses revenues increased 20.9% to $5.2 million versus $4.3 million in the prior-year period, while services revenues more than doubled to $3.8 million from $1.8 million the year before. On 4/27/99, the Company acquired Mobility.Net which added customizable Web applications server technology that supports Webmail, address book, calendar and task management applications. On 7/8/99, SWCM shipped WebEdged™ Mail and Calendar, a Web-based e-mail and calendaring server for small- and medium-sized service providers.

BUSINESS

SOFTWARE.COM, INC. is a developer and provider of messaging software applications for providers of Internet communications and services. The Company has developed a software platform using open Internet standards that enables its customers to deliver a variety of messaging services from a single platform. The messaging applications include Web browser-based e-mail, desktop client-based e-mail, outsourced or "managed" business messaging and Internet-based voicemail and faxmail messaging. The Company's customers include traditional telecommunications carriers, Internet service providers and wholesalers, cable-based Internet access providers, competitive local exchange telephone carriers, and Internet destination sites.

ANNUAL FINANCIAL DATA

	12/31/98	12/31/97	12/31/96
Earnings Per Share	d0.31	d0.46	d0.13
Cash Flow Per Share	d0.25	d0.42	d0.11
INCOME STATEMENT (IN THOUSANDS):			
Total Revenues	25,618	10,666	7,882
Costs & Expenses	30,470	21,157	10,696
Depreciation & Amort.	1,648	1,204	436
Operating Income	d6,500	d11,695	d3,250
Net Interest Inc./(Exp.)	d352	239	87
Income Before Income Taxes	d6,936	d11,456	d3,163
Income Taxes	446	1	...
Net Income	d7,382	d11,457	d3,163
Cash Flow	d6,559	d10,983	d2,907
Average Shs. Outstg.	26,649	26,235	25,419
BALANCE SHEET (IN THOUSANDS):			
Cash & Cash Equivalents	5,927	6,972	...
Total Current Assets	15,519	10,144	...
Net Property	3,264	3,533	...
Total Assets	19,032	13,931	...
Total Current Liabilities	15,650	10,677	...
Long-Term Obligations	100	340	...
Net Stockholders' Equity	d10,088	d9,924	...
Net Working Capital	d131	d533	...
Year-end Shs. Outstg.	27,052	26,436	...
STATISTICAL RECORD:			
Debt/Total Assets %	0.5	2.4	...
Statistics are as originally reported.			

REVENUES

(12/31/98)	($000)	(%)
Software Licenses	17,461	68.2
Services	8,157	31.8
Total	25,618	100.0

OFFICERS:
F. Perna, Chmn.
J. L. MacFarlane, C.E.O.
V. Koha, Pres.
J. S. Ingalls, Sr. V.P., C.F.O.

PRINCIPAL OFFICE: 525 Anacapa Street, Santa Barbara, CA 93101

TELEPHONE NUMBER: (805) 882-2470
FAX: (805) 882-2473
WEB: www.software.com

NO. OF EMPLOYEES: 252

SHAREHOLDERS: 298 (approx.)

ANNUAL MEETING: N/A

INCORPORATED: CA, Oct., 1994; reincorp., DE, Jun., 1999

INSTITUTIONAL HOLDINGS:
No. of Institutions: 4
Shares Held: 200,000
% Held: 0.5

INDUSTRY: Computer integrated systems design (SIC: 7373)

TRANSFER AGENT(S): EquiServe, Canton, MA

SPORTSLINE USA, INC.

YIELD ...
P/E RATIO ...

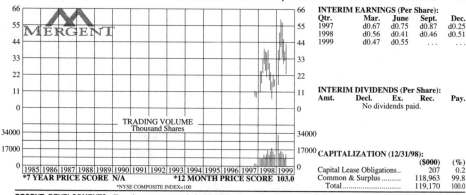

INTERIM EARNINGS (Per Share):

Qtr.	Mar.	June	Sept.	Dec.
1997	d0.67	d0.75	d0.87	d0.25
1998	d0.56	d0.41	d0.46	d0.51
1999	d0.47	d0.55	...	...

INTERIM DIVIDENDS (Per Share):

Amt.	Decl.	Ex.	Rec.	Pay.
	No dividends paid.			

*7 YEAR PRICE SCORE N/A ***12 MONTH PRICE SCORE 103.0**

*NYSE COMPOSITE INDEX=100

CAPITALIZATION (12/31/98):

	($000)	(%)
Capital Lease Obligations..	207	0.2
Common & Surplus	118,963	99.8
Total	119,170	100.0

RECENT DEVELOPMENTS: For the quarter ended 6/30/99, the Company reported a net loss of $12.4 million compared with a loss of $7.5 million in 1998. Total revenues jumped 85.7% to $13.0 million from $7.0 million in the prior-year period. Operating loss was $13.3 million compared with a loss of $8.7 million a year ago. Traffic on the Company's Web site grew 58.0%, averaging about 8.4 million page views per day for the second quarter of 1999 versus 5.3 million a year earlier. During the quarter, the Company was selected to produce and host the official Web sites of Major League Baseball and the NFL Europe league, as well as co-produce the official site of the PGA Tour. Separately, SportsLine Europe Limited, a majority-owned subsidiary of SPLN, unveiled sports.com, a series of sport sites created for fans of European sports. Also, SportsLine Europe Limited completed the acquisition of Infosis Group Limited's sports division.

BUSINESS

SPORTSLINE USA, INC. is an Internet-based sports media company that provides branded, interactive information and programming as well as merchandise to sports enthusiasts worldwide through a variety of Web sites. The Company produces and distributes original, interactive sports content, including editorials and analysis, radio shows, contests, games, fantasy league products and fan clubs. SPLN also distributes a broad range of up-to-date news, scores, player and team statistics and standings, photos, audio clips and video clips obtained from CBS and other leading sports news organizations. The Company generates revenues primarily through advertising and premium service subscriptions, as well as an on-line sports merchandise retail site.

ANNUAL FINANCIAL DATA

	12/31/98	12/31/97	12/31/96	12/31/95	12/31/94
Earnings Per Share	d1.94	d2.54	d1.92	d1.42	d0.19
Cash Flow Per Share	d1.01	d1.55	d1.80	d1.37	d0.19
Tang. Book Val. Per Share	5.86	2.51	5.43	...	...
INCOME STATEMENT (IN THOUSANDS):					
Total Revenues	30,551	10,327	2,437	52	...
Costs & Expenses	53,285	27,338	14,697	5,231	426
Depreciation & Amort.	17,104	10,284	824	193	16
Operating Income	d39,838	d27,296	d13,084	d5,372	d442
Net Interest Inc./(Exp.)	d118	d74	d136	d50	...
Income Before Income Taxes	d35,509	d26,535	d12,855	d5,330	d404
Net Income	d35,509	d26,535	d12,855	d5,330	d404
Cash Flow	d18,405	d16,250	d12,032	d5,137	d388
Average Shs. Outstg.	18,306	10,459	6,681	3,748	2,072
BALANCE SHEET (IN THOUSANDS):					
Cash & Cash Equivalents	59,075	32,158	13,994	184	...
Total Current Assets	74,720	37,560	14,947	320	...
Net Property	5,367	3,433	2,242	1,300	...
Total Assets	137,655	42,945	17,850	2,496	...
Total Current Liabilities	10,211	6,993	3,168	2,264	...
Long-Term Obligations	207	389	409	684	...
Net Stockholders' Equity	118,963	35,564	14,273	d452	...
Net Working Capital	64,509	30,567	11,779	d1,944	...
Year-end Shs. Outstg.	20,301	14,176	2,602	2,600	...
STATISTICAL RECORD:					
Debt/Total Assets %	0.2	0.9	2.3	27.4	...
Price Range	39⅝-6⅜	11½-7	...	...	...

Statistics are as originally reported.

REVENUES

(12/31/98)	($000)	(%)
Advertising	17,698	57.9
E-commerce	3,601	11.8
Membership & premium svc.	5,032	16.5
Content licensing & other......................	4,220	13.8
Total	30,551	100.0

OFFICERS:
M. Levy, Chmn., Pres., C.E.O.
K. W. Sanders, Sr. V.P., C.F.O.

PRINCIPAL OFFICE: 6340 N.W. 5th Way, Ft. Lauderdale, FL 33309

TELEPHONE NUMBER: (954) 351-2120
WEB: cbs.sportsline.com

NO. OF EMPLOYEES: 303

SHAREHOLDERS: 184 (record, approx.) 300 (beneficial, approx.)

ANNUAL MEETING: N/A

INCORPORATED: DE, Feb., 1994

INSTITUTIONAL HOLDINGS:
No. of Institutions: 70
Shares Held: 10,550,312
% Held: 47.0

INDUSTRY: Data processing and preparation (SIC: 7374)

TRANSFER AGENT(S): Continental Stock Transfer & Trust Company, New York, NY.

NASDAQ SYMBOL SPYG
Rec. Pr. 13½ (7/31/99)

SPYGLASS, INC.

YIELD ...
P/E RATIO ...

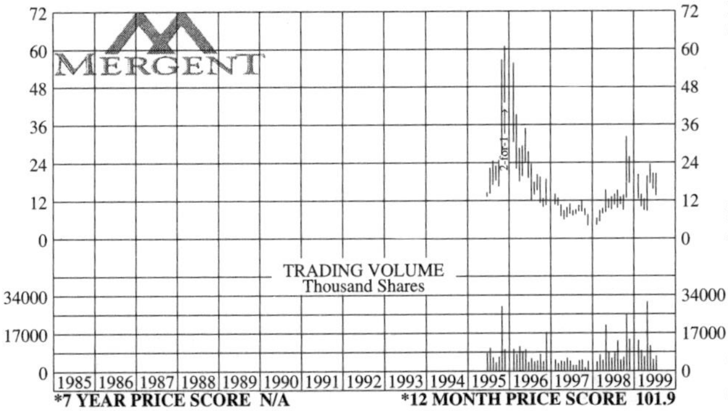

*7 YEAR PRICE SCORE N/A *12 MONTH PRICE SCORE 101.9

*NYSE COMPOSITE INDEX=100

INTERIM EARNINGS (Per Share):

Qtr.	Dec.	Mar.	June	Sept.
1995-96	0.07	0.06	0.07	0.08
1996-97	d0.12	0.16	d0.45	d0.38
1997-98	d0.28	d0.19	d0.09	d0.04
1998-99	d0.15	0.01	d0.04	...

INTERIM DIVIDENDS (Per Share):

Amt.	Decl.	Ex.	Rec.	Pay.

No dividends paid.

CAPITALIZATION (9/30/98):

	($000)	(%)
Common & Surplus	30,076	100.0
Total	30,076	100.0

RECENT DEVELOPMENTS: For the quarter ended 6/30/99, SPYG reported a net loss of $648,000 versus a net loss of $1.7 million in the comparable 1998 quarter. Earnings for the current quarter included one-time acquisition costs of $259,000. Total revenues increased 27.4% to $7.2 million from $5.7 million the year before. The increase in revenues, coupled with a decline in operating costs, led to the improvement in bottom-line results for 1999. Meanwhile, service revenues almost doubled to $4.8 million from $2.4 million in the prior-year quarter, while Internet technology revenues fell 24.9% to $2.4 million from $3.2 million the year before. The growth in services revenue was primarily due to a significant contribution from the Company's multi-year Solution Center contracts with Microsoft Corp. and General Instrument, both of which were executed earlier in fiscal 1999. Gross profit increased 11.6% to $4.6 million from $4.1 million in the previous year.

BUSINESS

SPYGLASS, INC. provides its customers with expertise, software and professional services intended to help them develop cost-effective Internet-enabled devices. SPYG's professional services include custom engineering for defining, developing and delivering complete, end-to-end Internet projects. The Company's products and technologies deliver the embedded Internet and infrastructure solutions needed to connect a wide variety of devices to the Internet.

ANNUAL FINANCIAL DATA

	9/30/98	9/30/97	9/30/96	9/30/95	9/30/94	9/30/93	9/30/92
Earnings Per Share	**[1] d0.60**	**[3] d0.81**	**0.27**	**[2] 0.25**	**[4] 0.08**	**d0.12**	**d0.15**
Cash Flow Per Share	**d0.32**	**d0.65**	**0.32**	**0.26**	**0.05**	**d0.21**	**d0.25**
Tang. Book Val. Per Share	**2.16**	**2.88**	**3.71**	**3.51**	...	...	...
INCOME STATEMENT (IN THOUSANDS):							
Total Revenues	20,494	21,295	22,307	10,350	3,629	1,375	918
Costs & Expenses	25,950	30,753	17,946	7,925	2,810	1,723	1,378
Depreciation & Amort.	3,782	1,899	694	260	68	40	24
Operating Income	d9,238	d11,357	3,667	3,028	752	d388	d484
Net Interest Inc./(Exp.)	...	...	...	...	23	28	46
Income Before Income Taxes	d8,016	d9,735	5,411	3,592	856	d320	d389
Income Taxes	...	...	1,951	1,415	325	...	...
Net Income	[1] d8,016	[3] d9,735	3,460	[2] 2,177	[4] 531	d320	d389
Cash Flow	d4,234	d7,836	4,154	2,246	341	d538	d621
Average Shs. Outstg.	13,395	12,090	12,838	8,636	6,898	2,514	2,520
BALANCE SHEET (IN THOUSANDS):							
Cash & Cash Equivalents	22,655	27,770	34,083	34,326	1,451	757	...
Total Current Assets	30,722	33,757	43,785	38,812	3,255	919	...
Net Property	3,585	5,037	3,377	1,055	319	179	...
Total Assets	34,575	40,580	48,769	42,448	5,297	1,167	...
Total Current Liabilities	4,449	4,913	4,668	3,505	1,407	258	...
Net Stockholders' Equity	30,076	35,567	43,891	37,238	d1,153	d2,227	...
Net Working Capital	26,273	28,844	39,117	35,307	1,848	661	...
Year-end Shs. Outstg.	13,935	12,363	11,820	10,619	2,532	2,530	...
STATISTICAL RECORD:							
Operating Profit Margin %	...	...	16.4	29.3	20.7	...	...
Net Profit Margin %	...	...	15.5	21.0	14.6	...	...
Return on Equity %	...	...	7.9	5.8	...	...	...
Return on Assets %	...	...	7.1	5.1	10.0	...	...
Price Range	32¼-4¼	14⅛-4$\frac{1}{16}$	55¾-10	61-13¼	...	...	...
P/E Ratio	...	...	206.4-37.0	243.9-53.0	...	...	...

Statistics are as originally reported. Adj. for stk. split: 2-for-1, 12/95 [1] Inc. acquistion pre-tax chrg. of $496,000. [2] Incl. gain of $863,000 on the sale of data visualization prod. line. [3] Incl. pre-tax restructuring chrg. of $900,000 [4] Excl. acctg. chrg. of $800,000.

OFFICERS:
D. P. Colbeth, Pres., C.E.O.
G. L. Vilchick, Exec. V.P., Fin., C.F.O.
T. S. Lewicki, Treas., Contr., Sec.

PRINCIPAL OFFICE: 1240 East Diehl Rd., Naperville, IL 60563

TELEPHONE NUMBER: (630) 505-1010
FAX: (630) 505-4944
WEB: www.spyglass.com

NO. OF EMPLOYEES: 127

SHAREHOLDERS: 625

ANNUAL MEETING: In Feb.

INCORPORATED: IL, Feb., 1990; reincorp., DE, May, 1995

INSTITUTIONAL HOLDINGS:
No. of Institutions: 29
Shares Held: 2,337,383
% Held: 15.5

INDUSTRY: Prepackaged software (SIC: 7372)

TRANSFER AGENT(S): American Stock Transfer and Trust Company, New York, NY

STERLING COMMERCE, INC.

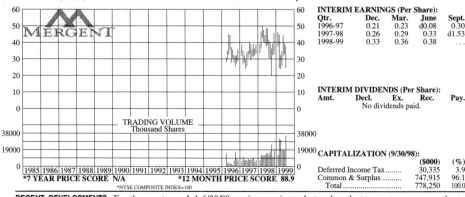

INTERIM EARNINGS (Per Share):

Qtr.	Dec.	Mar.	June	Sept.
1996-97	0.21	0.23	d0.08	0.30
1997-98	0.26	0.29	0.33	d1.53
1998-99	0.33	0.36	0.38	...

INTERIM DIVIDENDS (Per Share):

Amt.	Decl.	Ex.	Rec.	Pay.
No dividends paid.				

TRADING VOLUME
Thousand Shares

1985	1986	1987	1988	1989	1990	1991	1992	1993	1994	1995	1996	1997	1998	1999

*7 YEAR PRICE SCORE N/A   ***12 MONTH PRICE SCORE 88.9**

*NYSE COMPOSITE INDEX=100

CAPITALIZATION (9/30/98):

	($000)	(%)
Deferred Income Tax	30,335	3.9
Common & Surplus	747,915	96.1
Total	778,250	100.0

RECENT DEVELOPMENTS: For the quarter ended 6/30/99, net income grew 18.4% to $37.0 million from $31.2 million in the corresponding period of the previous year. Net income for the current quarter included a one-time net benefit of $2.5 million related to reorganization and unusual costs. Total revenue jumped 24.6% to $152.2 million from $122.1 million in the year-earlier quarter. Product revenue advanced 13.5% to $53.8 million, while product support revenue climbed 47.7% to $36.6 million. The increase in product and product support revenue was due to increased licensing of CONNECT software products, including remote and mobile management software products and related support not offered by the Company during the same period of 1998. SE reported services revenues of $61.8 million versus $49.9 million in 1998. The increase in services revenues was mostly due to growth in Managed Services and COMMERCE services customer volume, the addition of new customers and price increases.

BUSINESS

STERLING COMMERCE, INC. provides electronic commerce (EC) products and services based on Internet technology. The Company develops, markets and supports electronic commerce software products, and provides electronic services that enable businesses to engage in business-to-business electronic communications and transactions. The Company has been providing electronic commerce tools for over 25 years and has 42,000 customers spanned across many industries. SE has 37 office locations and more than 40 distributors worldwide. The products they offer include the CONNECT family, which provides the software infrastructure for moving and managing information inside and outside the enterprise; the COMMERCE family, which provides commerce community management services to help customers build, manage, and service global commerce business communities; the GENTRAN products, which provide business process integration software to automate the flow of internal and external business transactions; the VECTOR products, which provide banking application software and services for the automation of check flow and other financial transactions; and EC Managed Services, which include a full range of EC outsourcing services and consulting tools.

ANNUAL FINANCIAL DATA

	9/30/98	9/30/97	9/30/96	9/30/95	9/30/94	9/30/93
Earnings Per Share	⊡ d0.67	⊡ 0.64	0.77	0.59	...	...
Cash Flow Per Share	d0.22	1.03	1.08	0.83	0.58	...
Tang. Book Val. Per Share	6.28	5.97	1.25	0.15	0.07	...
INCOME STATEMENT (IN MILLIONS):						
Total Revenues	490.3	350.6	267.8	203.6	155.9	117.8
Costs & Expenses	470.7	247.8	150.6	114.0	95.0	82.3
Depreciation & Amort.	40.7	30.2	21.9	17.5	14.5	10.2
Operating Income	d21.2	72.6	95.2	72.0	46.4	25.4
Income Before Income Taxes	3.0	89.3	96.4	71.6	46.3	25.3
Income Taxes	64.1	33.8	38.0	28.6	18.5	10.1
Net Income	⊡ d61.2	⊡ 55.4	58.4	42.9	27.8	⊡ 15.2
Cash Flow	d20.4	85.7	80.3	60.4	42.3	25.4
Average Shs. Outstg. (000)	91,307	83,561	74,233	73,200	73,200	...
BALANCE SHEET (IN MILLIONS):						
Cash & Cash Equivalents	538.4	484.7	44.7	0.4	0.4	...
Total Current Assets	719.3	615.1	150.0	56.1	40.2	...
Net Property	74.4	59.7	43.2	25.8	17.0	...
Total Assets	967.0	748.6	241.7	129.0	100.6	...
Total Current Liabilities	174.2	123.3	72.8	52.4	38.0	...
Net Stockholders' Equity	747.9	600.9	138.2	53.2	43.1	...
Net Working Capital	545.1	491.8	77.2	3.7	2.2	...
Year-end Shs. Outstg. (000)	94,511	89,644	75,000	73,200	73,200	...
STATISTICAL RECORD:						
Operating Profit Margin %	...	20.7	35.6	35.4	29.8	21.5
Net Profit Margin %	...	15.8	21.8	21.1	17.8	12.9
Return on Equity %	...	9.2	42.3	80.7	64.5	...
Return on Assets %	...	7.4	24.2	33.3	27.6	...
Price Range	50¼-20⅛	40⁵/₁₆-24⅛	45-25½	...	...	...
P/E Ratio	...	63.0-37.7	58.4-33.1	...	...	...

Statistics are as originally reported. ⊡ Incl. non-recur. chgs. of $183.9 mill., 1998; $47.7 mill., 1997; $3.6 mill., 1993.

OFFICERS:
S. L. Williams, Chmn.
W. C. Blow, Pres., C.E.O.
S. P. Shiflet, Sr. V.P., C.F.O.
A. K. Hoover, Sr. V.P., Gen. Couns., Sec.

PRINCIPAL OFFICE: 300 Crescent Court, Suite 1200, Dallas, TX 75201

TELEPHONE NUMBER: (214) 981-1100
FAX: (214) 981-1215
WEB: www.sterlingcommerce.com

NO. OF EMPLOYEES: 2,300

SHAREHOLDERS: 1,130

ANNUAL MEETING: In Mar.

INCORPORATED: DE, Dec., 1995

INSTITUTIONAL HOLDINGS:
No. of Institutions: 236
Shares Held: 77,014,404
% Held: 80.8

INDUSTRY: Prepackaged software (SIC: 7372)

TRANSFER AGENT(S): The First National Bank of Boston, Boston, MA

STUDENT ADVANTAGE, INC.

YIELD ...
P/E RATIO ...

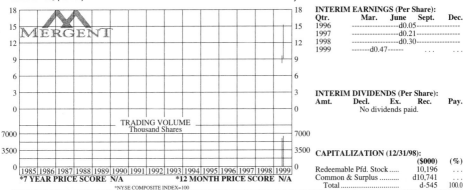

TRADING VOLUME
Thousand Shares

| 1985 | 1986 | 1987 | 1988 | 1989 | 1990 | 1991 | 1992 | 1993 | 1994 | 1995 | 1996 | 1997 | 1998 | 1999 |

*7 YEAR PRICE SCORE N/A   ***12 MONTH PRICE SCORE N/A**

*NYSE COMPOSITE INDEX=100

INTERIM EARNINGS (Per Share):

Qtr.	Mar.	June	Sept.	Dec.
1996	---------------- d0.05 ----------------			
1997	---------------- d0.21 ----------------			
1998	---------------- d0.30 ----------------			
1999	------- d0.47 ------		...	...

INTERIM DIVIDENDS (Per Share):

Amt.	Decl.	Ex.	Rec.	Pay.
No dividends paid.				

CAPITALIZATION (12/31/98):

	($000)	(%)
Redeemable Pfd. Stock	10,196	...
Common & Surplus	d10,741	...
Total	d-545	100.0

RECENT DEVELOPMENTS: For the quarter ended 6/30/99, the Company recorded a net loss of $5.4 million compared with a net loss of $2.3 million in the corresponding quarter the year before. Total revenues grew 31.3% to $4.8 million from $3.7 million in the comparable quarter a year earlier. Subscription revenue increased 4.0% to $2.4 million from $2.3 million in the equivalent 1998 quarter. Total costs and expenses jumped 71.7% to $10.2 million from $6.0 million in the previous year. Comparisons were made with restated prior-year figures. In June 1999, the Company acquired University Netcasting Inc., creator of The FANSOnly Network®, which is a major operator of official athletic Web sites for colleges, universities, and college sports associations. During the second quarter, the Company also acquired Mentor Interactive Corp., Rail Connection®, The Campus Agency, and Transaction Service Providers, Inc. These acquisitions are expected to enhance the Company's Internet and commerce-related business.

BUSINESS

STUDENT ADVANTAGE, INC. is a membership and media company, focused exclusively on the college market. The Company develops and supports partnerships between students, schools, and local and national sponsors through its membership program and Studentadvantage.com Web site. The Company offers its 1.0 million plus members throughout the U.S. an assortment of college-related goods and services, discounts on products and services, information on financial aid, and advice on finding a job.

ANNUAL FINANCIAL DATA

	12/31/98	12/31/97	12/31/96
Earnings Per Share	d0.30	d0.21	d0.05
Cash Flow Per Share	d0.27	d0.19	d0.04
INCOME STATEMENT (IN THOUSANDS):			
Total Revenues	17,443	3,792	1,730
Costs & Expenses	21,533	6,734	2,349
Depreciation & Amort.	1,027	239	37
Operating Income	d5,117	d3,181	d656
Net Interest Inc./(Exp.)	2	29	d1
Income Before Income Taxes	d5,115	d3,152	d657
Net Income	d5,115	d3,152	d657
Cash Flow	d4,088	d2,913	d620
Average Shs. Outstg.	15,424	15,295	14,184
BALANCE SHEET (IN THOUSANDS):			
Cash & Cash Equivalents	5,048	1,904	...
Total Current Assets	8,232	2,133	...
Net Property	1,085	235	...
Total Assets	9,934	2,745	...
Total Current Liabilities	10,479	6,969	...
Net Stockholders' Equity	d10,741	d4,335	...
Net Working Capital	d2,247	d4,836	...
Year-end Shs. Outstg.	16,134	14,907	...

Statistics are as originally reported.

QUARTERLY DATA

(12/31/98)($000)	Rev	INC
1st Quarter	3,396	-305
2nd Quarter	3,398	-928
3rd Quarter	5,682	-51
4th Quarter	4,967	-3,831

OFFICERS:
R. V. Sozzi Jr., Chmn., Pres. & C.E.O.
C. B. Andrews, V.P. & C.F.O.
R. J. Kos, C.O.O.

PRINCIPAL OFFICE: 280 Summer Street, Boston, MA 02210

TELEPHONE NUMBER: (617) 912-2011
WEB: www.studentadvantage.com

NO. OF EMPLOYEES: 175

SHAREHOLDERS: N/A

ANNUAL MEETING: N/A

INCORPORATED: DE, 1998

INSTITUTIONAL HOLDINGS:
No. of Institutions: 1
Shares Held: 10,250
% Held: 0.0

INDUSTRY: Information retrieval services (SIC: 7375)

TRANSFER AGENT(S): BankBoston, N.A., Boston, MA

NASDAQ SYMBOL SUNW
Rec. Pr. 67 7/8 (7/31/99)

SUN MICROSYSTEMS, INC.

YIELD ...
P/E RATIO 53.4

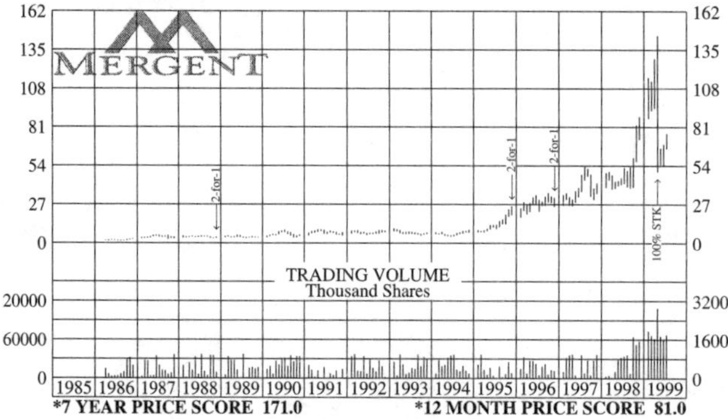

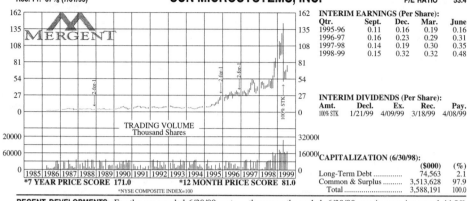

***7 YEAR PRICE SCORE 171.0** ***12 MONTH PRICE SCORE 81.0**

*NYSE COMPOSITE INDEX=100

INTERIM EARNINGS (Per Share):

Qtr.	Sept.	Dec.	Mar.	June
1995-96	0.11	0.16	0.19	0.16
1996-97	0.16	0.23	0.29	0.31
1997-98	0.14	0.19	0.30	0.35
1998-99	0.15	0.32	0.32	0.48

INTERIM DIVIDENDS (Per Share):

Amt.	Decl.	Ex.	Rec.	Pay.
100% STK	1/21/99	4/09/99	3/18/99	4/08/99

CAPITALIZATION (6/30/98):

	($000)	(%)
Long-Term Debt	74,563	2.1
Common & Surplus	3,513,628	97.9
Total	3,588,191	100.0

RECENT DEVELOPMENTS: For the year ended 6/30/99, net income increased 35.2% to $1.03 billion from $762.9 million the previous year. Net revenues advanced 19.8% to $11.73 billion from $9.79 billion the year before. Results were positively affected as a result of the Company's focus on network computing. Operating income rose 34.7% to $1.52 billion from $1.13 billion in the prior year. For the three months ended, 6/30/99, net income increased 44.8% to $395.2 million from $273.0 million in the corresponding period of the previous year. Net revenues climbed 22.0% to $3.51 billion from $2.88 billion in the prior-year quarter. Operating income advanced 40.1% to $563.8 million from $402.4 million the year before.

BUSINESS

SUN MICROSYSTEMS, INC. is a supplier of client-server computing services featuring networked workstations and servers that store, process, and distribute information for establishing enterprise-wide intranets and expanding the Internet. SUNW's product design philosophy is based on the use of industry-standard technologies such as the UNIX® operating system, NFS® file system, OpenWindows™ environment, and SPARC® microprocessor. SUNW has integrated these technologies in an open systems architecture and established a high-performance distributed computing environment. SUNW's systems currently are used in both commercial and technical applications, including financial services, telecommunications, electronic publishing, software engineering, computer-aided design, scientific research, and medical electronics.

ANNUAL FINANCIAL DATA

	6/30/98	6/30/97	6/30/96	6/30/95	6/30/94	6/30/93	6/30/92
Earnings Per Share	**[1] 0.97**	**[1] 0.98**	**[1] 0.61**	**0.46**	**0.25**	**0.19**	**0.21**
Cash Flow Per Share	**1.53**	**1.50**	**0.97**	**0.76**	**0.57**	**0.46**	**0.48**
Tang. Book Val. Per Share	**4.67**	**3.70**	**3.03**	**2.69**	**2.17**	**2.01**	**1.86**
INCOME STATEMENT (IN MILLIONS):							
Total Revenues	9,790.8	8,598.3	7,094.8	5,901.9	4,689.9	4,308.6	3,588.9
Costs & Expenses	8,220.8	7,230.1	6,135.7	5,160.9	4,164.4	3,835.8	3,112.4
Depreciation & Amort.	439.9	341.7	284.1	240.6	248.2	232.4	215.5
Operating Income	1,130.1	1,026.5	675.0	500.4	277.3	240.4	261.1
Net Interest Inc./(Exp.)	46.1	32.4	33.9	22.9	6.1	d1.5	d6.2
Income Before Income Taxes	1,176.2	1,121.2	708.9	523.3	283.4	223.9	254.9
Income Taxes	413.3	358.8	232.5	167.5	87.6	67.2	81.6
Net Income	[1] 762.9	[1] 762.4	[1] 476.4	355.8	195.8	156.7	173.3
Cash Flow	1,202.8	1,104.1	760.5	596.5	444.1	389.1	388.8
Average Shs. Outstg. (000)	788,548	736,852	786,760	787,400	774,112	841,000	813,120
BALANCE SHEET (IN MILLIONS):							
Cash & Cash Equivalents	1,298.5	1,112.8	989.6	1,228.0	882.8	1,138.7	1,220.1
Total Current Assets	4,147.5	3,728.5	3,033.7	2,934.4	2,305.1	2,272.3	2,148.4
Net Property	1,300.6	799.9	533.8	429.0	360.2	348.4	360.4
Total Assets	5,711.1	4,697.3	3,800.9	3,544.6	2,898.0	2,767.6	2,671.6
Total Current Liabilities	2,122.9	1,849.0	1,489.3	1,330.8	1,147.8	947.0	838.9
Long-Term Obligations	74.6	106.3	60.2	91.2	121.8	...	...
Net Stockholders' Equity	3,513.6	2,741.9	2,251.5	2,122.6	1,628.3	1,642.8	1,485.1
Net Working Capital	2,024.7	1,879.4	1,544.5	1,603.6	1,157.3	1,325.3	1,309.5
Year-end Shs. Outstg. (000)	752,608	740,972	743,928	788,112	750,808	816,896	800,016
STATISTICAL RECORD:							
Operating Profit Margin %	11.5	11.9	9.5	8.5	5.9	5.6	7.3
Net Profit Margin %	7.8	8.9	6.7	6.0	4.2	3.6	4.8
Return on Equity %	21.7	27.8	21.2	16.8	12.0	9.5	11.7
Return on Assets %	13.4	16.2	12.5	10.0	6.8	5.7	6.5
Debt/Total Assets %	1.3	2.3	1.6	2.6	4.2	...	...
Price Range	88 3/8-37 5/8	53 5/16-25 7/8	35 1/8-18	25 3/4-7 1/2	9 7/16-4 9/16	10 1/4-5 5/16	9 1/16-5 5/8
P/E Ratio	91.6-39.0	54.4-26.4	58.0-29.7	56.5-16.4	37.2-18.0	55.1-28.4	42.2-26.3

Statistics are as originally reported. Adj. for stk. splits: 2-for-1, 3/18/99; 2-for-1, 12/10/96; 2-for-1, 12/11/95 [1] Incl. non-recurr. chrg. 6/30/99: $120.7 mill.; chrg. 6/30/98: $176.4 mill.; credit 6/30/97: $39.3 mill.; chrg. 6/30/96: $57.9 mill.

OFFICERS:
S. G. McNealy, Chmn., C.E.O.
E. J. Zander, Pres., C.O.O.
M. E. Lehman, V.P., C.F.O.
A. D. Page, V.P., Treas.

PRINCIPAL OFFICE: 901 San Antonio Road, Palo Alto, CA 94303

TELEPHONE NUMBER: (650) 960-1300
FAX: (650) 336-0646
WEB: www.sun.com

NO. OF EMPLOYEES: 26,300 (approx.)

SHAREHOLDERS: 9,145

ANNUAL MEETING: In Nov.

INCORPORATED: CA, Feb., 1982; reincorp., DE, Jul., 1987

INSTITUTIONAL HOLDINGS:
No. of Institutions: 722
Shares Held: 479,179,799
% Held: 61.9

INDUSTRY: Electronic computers (SIC: 3571)

TRANSFER AGENT(S): Boston EquiServe LP, Boston MA.

NASDAQ SYMBOL SYBS
Rec. Pr. 10¼ (7/31/99)

SYBASE, INC.

YIELD ...
P/E RATIO 113.9

*7 YEAR PRICE SCORE 20.8   *12 MONTH PRICE SCORE 121.6
*NYSE COMPOSITE INDEX=100

TRADING VOLUME Thousand Shares

INTERIM EARNINGS (Per Share):

Qtr.	Mar.	June	Sept.	Dec.
1995	d0.25	d0.13	0.02	0.08
1996	d0.09	d0.33	d0.69	0.07
1997	d0.08	d0.23	d0.08	d0.32
1998	d1.01	0.01	0.03	d0.18
1999	0.07	0.17	...	...

INTERIM DIVIDENDS (Per Share):

Amt.	Decl.	Ex.	Rec.	Pay.
		No dividends paid.		

CAPITALIZATION (12/31/98):

	($000)	(%)
Long-Term Debt	2,011	0.7
Common & Surplus	301,072	99.3
Total	303,083	100.0

RECENT DEVELOPMENTS: For the quarter ended 6/30/99, net income jumped to $14.3 million compared with $450,000 in the corresponding quarter of the previous year. Total revenues slipped 3.5% to $210.2 million from $217.9 million the year before. Revenues from services increased to $114.5 million from $112.0 million in the prior year, while revenues from license fees decreased to $95.7 million from $105.9 million a year earlier. Operating income

soared to $21.2 million versus $1.6 million in the previous year. The increase in operating income primarily resulted from a 21.8% drop in sales and marketing expenses and a 7.1% decrease in cost of services, as well as a $5.6 million restructuring credit. During the quarter, the Company introduced Sybase® SQL Anywhere™ Studio, a mobile and embedded database for Linux.

BUSINESS

SYBASE, INC. develops, markets and supports a full line of relational database management software products and services for on-line applications in networked computing environments. The Company offers a broad range of relational database management system servers, application development tools and connectivity software and complements this product portfolio by providing consulting and integration services required to support enterprise-wide on-line applications. Sybase offers three major product families based upon its advanced client/server architecture: the SYBASE SQL Server family, SYBASE SQL Lifecycle tools and SYBASE connectivity interfaces and gateways. The Company markets its products and services worldwide through a direct sales force, distributors, value-added remarketers, systems integrators and original equipment manufacturers.

REVENUES

(12/31/98)	($000)	(%)
License Fees	421,454	48.6
Services	446,015	51.4
Total	867,469	100.0

ANNUAL FINANCIAL DATA

	12/31/98	12/31/97	12/31/96	12/31/95	12/31/94	12/31/93	12/31/92
Earnings Per Share	d1.15	d0.70	① d1.05	① d0.27	1.38	0.86	① 0.48
Cash Flow Per Share	0.18	0.63	0.25	0.78	2.11	1.33	0.82
Tang. Book Val. Per Share	3.27	4.09	4.25	4.95	6.30	3.82	2.48
INCOME STATEMENT (IN MILLIONS):							
Total Revenues	867.5	903.9	1,011.5	956.6	693.8	426.7	264.6
Costs & Expenses	846.5	845.6	987.9	904.8	537.8	332.8	210.2
Depreciation & Amort.	107.8	104.7	97.8	75.2	39.6	24.4	16.8
Operating Income	d86.8	d46.4	d74.2	d23.3	116.4	69.5	37.6
Net Interest Inc./(Exp.)	10.1	9.2	9.2	8.9	5.6	2.7	2.7
Income Before Income Taxes	d79.1	d40.8	d66.7	d14.7	121.3	71.2	39.5
Income Taxes	14.1	14.7	12.3	4.8	46.1	27.1	15.8
Net Income	d93.1	d55.4	① d79.0	① d19.5	75.2	44.1	① 23.7
Cash Flow	14.7	49.3	18.8	55.7	114.8	68.5	40.4
Average Shs. Outstg. (000)	80,893	78,794	75,160	71,292	54,422	51,432	49,211
BALANCE SHEET (IN MILLIONS):							
Cash & Cash Equivalents	248.6	236.0	174.5	223.7	197.1	138.1	75.0
Total Current Assets	477.7	475.7	445.3	461.5	384.0	257.3	167.1
Net Property	101.4	149.7	191.3	194.9	110.9	55.8	29.3
Total Assets	696.6	781.6	751.9	766.3	575.6	332.5	209.6
Total Current Liabilities	393.5	408.2	352.2	321.2	232.4	136.0	83.1
Long-Term Obligations	2.0	2.0	2.9	5.5	5.4	4.8	6.2
Net Stockholders' Equity	301.1	371.5	396.8	439.6	337.2	190.6	118.3
Net Working Capital	84.2	67.5	93.1	140.3	151.6	121.3	83.9
Year-end Shs. Outstg. (000)	81,169	79,998	76,609	72,646	51,647	47,780	44,929
STATISTICAL RECORD:							
Operating Profit Margin %	...	...	...	...	16.8	16.3	14.2
Net Profit Margin %	...	...	...	...	10.8	10.3	9.0
Return on Equity %	...	...	...	...	22.3	23.2	20.0
Return on Assets %	...	...	...	...	13.1	13.3	11.3
Debt/Total Assets %	0.3	0.3	0.4	0.7	0.9	1.4	3.0
Price Range	11¼-4½	23⅝-11½	37⅜-13½	55-19⅞	57-35¼	43½-22¾	24⅞-10¼
P/E Ratio	...	...	...	...	41.3-25.5	50.6-26.5	51.8-21.3

Statistics are as originally reported. Adj. for stk. split: 2-for-1, 11/22/93 ① Incl. non-recurr. chrg. $74.2 mill., 12/31/98; $49.2 mill., 12/31/96; $44.0 mill., 12/31/95; $2.2 mill., 12/31/92.

OFFICERS:
J. Chen, Chmn., Pres., C.E.O.
P. A. Van der Vorst, V.P., C.F.O.
M. L. Gaynor, V.P., Gen. Couns., Sec.

PRINCIPAL OFFICE: 6475 Christie Ave., Emeryville, CA 94608

TELEPHONE NUMBER: (510) 922-3500
FAX: (510) 922-3210
WEB: www.sybase.com

NO. OF EMPLOYEES: 4,196

SHAREHOLDERS: 2,066

ANNUAL MEETING: In May

INCORPORATED: CA, Nov., 1984; reincorp., DE, Jul., 1991

INSTITUTIONAL HOLDINGS:
No. of Institutions: 104
Shares Held: 47,629,428
% Held: 57.8

INDUSTRY: Prepackaged software (SIC 7372)

TRANSFER AGENT(S): EquiServe, Boston, MA

TELIGENT, INC.

YIELD ...
P/E RATIO ...

INTERIM EARNINGS (Per Share):

Qtr.	Mar.	June	Sept.	Dec.
1996	----------d0.29----------			
1997	d0.15	d0.99	d0.63	d1.17
1998	d0.73	d1.12	d1.49	d2.01
1999	d2.05	d2.34	...	...

INTERIM DIVIDENDS (Per Share):

Amt.	Decl.	Ex.	Rec.	Pay.
	No dividends paid.			

CAPITALIZATION (12/31/98):

	($000)	(%)
Long-Term Debt	576,058	94.9
Common & Surplus	31,053	5.1
Total	607,111	100.0

RECENT DEVELOPMENTS: For the quarter ended 6/30/99, the Company reported a net loss of $123.5 million compared with a net loss of $59.1 million in the equivalent 1998 quarter. Revenues were $4.0 million, up from $143,000 from a year earlier. Comparisons were made with restated 1998 results. The improvement in revenues was primarily attributed to Teligent's continued growth of its customer base and expansion into new markets. In July, TGNT launched lower-cost, high bandwidth communications services in Phoenix, Arizona. With its advanced, digital SmartWave™ technology, TGNT offers customers savings of up to 30% on local, long distance, high-speed data and Internet access services. With the addition of the Phoenix market, Teligent now serves business customers in 29 of the nation's top metropolitan areas. In June, TGNT announced the introduction of SmartWave™ DSL, a new, lower-cost, high-speed data service that enables small and mid-sized businesses to experience industrial strength service for as little as $149.00 a month.

BUSINESS

TELIGENT, INC. is a full-service, integrated communications company that is offering small and medium-sized business customers local, long distance, high-speed data and dedicated Internet services over its digital SmartWave™ local networks in 29 major markets. Eventually, Teligent will expand its service to 74 major metropolitan areas throughout the U.S. The Company's offerings of regulated services are subject to tariff approval.

QUARTERLY DATA

(12/31/98)($000)	Rev	Inc
1st Quarter	98	(38,558)
2nd Quarter	143	(59,136)
3rd Quarter	240	(78,545)
4th Quarter	479	(105,232)

ANNUAL FINANCIAL DATA

	12/31/98	12/31/97	12/31/96
Earnings Per Share	d5.35	d2.94	d0.29
Cash Flow Per Share	d4.55	d2.74	d0.29
Tang. Book Val. Per Share	...	4.07	...
INCOME STATEMENT (IN THOUSANDS):			
Total Revenues	960	3,311	1,386
Costs & Expenses	207,584	129,235	13,986
Depreciation & Amort.	42,073	9,513	164
Operating Income	d248,697	d135,437	d12,764
Net Interest Inc./(Exp.)	d66,880	d5,859	d879
Income Before Income Taxes	d281,471	d138,054	d13,633
Net Income	d281,471	d138,054	d13,633
Cash Flow	d239,398	d128,541	d13,469
Average Shs. Outstg.	52,597	46,951	46,258
BALANCE SHEET (IN THOUSANDS):			
Cash & Cash Equivalents	448,431	455,274	1,303
Total Current Assets	456,586	462,361	1,497
Net Property	180,726	8,186	3,545
Total Assets	763,434	596,380	5,145
Total Current Liabilities	154,178	21,045	8,427
Long-Term Obligations	576,058	300,000	...
Net Stockholders' Equity	31,053	274,146	d3,575
Net Working Capital	302,408	441,316	d6,930
Year-end Shs. Outstg.	52,633	52,583	...
STATISTICAL RECORD:			
Debt/Total Assets %	75.5	50.3	...
Price Range	35⅜-18¼	27¼-23½	...
Statistics are as originally reported.			

OFFICERS:
A. J. Mandl, Chmn., C.E.O.
A. L. Morris, Sr. V.P., C.F.O., Treas.

INVESTOR CONTACT: Michael S. Kraft,
V.P., Investor Relations, (703) 762-5264

PRINCIPAL OFFICE: 8065 Leesburg Pike,
Suite 400, Vienna, VA 22182

TELEPHONE NUMBER: (703) 762-5100
FAX: (703) 762-5200
WEB: www.teligent.com

NO. OF EMPLOYEES: 1,821

SHAREHOLDERS: 183 (Class A)

ANNUAL MEETING: In June
INCORPORATED: DE, Sept., 1997

INSTITUTIONAL HOLDINGS:
No. of Institutions: 62
Shares Held: 3,871,965
% Held: 46.6

INDUSTRY: Radiotelephone communications
(SIC: 4812)

TRANSFER AGENT(S): First Union National
Bank, Charlotte, NC

TERAYON COMMUNICATION SYSTEMS, INC.

YIELD ...
P/E RATIO ...

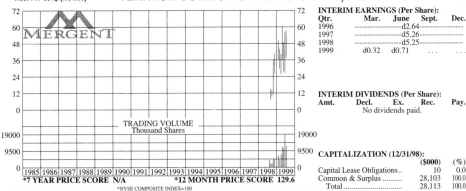

*7 YEAR PRICE SCORE N/A *12 MONTH PRICE SCORE 129.6
*NYSE COMPOSITE INDEX=100

INTERIM EARNINGS (Per Share):

Qtr.	Mar.	June	Sept.	Dec.
1996	------------------d2.64------------------			
1997	------------------d5.26------------------			
1998	------------------d5.25------------------			
1999	d0.32	d0.71	...	...

INTERIM DIVIDENDS (Per Share):

Amt.	Decl.	Ex.	Rec.	Pay.
		No dividends paid.		

CAPITALIZATION (12/31/98):

	($000)	(%)
Capital Lease Obligations..	10	0.0
Common & Surplus	28,103	100.0
Total	28,113	100.0

RECENT DEVELOPMENTS: For the quarter ended 6/30/99, the Company reported a net loss of $14.6 million versus a net loss of $5.6 million in the corresponding quarter of the previous year. Earnings in 1999 include a non-cash charge of $11.2 million related to the cost of two warrants to purchase common stock. Revenues more than doubled to $19.1 million from $6.9 million in the prior-year period due to increased shipments to new and existing customers. Gross profit totaled $3.8 million, up from a loss of $451,000 the year before, due to the introduction of TERN's lower cost, single-board modem and continued cost reduction efforts. Total expenses more than tripled to $19.7 million primarily due to costs of $11.2 million related to TERN's product development assistance agreement with Rogers Communications Inc. In July 1999, the Company agreed to acquire Imedia Corporation, a producer of routing and re-multiplexing systems for digital video.

BUSINESS

TERAYON COMMUNICATION SYSTEMS, INC. develops, markets and sells cable modem systems designed to enable cable operators to cost-effectively deploy reliable two-way broadband access services. The Company's cable modems support a broad range of residential and commercial data services across cable plants, ranging from all-coaxial systems to hybrid fiber/coax. The Company's systems incorporate sophisticated Quality of Service capability, allowing control of bandwidth in precise increments. This allows broadband service providers to offer tiered services to their subscribers, from residential Internet access to business services for data and telephony.

ANNUAL FINANCIAL DATA

	12/31/98	12/31/97	12/31/96	12/31/95
Earnings Per Share	d5.25	d5.26	d2.64	d1.02
Cash Flow Per Share	d4.98	d4.89	d2.43	d0.96
Tang. Book Val. Per Share	1.71	...	...	...
INCOME STATEMENT (IN THOUSANDS):				
Total Revenues	31,696	2,118	...	...
Costs & Expenses	52,960	23,220	10,120	3,531
Depreciation & Amort.	2,413	1,575	830	203
Operating Income	d23,677	d22,677	d10,950	d3,734
Net Interest Inc./(Exp.)	449	128	253	68
Income Before Income Taxes	d23,228	d22,549	d10,697	d3,666
Net Income	d23,228	d22,549	d10,697	d3,666
Cash Flow	d44,725	d20,974	d9,867	d3,463
Average Shs. Outstg.	8,986	4,289	4,054	3,589
BALANCE SHEET (IN THOUSANDS):				
Cash & Cash Equivalents	28,880	1,987	12,864	8,620
Total Current Assets	38,325	4,935	13,163	8,620
Net Property	3,593	3,615	2,572	...
Total Assets	42,146	8,778	15,978	8,620
Total Current Liabilities	13,903	9,782	3,192	...
Long-Term Obligations	10	44	1,255	439
Net Stockholders' Equity	28,103	d1,174	11,405	d3,917
Net Working Capital	24,422	d4,847	9,971	8,620
Year-end Shs. Outstg.	16,458	4,620	4,139	3,589
STATISTICAL RECORD:				
Debt/Total Assets %	...	0.5	7.9	5.1
Price Range	40½-7	...	...	...

Statistics are as originally reported.

REVENUES

12/31/98	($000)	(%)
Product Revenues......	19,150	60.4
Related Party Product Revenues	12,546	39.6
Total Revenues.........	31,696	100.0

OFFICERS:
S. Rakib, Chmn., Pres.
Z. Rakib, C.E.O.
R. M. Fritz, C.F.O.
D. J. Picker, C.O.O.

PRINCIPAL OFFICE: 2952 Bunker Hill Lane, Santa Clara, CA 95054

TELEPHONE NUMBER: (408) 727-4400
WEB: www.terayon.com
NO. OF EMPLOYEES: 130
SHAREHOLDERS: 248
ANNUAL MEETING: In May
INCORPORATED: CA, Jan., 1993; reincorp., DE, Jul., 1998

INSTITUTIONAL HOLDINGS:
No. of Institutions: 69
Shares Held: 5,477,210
% Held: 26.5

INDUSTRY: Telephone and telegraph apparatus (SIC: 3661)

TRANSFER AGENT(S): Boston Equiserve, Boston, MA

THEGLOBE.COM, INC.

YIELD ...
P/E RATIO ...

*7 YEAR PRICE SCORE N/A *12 MONTH PRICE SCORE N/A
*NYSE COMPOSITE INDEX=100

INTERIM EARNINGS (Per Share):

Qtr.	Mar.	June	Sept.	Dec.
1999	d0.30	d0.54	...	...

INTERIM DIVIDENDS (Per Share):

Amt.	Decl.	Ex.	Rec.	Pay.
2-for-1	4/08/99	5/17/99	5/03/99	5/14/99

CAPITALIZATION (12/31/98):

	($000)	(%)
Capital Lease Obligations..	2,006	6.2
Common & Surplus	30,301	93.8
Total	32,306	100.0

RECENT DEVELOPMENTS: For the three months ended 6/30/99, net loss totaled $13.1 million compared with a loss of $3.9 million in the previous year. Results in the current period were hampered by one-time pre-tax charges of $6.4 million stemming from the acquisitions of shop.theglobe.com, Inc. and Attitude Networks, Ltd. Reve- nues jumped to $4.1 million from $779,812 a year earlier. Gross profit advanced to $2.4 million from $514,583 the year before. Operating loss was $13.3 million compared with a loss of $4.1 million the prior year. On 5/19/99, the Company completed a secondary offering which generated proceeds of $65.0 million.

BUSINESS

THEGLOBE.COM, INC. is an on- line community with approximately 2.5 million members in the United States and abroad. The Company's Web site is a destination on the Internet where users are able to per- sonalize their on-line experience by publishing their own content and interacting with others having similar interests. TGLO provides various free services, including home page build- ing, discussion forums, chat rooms, e- mail and electronic commerce. Addi- tionally, the Company provides its users with news, business informa- tion, real-time stock quotes, weather, movie and music reviews, multi- player games and personals. The Company generates revenues prima- rily by selling advertisements, spon- sorship placements within its site, development fees and, to a lesser extent, from electronic commerce rev- enues and the sale of membership subscriptions for enhanced services.

ANNUAL FINANCIAL DATA

	12/31/98	12/31/97	12/31/96	12/31/95
Earnings Per Share	☐ d3.37	d1.56	d0.33	d0.03
Cash Flow Per Share	d3.22	d1.54	d0.31	d0.02
Tang. Book Val. Per Share	1.47	7.52	0.35	...
INCOME STATEMENT (IN THOUSANDS):				
Total Revenues	5,510	770	229	27
Costs & Expenses	21,653	4,593	954	82
Depreciation & Amort.	715	60	48	11
Operating Income	d16,859	d3,883	d772	d66
Net Interest Inc./(Exp.)	892	335	22	...
Income Before Income Taxes	d15,967	d3,548	d750	d66
Income Taxes	79	36	...	...
Net Income	☐ d16,046	d3,584	d750	d66
Cash Flow	d15,330	d3,524	d703	d55
Average Shs. Outstg.	4,762	2,294	2,250	2,250
BALANCE SHEET (IN THOUSANDS):				
Cash & Cash Equivalents	30,149	18,874	757	...
Total Current Assets	32,833	19,129	826	...
Net Property	3,563	326	137	...
Total Assets	38,130	19,462	973	...
Total Current Liabilities	5,824	2,011	178	...
Long-Term Obligations	2,006	99	...	...
Net Stockholders' Equity	30,301	17,352	795	...
Net Working Capital	27,009	17,117	648	...
Year-end Shs. Outstg.	20,625	2,309	2,250	...
STATISTICAL RECORD:				
Debt/Total Assets %	5.3	0.5	...	...
Price Range	48½-13½	...	...	...

Statistics are as originally reported. Adj. for 2-for-1 stk. split, 5/14/99. ☐ Incl. non- recurr. chrg. of $1.4 million.

THESTREET.COM, INC.

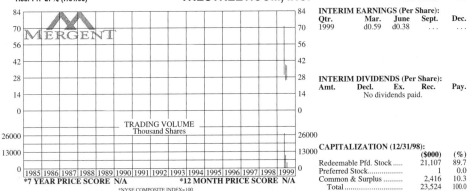

INTERIM EARNINGS (Per Share):

Qtr.	Mar.	June	Sept.	Dec.
1999	d0.59	d0.38	. . .	. . .

INTERIM DIVIDENDS (Per Share):

Amt.	Decl.	Ex.	Rec.	Pay.
	No dividends paid.			

CAPITALIZATION (12/31/98):

	($000)	(%)
Redeemable Pfd. Stock	21,107	89.7
Preferred Stock	1	0.0
Common & Surplus	2,416	10.3
Total	23,524	100.0

*7 YEAR PRICE SCORE N/A   *12 MONTH PRICE SCORE N/A
*NYSE COMPOSITE INDEX=100

RECENT DEVELOPMENTS: On 5/11/99, TSCM commenced an initial public offering of 5.5 million shares of its common stock at $19.00 per share. The IPO resulted in net proceeds of approximately $94.8 million. For the three months ended 6/30/99, the Company reported a net loss of $6.8 million compared with a loss of $4.7 million a year earlier. Total net revenues tripled to $3.3 million from $1.1 million in the previous year. Advertising revenues soared to $1.7 million from $586,000 a year ago. During the second quarter of 1999, 83 companies purchased advertising or sponsorships on TSCM's Web site versus 44 companies during the first quarter of 1999. Subscription revenues jumped to $934,000 from $448,000 the prior year. Gross profit totaled $1.2 million compared with $332,000 the year before. Loss from operations was $7.7 million versus a loss of $4.6 million in 1998.

BUSINESS

THESTREET.COM, INC. is a Web-based provider of original, timely and comprehensive financial news, commentary and information aimed at helping readers make informed investment decisions. The Company's editorial team, comprised of more than 65 experienced financial journalists and two dozen outside contributors, publishes approximately 40 original news stories and commentaries throughout each business day, including columns by James J. Cramer, Herb Greenberg and Adam Lashinsky. At 6/30/99, the Company had approximately 66,000 subscribers. The Company has established strategic alliances with Yahoo!, America Online, The New York Times Co., Fox News Network, Intuit, 3Com, E*TRADE, and DLJdirect, among others.

ANNUAL FINANCIAL DATA

	12/31/98	12/31/97	12/31/96
Earnings Per Share	d2.13	d0.95	d0.29
Cash Flow Per Share	d1.88	d0.92	d0.28
Tang. Book Val. Per Share	0.18	. . .	. . .
INCOME STATEMENT (IN THOUSANDS):			
Total Revenues	4,623	589	. . .
Costs & Expenses	20,510	5,789	1,697
Depreciation & Amort.	245	159	15
Operating Income	d16,131	d5,359	d1,712
Net Interest Inc./(Exp.)	d227	d406	d22
Net Income	d16,358	d5,764	d1,733
Cash Flow	d17,565	d5,606	d1,718
Average Shs. Outstg.	8,575	6,061	6,061
BALANCE SHEET (IN THOUSANDS):			
Cash & Cash Equivalents	24,612	157	. . .
Total Current Assets	26,774	315	. . .
Net Property	600	496	. . .
Total Assets	27,581	911	. . .
Total Current Liabilities	3,856	1,658	. . .
Long-Term Obligations	. . .	6,335	. . .
Net Stockholders' Equity	2,417	d7,157	. . .
Net Working Capital	22,918	d1,343	. . .
Year-end Shs. Outstg.	13,764	6,061	. . .
STATISTICAL RECORD:			
Debt/Total Assets %	. . .	695.5	. . .
Statistics are as originally reported.			

REVENUES

(12/31/1998)	($000)	(%)
Advertising		
Revenues	2,544	55.0
Subscription		
Revenues	1,685	36.5
Other Revenues	394	8.5
Total	4,623	100.0

OFFICERS:
K. W. English, Chmn., Pres., C.E.O.
P. Kothari, V.P., C.F.O.
M. S. Zuckert, V.P., Gen. Couns.

PRINCIPAL OFFICE: Two Rector Street, 14th Floor, New York, NY 10006

TELEPHONE NUMBER: (212) 271-4004
FAX: (212) 271-4005
WEB: www.thestreet.com

NO. OF EMPLOYEES: 138

SHAREHOLDERS: N/A

ANNUAL MEETING: N/A

INCORPORATED: DE, May, 1998

INSTITUTIONAL HOLDINGS:
No. of Institutions: 4
Shares Held: 60,103
% Held: 0.3

INDUSTRY: Data processing and preparation (SIC: 7374)

TRANSFER AGENT(S): American Stock Transfer & Trust Company, New York, NY

THINK NEW IDEAS, INC.

YIELD ...
P/E RATIO ...

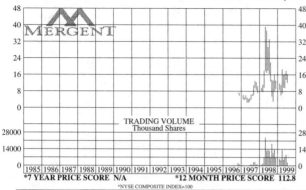

*7 YEAR PRICE SCORE N/A   *12 MONTH PRICE SCORE 112.8

INTERIM EARNINGS (Per Share):

Qtr.	Sept.	Dec.	Mar.	June
1996-97	d0.06	d0.19	d0.21	d1.17
1997-98	0.01	0.06	0.10	d4.54
1998-99	d0.17	d0.20	d0.18	...

INTERIM DIVIDENDS (Per Share):

Amt.	Decl.	Ex.	Rec.	Pay.
	No dividends paid.			

CAPITALIZATION (6/30/98):

	($000)	(%)
Capital Lease Obligations..	261	0.8
Common & Surplus	32,503	99.2
Total	32,764	100.0

RECENT DEVELOPMENTS: On 6/25/99, the Company agreed to be acquired by AnswerThink Consulting Group for approximately $231.0 million. The transaction is expected to close in the third quarter of 1999, subject to approval. For the quarter ended 3/31/99, THNK incurred a net loss of $1.6 million compared with net income of $660,257 in the equivalent 1998 quarter. Revenues were $12.8 million, up 16.9% from $11.0 million a year earlier. The decline in earnings was primarily attributed to a massive increase in expenses. During the quarter, THNK acquired Envision Group, a full-service Internet marketing and consulting firm, headquartered in Torrance, California. The purchase price for the acquisition included an initial payment of $3.5 million in THNK common stock and a potential earn-out, based on performance, of no more than an additional $5.5 million. In May, THNK was selected by JB Oxford Holdings, Inc., a provider of discount on-line brokerage services to clients nationwide, to design and implement its strategic marketing campaign.

BUSINESS

THINK NEW IDEAS, INC. provides integrated marketing, communications and technology services enabling clients to utilize the Internet and other interactive technologies to enhance their competitive positions. The Company's technology encompasses multiple system architectures, programming languages, broadband technologies, digital media applications, and communication networks utilizing Internet, intranet and extranet technologies. The Company's proprietary Internet and intranet tools include WEBMECHANIC, E-CORP, ASAP, and X-TRACKER. The Company maintains offices in New York, Los Angeles, San Francisco, Seattle, Stoneham (MA), Atlanta, London, and Sophia, Bulgaria.

ANNUAL FINANCIAL DATA

	6/30/98	6/30/97	6/30/96	6/30/95	6/30/94
Earnings Per Share	① d4.36	① d1.63	① d0.32	...	...
Cash Flow Per Share	d3.92	d1.28	d0.42	...	...
Tang. Book Val. Per Share	1.58	1.49	...	0.58	...
INCOME STATEMENT (IN THOUSANDS):					
Total Revenues	42,644	17,437	9,823	9,556	8,479
Costs & Expenses	67,229	23,295	10,389	8,894	8,609
Depreciation & Amort.	2,827	1,619	372	257	418
Operating Income	d27,412	d7,477	d937	405	d549
Net Interest Inc./(Exp.)	199	152	d373	d122	d82
Income Before Income Taxes	d27,213	d7,325	d1,274	290	d623
Income Taxes	340	246	141	232	cr104
Net Income	① d27,553	① d7,571	① d1,415	58	d519
Cash Flow	d24,726	d5,952	d1,043	314	d101
Average Shs. Outstg.	6,315	4,638	2,507	...	...
BALANCE SHEET (IN THOUSANDS):					
Cash & Cash Equivalents	7,654	4,773	430	334	...
Total Current Assets	26,256	17,121	3,342	2,666	...
Net Property	5,682	2,286	699	446	...
Total Assets	52,253	21,402	7,109	3,268	...
Total Current Liabilities	19,386	9,041	3,000	2,985	...
Long-Term Obligations	261	780	2,858	...	...
Net Stockholders' Equity	32,503	11,374	1,230	283	...
Net Working Capital	6,869	8,079	342	d319	...
Year-end Shs. Outstg.	8,434	6,537	2,895	492	488
STATISTICAL RECORD:					
Operating Profit Margin %	...	...	...	4.2	...
Net Profit Margin %	...	...	...	0.6	...
Return on Equity %	...	...	...	20.4	...
Return on Assets %	...	...	...	1.8	...
Debt/Total Assets %	0.5	3.6	40.2	...	...
Price Range	39¼-3	13-2½	7⅜-5⅞	...	...

Statistics are as originally reported. ① Incl. non-recurr. chrgs. $29.2 mill., 6/98; $1.7 mill., 6/97; $676,198, 6/96.

OFFICERS:
R. Bloom, Chmn., C.E.O.
M. Epstein, C.F.O., Sec.

PRINCIPAL OFFICE: 45 West 36th Street, 12th Floor, New York, NY 10018

TELEPHONE NUMBER: (212) 629-6800
WEB: www.thinkinc.com
NO. OF EMPLOYEES: 418 full-time; 56 part-time
SHAREHOLDERS: 166 shareholders of record; 400 approx. beneficial owners
ANNUAL MEETING: In Jan.
INCORPORATED: DE, Jan., 1996

INSTITUTIONAL HOLDINGS:
No. of Institutions: 19
Shares Held: 1,563,515
% Held: 15.5
INDUSTRY: Business services, nec (SIC: 7389)
TRANSFER AGENT(S): Continental Stock Transfer & Trust Company, New York, NY

NASDAQ SYMBOL COMS
Rec. Pr. 24⅛ (7/31/99)

3COM CORPORATION

YIELD	...
P/E RATIO	21.9

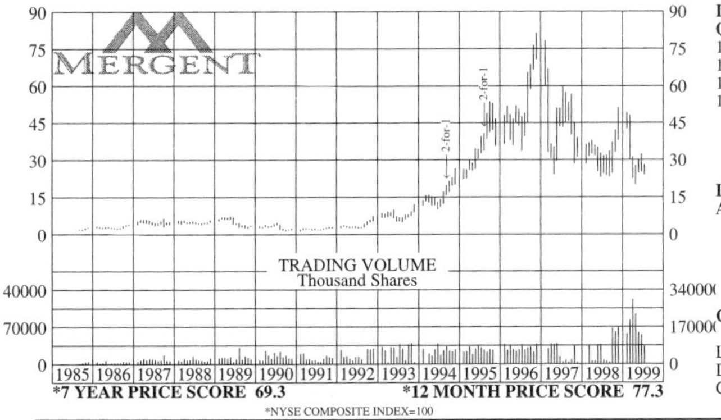
MERGENT
2-for-1
2-for-1
TRADING VOLUME
Thousand Shares
1985 1986 1987 1988 1989 1990 1991 1992 1993 1994 1995 1996 1997 1998 1999
*7 YEAR PRICE SCORE 69.3
*12 MONTH PRICE SCORE 77.3
*NYSE COMPOSITE INDEX=100

INTERIM EARNINGS (Per Share):

Qtr.	Aug.	Nov.	Feb.	May
1995-96	0.38	0.09	0.42	0.17
1996-97	0.52	0.57	0.47	0.48
1997-98	d0.43	0.04	0.04	0.17
1998-99	0.26	0.36	0.24	0.24

INTERIM DIVIDENDS (Per Share):

Amt.	Decl.	Ex.	Rec.	Pay.
		No dividends paid.		

CAPITALIZATION (5/31/98):

	($000)	(%)
Long-Term Debt	35,878	1.2
Deferred Income Tax	48,752	1.7
Common & Surplus	2,807,495	97.1
Total	2,892,125	100.0

RECENT DEVELOPMENTS: For the fiscal year ended 5/28/99, net income surged to $403.9 million from $30.2 million in the prior year. Earnings for fiscal 1999 included a pre-tax charge of $12.7 million for purchased in-process technology associated with the acquisitions of Smartcode Technologie, certain assests of ICS Networking, Inc. and NBX Corporation, and a net pre-tax credit of $21.8 million related to changes in previously recorded merger and restructuring expenses. Earnings for fiscal 1998 included a purchased in-process technology charge of $8.4 million associated with the acquisition of Lanworks and a net charge of $253.7 million primarily related to U.S. Robotics merger-related activities and the disposition of real estate. Sales advanced 6.5% to $5.77 billion from $5.42 billion the year before. On 7/27/99, COMS announced Transcend Network Control Services V1.1 for Windows NT, a tightly integrated suite of managment applications for the Company's networking system.

BUSINESS

3COM CORPORATION is a computer networking company, providing multi-vendor connectivity and information sharing for workgroups, departments and corporate environments. The Company designs, manufactures, markets and supports a wide range of networked client-server systems based on industry standards and an open systems architecture. 3Com's computer networking systems consist of products in three broad product categories: client-server systems, which include network operating software, dedicated workgroup servers and network workstations; internetwork or bridges and network control servers; and transmission products, which include network adapters, multi-media transmission systems and transceivers. COMS acquired Synernetics, Inc. and Centrum Communication, Inc. in the fiscal year ending 5/31/94 and Chipcom Corp. in 10/95. On 6/12/97, the Company completed the acquisition of U.S. Robotics Corp.

ANNUAL FINANCIAL DATA

	5/31/98	5/31/97	5/31/96	5/31/95	5/31/94	5/31/93	5/31/92
Earnings Per Share 1	**0.08**	**2.02**	**1.01**	**0.87**	**d0.23**	**0.31**	**0.04**
Cash Flow Per Share	**0.92**	**2.78**	**1.52**	**1.18**	**0.02**	**0.50**	**0.23**
Tang. Book Val. Per Share	**7.82**	**8.51**	**5.80**	**3.36**	**2.16**	**2.09**	**1.80**
INCOME STATEMENT (IN MILLIONS):							
Total Revenues	5,420.4	3,147.1	2,327.1	1,295.3	827.0	617.2	408.4
Costs & Expenses	5,020.5	2,443.2	1,934.5	1,053.1	793.4	531.1	381.4
Depreciation & Amort.	300.3	140.5	91.0	46.7	30.6	25.1	21.6
Operating Income	99.6	563.4	301.7	195.5	2.9	60.9	5.5
Income Before Income Taxes	116.5	584.3	308.5	198.4	19.5	60.2	5.2
Income Taxes	86.3	210.3	130.6	72.7	48.2	21.7	2.6
Equity Earnings/Minority Int.	...	...	...	...	...	...	1.5
Net Income 1	30.2	374.0	177.9	125.7	d28.7	38.6	4.2
Cash Flow	330.5	514.5	268.8	172.4	1.9	63.7	25.7
Average Shs. Outstg. (000)	360,262	185,316	176,517	145,618	125,240	126,496	112,752
BALANCE SHEET (IN MILLIONS):							
Cash & Cash Equivalents	1,076.1	889.9	499.3	323.5	129.7	117.2	78.7
Total Current Assets	3,134.7	1,831.3	1,239.7	707.6	361.1	304.4	228.6
Net Property	858.8	377.3	246.7	108.2	67.0	55.2	53.3
Total Assets	4,080.5	2,266.3	1,525.1	839.7	444.3	367.6	293.9
Total Current Liabilities	1,183.9	597.1	414.5	263.7	162.5	108.2	87.1
Long-Term Obligations	35.9	110.0	110.0	110.0	...	...	...
Net Stockholders' Equity	2,807.5	1,517.5	978.8	464.9	280.8	258.3	199.0
Net Working Capital	1,950.8	1,234.2	825.2	443.9	198.5	196.2	141.5
Year-end Shs. Outstg. (000)	358,870	178,374	168,800	138,462	130,104	123,400	110,392
STATISTICAL RECORD:							
Operating Profit Margin %	1.8	17.9	13.0	15.1	0.4	9.9	1.3
Net Profit Margin %	0.6	11.9	7.6	9.7	...	6.2	1.0
Return on Equity %	1.1	24.6	18.2	27.0	...	14.9	2.1
Return on Assets %	0.7	16.5	11.7	15.0	...	10.5	1.4
Debt/Total Assets %	0.9	4.9	7.2	13.1	...	...	...
Price Range	78¼-24	81⅜-33½	53⅝-22³⁄16	26⅝-10¹⁄16	12⅛-4¹⁵⁄16	7½-2⁷⁄16	3³⁄16-1⅜
P/E Ratio	N.M.	40.3-16.6	53.1-22.0	30.8-11.6	...	24.6-7.9	82.9-36.1

Statistics are as originally reported. Adj. for stk. splits: 2-for-1, 8/25/95; 2-for-1, 8/31/94

1 Incl. non-recurr. chrg. 5/31/98: $262.2 mill.; 5/31/97: $6.6 mill.; 5/31/96: $122.3 mill.; 5/31/95: $64.1 mill.; 5/31/94: $134.5 mill.; 5/31/93: $1.3 mill.; 5/31/92: $10.4 mill.

OFFICERS:
E. A. Benhamou, Chmn., C.E.O.
C. Cowell, Vice-Chmn.
B. L. Claflin, Pres., C.O.O.
C. B. Paisley, C.F.O., Sr. V.P., Fin.

INVESTOR CONTACT: Shirley Stacy, (408) 326-6301

PRINCIPAL OFFICE: 5400 Bayfront Plaza, Santa Clara, CA 95052

TELEPHONE NUMBER: (408) 326-5000
FAX: (408) 326-5001
WEB: www.3com.com

NO. OF EMPLOYEES: 12,920

SHAREHOLDERS: 7,100 (approx.)

ANNUAL MEETING: In Sept.

INCORPORATED: DE, Jun., 1979; reincorp., CA, Jun., 1997

INSTITUTIONAL HOLDINGS:
No. of Institutions: 372
Shares Held: 160,572,478
% Held: 44.4

INDUSTRY: Computer peripheral equipment, nec (SIC: 3577)

TRANSFER AGENT(S): Boston EquiServe, Boston, MA

TICKETMASTER ONLINE-CITYSEARCH, INC.

YIELD ...
P/E RATIO ...

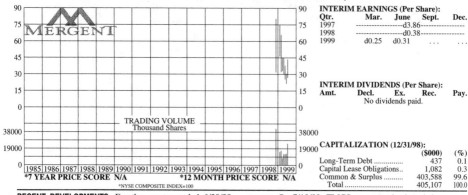

INTERIM EARNINGS (Per Share):

Qtr.	Mar.	June	Sept.	Dec.
1997	----------------d3.86----------------			
1998	----------------d0.38----------------			
1999	d0.25	d0.31	...	...

INTERIM DIVIDENDS (Per Share):

Amt.	Decl.	Ex.	Rec.	Pay.
	No dividends paid.			

CAPITALIZATION (12/31/98):

	($000)	(%)
Long-Term Debt	437	0.1
Capital Lease Obligations..	1,082	0.3
Common & Surplus	403,588	99.6
Total	405,107	100.0

RECENT DEVELOPMENTS: For the quarter ended 6/30/99, the Company reported a net loss of $22.9 million versus a net loss of $18.4 million in the comparable period of 1998. Results for the 1998 quarter are pro forma to reflect the merger of Ticketmaster Online and CitySearch. Total revenues almost tripled to $25.5 million from $8.9 million the year before. Revenues were enhanced by the growth in ticketing operations revenue to $17.8 million from $3.7 million, due to high profile concerts as well as sporting events. On 7/19/99, TMCS announced a broad, long-term relationship in which the Company will buy the entertainment city guide portion of MSN™ Sidewalk® for a combination of TMCS stock and warrants. TMCS will develop a version of its CitySearch local arts and entertainment city guide service to be delivered to consumers through a newly created MSN local channel and its current channel on MSN.com. Also, on 6/14/99, TMCS acquired Match.com, Inc., an Internet personals company.

BUSINESS

TICKETMASTER ONLINE-CITYSEARCH, INC. has combined CitySearch and Ticketmaster Online to create a major provider of local city guides, local advertising and live event ticketing on the Internet. The Company offers consumers up-to-date information on live entertainment events and a convenient means of purchasing tickets and related merchandise on the Web for live events in 43 states and in Canada and the United Kingdom. Consumers can access the Ticketmaster Online service at www.ticketmaster.com and from CitySearch owned and operated city guides at www.citysearch.com through numerous direct links from banners and event profiles. Ticketmaster Online is the exclusive agent for Ticketmaster Corp., a provider of live event automated ticketing services in the US, for the on-line sale of tickets to live events presented by Ticketmaster Corp.'s clients. On 3/29/99, the Company completed the acquisition of CityAuction Inc., a person-to-person on-line auction community. On 6/14/99, TMCS acquired Match.com, Inc., an Internet personals company.

ANNUAL FINANCIAL DATA

	12/31/98	12/31/97	12/31/96	12/31/95
Earnings Per Share	d0.38	d3.86	d1.58	d0.04
Cash Flow Per Share	...	d3.47	d1.50	d0.04
Tang. Book Val. Per Share	1.45	...	...	...
INCOME STATEMENT (IN THOUSANDS):				
Total Revenues	27,873	6,184	203	...
Costs & Expenses	24,784	39,169	13,568	308
Depreciation & Amort.	17,411	3,756	747	5
Operating Income	d14,322	d36,741	d14,112	d313
Net Interest Inc./(Exp.)	54	223	217	5
Income Before Income Taxes	d14,268	d36,518	d13,895	d308
Income Taxes	2,951	8	2	...
Net Income	d17,219	d36,526	d13,897	d308
Cash Flow	192	d32,770	d13,150	d303
Average Shs. Outstg.	45,201	9,452	8,786	7,895
BALANCE SHEET (IN THOUSANDS):				
Cash & Cash Equivalents	106,910	25,227	7,527	...
Total Current Assets	111,189	25,639	7,810	...
Net Property	5,893	6,016	3,645	...
Total Assets	416,725	31,655	13,370	...
Total Current Liabilities	11,618	6,264	3,553	...
Long-Term Obligations	1,519	1,340	82	...
Net Stockholders' Equity	403,588	d47,911	d11,943	...
Net Working Capital	99,571	19,375	4,257	...
Year-end Shs. Outstg.	71,459	9,540	8,814	...
STATISTICAL RECORD:				
Debt/Total Assets %	0.4	4.2	0.6	...
Price Range	80½-31¹³/₁₆	...	...	...
Statistics are as originally reported.				

OFFICERS:
A. Citron, Chmn.
C. Conn, C.E.O.
T. Layton, Pres., Treas.
B. Ramberg, C.F.O., Sec., V.P.

PRINCIPAL OFFICE: 790 E. Colorado Boulevard, Suite 200, Pasadena, CA 91101

TELEPHONE NUMBER: (626) 405-0050
FAX: (626) 405-9929
WEB: www.ticketmaster.com

NO. OF EMPLOYEES: 608

SHAREHOLDERS: N/A

ANNUAL MEETING: N/A

INCORPORATED: DE, Sep., 1998

INSTITUTIONAL HOLDINGS:
No. of Institutions: 62
Shares Held: 6,506,275
% Held: 9.4

INDUSTRY: Data processing and preparation (SIC: 7374)

TRANSFER AGENT(S): Chase Mellon Shareholder Services, L.L.C., Ridgefield Park, NJ

TMP WORLDWIDE INC.

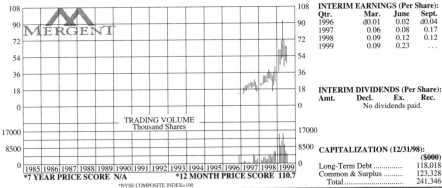

TRADING VOLUME
Thousand Shares

| | 1985 | 1986 | 1987 | 1988 | 1989 | 1990 | 1991 | 1992 | 1993 | 1994 | 1995 | 1996 | 1997 | 1998 | 1999 |

*7 YEAR PRICE SCORE N/A   ***12 MONTH PRICE SCORE 110.7**

*NYSE COMPOSITE INDEX=100

INTERIM EARNINGS (Per Share):

Qtr.	Mar.	June	Sept.	Dec.
1996	d0.01	0.02	d0.04	d2.61
1997	0.06	0.08	0.17	0.08
1998	0.09	0.12	0.12	d0.18
1999	0.09	0.23	...	...

INTERIM DIVIDENDS (Per Share):

Amt.	Decl.	Ex.	Rec.	Pay.
	No dividends paid.			

CAPITALIZATION (12/31/98):

	($000)	(%)
Long-Term Debt	118,018	48.9
Common & Surplus	123,328	51.1
Total	241,346	100.0

RECENT DEVELOPMENTS: For the three months ended 6/30/99, net income advanced 29.6% to $8.7 million from $6.7 million in the corresponding period of the previous year. The 1999 results include pre-tax merger and integration costs of $3.3 million. Total gross billings grew 4.2% to $417.4 million from $400.8 million in the prior-year quarter. Total commissions and fees increased 16.7% to $157.0 million from $134.6 million. Recruitment advertising commissions and fees totaled $43.3 million compared with $43.2 million the year before, while yellow page commissions and fees remained relatively flat at $26.6 million. Internet commissions and fees more than doubled to $26.0 million from $11.0 million the prior year. Search and selection commissions and fees increased 11.0% to $47.8 million from $43.0 million a year earlier, due to acquisitions in Europe and organic growth in Australia.

BUSINESS

TMP WORLDWIDE INC. provides advertising services including development of creative content, media planning, production and placement of corporate advertising, market research, direct marketing and other ancillary services and products. The Company primarily earns commission income for selling and placing yellow page and recruitment advertising for a large number of customers in many different industries, principally throughout North America, Europe and the Pacific Rim. In 1995, the Company began marketing Internet-based services as extensions of its core businesses. TMPW has several career Web sites that provide fee-based advertising services. The Company's Web sites include The Monster Board®, Online Career Center, Be the Boss and MedSearch. Each of these Web sites consists of a database of employment opportunities, resumes and a variety of other features.

BUSINESS LINE ANALYSIS

(12/31/1998)	REV (%)	INC (%)
Advertising	65.5	73.6
Internet	11.9	2.7
Search & Selection	22.6	(23.7)
Total	100.0	100.0

ANNUAL FINANCIAL DATA

	12/31/98	12/31/97	12/31/96	12/31/95	12/31/94	12/31/93
Earnings Per Share	① 0.14	0.38	① 0.11	0.15	d0.14	d0.27
Cash Flow Per Share	0.98	0.95	d2.21	0.49	0.18	d0.01
INCOME STATEMENT (IN THOUSANDS):						
Total Revenues	406,769	237,417	162,631	123,907	86,165	73,791
Costs & Expenses	356,511	196,150	187,965	98,365	73,134	66,732
Depreciation & Amort.	25,795	14,035	8,886	6,633	6,204	4,628
Operating Income	24,463	27,232	d34,220	18,909	6,827	2,431
Net Interest Inc./(Exp.)	d10,415	d8,772	d14,265	d10,894	d9,178	d7,652
Income Before Income Taxes	13,122	18,370	d48,649	8,165	d2,497	d5,607
Income Taxes	8,476	8,571	3,270	4,222	cr333	cr1,322
Equity Earnings/Minority Int.	d396	d176	d320	d714	d303	d341
Net Income	① 4,250	9,623	① d52,239	3,229	d2,467	d4,626
Cash Flow	30,045	23,535	d43,563	9,652	3,527	d208
Average Shs. Outstg.	30,673	24,735	19,732	19,516	19,226	17,772
BALANCE SHEET (IN THOUSANDS):						
Cash & Cash Equivalents	28,912	5,937	898	2,719	2,359	...
Total Current Assets	343,356	288,363	212,650	180,516	134,313	...
Net Property	53,525	37,760	20,562	11,937	15,392	...
Total Assets	608,059	495,206	331,753	258,094	198,965	...
Total Current Liabilities	359,517	282,496	224,577	186,247	146,124	...
Long-Term Obligations	118,018	115,852	70,799	88,070	72,008	...
Net Stockholders' Equity	123,328	96,858	31,295	d21,328	d24,320	...
Net Working Capital	d16,161	5,867	d11,927	d5,731	d11,811	...
Year-end Shs. Outstg.	30,013	26,083	23,393	19,064	19,064	...
STATISTICAL RECORD:						
Operating Profit Margin %	6.0	11.5	...	15.3	7.9	3.3
Net Profit Margin %	1.0	4.1	...	2.6	...	...
Return on Equity %	3.4	9.9	...	...	...	...
Return on Assets %	0.7	1.9	...	1.3	...	...
Debt/Total Assets %	19.4	23.4	21.3	34.1	36.2	...
Price Range	42⅝-15½	28¾-12⅞	14¼-12½	...	...	...
P/E Ratio	304.2-110.6	75.6-33.9	129.4-113.5	...	...	...

Statistics are as originally reported. ① Incl. non-recurr. chrg. $21.5 mill., 12/31/98; $52.0 mill., 12/31/96

OFFICERS:
A. J. McKelvey, Chmn., C.E.O.
T. G. Collison, Vice-Chmn., Sec.
B. W. Catalane, C.F.O.
M. F. Olesnyckyj, V.P., General Counsel

PRINCIPAL OFFICE: 1633 Broadway, 33rd Floor, New York, NY 10019

TELEPHONE NUMBER: (212) 977-4200
FAX: (212) 956-2142
WEB: www.tmpw.com

NO. OF EMPLOYEES: 5,200 (approx.)

SHAREHOLDERS: 498

ANNUAL MEETING: In May

INCORPORATED: DE, Aug., 1996

INSTITUTIONAL HOLDINGS:
No. of Institutions: 119
Shares Held: 16,037,875
% Held: 47.4

INDUSTRY: Advertising agencies (SIC: 7311)

TRANSFER AGENT(S): The Bank of New York, New York, NY.

TMSSEQUOIA

YIELD ...
P/E RATIO ...

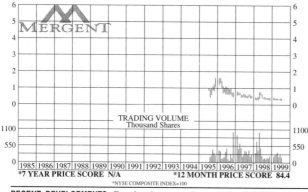

INTERIM EARNINGS (Per Share):

Qtr.	Nov.	Feb.	May	Aug.
1995-96	0.02	0.03	d0.01	Nil
1996-97	d0.01	0.01	Nil	Nil
1997-98	0.01	0.01	Nil	0.01
1998-99	d0.05	0.01	Nil	...

INTERIM DIVIDENDS (Per Share):

Amt.	Decl.	Ex.	Rec.	Pay.
	No dividends paid.			

TRADING VOLUME
Thousand Shares

1985 1986 1987 1988 1989 1990 1991 1992 1993 1994 1995 1996 1997 1998 1999

*7 YEAR PRICE SCORE N/A   *12 MONTH PRICE SCORE 84.4

*NYSE COMPOSITE INDEX=100

CAPITALIZATION (8/31/98):

	($000)	(%)
Long-Term Debt	310	6.7
Capital Lease Obligations..	79	1.7
Common & Surplus	4,245	91.6
Total	4,634	100.0

RECENT DEVELOPMENTS: For the three months ended 5/31/99, the Company reported net income of $41,935 compared with $24,211 in the previous year. Earnings benefited from the implementation of cost reduction and productivity enhancement initiatives. Total revenue slid 20.8% to $1.4 million from $1.7 million a year earlier. Licensing and royalties revenue fell 18.9% to $839,360, while software development services revenue advanced 52.7% to $397,352. Revenue from document conversion services dropped 70.8% to $123,345, reflecting the Company's decision in May 1998 to focus on electronic publishing of documents and discontinue large back-file conversion of documents for imaging and database management. As of 5/31/99, the Company's cash amounted to $721,870, and its current ratio was 4.86.

BUSINESS

TMS, INC., which does business as TMSSequoia™, designs, develops and markets software tools and applications for Internet imaging, image capture, enhancement, viewing, and forms processing. The Company also provides software development and document conversion services to corporations and government organizations worldwide to assist in the migration from paper to electronic information systems. The Company's product and service clients include BancTec, Caere, Caterpillar, Diamond Head Software, EDS, General Dynamics, General Motors, Hewlett Packard, Learjet, Minolta, PricewaterhouseCoopers, Ricoh, Toro, the U.S. Navy and Army, The World Bank, Xerox, Yamaha and others.

ANNUAL FINANCIAL DATA

	8/31/98	8/31/97 ①	8/31/96	8/31/95	8/31/94	8/31/93	8/31/92
Earnings Per Share	0.04	Nil	0.03	0.08	0.04	0.05	d0.04
Cash Flow Per Share	0.09	0.05	0.06	0.11	0.06	0.06	d0.03
Tang. Book Val. Per Share	0.27	0.25	0.24	0.24	0.17	0.12	0.05
INCOME STATEMENT (IN THOUSANDS):							
Total Revenues	7,355	5,665	5,613	4,221	3,437	2,801	2,124
Costs & Expenses	6,143	5,018	5,022	3,539	2,905	2,209	2,307
Depreciation & Amort.	734	613	418	246	192	152	95
Operating Income	478	35	172	436	340	440	d278
Net Interest Inc./(Exp.)	d29	d8	d15	d6	3	d16	d38
Income Before Income Taxes	442	67	212	456	352	434	d316
Income Taxes	cr47	24	cr171	cr316	2	4	...
Net Income	489	44	383	771	351	430	d316
Cash Flow	1,223	656	802	1,018	542	582	d221
Average Shs. Outstg.	13,841	14,067	14,016	9,188	9,012	9,093	7,978
BALANCE SHEET (IN THOUSANDS):							
Cash & Cash Equivalents	492	426	542	114	240	167	88
Total Current Assets	2,748	2,563	2,481	1,326	1,109	822	582
Net Property	1,660	1,546	1,482	1,447	603	377	319
Total Assets	5,286	4,847	4,708	3,132	1,782	1,310	1,039
Total Current Liabilities	652	768	642	499	326	242	282
Long-Term Obligations	389	334	356	378	...	...	181
Net Stockholders' Equity	4,245	3,746	3,710	2,254	1,457	1,069	500
Net Working Capital	2,096	1,795	1,838	827	784	580	300
Year-end Shs. Outstg.	13,319	13,137	13,214	8,405	8,219	8,030	8,145
STATISTICAL RECORD:							
Operating Profit Margin %	6.5	0.6	3.1	10.3	9.9	15.7	...
Net Profit Margin %	6.6	0.8	6.8	18.3	10.2	15.4	...
Return on Equity %	11.5	1.2	10.3	34.2	24.1	40.2	...
Return on Assets %	9.3	0.9	8.1	24.6	19.7	32.8	...
Debt/Total Assets %	7.4	6.9	7.6	12.1	...	...	17.4
Price Range	³⁄₄-¹⁄₄	¹³⁄₁₆-³⁄₈	1⁵⁄₈-¹⁄₂	1⁵⁄₈-⁷⁄₁₆	...	...	...
P/E Ratio	19.5-6.5	...	54.0-15.6	20.3-5.5	...	...	...

Statistics are as originally reported. ① Fins incl. Sequoia Computer Corp., acq. in 1996.

OFFICERS:
D. R. Allen, Chmn., Pres., C.E.O.
D. D. Mosier, C.F.O.

INVESTOR CONTACT: Investor Relations,
(405) 377-0880

PRINCIPAL OFFICE: 206 West Sixth Avenue,
Stillwater, OK 74076

TELEPHONE NUMBER: (405) 377-0880
FAX: (405) 377-9288
WEB: www.tmssequoia.com

NO. OF EMPLOYEES: 63 full-time; 5 part-time

SHAREHOLDERS: 1,730 (approx.)

ANNUAL MEETING: In Jan.

INCORPORATED: OK, Apr., 1990

INSTITUTIONAL HOLDINGS:
No. of Institutions: 1
Shares Held: 24,800
% Held: 0.2

INDUSTRY: Prepackaged software (SIC: 7372)

TRANSFER AGENT(S): American Securities Transfer, Inc., Lakewood, CO

TUT SYSTEMS INC

YIELD ...
P/E RATIO ...

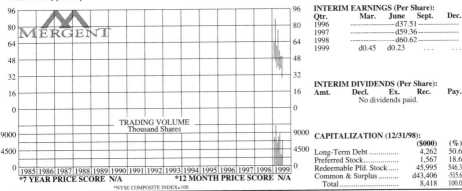

*7 YEAR PRICE SCORE N/A   *12 MONTH PRICE SCORE N/A

*NYSE COMPOSITE INDEX=100

INTERIM EARNINGS (Per Share):

Qtr.	Mar.	June	Sept.	Dec.
1996			d37.51	
1997			d59.36	
1998			d60.62	
1999	d0.45	d0.23	...	...

INTERIM DIVIDENDS (Per Share):

Amt.	Decl.	Ex.	Rec.	Pay.
	No dividends paid.			

CAPITALIZATION (12/31/98):

	($000)	(%)
Long-Term Debt	4,262	50.6
Preferred Stock.................	1,567	18.6
Redeemable Pfd. Stock	45,995	546.3
Common & Surplus	d43,406	-515.6
Total	8,418	100.0

RECENT DEVELOPMENTS: For the quarter ended 6/30/99, the Company reported a net loss of $2.7 million compared with a net loss of $3.8 million in the corresponding period of 1998. Total revenues leapt 88.8% to $5.0 million from $2.7 million in the prior year. Revenues benefited from strong demand for the Company's multi-tenant and service provider product lines. Product revenues nearly doubled to $4.7 million from $2.4 million in 1998. License and royalty revenues improved 8.3% to $275,000. Loss from operations amounted to $3.2 million versus a loss of $3.9 million a year earlier. The Company recently acquired PublicPort Inc., an Ann Arbor, Michigan-based networking company specializing in high-speed Internet applications for multi-tenant property owners. The acquisition is expected to accelerate TUT's product cycle and launch a subscriber management gateway system for service providers deploying Internet access tools.

BUSINESS

TUT SYSTEMS INC. designs, develops and markets advanced communications products that enable high-speed data access over the copper infrastructure of telephone companies, as well as the copper telephone wires in homes, businesses and other buildings. These products incorporate the Company's proprietary FASTCOPPER technology in a cost-effective, scalable and easy-to-deploy tool to exploit the underutilized bandwidth of copper telephone wires. The Company's products include EXPRESSO high bandwidth access multiplexers, associated modems and routers, XL ETHERNET extension products and integrated network management software. The Company's customers include large corporations, universities, independent telephone companies, Internet service providers, local exchange carriers, owners and operators of multiple dwelling units, and semiconductor, computer hardware and electronics manufacturers.

ANNUAL FINANCIAL DATA

	12/31/98	12/31/97	12/31/96
Earnings Per Share	d60.62	d59.36	d37.51
Cash Flow Per Share	d59.22	d57.90	d36.34
INCOME STATEMENT (IN THOUSANDS):			
Total Revenues	10,555	6,221	4,454
Costs & Expenses	24,109	15,326	8,876
Depreciation & Amort.	402	246	185
Operating Income	d13,956	d9,351	d4,607
Net Interest Inc./(Exp.)	d117	d61	d40
Income Before Income Taxes	d13,746	d9,156	d4,426
Income Taxes	1	1	1
Net Income	d13,747	d9,157	d4,427
Cash Flow	d15,929	d10,538	d5,379
Average Shs. Outstg.	269	182	148
BALANCE SHEET (IN THOUSANDS):			
Cash & Cash Equivalents	4,452	10,285	...
Total Current Assets	11,932	13,667	...
Net Property	1,790	1,345	...
Total Assets	15,257	15,168	...
Total Current Liabilities	4,759	2,601	...
Long-Term Obligations	4,262	140	...
Net Stockholders' Equity	d41,839	d26,444	...
Net Working Capital	7,173	11,066	...
Year-end Shs. Outstg.	1,445	1,316	1,240
STATISTICAL RECORD:			
Debt/Total Assets %	27.9	0.9	...

Statistics are as originally reported.

OFFICERS:
M. Taylor, Chmn., Sec.
S. D'Auria, Pres., C.E.O.
N. Caldwell, V.P., Fin., C.F.O.

PRINCIPAL OFFICE: 2495 Estand Way, Pleasant Hill, CA 94523

TELEPHONE NUMBER: (925) 682-6510
WEB: www.tutsys.com

NO. OF EMPLOYEES: 95 (avg.)

SHAREHOLDERS: 214

ANNUAL MEETING: In May

INCORPORATED: CA, Aug., 1983; reincorp., DE, Sep., 1998

INSTITUTIONAL HOLDINGS:
No. of Institutions: 26
Shares Held: 1,853,443
% Held: 16.9

INDUSTRY: Telephone and telegraph apparatus (SIC: 3661)

TRANSFER AGENT(S): American Stock Transfer & Trust Company, New York, NY

24/7 MEDIA, INC.

YIELD ...
P/E RATIO ...

*7 YEAR PRICE SCORE N/A   *12 MONTH PRICE SCORE 109.5
*NYSE COMPOSITE INDEX=100

INTERIM EARNINGS (Per Share):

Qtr.	Mar.	June	Sept.	Dec.
1997	d0.73	d1.32	d2.25	d0.59
1998	d0.76	d1.27	d0.51	d0.43
1999	d0.42	d0.37	...	...

INTERIM DIVIDENDS (Per Share):

Amt.	Decl.	Ex.	Rec.	Pay.
	No dividends paid.			

CAPITALIZATION (12/31/98):

	($000)	(%)
Capital Lease Obligations..	34	0.1
Common & Surplus	51,946	99.9
Total	51,980	100.0

RECENT DEVELOPMENTS: For the quarter ended 6/30/99, the Company reported a net loss of $7.2 million compared with a net loss of $10.0 million in the equivalent 1998 quarter. Revenues were $17.2 million, up from $4.0 million a year earlier. Increased revenues were driven by growth across TFSM's full range of Internet media offerings, which enabled TFSM to attract additional customers. On 8/10/99, TFSM agreed to acquire ConsumerNet.com, an on-line direct marketing and database company. In July, TFSM acquired Toronto-based ClickThrough Interactive, an Internet advertising sales network. ClickThrough represents more than 65 premium Canadian Web sites. Separately, TFSM acquired an email service, Sift, Inc., thus expanding its capabilities to include email-related services. Separately, TFSM partnered with NBC-Interactive Neighborhood to offer local market multimedia advertising for television and the Internet.

BUSINESS

24/7 MEDIA, INC. is an Internet advertising and direct marketing firm that enables both advertisers and Web publishers to capitalize on the many opportunities presented by Internet advertising, direct marketing and electronic commerce. TFSM generates revenue by selling advertisements and promotions for its Affiliated Web sites. Through its flagship networks, the Company represents more than 2.5 billion ad impressions per month on more than 30 high-profile sites globally. TFSM operates the 24/7 Network, a network of over 150 high-profile Affiliated Web sites to which TFSM delivered an aggregate of more than 900 million advertisements in December 1998; the ContentZone, a network of over 2,500 small to medium-sized Affiliated Web sites to which TFSM delivered an aggregate of more than 50 million advertisements in December 1998; and the 24/7 Media Europe Network, a network of over 60 Web sites that generated an aggregate of more than 200 million page views in December 1998, through TFSM's 60%-owned subsidiary, 24/7 Media Europe.

ANNUAL FINANCIAL DATA

	12/31/98	12/31/97	12/31/96	12/31/95
Earnings Per Share	d2.62	d4.88	d6.48	d2.78
Cash Flow Per Share	d1.96	d4.51	d6.17	d2.63
Tang. Book Val. Per Share	2.61	...	1.60	...
INCOME STATEMENT (IN THOUSANDS):				
Total Revenues	19,863	3,149	1,542	152
Costs & Expenses	38,918	7,951	7,981	1,261
Depreciation & Amort.	6,339	407	323	59
Operating Income	d25,394	d5,209	d6,762	d1,168
Net Interest Inc./(Exp.)	671	d96	d34	...
Income Before Income Taxes	d24,723	d5,306	d6,796	d1,168
Net Income	d24,723	d5,306	d6,796	d1,168
Cash Flow	d18,660	d4,899	d6,473	d1,109
Average Shs. Outstg.	9,533	1,087	1,049	421
BALANCE SHEET (IN THOUSANDS):				
Cash & Cash Equivalents	33,983	94	1,689	...
Total Current Assets	42,962	285	2,194	...
Net Property	2,022	591	1,678	...
Total Assets	62,716	1,039	3,951	...
Total Current Liabilities	10,736	1,450	2,201	...
Long-Term Obligations	34	2,317	...	...
Net Stockholders' Equity	51,946	d2,728	1,750	...
Net Working Capital	32,226	d1,165	d6	...
Year-end Shs. Outstg.	15,719	1,149	1,079	...
STATISTICAL RECORD:				
Debt/Total Assets %	0.1	223.0	...	...
Price Range	41¼-5	...	...	...
Statistics are as originally reported.				

OFFICERS:
R. T. Ammon, Chmn.
D. J. Moore, Pres., C.E.O.
C. A. Johns, Exec. V.P., C.F.O., Treas.

PRINCIPAL OFFICE: 1250 Broadway, New York, NY 10001

TELEPHONE NUMBER: (212) 231-7100
WEB: www.247media.com

NO. OF EMPLOYEES: 200 (avg.)

SHAREHOLDERS: 300 (approx.)

ANNUAL MEETING: In June

INCORPORATED: DE, Jan., 1998

INSTITUTIONAL HOLDINGS:
No. of Institutions: 33
Shares Held: 5,197,666
% Held: 25.8

INDUSTRY: Advertising agencies (SIC: 7311)

TRANSFER AGENT(S): The Bank of New York, New York, NY

UBID INC.

YIELD ...
P/E RATIO ...

INTERIM EARNINGS (Per Share):

Qtr.	Mar.	June	Sept.	Dec.
1997	------------------d0.04------------------			
1998	------------------d1.36------------------			
1999	d0.37	d0.56	...	...

INTERIM DIVIDENDS (Per Share):

Amt.	Decl.	Ex.	Rec.	Pay.
	No dividends paid.			

TRADING VOLUME
Thousand Shares

*7 YEAR PRICE SCORE N/A   *12 MONTH PRICE SCORE N/A
*NYSE COMPOSITE INDEX=100

CAPITALIZATION (12/31/98):

	($000)	(%)
Common & Surplus	18,633	100.0
Total	18,633	100.0

RECENT DEVELOPMENTS: For the three months ended 6/30/99, the Company reported a net loss of $5.2 million compared with a net loss of $993,000 in the corresponding period of the previous year. Net sales totaled $45.6 million compared with $6.8 million in the prior-year quarter. Gross profit totaled $4.0 million compared with $496,000 the year before. On 6/8/99, UBID's parent company, Creative Computers, Inc., completed the distribution to its stockholders of all of its 7,329,883 shares of UBID. The shareholders of Creative Computers received approximately 0.70488 shares of UBID for each share of Creative Computers held. On 7/23/99, UBID and Surplus Record, Inc., the world's largest directory of used and surplus machinery and equipment, formed an alliance to introduce real-time electronic bidding to industrial manufacturers throughout North America. On 8/2/99, UBID teamed up with Xerox Corporation to offer new and Xerox Certified Pre-Owned Copiers on-line.

BUSINESS

UBID INC. operates an on-line auction for excess merchandise. The Company offers closed-out and refurbished products to consumers and small- to medium-sized businesses. The auctions feature a rotating selection of brand name computer, consumer electronics and housewares, sports and recreation products, and jewelry, which typically sell at significant discounts to prices found at traditional retailers. The auctions are held seven days a week, offering on the average over 1,000 total items in each of its auctions.

ANNUAL FINANCIAL DATA

	12/31/98	① 12/31/97
Earnings Per Share	d1.36	d0.04
Cash Flow Per Share	d1.34	d0.04
Tang. Book Val. Per Share	2.04	...
INCOME STATEMENT (IN THOUSANDS):		
Total Revenues	48,232	9
Costs & Expenses	58,076	292
Depreciation & Amort.	155	4
Operating Income	d9,999	d287
Net Interest Inc./(Exp.)	d170	d26
Income Before Income Taxes	d10,169	d313
Net Income	d10,169	d313
Cash Flow	d10,014	d309
Average Shs. Outstg.	7,461	7,330
BALANCE SHEET (IN THOUSANDS):		
Cash & Cash Equivalents	26,053	...
Total Current Assets	34,106	31
Total Assets	34,625	358
Total Current Liabilities	12,661	...
Net Stockholders' Equity	18,633	d312
Net Working Capital	21,445	31
Year-end Shs. Outstg.	9,147	7,330
STATISTICAL RECORD:		
Price Range	189-30	...

Statistics are as originally reported. ① From inception April 1, 1997

OFFICERS:
G. K. Jones, Chmn., Pres., C.E.O.
T. E. Werner, V.P., C.F.O.

PRINCIPAL OFFICE: 2525 Busse Road, Elk Grove Village, IL 60007

TELEPHONE NUMBER: (847) 860-5000
FAX: (847) 616-0302
WEB: www.ubid.com
NO. OF EMPLOYEES: 74
SHAREHOLDERS: N/A
ANNUAL MEETING: In May
INCORPORATED: IL, Sep., 1997; reincorp., DE, Sep., 1997

INSTITUTIONAL HOLDINGS:
No. of Institutions: 24
Shares Held: 423,308
% Held: 4.8

INDUSTRY: Catalog and mail-order houses (SIC: 5961)

TRANSFER AGENT(S): LaSalle National Bank, Chicago, IL.

USINTERNETWORKING, INC.

YIELD ...
P/E RATIO ...

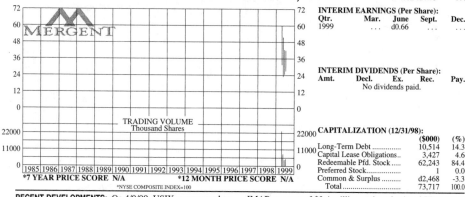

INTERIM EARNINGS (Per Share):

Qtr.	Mar.	June	Sept.	Dec.
1999	...	d0.66	...	...

INTERIM DIVIDENDS (Per Share):

Amt.	Decl.	Ex.	Rec.	Pay.
	No dividends paid.			

CAPITALIZATION (12/31/98):

	($000)	(%)
Long-Term Debt	10,514	14.3
Capital Lease Obligations..	3,427	4.6
Redeemable Pfd. Stock	62,243	84.4
Preferred Stock.................	1	0.0
Common & Surplus	d2,468	-3.3
Total	73,717	100.0

*7 YEAR PRICE SCORE N/A   *12 MONTH PRICE SCORE N/A

*NYSE COMPOSITE INDEX=100

RECENT DEVELOPMENTS: On 4/9/99, USIX commenced an initial public offering of 6.9 million shares of its common stock at $21.00 per share. The IPO resulted in net proceeds of approximately $132.8 million. For the three months ended 6/30/99, the Company reported a net loss of $23.6 million compared with a loss of $3.1 million a year earlier. Total revenue amounted to $6.7 million, comprised of IMAP revenue of $3.4 million and professional IT services revenue of $3.3 million. The Company was in its development stage during the same period in 1998 and generated no revenue. Operating loss totaled $23.9 million versus a loss of $3.1 million a year ago. For the six months ended 6/30/99, net loss totaled $41.3 million, while total revenue was $11.1 million.

BUSINESS

USINTERNETWORKING, INC. implements, operates, and supports packaged software applications that can be accessed and used over the Internet. The Company's Internet Managed Application Provider (IMAP) services are based on packaged applications from software vendors including Siebel, PeopleSoft, Sagent and BroadVision, and are designed for business functions such as sales force automation, customer support, e-commerce, and human resource and financial management. The Company implements these applications in its data centers, configures them to meet the needs of its customers, and packages them with security, Internet access, back-up and operational support.

ANNUAL FINANCIAL DATA

	12/31/98
Earnings Per Share	d60.96
Cash Flow Per Share	d55.87

INCOME STATEMENT (IN THOUSANDS):

Total Revenues	4,122
Costs & Expenses	31,082
Depreciation & Amort.	3,180
Operating Income	d30,140
Net Interest Inc./(Exp.)	d2,314
Net Income	d32,453
Cash Flow	d34,918
Average Shs. Outstg.	625

BALANCE SHEET (IN THOUSANDS):

Cash & Cash Equivalents	44,384
Total Current Assets	49,703
Net Property	21,640
Total Assets	106,516
Total Current Liabilities	27,152
Long-Term Obligations	13,941
Net Stockholders' Equity	d2,467
Net Working Capital	22,551
Year-end Shs. Outstg.	625

STATISTICAL RECORD:

Debt/Total Assets %	13.1

Statistics are as originally reported.

OFFICERS:
C. R. McCleary, Chmn., C.E.O.
S. E. McManus, Pres.
A. A. Stern, Exec. V.P., C.F.O.
W. T. Price, V.P., Sec., Gen. Couns.

INVESTOR CONTACT: Joanne Hellebrand Rasch, (410) 897-4532

PRINCIPAL OFFICE: One USi Plaza, Annapolis, MD 21401-7478

TELEPHONE NUMBER: (410) 897-4400
FAX: (410) 573-1906
WEB: www.usi.net

NO. OF EMPLOYEES: 450 (avg.)

SHAREHOLDERS: N/A

ANNUAL MEETING: N/A

INCORPORATED: DE, Jan., 1998

INSTITUTIONAL HOLDINGS:
No. of Institutions: 6
Shares Held: 201,235
% Held: 0.5

INDUSTRY: Data processing and preparation (SIC: 7374)

TRANSFER AGENT(S): American Stock Transfer & Trust Company, New York, NY

USWEB CORP.

NASDAQ SYMBOL USWB
Rec. Pr. 20¹⁵/₁₆ (7/31/99)

YIELD ...
P/E RATIO ...

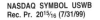

*7 YEAR PRICE SCORE N/A   ***12 MONTH PRICE SCORE 87.6**

*NYSE COMPOSITE INDEX=100

TRADING VOLUME Thousand Shares

INTERIM EARNINGS (Per Share):

Qtr.	Mar.	June	Sept.	Dec.
1997	d2.00	d3.43	d2.53	6.23
1998	d0.56	d1.81	d0.95	0.25
1999	d0.73	d0.29	...	...

INTERIM DIVIDENDS (Per Share):

Amt.	Decl.	Ex.	Rec.	Pay.
	No dividends paid.			

CAPITALIZATION (12/31/98):

	($000)	(%)
Capital Lease Obligations..	1,377	0.5
Common & Surplus	299,872	99.5
Total	301,249	100.0

RECENT DEVELOPMENTS: For the quarter ended 6/30/99, net loss amounted to $22.6 million compared with $61.1 million in the same period of 1998. Results included charges of $1.4 million in 1999 and $18.3 million in 1998 for acquired in-process technology. Revenues jumped 86.8% to $101.0 million from $54.0 million the prior year. Gross profit increased to $49.7 million, or 49.2% of net sales, from $7.2 million, or 13.3% the year before. Loss from operations was $22.7 million versus $60.0 million in 1998. USWB and Walgreens have completed an in-depth analysis of Walgreens' systems architecture, business process, supply-chain dynamics and brand, and are currently implementing the on-line pharmacy, which is expected to be launched in the fall at www.walgreens.com. The on-line pharmacy will be followed by the Walgreens on-line drug-store, which will offer non-perscription items and is scheduled for completion later this year.

BUSINESS

USWEB CORPORATION, also known as "USWeb/CKS," is a professional services firm with expertise in business strategy, marketing communications and Internet technology. The Company aims to help businesses differentiate their products and services, strengthen customer relationships, leverage human capital, and improve business efficiency in the digital economy. USBW provides a broad selection of services from brand development and advertising to business process automation and e-commerce tools, helping hundreds of businesses advance their marketing communications programs as well as their traditional IT and Internet systems. The Company is headquartered in Santa Clara, CA and has offices in Austria, Canada, France, Germany, Switzerland and the U.K.

ANNUAL FINANCIAL DATA

	12/31/98	12/31/97	12/31/96
Earnings Per Share	① d3.07	② d7.98	d0.53
Cash Flow Per Share	d1.74	d6.46	d0.52
Tang. Book Val. Per Share	1.88	1.41	...
INCOME STATEMENT (IN THOUSANDS):			
Total Revenues	228,600	19,278	1,820
Costs & Expenses	331,957	62,831	15,522
Depreciation & Amort.	81,487	10,940	263
Operating Income	d184,844	d54,493	d13,965
Net Interest Inc./(Exp.)	4,302	309	273
Income Before Income Taxes	d180,542	d58,184	d13,692
Income Taxes	7,739	...	...
Net Income	① d188,281	② d58,184	d13,692
Cash Flow	d106,794	d47,244	d13,429
Average Shs. Outstg.	61,329	7,312	26,017
BALANCE SHEET (IN THOUSANDS):			
Cash & Cash Equivalents	101,186	44,145	3,220
Total Current Assets	200,807	52,705	3,411
Net Property	18,880	6,202	1,084
Total Assets	403,174	79,250	7,482
Total Current Liabilities	101,925	12,189	3,338
Long-Term Obligations	1,377	372	436
Net Stockholders' Equity	299,872	66,689	d12,492
Net Working Capital	98,882	40,516	73
Year-end Shs. Outstg.	70,071	33,811	6,381
STATISTICAL RECORD:			
Debt/Total Assets %	0.3	0.5	5.8
Price Range	38³/₄-7³/₄	14⁵/₈-7¹/₁₆	...

Statistics are as originally reported. ① Incl. merger & integration costs $28.8 mill. and impairment of goodwill chrg. $11.1 mill. ② Incl. chrg. of $4 mill. for impair. of invested carried at cost.

QUARTERLY DATA

(12/31/98)($000)	REV	INC
1st	39,325	(15,255)
2nd	54,041	(61,112)
3rd	62,586	(27,765)
4th	72,648	(84,149)

OFFICERS:
M. Kvamme, Chmn.
R. Shaw, C.E.O.
T. Corey, Pres., C.O.O.
C. Aver, C.F.O.

PRINCIPAL OFFICE: 2880 Lakeside Drive, Suite 300, Santa Clara, CA 95054

TELEPHONE NUMBER: (408) 987-3200
WEB: www.usweb.com
NO. OF EMPLOYEES: 2,400
SHAREHOLDERS: 890 (approx.)
ANNUAL MEETING: In May
INCORPORATED: UT, Nov., 1995; reincorp., DE, Dec., 1997

V-ONE CORPORATION

YIELD ...
P/E RATIO ...

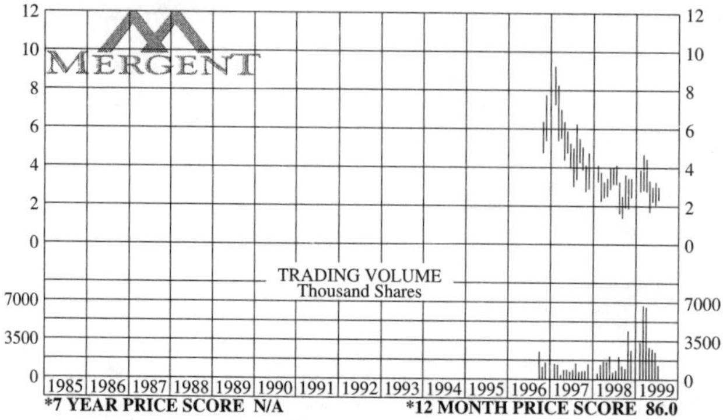

INTERIM EARNINGS (Per Share):

Qtr.	Mar.	Jun.	Sept.	Dec.
1996	d0.10	d0.34	d0.11	d0.11
1997	d0.07	d0.25	d0.03	d0.43
1998	d0.12	d0.02	d0.10	d0.16
1999	d0.13	d0.13	...	...

INTERIM DIVIDENDS (Per Share):

Amt.	Decl.	Ex.	Rec.	Pay.
		No dividends paid.		

TRADING VOLUME
Thousand Shares

1985 1986 1987 1988 1989 1990 1991 1992 1993 1994 1995 1996 1997 1998 1999
*7 YEAR PRICE SCORE N/A   *12 MONTH PRICE SCORE 86.0
*NYSE COMPOSITE INDEX=100

CAPITALIZATION (12/31/98):

	($000)	(%)
Capital Lease Obligations..	198	23.7
Common & Surplus	636	76.3
Total	834	100.0

RECENT DEVELOPMENTS: For the quarter ended 6/30/99, the Company reported a net loss of $2.2 million compared with a net loss of $2.6 million in the corresponding quarter the year before. Total revenues declined 19.0% to $1.0 million from $1.2 million in the prior-year quarter. Products revenues dropped 30.4% to $719,168 versus $1.0 million in the previous year. Consulting and services revenues jumped 37.5% to $287,500 compared with $209,108 a year earlier. Gross profit as percentage of revenues totaled 77.1% versus 59.0% in the prior-year quarter. Operating loss was $2.0 million compared with a loss of $2.6 million a year ago. The Company plans to launch several new products in the second half of 1999, including SmartGate VPN for Windows CE; AirSmartGate; SmartGate 4.0 and InstantExtranet Server. The product introductions follow a $1.9 million investment in research and development during the first six months of 1999.

BUSINESS

V-ONE CORPORATION develops, markets, and licenses a comprehensive suite of network security products that enable organizations to conduct secured electronic transactions and information exchange using private enterprise networks and public networks, such as the Internet. The Company's suite of products address network user authentication, perimeter security, access control and data integrity through the use of smart cards, tokens, digital certificates, firewalls and encryption technology. VONE's primary product is Smart-Gate®, a client/server Virtual Private Network technology which is used for establishing secure intranets to slash remote access and deploying secure business-to-business. The Company's principal market is the United States, with secondary markets located in Europe and Asia.

ANNUAL FINANCIAL DATA

	12/31/98	12/31/97	12/31/96	12/31/95	12/31/94	12/31/93
Earnings Per Share	d0.68	d0.78	d0.72	d0.12	d0.06	d0.01
Cash Flow Per Share	d0.63	d0.73	d0.71	d0.11	d0.06	d0.01
Tang. Book Val. Per Share	0.02	0.43	1.04	...	30.86	...
INCOME STATEMENT (IN THOUSANDS):						
Total Revenues	6,260	9,403	6,266	1,104	60	76
Costs & Expenses	14,876	18,525	12,438	2,139	504	139
Depreciation & Amort.	637	592	173	25	10	1
Operating Income	d9,253	d9,714	d6,345	d1,060	d455	d64
Net Interest Inc./(Exp.)	60	328	d351	d62	d2	d2
Income Before Income Taxes	d9,193	d9,386	d6,696	d1,122	d457	d66
Net Income	d9,193	d9,386	d6,696	d1,122	d457	d66
Cash Flow	d8,770	d9,406	d6,523	d1,097	d447	d65
Average Shs. Outstg.	13,898	12,869	9,245	9,568	8,047	6,187
BALANCE SHEET (IN THOUSANDS):						
Cash & Cash Equivalents	636	6,204	10,894	1,328	322	...
Total Current Assets	1,811	9,457	14,134	1,842	322	...
Net Property	875	1,002	757	198	72	...
Total Assets	3,922	11,860	15,697	2,051	395	...
Total Current Liabilities	3,088	1,598	1,491	2,011	77	...
Long-Term Obligations	198	301	135	127	...	...
Net Stockholders' Equity	636	6,158	13,994	d140	318	...
Net Working Capital	d1,277	7,859	12,643	d168	246	...
Year-end Shs. Outstg.	16,478	13,070	12,658	8,304	10	...
STATISTICAL RECORD:						
Debt/Total Assets %	5.0	2.5	0.9	6.2	...	...
Price Range	4⅛-1⅜	9¼-2¾	7¾-4¾	...	...	...
Statistics are as originally reported.						

REVENUES

(12/31/98)	($000)	(%)
Products.....................	5,799	92.6
Consulting & Services	461	7.4
Total	6,260	100.0

OFFICERS:
D. D. Dawson, Chmn., Pres., C.E.O.
C. B. Griffis, Sr. V.P., C.F.O., Treas.

PRINCIPAL OFFICE: 20250 Century Blvd., Suite 300, Germantown, MD 20874

TELEPHONE NUMBER: (301) 515-5200
FAX: (301) 515-5280
WEB: www.v-one.com
NO. OF EMPLOYEES: 68
SHAREHOLDERS: 124 (approx.)
ANNUAL MEETING: In May
INCORPORATED: MD, Feb., 1993; reincorp., DE, Feb., 1996

INSTITUTIONAL HOLDINGS:
No. of Institutions: 8
Shares Held: 1,259,981
% Held: 7.5

INDUSTRY: Computers, peripherals & software (SIC: 5045)

TRANSFER AGENT(S): American Stock Transfer & Trust Company, New York, NY

NASDAQ SYMBOL VUSA
Rec. Pr. 14⅝ (7/31/99)

VALUE AMERICA, INC.

YIELD ...
P/E RATIO ...

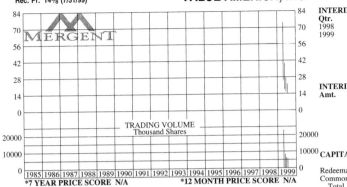

*7 YEAR PRICE SCORE N/A
*NYSE COMPOSITE INDEX=100
*12 MONTH PRICE SCORE N/A

INTERIM EARNINGS (Per Share):				
Qtr.	Mar.	Jun.	Sept.	Dec.
1998	----------------d2.79----------------			
1999	d2.72	d0.79	...	...

INTERIM DIVIDENDS (Per Share):

Amt.	Decl.	Ex.	Rec.	Pay.
	No dividends paid.			

CAPITALIZATION (12/31/98):

	($000)	(%)
Redeemable Pfd. Stock	37,821	604.5
Common & Surplus	d31,564	-504.5
Total	6,257	100.0

RECENT DEVELOPMENTS: For the quarter ended 6/30/99, the Company reported a net loss of $31.8 million compared with a net loss of $9.8 million in the corresponding quarter the year before. Total revenues skyrocketed to $35.8 million from $5.1 million in the prior-year quarter. The increase in revenues was mainly attributed to the increase in the Company's customer base, which grew 50.0% in the quarter to over 400,000 members. Operating loss was $28.1 million, up from $9.9 million in the 1998 quarter. Gross profit more than doubled to $1.3 million compared with $436,000 in the year-earlier quarter. On June 21, 1999, Company announced the acquisition of InService America, a customer service and acquisition company, for an undisclosed amount. InService America will become the Company's primary outreach partner for religious and non-profit customer acquisition.

BUSINESS

VALUE AMERICA, INC. is an on-line superstore that offers a one-stop shopping experience for consumers via the Internet. The Company offers a wide selection of technology, office and consumer products. The Company currently sells products in more than 40 industries from more than 2,000 brand manufacturers. The Company sells brand name goods from manufacturers such as Hewlett-Packard, IBM, Olympus, Panasonic and Weber.

QUARTERLY DATA

(12/31/98) ($000)	Rev	Inc
1st Quarter................	2,211	(3,540)
2nd Quarter................	5,073	(9,835)
3rd Quarter	15,324	(15,579)
4th Quarter................	18,936	(24,662)

ANNUAL FINANCIAL DATA

	12/31/98	12/31/97	① 12/31/96
Earnings Per Share	**d2.80**	**d0.09**	**d0.02**
Cash Flow Per Share	**d2.67**	**d0.09**	**d0.02**
INCOME STATEMENT (IN THOUSANDS):			
Total Revenues	41,544	133	...
Costs & Expenses	89,516	1,959	419
Depreciation & Amort.	2,920	46	9
Operating Income	d50,893	d1,871	d428
Net Interest Inc./(Exp.)	d2,723	18	3
Income Before Income Taxes	d53,616	d1,853	d425
Net Income	d53,616	d1,853	d425
Cash Flow	d61,855	d1,996	d416
Average Shs. Outstg.	23,154	22,616	22,500
BALANCE SHEET (IN THOUSANDS):			
Cash & Cash Equivalents	25,127	10,341	...
Total Current Assets	54,872	10,806	...
Net Property	2,062	168	...
Total Assets	60,098	10,994	...
Total Current Liabilities	52,827	1,477	...
Net Stockholders' Equity	d31,564	d1,310	...
Net Working Capital	2,046	9,329	...
Year-end Shs. Outstg.	23,778	23,153	22,500
STATISTICAL RECORD:			

Statistics are as originally reported. ① Period from 3/13/96 (inception) to 12/31/96

OFFICERS:
C. A. Winn, Chmn., Founder
R. Scatena, Vice-Chmn., Gen. Couns.
T. Morgan, C.E.O.
G. M. Dorchak, Pres., C.O.O.

PRINCIPAL OFFICE: 1560 Insurance Lane, Charlottesville, VA 22911

TELEPHONE NUMBER: (804) 817-7700
WEB: www.valueamerica.com

NO. OF EMPLOYEES: 332

SHAREHOLDERS: 118

ANNUAL MEETING: N/A

INCORPORATED: NV, Mar., 1996; reincorp., VA, Oct., 1997

INSTITUTIONAL HOLDINGS:
No. of Institutions: 2
Shares Held: 359,500
% Held: 0.8

INDUSTRY: Miscellaneous retail stores, nec (SIC: 5999)

TRANSFER AGENT(S): American Securities Transfer & Trust, Inc., Denver, CO

VERIO INC.

YIELD ...
P/E RATIO ...

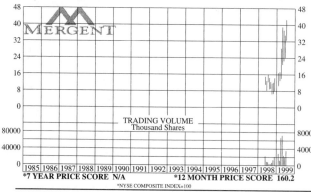

*7 YEAR PRICE SCORE N/A   *12 MONTH PRICE SCORE 160.2

*NYSE COMPOSITE INDEX=100

INTERIM EARNINGS (Per Share):

Qtr.	Mar.	June	Sept.	Dec.
1996	---------------d2.65---------------			
1997	d2.15	d4.16	d5.63	d8.31
1998	d7.23	d0.72	d0.52	d0.51
1999	d0.62	d0.61	...	...

INTERIM DIVIDENDS (Per Share):

Amt.	Decl.	Ex.	Rec.	Pay.
100% STK	7/22/99	8/23/99	8/03/99	8/20/99

CAPITALIZATION (12/31/98):

	($000)	(%)
Long-Term Debt	668,177	76.1
Capital Lease Obligations..	6,441	0.7
Minority Interest	361	0.0
Common & Surplus	202,681	23.1
Total	877,660	100.0

RECENT DEVELOPMENTS: For three months ended 6/30/99, the Company reported a net loss of $45.7 million compared with a net loss of $26.3 million in the corresponding period of the prior year. Total revenue more than doubled to $61.9 million from $28.5 million the previous year. Approximately 53.0% of revenues were attributed to Web hosting and other enhanced services versus 37.0% the year before. Gross profit as a percentage of revenues advanced to 67.0% due to improved efficiencies from VRIO's Tier 1 national network and regional networks. On 7/13/99, the Company completed the acquisition of digitalNATION, Inc. for $100.0 million in cash. This acquisition adds more than 1,200 dedicated servers and expands VRIO's business Web hosting services. In May 1999, the Company launched a media campaign with America Online that is driving substantial new business and brand-name recognition.

BUSINESS

VERIO INC. is a provider of comprehensive Internet services with an emphasis on serving the small- and medium-sized business markets. The Company provides its customers with telecommunications circuits that allows them to make connections to and transmissions over the Internet. The Company also hosts its customers' Web sites. In addition, the Company offers an expanding package of enhanced Internet tools, such as electronic commerce and virtual private networks. The Internet Corporation for Assigned Names and Numbers selected VRIO as an official registrar of Internet domain names. The Company serves as an official registrar of .com, .net and .org domain names internationally, which is the primary entry point for developing a Web presence.

ANNUAL FINANCIAL DATA

	12/31/98	12/31/97	12/31/96
Earnings Per Share	☐ d2.62	d20.23	d2.64
Cash Flow Per Share	d1.69	d15.59	d2.30
INCOME STATEMENT (IN THOUSANDS):			
Total Revenues	120,653	35,692	2,365
Costs & Expenses	87,343	65,357	2,164
Depreciation & Amort.	39,726	10,624	669
Operating Income	d91,018	d40,289	d6,280
Net Interest Inc./(Exp.)	d21,318	d5,746	478
Income Before Income Taxes	d112,336	d47,993	d5,802
Equity Earnings/Minority Int.	482	1,924	680
Net Income	☐ d111,854	d46,069	d5,122
Cash Flow	d72,215	d35,705	d4,476
Average Shs. Outstg.	42,752	2,290	1,944
BALANCE SHEET (IN THOUSANDS):			
Cash & Cash Equivalents	591,016	93,601	66,467
Total Current Assets	613,931	105,822	67,607
Net Property	50,446	28,213	4,487
Total Assets	933,712	246,471	82,628
Total Current Liabilities	56,052	31,137	7,469
Long-Term Obligations	674,618	142,321	106
Net Stockholders' Equity	202,681	d27,001	d4,055
Net Working Capital	557,879	74,685	60,138
Year-end Shs. Outstg.	66,292	2,510	2,180
STATISTICAL RECORD:			
Debt/Total Assets %	72.3	57.7	0.1
Price Range	15¹⁵/₁₆-6½	...	...

Statistics are as originally reported. Adj. for stk. split: 100% div., 8/20/99 ☐ Bef. extraord. chrg. $10.1 mill.

REVENUES

(12/31/98)	($000)	(%)
Dedicated Inter. Connect	1,100	46.5
Dial-up Internet Connect	1,139	48.2
Enhanced Services & Other	126	5.3
Total	2,365	100.0

OFFICERS:
S. C. Halstedt, Chmn.
J. L. Jaschke, C.E.O.
H. R. Hribar, Pres., C.O.O.
P. B. Fritzinger, C.F.O.

PRINCIPAL OFFICE: 8005 South Chester Street, Suite 200, Englewood, CO 80112

TELEPHONE NUMBER: (303) 645-1900
FAX: (303) 792-5644
WEB: www.verio.com

NO. OF EMPLOYEES: 1,360 (avg.)

SHAREHOLDERS: 425 (approx.)

ANNUAL MEETING: In Jun.

INCORPORATED: DE, Mar., 1996

INSTITUTIONAL HOLDINGS:
No. of Institutions: 100
Shares Held: 26,804,632 (Adj.)
% Held: 35.9

INDUSTRY: Data processing and preparation (SIC: 7374)

TRANSFER AGENT(S): Norwest Bank Minnesota, N.A., St. Paul, MN

VERISIGN INC.

YIELD ...
P/E RATIO ...

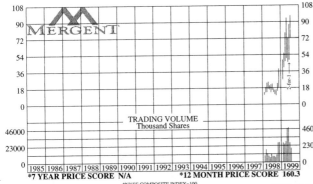

7 YEAR PRICE SCORE N/A   **12 MONTH PRICE SCORE 160.3**

*NYSE COMPOSITE INDEX=100

INTERIM EARNINGS (Per Share):

Qtr.	Mar.	June	Sept.	Dec.
1996	----------------d0.37----------------			
1997	d0.29	d0.28	d0.32	d0.42
1998	d0.16	d0.12	d0.17	d0.03
1999	d0.08	Nil	...	...

INTERIM DIVIDENDS (Per Share):

Amt.	Decl.	Ex.	Rec.	Pay.
2-for-1	3/31/99	6/01/99	5/14/99	5/28/99

CAPITALIZATION (12/31/98):

	($000)	(%)
Minority Interest	964	2.3
Common & Surplus	40,728	97.7
Total	41,692	100.0

RECENT DEVELOPMENTS: For the quarter ended 6/30/99, the Company reported a net loss of $152,000 compared with a net loss of $4.8 million in the corresponding period of the prior year. Revenues more than doubled to $18.7 million from $8.6 million the prior year. The Company reported an operating loss of $1.9 million versus an operating loss of $5.8 million the year before. VRSN added four new international service providers in Australia, Greece, the Middle East, and Canada to the VeriSign Trust Network^{SM}. The Company also formed a strategic relationship with Visa U.S.A. to allow any of Visa's 21,000 member banks to issue VeriSign SSL digital certificates to their merchant customers who wish to accept payments securely over the Internet. VRSN also launched its Go Secure!^{SM} Services for enterprise customers, designed to extend the value of the OnSite managed service, and accelerate the way organizations can deploy secure e-commerce applications.

BUSINESS

VERISIGN INC. provides Internet-based trust services and digital certificate tools needed by websites, enterprises, electronic commerce service providers and individuals to conduct trusted and secure electronic commerce and communication over the Internet, intranets and extranets, also known as IP networks. The Company has established strategic relationships with industry leaders to allow a widespread utilization of their digital certificate services and to assure their interoperability with a wide variety of applications and network equipment. The Company also offers a service which allows their customers to leverage the Company's trusted service infrastructure to develop and deploy customized digital certificate services for use by its employees, customers and business partners.

ANNUAL FINANCIAL DATA

	12/31/98	12/31/97	12/31/96
Earnings Per Share	d0.47	① d0.56	d0.37
Cash Flow Per Share	d0.38	d0.49	d0.35
Tang. Book Val. Per Share	0.88	0.87	2.24
INCOME STATEMENT (IN THOUSANDS):			
Total Revenues	38,930	9,382	1,351
Costs & Expenses	58,129	28,653	11,806
Depreciation & Amort.	3,946	2,611	559
Operating Income	d23,145	① d21,882	d11,014
Income Before Income Taxes	d21,025	20,733	d11,081
Equity Earnings/Minority Int.	1,282	1,538	838
Net Income	d19,743	① d19,195	d10,243
Cash Flow	d15,797	d16,584	d9,684
Average Shs. Outstg.	41,746	34,036	27,672
BALANCE SHEET (IN THOUSANDS):			
Cash & Cash Equivalents	41,745	11,894	29,983
Total Current Assets	53,688	14,918	31,520
Net Property	9,234	8,622	4,617
Total Assets	64,295	24,406	36,503
Total Current Liabilities	22,603	9,691	6,697
Net Stockholders' Equity	40,728	12,469	28,555
Net Working Capital	31,085	5,227	24,823
Year-end Shs. Outstg.	46,174	14,240	12,753
STATISTICAL RECORD:			
Price Range	38¾-9¹¹⁄₁₆	...	...

Statistics are as originally reported. Adj. for stk. split: 2-for-1, 5/28/99 ① Incl. non-recurr. chrg. $2.8 mill.

REVENUES

(12/31/98)	($000)	(%)
United States	33,650	86.4
All Other Countries ...	5,280	13.6
Total	38,930	100.0

OFFICERS:
S. D. Sclavos, Pres., C.E.O.
D. L. Evan, V.P. of Fin. & Admin., C.F.O.
J. S. Chaudhry, V.P., Gen. Man. of Security Services
T. Tomlinson, Sec.

PRINCIPAL OFFICE: 1390 Shorebird Way, Mountain View, CA 94043-1338

TELEPHONE NUMBER: (650) 961-7500
FAX: (650) 961-7300
WEB: www.verisign.com

NO. OF EMPLOYEES: 315

SHAREHOLDERS: 236 (of record)

ANNUAL MEETING: In May

INCORPORATED: DE, Apr., 1995

INSTITUTIONAL HOLDINGS:
No. of Institutions: 119
Shares Held: 32,738,453 (Adj.)
% Held: 65.3

INDUSTRY: Computer programming services (SIC: 7371)

TRANSFER AGENT(S): ChaseMellon Shareholder Services, L.L.C., South Hackensack, NJ

VERTICALNET, INC.

YIELD   . . .
P/E RATIO   . . .

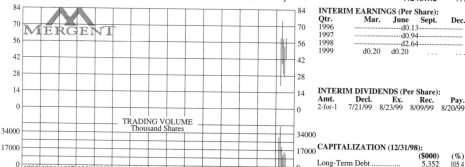

INTERIM EARNINGS (Per Share):

Qtr.	Mar.	June	Sept.	Dec.
1996	------------------d0.13------------------			
1997	------------------d0.94------------------			
1998	------------------d2.64------------------			
1999	d0.20	d0.20	. . .	. . .

INTERIM DIVIDENDS (Per Share):

Amt.	Decl.	Ex.	Rec.	Pay.
2-for-1	7/21/99	8/23/99	8/09/99	8/20/99

CAPITALIZATION (12/31/98):

	($000)	(%)
Long-Term Debt	5,352	105.4
Preferred Stock	78	1.5
Common & Surplus	d354	-7.0
Total	5,076	100.0

RECENT DEVELOPMENTS: For the quarter ended 6/30/99, the Company reported a net loss of $6.8 million compared with a loss of $2.9 million in 1998. Revenues soared to $3.6 million from $587,422 in the prior-year period. Revenue from storefront sites accounted for 40.0% of total revenues during the quarter. Meanwhile, sponsorship revenues represented 55.0% of revenues. Operating loss was $7.5 million compared with a loss of $2.9 million in the previous year. Results benefited from new revenue, new storefronts, and ongoing business improvements. During the quarter, the Company added eight new on-line sites, increasing the total to 43 global industrial communities. VERT acquired labX.com, a trading community for used and excess scientific laboratory equipment. LabX will be integrated with the Company's science industries group, which is comprised of BioResearch online, Drug Discovery online, and LaboratoryNetwork.com.

BUSINESS

VERTICALNET, INC. is an owner and operator of 43 vertical trade communities in 10 major industries that target business-to-business communities of commerce on the Internet. The vertical trade communities include Web sites that act as industry-specific sources of information, interaction, and electronic commerce. Vertical trade communities also combine product information, industry news, requests for proposals, directories, classifieds, job listings, discussion forums, electronic commerce opportunities for buyers and sellers, and online professional services for education courses. Revenue is mostly generated through Internet advertising, as well as Web site development fees. In June 1999, the Company acquired the Oillink Web site, the ElectricNet Web site, and Techspex, Inc.

ANNUAL FINANCIAL DATA

	12/31/98	12/31/97	12/31/96	12/31/95
Earnings Per Share	d2.64	d0.94	d0.13	d0.09
Cash Flow Per Share	d2.48	d0.87	d0.13	d0.09
Tang. Book Val. Per Share	. . .	. . .	0.02	. . .
INCOME STATEMENT (IN THOUSANDS):				
Total Revenues	3,135	792	285	16
Costs & Expenses	15,806	5,067	925	220
Depreciation & Amort.	838	388	62	6
Operating Income	d13,509	d4,664	d702	d210
Net Interest Inc./(Exp.)	d85	d115	d6	d1
Income Before Income Taxes	d13,594	d4,779	d709	d211
Net Income	d13,594	d4,779	d709	d211
Cash Flow	d12,757	d4,391	d647	d205
Average Shs. Outstg.	5,141	5,054	5,167	2,193
BALANCE SHEET (IN THOUSANDS):				
Cash & Cash Equivalents	5,663	755	329	. . .
Total Current Assets	8,206	1,592	515	. . .
Net Property	1,072	492	106	. . .
Total Assets	12,343	2,104	637	. . .
Total Current Liabilities	7,267	4,128	365	. . .
Long-Term Obligations	5,352	400	167	. . .
Net Stockholders' Equity	d276	d2,424	105	. . .
Net Working Capital	938	d2,536	150	. . .
Year-end Shs. Outstg.	5,269	4,731	4,731	3,925
STATISTICAL RECORD:				
Debt/Total Assets %	43.4	19.0	26.2	. . .

Statistics are as originally reported. Adj. for 2-for-1 split, 8/99.

QUARTERLY DATA

12/31/1998($000)	Rev	Inc
1st Quarter	377	(2,085)
2nd Quarter	587	(2,872)
3rd Quarter	897	(3,378)
4th Quarter	1,273	(5,260)

OFFICERS:
D. A. Alexander, Chmn.
M. L. Walsh, Pres., C.E.O.
G. S. Godick, V.P., C.F.O.
C. H. Low, C.T.O.

PRINCIPAL OFFICE: 700 Dresher Rd., Horsham, PA 19044

TELEPHONE NUMBER: (215) 328-6100
WEB: www.verticalnet.com

NO. OF EMPLOYEES: 220

SHAREHOLDERS: 99

ANNUAL MEETING: In Nov.

INCORPORATED: PA, Jul., 1995

INSTITUTIONAL HOLDINGS:
No. of Institutions: 49
Shares Held: 7,525,454 (Adj.)
% Held: 22.4

INDUSTRY: Information retrieval services (SIC: 7375)

TRANSFER AGENT(S): American Stock Transfer & Trust Company, New York, NY

VIANT CORPORATION

YIELD ...
P/E RATIO ...

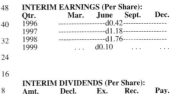

INTERIM EARNINGS (Per Share):

Qtr.	Mar.	June	Sept.	Dec.
1996	------------------d0.42------------------			
1997	------------------d1.18------------------			
1998	------------------d1.76------------------			
1999	...	d0.10	...	...

INTERIM DIVIDENDS (Per Share):

Amt.	Decl.	Ex.	Rec.	Pay.
	No dividends paid.			

TRADING VOLUME
Thousand Shares

7 YEAR PRICE SCORE N/A   *12 MONTH PRICE SCORE N/A*

*NYSE COMPOSITE INDEX=100

CAPITALIZATION (1/1/99):

	($000)	(%)
Long-Term Debt	603	2.8
Capital Lease Obligations..	1,634	7.5
Preferred Stock.................	32,136	146.7
Common & Surplus	d12,471	-56.9
Total	21,902	100.0

RECENT DEVELOPMENTS: For the three months ended 7/2/99, the Company reported a net loss of $1.8 million compared with a net loss of $904,000 in the corresponding period of the previous year. Revenues more than doubled to $11.0 million from $4.5 million the year before. Gross margin as a percentage of sales showed significant improvement to 49.0% from 43.0% in the year-ago quarter. The stronger results were propelled by a number of factors, including the addition of eight new accounts and several conversion and expansion projects within the Company's existing client base. For the six months ended 7/2/99, net loss was $3.9 million compared with a loss of $1.6 million the year before. Net revenues more than doubled to $18.9 million from $8.6 million in the corresponding prior-year period. The Company recently opened two new offices in London, England and Chicago, IL.

BUSINESS

VIANT CORPORATION is an Internet professional services firm providing strategic consulting, creative design and technology services to companies seeking to capitalize on the Internet. The Company's services include the design and development of: Internet strategies that help integrate a client's Internet projects and investments with its broader corporate strategies and business practices; electronic commerce tools that enable a company to attract new customers, and sell goods and services over a website; business partner tools, extranets that allow companies to share information and communicate with one another; internal information tools that improve a company's ability to capture, store, and distribute information to its employees; and new business ventures exclusively for the Internet. VIAN's clients include American Express Co., BankBoston Corp., Compaq Computer Corp., Kinko's Corp., Lucent Technologies Inc., Polo/Ralph Lauren Corp. and RadioShack.

ANNUAL FINANCIAL DATA

	1/1/99	12/31/97	[1] 12/31/96
Earnings Per Share	d1.76	d1.18	d0.42
Cash Flow Per Share	d1.47	d1.12	d0.40
INCOME STATEMENT (IN THOUSANDS):			
Total Revenues	20,043	8,808	642
Costs & Expenses	25,303	12,781	2,343
Depreciation & Amort.	1,065	205	49
Operating Income	d6,325	d4,178	d1,750
Net Interest Inc./(Exp.)	d137	135	91
Income Before Income Taxes	d6,487	d4,080	d1,659
Net Income	d6,487	d4,080	d1,659
Cash Flow	d5,422	d3,875	d1,610
Average Shs. Outstg.	3,681	3,468	3,981
BALANCE SHEET (IN THOUSANDS):			
Cash & Cash Equivalents	18,811	6,174	...
Total Current Assets	25,473	8,159	...
Net Property	4,048	2,011	...
Total Assets	29,753	10,318	...
Total Current Liabilities	7,851	3,642	...
Long-Term Obligations	2,237	670	...
Net Stockholders' Equity	19,665	6,006	...
Net Working Capital	17,622	4,517	...
Year-end Shs. Outstg.	3,762	3,556	...
STATISTICAL RECORD:			
Debt/Total Assets %	7.5	6.5	...

Statistics are as originally reported. [1] From period of inception, 4/10/96.

OFFICERS:
W. H. Davidow, Chmn.
R. L. Gett, Pres., C.E.O.
M. D. Nesmith, V.P., C.F.O.
M. J. Tubridy, V.P., Fin., Treas.

INVESTOR CONTACT: Investor Relations, 1-877-OWN-VIAN

PRINCIPAL OFFICE: Lincoln Plaza, 89 South Street, Boston, MA 02111

TELEPHONE NUMBER: (617) 531-3700
FAX: (617) 531-3803
WEB: www.viant.com

NO. OF EMPLOYEES: 300

SHAREHOLDERS: 99

ANNUAL MEETING: N/A

INCORPORATED: CA, Apr., 1996

INSTITUTIONAL HOLDINGS:
No. of Institutions: 5
Shares Held: 252,606
% Held: 1.2

INDUSTRY: Business services, nec (SIC: 7389)

TRANSFER AGENT(S): BankBoston, Boston, MA

VIGNETTE CORP.

YIELD . . .
P/E RATIO . . .

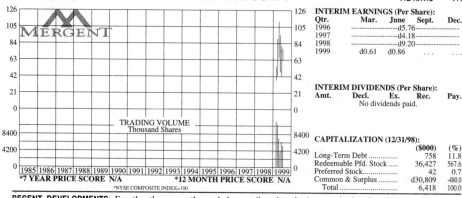

*7 YEAR PRICE SCORE N/A   *12 MONTH PRICE SCORE N/A

TRADING VOLUME
Thousand Shares

1985 1986 1987 1988 1989 1990 1991 1992 1993 1994 1995 1996 1997 1998 1999

*NYSE COMPOSITE INDEX=100

INTERIM EARNINGS (Per Share):

Qtr.	Mar.	June	Sept.	Dec.
1996			d5.76	
1997			d4.18	
1998			d9.20	
1999	d0.61	d0.86	. . .	. . .

INTERIM DIVIDENDS (Per Share):

Amt.	Decl.	Ex.	Rec.	Pay.
	No dividends paid.			

CAPITALIZATION (12/31/98):

	($000)	(%)
Long-Term Debt	758	11.8
Redeemable Pfd. Stock	36,427	567.6
Preferred Stock.................	42	0.7
Common & Surplus	d30,809	-480.0
Total	6,418	100.0

RECENT DEVELOPMENTS: For the three months ended 6/30/99, the Company reported a net loss of $21.5 million compared with a net loss of $8.1 million in the corresponding period of the previous year. The Company incurred charges for merger-related activities of $14.7 million and $2.1 million in the 1999 and 1998 periods, respectively. Total revenues soared to $14.9 million from $2.9 million the year before. The improvement in total revenues was attributed to the increase in the client base combined with an advancement in the average deal size of new customer orders. Product license revenues jumped to $7.6 million from $1.6 million in the prior-year period, while revenues from services climbed to $7.3 million from $1.3 million the year before. On 6/30/99, the Company completed the acquisition of Diffusion Inc., a producer of multi-channel information delivery tools.

BUSINESS

VIGNETTE CORP. is a provider of Internet Relationship Management (IRM) software products and services. IRM software is a new category of applications that enable mid- to large-sized enterprises to develop and manage on-line customer relationships for the purpose of increasing their Web-based revenues and market share. The Company has more than 225 global corporate customers.

REVENUES

(12/31/1998)	($000)	(%)
Product license	8,584	53.0
Services	7,621	47.0
Total	16,205	100.0

ANNUAL FINANCIAL DATA

	12/31/98	12/31/97
Earnings Per Share	① d9.20	d4.18
Cash Flow Per Share	d8.82	d4.07
INCOME STATEMENT (IN THOUSANDS):		
Total Revenues	16,205	3,024
Costs & Expenses	41,506	10,469
Depreciation & Amort.	1,068	198
Operating Income	d26,369	d7,643
Net Interest Inc./(Exp.)	264	198
Income Before Income Taxes	d26,197	d7,474
Net Income	① d26,197	d7,474
Cash Flow	d25,129	d7,276
Average Shs. Outstg.	2,849	1,788
BALANCE SHEET (IN THOUSANDS):		
Cash & Cash Equivalents	12,242	6,865
Total Current Assets	20,120	7,711
Net Property	1,754	744
Total Assets	22,781	8,499
Total Current Liabilities	16,363	3,456
Long-Term Obligations	758	833
Net Stockholders' Equity	d30,767	d9,248
Net Working Capital	3,757	4,255
Year-end Shs. Outstg.	5,507,352	3,492,093
STATISTICAL RECORD:		
Debt/Total Assets %	3.3	9.8

Statistics are as originally reported. ① Incl. non-recurr. chrg. $2.1 mill.

OFFICERS:
R. B. Garber, Chmn.
G. A. Peters, C.E.O., Pres.
J. F. Lynch, V.P., Fin. & Oper., Sec.

PRINCIPAL OFFICE: 901 South MoPac Expressway, Austin, TX 78746

TELEPHONE NUMBER: (512) 306-4300
FAX: (512) 306-4500
WEB: www.vignette.com

NO. OF EMPLOYEES: 310

SHAREHOLDERS: 150 (approx.)

ANNUAL MEETING: N/A

INCORPORATED: DE, Dec., 1995

INSTITUTIONAL HOLDINGS:
No. of Institutions: 69
Shares Held: 3,949,122
% Held: 14.4

INDUSTRY: Prepackaged software (SIC: 7372)

TRANSFER AGENT(S): ChaseMellon Shareholder Services, L.L.C., Ridgefield Park, NJ

NASDAQ SYMBOL VDAT
Rec. Pr. 15¼ (7/31/99)

VISUAL DATA CORPORATION

YIELD ...
P/E RATIO ...

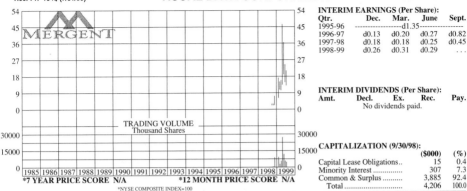

TRADING VOLUME
Thousand Shares

1985 1986 1987 1988 1989 1990 1991 1992 1993 1994 1995 1996 1997 1998 1999
*7 YEAR PRICE SCORE N/A   *12 MONTH PRICE SCORE N/A
*NYSE COMPOSITE INDEX=100

INTERIM EARNINGS (Per Share):

Qtr.	Dec.	Mar.	June	Sept.
1995-96	------------------d1.35-----------------			
1996-97	d0.13	d0.20	d0.27	d0.82
1997-98	d0.18	d0.18	d0.25	d0.45
1998-99	d0.26	d0.31	d0.29	...

INTERIM DIVIDENDS (Per Share):

Amt.	Decl.	Ex.	Rec.	Pay.
	No dividends paid.			

CAPITALIZATION (9/30/98):

	($000)	(%)
Capital Lease Obligations..	15	0.4
Minority Interest	307	7.3
Common & Surplus	3,885	92.4
Total	4,206	100.0

RECENT DEVELOPMENTS: For the quarter ended 6/30/99, the Company incurred a net loss of $1.9 million compared with a net loss of $810,283 in the corresponding period of the prior year. Revenue advanced to $1.2 million from $256,091 a year earlier. Results for the current quarter included revenues of approximately $905,000 from the Company's EDnet subsidiary. Going forward, VDAT should continue to achieve revenue growth through strate-gic alliances, acquisitions and expansion of its video library. On 5/24/99, the Company announced a business services, advertising and distribution partnership with Broadcast.com to create a new on-line travel video channel. Under the agreement, VDAT will provide travel-related video content for the channel and will sponsor the channel through the use of broadcast.com's multimedia advertising services.

BUSINESS

VISUAL DATA CORPORATION produces, markets and distributes original video and audio content for the Internet and eventually Interactive Television. The Company's video libraries cover a wide range of topics, including travel, business information, medicine and healthcare and entertainment. Through its subsidiary EDnet, Inc., the Company has estab-lished relationships throughout the motion picture and recording indus-tries. The Company's strategic part-nerships include PR Newswire, InterVu, TravelWeb, Interval Interna-tional, Broadcast.com, Rezsolutions, Physicians Online, and Intelihealth.

ANNUAL FINANCIAL DATA

	9/30/98	9/30/97	9/30/96	9/30/95
Earnings Per Share	d1.06	☐ d1.42	d1.35	d0.43
Cash Flow Per Share	d0.96	d1.40	d1.29	d0.42
Tang. Book Val. Per Share	1.04	1.07	...	0.34
INCOME STATEMENT (IN THOUSANDS):				
Total Revenues	1,881	193	112	...
Costs & Expenses	5,034	2,685	1,892	484
Depreciation & Amort.	309	64	85	9
Operating Income	d3,463	d2,556	d1,892	d502
Net Interest Inc./(Exp.)	d28	d1,012	d26	d8
Income Before Income Taxes	d3,410	d3,574	d1,892	d501
Equity Earnings/Minority Int.	d25	...	...	...
Net Income	d3,435	☐ d3,574	d1,892	d501
Cash Flow	d3,146	d3,510	d1,807	d491
Average Shs. Outstg.	3,254	2,509	1,405	1,173
BALANCE SHEET (IN THOUSANDS):				
Cash & Cash Equivalents	611	2,554	158	250
Total Current Assets	1,748	2,712	283	270
Net Property	3,535	1,861	272	194
Total Assets	6,394	4,588	1,329	483
Total Current Liabilities	2,188	366	402	103
Long-Term Obligations	15	975	738	81
Net Stockholders' Equity	3,885	3,247	189	298
Net Working Capital	d439	2,346	d119	166
Year-end Shs. Outstg.	3,732	3,038	1,166	873
STATISTICAL RECORD:				
Debt/Total Assets %	0.2	21.2	55.5	16.7
Price Range	7⁵⁄₁₆-2¹⁄₁₆	...	...	...

Statistics are as originally reported. ☐ Includes loss on write-off of property, plant & equipment of $6.3 million.

OFFICERS:
R. S. Selman, Pres., C.E.O., C.F.O.
A. M. Saperstein, V.P., Sec.
D. E. Goodman, Exec. V.P., C.O.O.

PRINCIPAL OFFICE: 1291 SW 29th Avenue, Suite 3A, Pompano Beach, FL 33069

TELEPHONE NUMBER: (954) 917-6655
FAX: (954) 917-6660
WEB: www.vdat.com

NO. OF EMPLOYEES: 41

SHAREHOLDERS: 206 (approx.)

ANNUAL MEETING: N/A

INCORPORATED: FL, May, 1993

INSTITUTIONAL HOLDINGS:
No. of Institutions: 6
Shares Held: 172,305
% Held: 2.6

INDUSTRY: Miscellaneous publishing (SIC: 2741)

TRANSFER AGENT(S): Interwest Transfer Co., Inc., Salt Lake City, UT

WAVO CORPORATION

YIELD   ...
P/E RATIO   ...

*7 YEAR PRICE SCORE N/A   *12 MONTH PRICE SCORE 74.4

TRADING VOLUME
Thousand Shares

INTERIM EARNINGS (Per Share):

Qtr.	Mar.	June	Sept.	Dec.
1994	----------------d0.57----------------			
1995	------- ------------d1.52----------------			
1996	----------------d0.64----------------			
1997	d0.21	d0.60	d0.18	d0.21
1998	d0.26	d0.23	d0.33	d0.44
1999	d0.19	d0.19	...	...

INTERIM DIVIDENDS (Per Share):

Amt.	Decl.	Ex.	Rec.	Pay.
	No dividends paid.			

CAPITALIZATION (12/31/98):

	($000)	(%)
Long-Term Debt	40	0.1
Preferred Stock	5,522	12.4
Common & Surplus	39,109	87.6
Total	44,670	100.0

RECENT DEVELOPMENTS: For the quarter ended 6/30/99, the Company reported a net loss of $5.6 million compared with a loss of $4.9 million in the corresponding quarter of 1998. Total revenues fell 11.4% to $6.0 million from $6.8 million in the prior-year period. Gross margin decreased 16.4% to $2.9 million compared with $3.5 million a year ago. Revenues were negatively affected by lower overseas sales of communication equipment. WAVO joined the Secure Digital Music Initiative, which includes over 100 companies from the music, consumer electronics and information technology industries that deliver digital music. The Company is planning to release JamCast, a Web site that provides a continuous broadcast of entertainment files over television airwaves. On 5/26/99, the Company changed its name to Wavo Corporation from WavePhore, Inc.

BUSINESS

WAVO CORPORATION (formerly Wavephore, Inc.) partners with providers of news, business, data, Internet-based content and multi-media programming to deliver selective content that enables people and enterprises to effectively receive, manage, and produce all types of information. The Company operates through five lines of business: WaveTop™, newscast, networks, eWatch, and WavePhore Labs. WaveTop™ is a free multimedia Internet broadcast service that enables a nationwide wireless broadcast medium for the personal computer. The newscast service is designed for information professionals in order to customize information profiles. The networks products and services provide wireless data broadcasting, network services and related equipment to providers of financial data and news. The eWatch service provides a subscription-based Internet monitoring service for business customers. WavePhore Labs provides in-house professional services aimed to deliver custom news and information integration solutions.

ANNUAL FINANCIAL DATA

	12/31/98	12/31/97	12/31/96	12/31/95	12/31/94	12/31/93	12/31/92
Earnings Per Share	② d1.31	① d1.19	d0.64	d1.52	d0.57	d0.68	d0.35
Cash Flow Per Share	d1.18	d1.08	d0.54	d1.52	d0.55	d0.62	d0.32
Tang. Book Val. Per Share	0.65	...	0.16	...	0.64	...	...
INCOME STATEMENT (IN THOUSANDS):							
Total Revenues	22,296	22,590	19,020	813	...	...	...
Costs & Expenses	42,469	39,407	25,198	16,231	4,190	4,427	3,101
Depreciation & Amort.	4,376	3,469	2,981	515	193	415	331
Operating Income	d24,549	d20,285	d9,159	d15,933	d4,383	d4,842	d3,433
Net Interest Inc./(Exp.)	665	501	545	477	d258	d270	d128
Income Before Income Taxes	d28,485	d19,784	d8,615	d15,456	d4,641	d5,112	d3,561
Net Income	② d28,485	① d19,784	d8,615	d15,456	d4,641	d5,112	d3,561
Cash Flow	d25,660	d18,024	d7,327	d15,493	d4,447	d4,696	d3,229
Average Shs. Outstg.	21,774	16,676	13,554	10,195	8,082	7,557	10,034
BALANCE SHEET (IN THOUSANDS):							
Cash & Cash Equivalents	17,719	11,553	11,793	10,945	10,325	264	21
Total Current Assets	26,038	24,971	20,846	17,296	11,850	350	35
Net Property	4,762	4,507	2,281	2,014	147	208	252
Total Assets	52,987	52,991	41,562	38,258	12,048	647	375
Total Current Liabilities	7,937	7,001	5,099	6,297	452	5,474	3,534
Long-Term Obligations	40	12	98	638	...	...	...
Net Stockholders' Equity	44,630	45,612	35,854	30,806	11,561	d4,914	d3,270
Net Working Capital	18,100	17,970	15,747	10,999	11,397	d5,124	d3,498
Year-end Shs. Outstg.	28,576	18,167	16,521	11,406	9,471	7,541	7,341
STATISTICAL RECORD:							
Debt/Total Assets %	0.1	...	0.2	1.7	...	...	...
Price Range	19 1/8-3 1/4	13-5 5/8	20 1/2-5	20 1/2-5	11 1/4-5 5/8	...	...

Statistics are as originally reported. ① Incl. $6.0 mill. chg. for purch. R&D. ② Incl. $4.6 mill. non-recur. chg. & $480,000 chg. for purch. R&D.

OFFICERS:
D. E. Deeds, Chmn., C.E.O.
P. White, Pres.
K. D. Swenson, Exec. V.P., C.F.O., Treas.
D. J. Reich, Sr. V.P., Couns., Sec.

PRINCIPAL OFFICE: 3131 E. Camelback Rd., Suite 320, Phoenix, AZ 85016

TELEPHONE NUMBER: (602) 952-5500
FAX: (602) 952-5517
WEB: www.wavo.com

NO. OF EMPLOYEES: 184

SHAREHOLDERS: 534 (approx.)

ANNUAL MEETING: In Apr.

INCORPORATED: AZ, 1983; reincorp., IN, Nov., 1990

INSTITUTIONAL HOLDINGS:
No. of Institutions: 26
Shares Held: 2,286,308
% Held: 8.0

INDUSTRY: Radio & TV communications equipment (SIC: 3663)

TRANSFER AGENT(S): American Securities Transfer & Trust, Inc., Lakewood, CO.

WEBTRENDS CORPORATION

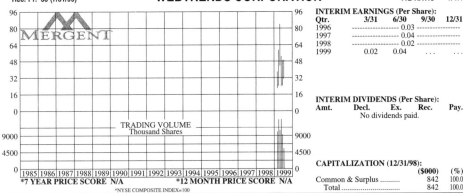

INTERIM EARNINGS (Per Share):

Qtr.	3/31	6/30	9/30	12/31
1996	------------------	0.03	------------------	
1997	------------------	0.04	------------------	
1998	------------------	0.02	------------------	
1999	0.02	0.04	...	...

INTERIM DIVIDENDS (Per Share):

Amt.	Decl.	Ex.	Rec.	Pay.
	No dividends paid.			

7 YEAR PRICE SCORE N/A *12 MONTH PRICE SCORE N/A*
*NYSE COMPOSITE INDEX=100

CAPITALIZATION (12/31/98):

	($000)	(%)
Common & Surplus	842	100.0
Total	842	100.0

RECENT DEVELOPMENTS: For the quarter ended 6/30/99, net income was $525,572 compared with $41,398 in the equivalent 1998 quarter. Total revenues more than doubled to $4.0 million from $1.8 million a year earlier. WEBT has exceeded its internal expectations and continues to grow its customer base. WEBT's Internet-based products grew 145.0% due to new customers using WEBT's enterprise products. Major new customers adopting WEBT's enterprise products during the quarter included Dell Computer, WebMD, America Online, NaviSite, Internetworking, XOOM.COM, Web Promote, Freddie Mac, Reel.Com, CheckFree, Sega, Circuit City, Deloitte & Touche, Merrill Lynch, Fidelity Investment, Morgan Stanley and Ameritech. In June, WebTrends announced CommerceTrends, a product that enables organizations to forecast, track and optimize their returns on investment for Web sites and marketing campaigns by quantifying visitor value.

BUSINESS

WEBTRENDS CORPORATION is a major provider of enterprise management and reporting solutions for Internet and intranet servers and firewalls. WebTrends offers organizations a comprehensive set of solutions that are integrated, scalable, modular, and easy-to-use. Products include WebTrends Enterprise Suite, WebTrends Enterprise Reporting Server, WebTrends CommerceTrends, WebTrends Log Analyzer, WebTrends Professional Suite, WebTrends Security Analyzer, and WebTrends for Firewalls and VPNs. The Company's customers include Internet service providers and corporate, government and educational institutions.

ANNUAL FINANCIAL DATA

	12/31/98	12/31/97	12/31/96
Earnings Per Share	0.02	0.04	0.03
Cash Flow Per Share	0.05	0.05	0.06
Tang. Book Val. Per Share	0.10	0.07	...
INCOME STATEMENT (IN THOUSANDS):			
Total Revenues	8,008	4,055	1,865
Costs & Expenses	7,547	3,539	1,438
Depreciation & Amort.	239	88	29
Operating Income	222	427	398
Net Interest Inc./(Exp.)	29	10	7
Income Before Income Taxes	251	438	405
Income Taxes	31	151	...
Net Income	219	287	405
Cash Flow	459	376	434
Average Shs. Outstg.	9,022	8,126	7,800
BALANCE SHEET (IN THOUSANDS):			
Cash & Cash Equivalents	1,099	807	...
Total Current Assets	2,742	1,555	...
Net Property	598	326	...
Total Assets	3,362	1,886	...
Total Current Liabilities	2,520	1,295	...
Net Stockholders' Equity	842	584	...
Net Working Capital	221	260	...
Year-end Shs. Outstg.	8,219	8,211	...
STATISTICAL RECORD:			
Operating Profit Margin %	2.8	10.5	21.3
Net Profit Margin %	2.7	7.1	21.7
Return on Equity %	26.1	49.2	...
Return on Assets %	6.1	15.2	...

Statistics are as originally reported.

REVENUES

(12/31/98)	($000)	(%)
Software Licenses	2,181	88.3
Support Services........	288	11.7
Total	2,469	100.0

OFFICERS:
E. Shapiro, Chmn., C.E.O.
W. G. Boyd, Pres., C.T.O.
J. T. Richardson, Sr. V.P., C.F.O., Sec.

PRINCIPAL OFFICE: 851 S.W. Sixth Avenue, Suite 1200, Portland, OR 97204

TELEPHONE NUMBER: (503) 294-7025
WEB: www.webtrends.com

NO. OF EMPLOYEES: 87

SHAREHOLDERS: 7

ANNUAL MEETING: N/A

INCORPORATED: DE, Aug., 1993; reincorp., OR, Jan., 1997

INDUSTRY: Data processing and preparation (SIC: 7374)

TRANSFER AGENT(S): BankBoston, N.A., Canton, MA

WHITE PINE SOFTWARE, INC.

YIELD ...
P/E RATIO ...

*7 YEAR PRICE SCORE N/A   ***12 MONTH PRICE SCORE 150.7**

*NYSE COMPOSITE INDEX=100

INTERIM EARNINGS (Per Share):

Qtr.	Mar.	June	Sept.	Dec.
1996	d0.16	d0.16	d0.16	d0.07
1997	d0.26	d0.27	d0.10	d0.12
1998	d0.21	d0.28	d0.18	d0.19
1999	d0.12	d0.12	...	...

INTERIM DIVIDENDS (Per Share):

Amt.	Decl.	Ex.	Rec.	Pay.
	No dividends paid.			

CAPITALIZATION (12/31/98):

	($000)	(%)
Long-Term Debt	7	0.1
Common & Surplus	12,415	99.9
Total	12,422	100.0

RECENT DEVELOPMENTS: For the quarter ended 7/2/99, the Company reported a net loss of $1.3 million compared with a net loss of $2.6 million in the equivalent 1998 quarter. Revenues were $2.6 million, up 54.1% from $1.7 million a year earlier. Revenue growth in the quarter was due primarily to 62.0% higher videoconferencing software server sales and 37.0% higher videoconferencing client revenues. Total sales benefited from strong growth in the Americas, increasing 67.0% year over year. During July, WPNE and Zoom Telephonics introduced a new Macintosh camera package for videoconferencing and videochat. Macintosh users can seamlessly interact and conference with people using CU-SeeMe Pro for Windows, Microsoft Netmeeting, or any other H.323 standards-based client by connecting through a MeetingPoint™ conference server. Separately, WPNE and Telecom MODUS, a joint venture between NEC Corporation of Japan and ERA Technology Ltd. in the UK, announced the first mobile multipoint videoconference over an Internet Protocol network.

BUSINESS

WHITE PINE SOFTWARE, INC. develops, markets and supports multi-platform browser-based internetworking software that facilitates worldwide video and audio communication and data collaboration across the Internet, intranets, extranets and other networks that use the Internet Protocol. WPNE's videoconferencing software products, CU-SeeMe Pro and MeetingPoint, create a client-server solution that allows users to participate in real-time, multi-point video, audio and data conferences over the Internet and intranets. WPNE's ClassPoint™ provides a complete solution for corporate training and distance learning.

REVENUES

12/31/1998	Rev($000)	(%)
Software license fees.	6,948	89.2
Service and Other......	845	10.8
Total	7,793	100.0

ANNUAL FINANCIAL DATA

	12/31/98	12/31/97	12/31/96	12/31/95
Earnings Per Share	d0.86	① d0.75	d0.55	① d0.65
Cash Flow Per Share	d0.75	d0.62	d0.40	d0.55
Tang. Book Val. Per Share	0.75	1.94	2.69	0.29
INCOME STATEMENT (IN THOUSANDS):				
Total Revenues	7,793	11,052	11,666	7,184
Costs & Expenses	15,648	17,683	14,483	10,279
Depreciation & Amort.	1,056	1,115	973	551
Operating Income	d8,911	d7,746	d3,790	d3,646
Net Interest Inc./(Exp.)	577	1,037	251	82
Income Before Income Taxes	d8,419	d6,819	d3,559	d3,496
Income Taxes	5	7	77	30
Net Income	d8,424	① d6,826	d3,637	① d3,526
Cash Flow	d7,368	d5,711	d2,664	d2,975
Average Shs. Outstg.	9,798	9,148	6,618	5,451
BALANCE SHEET (IN THOUSANDS):				
Cash & Cash Equivalents	6,421	14,704	23,298	1,774
Total Current Assets	9,045	18,583	26,414	3,560
Net Property	1,354	1,514	1,064	613
Total Assets	15,996	21,610	29,404	6,437
Total Current Liabilities	2,419	2,852	3,844	2,778
Long-Term Obligations	7	33	324	879
Net Stockholders' Equity	12,415	18,726	25,236	2,780
Net Working Capital	6,626	15,732	22,570	782
Year-end Shs. Outstg.	10,460	9,306	9,031	5,590
STATISTICAL RECORD:				
Debt/Total Assets %	...	0.2	1.1	13.7
Price Range	3⁹⁄₁₆-0¹¹⁄₁₆	7³⁄₈-1¾	9⁵⁄₈-6¼	...

Statistics are as originally reported. ① Incl. non-recurr. chrg. $660,871, 12/97; $3.2 mill., 12/95.

OFFICERS:
A. H. Bruno, Chmn.
K. A. Caballero, Pres., C.E.O.
C. J. Cox, V.P., C.F.O.
INVESTOR CONTACT: Investor Relations, (603) 886-0903-433
PRINCIPAL OFFICE: 542 Amherst St., Nashua, NH 03063

TELEPHONE NUMBER: (603) 886-9050
FAX: (603) 886-9051
WEB: www.wpine.com
NO. OF EMPLOYEES: 110
SHAREHOLDERS: 153
ANNUAL MEETING: In July
INCORPORATED: DE, Apr., 1992

INSTITUTIONAL HOLDINGS:
No. of Institutions: 6
Shares Held: 1,266,925
% Held: 12.0
INDUSTRY: Prepackaged software (SIC: 7372)
TRANSFER AGENT(S): BankBoston NA, Boston, MA

WINSTAR COMMUNICATIONS, INC.

YIELD ...
P/E RATIO ...

7 YEAR PRICE SCORE 144.7   **12 MONTH PRICE SCORE 133.2**

NYSE COMPOSITE INDEX=100

INTERIM EARNINGS (Per Share):

Qtr.	Mar.	June	Sept.	Dec.
1996	d0.39	d0.65	d0.75	d1.17
1997	d1.27	d1.85	d1.97	d2.18
1998	d2.54	d2.77	d2.83	d3.80
1999	d3.72	d3.53	...	...

INTERIM DIVIDENDS (Per Share):

Amt.	Decl.	Ex.	Rec.	Pay.
	No dividends paid.			

CAPITALIZATION (12/31/98):

	($000)	(%)
Long-Term Debt	1,396,635	98.6
Capital Lease Obligations..	49,354	3.5
Deferred Income Tax	18,500	1.3
Redeemable Pfd. Stock	401,478	28.3
Preferred Stock................	42	0.0
Common & Surplus	d449,534	-31.7
Total	1,416,475	100.0

RECENT DEVELOPMENTS: For the second quarter ended 6/30/99, the Company reported a net loss of $162.6 million. This compares with a loss from continuing operations of $93.8 million in the corresponding quarter the year before. Total operating revenues jumped 71.6% to $96.5 million from $56.2 million in the comparable quarter a year earlier. Total telecommunications services revenues soared 91.9% to $83.9 million from $43.7 million primarily due to accel-

erated Internet and data-related revenue growth. Information services revenues increased slightly to $12.6 million versus $12.5 million in the equivalent 1998 quarter. During the quarter, the Company added 69,000 lines bringing the total number of lines to 453,000. Gross margin improved to 24.0% due to the Company's on-net improvement and higher sales of enhanced services.

BUSINESS

WINSTAR COMMUNICATIONS, INC. provides business customers with broadband communications services, including local and long distance phone service, high-speed Internet access, and data and information services. The Company provides its Wireless Fiber(SM) service in more than 30 U.S. markets and in two markets outside the U.S. The Company has more than 450,000 installed lines serving more than 15,000 business customers.

REVENUES

(12/31/98)	($000)	(%)
Telecomm-		
commercial	141,466	57.9
Telecomm-residential	49,643	20.3
Information Services .	53,338	21.8
Total	244,447	100.0

ANNUAL FINANCIAL DATA

	12/31/98	12/31/97	12/31/96	12/31/95	2/28/95	2/28/94	2/28/93
Earnings Per Share	① d11.96	① d7.49	d3.00	② d0.70	d0.42	③ d1.09	d0.93
Cash Flow Per Share	d10.02	d6.51	d2.77	d0.64	d0.38	d1.10	d0.80
Tang. Book Val. Per Share	...	...	...	0.20	0.71	...	...
INCOME STATEMENT (IN MILLIONS):							
Total Revenues	244.4	79.6	68.0	29.8	25.6	15.6	11.3
Costs & Expenses	467.9	235.3	118.3	38.7	30.5	17.2	13.7
Depreciation & Amort.	75.0	32.4	6.3	1.3	0.7	0.5	0.7
Operating Income	d298.4	d188.0	d56.5	d10.3	d5.6	d2.1	d3.0
Net Interest Inc./(Exp.)	d126.8	d59.7	d27.2	d4.7	d0.3	d0.6	d0.5
Income Before Income Taxes	d425.2	d245.5	d83.7	d15.0	d6.1	d8.4	d4.7
Income Taxes	cr5.5	cr2.5	...	...	...	...	...
Equity Earnings/Minority Int.	...	...	...	d0.9	d1.1	...	...
Net Income	① d419.7	① d243.0	d83.7	d15.9	d7.2	③ d8.4	d4.7
Cash Flow	d387.8	d216.5	d77.4	d14.8	d6.6	d8.0	d4.1
Average Shs. Outstg. (000)	38,681	33,249	27,911	22,770	17,122	7,179	5,066
BALANCE SHEET (IN MILLIONS):							
Cash & Cash Equivalents	313.0	419.3	123.2	218.2	3.2	0.7	0.6
Total Current Assets	427.3	471.0	171.2	238.1	13.1	7.8	5.8
Net Property	639.7	284.8	63.3	15.9	2.7	1.3	0.4
Total Assets	1,663.2	976.4	290.2	285.4	29.5	14.6	8.9
Total Current Liabilities	234.1	104.9	55.6	23.2	6.1	6.8	6.0
Long-Term Obligations	1,446.0	790.3	284.3	240.5	5.2	3.1	1.2
Net Stockholders' Equity	d449.5	d118.4	d49.7	21.8	18.3	3.6	1.5
Net Working Capital	193.1	366.0	115.6	214.9	7.0	1.0	d0.2
Year-end Shs. Outstg. (000)	41,403	34,610	28,989	27,201	20,147	9,843	6,539
STATISTICAL RECORD:							
Debt/Total Assets %	86.9	80.9	98.0	84.3	17.5	21.1	13.5
Price Range	48⅛-10¼	29⅞-9¾	32½-12¾	23⅛-4⅝	9¾-2¾	3¾-0⅞	4⅜-1³⁄₁₆

Statistics are as originally reported. ① Bef. disc. oper. loss $25.0 mill., 12/31/98; $6.5 mill., 12/31/97. ② For 10 mos. due to fiscal year-end change. ③ Bef. extraord. credit $194,154

WIT CAPITAL GROUP, INC.

YIELD ...
P/E RATIO ...

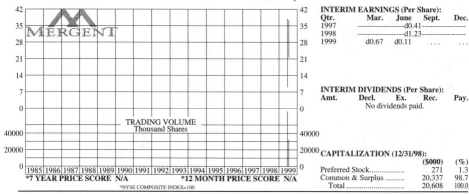

TRADING VOLUME
Thousand Shares

*7 YEAR PRICE SCORE N/A   ***12 MONTH PRICE SCORE N/A**
*NYSE COMPOSITE INDEX=100

INTERIM EARNINGS (Per Share):

Qtr.	Mar.	June	Sept.	Dec.
1997	------------------d0.41------------------			
1998	------------------d1.23------------------			
1999	d0.67	d0.11	...	...

INTERIM DIVIDENDS (Per Share):

Amt.	Decl.	Ex.	Rec.	Pay.
	No dividends paid.			

CAPITALIZATION (12/31/98):

	($000)	(%)
Preferred Stock..................	271	1.3
Common & Surplus	20,337	98.7
Total	20,608	100.0

RECENT DEVELOPMENTS: For the three months ended 6/30/99, the Company reported a net loss of $2.8 million compared with a net loss of $1.8 million in the corresponding period of the previous year. Total revenues surged to $11.3 million from $282,990 in the comparable 1998 quarter. Revenues from investment banking jumped to $8.2 million versus $180,330 the year before. Brokerage revenues were up to $1.6 million from $76,880 in the prior year. Interest revenues leapt to $1.2 million from $25,780, while the Company reported other revenues of $289,507. On 7/21/99, the Company announced that it will establish a Japanese Internet investment banking firm, to be known as Wit Capital Japan, with Mitsubishi Corporation and Trans Cosmos Inc. as initial joint venture partners. The new company will be based in Tokyo and is expected to be incorporated by the third quarter of 1999. Start-up of operations is targeted for early 2000.

BUSINESS

WIT CAPITAL GROUP, INC. is an Internet-based banking and brokerage firm that uses electronic mail and the Web to offer and sell shares in public offerings to individuals. With offices in New York and San Francisco, the Company offers investment banking services including public underwriting, private equity services, strategic advisory, and institutional quality research. WITC also offers individual investors on-line brokerage services which include access to IPOs and other securities offerings. The Company also advises corporate clients in connections with significant transactions like mergers and acquisitions, as well as assists companies with the development of Internet strategies and businesses and in raising funds from private sources. WITC completed its initial public offering on 6/4/99.

REVENUES

12/31/1998	($000)	(%)
Investment Banking...	1,515	74.4
Brokerage	294	14.4
Interest......................	183	9.0
Other.........................	45	2.2
Total	2,037	100.0

ANNUAL FINANCIAL DATA

	12/31/98	12/31/97	12/31/96
Earnings Per Share	**d1.23**	**d0.41**	**d0.33**
Cash Flow Per Share	**d1.11**	**d0.38**	**d0.33**
Tang. Book Val. Per Share	**1.66**	**0.39**	...
INCOME STATEMENT (IN THOUSANDS):			
Total Revenues	2,038	246	41
Costs & Expenses	9,901	2,986	1,790
Depreciation & Amort.	897	229	9
Operating Income	d8,760	d2,970	d1,758
Income Before Income Taxes	d8,760	d2,970	d1,758
Income Taxes	34	23	16
Net Income	d8,794	d2,993	d1,774
Cash Flow	d7,897	d2,763	d1,765
Average Shs. Outstg.	7,140	7,303	5,378
BALANCE SHEET (IN THOUSANDS):			
Cash & Cash Equivalents	18,868	1,651	...
Total Current Assets	19,132	3,370	...
Net Property	615	335	...
Total Assets	22,296	5,837	...
Total Current Liabilities	1,032	876	...
Net Stockholders' Equity	20,608	4,859	...
Net Working Capital	18,100	2,494	...
Year-end Shs. Outstg.	11,265	7,056	...
STATISTICAL RECORD:			

Statistics are as originally reported.

OFFICERS:
R. H. Lessin, Chmn., Co-C.E.O.
R. Readmond, Vice-Chmn., Pres., Co-C.E.O.
A. D. Klein, Vice-Chmn., Founder
M. B. Siegel, Sr. V.P., C.F.O.

PRINCIPAL OFFICE: 826 Broadway, Sixth Floor, New York, NY 10003

TELEPHONE NUMBER: (212) 253-4400
FAX: (212) 253-4428
WEB: www.witcapital.com

NO. OF EMPLOYEES: 138

SHAREHOLDERS: N/A

ANNUAL MEETING: N/A

INCORPORATED: DE, Mar., 1996

INSTITUTIONAL HOLDINGS:
No. of Institutions: 3
Shares Held: 231,000
% Held: 3.0

INDUSTRY: Security brokers and dealers (SIC: 6211)

TRANSFER AGENT(S): American Stock Transfer, New York, NY

WORLDGATE COMMUNICATIONS, INC

YIELD ...
P/E RATIO ...

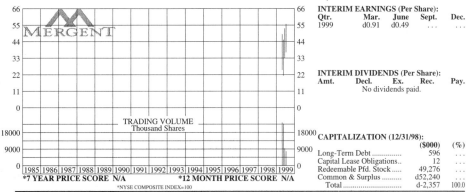

66 66
55 55
44 44
33 33
22 22
11 11
0 0

MERGENT

TRADING VOLUME
Thousand Shares

18000 18000
9000 9000
0 0

1985|1986|1987|1988|1989|1990|1991|1992|1993|1994|1995|1996|1997|1998|1999
*7 YEAR PRICE SCORE N/A   *12 MONTH PRICE SCORE N/A
*NYSE COMPOSITE INDEX=100

INTERIM EARNINGS (Per Share):

Qtr.	Mar.	June	Sept.	Dec.
1999	d0.91	d0.49	...	...

INTERIM DIVIDENDS (Per Share):

Amt.	Decl.	Ex.	Rec.	Pay.
	No dividends paid.			

CAPITALIZATION (12/31/98):

	($000)	(%)
Long-Term Debt	596	...
Capital Lease Obligations..	12	...
Redeemable Pfd. Stock	49,276	...
Common & Surplus	d52,240	...
Total	d-2,357	100.0

RECENT DEVELOPMENTS: For the second quarter ended 6/30/99, the Company reported a net loss of $9.2 million compared with a net loss of $5.0 million in the corresponding prior-year period. Total revenues surged to $741,000 from $182,000 in the previous year. The Company reported a loss from operations of $9.0 million versus $5.1 million a year earlier. On 6/10/99, the Company signed an agreement with The Hunan Multimedia Communications Bureau, a division of the People's Republic of China Hunan Provincial Telecommunications Authority's Posts and Telecommunications Administration, to deploy the WORLDGATE SERVICE. WGAT has received the initial purchase order for Changsha, capital of the Hunan province, and Hengyang, with additional cities possible in the Hunan province.

BUSINESS

WORLDWIDE COMMUNICA-TIONS, INC. provides a television-based Internet service, the WORLDGATE[SM] Service, that enables cable television subscribers to access the Internet through their televisions. The WORLDGATE Service is designed to operate with cable systems using advanced analog or current and future generation digital cable television set-top boxes. The Company's CHANNEL HYPERLINKING[TM] technology integrates the dynamics of the Internet with television's proven advertiser-sponsored entertainment model. This technology will enable a viewer watching a television program or advertisement to link within seconds to a related interactive Web site.

ANNUAL FINANCIAL DATA

	12/31/98	12/31/97	12/31/96
Earnings Per Share	d2.25	d1.81	d0.33
Cash Flow Per Share	d2.23	d1.81	d0.33
INCOME STATEMENT (IN THOUSANDS):			
Total Revenues	1,022	141	...
Costs & Expenses	28,144	14,559	2,929
Depreciation & Amort.	323	29	...
Operating Income	d27,444	d14,447	d2,929
Net Interest Inc./(Exp.)	322	406	6
Income Before Income Taxes	d27,122	d14,041	d2,923
Net Income	d27,122	d14,041	d2,923
Cash Flow	d32,944	d16,448	d2,998
Average Shs. Outstg.	14,786	9,101	9,101
BALANCE SHEET (IN THOUSANDS):			
Cash & Cash Equivalents	368	17,318	...
Total Current Assets	3,848	18,120	...
Net Property	643	249	...
Total Assets	5,621	18,412	...
Total Current Liabilities	7,097	1,938	...
Long-Term Obligations	607	404	...
Net Stockholders' Equity	d52,240	d19,177	...
Net Working Capital	d3,249	16,182	...
Year-end Shs. Outstg.	9,101	9,101	...
STATISTICAL RECORD:			
Debt/Total Assets %	10.8	2.2	...
Statistics are as originally reported.			

OFFICERS:
H. M. Krisbergh, Chmn. & C.E.O.
D. A. Dill, C.F.O.
R. J. Gort, V.P., Gen. Couns. & Sec.

PRINCIPAL OFFICE: 3190 Tremont Ave., Trevose, PA 19053

TELEPHONE NUMBER: (215) 354-5100
WEB: www.wgate.com.

NO. OF EMPLOYEES: 131

SHAREHOLDERS: N/A

ANNUAL MEETING: N/A

INCORPORATED: DE, 1996

INSTITUTIONAL HOLDINGS:
No. of Institutions: 3
Shares Held: 470,318
% Held: 2.3

INDUSTRY: Cable and other pay TV services (SIC: 4841)

TRANSFER AGENT(S): American Stock Transfer & Trust Company.

XOOM.COM INC.

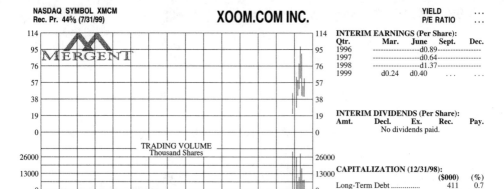

INTERIM EARNINGS (Per Share):

Qtr.	Mar.	June	Sept.	Dec.
1996		d0.89		
1997		d0.64		
1998		d1.37		
1999	d0.24	d0.40	...	...

INTERIM DIVIDENDS (Per Share):

Amt.	Decl.	Ex.	Rec.	Pay.
		No dividends paid.		

TRADING VOLUME
Thousand Shares

CAPITALIZATION (12/31/98):

	($000)	(%)
Long-Term Debt	411	0.7
Capital Lease Obligations..	117	0.2
Common & Surplus	60,332	99.1
Total	60,860	100.0

*7 YEAR PRICE SCORE N/A   ***12 MONTH PRICE SCORE N/A**

*NYSE COMPOSITE INDEX=100

RECENT DEVELOPMENTS: For the quarter ended 6/30/99, the Company reported a net loss of $6.8 million compared with a net loss of $2.3 million in the same period of 1998. Results included pre-tax charges of $2.6 million in 1999 and $330,000 in 1998 for purchased in-process research and development. Total net revenues more than tripled to $6.5 million from $1.7 million in the prior year. E-commerce revenues, which more than doubled to $3.3 million from $1.2 million in 1998, fueled top-line growth. Gross profit amounted to $3.8 million in 1999 compared with $1.1 million a year earlier. During the second quarter, the Company entered into an agreement to merge with several NBC Internet assets and Snap.com. Inc. to form the first publicly traded Internet company integrated with a major broadcaster. If approved by the stockholders and completed as proposed, the new company, to be called NBC Internet, Inc., will use Snap.com as its umbrella consumer brand, integrating broadcast, portal and e-commerce services.

BUSINESS

XOOM.COM INC. is a direct e-commerce company that offers consumers free services over the Web, including homepage building, chat rooms, message boards, HTML e-mail, on-line greeting cards, a Web page counter, clip art and downloadable software. The Company also offers services such as a travel club, long distance telephone services and a DVD club. XOOM.com sell its proprietary products, as well as third party products, to the Company's registered members. XOOM.com attempts to draw membership by offering consumers high-quality, free services over the Web. As of 8/3/99, the Company attracted more than 9.2 million members.

ANNUAL FINANCIAL DATA

	12/31/98	12/31/97	12/31/96
Earnings Per Share	① d1.37	① d0.64	d0.89
Cash Flow Per Share	d0.86	d0.54	d0.88
Tang. Book Val. Per Share	4.13	...	0.17
INCOME STATEMENT (IN THOUSANDS):			
Total Revenues	8,318	841	...
Costs & Expenses	13,619	3,471	437
Depreciation & Amort.	4,055	502	2
Operating Income	d9,356	d3,132	d440
Net Interest Inc./(Exp.)	d1,442	...	...
Income Before Income Taxes	d10,798	d3,132	d440
Net Income	① d10,798	① d3,132	d440
Cash Flow	d6,743	d2,630	d437
Average Shs. Outstg.	7,879	4,874	497
BALANCE SHEET (IN THOUSANDS):			
Cash & Cash Equivalents	54,575	6	1
Total Current Assets	58,573	255	301
Net Property	2,071	414	62
Total Assets	66,874	782	705
Total Current Liabilities	6,013	1,655	145
Long-Term Obligations	528	...	...
Net Stockholders' Equity	60,332	d873	560
Net Working Capital	52,560	d1,400	156
Year-end Shs. Outstg.	13,700	5,541	3,333
STATISTICAL RECORD:			
Debt/Total Assets %	0.8	...	...
Price Range	45⅛-21⅛	...	...

Statistics are as originally reported. ① Incl. non-recurr. chrg. $790,000, 1998; $1.2 mill. 1997.

REVENUES

(12/31/98)	($000)	(%)
Electronic Commerce	5,582	67.1
Advertising	2,144	25.8
License Fees & Other	592	7.1
Total	8,318	100.0

OFFICERS:
C. Kitze, Chmn.
L. Massa, C.E.O., Pres.
J. Harbottle, C.F.O., V.P., Fin.

PRINCIPAL OFFICE: 300 Montgomery Street, Suite 300, San Francisco, CA 94104

TELEPHONE NUMBER: (415) 288-2500
WEB: www.xoom.com

NO. OF EMPLOYEES: 71

SHAREHOLDERS: 90 (approx.)

ANNUAL MEETING: N/A

INCORPORATED: DE, Apr., 1996

INSTITUTIONAL HOLDINGS:
No. of Institutions: 35
Shares Held: 2,690,231
% Held: 16.8

INDUSTRY: Advertising agencies (SIC: 7311)

TRANSFER AGENT(S): BankBoston, N.A., Canton, Massachusetts.

NASDAQ SYMBOL YHOO		
Rec. Pr. 137⁷/₁₆ (7/31/99)	**YAHOO! INC.**	YIELD ...
		P/E RATIO N.M.

INTERIM EARNINGS (Per Share):

Qtr.	Mar.	June	Sept.	Dec.
1996	Nil	d0.01	d0.01	Nil
1997	d0.01	d0.25	0.01	d0.02
1998	0.02	d0.05	0.06	0.08
1999	0.08	d0.07	...	...

INTERIM DIVIDENDS (Per Share):

Amt.	Decl.	Ex.	Rec.	Pay.
3-for-2	7/29/97	9/02/97	8/11/97	8/29/97
2-for-1	7/08/98	8/03/98	7/17/98	7/31/98
2-for-1	1/12/99	2/08/99	1/22/99	2/05/99

TRADING VOLUME
Thousand Shares

1985 1986 1987 1988 1989 1990 1991 1992 1993 1994 1995 1996 1997 1998 1999

***7 YEAR PRICE SCORE N/A**   ***12 MONTH PRICE SCORE 112.6**

*NYSE COMPOSITE INDEX=100

CAPITALIZATION (12/31/98):

	($000)	(%)
Minority Interest	1,248	0.2
Common & Surplus	536,210	99.8
Total	537,458	100.0

RECENT DEVELOPMENTS: For the quarter ended 6/30/99, the Company reported a net loss of $15.1 million compared with a net loss of $14.2 million in the corresponding period of the previous year. The results included non-recurring charges of $56.1 million from acquisition-related activities in 1999 and non-recurring charges of $15.0 million for in-process research and development in 1998. Net revenues surged to $115.2 million from $44.9 million the year before. The improvement in revenues was due to the increasing number of advertisers purchasing space on the Company's on-line media properties as well as larger and longer-term purchases by certain advertisers. Gross profit was $96.8 million, or 84.0% of net revenues, versus $36.8 million, or 81.8% of net revenues, in the previous year. On 7/20/99, the Company completed the acquisition of broadcast.com, a publicly traded aggregator and broadcaster of media programming on the Internet, for approximately 28.6 million shares of stock.

BUSINESS

YAHOO! INC. is an Internet media company that helps Internet users navigate the World Wide Web. Under the Yahoo! brand, the Company provides contexed-based guides to on-line content, Web search capabilities, aggregated third-party content, email, and community and personalization features. The Company makes its properties available without charge to users, and generates revenue primarily through the sale of banner advertisements on short-term contracts. The Company is headquartered in Santa Clara, Calif., and has offices in Europe, the Asia-Pacific region and Canada. The Company acquired GeoCities on 5/28/99 and broadcast.com on 7/20/99.

ANNUAL FINANCIAL DATA

	12/31/98	12/31/97	12/31/96	12/31/95
Earnings Per Share	① 0.11	① d0.13	d0.01	Nil
Cash Flow Per Share	0.16	d0.12	0.01	...
Tang. Book Val. Per Share	2.69	0.65	0.64	0.09
INCOME STATEMENT (IN THOUSANDS):				
Total Revenues	203,270	67,411	19,073	1,363
Costs & Expenses	164,287	93,453	25,488	1,910
Depreciation & Amort.	10,215	2,554	390	133
Operating Income	28,768	d28,596	d6,805	d680
Income Before Income Taxes	43,415	d23,614	d2,874	d634
Income Taxes	17,827	...	...	...
Equity Earnings/Minority Int.	68	727	540	...
Net Income	① 25,588	① d22,887	d2,334	d634
Cash Flow	35,803	d20,333	d1,944	d501
Average Shs. Outstg.	224,100	174,332	152,664	135,246
BALANCE SHEET (IN THOUSANDS):				
Cash & Cash Equivalents	433,499	90,310	92,554	5,297
Total Current Assets	467,239	107,189	97,555	6,112
Net Property	15,189	7,035	2,223	186
Total Assets	621,884	141,884	110,255	6,298
Total Current Liabilities	79,983	23,456	7,670	751
Long-Term Obligations	...	...	...	97
Net Stockholders' Equity	536,210	117,712	102,075	5,450
Net Working Capital	387,256	83,733	89,885	5,361
Year-end Shs. Outstg.	199,019	180,050	159,462	61,518
STATISTICAL RECORD:				
Operating Profit Margin %	14.2	...	...	...
Net Profit Margin %	12.6	...	...	...
Return on Equity %	4.8	...	...	...
Return on Assets %	4.1	...	...	...
Debt/Total Assets %	...	...	...	1.5
Price Range	143-14⁷/₁₆	17³/₄-2¹³/₁₆	7³/₁₆-2⁹/₁₆	...
P/E Ratio	N.M.-130.8	...	...	...

Statistics are as originally reported. Adj. for stk. splits: 2-for-1, 2/5/99; 2-for-1, 7/31/98; 3-for-2, 8/29/97 ① Incl. non-recurr. chrg. 12/31/98: $19.4 mill.; 12/31/97: $25.1 mill.

OFFICERS:
T. Koogle, Chmn., C.E.O.
J. Mallet, Pres., C.O.O.
G. Valenzuela, Sr. V.P., C.F.O.
J. Place, Sec., Gen. Couns.

INVESTOR CONTACT: Gary Valenzuela, Sr. V.P., C.F.O., (408) 731-3350

PRINCIPAL OFFICE: 3420 Central Expressway, Santa Clara, CA 95051-0703

TELEPHONE NUMBER: (408) 731-3300
FAX: (408) 731-3301
WEB: www.yahoo.com

NO. OF EMPLOYEES: 803

SHAREHOLDERS: 2,350 (approx.)

ANNUAL MEETING: In May

INCORPORATED: CA, Mar., 1995

INSTITUTIONAL HOLDINGS:
No. of Institutions: 302
Shares Held: 47,278,900
% Held: 20.9

INDUSTRY: Computer integrated systems design (SIC: 7373)

TRANSFER AGENT(S): Boston EquiServe, Boston, MA

ZIFF-DAVIS, INC.

YIELD ...
P/E RATIO ...

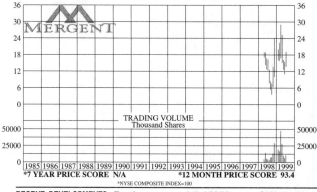

INTERIM EARNINGS (Per Share):

Qtr.	Mar.	June	Sept.	Dec.
1998	d0.05	d0.75	d0.04	0.08
1999	d0.37	d0.03	...	...

TRADING VOLUME
Thousand Shares

INTERIM DIVIDENDS (Per Share):

Amt.	Decl.	Ex.	Rec.	Pay.
		No dividends paid.		

1985 1986 1987 1988 1989 1990 1991 1992 1993 1994 1995 1996 1997 1998 1999
*7 YEAR PRICE SCORE N/A   *12 MONTH PRICE SCORE 93.4
*NYSE COMPOSITE INDEX=100

CAPITALIZATION (12/31/98):

	($000)	(%)
Long-Term Debt	1,539,322	50.4
Deferred Income Tax	165,082	5.4
Common & Surplus	1,352,598	44.2
Total	3,057,002	100.0

RECENT DEVELOPMENTS: For the quarter ended 6/30/99, the Company reported a net loss of $3.3 million compared with a loss of $76.6 million in the corresponding quarter of the previous year. Total revenues declined slightly to $257.6 million from $264.2 million in the prior-year quarter. The decline in revenues was due primarily to lower advertising revenue in certain business publications as well as the absence of revenue from publications that were discontinued in October 1998. Publishing revenues fell 10.1%

to $178.4 million from $198.4 million. Event revenues were $75.6 million, an increase of 14.9% from $65.8 million. Television revenue totaled $3.6 million. Going forward, the Company will continue to explore strategic alternatives to maximize shareholder value. Such strategic alternatives include possible alliances, mergers, and the sale or joint venture of all or some of the Company's businesses.

BUSINESS

ZIFF-DAVIS, INC. provides information on computing and technology, including the Internet. The Company is focused on the businesses of print publishing, trade shows and conferences, Internet, market research, education and television. ZD provides technology companies worldwide with marketing strategies for reaching key decision-makers. The Comany operates in four primary business segments. The publishing segment is a computer-related magazine publisher with 26 primary U.S. and international titles. The events segment is engaged in the production of trade shows, conferences, and customized marketing and educational programs for the computer industry in the U.S. The Internet segment represents ZDNet, which is the Company's online division. In February 1999, the Company added the television segment, ZDTV, which launched its first 24-hour cable television channel and integrated Web site focused exclusively on computers, technology and the Internet.

ANNUAL FINANCIAL DATA

	12/31/98	12/31/97	12/31/96	12/31/95
Earnings Per Share	d0.78	...	...	...
Cash Flow Per Share	0.77	...	...	...
INCOME STATEMENT (IN THOUSANDS):				
Total Revenues	1,108,892	1,153,761	955,139	202,729
Costs & Expenses	922,838	889,589	728,222	115,749
Depreciation & Amort.	154,974	154,940	139,736	24,305
Operating Income	31,080	109,232	87,181	62,675
Net Interest Inc./(Exp.)	d143,547	d190,445	d120,646	d44,005
Income Before Income Taxes	d104,236	d72,491	d27,124	22,869
Income Taxes	cr26,427	cr1,312	24,957	11,924
Net Income	d77,809	d71,179	d52,081	10,945
Cash Flow	77,165	83,761	87,655	35,250
Average Shs. Outstg.	100,000	...	...	...
BALANCE SHEET (IN THOUSANDS):				
Cash & Cash Equivalents	32,566	30,301	29,915	...
Total Current Assets	386,231	447,448	371,654	...
Net Property	91,189	53,536	53,561	...
Total Assets	3,433,803	3,546,646	3,584,173	...
Total Current Liabilities	350,698	818,588	418,406	...
Long-Term Obligations	1,539,322	2,408,240	2,522,252	...
Net Stockholders' Equity	1,352,598	126,130	447,756	...
Net Working Capital	35,533	d371,140	d46,752	...
Year-end Shs. Outstg.	100,000	100,000	...	...
STATISTICAL RECORD:				
Operating Profit Margin %	2.8	9.5	9.1	30.9
Net Profit Margin %	...	...	...	5.4
Debt/Total Assets %	44.8	67.9	70.4	...
Price Range	23¹⁵/₁₆-3⅝	...	...	...
Statistics are as originally reported.				

REVENUES

(12/31/98)	($000)	(%)
Publishing	782,882	70.6
Events	269,867	24.3
Internet	56,143	5.1
Total	1,108,892	100.0

OFFICERS:
E. Hippeau, Chmn., C.E.O.
T. C. O'Brien, C.F.O.
T. L. Wright, V.P., Treas.
J. M. Morris, Sr. V.P., Gen. Couns.

PRINCIPAL OFFICE: One Park Avenue, New York, NY 10016

TELEPHONE NUMBER: (212) 503-3500
WEB: www.ziffdavis.com
FAX: (212) 503-4599

NO. OF EMPLOYEES: 3,205

SHAREHOLDERS: 315

ANNUAL MEETING: In May

INCORPORATED: DE, Feb., 1998

INSTITUTIONAL HOLDINGS:
No. of Institutions: 58
Shares Held: 14,871,838
% Held: 14.4

INDUSTRY: Periodicals (SIC: 2721)

TRANSFER AGENT(S): The Bank of New York, New York, NY.